PENGUIN  CLASS... W9-ARZ-872

LIVING MY LIFE

EMMA GOLDMAN (1869–1940) was a Russian-Jewish anarchist lecturer and writer who rose to prominence in the United States, the home to which she had immigrated as a young woman. A passionate orator, a defender of the struggles of labor for better working conditions, Goldman crossed America to advocate resistance to the tyranny of any form of government. Dismissive of the woman suffrage campaign, Goldman lent her support to the birth control and free-love movements. With the proceeds of her popular lectures on modern drama, she supported *Mother Earth,* the newspaper she founded in 1905. *Mother Earth* was a primary platform for anarchist theory until it was closed down in 1917, a victim of the Espionage Act of that year, making it illegal to speak disloyally of the military or to obstruct the draft. After frequent imprisonments for inciting to riot and speaking against the American entry into World War I, Goldman was deported as an "alien" in 1919. After her deportation, she resided temporarily in the Soviet Union, whose Bolshevik Revolution she came to regard as a tragic failure. She lived in Europe as a stateless exile, finding refuge finally in Canada at the end of her life.

MIRIAM BRODY is the editor of the Penguin edition of Mary Wollstonecraft's *A Vindication of the Rights of Woman.* She has written biographies of Mary Wollstonecraft (2000) and the nineteenth-century American free-love advocate Victoria Woodhull (2003). Her other works include *Manly Writing: Gender, Rhetoric, and the Rise of Composition* (1993). She resides in Ithaca, New York.

EMMA GOLDMAN

Living My Life

ABRIDGED

Introduction and Notes by
MIRIAM BRODY

PENGUIN BOOKS

PENGUIN BOOKS

Published by the Penguin Group
Penguin Group (USA) Inc., 375 Hudson Street, New York, New York 10014, U.S.A.
Penguin Group (Canada), 90 Eglinton Avenue East, Suite 700, Toronto,
Ontario, Canada M4P 2Y3 (a division of Pearson Penguin Canada Inc.)
Penguin Books Ltd, 80 Strand, London WC2R oRL, England
Penguin Ireland, 25 St Stephen's Green, Dublin 2, Ireland (a division of Penguin Books Ltd)
Penguin Group (Australia), 250 Camberwell Road, Camberwell, Victoria 3124, Australia
(a division of Pearson Australia Group Pty Ltd)
Penguin Books India Pvt Ltd, 11 Community Centre,
Panchsheel Park, New Delhi - 110 017, India
Penguin Group (NZ), 67 Apollo Drive, Rosedale, North Shore 0745, Auckland, New Zealand
(a division of Pearson New Zealand Ltd)
Penguin Books (South Africa) (Pty) Ltd, 24 Sturdee Avenue, Rosebank,
Johannesburg 2196, South Africa

Penguin Books Ltd, Registered Offices:
80 Strand, London WC2R oRL, England

First published in the United States of America in two volumes by Alfred A. Knopf, Inc. 1931
This condensed edition with an introduction and notes by Miriam Brody
published in Penguin Books 2006

12 14 16 18 20 19 17 15 13 11

Condensation, introduction, and notes copyright © Miriam Brody, 2006
All rights reserved

LIBRARY OF CONGRESS CATALOGING IN PUBLICATION DATA
Goldman, Emma, 1869–1940.
Living my life / Emma Goldman ; introduction and notes by Miriam Brody.
p. cm.
Abridgement of author's 2 vol. Work originally published: New York : Knopf, 1931.
Includes bibliographical references
ISBN 978-0-14-243785-8
1. Goldman, Emma, 1869–1940. 2. Anarchists—United States—Biography. I. Title.
HX843.7.G65A3 2006
355'.83092—dc22
[B] 2005054420

Printed in the United States of America
Set in Adobe Sabon

Contents

LIVING MY LIFE

Introduction

1. "RED EMMA" WRITES HER LIFE

"The most dangerous woman in America," as J. Edgar Hoover described her, took pen in hand in June 1928 to write the events of her tumultuous life. "Red Emma" Goldman, who the popular press claimed owned no God, had no religion, would kill all rulers, and overthrow all laws, chose to begin her autobiography on her fifty-ninth birthday, a task she would later say was the "hardest and most painful" she had ever undertaken (Goldman, *Nowhere at Home*, 145). As she wrote about her life, she confronted not only her own loneliness but also the disappointment of her political hopes, the dream that anarchism, which she called her "beautiful ideal," would take root in her lifetime among the people whose benefit she believed she served.

Others had urged her to begin her memoir years before, but she had been busy traversing the country, lecturing, organizing, writing, or if in prison, forging bonds with other inmates, protesting conditions, or alerting vast networks of supporters and friends to crises imminent or arrived. Now in a borrowed cottage in the south of France, years advancing, living on funds raised by friends and a generous advance from her American publisher, Emma Goldman began a labor that would require three years to complete, writing in longhand by night and dictating to a typist by day. "I am anxious to reach the mass of the American reading public," she wrote to a friend, "not so much because of the royalties, but because I have always worked for the mass" (Drinnon, 269). In fact, she was writing also in her own interest, hoping to win the sympathy of American readers who might help reverse the decision to deport her that had left her a stateless exile.

Eight years earlier, in 1920, America, her adopted country, had deported her as a subversive, leaving her feeling "an alien everywhere," as she wrote to her friend in exile Alexander Berkman (*Nowhere at Home,* 170). A permanent, often unwelcome guest in someone else's country, she would infuse her writing with a sense of loneliness and despair. To Berkman she wrote "hardly anything has come of our years of effort" (ibid., 49). On the eve of fascist victories in Europe, she felt as well the nearness of catastrophe, the likelihood that once again, as it had in 1914, Europe would be convulsed by war.

Underlying this sense of impending disaster, she was aware that political radicals on the left were embracing the Bolshevik Revolution in Russia, a revolution she believed had betrayed the expectations of the Russian peasants and workers in whose name Lenin's government served. She had spent two years in the new Soviet state, having gone there as an anarchist victim of the infamous Palmer raids that launched the first widespread "red scare" at the time of America's entry into World War I. Instead of meeting the intoxication of a liberated society that had thrown off the shackles of czarist autocracy, Emma Goldman found, she believed, a dispirited and growing Bolshevik state. To her dismay, the state was consolidating its powers, responding, she felt, incompetently and calamitously to its economic and political crises and, to compound the disaster, imprisoning and executing its dissidents.

Russia had been her birthplace in 1869, but more important, Russia had nurtured the revolutionary beliefs she had taken as a young immigrant girl to America. At sixteen, she had joined the thousands of refugees from eastern Europe, many fleeing the Russian anti-Semitism that broke out in violent pogroms in the eastern "pale of settlement" after terrorists assassinated Czar Alexander II. Now disappointed by Russia, Emma Goldman trained her hopes once more on the American shores, where she had left behind friends and family.

Writing her life story might have proved difficult. She had kept no diary. Although there had been a vast record of her writing and lecturing stored in the offices of *Mother Earth*, the journal she founded in 1905 and maintained through many busy years, these records had been destroyed by federal agents who systematically ransacked and looted the property of political radicals. Fortunately she had been a faithful and copious letter writer, and in response to her request more than a thousand of these were returned to her. Some letters to friends were meticulous accounts of her prison years—what she read, what she was fed, the gifts sent to her by loyal supporters, the campaigns she carried on for better conditions, the relations formed with other inmates. Other letters could provide testimony enough for her to recall her public life, years in which she was both witness to and a principal actor in the political convulsions that defined her time—workers' strikes, riots, assassinations, the women's rights movement, political repression, revolution, and exile. Five hundred more letters came from Ben Reitman, the man who had been for many years her publicist, road manager, and lover. In these she chronicled a response to a love affair in which she berated Reitman for betrayal, soothed his vanity when he was snubbed by the anarchist luminaries he hoped to impress, or frankly recalled the pleasures of his bed.

Goldman's was a rich life to chronicle, the story of an intellectual and emotional journey of a Russian woman who became an American original, someone who combined the radical political traditions of nineteenth-century Europe with the insurgent individualism of the young American republic. The fusion she sought was an anarchism responsive to the changes in America in the early twentieth century, an anarchism that would transform the conditions of public and private life. To the call for radical reorganization of work life she inherited from European political tradition and to the conviction in the supremacy of individual liberty she found in the American literature of Emerson, Thoreau, and Whitman, Goldman added advocacy of the birth control and free-love movements that had emerged out of nineteenth-century American anarchist and utopian communities. Without such reforms, she would argue, there would be no egalitarian emancipation of the whole of humanity.

The foundations of these beliefs, Goldman claimed in her autobiography, were laid in her earliest years in Russia when, as a child, her sympathies were stirred by the oppression of the peasants of her native Lithuania and the suffering of the political rebels, communists or anarchists, imprisoned or executed by the czars. While a young teenager in Russia, Emma Goldman had read Nikolai Chernyshevsky's widely influential 1863 novel, *What Is to Be Done?*, in which a young woman from the propertied Russian gentry escapes from the constraints of bourgeois marriage to claim romantic love and economic independence. Chernyshevsky's heroine allies herself with the young radicals influenced by the European revolutions of 1848, rebels who sought to redress the great disparities of wealth in their own native Russia. To the young Emma Goldman, this sexually and materially emancipated model of womanhood was inspiring, chafing as Goldman was under the authoritarian rule of a patriarchal and often violent father.

In 1886, after she joined some of her family who had come earlier to Rochester, New York, Goldman's sympathy for victims of social injustice was stirred into a lifelong commitment to political action by events in Chicago that became known to the world as the Haymarket Massacre. Four American anarchist revolutionaries, hanged in Chicago, had been held responsible without evidence for throwing a bomb that killed seven policemen. As the police opened fire, perhaps three times as many more workers who were rallying for the eight-hour workday were killed. Goldman revered the memory of the eloquent and brave "Haymarket martyrs," who had gone to their death believing that their own executions would rouse the anger of the laboring classes whom they hoped to liberate.

Awakened to a political life by the Haymarket affair, Goldman left her factory work and an early failed marriage in Rochester for the street corner, café, and saloon society of lower Manhattan, where she found a home among the European immigrants who had brought their anarchism and socialism with them to the new country. Emma Goldman's work would carry the ideals of these immigrants from the self-imposed isolation of their insular community, where they preached to one another in their native tongues, into the mainstream of American intellectual debate.

She was not, in fact, the bomb-toting virago depicted by the popular press. But though she loathed violence, she would not condemn the radicals who practiced it, remaining loyal to the unsuccessful *attentat,* or revolutionary act of violence, committed by Alexander "Sasha" Berkman, her pal, as she called him—her lover, confidant, and lifelong friend. In 1892, when she was twenty-three, as she described fully in her memoir for the first time, Goldman helped Berkman plan and carry out an attempt on the life of Henry Clay Frick, the Carnegie Steel plant manager who presided over the bloody confrontation between Pinkerton guards and strikers in Homestead, Pennsylvania. As she described in her autobiography, Goldman made an awkward and unsuccessful attempt to procure funds for Berkman's attack by walking the streets one night as a prostitute. But for lack of funds to buy the railroad ticket to Pittsburgh, Goldman might well have been by Berkman's side when he fired his gun. While Frick survived his bullet wounds, Goldman endured Berkman's long and often brutal imprisonment as a personal vigil. Faithful to her friend, as she described in her autobiography, she once ascended a lecturer's dais and lashed her fellow anarchist and former mentor Johann Most with a horsewhip because he had ridiculed and disparaged Berkman's act.

Although Emma Goldman was never connected to the attempt on Frick's life, nine years later in 1901 her notoriety as a dangerous rebel was sealed when the young Polish immigrant Leon Czolgosz shot and killed President William McKinley. Czolgosz, who acted alone and whose connection to anarchism was vague, was alleged to have told reporters "I am a disciple of Emma Goldman. Her words set me on fire." Goldman herself called the statement "a police fabrication." Although she had met Czolgosz briefly, and he had indeed heard her speak, "no living soul ever heard Czolgosz make that statement," she wrote, "nor is there a single written word to prove that the boy ever breathed the accusation" (*Anarchism and Other Essays,*

88). Still, the association with assassination was indelible, and named a firebrand, she came to know the insides of many jails, charged with inciting to riot or for disseminating birth control information in violation of the Comstock laws, laws that had since 1873 defined all public discussions of human sexuality as obscene and illegal. But it was not until she counseled young men to resist the draft in the wave of jingoism accompanying the United States' entry into World War I that she encountered the full weight of the justice system of her adopted country, a system that ultimately found reasons to nullify her citizenship and deport her.

2. THE "BEAUTIFUL IDEAL"— EMMA GOLDMAN'S ANARCHISM

As an anarchist, Emma Goldman would have brooked no illusions about the state and its agent, U.S. Attorney General Alexander Palmer, nor anticipated from it any admirable administration of social justice. The founding principle of anarchism, she claimed, "is the theory that all forms of government rest on violence, and are therefore wrong and harmful as well as unnecessary" (Anarchism and Other Essays, 50). It made no difference if a government were run by kings or parliaments, the fabric of its laws constrained and fettered the liberty of individuals. She had found injustice not only in czarist Russia but also in the American republic. Newly arrived in New York City, Goldman carried angry memories of a factory owner in Rochester refusing her request for fair pay. As she joined the throngs of young, articulate, and combative newcomers, many of them Jewish immigrants from eastern Europe, she was drawn to the anarchist movement of her Haymarket heroes, particularly to the lectures of German immigrant Johann Most, the social democrat turned anarchist, whose exhortations to violence in his newspaper Die Freiheit and publication of a bomb-making handbook helped to harden the police arm of the state into active repression.

It was a congenial, conversational, and activist community in which she found herself in lower Manhattan in the late 1880s. The young people who crowded the teashops and cafeterias of the Lower East Side were often well-educated newcomers, compelled to abandon their professional lives in Russia by anti-Semitic prohibitions and pogroms instigated by the czar. In a lyrical description of the Lower East Side at the end of the nineteenth century, one activist reformer recalled the summer evenings when young men and women, weary from work in the city's sweatshops and factories, escaped the heat of the crowded tenement streets by climbing to the roofs. In pleasant congregation from rooftop to rooftop they raised voices in German, Russian, or Yiddish debating responses to the oppression of the capitalist owners, their politics shaped by the revolutions in Europe, revolutions that witnessed the formation of new nation-states on the ashes of the houses of Bourbon/Orleans and Hapsburg monarchies (Hillquit 1–2).

Although anarchism flourished among the newcomers, by the time Emma Goldman arrived in New York City in 1889, the appeal to native American workers of this radical alternative had waned, a popular animus against it raised by the Haymarket violence and fanned by a hostile press. Where kept alive, anarchism found its home among the immigrant Italian, Slavic, and Jewish communities in larger cities, as in New York's Lower East Side. Goldman would become anarchism's most spirited spokesperson in America, although, eclectic and pragmatic in her adaptation, she would raise the sharp incisive wit of her oratory to advance as well the sexual liberation of women and the redemptive force of aestheticism, advocacies that took her beyond the conceptual borders of the movement as it was defined by its European male architects. While she shaped the tradition she received to her own purposes, it was European anarchism that had nurtured her intellectual development and remained the "beautiful ideal" against which she would measure all political struggles.

Emma Goldman grounded her political belief on a fundamental repudiation of all states and governments. As did socialists, anarchists called for the end to private ownership of the means of production that involved the exploitation of labor. But while anarchists and Marxists merged in the coffeehouses, saloons, and street corners of lower Manhattan, joining forces to swell a protest or support a strike, a profoundly different response to the revolutionary changes in Europe divided them. So serious, in fact, was this division that in 1872, Karl Marx evicted the followers of the revolutionary anarchist Michael Bakunin from the First International, dividing the leftist enemies of capitalism into two irreconcilable camps.

In theory the goals of anarchists and socialists seemed similar: after destroying the capitalist class and ending its exploitation of labor, workers would share the product of their labor with one another in a stateless, communal society. But the Marxist commitment to the end of the state was theoretical, the positioning of an imagined and distant terminus, the process a slow "withering away" of a state apparatus after a protracted postrevolutionary period of political centralization. Following a Marxist revolution, the nation-state, although "temporary," would still be alive and well, in principle working in the interests of the proletariat, whose well-being the new possessors of state power would advance and protect.

The anarchist followers of Bakunin, by contrast, continuing the tradition begun by the French printer and journalist Pierre Proudhon, sought the total and immediate elimination of the state after revolution. In its place, free federations of autonomous groups would emerge, networks of workers joined voluntarily into syndicalist associations, without any centralized administrative apparatus. Proudhon had conceived of the free individual as the basic unit of society. Rather than contracting with governments to ensure his well-being, as in the Lockean tradition that informed the American Declaration of Independence, the individual liberated from state tyranny enters into free associations with other individuals, these associations forming the social networks of public life. Although this new collectivity has its own force or character, Proudhon wrote, it must never become a monolithic totality in which individual differences are merged.

A whiff of nostalgia accompanies the anarchist vision, as it repudiates the new centralized nation-states that demanded allegiance from the smaller communities of premodern Europe. Anarchism looks backward for its model to the medieval city-state as a smaller, autonomous unit in a network of mutual interest with other such cities. Insisting on the liberty of individuals and preferring the ideal of small, autonomous groups of workers, perhaps at a printing press distributing political tracts, anarchism positions itself in libertarian resistance to authoritarian Marxism, opposing its call for a postrevolutionary centralized state, even when that is depicted as a transitional necessity.

Anarchists after Proudhon retained his notion of "mutualism" while becoming less clear about the constitution of the stateless collective that would replace nation-states, particularly as Proudhon's world of peasants and small craftsmen gave way to large concentrations of industrial workers. As the great Russian anarchist theorists Bakunin and Peter Kropotkin coped with industrialization, the idea of a federation of workers' collectives as the basic unit of social organization replaced the notion of individuals in association. Still, when pressed for details about such an anarchist community, Goldman claimed, with other anarchists, that she was less interested in distant outcomes than in correcting present ills, since no future community should be constrained by the imaginings of present planners, fettered as they were by the bonds of government.

By the time Emma Goldman had arrived in New York City, the work of the Russian aristocrat Kropotkin, elegant, lucid, and optimistic, dominated the direction of anarchist thought. A university-trained scientist whom many of his contemporaries regarded as saintly, Kropotkin believed that a spirit of cooperation was native to human beings, indeed to the animal world as well. Social organization among all species evolved in response to natural conditions. Human beings, like other natural creatures, adapted themselves in cooperative ways to serve their own interests in survival and would continue to do so without artificial regulations like the laws of government. Wedding this Darwinian framework, although in cooperative not competitive terms, to the philosophy of anarchism, Kropotkin described human beings learning to rely on "mutual aid" in their struggle to survive the vicissitudes of natural and social adversity. That such an intrinsic spirit of cooperation could be tapped in the struggle to form workers' collectives was at the heart of his optimistic anarchist vision.

Goldman called Kropotkin the father of modern anarchism, not only because he had brought the discipline of Darwinian science to political philosophy, giving the stamp of a species' inevitability to the Proudhonian vision of voluntary association, but because he became a theoretician as well of the modern industrial state. Rather than looking back to agrarian and craft communities as the model for social organization, Kropotkin admired the power of industrial production, on which achievement anarchist collectives might build and improve without wasting labor, as he argued, "in keeping up the stables, the kennels, and the retinue of the rich" (*The Conquest of Bread,* 24). Although Goldman revered Kropotkin, admiring his gentle and generous nature, as she described in meetings with him in her autobiography, privately she believed he was bookish, isolated from the real world, an isolation that may have explained his confidence in the intrinsic cooperativeness and generosity of human nature. While this did not lead her to Bakunin's rather grim vision of cutthroat competitiveness, Goldman would become quite contemptuous of the "masses," particularly as they failed to rise in defense of Berkman. His attempt on the life of Frick did not lead, as he and she had hoped, to wide-scale protests from the Homestead strikers he was defending. "The mass is really hopeless as far as real progress and freedom is concerned," she wrote later in life to Berkman (*Nowhere at Home,* 49). "The mass unfortunately cannot be depended upon" (ibid., 106).

Such hopes as Berkman and Goldman entertained as they planned the assassination of Frick were derived from a strategy of revolution that came to be known in the 1880s as an *attentat,* or "propaganda by the deed." The path to anarchist revolution had never been certain. Before Kropotkin, the principal anarchist theorists Proudhon and Bakunin had offered dramatically contrasting narratives of social change. Rather than the revolutionary violence Marx predicted, Proudhon foresaw incremental alterations in the political economy as associations of workers, educating the proletariat, took over production, workshop by workshop. The revolutionary Bakunin, on the other hand, envisaged an apocalyptic breakdown of society, a purifying and regenerating baptism by fire out of which, phoenixlike, the voluntary and autonomous network of workers' federations would emerge. Kropotkin assumed that the path to revolution was a natural process, arising out of a clash that obeyed the inexorable laws of social development, although later in life he recoiled from violence and hoped for social progress through peaceful development.

And yet it had been Kropotkin who became identified with the theory of the violent revolutionary act as a tool of anarchist social change. Kropotkin's newspaper *Le Révolté* had given a legitimacy to political terror that Kropotkin himself hesitated to endorse wholly: "Permanent revolt by word of mouth, in writing, by the dagger, the rifle, dynamite. Everything is good for us which goes beyond legality" (Miller, *Selected Writings*, 20). With few recourses for democratic protest, the *attentat* was an attractive strategy in repressive regimes like czarist Russia's, where nihilists had conspired to achieve the assassination of Czar Alexander II and had, indeed, sent seismic convulsions through the political landscape.

On the Lower East Side in New York, the convulsions of the Haymarket murders and, later, the violence against the Homestead steelworkers had inspired talk of striking back. As a memoir writer of the period recalled the young radical immigrants in New York, "the judicial murder of the heroic anarchist leaders in November 1886 was still fresh in their minds and . . . they were full of bitterness. It was amusing to hear these mild-mannered and soft-spoken boys and girls talk glibly about blowing up buildings and killing tyrants. But it was all theory with them" (Hillquit 5). But for young Emma Goldman, enthralled by the call to self-sacrifice the anarchist revolutionary movement inspired in her, theory alone was inadequate. In a fusion of romantic and political passion, Emma Goldman and her young lover Alexander Berkman pledged themselves "to die together if necessary, or to continue to live and work for the ideal for which one of us might have to give his life" (*Living My Life*, 47).

Their early hopes were that the *attentat* would provoke revolutionary uprising, a hope given luminous expression by Haymarket martyr August Spies's death-house prophecy that "Here you will tread upon a spark, but there and there, and behind you and in front of you, and everywhere, flames will blaze up" (Falk 23). Anarchists reasoned that not only would such individual acts of resistance, the *attentats* of Berkman and Czolgosz, for example, illuminate the social misery that compelled the assassin to violence, the acts must also humiliate existing authorities, revealing the limitations of their power by exposing their vulnerability. But even as Kropotkin himself regretted acts of violence, while never failing to sympathize with the conditions that impelled the actor to strike, Goldman too came to despair that any single *attentat* might illuminate the injustices that had nurtured the act. "Acts of violence, except as demonstrations of a sensitive human soul, have proved utterly useless," she wrote to Berkman later, when both were exiled and living with the disappointments of their political hopes (*Nowhere at Home*, 95).

By the time of the publication of her collected essays in 1910, Goldman's confidence in workers' uprisings was deflated. In her essay "Minorities Versus Majorities," she is skeptical of the revolutionary potential of the "masses" and convinced instead of their "inertia, the cravenness, the utter submission of the mass" (*Anarchism and Other Essays*, 71). "The mass," she regretted, "clings to its masters, loves the whip, and is the first to cry Crucify!" (ibid., 77). Change would come, she claimed, citing Ralph Waldo Emerson, as the masses were "schooled" (ibid., 78). Rather than believing in an epiphany of understanding jolting the "masses" into a revolutionary fervor, she placed her faith increasingly in an educated vanguard, the middle-class audiences to whom she lectured.

Goldman recalled, in her autobiography, the force of her conviction that she must continue her political work in English, among America's native born. She was twenty-five years old, nine years in America. Her beloved Sasha was serving

a twenty-two-year term for attempting to kill Frick. Newly released from a year's imprisonment for "inciting to riot," she
found herself taken up by liberal middle-class sympathizers as
a celebrated victim of political repression. Americans, too, she
wrote, were "as capable of idealism and sacrifice as my Russian heroes and heroines . . . From now on I meant to devote myself to propaganda in English among the American people. . . .
Real social changes could be accomplished only by the natives"
(*Living My Life*, 106).

Educating mainstream America in anarchist ideals was uphill
work. Against her was the popular prejudice toward anarchism, fed by the violent acts of Berkman and Czolgosz.
Against her as well was the failure of anarchism to provide a
clear picture of the kind of anarchist society that would replace
capitalism. Nor did the unwillingness of anarchists to embrace
piecemeal reform on the way to a vaguely depicted paradise of
mutual-aid societies sit well with the American working class
struggling for the eight-hour workday. Goldman recounts some
rueful struggling with such "crimes . . . against the workers" in
anarchist theory and resolves to do some "independent thinking"
(ibid., 40).

As she became a more proficient English speaker and addressed audiences beyond the immigrant communities of the
eastern seaboard, Goldman became increasingly a spokesperson for the reforms she believed were necessary to an emancipated, fully realized humanity. At the same time she embedded
the ideals of European anarchism in the rich individualist tradition of America's native soil—the revolutionary pamphlets of the
insurrectionist patriot Tom Paine, the antipathy to the state and
its liberty-crushing laws of the transcendentalist essayist Emerson, and, above all, the defiant individualism of Henry David
Thoreau, whom Goldman called "the greatest American anarchist" (*Anarchism and Other Essays*, 56).

Thoreau's essay *Walden*, recounting his two years of living
simply and modestly in a natural setting, modeled the anarchist ideal of giving up unnecessary material possessions and
dwelling in harmony with natural laws. Thoreau's 1849 essay
"On the Duty of Civil Disobedience" argued for the primacy of

individual conscience over the tyranny of authority, a primacy which Emma Goldman understood as anarchist and revolutionary. She applauded Thoreau's great admiration for John Brown, who led the insurrection of slaves at Harpers Ferry (*Living My Life*, 330).

Goldman was drawn to notions of the individual capable of triumph in heroic combat with crushing authority. During her residence in 1895 in Vienna, where she studied nursing and midwifery, Goldman discovered the work of Friedrich Nietzsche, a philosopher whom she described as hurling his anathemas against old values. Earlier, she admired the German philosopher Max Stirner's notion of the paramount drive of individuals to seek their own self-interest, an "egoism" that positioned the fully free individuals in a permanent stance of resistance to that which threatens to thwart their will. Out of this conviction that the individual will is impelled by profound forces to assert its own needs, Emma Goldman explained the psychological conditions that result in political violence and the baleful effects of sexual repression. Convinced that a social revolution must be preceded by the education of the masses, Goldman ultimately laid the failure of the Russian revolution and progressive European and American political movements on the failure of the will of the masses to insist upon their own interests (*Nowhere at Home*, 82).

3. NO "DENIAL OF LIFE AND JOY"—
SEXUAL LIBERATION AND
AESTHETIC PASSION

As Emma Goldman folded the American individualist tradition into European anarchism, she also expanded the notion of the essential liberty of the autonomous individual—an anarchist axiom—to include the fundamental rights of sexual expression. Although anarchists urged equality between the sexes in their resistance to all forms of authoritarianism, in practice they were reluctant to spend their political capital advocating sexual freedom. When Emma Goldman became a spokesperson for birth control reform, sex education, and the free-love movement, ideas which she found in proselytizers like the American free-love advocate Moses Harman, not all anarchists were willing to share such platforms with her. At the international meeting in Paris in 1900 she was rebuffed by anarchists who would not allow her to add sexual freedom to their political agenda (*Living My Life*, 163).

To be sure, she had sensed a breach earlier between her understanding of her own desires and what she came to recognize as puritanism among her revolutionary comrades, a sexual puritanism that went hand in hand with a more general ascetic disdain for pleasure. Her own beloved Sasha, for example, had responded angrily to the extravagance of her taste for flowers. Another comrade reproached her for the vivacity of her dancing at a party following a political meeting, to which the young Goldman responded angrily: "I did not believe that a Cause which stood for a beautiful ideal, for anarchism, for release and freedom from conventions and prejudice, should demand the denial of life and joy. I insisted that our Cause could not expect me to become a nun and that the movement should not be turned into a cloister" (ibid., 42).

Challenged at such moments, Emma Goldman defended impulses in her own nature that seemed at once profound and immutable, but she was nonetheless troubled. Her response to aesthetic and physical pleasure seemed to yoke her to her own personal desires, while the more self-denying Sasha burned with an altruistic and purifying zeal. Comparing herself to her friend, Goldman wrote in her autobiography, "I was woven of many skeins, conflicting in shade and texture. To the end of my days, I should be torn between the yearning for a personal life and the need of giving all to my ideal" (ibid., 104).

In 1885 in Vienna, a city she found "fascinating," "lighthearted," "gorgeous" (ibid., 113), she attended a series of lectures given by the young neurologist Sigmund Freud. Only the year before, Freud had published *Studies in Hysteria*, beginning his inquiry into the composition of the unconscious mind that established the modern school of psychoanalysis. As Freud lectured, Goldman described a "feeling of being led out of a dark cellar into broad daylight. For the first time," she continued in her autobiography, "I grasped the full significance of sex repression and its effect on human thought and action. He helped me to understand myself, my own needs" (ibid., 114). Later readings of the European sexologists Havelock Ellis, Richard Krafft-Ebing, and Edward Carpenter, whose works she encountered during travels in Europe in 1895, added to her understanding of the baleful effects of sexual repression. Years after first hearing Freud lecture, Goldman traveled up from New York to Worcester, Massachusetts, a city where she had once sold ice cream with Alexander Berkman, to hear the Viennese psychoanalyst deliver his American lectures at Clark University. In her autobiography, the reconstruction of her childhood memories bears the imprint of Freud's teaching. She renders early childhood memory as idyllic and erotic scenes. She recalls feeling a guilty repression of sexual desire after her mother's admonitions, and a violent first sexual encounter leaves her feeling both desire and revulsion. Just as candidly, she narrates her sexual response to adult love affairs. The expression of sexuality was important to her as a liberation of consciousness, a value in its own right, but also one that would nurture both political and aesthetic self-realization.

As she learned to distinguish repression in her personal history, Goldman no longer allowed herself to be chastened by what she regarded as the sexual puritanism of her comrades, a puritanism that she believed destroyed natural and healthy impulses. Years after hearing Freud lecture, in an illuminating encounter with Kropotkin—whose belief in the anarchist ideal of mutual assistance rose out of a conviction that cooperation was a Darwinian trait hewn for survival—Goldman challenged his dismissal of the free-love interests of some American anarchists. When Kropotkin complained that an anarchist publication shouldn't "waste so much space discussing sex," Goldman quarreled with him energetically, saying, "All right, dear comrade, when I have reached your age, the sex question may no longer be of importance to me. But it is now" (*Living My Life*, 152).

Goldman believed that sexuality, if unfettered by convention, prejudice, and repressive state institutions, was an agency that could produce the social harmony that Kropotkin argued was an adaptive strategy for human survival. "Love," she wrote, "should be the impetus for the harmonious blending of two beings" (*Traffic in Women*, 149). "If the world is ever to give birth to true companionship and oneness . . . love will be the parent" (ibid., 213). Anarchism, her "beautiful ideal" of autonomous individuals living in social networks of mutual respect, rested on a reading of human nature in which Goldman, inspired by Freud, considered sexual desire an ameliorative force. "Every stimulus which quickens the imagination and raises the spirits is as necessary to life as air. It invigorates the body and deepens our vision of human fellowship" (ibid., 157).

But until the unnatural constraints imposed on sexual desire by government, religion, and traditional conventions were lifted, this more profound vision of human fellowship would not be realized. Becoming a spokesperson for reforms in private life, Goldman recommended the radical reorganization of domestic life that became foundational in later feminist platforms in the 1960s and 1970s that assigned childcare to both parents, not simply the woman. While Kropotkin had argued that woman's apparent inferiority could be remedied by making her man's intellectual equal, Goldman insisted she must become as free as men sexually as well, unhampered by the Victorian convention of celibacy before marriage. "Can there be anything more outrageous," she asks, "than the idea that a healthy, grown woman, full of life and passion, must deny nature's demand, must subdue her most intense craving, undermine her health and break her spirit, must stunt her vision, abstain from the depth and glory of sex experience until a 'good' man comes along to take her unto himself as a wife" (*Anarchism and Other Essays*, 231).

While Freud's lectures had provided the illuminating moment when she understood the harmful effects of sexual repression, her work on the Lower East Side taught her the necessity of birth control. Marriage itself she understood, as did all anarchists, Marxists, and nineteenth-century free-love advocates, as an "economic arrangement," an "insurance pact" for women, although for many a vastly unsatisfactory one. Marriage, "that poor little State- and Church-begotten weed," had little to do with love, but alas much to do with the misery of woman's condition in poverty and the ill health of so many of her children (ibid., 236).

Because Goldman had herself refused an operation that would have permitted her to bear a child, she entered into love affairs with a freedom from fear of unwanted pregnancies that most women did not enjoy. As a nurse and midwife practicing in the tenements of the Lower East Side, she recalled the misery of the squalid rooms in which a woman labored, often with "sickly and ill-nourished," "ill-born, ill-kept, and unwashed" children trailing at her feet as she helped "another poor creature into the world" (*Living My Life*, 121). One progressive physician's opinion that as woman used her brains more, "her procreative organs will function less," did not ease the anguish of ceaseless childbirth. "I saw," Goldman wrote, "that it was mockery to expect them to wait until the social revolution arrives in order to right injustice" (ibid., 127).

Goldman's nursing work was not confined to the desperately poor living in Lower East Side tenements. As her professional work grew, she addressed physical complaints of unmarried middle-class women as well, many of whom were self-supporting and in principle freed from the economic dependency of conventional marriage. From these women and what she understood as their enforced celibacy, Goldman derived what she called the "tragedy of women's emancipation," a tragedy she believed began in their stunted and repressed sexual lives. Emancipation for women, as she imagined such liberation, would follow not access to the ballot box but resistance to all forms of prejudice, convention, and authority that thwarted individual liberty.

As an anarchist Goldman was not an advocate of woman suffrage. She considered the ballot a dubious privilege, its having led to no discernible improvement in the lives of women or workers in the few states where voting was extended to women. She called universal suffrage "our modern fetish" (*Anarchism and Other Essays*, 195), "an evil that enslaves people," "the new idol" (ibid., 197), and was frankly contemptuous of the American woman's suffrage movement, which she called "a parlor affair absolutely detached from the needs of the people." In fact, debased by dependency, corrupted by puritanism into another Mrs. Grundy, the American woman, Goldman believed, was a "danger to liberty wherever she has political power" (ibid., 204): disenfranchising prostitutes in Idaho (ibid., 203), an enemy of free speech in a prudish support of the Comstock laws, and a supporter of Prohibition "which sanctions the spread of drunkenness among men and women of the rich class and yet keeps vigilant watch on the only place left to the poor man" (ibid., 204).

Goldman was impressed with the work of only a "handful of women" in the women's rights movement, a few lone individuals who issued a manifesto called the Declaration of Sentiments at a Conference in Seneca Falls, New York, in 1848, a manifesto that had opened higher education and professional life to women. Goldman accepted that the "main evil today is an economic one," but she added that the "solution of that evil can be brought about only through the consideration of every phase of life—individual, as well as collective; the internal, as well as the external phases" (ibid., 50). It is this "individual" and "internal" liberation that she demands, drawn from her readings of Nietzsche and Stirner, claiming "if society is ever to become free, it will be so through liberated individuals" (ibid., 44). Of woman's liberation she writes:

> Her development, her freedom, her independence, must come from and through herself. First, by asserting herself as a personality, and not as a sex commodity. Second, by refusing the right to anyone over her body; by refusing to bear children, unless she wants them; by refusing to be a servant to God, the State, society, the husband, the family, etc., by making her life simpler, but deeper and richer. (*Anarchism and Other Essays*, 211)

With sexuality no longer confined to a private realm but instead shaped and constrained by social conventions and institutions, Goldman argued that sexual liberation must ultimately

challenge and transform church and state, the very edifices that
protect sexual repression (Haaland 136). As the *attentats* of
bullet and bomb might injure and humiliate authorities, so too
individual acts of flouting sexual conventions might undermine
state institutions. Goldman insists vehemently that anarchism
engages "every phase" (*Anarchism and Other Essays*, xiii), the
"internal" as well as the "external," and that the liberation of
sexual repression could be a "force hitherto unknown in the
world" (ibid., 211).

4. "EVERYBODY'S RIGHT TO BEAUTIFUL, RADIANT THINGS"—AESTHETICISM AND MODERN DRAMA

During the early years of the twentieth century, Emma Goldman became a popular lecturer, welcomed to venues of middle-
class respectability like the Manhattan Liberal Club and the
Brooklyn Philosophical Society, where she spoke to audiences
considerably different from the crowds of workers who hur-
rahed her impromptu speeches from carts in Union Square or
crowded into the back rooms of Lower East Side cafés. To be
sure, some of her radical political comrades were suspicious
of her willingness to carry her message into the more respectable venues of the liberal middle class. Communist leader
Elizabeth Gurley Flynn, for example, reflecting on this period,
wrote that "As long as Emma Goldman spoke to poor people
in the small halls with sawdust on the floor there was an agi-
tational vibrance in her speeches," a vibrancy Flynn found
missing when Goldman became "the idol of middle-class liberals" (50).

Goldman intended, however, to carry her message—anarchism,
birth control, free love, free speech—into the American mainstream. She had gone through a period of anguish and depression
following the assassination of President McKinley in 1901.
When she was falsely accused of assisting the assassin Czolgosz, Goldman was hunted down, bloodied by police, and

briefly jailed. Alone among her anarchist comrades she sympathized with the young anarchist Czolgosz, whom she had briefly met; and she was stunned when Berkman wrote to her from prison that Czolgosz's act had been ill conceived, directed mistakenly against a political foe rather than an economic one, an *attentat* therefore, without any social importance. Years later Goldman and Berkman, reliving their American activism while in exile in Europe, were still quarreling over Berkman's response to Czolgosz, whom Goldman regarded as a well-intentioned unfortunate (*Nowhere at Home*, 95). Goldman defended the "Buffalo tragedy" in her essay "The Psychology of Political Violence," again disavowing the political effectiveness of violence but ascribing the greater violence to those conditions that led such tortured young men as Czolgosz to act. "Poor Leon Czolgosz," she wrote, ". . . your crime consisted of too sensitive a social consciousness. Unlike your idealless and brainless American brothers, your ideals soared above the belly and the bank account" (*Anarchism and Other Essays*, 90). As for Alexander Berkman, it was "the brutal slaughter of the eleven steel workers" that impelled him to take up arms against Frick (ibid., 93).

She was jolted from what she called "spiritual death" after the execution of Czolgosz (*Living My Life*, 206) by events in Russia, where the czar was violently repressing insurgents. Awakened out of her depressive lethargy by a sense that in her motherland others were struggling against tyranny, she resolved that she would use her "greater access to the American mind," her steadily growing confidence as an English speaker, to "plead the heroic cause of revolutionary Russia." She had befriended politically engaged American reformers such as the settlement worker Lillian Wald and the patrician reformer Lucy Stone Blackwell. At the same time new Progressive era sentiment was more responsive to political dissent, directing its fire against urban political corruption and the appalling conditions among the poor, crowded into the cities' tenement slums. When the suffering of the Russian revolutionaries promoted some sympathy for socialists among middle-class liberals, Goldman was able to arrange lectures in New York for the "grandmother" of the Russian revolution, Catherine Breshkovskaya. The prominent Republican William Dudley Foulke became president of the newly reorganized Society of the Friends of Russian Freedom.

Goldman was meeting rich and influential people as well through her sponsorship of a progressive Russian theater group whose American tour she had arranged. Disguised as a Russian gentlewoman in reduced circumstances, she played her part in many tea parties in Chicago, where none of the fashionable theater patrons understood they were entertaining the notorious anarchist. Not all of Goldman's friends were pleased by her new prominence. Like Elizabeth Gurley Flynn, some of her comrades believed she was too easily accommodating the middle class. When Berkman was at last released from prison in 1906 and reunited with Goldman, he discovered the girl he remembered changed in uncongenial ways: "Her mind has matured, but her wider interests antagonize my old revolutionary traditions. . . . Her friends and admirers crowd her home and turn it into a sort of salon. They talk art and literature . . . even she has been infected by the air of intellectual aloofness" (493). Indeed the familiar Lower East Side neighborhood of immigrant kaffeeklatsches in backroom saloons was vanishing. But Goldman might have quarreled with him that these literary and artistic interests were new. Aesthetic passion was as real to her as sexual response, and she traced the provenance of her interests again to early childhood.

In a revealing anecdote Goldman offers in her autobiography (39), she describes a visit to the opera with anarchist Johann Most, in the early days of her romantic infatuation with him. Moved by the music, Goldman recalls her earlier encounter with opera as a child, so impressing Most with the passionate delivery of her memory that Most prophesies that she will replace him one day as a great public speaker (40). Listening to the young Emma Goldman, Most had heard a compelling force of conviction in her voice, one that would infuse her oratory with passion in the service of anarchism. Most, as Goldman recalls him, seems to have understood that the wellsprings of her political idealism nurtured as well a love of beauty. To the comrade who reproached her for spirited dancing at a party after a political meeting, Goldman responded: "I want freedom, the right to self-expression, everybody's right to beautiful, radiant things" (ibid., 42). For Goldman the right to beauty was as important as the right to freedom itself. Just as physical passion was a force of self-expression, so too was aesthetic passion. "I cannot imagine a free society without beauty," she wrote in exile to a friend, "for of what use liberty, if not to strive for beauty?" (*Nowhere at Home,* 99). Just as sexuality provided the adhesion that fixed individuals in social relations with one another, so too Goldman believed that the aesthetic response could be the conduit by which the "beautiful ideal" of anarchist values passed from the consciousness of one liberated individual into the minds of the members of a community.

In her essay "The Modern Drama," Goldman denies that propagandistic literature can adequately represent "modern, conscious social unrest" (*Anarchism and Other Essays,* 241) and turns to the theater for the "leaven of radical thought and the disseminator of new values" (ibid., 242). The middle class might be able to insulate itself against the sufferings of the poor and against the hypocrisies and stultifying repressive force of its own prejudice and conventions; but the stage and its living representation of social misery bring home this painful reality even to self-satisfied audiences. For example, Goldman argues, when George Bernard Shaw's character Undershaft declares that "the worst of crimes is poverty" and that "all the other crimes are virtues beside it," his play is far more effective as political instruction than all of Shaw's socialist tracts (ibid., 261). Other modern playwrights achieve similar force. Ibsen, "the supreme hater of all social shams," wars against all false idols, paving the way for woman's emancipation in *A Doll's House,* performing "the last funeral rites over a decaying and dying social system" (ibid., 257) in *An Enemy of the People,* with "the regenerated individual, the bold and daring rebel" rising out of its ashes.

Lecturing on the social significance of modern drama, Emma Goldman had fixed yet another string to her bow. The comprehensiveness of her reform vision was enthralling. One young woman who became a social reform worker wrote, "Can you imagine the effect she had on an East Side girl of seventeen who knew nothing of the world of culture? She introduced me to Strindberg, Shaw, and Ibsen. I used to travel clear across town to hear her lecture Sunday nights on literature, birth control, and women" (*Anarchism and Other Essays*, vii). While all of her interests cohered in the primary value she placed on individual freedom, she insisted that such freedom was in essence aesthetic, political, and sexual, a mixed brew all her own.

5. MOTHER EARTH— "THE DEAREST CHILD"

While she was establishing a national reputation on the lecture circuit, Emma Goldman fulfilled a long-standing ambition and founded her own journal. Like herself, *Mother Earth* was "woven of many skeins," an anarchist journal of impressive range and breadth that, with "Yiddish perseverance and boundless enthusiasm" (*Living My Life*, 312), she brought before the public in 1905. With revenues from her lecture tours, where she was finding a sympathetic audience willing to hear her out now that the McKinley assassination taint was fading, Goldman was able to supply the funding that kept the always financially precarious journal in print for more than a decade. Publishing *Mother Earth* represented a milestone for her. Bringing this dream for "an independent radical spokesman in the United States" (ibid., 312) to fruition signaled a personal victory over the depressive inactivity that followed the McKinley assassination. At the same time, the journal provided a means of constructing an anarchist platform that combined Goldman's interest in social and cultural issues. Through *Mother Earth* and the community of activists it gathered, Goldman became the spokesperson for her kind of American anarchism, one that kept alive the theoretical insights of the European anarchists, but was free of a single-minded focus on propaganda for working-class consciousness and insurrection that had been the earlier focus of the immigrant communities.

As she so often had reason to observe, her kind of anarchism was as interested in the "internal" as well as the "external," in psychological well-being as well as economic improvement. She intended to keep *Mother Earth* "free from party politics," "to voice without fear every unpopular progressive cause, and to aim for unity between revolutionary effort and artistic expression" (ibid., 312).

No surprise, then, that when he emerged from fourteen years in prison, Alexander Berkman noticed with unease that Goldman had moved beyond the single-minded focus of the German-, Russian-, and Yiddish-speaking immigrants of the East Coast. Goldman was addressing the liberal audiences of native-born reform-minded professionals—doctors, lawyers, teachers, journalists, many of them affluent and aristocratic patrons, now including communities on both coasts and in the midlands. These were the liberal intelligentsia of the professional middle class whom Goldman now considered in the vanguard of social change. She had learned the influence wealthy liberals could wield, an influence that helped keep alive the American anarchism she preached. A well-placed complaint in the ears of socially prominent liberals in any far-flung city could halt the kind of repressive police injunction against the "notorious" Emma Goldman's speaking that might spoil the best-planned lecture tour. These tours were where audiences filled the coffers that fed *Mother Earth* not only by paying the price of admission but also by buying up the pamphlets of anarchist essays Goldman brought with her. Goldman was educating the middle class.

Mother Earth went to press with a "nest egg" of $250 from the progressive Russian theater troupe Goldman had sponsored in America (*Living My Life*, 312). Subtitled "a monthly magazine devoted to social science and literature," the magazine's cover offered a picture of the backs of a fanciful Adam and Eve, standing under the tree of knowledge. With their chains cast off behind them, they greeted a rising sun on the distant horizon, their feet on the open road that led to the new dawn. The mission statement of the opening issue extended the embrace of anarchism to all free thinkers, libertarians, and socially conscious aesthetes: "*Mother Earth*," announced the first issue, "will endeavor to attract and appeal to all those who oppose encroachment on public and individual life. It will appeal to those who strive for something higher, weary of the commonplace . . . to those who long for the tender shade of a new dawn for humanity free from the dread of want, the dread of starvation in the face of mountains of riches (*Mother Earth,* Mar. 1906, 4).

The journal, Goldman's "dearest child," as she often referred to it, also provided its peripatetic publisher with a "family," including, among others, fellow publisher and radical anarchist journalist Max Baginski; Harry Kelly, a printer with a union background; American anarchist Leonard Abbott; Czech anarchist Hippolyte Havel; the anarchist theorist Voltairine de Cleyre; and, of course, Alexander Berkman, whose painful reentry to life outside prison began with writing for *Mother Earth*. With some of these comrades, she experimented in collective living arrangements, although the ideal of honoring individual wills and mutual needs proved impracticable. Other problems in the extended family of anarchists and artists were perhaps also inevitable. The loss of a primary focus on economic materialism and the defense of middle-class liberals as an embryonic vanguard made Goldman seem less revolutionary than other anarchists liked. At the same time her literary taste, formed by nineteenth-century realism in her youth, was too conservative for many new modern writers, whose experiments in atonality, abstraction, and anomie were unsatisfying to her. Goldman published, among others, the nineteenth-century poetry of Samuel Butler, Matthew Arnold, Walt Whitman, Rudyard Kipling, James Russell Lowell, and Ralph Waldo Emerson. She gave space to poems by Anna Louise Strong and to Alice Stone Blackwell's translations of Maxim Gorky's poetry. Believing that literature claimed its importance as it exposed social problems, she chastised the "art for art's sake" escapism of the New York literati. As *Mother Earth* bequeathed the voice of literary experimentalism to other journals, Max Eastman's *The Masses* published the leftist literary avant-garde in America.

These criticisms aside, *Mother Earth* was a brave, dissident voice, preaching political and social change, while those who lectured to sustain its publication risked imprisonment for violation of the Comstock laws or, as anarchists, the violence of police raids, brutal arrests, and the threat of deportation. The journal itself was under constant surveillance. On one occasion when Goldman published a lecture on the importance of sexual education for women, disguised decorously with references to the "function of the most important part of her life," the New York postmaster impounded issues and held up delivery for days.

As the foremost anarchist publication in the English language in America, the journal hosted an ongoing forum in which such theorists as Goldman, Berkman, de Cleyre, Baginski, Coryell, and Kelly defined anarchism and anarchist communism, criticized statist socialism, and explained anarchism's position on "defensive violence"; it offered regular excerpts from major libertarian writings, from the anarchist Kropotkin to the philosopher Nietzsche and the writer Oscar Wilde. Works that might otherwise have reached far fewer readers, like the educator and anarchist Francisco Guardia Ferrer's journal *The Modern School,* were excerpted. In 1910 *Mother Earth* published Goldman's own collected essays. Two years later, when no other publisher for Alexander Berkman's finely hewn *Prison Memoirs of an Anarchist* could be found, the Mother Earth publishing company found the money.

The magazine published commentaries on pressing current issues such as free speech, child labor, education, white slave traffic, Zionism, and legal defense for radicals under indictment. It was alone in exposing the brutality of America's jails, with firsthand accounts by those who had been there. The magazine flourished also as a form of anarchist bulletin board with reports of state trials of anarchists from all over the world, as well as reports of international and national anarchist meetings, notes coming in from Spain, Portugal, Italy, Germany, Switzerland, Austria, England, Russia, Argentina, China, and Japan.

While she traveled, Goldman remained in continual contact with the magazine's home office, posting accounts of her lectures at various sites across America; in many of these reports her inimitable voice gave *Mother Earth* the feeling of a family letter. From St. Louis, she complained about some comrade's regrettable indifference to "cleanliness and beauty," ending "I cannot even for her sake [raising funds for *Mother Earth*] speak in dingy little halls, dark and gloomy, with the dust and smoke making it impossible to breathe" (*Mother Earth*, May 1907, 132).

Occasionally family quarrels that broke out on its pages revealed the fault lines of more serious divisions. One quarrel surfaced when Ben Reitman, Goldman's road manager and lover, reported a London meeting with Peter Kropotkin, who worried aloud that the American anarchists were becoming too "utilitarian," too "respectable" (ibid., Oct. 1910, 252). Two months later Voltairine de Cleyre complained in the same pages that she had been booked into "respectable halls" during her lecture tour to address the professional middle class, halls whose rentals required a ticket of admission that few working people could afford. De Cleyre, who chose a life of spartan simplicity, insisted that anarchists take their message to the working class and implied that she might cheerfully breathe the "dust and smoke" that offended Goldman in service of that greater good (ibid., Dec. 1910, 323).

In response to de Cleyre, Goldman defended the "respectable halls" she had come to know, and with them defended the middle-class liberals as a vanguard. "The pioneers of every new thought rarely come from the ranks of the workers," she wrote in a letter to *Mother Earth*, suggesting that the economic exigencies of their daily lives made them less likely to grasp theoretical truths. "Besides," she added, in an ironic reference to the Marxist call to workers' revolution, "it is an undisputed fact that those who have but their chains to lose cling tenaciously to them. The men and women who first take up the banner of a new liberating idea generally emanate from the so called respectable classes" (ibid., 326).

Meanwhile, Emma Goldman and her comrades watched with mounting alarm as the drumroll of militarism in the United States intensified following the outbreak of World War I in Europe. In December 1915 *Mother Earth* denounced this swelling of patriotic fervor that was calling for intervention in Europe, and Goldman lectured widely across the country on "Prepared-ness to the Road to Universal Slaughter." As Wilson's govern-ment inched closer to war, calling it "the war to end all wars" and "the war to make the world safe for democracy," *Mother Earth* called on the American working class to resist: "Workers alone can avert the impending war; in fact all wars; if they will refuse to be a party to them" (ibid., Mar. 1917, 10). Goldman told her audiences that the capitalist war was fought to enrich "the privileged few and help them to subdue, to enslave and crush labor" (Morton, 84).

In spite of the war propaganda maintained by a cooperative mainstream press, men did not immediately volunteer to join the hostilities. With war declared and a million-man army sought, only 73,000 men responded in the first six weeks, a lack of enthusiasm that made the antiwar efforts of the small dissident minority seem even more threatening. While Congress was debating Selective Service legislation, Goldman and Berk-man organized a No Conscription League with branches in many American cities, the meetings often scenes of near-violent clashes with soldiers and sailors charging the platforms. When the Selective Service Act was passed in June 1917, requiring all men between the ages of twenty and thirty to register for the draft, *Mother Earth* was published with black borders, and men crowded the journal's office in New York City to ask for advice. At such times the warnings of J. Edgar Hoover, the Justice De-partment's new director of a radical-surveillance branch, that Emma Goldman was "the most dangerous woman in America" may have seemed prescient.

The Espionage Act of June 1917 made it illegal to encourage disloyalty to the military or to obstruct the draft, and issues of *Mother Earth* were impounded by the postal authorities. Along with other radical publications like Max Eastman's *The Masses* and Berkman's own publication the *Blast,* published out of San Francisco, *Mother Earth* ceased publishing. Its last issue of Au-gust 1917 never reached subscribers. The cessation of publica-tion was painful for Goldman, who wrote, "A struggle of over a decade, exhausting tours for its supports, much worry and grief . . . and now with one blow its life has been snuffed out"

(*Living My Life*, 642). A more modest publication, the *Mother Earth Bulletin*, kept some avenues of communication open within the radical community from October 1917 to May 1918, when it too was banned from the mail. In these pages the anarchist Goldman defended the Russian Marxist Bolshevik October Revolution, which swept Alexander Kerensky's provisional government from power in 1917. Although apprehensive that in Soviet Russia "the same monster is being set up" and that "in the end it will be the same delusion," she urged anarchists to rally to defend the infant revolutionary government from being attacked by "capitalistic and imperialistic bloodhounds" (Wexler, *Emma Goldman in Exile*, 261).

In 1918, Congress passed the Sedition Act, prohibiting "disloyal, scurrilous and abusive language about the government." Some nine hundred people would be imprisoned for violation of the congressional acts passed to quell dissent during wartime, among them the progressive reformer and socialist Eugene Debs, who was not released until 1921. Among the first to be arrested were Emma Goldman and Alexander Berkman, who were imprisoned for conspiracy to encourage others to avoid the draft.

If anarchist agitators were not enough, established authority had additional reason to be fearful in those years. First the Bolshevik Revolution in Russia raised alarm, followed by labor unrest that spread across America with the end of the war. In 1919, a general strike was declared in Seattle that brought the city to a halt. Across the country, 250,000 AFL workers joined 100,000 union workers striking the steel industry in western Pennsylvania, where men worked exhausting twelve-hour days, six days a week, in brutal heat. The following year 120,000 textile workers struck in New England and New Jersey. In Boston, the police went out on strike. Class antagonism and civil unrest never seemed so high, with militant labor organizations like the Industrial Workers of the World (IWW) attracting sympathy and followers from among socialists, anarchists, and radical trade unionists all over the United States.

In the summer of 1919, a bomb exploded in Washington outside the home of Attorney General A. Mitchell Palmer, an act which fueled a new aggressive stage in government reprisal. Palmer began his notorious series of "raids" on immigrants who were not American citizens, enabled by a new federal law that permitted the deportation of foreign-born dissidents described as aliens. On December 21, 1919, Palmer's men arrested Emma Goldman and Alexander Berkman, only recently released from a two-year prison sentence for their antiwar work. Goldman and Berkman were summarily deported along with 249 other "aliens," crowded onto the ship the *Buford* for transport ultimately to the new Soviet Union, where the Bolsheviki were in the early days of making a proletarian revolution.

6. DISILLUSIONMENT IN RUSSIA

Goldman gives a riveting account of her residence in Russia, a story of a passage from hopeful expectation to profound disillusionment. In her two years' residency, amply and dramatically narrated in *Living My Life,* Goldman traveled widely in Soviet cities and the countryside. She met defenders and critics of the Bolshevik revolution among government officials, revolutionists, artists, and writers, while touring factories, health facilities, schools, and prisons. Two years after their arrival, Goldman and Berkman left Russia, traveling without visas to an anarchist conference in Germany, resolved to tell the world they had found only misery and repression, not the social and economic revolution they had anticipated.

Goldman may have felt a special imperative to make her disclosure. Her 1917 pamphlet published by *Mother Earth* supporting the young Bolshevik revolution and urging anarchists to do likewise may have encouraged many anarchists to travel to join the revolution, a decision some paid for with arrest and execution. From prison in America, she had written an impassioned letter to her beloved "Babushka," the Russian anarchist Catherine Breshkovskaya, asking her to recant her recent repudiation of the Bolsheviks. "They are flesh of our flesh, blood of our blood," Goldman wrote (Wexler, *Emma Goldman in Exile,* 260). Although in the early days after the October Revolution,

Lenin had welcomed the participation of anarchists, some even joining the government, the anarchists became the target of repression by the Cheka, the state police, as they criticized the growing state power of the Bolsheviks.

In Berlin in July 1922, needing money, and eager to share her story with the mainstream American liberals whom she had so long cultivated, Goldman told her story first to the New York *World,* which published her reflections on her two-year residency as a series of seven articles from late March to early April. Goldman's chronicle of corruption, special privileges, widespread mismanagement, hunger, and police terror provoked outcries of disbelief from some on the left in America. Rose Pastor Stokes, with whom Goldman had worked in the birth control movement, suggested she be hanged "at least in effigy" (Morton 121).

In response to a suggestion from an American publisher that she turn the articles into a book, Goldman accepted an advance from Doubleday and Page, who, to her dismay, published her manuscript "My Two Years in Russia" with the altered and more sensational title *My Disillusionment in Russia.* Goldman felt the new title was misleading, as her disillusion had been with the Bolsheviks, not with the Russian revolution. Even more disturbing, the last twelve chapters of the book had become detached from the manuscript in transmission, and the work went to press without them or the afterword, in which Goldman offered an analysis of the failure of the Soviet state. A second volume containing the missing material was published in 1924, but Goldman could not escape the regret that she had been misrepresented to the American reading public.

In fact, the book with its preface and afterword serves as a concise and informative anarchist response to the events of the Russian revolution. Her witness to the historic experiment taking place in Russia is prescient in its unforgiving repudiation of political repression. Of her earlier support for Bolshevism, Goldman wrote, "For 30 years I fought the Marxian theory as a cold, mechanistic, enslaving formula. . . . But the Allied attack upon them made them the symbol of the Russian Revolution, and brought me to their defence" (*Disillusionment in Russia,* x).

She accused the Bolsheviks of betraying the Russian revolution, replacing one state power with another.

Goldman offers Kropotkin's distinction between the Russian revolution, which she wrote was inspired by "libertarian principles," and the Bolshevik ascendancy, which ruled by "coercion" (ibid., 157). "The *actual* Russian Revolution," she wrote, "took place in the summer months of 1917. During that period the peasants possessed themselves of the land, the workers of the factories, thus demonstrating that they knew well the meaning of social revolution" (ibid., ix). Indeed, these workers "were virtually in control of the economic life of Russia" (ibid., xvii). "But after the high tide of revolutionary enthusiasm had carried them into power, the Bolsheviki discarded their false plumes" (ibid., ix), broke up the "shop committees" that had formed under direct worker control in the factories, and crushed them "under the iron yoke of the Bolshevik state" (ibid., xvii).

She had not, she wrote, expected to see individual liberty immediately extended. "I should have been content if the Russian workers and peasants as a whole had derived social betterment as a result of the Bolshevik regime" (ibid., xvi). Instead, fuel lay untapped sixty-five miles from St. Petersburg while the city workers froze; farm implements lay stacked in warehouses of Kharkov, waiting for orders from Moscow for their distribution, while peasants in the Ukraine were unable to cultivate their land (*My Further Disillusionment,* 162). All this mismanagement, she believed, might have been rectified if independent units of workers had been free to establish networks of mutual aid. "The industrial power of the masses," she wrote, "expressed through their libertarian associations—Anarcho-syndicalism—is alone able to organize successfully the economic life" (ibid., 163). Meanwhile, claiming the need to defend itself, the Bolshevik state strengthened its police arm and violently suppressed dissent.

The Russian revolution, the true libertarian revolution, failed, she wrote, because the Russian people, so long repressed by the czar, were inexperienced "in the political game and [had] a naïve faith in the miraculous power of the party that talked the loudest and made the most promises" (ibid., 159). Russian anarchists who might have led the masses to a consciousness of their own political and economic power had been themselves victims of suppression and were "too few," and too engaged in "limited group activities of individualistic endeavour" (ibid., 159).

The field had been left to Lenin, whom Goldman met personally in Russia and whom she assessed: "he was a shrewd politician who knew exactly what he was about and . . . would stop at nothing to achieve his ends" (ibid., 151). There were, she wrote, "an all-powerful, centralized Government with State Capitalism as its economic expression," with the transfer of wealth from workers to the new Soviet bureaucracy, an elite that maintained itself with privileges never imagined in "true communism" (ibid., 153).

Finally Goldman unequivocally repudiated the justification of human misery as a means to an end. While violence attends revolution, "if it is to result only in a change of dictatorship . . . then it is hardly worth while. It is surely not worth all the struggle and sacrifice, the stupendous loss in human life and cultural values that result from every revolution" (ibid., 170). She had witnessed true revolutionary values, "the sense of justice and equality, the love of liberty and of human brotherhood," dismissed as "weak sentimentalizing" or "bourgeois superstition," the sanctity of life itself disregarded as "unrevolutionary."

The mainstream press in the United States received the work with predictable favor, but again some former comrades were vituperative. The IWW's "Big Bill" Haywood who escaped imprisonment in America by fleeing to Russia and Communist William Foster suggested she was in the pay of the U.S. government (Morton 123). A reviewer for *The Nation* wrote that Goldman's responses to Russia were not to be trusted, rising out of her "deep-seated antagonism" for Marxism. "Violent inner conflicts are not the soil out of which sprout unbiased opinion," the reviewer wrote (18 Feb. 1925, 189–90). *The Nation* wryly suggested Goldman was being disingenuous in traveling to Russia, as if anticipating the Promised Land of "a cooperative decentralized Anarchist commonwealth" (ibid., 189). "They are

Marxists," reminded *The Nation,* "at the opposite pole from Anarchists." Goldman anticipated the criticism: "Just because I am a revolutionist," she wrote in her preface, "I refuse to side with the master class, which in Russia is called the Communist Party" (*My Further Disillusionment,* xix).

7. *LIVING MY LIFE* AND AFTER

When the reviews of her autobiography came out in 1931, the praise from the mainstream press may have made Emma Goldman feel somewhat uncomfortable. Used to being caricatured as demonic, bomb-throwing, and foreign, Goldman found herself the author of "one of the finest autobiographies of its kind," according to the reviewer in *The New York Times,* although at the same time the review suggested that the kind referred to was memoirs of ages so safely bygone that their authors may be considered to have already been embalmed (R. L. Duffus, 10/25/31). Reviewers from the left-wing press were less generous. Goldman had written frankly and lengthily about her lovers, some romances fleeting and others long-standing, and the candor disturbed some of her friends, who wondered why they needed to be subjected to such intimate confessions. Goldman's friend Mollie Steimer, also unhappy with the revelations about Reitman when they were published, complained to Goldman that she had tipped the scales heavily in favor of romance, rather than describing her life in such a way that the cause of anarchism itself would be served (Falk, *Love, Anarchy,* xvi–xvii). It seemed to many that Goldman's emotionally wrought narrative must reinforce the popular conception of the anarchist as a political enthusiast, an irrational and intemperate zealot.

But no reader, sympathetic or not, could have denied how intensely readable Goldman's autobiography was. In it she describes her great service to anarchism as less an intellectual exercise in which principles are tested against practical realities and more as an affective state of discovery, commitment, and, perhaps, martyrdom. In this sense the autobiography that

Goldman completed in 1931 took on the shape of a heroic journey, a quest for social justice in the service of the "beautiful ideal" she discovered as a girl when the Haymarket martyrs died in Chicago, an ideal she carried through the fire of America's prisons and Lenin's Russia, and whose flame she tended alone and solitary in exile in Europe. She imagined her work as a missionary, writing, "Perhaps it will help the young generations to see that no life is worth anything which does not contain a great ideal" (Falk 9). No one who had attended her lectures on anarchism, literary criticism, or birth control should have been surprised by the persona that Goldman crafted in her autobiography. The sense of herself she offered as she mined memory and archive for the personhood of Emma Goldman was utterly consistent with the figure who lectured from so many public platforms that the aesthetic, sexual, and political responses to life's challenges were inseparable and mutually nurturing.

As she discussed her autobiography before she began to write, she expressed concern to friends about the project before her. While she recognized that she was writing about "the life of EG, the public person, not the private individual," she wished at the same time to be faithful to "the other side, the woman, the personality in quest for the unattainable" (ibid., 3). Her friend Frank Harris, who had included a short biography of her in his book *Contemporary Portraits,* had written an erotic autobiography, *My Life and Loves,* which Goldman admired and Harris suggested she imitate: "We want a woman's view of life and freedom in sex matters, want it badly" (Wexler, *Emma Goldman in Exile,* 146).

In the end, however, Goldman chose not to write graphically about her sexual intimacies. She had taken from Freud a sense that sexual feeling was important and legitimate, but she did not find the modernist style of detachment and abstraction sympathetic. "I do not consider the mere physical fact sufficient to convey the tremendous effect it has upon human emotions and sensations," she wrote to Frank Harris (*Nowhere at Home,* 128). Instead, as Alice Wexler has noted, when Goldman described her love affairs, she did so in the sentimental and melodramatic vocabulary of popular romance novels and with the spiritualist and otherworldly principles of the nineteenth-century free-love movement (*Emma Goldman in Exile,* 147). Moreover, the commitment to write about her personal life was far more easily made than realized. She worried about disclosing the nature of her relationship with Ben Reitman, the "hobo" doctor who became the manager of her lecture tours, confiding to Berkman that "the world would stand aghast that I, Emma Goldman, the strong revolutionist, the daredevil . . . should have been as helpless as a ship-wrecked crew on a foaming ocean" (Falk 4). Reitman, called a hobo for his work organizing the unemployed, is depicted as weak and foolish and Goldman in a continual state of summoning the resolve to cast him adrift, a resolve she ultimately achieves.

In fact Goldman may have been ungenerous to Reitman, who was devastated by her treatment of him when he read the autobiography. After parting from Goldman, Reitman published a well-respected work on prostitution and worked for the prevention and treatment of venereal disease, doing notable work promoting public health among prostitutes and the homeless in Chicago. While it is certain that this American maverick struck the lower Manhattan anarchist intelligentsia as a buffoon, Goldman was lavish in *Mother Earth* in her praise of Reitman's business management of her lecture tours, praise that preceded the demise of their relationship. Another former friend, Johann Most, also fared poorly in *Living My Life*. Goldman regarded Most's scornful denunciation of Alexander Berkman's *attentat* against Frick as apostasy, although in fact Most had begun to withdraw his advocacy of sabotage and assassination years before Berkman acted. It was indeed Alexander Berkman who had always regarded Ben Reitman as a fool, and Berkman who registered angry incredulity at Most's apparent defection in his prison memoir (Berkman 101).

Goldman's work bears the imprimatur of her old "pal." She had mailed her manuscript in chapters to Berkman while she was writing and received the pages back from him with red ink prominently in evidence. Berkman wrote of his editing, "the Mss., after I correct it, looks worse than an ordinary battle-field" (Wexler, *Emma Goldman,* xviii). Berkman gave Goldman reassurance while she wrote and praised the finished work as "one of the greatest autobiographies," if also "very feminine" (ibid., 153, 135). Although she had omitted Berkman from her narrative essay *My Disillusionment in Russia,* when she wrote her life, Emma Goldman accorded the status of life-long confidant and soul mate to Berkman. They had not resumed their earlier love affair after Berkman was released from prison, but in her final years, with ties to country and comrades severed by deportation and statelessness, she found solace and continuity in this friendship that had been sealed in blood when they were younger. Alice Wexler has called *Living My Life* a "love letter" to Alexander Berkman (*Emma Goldman in Exile,* 152). As for Berkman, the prison memoirs he wrote years before her autobiography are in part a love letter to Emma Goldman, the unnamed "Girl," the "immutable," in whom he idealized the memory of shared political passion, a memory that sustained him through his long incarceration.

Alexander Berkman was not alone in finding an essential womanliness in the autobiography. The *New York Herald Tribune* called the book "a great woman's story" (ibid., 154). Less favorably, the *Boston Transcript* said of Goldman that she "is lovable even where she is unintelligent—and frequently she seems so wrongheaded as to be laughable" (Nov. 21, 1931, 3). Perhaps the writer who was most able to receive both the confessional and intellectual dimensions of the autobiography as they had been intended was *Nation* reviewer Freda Kirchwey, who wrote:

Her personal affairs and emotions should in no way be segregated from her more public ones. Emma Goldman displays a complete incapacity for disinterest in the usual sorts of differentiation. The emotion that drove her was a single force, whether it was directed against the might of government of Russia or toward the fulfillment of personal passion. The excitement of a mass meeting was akin to the thrill of an embrace. . . . Herein lies her undeniable power. Her emotion is both intense and universal; her expression of it in words and action—unrestrained, her courage completely instinctive. She is contemptuous of any intellectualizing that stands in the way of faith and action. Always she feels first and thinks later. (*Nation*, 614)

Goldman thought Kirchwey's the best of the reviews written, although she bridled at the suggestion that her feelings impaired her thinking clearly. She preferred the compliment of a friend who told her she was "among the few women who can think without having lost anything of [her] femininity" (*Nowhere at Home*, 101).

Although the reviews were favorable, the published work did less well at the bookstores than Goldman hoped. She had quarreled with Knopf over its length, wanting to conclude her chronicle with her deportation to Russia. When Knopf insisted that she narrate the events of her life up to the present moment, the book swelled to more than a thousand pages, coming out in two volumes for $7.50, a price greater than Goldman had originally agreed upon and one, she feared, that would place the book beyond the buying power of many readers in the Depression economy of 1931. Goldman considered her work to have been a failure because of the disappointing sales. But in fact, judged by library demands, the book was read widely, passed from hand to hand.

Disappointments from the publication aside, Goldman was soon distracted by the tumultuous turn of European politics. In 1933, Adolf Hitler was appointed chancellor in Germany, and with him commenced the fateful challenge of fascism to democracy that would lead to World War II. Emma Goldman had always been granted dubious welcome in the countries she visited or in which she tentatively resided, her visits often preceded by clandestine warnings from the United States government that she should be considered a grave risk to security. But now with Nazism insurgent in Germany, she was subject to real threats and expulsion when she visited there. "The whole world is a prison and most people have turned into jailors," she wrote to a friend (Falk 400). In Berlin, thugs on the street threatened her with the fate of the murdered revolutionary Rosa Luxemburg. Holland, fearful of antagonizing its near neighbor, had permitted her entry under condition she not speak out against Nazism, expelling her after she delivered an anti-Nazi lecture in Amsterdam. English reserve had never attracted her, and she must have been amused at British consternation when the loyal toast to King George (a traditional staple at English banquets) was omitted from the celebration of her autobiography in London, the omission in deference to her anarchist sentiments. Nor did she feel part of the political life in France, where she lived in a small community of exiles. To Berkman she wrote, "I . . . feel an alien everywhere" (*Nowhere at Home,* 171).

Home, if she had one, was America, where she had left behind family and friends who supported her financially and emotionally. To an American friend she wrote about her desire to return to the home she missed. That home was among the polyglot socialist and libertarian immigrant communities, among liberal settlement workers and reformers whose America, she believed, permitted "adventure, innovations, experimental daring, which, except for Russia, no European country does. . . . It is this surcharged, electric, and dynamic atmosphere which permeates its writers, poets, and dramatists," she wrote to Berkman. "Europe is hoary with age; it sticks in its centuries of traditions; it dares nothing" (*Nowhere at Home,* 235). Most of her efforts to return had been fruitless. But after an impressive roster of artists and scholars intervened on her behalf—among others, John Dewey, Theodore Dreiser, H. L. Mencken, Sherwood Anderson, and Sinclair Lewis—she was granted a ninety-day visa in 1934, albeit with conditions that she confine her lectures to literature. Emma Goldman crossed the border in February 1934 at Niagara Falls, where a customs official noticed "a grandmotherly person with a blue twinkling eye" (Chalberg 1).

Although the initial welcome home was encouraging, the lecture tour was poorly handled, with bookings into large, expensive halls where at times only a handful of rows were occupied and those by the middle aged and middle class, a younger audience kept out by the ticket price. Still echoing sentiments that accompanied the reviews of her autobiography, some friendly mainstream press seemed to suggest that as the old anarchist tiger had been defanged by failure and passing years, kindness was appropriate. The *New York Herald Tribune* called her "our old friend," and the *Washington Herald* observed that her legendary wit had become "more nimble with increasing age" (Drinnon 280). The Communists, whom she had enraged with her criticism of the Soviet Union, were unforgiving, suggesting not only that she was lecturing to fill coffers to feed a lavish exile in the south of France, but also that her "reactionary" politics would smooth the way for fascism in the United States. But even as she was being reviled by the Communist *Daily Worker,* one of the Hearst chain, in an excess of ignorance, reminded its readers that "Red Emma" was "for many years the leading Communist in the United States" (ibid., 280).

Goldman's tour revealed the anomalies of her situation—that in her anarchist opposition to centralized state power, she would draw fire from entrenched positions at opposite ends of the political spectrum. A writer for *The Nation* defined the irony of this stance. Saying nay to the twin behemoths of capitalism and communism, Goldman had become "a symbol of the ultimate social cleavage, of differences that cannot be bridged" (3/21/34, 320). The disappointment over audiences aside, America had become home, and Goldman was desolate when at the end of her ninety-day visa, despite efforts made on her behalf, she was compelled to leave the United States. To one friend she wrote, "for a revolutionist and internationalist it is indeed disgraceful to be rooted to the soil of one country. Perhaps one can not adjust oneself easily in later years as one does in one's youth. Whatever the reason I have to admit defeat. The ninety days of my return dispelled whatever doubts I had on that score. I know now I will remain an alien abroad for the rest of my life" (Drinnon 290).

A year after Goldman penned these reflections, she bore a greater loss. Alexander Berkman, terminally ill and in great pain, took his own life in Nice. Her lifelong friend, he had been her comrade in exile, a second self with whom to share the disappointments when the anarchist ideal they served failed to take fire in the masses they attempted to instruct. In correspondence with each other Goldman and Berkman voiced despair as they watched Stalinism and Nazism overcome and brutally destroy anarchist positions where they had taken root. Finally Goldman and Berkman believed it was not Stalin, Mussolini, or Hitler who defeated anarchism, but the inadequacy of the people themselves. In such a mood of political hopelessness and personal loss, Emma Goldman was hardly likely to have anticipated that she might be revitalized. She was sixty-seven years old, separated by an ocean from family and friends on whom she was wholly financially dependent, and contrary to the innuendos of the *Daily Worker,* barely able to eke out a living on the proceeds of lecture tours, subject to continual harassment from governments that might find it politically inexpedient to tolerate her. The image of a society formed by workers in a benevolent network of mutual-aid associations could not have seemed more remote in Europe in 1936, a time when European democracies were busy making their peace with fascism, a menace that, even as she mourned Berkman's death, was acquiring its most virulent shape.

Civil war in Spain shook Goldman free of the grief that followed Berkman's death. While the working class in Germany and Italy had succumbed ignobly to fascism, here at last, it seemed, a brave people were resisting tyranny in the name of the "beautiful ideal" to which Emma Goldman had dedicated her life. Five years earlier in 1931 a popular vote in Spain supplanted the Spanish monarchy with a republic, a republic that was liberal, left-leaning, and supported by militant anarchists, who had learned their antipathy to repressive governments from a Spanish follower of Bakunin in the mid-nineteenth century. Consistent with some of the apocalyptic militancy of Bakunin, the anarchists had staged a series of violent insurrections in hopes of preparing the ground for social revolution. By 1933, grown contemptuous of the government they had intitially supported, Spanish anarchists boycotted elections, permitting a more conservative government to come into power. Although a tentative popular-front government emerged to unite the left, the government faced opposition from both flanks. Meanwhile, forces of reaction, a powerful coalition of reactionary church leaders, landowners, conservative industrialists, and the military, had taken alarm.

In July 1936, the right struck with an army coup that divided Spain in two. In the northern provinces of industrial Spain and in the great southwestern estates of Andalucía and Estremadura, the coup was defeated by the spontaneous action of workers. In the industrial city of Barcelona, where workers toiled in appalling misery in airless textile mills, and among the miners in the northern provinces of Asturias and Oviedo, an uprising of militant trade unionists in the first few days of the war resulted in a massive collectivization of industry. Trade unions and political parties formed armed militias democratically organized without rank and privilege to defend themselves against the "Nationalists," fascist brigades under the leadership of Francisco Franco. In the countryside, particularly in Aragon where agrarian workers had labored in unrelenting poverty, a collectivization of the land ensued with stunning rapidity after the fascist uprising was put down. Against all expectation, an anarchist social revolution had taken place and, for a few months, was declaring itself to the world in northern Spain and along its eastern coast.

Emma Goldman was ecstatic. In August 1936, she was invited by the Spanish trade unionists, the CNT (Confederación Nacional del Trabajo) and the more militant FAI (Federación Anarquista Ibérica), to Barcelona to undertake English language propaganda for the anarchists. "At last," she wrote, "I will be on the scene of revolutionary action" (Wexler, *Emma Goldman in Exile*, 201). "I have come to you as to my own," she told the thousands of comrades who welcomed her at a mass meeting, "for your ideal has been my ideal for forty-five years and it will remain to my last breath" (Drinnon 302). To understand the Spanish social revolution and report on its progress, she toured factory and countryside, pleased that worker control was succeeding without the apparatus of state bureaucracy and police that she believed had destroyed the fledgling Russian revolt.

She traveled to the front in Aragon, within hearing of fascist gunfire in the trenches of Madrid, to see for herself if a volunteer workers' army had succumbed to hierarchy and discipline, relieved to find, as she sat in trenches with anarchist troops, that no special privileges separated officer from foot soldier. "Your revolution," she told a meeting of FAI youth, "will destroy forever [the notion] that anarchism stands for chaos" (ibid., 303).

These moments of exhilaration were painfully short-lived. Mounting internal and external threats seemed to conspire against the young anarchist experiment. Within months of her confident public affirmations, Goldman worried privately to friends that power in anarchist strongholds was already shifting from the local revolutionary associations, whose autonomy was precious to anarchist principles, to the centralized republican government of the popular front. When leading figures in the CNT/FAI groups consented to take up offices in the popular front government, Goldman believed the "spirit" and "tradition" of their anarchism was succumbing to "pitfalls." Of one woman anarchist leader whom she distrusted, she wrote privately to a friend that she was a "Lenin in skirts" (Wexler, *Emma Goldman in Exile*, 207).

While schisms within the Spanish republic widened and deepened, the European democracies and the international labor movement itself were ominously passive, while the fascist governments of Italy and Germany readied sophisticated military arms to meet the untrained militias of the republic. Back in England, where Goldman traveled in 1937 to rally financial support for Spain, the Tory government's Non-Intervention Pact claimed neutrality while actually sabotaging republican military capacity by closing the ports of Tangier and Gibraltar to their forces and imposing strict laws prohibiting the sale of arms to the republicans. England's extensive mining interests in Spain encouraged its keeping a wary eye on a social revolution that threatened its own economic interests. Other countries, including France and the isolationist United States, joined the Non-Intervention Pact. Meanwhile Nazi Germany and Mussolini's Italy passed arms into Franco's arsenals without restraint.

Only the Soviet Union came to the support of the republic with arms for its fight against fascism, although the support came with a heavy price tag. Stalin, a shrewd political strategist, embarked on a program of dismantling the social revolution in Spain, telling comrades that the time was not right for such change. In fact, Stalin was determined to preserve an antifascist alliance with England and France as long as possible, well aware that while these governments might tolerate a Spanish bourgeois democracy, they would no more tolerate social revolution in southern Europe than they had been willing to see the Bolsheviks prevail in eastern Europe.

It was no surprise that Emma Goldman would recoil at the new influence of Stalin's foot soldiers in Spain. With her memory firmly fixed on Bolshevik prisons, the oppression by the Cheka, the special privileges of a new Soviet elite, Goldman appealed to Barcelona youth to consider that their enemies were not only among the fascists: "All those who talk of the necessity of new governments, of new rules, are making ready to forge new chains for your enslavement. They are trying . . . to lead your glorious Revolution into channels that will inevitably end in a new form of dictatorship" (Wexler, *Emma Goldman in Exile*, 209). Stirring words, yet with her bleak forebodings of malign Soviet influence, her old friends in the CNT/FAI were not uniformly pleased at the direction their propagandist was taking. She was asked to mute her criticism of both the communists and the popular front, lest supporters in Europe and abroad believe the Spanish cause was either hopelessly compromised by the Bolsheviks or hopelessly ineffective because of its ideological purity.

Meanwhile, it must have seemed tragic to Goldman that so many forces conspired to defeat the revolution: the European democracies averted their eyes; the international working class remained strangely silent; the fascist enemies prepared their assault; while the Spanish revolution was being devoured from within by deadly fighting among socialists, anarchists, and communists. In response, Goldman was not consistent with her advice, publicly making urgent appeals for support for the republic, no matter their mistakes or friends, privately alternately

excoriating anarchists for making common cause with the popular government or accepting its strategic necessity, loathing the
centralization of the military with its accompanying hierarchies
while at the same time regretting the naïveté of the volunteer
militias, so hopelessly less skilled and less well armed than their
fascist enemies.

In May 1937 the storm that had long been brewing surfaced. As part of a campaign to centralize command, the popular front government, attempting to take control of the
telephone exchange in Barcelona, met armed resistance from
anarchists and socialists in the streets. Under pressure from
the communists, brigades advanced into Barcelona from Va-
lencia. Socialists and anarchists who resisted died in the
streets; thousands more were later imprisoned and socialist
leaders murdered. Meanwhile, enacting Stalin's strategy of re-
versing the social revolution, military forces under communist
leadership were sent into Aragon to disassemble the agricultural collectives and to return land to former owners. Franco
had not yet ended the Spanish civil war, but in those regions
of northern and eastern Spain where the CNT/FAI had held
sway, the anarchist social revolution was effectively shut
down. Goldman wrote to a friend, "Spain has again proven
that nothing remains of anarchism when one is forced to
make concessions that undermine the ideal" (Wexler, *Emma
Goldman in Exile*, 220).

Barcelona surrendered to Franco in 1938. Emma Goldman
was in London still rallying the faithful to her "beautiful
ideal." "I wish I had remained in Spain," she wrote. "I have
lived long enough. The agony over the debacle of the Russian
Revolution was enough for one life. Now the Spanish revolution is to be crushed. Life holds nothing else" (Falk 491).
Goldman blamed the surrender of Barcelona on the Communists, who she believed betrayed the anarchists, who unwittingly or not were complicit in the Communist program to
reverse the radical progression of the revolution. Mariano
Vásquez of the CNT responded to Goldman's reproach that the
anarchists had been "childlike" in their relationship with the

Communists, writing, "Nobody has betrayed anybody" (Wexler, *Emma Goldman in Exile,* 229). The death blow had been "the lack of arms brought about by the attitude of the Democracies. The fact is," finished Vásquez, "that one country alone cannot fight against the whole world" (ibid., 230). In this gallant fight, however ill destined, Emma Goldman, Vásquez insisted, had played a magnificent role. He cabled Goldman on her seventieth birthday, naming her their "spiritual mother." "You have understood us," he wrote, "and our aim as few who came to our shores have understood us" (ibid., 232). No other accolade, among the many she had received in a long lifetime, pleased her half so well. While the revolution had flourished, Emma Goldman had made Spain her spiritual home. Its death had been tragic but not ignoble. And as with the Haymarket martyrs, whose sacrifice she had enshrined a half century earlier, she would be faithful to the memory of "the first example in history how Revolutions should be made" (ibid., 232).

In May 1940, Emma Goldman died in Canada, where she had gone to settle and to carry on her work now for Spanish refugees. She died from the aftereffects of a stroke she'd suffered some months earlier, her last words to card-playing friends who waited with her for a libertarian meeting to begin, "God damn it, why did you lead that?" (Falk 513). She was bellicose and vigorous to the end, no one having sensed that her health was badly declining. The last few months she had exhausted herself working on behalf of an Italian anarchist in Canada at risk of deportation to Mussolini's Italy. As her friends and family gathered at her deathbed, disaster was overtaking Europe.

In the last two years of Goldman's life, Adolf Hitler captured Warsaw, marched into Paris, and began his campaign of genocide against European Jewry. The Russian Jew Emma Goldman was no pacifist, but she responded to anti-Nazi militarism by adhering to positions on warring capitalist states that she had taken in opposition to World War I. "Much as I loathe Hitler, Mussolini, Stalin, and Franco," she wrote, "I would not support a war against them and for the democracies which, in the last analysis, are only Fascist in disguise. If I have supported civil war in Spain, it was only because the social revolution was at stake" (Wexler, *Emma Goldman in Exile,* 236).

Unlike other Jewish anarchist immigrants in Canada and the United States who were outspoken for intervention against German fascism, Goldman believed that Jewish emancipation depended on their joining an international movement like anarchism. Although she supported Jewish rights for asylum in Palestine or in any other country, as she would other refugees, and condemned Britain's turning away the ship *St. Louis* filled with desperate Jewish refugees from Nazism, she rejected Jewish nationalism. As an anarchist, she placed no more faith in the goodness of a Jewish state than in any other, since all governments led to repression.

In 1939 and 1940, Emma Goldman was not alone in woefully misunderstanding the nature of Hitler's war against the Jews, nor alone in failing to predict the scale of the catastrophe about to descend on those still trapped within the charnel house that Europe had become. Like others, she may have assumed Hitler's anti-Semitism, like Russian pogroms, would fall short of the cataclysmic annihilation planned. Then again, in her mind Europe was already the graveyard of Spanish anarchists, heroes left to perish because of European betrayal or indifference. In 1939 and 1940, these were the deaths she regretted and theirs the wrong she wished to memorialize. Like the complex political realities in Spain that required her to evaluate the worthiness of anarchist principles against the exigencies of immediate conditions, the fateful years at the close of Goldman's life required a balancing of principles she did not live to undertake. But in 1940, she would not differentiate among the faces of her enemy, nor believe in such distinctions among them that might excuse more violence.

She was laid to rest at Waldheim Cemetery in Chicago, near the graves of the Haymarket martyrs whose deaths had called her into the service of anarchism when she was young. Denied residence for two decades while she was alive, Emma Goldman's body was brought back to the United States for burial with a Spanish anarchist banner draping her coffin.

8. THE LEGACY OF EMMA GOLDMAN

When Emma Goldman's friends attended her bedside as she lay dying, they were most struck by her silence. The cerebral hemorrhage had accomplished what no one had been able to do hitherto—Emma Goldman was unable to speak. Speech had been her most formidable political asset. Indeed, as Alexander Berkman had noted, it was "the platform, not the pen" that was her forte (*Nowhere at Home,* 27). Her oratory was passionate, electric, accusatory, sarcastic, humorous—and delivered with a bulldog determination, all the more remarkable because in appearance she was the least consequential of persons. A small, square-chinned, gray-haired, thickset woman, she would have been easy to overlook in a crowd had she not always been center stage, eyewitness to and participant in the historical cataclysms of her time. Nothing in these bravura public performances suggested the loneliness, the ambivalence, or uncertainty of some of her private correspondence. If in her peripatetic wanderings over the face of Europe she came to symbolize the deracination of the twentieth-century refugee, she bore this anguish with an indomitable spirit. She was not capable of being crushed.

Less certain is the legacy she left behind her as a critic of the two central forces that shaped the political profile of the twentieth century, capitalism and communism. One of her detractors on the left said acidly of her that she was "not paralyzed by seeing too many sides of the problem" (Wexler, *Emma Goldman in Exile,* 85). Yet even with the benefit of historical hindsight, good people may differ about the impartiality with which she reached her early indictment of the infant Bolshevik state. To some the moral clarity with which she condemned Soviet elitism and the growth of a Soviet police state stood in luminous contrast to the paralysis of other left liberals, who too long remained apologists for Soviet oppression and bloodshed. To others her early and unconditional repudiation of the Bolshevik revolution, made before Stalin took power, may have failed to account sufficiently for the exigencies of the fragile state surrounded by enemies and the emergency measures needed to sustain a war economy. More fatefully, as Alice Wexler has suggested, for the decades that followed the close of World War II, Goldman's easy conflation of Marxism, Bolshevism, and Stalinism lent legitimacy to the "continuity theory," a Cold War ideology that rendered all forms of socialism in whole cloth and homogenized, as if they were necessarily embryonic Stalinist tyrannies.

As a blueprint for social revolution, anarchism itself suffered from the very conditions of its extraordinary appeal. Its fidelity to the principle of individual autonomy and mutual cooperation limited its response to the more complex operations of large nation-states. As the immigrant communities who had brought anarchism with them to the United States aged, the "beautiful ideal" of no state became less and less the choice of radical social activists, who looked increasingly to government welfare programs for redress of social inequities. If one searches for an enduring legacy of anarchism in the twentieth century, it is to be found perhaps in its having represented an appealing alternative to those structures of powers which, in their very massive, impersonal, and centralized constitution, felt overbearing, inhibiting, and destructive. When other left alternatives to capitalist expansion were found wanting or discredited, the "beautiful ideal" of Emma Goldman's remained on the drawing board of American political possibility.

Small wonder, then, that a resurgence of anarchism accompanied the political activism of the cultural revolution of the 1960s and 1970s, initiated by the civil rights movements and opposition to the unpopular war in Vietnam. A new generation of antiwar activists and advocates of free speech and free love found common ground in Emma Goldman's anarchism. Her face adorned T-shirts, posters, and banners. A clinic in Iowa City was named for her, as was a theater troupe in New York. Screenplays, stage plays, and even an opera were written about her, as a generation rejecting the militarism, corporatism, and industrialism of the mainstream capitalist West found the antihierarchical and antiauthoritarian principles of anarchism congenial. If anarchism had seemed less and less relevant to America in the 1930s, with New Deal centralism promising a more beneficent role for government than anarchism allowed, to a generation disavowing the ideological disputes of the "old Left," the purity of the anarchist ideal, with its invitations to form local associations, day-care centers, clinics, and small agricultural collectives, was alluring.

The allure was particularly appealing to feminists in the 1970s, who could plausibly assign to Emma Goldman an early enunciation of the feminist doctrine that "the personal is political." Goldman positioned her feminism within her anarchism, insisting that no woman's freedom could be found by appealing to a state government for redress of grievance. But at the same time she redefined the male-centered anarchism she inherited by insisting that sexual liberation be included in its agenda. Insufficiently accredited as an original thinker, Emma Goldman in her battle against sexual repression in radical political thinking made an important contribution to twentieth-century political thought. Sexual liberation, on her terms, was not only a fundamental human right, it was foundational to the creativity necessary for social revolution itself. The flouting of repressive sexual taboos, found among the puritans of the left or right, was, she believed, a strategy for political change, an *attentat* to shock and humiliate authorities. Quite appropriately, a contemporary greeting card bearing her name records her challenge: "If I can't dance, I don't want to be part of your revolution." These were not the words engraved on her tombstone at Waldheim Cemetery in Chicago. But they might have been.

In 2003, when once again a military drumbeat was sounding in her adopted country, America, the words of that old anarchist warhorse Emma Goldman were stirred into life on the front pages of *The New York Times*. Apparently a letter to subscribers to the Emma Goldman Archive housed at the University of California at Berkeley included Goldman's early-twentieth-century jeremiad against the impending slaughter. Underneath the letterhead of the university archive, her angry words rang out: those "not yet overcome by war madness [must] raise their voice of protest to call the attention of the people to the crime and outrage which are about to be perpetrated on them." Learning of the contents, the University of California vice chancellor for research took alarm and suppressed the letter; but front-page headlines in America's foremost newspaper reported the story with its worrisome implications for the suppression of free speech. So doing, the newspaper gave Goldman's jeremiad national coverage, a more powerful sounding board against, yet again, another war. Had she been granted prescience to foresee her twenty-first-century rebirth, she would have, as she had so many times, thanked those who wished to silence her for giving her voice so much more public notice than she might ever have achieved on her own.

Not much later, when the American hostilities broke out against Iraq, graffiti artists painted Goldman's antiwar declarations on the cliffs above a San Francisco beach. There, where only the wind and tide might erase the words her pen preserved, Emma Goldman still hurled her own anathemas against the malignancies of indifferent states.

Works Cited

Berkman, Alexander. *Prison Memoirs of an Anarchist*. New York: Mother Earth Publishing, 1912.

Chalberg, John. *Emma Goldman: American Individualist*. New York: HarperCollins, 1991.

Chernyshevsky, Nikolai. *What Is to Be Done?* (1863). Ann Arbor, Mich.: Ardis Publishers, 1986.

Drinnon, Richard. *Rebel in Paradise: A Biography of Emma Goldman*. Chicago: University of Chicago Press, 1961.

Duffus, R. L. "Review of *Living My Life* by Emma Goldman." *The New York Times,* October 25, 1931, p. 1.

"Emma Goldman." *The Nation* 138 (March 21, 1934): 320.

Falk, Candace. *Love, Anarchy, and Emma Goldman*. New York: Holt, Rinehart, and Winston, 1984.

Flynn, Elizabeth Gurley. *The Rebel Girl*. New York: International Publishers, 1955.

Goldman, Emma. *Anarchism and Other Essays*. Edited by Richard Drinnon. New York: Dover, 1969.

———. *Emma Goldman, A Documentary History of the American Years*. Vol. 1, *Made for America, 1890–1901*. Edited by Candace Falk, Barry Pateman, and Jessica Moran. Berkeley: University of California Press, 2003.

———. *Living My Life*. New York: Dover, 1970.

———. *Mother Earth*. New York. Vols. 1–12, March 1906–August 1917.

———. *My Disillusionment in Russia*. New York: Doubleday, Page, 1923.

———. *My Further Disillusionment in Russia*. New York: Doubleday, Page, 1924.

————. *Nowhere at Home: Letters from Exile of Emma Goldman and Alexander Berkman*. Edited by Richard and Anna Maria Drinnon. New York: Schocken Books, 1975.

————. *Traffic in Women and Other Essays on Feminism*. Edited by Alix Kates Shulman. Albion, Calif.: Times Change Press, 1970.

Haaland, Bonnie. *Emma Goldman: Sexuality and the Impurity of the State*. Montreal and New York: Black Rose Books, 1993.

Harris, Frank. "Emma Goldman, the Famous Anarchist," in *Contemporary Portraits*. New York: Brentano's Publishers, 1923.

————. *My Life and Loves*. Edited by John Gallagher. New York: Grove Press, 1963.

Hillquit, Morris. *Loose Leaves from a Busy Life*. New York: Macmillan, 1934.

Kirchwey, Freda. "Review of *Living My Life* by Emma Goldman." *The Nation* 133 (December 2, 1931): 612–14.

Kropotkin, Peter. *The Conquest of Bread and Other Writings*. Edited by Marshall Shatz. Cambridge, UK: Cambridge University Press, 1995.

————. *Selected Writings on Anarchism and Revolution*. Edited by Martin A. Miller. Cambridge, Mass.: MIT Press, 1970.

Morton, Marian J. *Emma Goldman and the American Left*. New York: Twayne Publishers, 1992.

The New York Times, "Old Words on War Stirring a New Dispute at Berkeley," January 14, 2003, 1, A16.

Wexler, Alice. *Emma Goldman in America*. Boston: Beacon Press, 1984.

————. *Emma Goldman in Exile*. Boston: Beacon Press, 1989.

Suggestions for Further Reading

1. WORKS BY EMMA GOLDMAN

Anarchism on Trial: Speeches of Alexander Berkman and Emma Goldman Before the United States District Court in the City of New York, July 1917. New York: Mother Earth Publishing, 1917.

Anarchism and Other Essays. Edited with introduction by Richard Drinnon, including biographical sketch by Hippolyte Havel (1910). New York: Dover, 1969.

Emma Goldman: A Documentary History of the American Years. Vol. 1, *Made for America, 1890–1901.* Edited by Candace Falk, Barry Pateman, and Jessica Moran. Berkeley: University of California Press, 2003.

Living My Life. 2 vols. New York: Dover, 1970 (an unabridged reproduction of the original 1931 publication).

Mother Earth (New York). Vols. 1–12, March 1906–August 1917.

Mother Earth Bulletin (New York). Vols. 1–7, October 1917–18.

My Disillusionment in Russia. New York: Doubleday, Page, 1923.

My Further Disillusionment in Russia. New York: Doubleday, Page, 1924.

Nowhere at Home: Letters from Exile of Emma Goldman and Alexander Berkman. Edited by Richard Drinnon and Anna Maria Drinnon. New York: Schocken Books, 1975.

Red Emma Speaks: An Emma Goldman Reader. Compiled and edited by Alix Kates Shulman. Atlantic Highlands, N.J.: Humanities Press, 1996.

The Social Significance of Modern Drama. Boston: R. G. Badger, 1914.

Traffic in Women and Other Essays on Feminism. Compiled and with biographical essay by Alix Kates Shulman. Albion, Calif.: Times Change Press, 1970.

Vision on Fire: Emma Goldman on the Spanish Revolution. Edited with introduction by David Porter. New Paltz, N.Y.: Commonground Press, 1983.

2. BIOGRAPHIES

Chalberg, John. *Emma Goldman: American Individualist.* New York: HarperCollins, 1991.

Drinnon, Richard. *Rebel in Paradise.* Chicago: University of Chicago Press, 1961.

Falk, Candace. *Love, Anarchy, and Emma Goldman.* New York: Holt, Rinehart, and Winston, 1984.

Ganguli, B. N. *Emma Goldman: Portrait of a Rebel Woman.* New Delhi: Allied, 1979.

Harris, Frank. "Emma Goldman, the Famous Anarchist," in *Contemporary Portraits.* New York: Brentano's Publishers, 1923.

Shulman, Alix Kates. *To the Barricades: The Anarchist Life of Emma Goldman.* New York: Crowell, 1971.

Solomon, Martha. *Emma Goldman.* Boston: Twayne Publishers, 1987.

Wexler, Alice. *Emma Goldman in America.* Boston: Beacon Press, 1984.

———. *Emma Goldman in Exile.* Boston: Beacon Press, 1989.

3. READINGS IN ANARCHISM AND HISTORICAL CONTEXT

Berkman, Alexander. *Prison Memoirs of an Anarchist.* New York: Mother Earth Publishing, 1912.

Daily Bleed's Anarchist Encyclopedia. http://recollectionbooks
.com/bleed/gallery/galleryindex.htm.

Haaland, Bonnie. *Emma Goldman: Sexuality and the Impurity
of the State.* Montreal and New York: Black Rose Books,
1993.

Joll, James. *The Anarchists.* New York: Grosset and Dunlap,
1966.

Kropotkin, Peter. *The Conquest of Bread and Other Writings.*
Edited by Marshall Shatz. Cambridge, UK: Cambridge University Press, 1995.

———. *Selected Writings on Anarchism and Revolution.* Edited
by Martin A. Miller. Cambridge, Mass.: MIT Press, 1970.

Morton, Marian J. *Emma Goldman and the American Left.*
New York: Twayne Publishers, 1992.

Pyziar, Eugene. *The Doctrine of Anarchism of Michael A.
Bakunin.* Chicago: Henry Regnery, 1968.

Ritter, Alan. *The Political Thought of Pierre-Joseph Proudhon.*
Princeton, N.J.: Princeton University Press, 1969.

Shatz, Marshall S., ed. *The Essential Works of Anarchism.*
New York: Bantam, 1971.

Taylor, Michael. *Community, Anarchy, and Liberty.* Cambridge, UK: Cambridge University Press, 1982.

Wolff, Robert Paul. *In Defense of Anarchism.* New York:
Harper & Row, 1970.

Woodcock, George. *Anarchism: A History of Libertarian Ideas
and Movements.* Cleveland: World Publishing, 1962.

———, and Ivan Akaumovic. *The Anarchist Prince: Peter
Kropotkin.* New York: Schocken Books, 1971.

A Note on the Text

Emma Goldman was concerned that the length of her autobiography placed it beyond the reach of the pocketbooks of most readers during the Depression year of 1931. She would have been pleased by an abridgment of her original two-volume, one-thousand-page work if a wider audience of readers became acquainted with her life's story. In shaping a condensation as faithful as possible in tone and substance to Goldman's original, this editor has been careful to retain its basic architecture: her foundational years in Russia, which laid the basis, she believed, for her lifelong crusade against sexual repression and political tyranny; her awakening to the political ideal of anarchism in her early youth, inseparable from her romantic friendship with Alexander Berkman, with whom she planned the assassination of the steel baron Henry Clay Frick; the accounts of her trials and imprisonments; her passionate relationship with her longtime lover Ben Reitman; her political work against the draft during World War I, leading to her deportation, to her travels in the Soviet Union, and to her exile in Europe. In its condensation this abridgment has also endeavored to retain as much as possible Goldman's kaleidoscopic commentary as she traveled as a lecturer for anarchism, appraising the liberal reformers, Marxist and Leninist revolutionaries, and free-love advocates who were sometimes political allies. When the interests of a condensed text demanded exclusions, every attempt was made to confine omissions to redundancies in narrative or to commentary on meetings with political comrades no longer familiar to contemporary readers. While some color and flavor of Goldman's tumultuous life are unfortunately lost in the omissions, great care has been taken to render the abridgment as true as possible to the shape and spirit of the original work.

Living My Life

In Appreciation

Suggestions that I write my memoirs came to me when I had barely begun to live, and continued all through the years. But I never paid heed to the proposal. I was living my life intensely—what need to write about it? Another reason for my reluctance was the conviction I entertained that one should write about one's life only when one had ceased to stand in the very torrent of it. "When one has reached a good philosophic age," I used to tell my friends, "capable of viewing the tragedies and comedies of life impersonally and detachedly—particularly one's own life—one is likely to create an autobiography worth while." Still feeling adolescently young in spite of advancing years, I did not consider myself competent to undertake such a task. Moreover, I always lacked the necessary leisure for concentrated writing.

My enforced European inactivity left me enough time to read a great deal, including biographies and autobiographies. I discovered, much to my discomfiture, that old age, far from ripening wisdom and mellowness, is too often fraught with senility, narrowness, and petty rancour. I would not risk such a calamity, and I began to think seriously about writing my life.

The great difficulty that faced me was lack of historical data for my work. Almost everything in the way of books, correspondence, and similar material that I had accumulated during the thirty-five years of my life in the United States had been confiscated by the Department of Justice raiders and never returned. I lacked even my personal set of the *Mother Earth* magazine, which I had published for twelve years. It was a problem I could see no solution for. Sceptic that I am, I had overlooked the magic power of friendship, which had so often in my life made mountains move. My staunch friends Leonard D. Abbott, Agnes Inglis, W. S. Van Valkenburgh, and others soon put my doubts to shame. Agnes, the founder of the Labadie Library in Detroit, containing the richest collection of radical and revolutionary material in America, came to my aid with her usual readiness. Leonard did his share, and Van spent all his free time in research work for me.

In the matter of European data I knew I could turn to the two best historians in our ranks: Max Nettlau and Rudolf Rocker. No further need to worry with such an array of co-workers.

Still I was not appeased. I needed something that would help me re-create the atmosphere of my own personal life: the events, small or great, that had tossed me about emotionally. An old vice of mine came to my rescue: veritable mountains of letters I had written. Often I had been chided by my pal Sasha, otherwise known as Alexander Berkman, and by my other friends, for my proclivity to spread myself in letters. Far from virtue bringing reward, it was my iniquity that gave me what I needed most— the true atmosphere of past days. Ben Reitman, Ben Capes, Jacob Margolis, Agnes Inglis, Harry Weinberger, Van, my romantic admirer Leon Bass, and scores of other friends readily responded to my request to send me my letters. My niece, Stella Ballantine, had kept everything I had written her during my imprisonment in the Missouri penitentiary. She, as well as my dear friend M. Eleanor Fitzgerald, had also preserved my Russian correspondence. In short, I was soon put into possession of over one thousand specimens of my epistolary effusions. I confess that most of them were painful reading, for at no time does one reveal oneself so much as in one's intimate correspondence. But for my purpose they were of utmost value.

Thus supplied, I started for Saint-Tropez, a picturesque fisher nest in the south of France, in company of Emily Holmes Coleman, who was to act as my secretary. Demi, as she is familiarly called, was a wild wood-sprite with a volcanic temper. But she was also the tenderest of beings, without any guile or rancour. She was essentially the poet, highly imaginative and sensitive. My world of ideas was foreign to her, natural rebel and anarchist though she was. We clashed furiously, often to the point of wishing each other in Saint-Tropez Bay. But it was nothing compared to her charm, her profound interest in my work, and her fine understanding for my inner conflicts.

Writing had never come easy to me, and the work at hand did not mean merely writing. It meant reliving my long-forgotten past, the resurrection of memories I did not wish to dig out from the deeps of my consciousness. It meant doubts in my creative ability, depression, and disheartenings. All through that period Demi held out bravely and by her faith and encouragement proved the comfort and inspiration of the first year of my struggle.

Altogether I was very fortunate in the number and devotion of friends who exerted themselves to smooth the way for *Living My Life*. The first to start the fund to secure me from material anxiety was Peggy Guggenheim. Other friends and comrades followed suit, giving without stint from their limited economic means. Miriam Lerner, a young American friend, volunteered to take Demi's place when the latter had to leave for England. Dorothy Marsh, Betty Markow, and Emmy Eckstein typed part of my manuscript as a labour of love. Arthur Leonard Ross, kindest and most lavish of men, gave me his untiring efforts as legal representative and adviser. How could such friendship ever be rewarded?

And Sasha? Many misgivings beset me when we began the revision of my manuscript. I feared he might resent seeing himself pictured through my eyes. Would he be detached enough, I wondered, sufficiently objective for the task? I found him remarkably so for one who is so much a part of my story. For eighteen months Sasha worked side by side with me as in our old days. Critical, of course, but always in the finest and broadest spirit. Sasha also it was who suggested the title, *Living My Life*.

My life as I have lived it owes everything to those who had come into it, stayed long or little, and passed out. Their love, as well as their hate, has gone into making my life worth while.

Living My Life is my tribute and my gratitude to them all.

EMMA GOLDMAN

Saint-Tropez, France
January 1931

Living My Life

CHAPTER I

It was the 15th of August 1889, the day of my arrival in New York City. I was twenty years old. All that had happened in my life until that time was now left behind me, cast off like a worn-out garment. A new world was before me, strange and terrifying. But I had youth, good health, and a passionate ideal. Whatever the new held in store for me I was determined to meet unflinchingly.

How well I remember that day! It was a Sunday. The West Shore train, the cheapest, which was all I could afford, had brought me from Rochester, New York, reaching Weehawken at eight o'clock in the morning. Thence I came by ferry to New York City. I had no friends there, but I carried three addresses, one of a married aunt, one of a young medical student I had met in New Haven a year before, while working in a corset factory there, and one of the *Freiheit*, a German anarchist paper published by Johann Most.[1]

My entire possessions consisted of five dollars and a small hand-bag. My sewing-machine, which was to help me to independence, I had checked as baggage. Ignorant of the distance from West Forty-second Street to the Bowery, where my aunt lived, and unaware of the enervating heat of a New York day in August, I started out on foot. How confusing and endless a large city seems to the new-comer, how cold and unfriendly!

After receiving many directions and misdirections and making frequent stops at bewildering intersections, I landed in three hours at the photographic gallery of my aunt and uncle. Tired and hot, I did not at first notice the consternation of my relatives at my unexpected arrival. They asked me to make myself at home, gave me breakfast, and then plied me with questions. Why did I come to New York? Had I definitely broken with my husband? Did I have money? What did I intend to do? I was told that I could, of course, stay with them. "Where else could you go, a young woman alone in New York?" Certainly, but I would have to look for a job immediately. Business was bad, and the cost of living high.

I heard it all as if in a stupor. I was too exhausted from my wakeful night's journey, the long walk, and the heat of the sun, which was already pouring down fiercely. The voices of my relatives sounded distant, like the buzzing of flies, and they made me drowsy. With an effort I pulled myself together. I assured them I did not come to impose myself on them; a friend living on Henry Street was expecting me and would put me up. I had but one desire—to get out, away from the prattling, chilling voices. I left my bag and departed.

The friend I had invented in order to escape the "hospitality" of my relatives was only a slight acquaintance, a young anarchist by the name of A. Solotaroff, whom I had once heard lecture in New Haven.[2] Now I started out to find him. [. . .] The oppressive day was drawing to a close. At last, when I was about to give up the search, I discovered him on Montgomery Street, on the fifth floor of a tenement house seething with humanity.

A year had passed since our first meeting, but Solotaroff had not forgotten me. His greeting was genial and warm, as of an old friend. He told me that he shared his small apartment with his parents and little brother, but that I could have his room; he would stay with a fellow-student for a few nights. He assured me that I would have no difficulty in finding a place; in fact, he knew two sisters who were living with their father in a two-room flat. [. . .]

Later Solotaroff took me to Sachs's café on Suffolk Street, which, as he informed me, was the headquarters of the East Side radicals, socialists, and anarchists, as well as of the young Yiddish writers and poets. "Everybody forgathers there," he remarked; "the Minkin sisters will no doubt also be there."

For one who had just come away from the monotony of a provincial town like Rochester and whose nerves were on edge from a night's trip in a stuffy car, the noise and turmoil that greeted us at Sachs's were certainly not very soothing. The place consisted of two rooms and was packed. Everybody talked, gesticulated, and argued, in Yiddish and Russian, each competing with the other. I was almost overcome in this strange human medley. My escort discovered two girls at a table. He introduced them as Anna and Helen Minkin.

They were Russian Jewish working girls. Anna, the older, was about my own age; Helen perhaps eighteen. Soon we came to an understanding about my living with them, and my anxiety and uncertainty were over. I had a roof over my head; I had found friends. The bedlam at Sachs's no longer mattered. I began to breathe freer, to feel less of an alien.

While the four of us were having our dinner, and Solotaroff was pointing out to me the different people in the café, I suddenly heard a powerful voice call: "Extra-large steak! Extra cup of coffee!" My own capital was so small and the need for economy so great that I was startled by such apparent extravagance. Besides, Solotaroff had told me that only poor students, writers, and workers were the clients of Sachs. I wondered who that reckless person could be and how he could afford such food. "Who is that glutton?" I asked. Solotaroff laughed aloud. "That is Alexander Berkman.[3] He can eat for three. But he rarely has enough money for much food. When he has, he eats Sachs out of his supplies. I'll introduce him to you."

We had finished our meal, and several people came to our table to talk to Solotaroff. The man of the extra-large steak was still packing it away as if he had gone hungry for weeks. Just as we were about to depart, he approached us, and Solotaroff introduced him. He was no more than a boy, hardly eighteen, but with the neck and chest of a giant. His jaw was strong, made more pronounced by his thick lips. His face was almost severe, but for his high, studious forehead and intelligent eyes. A determined youngster, I thought. Presently Berkman remarked to me: "Johann Most is speaking tonight. Do you want to come to hear him?"

How extraordinary, I thought, that on my very first day in New York I should have the chance to behold with my own eyes and hear the fiery man whom the Rochester press used to portray as the personification of the devil, a criminal, a blood-thirsty demon! I had planned to visit Most in the office of his newspaper some time later, but that the opportunity should present itself in such an unexpected manner gave me the feeling that something wonderful was about to happen, something that would decide the whole course of my life.

On the way to the hall I was too absorbed in my thoughts to hear much of the conversation that was going on between Berk-man and the Minkin sisters. Suddenly I stumbled. I should have fallen had not Berkman gripped my arm and held me up. "I have saved your life," he said jestingly. "I hope I may be able to save yours some day," I quickly replied.

The meeting-place was a small hall behind a saloon, through which one had to pass. It was crowded with Germans, drink-ing, smoking, and talking. Before long, Johann Most entered. My first impression of him was one of revulsion. He was of medium height, with a large head crowned with greyish bushy hair; but his face was twisted out of form by an apparent dislo-cation of the left jaw. Only his eyes were soothing; they were blue and sympathetic.

His speech was a scorching denunciation of American condi-tions, a biting satire on the injustice and brutality of the domi-nant powers, a passionate tirade against those responsible for the Haymarket tragedy and the execution of the Chicago anarchists in November 1887. He spoke eloquently and picturesquely. As if by magic, his disfigurement disappeared, his lack of physical dis-tinction was forgotten. He seemed transformed into some primi-tive power, radiating hatred and love, strength and inspiration. The rapid current of his speech, the music of his voice, and his sparkling wit, all combined to produce an effect almost over-whelming. He stirred me to my depths.

Caught in the crowd that surged towards the platform, I found myself before Most. Berkman was near me and intro-duced me. But I was dumb with excitement and nervousness, full of the tumult of emotions Most's speech had aroused in me.

That night I could not sleep. Again I lived through the events of 1887. Twenty-one months had passed since the Black Friday of

November 11, when the Chicago men had suffered their martyrdom, yet every detail stood out clear before my vision and affected
me as if it had happened but yesterday. My sister Helena and I
had become interested in the fate of the men during the period of
their trial. The reports in the Rochester newspapers irritated, confused, and upset us by their evident prejudice. The violence of the
press, the bitter denunciation of the accused, the attacks on all
foreigners, turned our sympathies to the Haymarket victims.

We had learned of the existence in Rochester of a German
socialist group that held sessions on Sunday in Germania Hall.
We began to attend the meetings, my older sister, Helena, on a
few occasions only, and I regularly. The gatherings were generally uninteresting, but they offered an escape from the grey
dullness of my Rochester existence. There one heard, at least,
something different from the everlasting talk about money and
business, and one met people of spirit and ideas.

One Sunday it was announced that a famous socialist speaker
from New York, Johanna Greie, would lecture on the case then
being tried in Chicago. On the appointed day I was the first in
the hall. The huge place was crowded from top to bottom by
eager men and women, while the walls were lined with police. I
had never before been at such a large meeting. I had seen *gendarmes* in St. Petersburg disperse small student gatherings. But
that in the country which guaranteed free speech, officers
armed with long clubs should invade an orderly assembly filled
me with consternation and protest.

Soon the chairman announced the speaker. She was a woman
in her thirties, pale and ascetic-looking, with large luminous
eyes. She spoke with great earnestness, in a voice vibrating with
intensity. Her manner engrossed me. I forgot the police, the audience, and everything else about me. I was aware only of the
frail woman in black crying out her passionate indictment
against the forces that were about to destroy eight human lives.

The entire speech concerned the stirring events in Chicago.
She began by relating the historical background of the case. She
told of the labour strikes that broke out throughout the country
in 1886, for the demand of an eight-hour workday. The centre
of the movement was Chicago, and there the struggle between

the toilers and their bosses became intense and bitter. A meeting of the striking employees of the McCormick Harvester Company in that city was attacked by police; men and women were beaten and several persons killed. To protest against the outrage a mass meeting was called in Haymarket Square on May 4. It was addressed by Albert Parsons, August Spies, Adolph Fischer, and others, and was quiet and orderly. [. . .] Then something flashed through the air and exploded, killing a number of police officers and wounding a score of others. It was never ascertained who the actual culprit was, and the authorities apparently made little effort to discover him. Instead orders were immediately issued for the arrest of all the speakers at the Haymarket meeting and other prominent anarchists. The entire press and *bourgeoisie* of Chicago and of the whole country began shouting for the blood of the prisoners. [. . .] The incited state of the public mind, and the general prejudice against anarchists, coupled with the employers' bitter opposition to the eight-hour movement, constituted the atmosphere that favoured the judicial murder of the Chicago anarchists. Five of them—Albert Parsons, August Spies, Louis Lingg, Adolph Fischer, and George Engel—were sentenced to die by hanging; Michael Schwab and Samuel Fielden were doomed to life imprisonment; Neebe received fifteen years' sentence. The innocent blood of the Haymarket martyrs was calling for revenge.

At the end of Greie's speech I knew what I had surmised all along: the Chicago men were innocent. They were to be put to death for their ideal. But what was their ideal? Johanna Greie spoke of Parsons, Spies, Lingg, and the others as socialists, but I was ignorant of the real meaning of socialism. What I had heard from the local speakers had impressed me as colourless and mechanistic. On the other hand, the papers called these men anarchists, bomb-throwers. What was anarchism? It was all very puzzling. But I had no time for further contemplation. The people were filing out, and I got up to leave. Greie, the chairman, and a group of friends were still on the platform. As I turned towards them, I saw Greie motioning to me. I was startled, my heart beat violently, and my feet felt leaden. When I approached her, she took me by the hand and said: "I never saw a face that reflected such a tumult of emotions as yours. You must be feeling the impending tragedy intensely. Do you know the men?" In a trembling voice I replied: "Unfortunately not, but I do feel the case with every fibre, and when I heard you speak, it seemed to me as if I knew them." She put her hand on my shoulder. "I have a feeling that you will know them better as you learn their ideal, and that you will make their cause your own."

I walked home in a dream. Sister Helena was already asleep, but I had to share my experience with her. I woke her up and recited to her the whole story, giving almost a verbatim account of the speech. I must have been very dramatic, because Helena exclaimed: "The next thing I'll hear about my little sister is that she, too, is a dangerous anarchist."

[. . .] I began to read *Die Freiheit* regularly. I sent for the literature advertised in the paper and I devoured every line on anarchism I could get, every word about the men, their lives, their work. I read about their heroic stand while on trial and their marvellous defence. I saw a new world opening before me.

The terrible thing everyone feared, yet hoped would not happen, actually occurred. Extra editions of the Rochester papers carried the news: the Chicago anarchists had been hanged!

We were crushed, Helena and I. The shock completely unnerved my sister; she could only wring her hands and weep silently. I was in a stupor; a feeling of numbness came over me, something too horrible even for tears. In the evening we went to our father's house. Everybody talked about the Chicago events. I was entirely absorbed in what I felt as my own loss. Then I heard the coarse laugh of a woman. In a shrill voice she sneered: "What's all this lament about? The men were murderers. It is well they were hanged." With one leap I was at the woman's throat. Then I felt myself torn back. Someone said: "The child has gone crazy." I wrenched myself free, grabbed a pitcher of water from a table, and threw it with all my force into the woman's face. "Out, out," I cried, "or I will kill you!" The terrified woman made for the door and I dropped to the ground in a fit of crying. I was put to bed, and soon I fell into a deep sleep. The next morning I woke as from a long illness, but free from the numbness and the depression of those harrowing weeks of waiting, ending with the final shock. I had a distinct sensation that something new and wonderful had been born in my soul. A great ideal, a burning faith, a determination to dedicate myself to the memory of my martyred comrades, to make their cause my own, to make known to the world their beautiful lives and heroic deaths. Johanna Greie was more prophetic than she had probably realized.

My mind was made up. I would go to New York, to Johann Most. He would help me prepare myself for my new task. But my husband, my parents—how would they meet my decision?

I had been married only ten months. The union had not been happy. I had realized almost from the beginning that my husband and I were at opposite poles, with nothing in common, not even sexual blending. The venture, like everything else that had happened to me since I had come to America, had proved most disappointing. America, "the land of the free and the home of the brave"—what a farce it now seemed to me! Yet how I had fought with my father to get him to let me go to America with Helena! In the end I had won, and late in December 1885, Helena and I had left St. Petersburg for Hamburg, there embarking on the steamer *Elbe* for the Promised Land.

[. . .] I left without regrets. Since my earliest recollection, home had been stifling, my father's presence terrifying. My mother, while less violent with the children, never showed much warmth. It was always Helena who gave me affection, who filled my childhood with whatever joy it had. She would continually shoulder the blame for the rest of the children. Many blows intended for my brother and me were given Helena. Now we were completely together—nobody would separate us.

[. . .] The last day of our journey comes vividly to my mind. Everybody was on deck. Helena and I stood pressed to each other, enraptured by the sight of the harbour and the Statue of Liberty suddenly emerging from the mist. Ah, there she was, the symbol of hope, of freedom, of opportunity! She held her torch high to light the way to the free country, the asylum for the oppressed of all lands. We, too, Helena and I, would find a place in the generous heart of America. Our spirits were high, our eyes filled with tears.

[. . .] We had heard that Rochester was the "Flower City" of New York, but we arrived there on a bleak and cold January morning. My sister Lena, heavy with her first child, and Aunt Rachel met us.[4] Lena's rooms were small, but they were bright and spotless. The room prepared for Helena and myself was filled with flowers. Throughout the day people came in and out—relatives I had never known, friends of my sister and of her husband, neighbours. All wanted to see us, to hear about the old country. They were Jews who had suffered much in Russia; some of them had even been in pogroms. Life in the new country, they said, was hard; they were all still possessed by nostalgia for their home that had never been a home.

[. . .] One coarse-looking fellow concentrated his attention on me. He kept staring at me all the evening, scanning me up and down. He even came over and tried to feel my arms. It gave me the sensation of standing naked on the market-place. I was outraged, but I did not want to insult my sister's friends. I felt utterly alone and I rushed out of the room. A longing possessed me for what I had left behind—St. Petersburg, my beloved Neva, my friends, my books and music. I became aware of loud voices in the next room. I heard the man who had enraged me say: "I can get her a job at Garson and Mayer's. The wages will be small, but she will soon find a feller to marry her. Such a buxom girl, with her red cheeks and blue eyes, will not have to work long. Any man will snatch her up and keep her in silks and diamonds." I thought of Father. He had tried desperately to marry me off at the age of fifteen. I had protested, begging to be permitted to continue my studies. In his frenzy he threw my French grammar into the fire, shouting: "Girls do not have to learn much! All a Jewish daughter needs to know is how to prepare *gefüllte* fish, cut noodles fine, and give the man plenty of children." I would not listen to his schemes; I wanted to study, to know life, to travel. Besides, I never would marry for anything but love, I stoutly maintained. It was really to escape my father's plans for me that I had insisted on going to America. Now attempts to marry me off pursued me even in the new land. I was determined not to be bartered: I would go to work. [. . .]

CHAPTER II

I had worked in factories before, in St. Petersburg. In the winter of 1882, when Mother, my two little brothers, and I came from Königsberg to join Father in the Russian capital, we found that he had lost his position. He had been manager of his cousin's dry-goods store; but, shortly before our arrival, the business failed. The loss of his job was a tragedy to our family, as Father had not managed to save anything. The only bread-winner then was Helena. Mother was forced to turn to her brothers for a loan. The three hundred roubles they advanced were invested in a grocery store. The business yielded little at first, and it became necessary for me to find employment.

[. . .] Father's cousin who had failed in the dry-goods business now owned a glove factory. He offered to teach me the trade and give me work. The factory was far from our place. One had to get up at five in the morning to be at work at seven. The rooms were stuffy, unventilated, and dark. Oil lamps gave the light; the sun never penetrated the work-room. There were six hundred of us, of all ages, working on costly and beautiful gloves day in, day out, for very small pay. But we were allowed sufficient time for our noon meal and twice a day for tea. We could talk and sing while at work; we were not driven or harassed. That was in St. Petersburg, in 1882.

Now I was in America, in the Flower City of the State of New York, in a model factory, as I was told. Certainly, Garson's clothing-works were a vast improvement on the glove factory on the Vassilevsky Ostrov. The rooms were large, bright, and airy. One had elbow space. There were none of those ill-smelling odours that used to nauseate me in our cousin's shop.

Yet the work here was harder, and the day, with only half an hour for lunch, seemed endless. The iron discipline forbade free movement (one could not even go to the toilet without permission), and the constant surveillance of the foreman weighed like stone on my heart. The end of each day found me sapped, with just enough energy to drag myself to my sister's home and crawl into bed. [. . .]

The next morning the enervating routine started all over again, continuing for weeks and months, broken only by the new arrival in our family, a baby girl. The child became the one interest in my dull existence. Often, when the atmosphere in Garson's factory threatened to overcome me, the thought of the lovely mite at home revived my spirit. The evenings were no longer dreary and meaningless. But, while little Stella brought joy into our household, she added to the material anxiety of my sister and my brother-in-law.[1]

Lena never by word or deed made me feel that the dollar and fifty cents I was giving her for my board (the car fare amounted to sixty cents a week, the remaining forty cents being my pin-money) did not cover my keep. But I had overheard my brother-in-law grumbling over the growing expenses of the house. I felt he was right. I did not want my sister worried, she was nursing her child. I decided to apply for a rise. I knew it was no use talking to the foreman and therefore I asked to see Mr. Garson.

I was ushered into a luxurious office. American Beauties were on the table. Often I had admired them in the flower shops, and once, unable to withstand the temptation, I had gone in to ask the price. They were one dollar and a half apiece—more than half of my week's earnings. The lovely vase in Mr. Garson's office held a great many of them.

I was not asked to sit down. For a moment I forgot my mission. The beautiful room, the roses, the aroma of the bluish smoke from Mr. Garson's cigar, fascinated me. I was recalled to reality by my employer's question: "Well, what can I do for you?"

I had come to ask for a rise, I told him. The two dollars and a half I was getting did not pay my board, let alone anything else, such as an occasional book or a theatre ticket for twenty-five cents. Mr. Garson replied that for a factory girl I had rather extravagant tastes, that all his "hands" were well satisfied, that they seemed to be getting along all right—that I, too, would have to manage or find work elsewhere. "If I raise your wages, I'll have to raise the others' as well and I can't afford that," he said. I decided to leave Garson's employ.

A few days later I secured a job at Rubinstein's factory at four dollars a week. It was a small shop, not far from where I lived. The house stood in a garden, and only a dozen men and women were employed in the place. The Garson discipline and drive were missing.

Next to my machine worked an attractive young man whose name was Jacob Kershner. He lived near Lena's home, and we would often walk from work together. Before long he began calling for me in the morning. We used to converse in Russian, my English still being very halting. His Russian was like music to me; it was the first real Russian, outside of Helena's, that I had had an opportunity to hear in Rochester since my arrival. [. . .]

The late fall of 1886 brought the rest of our family to Rochester—Father, Mother, my brothers, Herman and Yegor. Conditions in St. Petersburg had become intolerable for the Jews, and the grocery business did not yield enough for the ever-growing bribery Father had to practise in order to be allowed to exist. America became the only solution.

Together with Helena I had prepared a home for our parents, and on their arrival we went to live with them. Our earnings soon proved inadequate to meet the household expenses. Jacob Kershner offered to board with us, which would be of some help, and before long he moved in. [. . .]

On nearer acquaintance I had grown to understand that we were too different. His interest in books, which had first attracted me to him, had waned. He had fallen into the ways of his shopmates, playing cards and attending dull dances. I, on the contrary, was filled with striving and aspirations. In spirit I was still in Russia, in my beloved St. Petersburg, living in the world of the books I had read, the operas I had heard, the circle of the students I had known. I hated Rochester even more than before. But Kershner was the only human being I had met since my arrival. He filled a void in my life, and I was strongly attracted to him. In February 1887 we were married in Rochester by a rabbi, according to Jewish rites, which were then considered sufficient by the law of the country.

My feverish excitement of that day, my suspense and ardent anticipation gave way at night to a feeling of utter bewilderment. Jacob lay trembling near me; he was impotent.

The first erotic sensations I remember had come to me when I was about six. My parents lived in Popelan then, where we children had no home in any real sense. Father kept an inn, which was constantly filled with peasants, drunk and quarrelling, and government officials. [. . .] I was left to myself most of the day. Among the stable help there was a young peasant, Petrushka, who served as shepherd, looking after our cows and sheep. Often he would take me with him to the meadows, and I would listen to the sweet tones of his flute. In the evening he would carry me back home on his shoulders, I sitting astride. He would play horse—run as fast as his legs could carry him, then suddenly throw me up in the air, catch me in his arms, and press me to him. It used to give me a peculiar sensation, fill me with exultation, followed by blissful release.

I became inseparable from Petrushka. I grew so fond of him that I began stealing cake and fruit from Mother's pantry for him. To be with Petrushka out in the fields, to listen to his music, to ride on his shoulders, became the obsession of my waking and sleeping hours. One day Father had an altercation with Petrushka, and the boy was sent away. The loss of him was one of the greatest tragedies of my child-life. For weeks afterwards I kept on dreaming of Petrushka, the meadows, the music, and reliving the joy and ecstasy of our play. One morning I felt myself torn out of sleep. Mother was bending over me, tightly holding my right hand. In an angry voice she cried: "If ever I find your hand again like that, I'll whip you, you naughty child!"

The approach of puberty gave me my first consciousness of the effect of men on me. I was eleven then. Early one summer day I woke up in great agony. My head, spine, and legs ached as if they were being pulled asunder. I called for Mother. She drew back my bedcovers, and suddenly I felt a stinging pain in my face. She had struck me. I let out a shriek, fastening on Mother terrified eyes. "This is necessary for a girl," she said, "when she becomes a woman, as a protection against disgrace." She tried to take me in her arms, but I pushed her back. I was writhing in pain and I was too outraged for her to touch me. "I am going to die," I howled, "I want the *Feldscher*" (assistant doctor). The *Feldscher* was sent for. He was a young man, a new-comer in our village. He examined me and gave me something to put me to sleep. Thenceforth my dreams were of the *Feldscher*.

When I was fifteen, I was employed in a corset-factory in the Hermitage Arcade in St. Petersburg. After working hours, on leaving the shop together with the other girls, we would be waylaid by young Russian officers and civilians. Most of the girls had their sweethearts; only a Jewish girl chum of mine and I refused to be taken to the *konditorskaya* (pastry shop) or to the park.

Next to the Hermitage was a hotel we had to pass. One of the clerks, a handsome fellow of about twenty, singled me out for his attentions. At first I scorned him, but gradually he began to exert a fascination on me. [. . .]

For several months my admirer and I met clandestinely. One day he asked me whether I should not like to go through the hotel to see the luxurious rooms. I had never been in a hotel before—the joy and gaiety I fancied behind the gorgeous windows used to fascinate me as I would pass the place on my way from work.

The boy led me through a side entrance, along a thickly carpeted corridor, into a large room. It was brightly illumined and beautifully furnished. A table near the sofa held flowers and a tea-tray. We sat down. The young man poured out a golden-coloured liquid and asked me to clink glasses to our friendship. I put the wine to my lips. Suddenly I found myself in his arms, my waist torn open—his passionate kisses covered my face, neck, and breasts. Not until after the violent contact of our bodies and the excruciating pain he caused me did I come to my senses. I screamed, savagely beating against the man's chest with my fists. Suddenly I heard Helena's voice in the hall. "She must be here—she must be here!" I became speechless. The man, too, was terrorized. His grip relaxed, and we listened in breathless silence. After what seemed to me hours, Helena's voice receded. The man got up. I rose mechanically, mechanically buttoned my waist and brushed back my hair.

Strange, I felt no shame—only a great shock at the discovery that the contact between man and woman could be so brutal and so painful. I walked out in a daze, bruised in every nerve.

When I reached home I found Helena fearfully wrought up. [. . .] The shame I did not feel in the arms of the man now overwhelmed me. I could not muster up courage to tell Helena of my experience. After that I always felt between two fires in the presence of men. Their lure remained strong, but it was always mingled with violent revulsion. I could not bear to have them touch me. These pictures passed through my mind vividly as I lay alongside my husband on our wedding night. He had fallen fast asleep.

The weeks went on. There was no change. I urged Jacob to consult a doctor. At first he refused, pleading diffidence, but finally he went. He was told it would take considerable time to "build up his manhood." My own passion had subsided. The material anxiety of making ends meet excluded everything else. I had stopped work: it was considered disgraceful for a married woman to go to the shop. Jacob was earning fifteen dollars a week. He had developed a passion for cards, which swallowed up a considerable part of our income. He grew jealous, suspecting everyone. Life became insupportable. I was saved from utter despair by my interest in the Haymarket events.

After the death of the Chicago anarchists I insisted on a separation from Kershner. He fought long against it, but finally consented to a divorce. It was given to us by the same rabbi who had performed our marriage ceremony. Then I left for New Haven, Connecticut, to work in a corset-factory. [. . .]

In New Haven I met a group of young Russians, students mainly, now working at various trades. Most of them were socialists and anarchists. They often organized meetings, generally

inviting speakers from New York, one of whom was
A. Solotaroff. Life was interesting and colourful, but gradually
the strain of the work became too much for my depleted vitality.
Finally I had to return to Rochester.

I went to Helena. She lived with her husband and child over
their little printing shop, which also served as an office for their
steamship agency. But both occupations did not bring in
enough to keep them from dire poverty. Helena had married Jacob Hochstein, a man ten years her senior. He was a great Hebrew scholar, an authority on the English and Russian classics.
[. . .] His income was insufficient for the needs of the family,
and the one to worry and fret most about it was my poor Helena. She was pregnant with her second child and yet had to
drudge from morning till night to make ends meet, with never a
word of complaint. But, then, she had been that way all her life,
suffering silently, always resigned. [. . .]

On my return from New Haven Helena received me, as always,
with tenderness and with the assurance that her home was also
mine. It was good to be near my darling again, with little Stella
and my young brother Yegor. But it did not take me long to discover the pinched condition in Helena's home. I went back to
the shop.

Living in the Jewish district, it was impossible to avoid those
one did not wish to see. I ran into Kershner almost immediately
after my arrival. Day after day he would seek me out. He began
to plead with me to go back to him—all would be different.
One day he threatened suicide—actually pulled out a bottle of
poison. Insistently he pressed me for a final answer.

[. . .] Kershner's threat frightened me: I could not be responsible for his death. I remarried him. My parents rejoiced and so
did Lena and her husband, but Helena was sick with grief. Without Kershner's knowledge I took up a course in dressmaking, in
order to have a trade that would free me from the shop. During
three long months I wrestled with my husband to let me go my
way. I tried to make him see the futility of living a patched life,
but he remained obdurate. Late one night, after bitter recrimina-
tions, I left Jacob Kershner and my home, this time definitely.

I was immediately ostracized by the whole Jewish population of Rochester. I could not pass on the street without being held up to scorn. My parents forbade me their house, and again it was only Helena who stood by me. Out of her meagre income she even paid my fare to New York.

So I left Rochester, where I had known so much pain, hard work, and loneliness, but the joy of my departure was marred by separation from Helena, from Stella, and the little brother I loved so well.

The break of the new day in the Minkin flat still found me awake. The door upon the old had now closed for ever. The new was calling, and I eagerly stretched out my hands towards it. I fell into a deep, peaceful sleep.

I was awakened by Anna Minkin's voice announcing the arrival of Alexander Berkman. It was late afternoon.

CHAPTER III

Helen Minkin was away at work. Anna was out of a job just then. She prepared tea, and we sat down to talk. Berkman inquired about my plans for work, for activity in the movement. Would I like to visit the *Freiheit* office? Could he be of help in any way? He was free to take me about, he said; he had left his job after a fight with the foreman. "A slave-driver," he commented; "he never dared drive me, but it was my duty to stand up for the others in the shop." It was rather slack now in the cigar-making trade, he informed us, but as an anarchist he could not stop to consider his own job. Nothing personal mattered. Only the Cause mattered. Fighting injustice and exploitation mattered.

How strong he was, I thought; how wonderful in his revolutionary zeal! Just like our martyred comrades in Chicago.

I had to go to West Forty-second Street to get my sewing-machine out of the baggage-room. Berkman offered to accompany me. He suggested that on our way back we might ride down to Brooklyn Bridge on the Elevated and then walk over to William Street, where the *Freiheit* office was located.

I asked him whether I could hope to establish myself in New York as a dressmaker. I wanted so much to free myself from the dreadful grind and slavery of the shop. I wanted to have time for reading, and later I hoped to realize my dream of a co-operative shop. "Something like Vera's venture in *What's to be Done?*" I explained.[1] "You have read Chernishevsky?" Berkman inquired, in surprise; "surely not in Rochester?" "Surely not," I replied, laughing; "besides my sister Helena, I found no one there who would read such books. No, not in that dull

town. In St. Petersburg." He looked at me doubtfully. "Chernishevsky was a Nihilist," he remarked, "and his works are prohibited in Russia. Were you connected with the Nihilists? They
are the only ones who could have given you the book." I felt indignant. How dared he doubt my word! I repeated angrily that
I had read the forbidden book and other similar works, such as
Turgeniev's *Fathers and Sons,* and *Obriv (The Precipice)* by
Gontcharov.² My sister had got them from students and she let
me read them. "I am sorry if I hurt you," Berkman said in a soft
tone. "I did not really doubt your word. I was only surprised to
find a girl so young who had read such books." [. . .]

In an old building, up two dark and creaking flights, was the office of the *Freiheit.* Several men were in the first room setting
type. In the next we found Johann Most standing at a high desk,
writing. With a side-glance he invited us to sit down. "My
damned torturers there are squeezing the blood out of me," he
declared querulously. "Copy, copy, copy! That's all they know!
Ask them to write a line—not they. They are too stupid and too
lazy." A burst of good-natured laughter from the composing-
room greeted Most's outburst. His gruff voice, his twisted jaw,
which had so repelled me on my first meeting him, recalled to
me the caricatures of Most in the Rochester papers. I could not
reconcile the angry man before me with the inspired speaker of
the previous evening whose oratory had so carried me away.

Berkman noticed my confused and frightened look. He whispered in Russian not to mind Most, that he was always in such
a mood when at work. I got up to inspect the books which covered the shelves from floor to ceiling, row upon row. How few
of them I had read, I mused. [. . .]

Most approached me. His deep blue eyes looked searchingly
into mine. "Well, young lady," he said, "have you found anything
you want to read? Or don't you read German and English?" The
harshness of his voice had changed to a warm, kindly texture.
"Not English," I said, soothed and emboldened by his tone, "German." He told me I could have any book I wanted. [. . .] I was
deeply touched by the interest of this man in me, a perfect
stranger. I explained that New York had lured me because it

was the centre of the anarchist movement, and because I had read of him as its leading spirit. I had really come to him for suggestions and help. I wanted very much to talk to him. [. . .]

He suggested that I come next Wednesday, to help with expediting the *Freiheit,* to write addresses and fold the papers— "and afterwards we may be able to talk." With several books under my arm and a warm handshake, Most sent me off. Berkman left with me. [. . .]

It was late in the evening when we parted. Berkman had told me little about himself, except that he had been expelled from the *Gymnasium* for an anti-religious essay he had composed, and that he had left home for good. He had come to the United States in the belief that it was free and that here everyone had an equal chance in life. He knew better now. He had found exploitation more severe, and since the hanging of the Chicago anarchists he had become convinced that America was as despotic as Russia.

"Lingg was right when he said: 'If you attack us with cannon, we will reply with dynamite.' Some day I will avenge our dead," he added with great earnestness. "I too! I too!" I cried; "their death gave me life. It now belongs to their memory—to their work." He gripped my arm until it hurt. "We are comrades. Let us be friends, too—let us work together." His intensity vibrated through me as I walked up the stairs to the Minkin flat.

The following Friday, Berkman invited me to come to a Jewish lecture by Solotaroff at 54 Orchard Street, on the East Side. [. . .] After the meeting Berkman introduced me to a number of people, "all good active comrades," as he put it. "And here is my chum Fedya,"[3] he said, indicating a young man beside him; "he is also an anarchist, of course, but not so good as he should be."

The young chap was probably of the same age as Berkman, but not so strongly built, nor with the same aggressive manner about him. His features were rather delicate, with a sensitive mouth, while his eyes, though somewhat bulging, had a dreamy expression. He did not seem to mind in the least the banter of his friend. He smiled good-naturedly and suggested that we retire to Sachs's, "to give Sasha a chance to tell you what a good anarchist is."

Berkman did not wait till we reached the café. "A good anarchist," he began with deep conviction, "is one who lives only for the Cause and gives everything to it. My friend here"—he indicated Fedya—"is still too much of a *bourgeois* to realize that. He is a *mamenkin sin* (mother's spoilt darling), who even accepts money from home." He continued to explain why it was inconsistent for a revolutionary to have anything to do with his *bourgeois* parents or relatives. His only reason for tolerating his friend Fedya's inconsistency, he added, was that he gave most of what he received from home to the movement. "If I'd let him, he'd spend all his money on useless things—'beautiful,' he calls them. Wouldn't you, Fedya?" He turned to his friend, patting him on the back affectionately.

The café was crowded, as usual, and filled with smoke and talk. For a little while my two escorts were much in demand, while I was greeted by several people I had met during the week. Finally we succeeded in capturing a table and ordered some coffee and cake. I became aware of Fedya watching me and studying my face. To hide my embarrassment I turned to Berkman. "Why should one not love beauty?" I asked; "flowers, for instance, music, the theatre—beautiful things?"

"I did not say one should not," Berkman replied; "I said it was wrong to spend money on such things when the movement is so much in need of it. It is inconsistent for an anarchist to enjoy luxuries when the people live in poverty."

"But beautiful things are not luxuries," I insisted; "they are necessaries. Life would be unbearable without them." Yet, at heart, I felt that Berkman was right. Revolutionists gave up even their lives—why not also beauty? Still the young artist struck a responsive chord in me. I, too, loved beauty. Our poverty-stricken life in Königsberg had been made bearable to me only by the occasional outings with our teachers in the open. The forest, the moon casting its silvery shimmer on the fields, the green wreaths in our hair, the flowers we would pick—these made me forget for a time the sordid home surroundings. [. . .]

The next day Fedya took me to Central Park. Along Fifth Avenue he pointed out the various mansions, naming their owners. I had read about those wealthy men, their affluence

and extravagance, while the masses lived in poverty. I expressed
my indignation at the contrast between those splendid palaces
and the miserable tenements of the East Side. "Yes, it is a crime
that the few should have all, the many nothing," the artist said.
"My main objection," he continued, "is that they have such
bad taste—those buildings are ugly." Berkman's attitude to
beauty came to my mind. "You don't agree with your chum on
the need and importance of beauty in one's life, do you?" I
asked. "Indeed I do not. But, then, my friend is a revolutionist
above everything else. I wish I could also be, but I am not." I
liked his frankness and simplicity. He did not stir me as Berkman did when speaking of revolutionary ethics; Fedya awakened in me the mysterious yearning I used to feel in my
childhood at sight of the sunset turning the Popelan meadows
golden in its dying glow, as the sweet music of Petrushka's flute
did also.

The following week I went to the *Freiheit* office. Several people were already there, busy addressing envelopes and folding
the papers. Everybody talked. Johann Most was at his desk. I
was assigned a place and given work. I marvelled at Most's capacity to go on writing in that hubbub. Several times I wanted
to suggest that he was being disturbed, but I checked myself.
After all, they must know whether he minded their chatter.

In the evening Most stopped writing and gruffly assailed the
talkers as "toothless old women," "cackling geese," and other ap-
pellations I had hardly ever before heard in German. He snatched
his large felt hat from the rack, called to me to come along, and
walked out. I followed him and we went up on the Elevated. "I'll
take you to Terrace Garden," he said; "we can go into the theatre
there if you like. They are giving *Der Zigeunerbaron* tonight. Or
we can sit in some corner, get food and drink, and talk." I
replied that I did not care for light opera, that what I really
wanted was to talk to him, or rather have him talk to me. "But
not so violently as in the office," I added.

He selected the food and the wine. Their names were strange
to me. The label on the bottle read: *Liebfrauenmilch*. "Milk of
woman's love—what a lovely name!" I remarked. "For wine,
yes," he retorted, "but not for woman's love. The one is always

poetic—the other will never be anything but sordidly prosaic. It leaves a bad taste."

I had a feeling of guilt, as if I had made some bad break or had touched a sore spot. I told him I had never tasted any wine before, except the kind Mother made for Easter. Most shook with laughter, and I was near tears. He noticed my embarrassment and restrained himself. He poured out two glassfuls, saying: "*Prosit,* my young, naïve lady," and drank his down at a gulp. Before I could drink half of mine, he had nearly finished the bottle and ordered another.

He became animated, witty, sparkling. There was no trace of the bitterness, of the hatred and defiance his oratory had breathed on the platform. Instead there sat next to me a transformed human being, no longer the repulsive caricature of the Rochester press or the gruff creature of the office. He was a gracious host, an attentive and sympathetic friend. He made me tell him about myself and he grew thoughtful when he learned the motive that had decided me to break with my old life. He warned me to reflect carefully before taking the plunge. "The path of anarchism is steep and painful," he said; "so many have attempted to climb it and have fallen back. The price is exacting. Few men are ready to pay it, most women not at all." [. . .]

I inquired whether the anarchist movement in America had no outstanding woman. "None at all, only stupids," he replied; "most of the girls come to the meetings to snatch up a man; then both vanish, like the silly fishermen at the lure of the Lorelei." There was a roguish twinkle in his eye. He didn't believe much in woman's revolutionary zeal. But I, coming from Russia, might be different and he would help me. If I were really in earnest, I could find much work to do. "There is great need in our ranks of young, willing people—ardent ones, as you seem to be—and I have need of ardent friendship," he added with much feeling.

"You?" I questioned; "you have thousands in New York—all over the world. You are loved, you are idolized." "Yes, little girl, idolized by many, but loved by none. One can be very lonely among thousands—did you know that?" Something gripped my heart. I wanted to take his hand, to tell him that I would be his friend. But I dared not speak out. What could I give this man—I, a factory girl, uneducated; and he, the famous Johann Most, the leader of the masses, the man of magic tongue and powerful pen? [. . .]

The next day, when Berkman called, I related to him my wonderful evening with Most. His face darkened. "Most has no right to squander money, to go to expensive restaurants, drink expensive wines," he said gravely; "he is spending the money contributed for the movement. He should be held to account. I myself will tell him."

"No, no, you musn't," I cried. "I couldn't bear to be the cause of any affront to Most, who is giving so much. Is he not entitled to a little joy?" Berkman persisted that I was too young in the movement, that I didn't know anything about revolutionary ethics or the meaning of revolutionary right and wrong. I admitted my ignorance, assured him I was willing to learn, to do anything, only not to have Most hurt. He walked out without bidding me good-bye. [. . .]

For a whole week Berkman did not show up. When he came back again, it was to invite me for an outing in Prospect Park. He liked it better than Central Park, he said, because it was less cultivated, more natural. We walked about a great deal, admiring its rough beauty, and finally selected a lovely spot in which to eat the lunch I had brought with me.

We talked about my life in St. Petersburg and in Rochester. I told him of my marriage to Jacob Kershner and its failure. He wanted to know what books I had read on marriage and if it was their influence that had decided me to leave my husband. I had never read such works, but I had seen enough of the horrors of married life in my own home. Father's harsh treatment of Mother, the constant wrangles and bitter scenes that ended in Mother's fainting spells. I had also seen the debasing sordidness of the life of my married aunts and uncles, as well as in the homes of acquaintances in Rochester. Together with my own marital experiences they had convinced me that binding people for life was wrong. The constant

proximity in the same house, the same room, the same bed, revolted me.

"If ever I love a man again, I will give myself to him without
being bound by the rabbi or the law," I declared, "and when
that love dies, I will leave without permission."

My companion said he was glad to know that I felt that way.
All true revolutionists had discarded marriage and were living
in freedom. That served to strengthen their love and helped
them in their common task. He told me the story of Sophia Perovskaya and Zhelyabov.[4] They had been lovers, had worked in
the same group, and together they elaborated the plan for the
execution of Alexander II. After the explosion of the bomb Perovskaya vanished. She was in hiding. She had every chance to
escape, and her comrades begged her to do so. But she refused.
She insisted that she must take the consequences, that she
would share the fate of her comrades and die together with
Zhelyabov. "Of course, it was wrong of her to be moved by
personal sentiment," Berkman commented; "her love for the
Cause should have urged her to live for other activities." Again
I found myself disagreeing with him. I thought that it could not
be wrong to die with one's beloved in a common act—it was
beautiful, it was sublime. He retorted that I was too romantic
and sentimental for a revolutionist, that the task before us was
hard and we must become hard.

I wondered if the boy was really so hard, or was he merely
trying to mask his tenderness, which I intuitively sensed in him.
I felt myself drawn to him and I longed to throw my arms
around him, but I was too shy.

The day ended in a glowing sunset. Joy was in my heart. All
the way home I sang German and Russian songs, *Veeyut, vitri,
veeyut booyniy,* being one of them. "That is my favorite song,
Emma, *dorogaya* (dear)," he said. "I may call you that, may I
not? And will you call me Sasha?" Our lips met in a spontaneous embrace. [. . .]

Most had gone on a lecture tour. From time to time he would
send me a few lines, witty and caustic comments on the people he
was meeting, vitriolic denunciation of reporters who interviewed

him and then wrote vilifying articles about him. Occasionally he would include in his letters the caricatures made of him, with his own marginal comments: "Behold the wife-killer!" or "Here's the man who eats little children." [. . .]

When Most returned from his tour, we all went to hear his report. He was more masterly, more witty and defiant against the system than on any previous occasion. He almost hypnotized me. I could not help going up after the lecture to tell him how splendid his talk was. "Will you go with me to hear *Carmen* Monday at the Metropolitan Opera House?" he whispered. He added that Monday was an awfully busy day because he had to keep his devils supplied with copy, but that he would work ahead on Sunday if I would promise to come. "To the end of the world!" I replied impulsively.

We found the house sold out—no seats to be had at any price. We should have to stand. I knew that I was in for torture. Since childhood I had had trouble with the small toe of my left foot; new shoes used to cause me suffering for weeks, and I was wearing new shoes. But I was too ashamed to tell Most, afraid he would think me vain. I stood close to him, jammed in by a large crowd. My foot burned as if it were being held over a fire. But the first bar of the music, and the glorious singing, made me forget my agony. After the first act, when the lights went on, I found myself holding on to Most for dear life, my face distorted with pain. "What's the matter?" he asked. "I must get off my shoe," I panted, "or I shall scream out." Leaning against him, I bent down to loosen the buttons. The rest of the opera I heard supported by Most's arm, my shoe in my hand. I could not tell whether my rapture was due to the music of *Carmen* or the release from my shoe!

We left the Opera House arm in arm, I limping. We went to a café, and Most teased me about my vanity. But he was rather glad, he said, to find me so feminine, even if it was stupid to wear tight shoes. He was in a golden mood. He wanted to know if I had ever before heard an opera and asked me to tell him about it.

Till I was ten years of age I had never heard any music, except the plaintive flute of Petrushka, Father's stable-boy. The

screeching of the violins at the Jewish weddings and the pound-
ings of the piano at our singing lessons had always been hateful
to me. When I heard the opera *Trovatore*[5] in Königsberg, I first
realized the ecstasy music could create in me. My teacher may
have been largely responsible for the electrifying effect of that experience: she had imbued me with the romance of her favourite
German authors and had helped to rouse my imagination about
the sad love of the Troubadour and Leonore. The tortuous suspense of the days before Mother gave her consent to my accompanying my teacher to the performance aggravated my tense
expectancy. We reached the Opera a full hour before the beginning, myself in a cold sweat for fear we were late. Teacher, always in delicate health, could not keep up with my young legs
and my frenzied haste to reach our places. I flew up to the top
gallery, three steps at a time. The house was still empty and
half-lit, and somewhat disappointing at first. As if by magic, it
soon became transformed. Quickly the place filled with a vast
audience—women in silks and velvets of gorgeous hue, with
glistening jewels on their bare necks and arms, the flood of light
from the crystal chandeliers reflecting the colours of green, yellow, and amethyst. It was a fairyland more magnificent than any
ever pictured in the stories I had read. I forgot the presence of
my teacher, the mean surroundings of my home; half-hanging
over the rail, I was lost in the enchanted world below. The orchestra broke into stirring tones, mysteriously rising from the
darkened house. They sent tremors down my back and held me
breathless by their swelling sounds. Leonore and the Troubadour made real my own romantic fancy of love. I lived with
them, thrilled and intoxicated by their passionate song. [. . .]

When I had finished relating this to Most, I noticed that his
gaze was far away in the distance. He looked up as if from a
dream. He had never heard, he remarked slowly, the stirrings of
a child more dramatically told. I had great talent, he said, and I
must begin soon to recite and speak in public. He would make
me a great speaker—"to take my place when I am gone," he
added.

I thought he was only making fun, or flattering me. He could
not really believe that I could ever take his place or express his

fire, his magic power. I did not want him to treat me that way—
I wanted him to be a true comrade, frank and honest, without
silly German compliments. Most grinned and emptied his glass
to my "first public speech."

After that we went out together often. He opened up a new
world to me, introduced me to music, books, the theatre. But
his own rich personality meant far more to me—the alternating
heights and depths of his spirit, his hatred of the capitalist system, his vision of a new society of beauty and joy for all.

Most became my idol. I worshipped him.

CHAPTER IV

The 11th of November was approaching, the anniversary of the Chicago martyrdoms. Sasha and I were busy with preparations for the great event of so much significance to us. Cooper Union had been secured for the commemoration. The meeting was to be held jointly by anarchists and socialists, with the co-operation of advanced labour organizations.

Every evening for several weeks we visited various trade unions to invite them to participate. This involved short talks from the floor, which I made. I always went in trepidation. On previous occasions, at German and Jewish lectures, I had mustered up courage to ask questions, but every time I would experience a kind of sinking sensation. While I was listening to the speakers, the questions would formulate themselves easily enough, but the moment I got up on my feet, I would feel faint. Desperately I would grip the chair in front of me, my heart throbbing, my knees trembling—everything in the hall would turn hazy. Then I would become aware of my voice, far, far away, and finally I would sink back in my seat in a cold sweat.

When I was first asked to make short speeches, I declined; I was sure I could never manage it. But Most would accept no refusal, and the other comrades sustained him. For the Cause, I was told, one must be able to do everything, and I so eagerly wanted to serve the Cause.

My talks used to sound incoherent to me, full of repetitions, lacking in conviction; and always the dismal feeling of sinking would be upon me. I thought everyone must see my turmoil, but apparently no one did. Even Sasha often commented on my calm and self-control. I do not know whether it was due to my being a beginner, to my youth, or to my intense feeling for the martyred men, but I never once failed to interest the workers I had been sent to invite. [. . .]

At last the long-awaited evening arrived—my first public meeting in memory of the martyred men. Since I had read the accounts in the Rochester papers of the impressive march to Waldheim—the five-mile line of workers who followed the great dead to their last resting-place—and the large meetings that had since been held all over the world, I had ardently looked forward to being present at such an event. Now the moment had at last come. I went with Sasha to Cooper Union.

We found the historic hall densely packed, but with our wreath held high over our heads we finally managed to get through. Even the platform was crowded. I was bewildered until I saw Most standing next to a man and a woman; his presence made me feel at ease. [. . .]

Then Most ascended the platform, and everything else seemed blotted out. I was caught in the storm of his eloquence, tossed about, my very soul contracting and expanding in the rise and fall of his voice. It was no longer a speech, it was thunder interspersed with flashes of lightning. It was a wild, passionate cry against the terrible thing that had happened in Chicago—a fierce call to battle against the enemy, a call to individual acts, to vengeance.

The meeting was at an end. Sasha and I filed out with the rest. I could not speak; we walked on in silence. When we reached the house where I lived, my whole body began to shake as in a fever. An overpowering yearning possessed me, an unutterable desire to give myself to Sasha, to find relief in his arms from the fearful tension of the evening.

My narrow bed now held two human bodies, closely pressed together. My room was no longer dark; a soft, soothing light seemed to come from somewhere. As in a dream I heard sweet, endearing words breathed into my ear, like the soft, beautiful Russian lullabies of my childhood. I became drowsy, my thoughts in confusion.

[. . .] . . . Johann Most . . . the force and wonder of his speech, his call to extermination—[. . .] Could idealists be cruel?

The enemies of life and joy and beauty are cruel. They are relentless, they have killed our great comrades. But must we, too, exterminate?

I was roused from my drowsiness as if by an electric current. I felt a trembling, shy hand tenderly glide over me. Hungrily I reached for it, for my lover. We were engulfed in a wild embrace. Again I felt terrific pain, like the cut of a sharp knife. But it was numbed by my passion, breaking through all that had been suppressed, unconscious, and dormant.

The morning still found me eagerly reaching out, hungrily seeking. My beloved lay at my side, asleep in blissful exhaustion. I sat up, my head resting on my hand. Long I watched the face of the boy who had so attracted and repelled me at the same time, who could be so hard and whose touch was yet so tender. Deep love for him welled up in my heart—a feeling of certainty that our lives were linked for all time. I pressed my lips to his thick hair and then I, too, fell asleep.

The people from whom I rented my room slept on the other side of the wall. Their nearness always disturbed me, and now in Sasha's presence it gave me a feeling of being seen. He also had no privacy where he lived. I suggested that we find a small apartment, and he consented joyfully. When we told Fedya of our plan, he asked to be taken in. The fourth of our little commune was Helen Minkin. The friction with her father had become more violent since I had moved out, and she could not endure it. She begged to come with us. We rented a four-room flat on Forty-second Street and we all felt it a luxury to have our own place.

From the very first we agreed to share everything, to live like real comrades. Helen continued to work in the corset-factory, and I divided my time between sewing silk waists and keeping house. Fedya devoted himself to painting. The expense of his oils, canvases, and brushes often consumed more than we could afford, but it never occurred to any one of us to complain. From time to time he would sell a picture to some dealer for fifteen or twenty-five dollars, whereupon he would bring an armful of flowers or some present for me. Sasha would upbraid him for it: the idea of spending money for such things, when the movement needed it so badly, was intolerable to him. His anger had no effect on Fedya. He would laugh it off, call him a fanatic, and say he had no sense of beauty. [. . .]

One morning Fedya asked me to pose for him. I experienced no sense of shame at standing naked before him. He worked away for a time, and neither of us talked. Then he began to fidget about and finally said he would have to stop: he could not concentrate, the mood was gone. I went back behind the screen to dress. I had not quite finished when I heard violent weeping. I rushed forward and found Fedya stretched on the sofa, his head buried in the pillow, sobbing. As I bent over him, he sat up and broke loose in a torrent—said he loved me, that he had from the very beginning, though he had tried to keep in the background for Sasha's sake; he had struggled fiercely against his feeling for me, but he knew now that it was of no use. He would have to move out.

I sat by him, holding his hand in mine and stroking his soft wavy hair. Fedya had always drawn me to him by his thoughtful attention, his sensitive response, and his love of beauty. Now I felt something stronger stirring within me. Could it be love for Fedya, I wondered. Could one love two persons at the same time? I loved Sasha. At that very moment my resentment at his harshness gave way to yearning for my strong, arduous lover. Yet I felt Sasha had left something untouched in me, something Fedya could perhaps waken to life. Yes, it must be possible to love more than one! All I had felt for the boy artist must have really been love without my being aware of it till now, I decided.

I asked Fedya what he thought of love for two or even for more persons at once. He looked up in surprise and said he did not know, he had never loved anyone before. His love for me had absorbed him to the exclusion of anyone else. He knew he could not care for another woman while he loved me. And he was certain that Sasha would never want to share me; his sense of possession was too strong.

I resented the suggestion of sharing. I insisted that one can only respond to what the other is able to call out. I did not believe that Sasha was possessive. One who so fervently wanted freedom and preached it so whole-heartedly could never object to my giving myself to someone else. We agreed that, whatever happened, there must be no deception. We must go to Sasha and tell him frankly how we felt. He would understand.

That evening Sasha returned straight from work. The four of us sat down, as usual, to our supper. We talked about various things. No reference was made to Sasha's long absence and there was no chance to speak to him alone about the new light that had come into my life. We all went to Orchard Street to a lecture.

After the meeting Sasha went home with me, Fedya and Helen remaining behind. In our flat he asked permission to come to my room. Then he began to talk, pouring out his whole soul. He said he loved me dearly, that he wanted me to have beautiful things; that he, too, loved beauty. But he loved the Cause more than anything else in the world. For that he would forgo even our love. Yes, and his very life.

He told me about the famous Russian revolutionary catechism that demanded of the true revolutionist that he give up home, parents, sweetheart, children, everything dear to one's being. He agreed with it absolutely and he was determined to allow nothing to stand in the way. "But I do love you," he repeated. His intensity, his uncompromising fervour, irritated and yet drew me like a magnet. Whatever longing I had experienced when near Fedya was silent now. Sasha, my own wonderful, dedicated, obsessed Sasha, was calling. I felt entirely his.

Later in the day I had to meet Most. He had spoken to me about a short lecture tour he was planning for me, but though I did not take it seriously, he had asked me to come to see him about it.

The *Freiheit* office was crowded. Most suggested a near-by saloon, which he knew to be quiet in the early afternoon. We went there. He began to explain his plans for my tour; I was to visit Rochester, Buffalo, and Cleveland. It threw me into a panic. "It is impossible!" I protested; "I don't know a thing about lecturing." He waved my objections aside, declaring that everybody felt that way in the beginning. He was determined to make a public speaker of me, and I would simply have to begin. He had already chosen the subject for me and he would help me prepare it. I was to speak on the futility of the struggle for the eight-hour workday, now again much discussed in labour ranks. He pointed out that the eight-hour campaigns in '84, '85, and '86 had already taken a toll far beyond the value of the "damned thing." "Our comrades in Chicago lost their lives for it, and the workers still work long hours." But even if the eight-hour day were established, there would be no actual gain, he insisted. On the contrary, it would serve only to distract the masses from the real issue—the struggle against capitalism, against the wage system, for a new society. [. . .]

When I got home, away from Most's presence, I again experienced the sinking feeling that had come upon me when I had first tried to speak in public. I still had three weeks in which to read up, but I was sure I never could go through with it. [. . .]

My three good friends insisted that I stop work to have more time for study. They would also relieve me of every domestic responsibility. I devoted myself to reading. Now and then Fedya would come with flowers. He knew that I had not yet spoken to Sasha. He never pressed me, but his flowers spoke more appealingly than anything he could have said. Sasha no longer scolded him for wasting money. "I know you love flowers," he would say; "they may inspire you in your new work."

I read up a great deal on the eight-hour movement, went to every meeting where the matter was to be discussed; but the more I studied the subject, the more confused I became. "The iron law of wages," "supply and demand," "poverty as the only leaven of revolt"—I could not follow it all. It left me as cold as the mechanistic theories I used to hear expounded in the Rochester Socialist local. But when I read Most's notes, everything seemed clear. [. . .]

The day of my departure for Rochester arrived. I met Most for a last talk; I came in a depressed mood, but a glass of wine and Most's spirit soon lifted the weight. He talked long and ardently, made numerous suggestions, and said I must not take the audiences too seriously; most of them were dullards, anyway. [. . .]

He took me to the Grand Central in a cab. On the way he moved close to me. He yearned to take me in his arms and asked if he might. I nodded, and he held me pressed to him. Conflicting thoughts and emotions possessed me; the speeches

I was going to make, Sasha, Fedya, my passion for the one, my budding love for the other. But I yielded to Most's trembling embrace, his kisses covering my mouth as of one famished with thirst. I let him drink; I could have denied him nothing. He loved me, he said; he had never known such longing for any woman before. Of late years he had not even been attracted to anyone. A feeling of growing age was overcoming him, and he felt worn from the long struggle and the persecution he had endured. More depressing even was the consciousness that his best comrades misunderstood him. But my youth had made him young, my ardour had raised his spirit. My whole being had awakened him to a new meaning in life. I was his *Blondkopf*, his "blue eyes"; he wanted me to be his own, his helpmate, his voice. [. . .]

At the station my three friends were already waiting for me. Sasha held out an American Beauty rose to me. "As a token of my love, *Dushenka*, and as a harbinger of luck on your first public quest." [. . .]

The train sped on towards Rochester. Only six months had passed since I had cut loose from my meaningless past. I had lived years in that time.

CHAPTER V

[. . .] When I faced the audience the next evening, my mind was a blank. I could not remember a single word of my notes. I shut my eyes for an instant; then something strange happened. In a flash I saw it—every incident of my three years in Rochester: the Garson factory, its drudgery and humiliation, the failure of my marriage, the Chicago crime. The last words of August Spies rang in my ears: "Our silence will speak louder than the voices you strangle today."

I began to speak. Words I had never heard myself utter before came pouring forth, faster and faster. They came with passionate intensity; they painted images of the heroic men on the gallows, their glowing vision of an ideal life, rich with comfort and beauty: men and women radiant in freedom, children transformed by joy and affection. The audience had vanished, the hall itself had disappeared; I was conscious only of my own words, of my ecstatic song.

I stopped. Tumultuous applause rolled over me, the buzzing of voices, people telling me something I could not understand. Then I heard someone quite close to me: "It was an inspired speech; but what about the eight-hour struggle? You've said nothing about that." I felt hurled down from my exalted heights, crushed. I told the chairman I was too tired to answer questions, and I went home feeling ill in body and mind. I let myself quietly into Helena's apartment and threw myself on the bed in my clothes.

Exasperation with Most for forcing the tour on me, anger with myself for having so easily succumbed to his influence, the conviction that I had cheated the audience—all seethed in my mind together with a new revelation. I could sway people with words! Strange and magic words that welled up from within me, from some unfamiliar depth. I wept with the joy of knowing.

I went to Buffalo, determined to make another effort. The preliminaries of the meeting threw me into the same nervous tension, but when I faced the audience, there were no visions to inflame my mind. In an endless, repetitive manner I made my speech about the waste of energy and time the eight-hour struggle involved, scoffing at the stupidity of the workers who fought for such trifles. At the end of what seemed to me several hours I was complimented on my clear and logical presentation. Some questions were asked, and I answered them with a sureness that brooked no gainsaying. But on the way home from the meeting my heart was heavy. No words of exaltation had come to me, and how could one hope to reach other hearts when one's own remained cold? I decided to wire Most the next morning, begging him to relieve me of the necessity of going to Cleveland. I could not bear to repeat once more the meaningless prattle.

After a night's sleep my decision seemed childish and weak. How could I give up so soon? Would Most have given up like that? Would Sasha? Well, I, too, would go on. I took the train for Cleveland.

The meeting was large and animated. It was a Saturday night, and the workers attended with their wives and children. Everybody drank. I was surrounded by a group, offered refreshments, and asked questions. How did I happen to come into the movement? Was I German? What was I doing for a living? The petty curiosity of people supposed to be interested in the most advanced ideas reminded me of the Rochester grilling on the day of my arrival in America. It made me thoroughly angry.

The gist of my talk was the same as in Buffalo, but the form was different. It was a sarcastic arraignment, not of the system or of the capitalists, but of the workers themselves—their readiness to give up a great future for some small temporary gains. The audience seemed to enjoy being handled in such an outspoken manner. They roared in some places, and in others vigorously applauded. It was not a meeting; it was a circus, and I was the clown!

A man in the front row who had attracted my attention by his white hair and lean, haggard face rose to speak. He said that he understood my impatience with such small demands as a few hours less a day, or a few dollars more a week. It was legitimate for young people to take time lightly. But what were men of his age to do? They were not likely to live to see the ultimate overthrow of the capitalist system. Were they also to forgo the release of perhaps two hours a day from the hated work? That was all they could hope to see realized in their lifetime. Should they deny themselves even that small achievement? Should they never have a little more time for reading or being out in the open? Why not be fair to people chained to the block?

The man's earnestness, his clear analysis of the principle involved in the eight-hour struggle, brought home to me the falsity of Most's position. I realized I was committing a crime against myself and the workers by serving as a parrot repeating Most's views. I understood why I had failed to reach my audience. I had taken refuge in cheap jokes and bitter thrusts against the toilers to cover up my own inner lack of conviction. My first public experience did not bring the result Most had hoped for, but it taught me a valuable lesson. It cured me somewhat of my childlike faith in the infallibility of my teacher and impressed on me the need of independent thinking.

In New York my friends had prepared a grand reception for me; our flat was spotlessly clean and filled with flowers. They were eager for an account of my tour and they felt apprehensive of the effect upon Most of my changed attitude.

The next evening I went out with Most, again to Terrace Garden. He had grown younger during my two weeks' absence: his rough beard was trimmed neatly and he wore a natty new grey suit, a red carnation in his buttonhole. He joined me in a gay mood, presenting me with a large bouquet of violets. The two weeks of my absence had been unbearably long, he said, and he had reproached himself for having let me go just when we had grown so close. But now he would never again let me go—not alone, anyhow.

I tried several times to tell him about my trip, hurt to the

quick that he had not asked about it. He had sent me forth
against my will, he had been so eager to make a great speaker
of me; was he not interested to know whether I had proved an
apt pupil?

Yes, of course, he replied. But he had already received the reports from Rochester that I had been eloquent, from Buffalo
that my presentation had silenced all opponents, and from
Cleveland that I had flayed the dullards with biting sarcasm.
"What about my own reactions?" I asked. "Don't you want me
to tell you about that?" "Yes, another time." Now he wanted
only to feel me near—his *Blondkopf*, his little girl-woman.

I flared up, declaring I would not be treated as a mere female.
I blurted out that I would never again follow blindly, that I had
made a fool of myself, that the five-minute speech of the old
worker had convinced me more than all his persuasive phrases.
I talked on, my listener keeping very silent. When I had finished, he called the waiter and paid the bill. I followed him out.

On the street he burst out in a storm of abuse. He had reared
a viper, a snake, a heartless coquette, who had played with him
like a cat with a mouse. He had sent me out to plead his cause
and I had betrayed him. I was like the rest, but he would not
stand for it. He would rather cut me out of his heart right now
than have me as a lukewarm friend. "Who is not with me is
against me," he shouted; "I will not have it otherwise!" A great
sadness overwhelmed me, as if I had just experienced an irreparable loss. [. . .]

Soon a new call came to me, of workers on strike, and I followed it eagerly. It came from Joseph Barondess,[1] whom I had
previously met; he was of the group of young Jewish socialists
and anarchists who had organized the cloakmakers and other
Yiddish unions. [. . .] Barondess was now at the head of the
union, directing the cloakmakers' strike. [. . .]

I threw myself into the work with all the ardour of my being
and I became absorbed in it to the exclusion of everything else.
My task was to get the girls in the trade to join the strike. For that
purpose meetings, concerts, socials, and dances were organized.
At these affairs it was not difficult to press upon the girls the

need of making common cause with their striking brothers. I
had to speak often and I became less and less disturbed when
on the platform. My faith in the justice of the strike helped me
to dramatize my talks and to carry conviction. Within a few
weeks my work brought scores of girls into the ranks of the
strikers.

I became alive once more. At the dances I was one of the
most untiring and gayest. One evening a cousin of Sasha, a
young boy, took me aside. With a grave face, as if he were
about to announce the death of a dear comrade, he whispered
to me that it did not behoove an agitator to dance. Certainly
not with such reckless abandon, anyway. It was undignified for
one who was on the way to become a force in the anarchist
movement. My frivolity would only hurt the Cause.

I grew furious at the impudent interference of the boy. I told
him to mind his own business, I was tired of having the Cause
constantly thrown into my face. I did not believe that a Cause
which stood for a beautiful ideal, for anarchism, for release and
freedom from conventions and prejudice, should demand the
denial of life and joy. I insisted that our Cause could not expect
me to became a nun and that the movement should not be
turned into a cloister. If it meant that, I did not want it. "I want
freedom, the right to self-expression, everybody's right to beautiful, radiant things." Anarchism meant that to me, and I would
live it in spite of the whole world—prisons, persecution, everything. Yes, even in spite of the condemnation of my own closest
comrades I would live my beautiful ideal. [. . .]

The strenuous weeks of the strike now gave way to less arduous activities: lectures, evenings at the Netters'[2] or at our flat,
and efforts to secure employment again. Fedya had begun to
work with crayons, enlarging photographs; he declared that he
could not keep on wasting our money, Helen's and mine, on
paints. He felt he would never become a great painter, anyway.
I suspected it was something else: no doubt his desire to earn
money so that he could relieve me of hard work.

I had not been feeling very well, especially during periods, on
which occasions I always had to take to bed, in excruciating
pain for days. It had been so since my great shock when Mother

slapped my face. It grew worse when I caught a cold on our way from Königsberg to St. Petersburg. We had to be smuggled across the border, Mother, my two brothers, and I. It was in the latter part of 1881 and the winter was particularly severe. The smugglers had told Mother that we would have to wade through deep snow, even across a half-frozen brook. Mother worried about me because I was taken sick a few days earlier than my time, owing to the excitement of our departure from Königsberg. At five in the morning, shivering with cold and fear, we started out. Soon we reached the brook that separated the German and Russian frontiers. The very anticipation of the icy water was paralysing, but there was no escape; we had to plunge in or be overtaken and perhaps shot by soldiers patrolling the border. A few roubles finally induced them to turn their backs, but they had cautioned us to be quick.

We plunged in, Mother loaded with bundles and I carrying my little brother. The sudden chill froze my blood; then I felt a stinging sensation in my spine, abdomen, and legs, as if I were being pierced with hot irons. I wanted to scream, but terror of the soldiers checked me. Soon we were over, and the stinging ceased; but my teeth kept chattering and I was in a hot sweat. We ran as fast as we could to the inn on the Russian side. I was given hot tea with *maliny*, packed in hot bricks, and covered with a large feather bed. I felt feverish all the way to St. Petersburg, and the pain in my spine and legs was racking. I was laid up for weeks, and my spine remained weak for years afterwards.

In America I had consulted Solotaroff about my trouble, and he took me to a specialist, who urged an operation. He seemed surprised that I could have stood my condition so long and that I had been at all able to have physical contact. My friends informed me that the physician had said I would never be free from pain, or experience full sexual release, unless I submitted to the operation.

Solotaroff asked me whether I had ever wanted a baby. "Because if you have the operation," he explained, "you will be able to have a child. So far your condition has made that impossible." [. . .]

A cruel hand clutched at my heart. My ghastly childhood stood before me, my hunger for affection, which Mother was unable to satisfy. Father's harshness towards the children, his violent outbreaks, his beating my sisters and me. Two frightful experiences were particularly fresh in my mind: Once Father lashed me with a strap so that my little brother Herman, awakened by my cries, came running up and bit Father on the calf. The lashing stopped. Helena took me to her room, bathed my bruised back, brought me milk, held me to her heart, her tears mingling with mine, while Father outside was raging: "I'll kill her! I will kill that brat! I will teach her to obey!" [. . .]

One day I was given a low mark for bad behaviour. I went home in trembling fear. I could not face Father—I showed my paper to Mother. She began to cry, said that I would be their ruin, that I was an ungrateful and wilful child, and that she would have to let Father see the paper. But she would plead with him for me, although I did not deserve it. I walked away from her with a heavy heart. At our bay window I looked out over the fields in the distance. Children were playing there; they seemed to belong to another world—there never had been much play in my life. A strange thought came to me: how wonderful it would be if I were stricken with some consuming disease! It would surely soften Father's heart. I had never known him soft save on *Sukkess,* the autumnal holiday of rejoicing. Father did not drink, except a little on certain Jewish fêtes, on this day especially. Then he would grow jolly, gather the children about him, promise us new dresses and toys. It was the one bright spot in our lives and we always eagerly looked forward to it. It happened only once a year. As long as I could think back, I remembered his saying that he had not wanted me. He had wanted a boy, the pig woman had cheated him.[3] Perhaps if I should become very ill, near death, he would become kind and never beat me again or let me stand in the corner for hours, or make me walk back and forth with a glass of water in my hand. "If you spill a drop, you will get whipped!" he would threaten. The whip and the little stool were always at hand. They symbolized my shame and my tragedy. After many attempts and considerable punishment I had learned to carry the glass without spilling the water. The process used to unnerve me and make me ill for hours after.

My father was handsome, dashing, and full of vitality. I loved him even while I was afraid of him. I wanted him to love me, but I never knew how to reach his heart. His hardness served only to make me more contrary. Why was he so hard, I was wondering, as I looked out of the bay window, lost in recollections.

Suddenly I felt a terrific pain in my head, as if I had been struck with an iron bar. It was Father's fist that had smashed the round comb I wore to hold my unruly hair. He pounded me and pulled me about, raging: "You are my disgrace! You will always be so! You can't be *my* child; you don't look like me or like your mother; you don't act like us!"

Sister Helena wrestled with him for my life. She tried to tear me away from his grip, and the blows intended for me fell upon her. At last Father became tired, grew dizzy, and fell headlong to the floor. Helena shouted to Mother that Father had fainted. She hurried me along to her room and locked the door.

All my love and longing for my father were turned to hatred. After that I avoided him and never talked to him, unless in answer. I did what I was told mechanically; the gulf between us widened with the years. My home had become a prison. Every time I tried to escape, I was caught and put back in the chains forged for me by Father. From St. Petersburg to America, from Rochester to my marriage, there were repeated attempts to escape. The last and final one was before I left Rochester for New York.

Mother had not been feeling well and I went over to put her house in order. I was on the floor scrubbing while Father was nagging me for having married Kershner, for having left him, and again for returning to him. "You are a loose character," he kept on saying; "you have always disgraced yourself in the family." He talked, while I continued scrubbing.

Then something snapped within me; my lone and woeful childhood, my tormented adolescence, my joyless youth—I flung them all into Father's face. He stood aghast as I denounced him, emphasizing every charge by beating my scrubbing-brush on the floor. Every cruel incident of my life stood out in my arraignment. Our large barn of a home, Father's angry voice resounding through it, his ill-treatment of the servants, his iron grip on my mother—everything that had haunted my days and terrorized my nights I now recalled in my bitterness. I told him that if I had not become the harlot he repeatedly called me, it was not his fault. I had been on the verge even of going on the street more than once. It was Helena's love and devotion that had saved me.

My words rushed on like a torrent, the brush pounding the floor with all the hatred and scorn I felt for my father. The terrible scene ended with my hysterical screams. My brothers carried me up and put me to bed. The next morning I left the house. I did not see Father again before I went to New York.

I had learned since then that my tragic childhood had been no exception, that there were thousands of children born unwanted, marred and maimed by poverty and still more by ignorant misunderstanding. No child of mine should ever be added to those unfortunate victims.

There was also another reason: my growing absorption in my newfound ideal. I had determined to serve it completely. To fulfil that mission I must remain unhampered and untied. Years of pain and of suppressed longing for a child—what were they compared with the price many martyrs had already paid? I, too, would pay the price, I would endure the suffering, I would find an outlet for my mother-need in the love of *all* children. The operation did not take place.

Several weeks' rest and the loving care of my friends—of Sasha, who had returned to the house, the Minkin sisters, Most, who called often and sent flowers, and, above all, the artist boy—gave me back to health. I rose from my sick-bed renewed in faith in my own strength. Like Sasha I now felt that I, too, could overcome every difficulty and face every test for my ideal. Had I not overcome the strongest and most primitive craving of a woman—the desire for a child?

During those weeks Fedya and I became lovers. It had grown clear to me that my feelings for Fedya had no bearing on my love for Sasha. Each called out different emotions in my being, took me into different worlds. They created no conflict, they only brought fulfilment.

I told Sasha about my love for Fedya. His response was bigger and more beautiful than I had expected. "I believe in your freedom to love," he said. He was aware of his possessive tendencies and hated them like everything else he had got from his *bourgeois* background. Perhaps if Fedya were not his friend, he might be jealous; he knew he had a large streak of jealousy in his make-up. But not only was Fedya his friend, he was his comrade in battle; and I was more to him than merely a woman. His love for me was intense, but the revolutionist and the fighter meant more to him.

When our artist friend came home that day, the boys embraced. Late into the night we talked of our plans for further activities. When we separated, we had made a pact—to dedicate ourselves to the Cause in some supreme deed, to die together if necessary, or to continue to live and work for the ideal for which one of us might have to give his life.

The days and weeks that followed were illumined by the glorious new light in us. We became more patient with each other, more understanding.

CHAPTER VI

Most had told me that he was planning a short lecture tour through the New England States. Now he informed me that he was about to leave, and he invited me to accompany him. He said that I looked worn and thin and that a change of scene would do me good. I promised to consider his invitation.

The boys urged me to go; Fedya stressed the need of getting away from household duties, while Sasha said it would help me to get acquainted with the comrades and open up a way for further activities. Two weeks later I went with Most by the Fall River Line to Boston. [. . .]

Most spoke interestingly of his past and he also wanted to know about my childhood and youthful life. All that had preceded my coming to New York seemed to me insignificant, but Most disagreed with me about it. He insisted that early environment and conditions are powerful factors in moulding one's life. He wondered whether my awakening to social problems was due entirely to the shock the Chicago tragedy had given me, or whether it was the flowering of what had its roots in myself, in the past and in the conditions of my childhood.

I related to him incidents of my recollections—some experiences of my schooldays, which seemed particularly to interest him.

When I was eight years of age, Father sent me to Königsberg to live with my grandmother and go to school there. Grandmother was the owner of a hairdressing parlour managed by her three daughters, while she herself continued to ply the trade of smuggler. Father took me as far as Kovno, where we were met by Grandmother. On the way he sternly impressed upon my mind what a sacrifice it was going to be for him to pay forty roubles a month for my board and schooling. I was going to be in a private school, as he would not permit his child in the *Volkschule*. He was willing to do anything for me if I would be a good girl, study hard, obey my teachers, grandmother, aunts, and uncles. He would never take me back if there should be any complaint against me and he would come to Königsberg to thrash me. My heart was heavy with fear of my father. I was even too miserable to care for Grandmother's loving reception. I had only one desire, to get away from Father. [. . .]

From the very first I took a violent dislike to my uncle. I missed our large yard, the fields, and the hills. I felt stifled and alone in the world. Before long I was sent to school. I made friends there with the other children and began to feel a little less lonely. All went well for a month; then Grandmother had to go away indefinitely. Almost immediately my purgatory began. Uncle insisted that it was no use wasting money on my schooling, and that forty roubles were barely enough for my keep. My aunts protested, but to no purpose. They were afraid of the man who bullied them all. I was taken out of school and put to work in the house.

From early morning, when I had to fetch the rolls, milk, and chocolate for our breakfast, until late at night I was kept busy, making beds, cleaning boots, scrubbing floors, and washing clothes. After a while I was even put to cooking, but my uncle was never satisfied. His gruff voice shouting orders all day long would send cold shivers down my spine. I drudged on. At night I would weep myself to sleep.

I became thin and pale; my shoes were run down at the heels, my clothes were threadbare, and I had no one to go to for comfort. [. . .] One afternoon, after an especially hard day's work and endless errands, Uncle came into the kitchen to say that I would have to deliver one more parcel. I knew by the address that it was far away. Whether from fatigue or because I disliked the man so violently, I took the courage to say that I could not make the journey; my feet hurt me too much. He

slapped me full in the face, shouting: "You are not earning your
keep! You are lazy!" When he left the room, I went out into the
corridor, sat down on the stairs, and began to cry bitterly. All of
a sudden I felt a kick in the back. I tried to grab the banister as I
rolled to the bottom, landing below in a heap. The clatter roused
the sisters, who came running to see what had happened. *"Das
Kind is tot!"* they screamed. "The scoundrel has killed her!"
They took me to their room and I clung to them, beseeching
them not to let me go back to my uncle. A doctor was called,
who found no bones broken, but my ankle was sprained. I was
put to bed, nursed and petted as I had never been before, except
by my own Helena. [. . .]

Soon my father and grandmother arrived. Aunt Yetta had
telegraphed them to come. Father was shocked by my appearance; he actually took me in his arms and kissed me. Such a
thing had not happened since I was four. There was a terrible
scene between Grandmother and her son-in-law, which ended
in his moving out of the house with his wife. Before long, Father took me back to Popelan. I then discovered that he had
been sending forty roubles regularly every month, and that my
uncle had just as regularly been reporting to him that I was doing splendidly at school.

Most was deeply moved by my story. He patted my head and
kissed my hands. *"Armes Aschenprödelchen,"*[1] he kept on saying; "your childhood was like mine after that beast of a step-
mother came to our house." He was now more convinced than
ever, he told me, that it was the influence of my childhood that
had made me what I was.

[. . .] In the winter of that year (1890) the radical ranks were
aroused over the report brought from Siberia by George Kennan,
an American journalist. His account of the harrowing conditions
of the Russian political prisoners and exiles moved even the
American press to lengthy comments. We on the East Side had
all along known of the horrors through underground messages.
A year before, fearful things had taken place in Yakutsk. Politicals who had protested against the maltreatment of their comrades were lured into the prison yard and fired upon by guards;

a number of prisoners were killed, among them women, while several others were subsequently hanged in the prison for "inciting an outbreak." We knew of other cases equally terrible, but the American press had kept silent on the inhumanities committed by the Tsar. [. . .]

When we first learned of the Yakutsk outrage, Sasha and I began discussing our return to Russia. What could we hope to achieve in barren America? It would require years to acquire the language thoroughly, and Sasha had no aspirations to become a public speaker. In Russia we could engage in conspiratorial work. We belonged to Russia. For months we went about nursing the idea, but the lack of necessary funds compelled us to give it up. But now, with George Kennan's *exposé* of the Russian horrors, our plans were revived. We decided to speak to Most about them. He became enthusiastic over the idea. "Emma is fast developing into a good speaker," he said; "when she will have mastered the language, she will become a force here. But you can do more in Russia," he agreed with Sasha. He would issue a confidential appeal for funds to some trustworthy comrades in order to equip Sasha for his trip and for his work afterwards. In fact, Sasha himself could help draw up the document. Most also suggested that it would be advisable for Sasha to learn the printing trade so as to enable him to start a secret press for anarchist literature in Russia. [. . .]

In New York we rented a flat on Forsythe Street. Fedya continued to make crayon enlargements whenever he was lucky enough to get orders. I again took up piece-work. Sasha worked as compositor on the *Freiheit,* still clinging to the hope that Most would enable him to go to Russia. The appeal for funds, composed by Most and Sasha, had been sent out, and we anxiously awaited the results.

I spent much time in the *Freiheit* office, where the tables were piled high with European exchanges. One of them particularly attracted my attention. It was *Die Autonomie,* a German anarchist weekly published in London. While not comparable with the *Freiheit* in force and picturesqueness of language, it nevertheless seemed to me to express anarchism in a clearer and more convincing manner. One time, when I had mentioned the publication to Most, he became enraged. He told me curtly that the people behind the venture were shady characters, that they had been mixed up with "the spy Peukert, who betrayed John Neve, one of our best German comrades, into the hands of the police."[2] It had never occurred to me then to doubt Most and I ceased reading the *Autonomie*.

But nearer acquaintance with the movement and my other experiences showed me Most's partiality. I began to read the *Autonomie* again. Soon I came to the conclusion that, however correct Most might be about the personnel of the paper, its tenets were much closer to what anarchism had come to mean to me than those of the *Freiheit*. The *Autonomie* stressed more the freedom of the individual and the independence of groups. Its entire tone held a powerful appeal for me. My two friends felt the same way. Sasha suggested that we get in touch with the comrades in London.

Before long we learned of the existence of the Group *Autonomic* in New York. Its weekly gatherings were on Saturdays, and we decided to visit the place on Fifth Street. It bore the peculiar name *Zum Groben Michel*, which well corresponded with the rough exterior and gruff manner of its giant owner. The leading spirit of the group was Joseph Peukert. [. . .]

Having been influenced by Most against Peukert, we long fought the [former's] version of the story that held him responsible for the arrest and imprisonment of Neve. But after months of association with Peukert we became convinced that, whatever might have been his share in that terrible affair, he could not have been a deliberate party to treachery. [. . .]

I went to the *Freiheit* office to see Most. [. . .] We went to a café on Sixth Avenue and Forty-second Street. It was a famous gathering-place for theatrical people, gamblers, and prostitutes. He chose the place because comrades never frequented it.

It was a long time since we had been out together, since I had watched the wonderful transformation that Most always underwent after a few glasses of wine. His changed mood would transport me to a different world, a world without discord and strife, without a Cause to bind one, or opinions of comrades to consider. All differences were forgotten. When we separated, I had not spoken to him about the Peukert case.

The next day I received a letter from Most, enclosing data on the Peukert affair. I read the letter first. Again he poured out his heart as on our trip to Boston. His plaint was love, and why it must end; it was not only that he could not continue to share me with another, but that he could no longer support the increasing differences between us. He was sure that I would go on growing, becoming an ever-increasing force in the movement. But this very assurance convinced him that our relations were bound to lack permanence. A home, children, the care and attention ordinary women can give, who have no other interest in life but the man they love and the children they bear him—that was what he needed. [. . .]

I read and reread the letter, locked in my room. I wanted to be alone with all that Most had meant to me, all he had given me. What had I given him? Not so much as even the ordinary woman gives the man she loves. I hated to admit, even to myself, that I lacked what he wanted so much. I knew I could bring him children if I would have the operation. How wonderful it would be to have a child by this unique personality! I sat lost in the thought. But soon something more insistent awakened in my brain—Sasha, the life and work we had together. Would I give it all up? No, no, that was impossible, that should never be! But why Sasha rather than Most? To be sure, Sasha had youth and indomitable zeal. Ah, yes, his zeal—was not that the cement that had bound me to him? But suppose Sasha, too, should want a wife, home, children. What then? Should I be able to give him that? But Sasha would never expect such a thing—he lived only for the Cause and he wanted me also to live only for it.

An agonized night followed that day. I could find no answer and no peace.

CHAPTER VII

At the International Socialist Congress held in Paris in 1889 the decision had been made to turn the first of May into a world-wide holiday of labour. The idea caught the imagination of the progressive workers in every land. The birth of spring was to mark the reawakening of the masses to new efforts for emancipation. In this year, 1891, the decision of the Congress was to find wide application. On the first of May the toilers were to lay down their tools, stop their machines, leave the factories and mines. In festive attire they were to demonstrate with their banners, marching to the inspiring strains of revolutionary music and song. Everywhere meetings were to take place to articulate the aspirations of labour. [. . .]

The celebration in New York was arranged by the socialists. They secured Union Square and promised to permit the anarchists to speak from their own platform. But at the last moment the socialist organizers refused to let us erect our platform on the square. Most did not arrive on time, but I was there with a group of young people, including Sasha, Fedya, and several Italian comrades. We were determined to have our say on this great occasion. When it became evident that we could not have our platform, the boys lifted me up on one of the socialist trucks. I began to speak. The chairman left, but in a few minutes he returned with the owner of the wagon. I continued to speak. The man hitched his horse to the truck and started off at a trot. I still continued to speak. The crowd, failing to take in the situation, followed us out of the square for a couple of blocks while I was speaking.

Presently the police appeared and began beating back the

crowd. The driver stopped. Our boys quickly lifted me off and hurried me away. The morning papers were filled with a story about a mysterious young woman on a truck who had waved a red flag and urged revolution, "her high-pitched voice putting the horse to flight." [. . .]

During the winter Fedya left for Springfield, Massachusetts, to work for a photographer. After a while he wrote that I could have a job at the same place, taking care of the orders. I was glad of the chance; it would take me away from New York, from the everlasting grind of the sewing-machine. Sasha and I had been supporting ourselves with piece-work on boys' jumpers. Often we worked eighteen hours a day in the one light room of our flat, and I had to do the cooking and the house-work besides. Springfield would be a change and a relief. [. . .]

Fedya was so successful with his work that it seemed folly to keep on enriching our employer. It occurred to us that we might start out for ourselves and have Sasha with us. Though Sasha had never complained, I could sense in his letters that he was not happy in New York. Fedya suggested that we open our own studio. We decided to go to Worcester, Massachusetts, and to invite Sasha to join us.

We fixed up an office, put out a sign, and waited for customers. But none came, and our little savings were dwindling. We hired a horse and buggy to enable us to visit near-by country places and secure orders from the farmers for crayon enlargements of family photographs. Sasha would drive, and whenever we bumped into trees and sidewalks, he would dilate on the natural cussedness of our horse. Often we traveled for hours before securing any work. [. . .]

Frequently we were on the point of giving up. The family we lived with used to advise us to open a lunch-room or ice-cream parlour. The suggestion at first seemed to us absurd; we had neither funds nor aspirations for such a venture. Besides, it was against our principles to engage in business.

Just at that time the radical press was again aroused by new atrocities in Russia. The old yearning took hold of us to return to our native country. But where get enough money for the purpose?

The private call sent out by Most had found no adequate response. Then it occurred to us that an ice-cream parlour might prove the means to our end. The more we thought of it, the more convinced we became that it offered the only solution.

Our savings consisted of fifty dollars. Our landlord, who had suggested the idea, said he would lend us a hundred and fifty dollars. We secured a store, and within a couple of weeks Sasha's skill with hammer and saw, Fedya's with his paint and brush, and my own good German housekeeping training succeeded in turning the neglected ramshackle place into an attractive lunch-room. It was spring and not yet warm enough for an ice-cream rush, but the coffee I brewed, our sandwiches and dainty dishes, were beginning to be appreciated, and soon we were kept busy till early morning hours. Within a short time we had paid back our landlord's loan and were able to invest in a soda-water fountain and some lovely coloured dishes. We felt we were on the way to the realization of our long-cherished dream.

CHAPTER VIII

It was May 1892. News from Pittsburgh announced that trouble had broken out between the Carnegie Steel Company and its employees organized in the Amalgamated Association of Iron and Steel Workers. It was one of the biggest and most efficient labour bodies of the country, consisting mostly of Americans, men of decision and grit, who would assert their rights. The Carnegie Company, on the other hand, was a powerful corporation, known as a hard master. It was particularly significant that Andrew Carnegie,[1] its president, had temporarily turned over the entire management to the company's chairman, Henry Clay Frick,[2] a man known for his enmity to labour. Frick was also the owner of extensive coke-fields, where unions were prohibited and the workers were ruled with an iron hand.

The high tariff on imported steel had greatly boomed the American steel industry. The Carnegie Company had practically a monopoly of it and enjoyed unprecedented prosperity. Its largest mills were in Homestead, near Pittsburgh, where thousands of workers were employed, their tasks requiring long training and high skill. Wages were arranged between the company and the union, according to a sliding scale based on the prevailing market price of steel products. The current agreement was about to expire, and the workers presented a new wage schedule, calling for an increase because of the higher market prices and enlarged output of the mills.

The philanthropic Andrew Carnegie conveniently retired to his castle in Scotland, and Frick took full charge of the situation. He declared that henceforth the sliding scale would be abolished. The company would make no more agreements with the Amalgamated Association; it would itself determine the wages to be paid. In fact, he would not recognize the union at all. He would not treat with the employees collectively, as before. He would close the mills, and the men might consider themselves discharged. Thereafter they would have to apply for work individually, and the pay would be arranged with every worker separately. Frick curtly refused the peace advances of the workers' organization, declaring that there was "nothing to arbitrate." Presently the mills were closed. "Not a strike, but a lock-out," Frick announced. It was an open declaration of war.

Feeling ran high in Homestead and vicinity. The sympathy of the entire country was with the men. Even the most conservative part of the press condemned Frick for his arbitrary and drastic methods. They charged him with deliberately provoking a crisis that might assume national proportions, in view of the great numbers of men locked out by Frick's action, and the probable effect upon affiliated unions and on related industries. [. . .]

Far away from the scene of the impending struggle, in our little ice-cream parlour in the city of Worcester, we eagerly followed developments. To us it sounded the awakening of the American worker, the long-awaited day of his resurrection. The native toiler had risen, he was beginning to feel his mighty strength, he was determined to break the chains that had held him in bondage so long, we thought. Our hearts were fired with admiration for the men of Homestead. [. . .]

One afternoon a customer came in for an ice-cream, while I was alone in the store. As I set the dish down before him, I caught the large headlines of his paper: "LATEST DEVELOPMENTS IN HOMESTEAD—FAMILIES OF STRIKERS EVICTED FROM THE COMPANY HOUSES—WOMAN IN CONFINEMENT CARRIED OUT INTO STREET BY SHERIFFS." I read over the man's shoulder Frick's dictum to the workers: he would rather see them dead than concede to their demands, and he threatened to import Pinkerton detectives. The brutal bluntness of the account, the inhumanity of Frick towards the evicted mother, inflamed my mind. Indignation swept my whole being. I heard the man at the table ask: "Are you sick, young lady? Can I do anything for you?" "Yes, you can let me have your paper," I blurted out.

"You won't have to pay me for the ice-cream. But I must ask you to leave. I must close the store." The man looked at me as if I had gone crazy.

I locked up the store and ran full speed the three blocks to our little flat. It was Homestead, not Russia; I knew it now. We belonged in Homestead. The boys, resting for the evening shift, sat up as I rushed into the room, newspaper clutched in my hand. "What has happened, Emma? You look terrible!" I could not speak. I handed them the paper.

Sasha was the first on his feet. "Homestead!" he exclaimed. "I must go to Homestead!" I flung my arms around him, crying out his name. I, too, would go. "We must go tonight," he said; "the great moment has come at last!" Being internationalists, he added, it mattered not to us where the blow was struck by the workers; we must be with them. We must bring them our great message and help them see that it was not only for the moment that they must strike, but for all time, for a free life, for anarchism. Russia had many heroic men and women, but who was there in America? Yes, we must go to Homestead, tonight!

I had never heard Sasha so eloquent. He seemed to have grown in stature. He looked strong and defiant, an inner light on his face making him beautiful, as he had never appeared to me before.

We immediately went to our landlord and informed him of our decision to leave. He replied that we were mad; we were doing so well, we were on the way to fortune. If we would hold out to the end of the summer, we would be able to clear at least a thousand dollars. But he argued in vain—we were not to be moved. We invented the story that a very dear relative was in a dying condition, and that therefore we must depart. We would turn the store over to him; all we wanted was the evening's receipts. We would remain until closing-hours, leave everything in order, and give him the keys.

That evening we were especially busy. We had never before had so many customers. By one o'clock we had sold out everything. Our receipts were seventy-five dollars. We left on an early morning train.

On the way we discussed our immediate plans. First of all,

we would print a manifesto to the steel-workers. We would
have to find somebody to translate it into English, as we were
still unable to express our thoughts correctly in that tongue. We
would have the German and English texts printed in New York
and take them with us to Pittsburgh. With the help of the German comrades there, meetings could be organized for me to
address. Fedya was to remain in New York till further developments. [. . .]

A few days after our return to New York the news was
flashed across the country of the slaughter of steel-workers by
Pinkertons. Frick had fortified the Homestead mills, built a
high fence around them. Then, in the dead of night, a barge
packed with strike-breakers, under protection of heavily armed
Pinkerton thugs, quietly stole up the Monongahela River. The
steel-men had learned of Frick's move. They stationed themselves along the shore, determined to drive back Frick's hirelings.
When the barge got within range, the Pinkertons had opened
fire, without warning, killing a number of Homestead men on
the shore, among them a little boy, and wounding scores of
others. [. . .]

We were stunned. We saw at once that the time for our manifesto had passed. Words had lost their meaning in the face of
the innocent blood spilled on the banks of the Monongahela.
Intuitively each felt what was surging in the heart of the others.
Sasha broke the silence. "Frick is the responsible factor in this
crime," he said; "he must be made to stand the consequences."
It was the psychological moment for an *Attentat*;[3] the whole
country was aroused, everybody was considering Frick the per-
petrator of a coldblooded murder. A blow aimed at Frick would
re-echo in the poorest hovel, would call the attention of the
whole world to the real cause behind the Homestead struggle. It
would also strike terror in the enemy's ranks and make them realize that the proletariat of America had its avengers.

Sasha had never made bombs before, but Most's *Science of
Revolutionary Warfare*[4] was a good text-book. He would procure dynamite from a comrade he knew on Staten Island. He
had waited for this sublime moment to serve the Cause, to give
his life for the people. He would go to Pittsburgh.

"We will go with you!" Fedya and I cried together. But Sasha would not listen to it. He insisted that it was unnecessary and criminal to waste three lives on one man.

We sat down, Sasha between us, holding our hands. In a quiet and even tone he began to unfold to us his plan. He would perfect a time regulator for the bomb that would enable him to kill Frick, yet save himself. Not because he wanted to escape. No; he wanted to live long enough to justify his act in court, so that the American people might know that he was not a criminal, but an idealist.

"I will kill Frick," Sasha said, "and of course I shall be condemned to death. I will die proudly in the assurance that I gave my life for the people. But I will die by my own hand, like Lingg. Never will I permit our enemies to kill me."

I hung on his lips. His clarity, his calmness and force, the sacred fire of his ideal, enthralled me, held me spellbound. Turning to me, he continued in his deep voice. I was the born speaker, the propagandist, he said. I could do a great deal for his act. I could articulate its meaning to the workers. I could explain that he had had no personal grievance against Frick, that as a human being Frick was no less to him than anyone else. Frick was the symbol of wealth and power, of the injustice and wrong of the capitalistic class, as well as personally responsible for the shedding of the workers' blood. Sasha's act would be directed against Frick, not as a man, but as the enemy of labour. Surely I must see how important it was that I remain behind to plead the meaning of his deed and its message throughout the country. [. . .]

"I will go with you, Sasha," I cried; "I must go with you! I know that as a woman I can be of help. I could gain access to Frick easier than you. I could pave the way for your act. Besides, I simply must go with you. Do you understand, Sasha?"

We had a feverish week. Sasha's experiments took place at night when everybody was asleep. While Sasha worked, I kept watch. I lived in dread every moment for Sasha, for our friends in the flat, the children, and the rest of the tenants. What if anything should go wrong—but, then, did not the end justify the means? Our end was the sacred cause of the oppressed and exploited people. It was for them that we were going to give our lives. What if a few should have to perish?—the many would be made free and could live in beauty and in comfort. Yes, the end in this case justified the means.

After we had paid our fare from Worcester to New York, we had about sixty dollars left. Twenty had already been used up since our arrival. The material Sasha bought for the bomb had cost a good deal and we still had another week in New York. Besides, I needed a dress and shoes, which, together with the fare to Pittsburgh, would amount to fifty dollars. I realized with a start that we required a large sum of money. I knew no one who could give us so much; besides, I could never tell him the purpose. After days of canvassing in the scorching July heat I succeeded in collecting twenty-five dollars. Sasha finished his preparatory work and went to Staten Island to test the bomb. When he returned, I could tell by his expression that something terrible had happened. I learned soon enough; the bomb had not gone off.

Sasha said it was due either to the wrong chemical directions or to the dampness of the dynamite. The second bomb, having been made from the same material, would most likely also fail. A week's work and anxiety and forty precious dollars wasted! What now? We had no time for lamentations or regrets; we had to act quickly. [. . .]

Sasha said that the act must be carried out, no matter how we got the money. It was now clear that the two of us would not be able to go. I would have to listen to his plea and let him go alone. He reiterated his faith in me and in my strength and assured me of the great joy I had given him when I insisted upon going with him to Pittsburgh. "But," he said, "we are too poor. Poverty is always a deciding factor in our actions. Besides, we are merely dividing our labours, each doing what he is best fitted for." He was not an agitator; that was my field, and it would be my task to interpret his act to the people. I cried out against his arguments, though I felt their force. We had no money. I knew that he would go in any event; nothing would stop him, of that I was certain.

Our whole fortune consisted of fifteen dollars. That would

take Sasha to Pittsburgh, buy some necessaries, and still leave him a dollar for the first day's food and lodging. Our Allegheny comrades Nold and Bauer,[5] whom Sasha meant to look up, would give him hospitality for a few days until I could raise more money. Sasha had decided not to confide his mission to them; there was no need for it, he felt, and it was never advisable for too many people to be taken into conspiratorial plans. He would require at least another twenty dollars for a gun and a suit of clothes. He might be able to buy the weapon cheap at some pawnshop. I had no idea where I could get the money, but I knew that I would find it somehow.

Those with whom we were staying were told that Sasha would leave that evening, but the motive for his departure was not revealed. There was a simple farewell supper, everyone joked and laughed, and I joined in the gaiety. I strove to be jolly to cheer Sasha, but it was laughter that masked suppressed sobs. Later we accompanied Sasha to the Baltimore and Ohio Station. Our friends kept in the distance, while Sasha and I paced the platform, our hearts too full for speech.

The conductor drawled out: "All aboard!" I clung to Sasha. He was on the train, while I stood on the lower step. His face bent low to mine, his hand holding me, he whispered: "My sailor girl" (his pet name for me), "comrade, you will be with me to the last. You will proclaim that I gave what was dearest to me for an ideal, for the great suffering people."

The train moved. Sasha loosened my hold, gently helping me to jump off the step. I ran after the vanishing train, waving and calling to him: "Sasha, Sashenka!" The steaming monster disappeared round the bend and I stood glued, straining after it, my arms outstretched for the precious life that was being snatched away from me.

I woke up with a very clear idea of how I could raise the money for Sasha. I would go on the street. I lay wondering how such a notion could have come to me. I recollected Dostoyevsky's *Crime and Punishment*,[6] which had made a profound impression on me, especially the character of Sonya, Marmeladov's daughter. She had become a prostitute in order to support her little brothers and sisters and to relieve her consumptive step-mother of worry. I visioned Sonya as she lay on her cot, face to the wall, her shoulders twitching. I could almost feel the same way. Sensitive Sonya could sell her body; why not I? My cause was greater than hers. It was Sasha—his great deed—the people. But should I be able to do it, to go with strange men—for money? The thought revolted me. I buried my face in the pillow to shut out the light. "Weakling, coward," an inner voice said. "Sasha is giving his life, and you shrink from giving your body, miserable coward!" It took me several hours to gain control of myself. When I got out of bed my mind was made up.

My main concern now was whether I could make myself attractive enough to men who seek out girls on the street. I stepped over to the mirror to inspect my body. I looked tired, but my complexion was good. I should need no make-up. My curly blond hair showed off well with my blue eyes. Too large in the hips for my age, I thought; I was just twenty-three. Well, I came from Jewish stock. Besides, I would wear a corset and I should look taller in high heels (I had never worn either before).

Corsets, slippers with high heels, dainty underwear—where should I get money for it all? I had a white linen dress, trimmed with Caucasian embroidery. I could get some soft flesh-coloured material and sew the underwear myself. I knew the stores on Grand Street carried cheap goods.

I dressed hurriedly and went in search of the servant in the apartment who had shown a liking for me, and she lent me five dollars without any question. I started off to make my purchases. When I returned, I locked myself in my room. I would see no one. I was busy preparing my outfit and thinking of Sasha. What would he say? Would he approve? Yes, I was sure he would. He had always insisted that the end justified the means, that the true revolutionist will not shrink from anything to serve the Cause.

Saturday evening, July 16, 1892, I walked up and down Fourteenth Street, one of the long procession of girls I had so often seen plying their trade. I felt no nervousness at first, but when I looked at the passing men and saw their vulgar glances and their manner of approaching the women, my heart sank. I wanted to take flight, run back to my room, tear off my cheap finery, and scrub myself clean. But a voice kept on ringing in my ears: "You must hold out; Sasha—his act—everything will be lost if you fail."

I continued my tramp, but something stronger than my reason would compel me to increase my pace the moment a man came near me. One of them was rather insistent, and I fled. By eleven o'clock I was utterly exhausted. My feet hurt from the high heels, my head throbbed. I was close to tears from fatigue and disgust with my inability to carry out what I had come to do.

I made another effort. I stood on the corner of Fourteenth Street and Fourth Avenue, near the bank building. The first man that invited me—I would go with him, I had decided. A tall, distinguished-looking person, well dressed, came close. "Let's have a drink, little girl," he said. His hair was white, he appeared to be about sixty, but his face was ruddy. "All right," I replied. He took my arm and led me to a wine house on Union Square which Most had often frequented with me. "Not here!" I almost screamed; "please, not here." I led him to the back entrance of a saloon on Thirteenth Street and Third Avenue. I had once been there in the afternoon for a glass of beer. It had been clean and quiet then.

That night it was crowded, and with difficulty we secured a table. The man ordered drinks. My throat felt parched and I asked for a large glass of beer. Neither of us spoke. I was conscious of the man's scrutiny of my face and body. I felt myself growing resentful. Presently he asked: "You're a novice in the business, aren't you?" "Yes, this is my first time—but how did you know?" "I watched you as you passed me," he replied. He told me that he had noticed my haunted expression and my increased pace the moment a man came near me. He understood then that I was inexperienced; whatever might have been the reason that brought me to the street, he knew it was not mere looseness or love of excitement. "But thousands of girls are driven by economic necessity," I blurted out. He looked at me in surprise. "Where did you get that stuff?" I wanted to tell him all about the social question, about my ideas, who and what I was, but I checked myself. I must not disclose my identity: it would be too dreadful if he should learn that Emma Goldman, the anarchist, had been found soliciting on Fourteenth Street. What a juicy story it would make for the press!

He said he was not interested in economic problems and did not care what the reason was for my actions. He only wanted to tell me that there was nothing in prostitution unless one had the knack for it. "You haven't got it, that's all there is to it," he assured me. He took out a ten-dollar bill and put it down before me. "Take this and go home," he said. "But why should you give me money if you don't want me to go with you?" I asked. "Well, just to cover the expenses you must have had to rig yourself out like that," he replied; "your dress is awfully nice, even if it does not go with those cheap shoes and stockings." I was too astounded for speech.

I had met two categories of men: vulgarians and idealists. The former would never have let an opportunity pass to possess a woman and they would give her no other thought save sexual desire. The idealists stoutly defended the equality of the sexes, at least in theory, but the only men among them who practised what they preached were the Russian and Jewish radicals. This man, who had picked me up on the street and who was now with me in the back of a saloon, seemed an entirely new type. He interested me. He must be rich. But would a rich man give something for nothing? The manufacturer Garson came to my mind; he would not even give me a small raise in wages.

Perhaps this man was one of those soul-savers I had read about, people who were always cleansing New York City of vice. I asked him. He laughed and said he was not a professional busybody. If he had thought that I really wanted to be on the street, he would not have cared. "Of course, I may be entirely mistaken," he added, "but I don't mind. Just now I am convinced that you are not intended to be a streetwalker, and that even if you do succeed, you will hate it afterwards." If he were not convinced of it, he would take me for his mistress. "For always?" I cried. "There you are!" he replied; "you are scared by the mere suggestion and yet you hope to succeed on the street. You're an awfully nice kid, but you're silly, inexperienced, childish." "I was twenty-three last month," I protested, resentful of being treated like a child. "You are an old lady," he said with a grin, "but even old folks can be babes in the woods. Look at me; I'm sixty-one and I often do foolish things." "Like believing in my innocence, for instance," I retorted. The simplicity of his manner pleased me. I asked for his name and address so as to be able to return his ten dollars some day. But he refused to give them to me. He loved mysteries, he said. On the street he held my hand for a moment, and then we turned in opposite directions.

That night I tossed about for hours. My sleep was restless; my dreams were of Sasha, Frick, Homestead, Fourteenth Street, and the affable stranger. Long after waking the next morning the dream pictures persisted. Then my eye caught my little purse on the table. I jumped up, opened it with trembling hands—it did contain the ten dollars! It had actually happened, then!

On Monday a short note arrived from Sasha. He had met Carl Nold and Henry Bauer, he wrote. He had set the following Saturday for his act, provided I could send some money he needed at once. He was sure I would not fail him. I was a little disappointed by the letter. Its tone was cold and perfunctory, and I wondered how the stranger would write to the woman he loved. With a start I shook myself free. It was crazy to have such thoughts when Sasha was preparing to take a life and lose his own in the attempt. How could I think of that stranger and Sasha in the same breath? I must get more money for my boy.

I would wire Helena for fifteen dollars. I had not written my dear sister for many weeks, and I hated to ask her for money, knowing how poor she was. It seemed criminal. Finally I wired her that I had been taken ill and needed fifteen dollars. I knew that nothing would prevent her from getting the money if she thought that I was ill. But a sense of shame oppressed me, as once before, in St. Petersburg, when I had deceived her.

I received the money from Helena by wire. I sent twenty dollars to Sasha and returned the five I had borrowed for my finery.

CHAPTER IX

[. . .] In the early afternoon of Saturday, July 23, Fedya rushed into my room with a newspaper. There it was, in large black letters: "Young man by the name of Alexander Bergman shoots Frick—assassin overpowered by working-men after desperate struggle."

Working-men, working-men overpowering Sasha? The paper was lying! He did the act for the working-men; they would never attack him.

Hurriedly we secured all the afternoon editions. Every one had a different description, but the main fact stood out—our brave Sasha had committed the act! Frick was still alive, but his wounds were considered fatal. He would probably not survive the night. And Sasha—they would kill him. They were going to kill him, I was sure of it. Was I going to let him die alone? Should I go on talking while he was being butchered? I must pay the same price as he—I must stand the consequences— I must share the responsibility! [. . .]

In feverish excitement we read the detailed story about the "assassin Alexander Berkman." He had forced his way into Frick's private office on the heels of the Negro porter who had taken in his card. He had immediately opened fire, and Frick had fallen to the ground with three bullets in his body. The first to come to his aid, the paper said, was his assistant Leishman, who was in the office at the time. Working-men, engaged on a carpenter job in the building, rushed in, and one of them felled Berkman to the ground with a hammer. At first they thought Frick dead. Then a cry was heard from him. Berkman had crawled over and got near enough to strike Frick with a dagger in the thigh. After that he was pounded into unconsciousness. He came to in the station-house, but he would answer no questions. One of the detectives grew suspicious about the appearance of Berkman's face and he nearly broke the young man's jaw trying to open his mouth. A peculiar capsule was found hidden there. When asked what it was, Berkman replied with defiant contempt: "Candy." On examination it proved to be a dynamite cartridge. The police were sure of conspiracy. They were now looking for the accomplices, especially for "a certain Bakhmetov, who had registered at one of the Pittsburgh hotels." [. . .]

The daily press carried on a ferocious campaign against the anarchists. They called for the police to act, to round up "the instigators, Johann Most, Emma Goldman, and their ilk." My name had rarely before been mentioned in the papers, but now it appeared every day in the most sensational stories. The police got busy; a hunt for Emma Goldman began.

My friend Peppie, with whom I was living, had a flat on Fifth Street and First Avenue, round the corner from the police station. I used to pass the latter frequently, going about openly and spending cosiderable time at the headquarters of the *Autonomie*. Yet the police seemed unable to find me. One evening, while we were away at a meeting, the police, having discovered my whereabouts at last, broke into the flat through the fire-escape and stole everything they could lay their hands on. My fine collection of revolutionary pamphlets and photographs, my entire correspondence, vanished with them. But they did not find what they came to look for. At the first mention of my name in the papers I had disposed of the material left over from Sasha's experiments. [. . .]

Several days after the *Attentat* militia regiments were marched into Homestead. The more conscious of the steel-workers opposed the move, but they were overruled by the conservative labour element, who foolishly saw in the soldiers protection against new attacks by Pinkertons. The troops soon proved whom they came to protect. It was the Carnegie mills, not the Homestead workers.

However, there was one militiaman who was wide awake enough to see in Sasha the avenger of labour's wrongs. This brave boy gave vent to his feelings by calling in the ranks for "three cheers for the man who shot Frick." He was court-martialled and strung up by his thumbs, but he stuck to his cheers. This incident was the one bright moment in the black and harassing days that followed Sasha's departure.

After a long, anxious wait a letter came from Sasha. He had been greatly cheered by the stand of the militiaman, W. L. Iams, he wrote. It showed that even American soldiers were waking up. Could I not get in touch with the boy, send him anarchist literature? He would be a valuable asset to the movement. I was not to worry about himself; he was in fine spirits and already preparing his court speech—not as a defence, he emphasized, but in explanation of his act. Of course, he would have no lawyer; he would represent his own case as true Russian and other European revolutionists did. Prominent Pittsburgh attorneys had offered their services free of charge, but he had declined. It was inconsistent for an anarchist to employ lawyers; I should make his attitude on the matter clear to the comrades. [. . .]

I pressed the letter to my heart, covering it with kisses. I knew how intensely my Sasha felt, although he had said not one word about his love and his thoughts of me.

I was considerably alarmed about his decision to represent his own case. I loved his beautiful consistency, but I knew that his English, like my own, was too poor to be effective in court. I feared he would have no chance. But Sasha's wish, now more than ever, was sacred to me, and I consoled myself with the hope that he would have a public trial, that I could have his speech translated, and that we might give the whole proceedings countrywide publicity. I wrote him that I agreed with his decision, and that we were preparing a large meeting where his act would be fully explained and his motives properly presented. [. . .]

We began to prepare for the large meeting on behalf of Sasha. [. . .] Our large red posters announcing the mass meeting roused the ire of the press. Were the authorities not going to interfere? The police came out with the threat that our gathering would be stopped, but on the appointed evening the audience was so large and looked so determined that the police did nothing.

I acted as chairman, a new experience for me; but we could get no one else. The meeting was very spirited, every one of the speakers paying the highest tribute to Sasha and his deed. My hatred of conditions which compelled idealists to acts of violence made me cry out in passionate strains the nobility of Sasha, his selflessness, his consecration to the people.

"Possessed by a fury," the papers said of my speech the next morning. "How long will this dangerous woman be permitted to go on?" Ah, if they only knew how I yearned to give up my freedom, to proclaim loudly my share in the deed—if only they knew! [. . .]

The papers began reporting that Frick was recovering from his wounds. Comrades visiting me expressed the opinion that Sasha, "had failed." Some even had the effrontery to suggest that Most might have been right in saying that "it was a toy pistol."[1] I was stung to the quick. I knew that Sasha had never had much practice in shooting. Occasionally, at German picnics, he would take part in target-shooting, but was that sufficient? I was sure Sasha's failure to kill Frick was due to the cheap quality of his revolver—he had lacked enough money to buy a good one.

Perhaps Frick was recovering because of the attention he was getting? The greatest surgeons of America had been called to his bedside. Yes, it must be that; after all, three bullets from Sasha's revolver had lodged in his body. It was Frick's wealth that was enabling him to recover. I tried to explain this to the comrades, but most of them remained unconvinced. Some even hinted that Sasha was at liberty. I was frantic—how dared they doubt Sasha? I would write him! I would ask him to send me word that would stop the horrible rumours about him.

Soon a letter arrived from Sasha, written in a curt tone. He was provoked that I could even ask for an explanation. Did I not know that the vital thing was the motive of his act and not its physical success or failure? My poor, tortured boy! I could read between the lines how crushed he was at the realization that Frick remained alive. But he was right: the important thing was his motives, and these no one could doubt.

Weeks passed without any indication of when Sasha's trial

would begin. He was still kept on "Murderers' Row" in the Pittsburgh jail, but the fact that Frick was improving had considerably changed Sasha's legal status. He could not be condemned to death. Through comrades in Pennsylvania I learned that the law called for seven years in prison for his attempt. Hope entered my heart. Seven years are a long time, but Sasha was strong, he had iron perseverance, he could hold out. I clung to the new possibility with every fibre of my being.

My own life was full of misery. [. . .] I went in search of a room, but my name seemed to frighten the landlords. My friends suggested that I give an assumed name, but I would not deny my identity. [. . .]

On Fourth Street near Third Avenue I had often passed a house which always had a sign out: "Furnished Room to Rent." One day I went in. No questions were asked about my identity. The room was small, but the rent was high, four dollars a week. The surroundings looked rather peculiar, but I hired the room.

In the evening I discovered that the whole house was tenanted by girls. I paid no attention at first, being busy putting my belongings in order. Weeks had passed since I had unpacked my clothes and books. It was such a comforting sensation to be able to take a scrub, to lie down on a clean bed. I retired early, but was awakened at night by someone knocking on my door. "Who is it?" I called, still heavy with sleep. "Say, Viola, ain't you goin' to let me in? I've been knockin' for twenty minutes. What the hell is up? You said I could come tonight." "You're in the wrong place, mister," I replied; "I'm not Viola."

Similar episodes happened every night for some time. Men called for Annette, for Mildred, or Clothilde. It finally dawned on me that I was living in a brothel.

The girl in the room next to mine was a sympathetic-looking youngster, and one day I invited her for coffee. I learned from her that the place was not a "regular dump, with a Madam," but that it was a rooming-house where girls were allowed to bring their men. She asked if I was doing good business, as I was so young. When I told her that I was not in the business, that I was only a dressmaker, the girl jeered. It took me some time to convince her that I was not looking for men customers.

What better place could I have found than this house full of girls who must need dresses? I began to consider whether to remain in the house or move out. [. . .]

Before the week was over, I had become the confidante of most of the girls. They competed with one another in being kind to me, in giving me their sewing to do and helping in little ways. For the first time since my return from Worcester I was able to earn my living. I had my own corner and I had made new friends. But my life was not destined to run smoothly for long.

The feud between Most and our group continued.[2] Hardly a week passed without some slur in the *Freiheit* against Sasha or myself. It was painful enough to be called vile names by the man who had once loved me, but it was beyond endurance to have Sasha slandered and maligned. Then came Most's article "*Attentats-Reflexionen* (Reflections on Propaganda by Deed)" in the *Freiheit* of August 27, which was a complete reversal of everything that Most had till then persistently advocated. Most, whom I had heard scores of times call for acts of violence, who had gone to prison in England for his glorification of tyrannicide—Most, the incarnation of defiance and revolt, now deliberately repudiated the *Tat*! [. . .]

I resolved to challenge him publicly to prove his insinuations, to compel him to explain his sudden reversal of attitude in the face of danger. I replied to his article, in the *Anarchist*, demanding an explanation and branding Most as a traitor and a coward. I waited for two weeks for a reply in the *Freiheit*, but none appeared. There were no proofs, and I knew that he could not justify his base accusations. I bought a horsewhip.

At Most's next lecture I sat in the first row, close to the low platform. My hand was on the whip under my long, grey cloak. When he got up and faced the audience, I rose and declared in a loud voice: "I came to demand proof of your insinuations against Alexander Berkman."

There was instant silence. Most mumbled something about "hysterical woman," but he said nothing else. I then pulled out my whip and leaped towards him. Repeatedly I lashed him across the face and neck, then broke the whip over my knee and threw the pieces at him. It was all done so quickly that no one had time to interfere.

Then I felt myself roughly pulled back. "Throw her out! Beat her up!" people yelled. I was surrounded by an enraged and threatening crowd and might have fared badly had not Fedya, Claus, and other friends come to my rescue. They lifted me up bodily and forced their way out of the hall. [...]

Meanwhile we were anxiously waiting for the date of Sasha's trial to be set, but no information was forthcoming. In the second week of September I was invited to speak in Baltimore, my lecture being scheduled for Monday, the 19th. As I was about to ascend the platform, a telegram was handed to me. The trial had taken place that very day and Sasha had been condemned to twenty-two years in prison! Railroaded to a living death! The hall and the audience began to swim before my eyes. Someone took the telegram out of my hands and pushed me into a chair. A glass of water was held to my lips. The meeting must be called off, the comrades said.

I looked wildly about me, gulped down some water, snatched up the telegram, and leaped to the platform. The yellow piece of paper in my hand was a glowing coal, its fire searing my heart and flaming it into passionate expression. It caught the audience and raised it to ferment. Men and women jumped to their feet, calling for vengeance against the ferocious sentence. Their burning fervour in the cause of Sasha and his act resounded like thunder through the great hall.

The police burst in with drawn clubs and drove the audience out of the building. I remained on the platform, the telegram still in my hand. Officers came up and put the chairman and me under arrest. On the street we were pushed into a waiting patrol wagon and driven to the station-house, followed by the incensed crowd.

I had been surrounded by people from the moment the crushing news had come, compelled to suppress the turmoil in my soul and force back the hot tears that kept swelling in my throat. Now, free from intrusion, the monstrous sentence loomed up before me in all its horror. Twenty-two years! Sasha was twenty-one, at the most impressionable and vivid age. The life he had not yet lived was before him, holding out the charm and beauty his intense nature could extract. And now he was cut down like a strong young tree, robbed of sun and of light. And Frick was alive, almost recovered from his wounds and now recuperating in his palatial summer house. He would go on spilling the blood of labour. Frick was alive, and Sasha doomed to twenty-two years in a living tomb. The irony, the bitter irony of the thing, struck me full in the face.

If only I could shut out the ghastly picture and give vent to tears, find forgetfulness in everlasting sleep! But there were no tears, there was no sleep. There was only Sasha—Sasha in convict's clothes, captive behind stone walls—Sasha with his pale set face pressed to the iron bars, his steady eyes gazing intently upon me, bidding me go on.

No, no, no, there must be no despair. I would live, I would fight for Sasha. I would rend the black clouds closing on him, I would rescue my boy, I would bring him back to life!

CHAPTER X

When I returned to New York two days later, having been discharged by the Baltimore police magistrate with a strong admonition never again to come back to the city, a letter from Sasha was awaiting me. It was written in very small but distinct script and gave the details of the Monday in court. He had repeatedly tried to learn the date of his trial, the letter read, but he could not procure any information about it. On the morning of the 19th he was suddenly ordered to get ready. He had barely time to gather up the sheets of his speech. Strange and antagonistic faces met him in the court-room. In vain he strained his eye for the sight of his friends. He realized that they, too, must have been kept in ignorance of the day of the trial. Yet he hoped against hope for the miracle. But there was not a friendly face anywhere. He was confronted with six indictments, all manufactured from the one act, and among them one charging him with an attempt on the life of John G. A. Leishman, Frick's assistant. Sasha declared that he knew nothing of Leishman; it was Frick whom he had come to kill. He demanded that he be tried on that charge alone, and that the other indictments be quashed, because they were all involved in the major charge. But his objection was overruled.

The jurors were selected in a few minutes, Sasha making no use of his right of challenge. What difference did it make? They were all alike, and he would be convicted anyhow. He declared to the Court that he scorned to defend himself; he wanted only to explain his act. The interpreter assigned to him translated haltingly and wrongly, and after several attempts to correct him Sasha discovered to his horror that the man was blind, as blind as justice in the American courts. He then tried to address the jury in English, but he was impatiently stopped by Judge McClung, who declared that "the prisoner has said enough already." Sasha protested, but in vain. The District Attorney stepped into the jury-box and held a low conversation with the talesmen, whereupon they brought in a verdict of guilty without even leaving their seats. The Judge was curt and denunciatory. He passed sentence on each count separately, including three indictments for "entering a building with felonious intent," giving the prisoner the maximum on each charge. The total amounted to twenty-one years in the Western Penitentiary of Pennsylvania, at the expiration of which time an additional year was to be served in the Allegheny County Workhouse for "carrying concealed weapons."

Twenty-two years of slow torture and death! He had done his duty, Sasha's letter concluded, and now the end had come. He would depart as he had determined, by his own will and hand. He wanted no effort made in his behalf. It would be of no use and he could not give his consent to an appeal to the enemy. No need of further help for him; whatever campaign could be made must be for his act, and I was to see to that. He was sure that no one else felt and understood his motives so well, no one else could clarify the meaning of his deed with the same conviction. His one deep longing now was for me. If he could only look into my eyes once more and press me to his heart— but as that was denied him, he would keep on thinking of me, his friend and comrade. No power on earth could take that away from him. [. . .]

His letters were dispiriting, but I held on grimly. I knew his indomitable will and his iron strength of character. I clung tenaciously to the hope that he would arouse himself and not allow himself to be crushed. That hope alone gave me the courage to go on. I joined the newly organized efforts for him. Night after night I was at some meeting voicing the meaning and message of Sasha's act.

Early in November came the first sign of Sasha's reawakened interest in life. His letter informed me that he might have the privilege of a visitor. Prisoners were entitled to one visit a month, but only from a near relative. Could I get his sister from Russia to come to see him? I understood what he meant and wrote him immediately to get the pass.

I had been invited by anarchist groups in Chicago and St. Louis to speak at the approaching anniversary of the 11th of November[1] and I decided to combine the trip with a visit to Sasha. I would go as his married sister, under the name of Niedermann. I was certain that the prison authorities knew nothing about Sasha's sister in Russia. I would impersonate her and they would never suspect my identity. I was hardly known then. The pictures of me in the papers in connexion with Sasha's act were so unlike me that no one could have recognized me from them. To see my boy again, to press him to my heart, to bring him hope and courage—I lived for nothing else during the weeks and days before the visit.

In a fever I made my preparations. My first stop was to be St. Louis; then Chicago; finally Pittsburgh. A letter from Sasha arrived a few days before my departure. It contained a pass from the Chief Prison Inspector of the Western Penitentiary for Mrs. E. Niedermann, sister of Prisoner A-7, for a visit on the 26th of November. [. . .]

I arrived in Pittsburgh early on the morning of Thanksgiving Day. I was met by Carl Nold and Max Metzkow, the latter a German comrade who had faithfully stood by Sasha. [. . .][2] In the afternoon I went out to Allegheny. [. . .]

The grey stone building, the high forbidding walls, the armed guards, the oppressive silence in the hall where I was told to wait, and the minutes creeping into endless time settled on my heart with the weight of a nightmare. In vain I tried to shake myself free. At last a harsh voice called: "This way, Mrs. Niedermann." I was taken through several iron doors, along twisting corridors, into a small room. Sasha was there, a tall guard beside him.

My first impulse was to rush up to him and cover him with kisses, but the presence of the guard checked me. Sasha approached me and put his arms around me. As he bent over to kiss me, I felt a small object pass into my mouth.

For weeks I had been looking forward eagerly, anxiously to

this visit. A thousand times I had gone over in my mind all I would say to him of my love and undying devotion, of the struggle I was making for his release, but all I could do was to press his hand and look into his eyes.

We began to speak in our beloved Russian, but we were stopped immediately by the cold command of the guard: "Talk English. No foreign languages here." His lynx-like eyes followed our every movement, watched our lips, crept into our very minds. I became tongue-tied, numb in every nerve. Sasha, too, was mute; his fingers kept on playing with my watch-chain and he seemed to hold on to it as a drowning man to a straw. Neither of us could utter a word, but our eyes spoke to each other—of our fears, our hopes, our yearnings.

The visit lasted twenty minutes. Another embrace, another touch of our lips, and our "time was up." I whispered to him to hold on, to hold out, and then I found myself on the prison steps. The iron gate clattered shut behind me.

I wanted to scream, to throw my weight against the door, to pound it with my fists. But the gate stared back at me and mocked. I walked along the front of the prison and into the street. I walked, silently weeping, towards the spot where I had left Metzkow. His presence brought me back to reality and made me conscious of the object Sasha had given me with his kiss. I took it out of my mouth—a small roll tightly wrapped. We went into the back room of a saloon and I unwound the several layers of paper. At last appeared a note with Sasha's diminutive handwriting, each word standing out like a pearl before me. "You must go to Inspector Reed," it read; "he promised me a second pass. Go to his jewellery shop tomorrow. I am counting on you. I'll give you another message of importance— the same way."

I went to Reed's store the next day. I looked shabby in my threadbare coat amid the sparkling jewellery, silver, and gold. I I asked to see Mr. Reed. He was a tall, emaciated, thin-lipped creature, with hard and piercing eyes. No sooner had I given my name than he exclaimed: "So this is Berkman's sister!" Yes, he had promised him a second visit, though he did not deserve any kindness. Berkman was a murderer, he had tried to kill a good Christian man. I held on to myself by sheer force; my chance to see Sasha again was at stake. He would call up the prison, Reed continued, to find out at what time I could be admitted. I was to return in an hour.

My heart sank. I had a distinct premonition that there would be no more visits for Sasha. But I came back as directed. As soon as Mr. Reed saw me, his face turned purple and he fairly leaped at me. "You deceiver!" he yelled. "You have already been at the penitentiary! You sneaked in under a false name as his sister. You don't get away with such lies here—you have been recognized by a guard! You are Emma Goldman, that criminal's mistress! There will be no more visits. You might as well make up your mind about it—Berkman will never get out alive!"

He had gone behind the glass counter, which was covered with silverware. In my indignation and rage I swept everything to the floor—plates, coffee-pots and pitchers, jewellery and watches. I seized a heavy tray and was about to throw it at him when I was pulled back by one of the clerks, who shouted to someone to run for the police. Reed, white with fear and frothing at the mouth, signalled to the clerk. "No police," I heard him say; "no scandal. Just kick her out." The clerk advanced towards me, then stopped. "Murderer, coward!" I cried; "if you harm Berkman, I will kill you with my own hands!"

No one moved. I walked out and boarded a street-car. [. . .] I was shocked by the thought that Sasha might indeed have to suffer as a result of my outbreak. But the threat of the Inspector that Sasha would never come out of prison alive had been too much for me. I was sure Sasha would understand.

The night was black as I walked with Nold to the station to take the train for New York. The steel-foundries belched huge flames that reflected the Allegheny hills blood-red and filled the air with soot and smoke. We made our way past the sheds where human beings, half man, half beast, were working like the galley-slaves of an era long past. Their naked bodies, covered only with small trunks, shone like copper in the glare of the red-hot chunks of iron they were snatching from the mouths of the flaming monsters. From time to time the steam rising from the water thrown on the hot metal would completely envelop the men; then they would emerge again like shadows. "The children of hell," I said, "damned to the everlasting inferno of heat and noise." Sasha had given his life to bring joy to these slaves, but they had remained blind and continued in the hell of their own forging. "Their souls are dead, dead to the horror and degradation of their lives." [. . .]

Far in the distance, as the train sped on, I could still see the belching flames shoot against the black sky, lighting up the hills of Allegheny. Allegheny, which held what was most precious to me immured perhaps for ever! I had planned the *Attentat* together with him; I had let him go alone; I had approved of his decision to have no lawyer. I strove to shake off the consciousness of guilt, but it would give me no rest until I found forgetfulness in sleep.

CHAPTER XI

Our work for the commutation of Sasha's sentence continued. At one of our weekly meetings, in the latter part of December, I became conscious of the steady gaze of a man in the audience. [...] I learned that his name was Edward Brady[1] and that he had just arrived from Austria after completing a term of ten years in prison for the publication of illegal anarchist literature. I found him the most scholarly person I had ever met. His field was not limited, like Most's, to social and political subjects; in fact, he rarely talked about them to me. He introduced me to the great classics of English and French literature. [...]

He asked about my childhood and schooldays. [...] I had only had three and a half years of *Realschule* in Königsberg, I told him. The régime was harsh, the instructors brutal; I learned scarcely anything. [...]

Two of my teachers had been altogether terrible. One, a German Jew, was our instructor in religion; the other taught geography. I hated them both. Occasionally I would avenge myself on the former for his constant beatings, but I was too terrorized by the other even to complain at home.

The great joy of our religious instructor used to be to beat the palms of our hands with a ruler. I used to organize schemes to annoy him: stick pins in his upholstered chair, stealthily tie his long coat-tails to the table, put snails in his pockets—anything I could think of to pay him back for the pain of his ruler. He knew I was the ring-leader and he beat me the more for it. But it was a frank feud that could be met in the open.

Not so with the other man. His methods were less painful, but more dreadful. Every afternoon he would keep one or two of the girls after school-hours. When everybody had left the building, he would send one girl to the next class-room, then force the other on his knee and grasp her breasts or put his hands between her legs. He would promise her good marks if she kept quiet and threaten instant dismissal if she talked. The girls were terrorized into silence. I did not know for a long time about these things, until one day I found myself on his knee. I screamed, reached for his beard, and pulled it violently in my attempt to wriggle out of his hold. He jumped up, and I fell to the floor. He ran to the door to see if anyone was coming in response to my cry; then he hissed into my ear: "If you breathe one word, I'll kick you out of school."

For several days I was too sick with fright to return to school, but I would not say anything. The dread of being dismissed brought back the remembrance of Father's fury whenever I returned with bad marks. I went back to school at last, and for some days the geography lessons passed without incident. Because of my poor eyesight I had to stand close to the map. One day the teacher whispered to me: "You will remain behind." "I will not!" I whispered back. The next moment I felt a stinging pain in my arm. He had stuck his nails into my flesh. My cries broke up the class and brought other instructors to the room. I heard our teacher telling them that I was a dullard, that I never knew my lessons and therefore he had to punish me. I was sent home.

At night my arm hurt a great deal. Mother noticed that it was all swollen and she sent for the doctor, who questioned me. His kindly manner led me to tell him the whole story. "Terrible!" he exclaimed; "the fellow belongs to the madhouse." A week later when I returned to school our geography-teacher was no longer there. He had gone on a journey, we were told. [. . .]

The sweet companionship with Ed did not eliminate Sasha from my mind. Ed was also deeply interested in him and he joined the groups that were carrying on a systematic campaign in Sasha's behalf. [. . .]

I wanted Sasha to feel that whatever happened in my life, whoever entered it, he would remain in it always. My letters left me dissatisfied and unhappy. But life went on. I had to work ten, sometimes twelve hours a day at the sewing-machine to earn my living. Almost nightly meetings and the need of improving my neglected education kept me engaged all the time. Somehow Ed made me feel that need more than anyone else had done.

Our friendship gradually ripened into love. Ed became indispensable to me. I had known for a long time that he also cared for me. Of unusual reserve, he had never spoken of his love, but his eyes and his touch were eloquent of it. He had had women in his life before. One of them had given him a daughter, who was living with her mother's parents. He felt grateful to those women, he would often say. They had taught him the mysteries and subtleties of sex. I could not follow Ed when he spoke of these matters, and I was too shy to ask for an explanation. But I used to wonder what he meant. Sex had seemed a simple process to me. My own sex life had always left me dissatisfied, longing for something I did not know. I considered love more important than all else, love which finds supreme joy in selfless giving.

In the arms of Ed I learned for the first time the meaning of the great life-giving force. I understood its full beauty, and I eagerly drank its intoxicating joy and bliss. [. . .] I would cling to Ed with a trembling heart. He would hold me close and his unfailing cheer and humour would dispel my dark thoughts. "You are overworked," he would say. "The machine and your constant anxiety about Sasha are killing you."

In the spring I fell ill, began to lose weight, and grew too weak to walk across the room. Physicians ordered immediate rest and a change of climate. My friends persuaded me to leave New York and I went to Rochester, accompanied by a girl who volunteered as nurse.

My sister Helena thought her place too cramped for a patient and she secured for me a room in a house with a large garden. She spent every spare moment with me, unfailing in her love and care. She took me to a lung-specialist who discovered an early stage of tuberculosis and put me on a special diet. Presently I began to improve, and within two months I had recovered sufficiently to take walks. My doctor was planning to send me for the winter to a sanatorium, when developments in New York gave a different turn to the situation.

The industrial crisis of that year had thrown thousands out of employment, and their condition now reached an appalling state. Worst of all was the situation in New York. Jobless workers were being evicted; suffering was growing and suicides multiplying. Nothing was being done to alleviate their misery.

I could no longer remain in Rochester. My reason told me it was reckless to go back in the middle of my cure. I had grown much stronger and had gained weight. I coughed less and the hæmorrhages had stopped. I knew, however, that I was far from well. But something stronger than reason was drawing me back to New York. I longed for Ed; but more compelling was the call of the unemployed, of the workers of the East Side who had given me my labour baptism. I had been with them in their previous struggles; I could not stay away from them now. I left notes behind for the physician and Helena; I did not have the heart to face them.

I had wired Ed and he met me joyously. But when I told him that I had returned to devote myself to the unemployed, his mood changed. It was insanity, he urged; it would mean the loss of everything I had gained in health through my rest. It might even prove fatal. He would not permit it—I was his now—his, to love and protect and watch over.

It was bliss to know that someone cared so much for me, but I felt it at the same time a handicap. His "to hold and protect"? Did he consider me his property, a dependent or a cripple who had to be taken care of by a man? I had thought he believed in freedom, in my right to do as I wished. It was anxiety about me, fear for my health, he assured me, that prompted his words. But if I was determined to resume my efforts, he would help. He was no speaker, but he could be useful in other ways.

Committee sessions, public meetings, collection of foodstuffs, supervising the feeding of the homeless and their numerous children, and, finally, the organization of a mass meeting on Union Square entirely filled my time.

The meeting at Union Square was preceded by a demonstration, the marching columns counting many thousands. The girls and women were in front, I at their head carrying a red banner. Its crimson waved proudly in the air and could be seen for blocks. My soul, too, vibrated with the intensity of the moment.

I had prepared my speech in writing and it seemed to me inspiring, but when I reached Union Square and saw the huge mass of humanity, my notes appeared cold and meaningless. [. . .]

"Men and women," I began amidst sudden silence, "do you not realize that the State is the worst enemy you have? It is a machine that crushes you in order to sustain the ruling class, your masters. Like naïve children you put your trust in your political leaders. You make it possible for them to creep into your confidence, only to have them betray you to the first bidder. But even where there is no direct betrayal, the labour politicians make common cause with your enemies to keep you in leash, to prevent your direct action. The State is the pillar of capitalism, and it is ridiculous to expect any redress from it. Do you not see the stupidity of asking relief from Albany with immense wealth within a stone's throw from here? Fifth Avenue is laid in gold, every mansion is a citadel of money and power. Yet there you stand, a giant, starved and fettered, shorn of his strength. [. . .] You, too, will have to learn that you have a right to share your neighbour's bread. Your neighbours—they have not only stolen your bread, but they are sapping your blood. They will go on robbing you, your children, and your children's children, unless you wake up, unless you become daring enough to demand your rights. Well, then, demonstrate before the palaces of the rich; demand work. If they do not give you work, demand bread. If they deny you both, take bread. It is your sacred right!"

Uproarious applause, wild and deafening, broke from the stillness like a sudden storm. The sea of hands eagerly stretching out towards me seemed like the wings of white birds fluttering.

The following morning I went to Philadelphia to secure relief and help organize the unemployed there. The afternoon papers carried a garbled account of my speech. I had urged the crowd to revolution, they claimed. "Red Emma has great swaying power; her vitriolic tongue was just what the ignorant mob needed to tear down New York." They also stated that I had been spirited away by some husky friends, but that the police were on my track. [. . .]

The streets near by were blocked with people. No one recognized me as I walked up the flight of steps leading to the meeting-place. Then one of the anarchists greeted me: "Here's Emma!" I waved him aside, but a heavy hand was immediately on my shoulder, and a voice said: "You're under arrest, Miss Goldman." There was a commotion, people ran towards me, but the officers drew their guns and held back the crowd. A detective gripped my arm and pulled me down the stairs into the street. [. . .] I was taken to police headquarters, in the tower of the City Hall, and locked up for the night. In the morning I was asked whether I was willing to go back with the detectives to New York. "Not of my own free will," I declared. [. . .]

Many comrades visited me in the jail, and from them I learned that the meeting had been allowed to proceed after my arrest. Voltairine de Cleyre[2] had taken my place and had protested vigorously against my suppression. [. . .]

The second morning after my arrest I was transferred to Moyamensing Prison to await extradition. I was put into a fairly large cell, its door of solid sheet iron, with a small square in the centre opening from the outside. The window was high and heavily barred. The cell contained a sanitary toilet, running water, a tin cup, a wooden table, a bench, and an iron cot. A small electric lamp hung from the ceiling. From time to time the square in the door would open and a pair of eyes would look in, or a voice would call for the cup and it would be passed back to me filled with tepid water or soup and a slice of bread. Except for such interruptions silence prevailed.

After the second day the stillness became oppressive and the hours crept on endlessly. I grew weary from constant pacing between the window and the door. My nerves were tense with the strain for some human sound. I called for the matron, but no one answered. I banged my tin cup against the door. Finally it brought response. My door was unlocked and a large woman with a hard face came into the cell. It was against the rules to make so much noise, she warned me. If I did it again, she would have to punish me. What did I want? I wanted my mail, I told her. I was sure there was some from my friends, and I also wanted books to read. She would bring a book, but there was no mail, the matron said. I knew she was lying, for I was certain Ed had written, even if no one else. She went out, locking the door after her. Presently she returned with a book. It was the Bible and it recalled to my mind the cruel face of my religious instructor in school. Indignantly I flung the volume at the matron's feet. I had no need of religious lies; I wanted some human book, I told her. For a moment she stood horror-stricken; then she began raging at me. I had desecrated God's word; I would be put in the dungeon; later on I would burn in hell. I replied heatedly that she did not dare punish me, because I was a prisoner of the State of New York, that I had not yet been tried and therefore still had some civil rights. She flung out, slamming the door after her.

In the evening I had a violent headache, caused by the electric light scorching my eyes. I again knocked on the door and demanded to see the doctor. Another woman came, the prison physician. She gave me some medicine and I asked her for some reading-matter, or at least some sewing. Next day I was given towels to hem. Eagerly I stitched by the hour, my thoughts with Sasha and Ed. With crushing clarity I saw what Sasha's life in prison meant. Twenty-two years! I should go mad in a year.

One day the matron came to announce that extradition had been granted and that I was to be taken to New York. I followed her into the office, where I was handed a large package of letters, telegrams, and papers. I was informed that several boxes of fruit and flowers had come for me, but that it was against the rules for prisoners to have such things. Then I was handed over to a heavy-set man. A cab waited outside the prison and we were driven to the station.

We travelled in a Pullman car, and the man introduced himself as Detective-Sergeant ——. He excused himself, saying he was only doing his duty; he had six children to support. I asked him why he had not chosen a more honourable occupation and why he had to bring more spies into the world. If *he* did not do

it, someone else would, he replied. The police force was necessary; it protected society. Would I have dinner? He would have
it brought to the car to save my going to the diner. I consented.
I had not eaten anything decent for a week; besides, the City of
New York was paying for the unsolicited luxury of my journey.

Over the dinner the detective referred to my youth and the
life "such a brilliant girl, with such abilities" had before her.
He went on to say that I never would earn anything by the work
I was doing, not even my salt. Why shouldn't I be sensible and
"look out for number one" first? He felt for me because he was
a *Yehude* himself. He was sorry to see me go to prison. He
could tell me how to get free, even to receive a large sum of
money, if I would only be sensible.

"Out with it," I said; "what's on your mind?"

His chief had instructed him to tell me that my case would be
quashed and a substantial sum of money presented to me if I
would give way a little. Nothing much, just a short periodic report of what was going on in radical circles and among the
workers on the East Side.

A horrible feeling came over me. The food nauseated me. I
gulped down some ice-water from my glass and threw what was
left into the detective's face. "You miserable cur!" I shouted;
"not enough that you act as a Judas, you try even to turn me
into one—you and your rotten chief! I'll take prison for life,
but no one will ever buy me!"

"All right, all right," he said soothingly; "have it your own
way."

From the Pennsylvania Station I was driven to the Mulberry
Street Police Station, where I was locked up for the night. [. . .]
The next morning I was taken before the Chief. The detective
had told him everything and he was furious. [. . .]

My trial was set for the 28th of September; my bail, to the
amount of five thousand dollars, was given by Dr. Julius Hoffmann. In triumph my friends took me to Justus's den.[3]

In my accumulated mail I found an underground letter from
Sasha. He had read about my arrest. "Now you are indeed my
sailor girl," he wrote. He had at last established communication

with Nold and Bauer and they were arranging a *sub rosa* prison publication. They had already chosen a name; it was to be called "*Gefängniss-Blüthen* (Prison Blossoms)." I felt a weight lifted off my heart. Sasha had come back, he was beginning to take an interest in life, he would hold out! At most he would have to serve seven years on the first charge. We must work energetically to get his sentence commuted. I was light-hearted and happy in the thought that we might yet succeed in wrenching Sasha from his living grave.

Justus's place was crowded. People I had never before seen now came to express their sympathy. I had suddenly become an important personage, though I could not understand why, since I had done or said nothing that merited distinction. But I was glad to see so much interest in my ideas. I never doubted for a moment that it was the social theories I represented, and not I personally, that was attracting attention. My trial would give me a wonderful chance for propaganda. I must prepare for it. My defence in open court should carry the message of anarchism to the whole country. [. . .]

My trial began on the 28th of September. [. . .] When I took the stand in my own behalf, District Attorney MacIntyre persisted in questioning me on everything under the sun except my Union Square speech. Religion, free love, morality—what were my opinions on those subjects? I attempted to unmask the hypocrisy of morality, the Church as an instrument for enslavement, the impossibility of love that is forced and not free. Constant interruptions by MacIntyre and orders from the Judge to reply only with yes or no finally compelled me to give up the task. [. . .]

The Judge enlarged on law and order, the sanctity of property, and the need of protecting "free American institutions." The jury deliberated for a long time; it was evidently loath to convict. Once the foreman came back for instructions: the jury seemed especially impressed by the testimony of one of my witnesses, a young reporter on the New York *World*. He had been at the meeting and had written a detailed account of it. When he saw his story in the paper the following morning, it was so garbled that he had at once offered to testify to the actual facts. While he was on the witness-stand, Jacobs bent over to MacIntyre, whispered something, and a court attendant was sent out. He soon returned with a copy of the *World* of the morning after the meeting. The reporter could not charge some desk editor in open court with having tampered with his account. He became embarrassed, confused, and obviously very miserable. His report as printed in the *World,* and not as testified to by him on the witness-stand, decided my fate. I was found guilty.

My attorney insisted on an appeal to the higher court, but I refused. The farce of my trial had strengthened my opposition to the State and I would ask no favours from it. I was ordered back to the Tombs until the 18th of October, the day set for sentence. [. . .][4]

On the way from the Tombs to the court New York looked as if it were under martial law. The streets were lined with police, the buildings surrounded by heavily armed cordons, the corridors of the court-house filled with officers. I was called to the bar and asked if I had "anything to say why sentence should not be passed." I had considerable to say; should I be given the chance? No, that was impossible; I could only make a very brief statement. Then I would say only that I had expected no justice from a capitalist court. The Court might do its worst, but it was powerless to change my views, I said.

Judge Martin sentenced me to one year in Blackwell's Island Penitentiary.[5] On my way to the Tombs I heard the news-boys shout: "Extra! Extra! Emma Goldman's speech in court!" and I felt glad that the *World* had kept its promise. I was at once placed in the Black Maria and taken to the boat that delivers prisoners to Blackwell's Island.

It was a bright October day, the sun playing on the water as the barge sped on. Several newspaper men accompanied me, all pressing me for an interview. "I travel in queenly state," I remarked in light mood; "just look at my satraps." "You can't squelch that kid," a young reporter kept on saying, admiringly. When we reached the island, I bade my escorts good-bye, admonishing them not to write any more lies than they could help. I called out to them gaily that I would see them again within a year and then followed the Deputy Sheriff along the broad, tree-lined gravel walk to the prison entrance. There I turned towards the river, took a last deep breath of the free air, and stepped across the threshold of my new home.

CHAPTER XII

I was called before the head matron, a tall woman with a stolid face. She began taking my pedigree. "What religion?" was her first question. "None, I am an atheist." "Atheism is prohibited here. You will have to go to church." I replied that I would do nothing of the kind. I did not believe in anything the Church stood for and, not being a hypocrite, I would not attend. Besides, I came from Jewish people. Was there a synagogue?

She said curtly that there were services for the Jewish convicts on Saturday afternoon, but as I was the only Jewish female prisoner, she could not permit me to go among so many men.

After a bath and a change into the prison uniform I was sent to my cell and locked in.

I knew from what Most had related to me about Blackwell's Island[1] that the prison was old and damp, the cells small, without light or water. I was therefore prepared for what was awaiting me. But the moment the door was locked on me, I began to experience a feeling of suffocation. In the dark I groped for something to sit on and found a narrow iron cot. Sudden exhaustion overpowered me and I fell asleep.

I became aware of a sharp burning in my eyes, and I jumped up in fright. A lamp was being held close to the bars. "What is it?" I cried, forgetting where I was. The lamp was lowered and I saw a thin, ascetic face gazing at me. A soft voice congratulated me on my sound sleep. It was the evening matron on her regular rounds. She told me to undress and left me.

But there was no more sleep for me that night. The irritating feel of the coarse blanket, the shadows creeping past the bars, kept me awake until the sound of a gong again brought me to my feet. The cells were being unlocked, the doors heavily thrown open. Blue and white striped figures slouched by, automatically forming into a line, myself a part of it. "March!" and the line began to move along the corridor down the steps towards a corner containing wash-stands and towels. Again the command: "Wash!" and everybody began clamouring for a towel, already soiled and wet. Before I had time to splash some water on my hands and face and wipe myself half-dry, the order was given to march back.

Then breakfast: a slice of bread and a tin cup of warm brownish water. Again the line formed, and the striped humanity was broken up in sections and sent to its daily tasks. With a group of other women I was taken to the sewing-room.

The procedure of forming lines—"Forward, march!"—was repeated three times a day, seven days a week. After each meal ten minutes were allowed for talk. A torrent of words would then break forth from the pent-up beings. Each precious second increased the roar of sounds; and then sudden silence.

The sewing-room was large and light, the sun often streaming through the high windows, its rays intensifying the whiteness of the walls and the monotony of the regulation dress. In the sharp light the figures in baggy and ungainly attire appeared more hideous. Still, the shop was a welcome relief from the cell. Mine, on the ground floor, was grey and damp even in the daytime; the cells on the upper floors were somewhat brighter. Close to the barred door one could even read by the help of the light coming from the corridor windows.

The locking of the cells for the night was the worst experience of the day. The convicts were marched along the tiers in the usual line. On reaching her cell each left the line, stepped inside, hands on the iron door, and awaited the command. "Close!" and with a crash the seventy doors shut, each prisoner automatically locking herself in. More harrowing still was the daily degradation of being forced to march in lock-step to the river, carrying the bucket of excrement accumulated during twenty-four hours.

I was put in charge of the sewing-shop. My task consisted in cutting the cloth and preparing work for the two dozen women employed. In addition I had to keep account of the incoming material and the outgoing bundles. I welcomed the work. It helped me to forget the dreary existence within the prison. But the evenings were torturous. The first few weeks I would fall asleep as soon as I touched the pillow. Soon, however, the nights found me restlessly tossing about, seeking sleep in vain. The appalling nights—even if I should get the customary two months' commutation time, I still had nearly two hundred and ninety of them. Two hundred and ninety—and Sasha? I used to lie awake and mentally figure in the dark the number of days and nights before him. Even if he could come out after his first sentence of seven years, he would still have more than twenty-five hundred nights! Dread overcame me that Sasha could not survive them. Nothing was so likely to drive people to madness, I felt, as sleepless nights in prison. Better dead, I thought. Dead? Frick was not dead, and Sasha's glorious youth, his life, the things he might have accomplished—all were being sacrificed—perhaps for nothing. But—was Sasha's *Attentat* in vain? Was my revolutionary faith a mere echo of what others had said or taught me? "No, not in vain!" something within me insisted. "No sacrifice is lost for a great ideal."

One day I was told by the head matron that I would have to get better results from the women. They were not doing so much work, she said, as under the prisoner who had had charge of the sewing-shop before me. I resented the suggestion that I become a slave-driver. It was because I hated slaves as well as their drivers, I informed the matron, that I had been sent to prison. I considered myself one of the inmates, not above them. I was determined not to do anything that would involve a denial of my ideals. I preferred punishment. [. . .]

News in prison travels with amazing rapidity. Within twenty-four hours all the women knew that I had refused to act as a slave-driver. They had not been unkind to me, but they had kept aloof. They had been told that I was a terrible "anarchist" and that I didn't believe in God. They had never seen me in church and I did not participate in their ten-minute gush of talk. I was a freak in their eyes. But when they learned that I had refused to play the boss over them, their reserve broke down. Sundays after church the cells would be opened to permit the women an hour's visit with one another. The next Sunday I received visits from every inmate on my tier. They felt I was their friend, they assured me, and they would do anything for me. Girls working in the laundry offered to wash my clothes, others to darn my stockings. [. . .]

Among the seventy inmates, there were no more than half a dozen who showed any intelligence whatever. The rest were outcasts without the least social consciousness. Their personal misfortunes filled their thoughts; they could not understand that they were victims, links in an endless chain of injustice and inequality. From early childhood they had known nothing but poverty, squalor, and want, and the same conditions were awaiting them on their release. Yet they were capable of sympathy and devotion, of generous impulses. I soon had occasion to convince myself of it when I was taken ill.

The dampness of my cell and the chill of the late December days had brought on an attack of my old complaint, rheumatism. For some days the head matron opposed my being taken to the hospital, but she was finally compelled to submit to the order of the visiting physician.

Blackwell's Island Penitentiary was fortunate in the absence of a "steady" physician. The inmates were receiving medical attendance from the Charity Hospital, which was situated near by. That institution had six weeks' post-graduate courses, which meant frequent changes in the staff. They were under the direct supervision of a visiting physician from New York City, Dr. White, a humane and kindly man. The treatment given the prisoners was as good as patients received in any New York hospital.

The sick-ward was the largest and brightest room in the building. Its spacious windows looked out upon a wide lawn in front of the prison and, farther on, the East River. In fine weather the sun streamed in generously. A month's rest, the kindliness of the physician, and the thoughtful attention of my fellow prisoners relieved me of my pain and enabled me to get about again.

During one of his rounds Dr. White picked up the card hanging at the foot of my bed giving my crime and pedigree. "Inciting to riot," he read. "Piffle! I don't believe you could hurt a fly. A fine inciter you would make!" he chuckled, then asked me if I should not like to remain in the hospital to take care of the sick. "I should, indeed," I replied, "but I know nothing about nursing." He assured me that neither did anyone else in the prison. He had tried for some time to induce the city to put a trained nurse in charge of the ward, but he had not succeeded. For operations and grave cases he had to bring a nurse from the Charity Hospital. I could easily pick up the elementary things about tending the sick. He would teach me to take the pulse and temperature and to perform similar services. He would speak to the Warden and the head matron if I wanted to remain.

Soon I took up my new work. The ward contained sixteen beds, most of them always filled. The various diseases were treated in the same room, from grave operations to tuberculosis, pneumonia, and childbirth. My hours were long and strenuous, the groans of the patients nerve-racking; but I loved my job. It gave me opportunity to come close to the sick women and bring a little cheer into their lives. I was so much richer than they: I had love and friends, received many letters and daily messages from Ed. Some Austrian anarchists, owners of a restaurant, sent me dinners every day, which Ed himself brought to the boat. Fedya supplied fruit and delicacies weekly. I had so much to give; it was a joy to share with my sisters who had neither friends nor attention. There were a few exceptions, of course; but the majority had nothing. They never had had anything before and they would have nothing on their release. They were derelicts on the social dung-heap.

I was gradually given entire charge of the hospital ward, part of my duties being to divide the special rations allowed the sick prisoners. They consisted of a quart of milk, a cup of beef tea, two eggs, two crackers, and two lumps of sugar for each invalid. On several occasions milk and eggs were missing and I reported the matter to a day matron. Later she informed me that a head matron had said that it did not matter and that certain patients were strong enough to do without their extra rations. I had had considerable opportunity to study this head matron, who felt a violent dislike of everyone not Anglo-Saxon. Her special targets were the Irish and the Jews, against whom she discriminated habitually. I was therefore not surprised to get such a message from her.

A few days later I was told by the prisoner who brought the hospital rations that the missing portions had been given by this head matron to two husky Negro prisoners. That also did not surprise me. I knew she had a special fondness for the coloured inmates. She rarely punished them and often gave them unusual privileges. In return her favourites would spy on the other prisoners, even on those of their own colour who were too decent to be bribed. I myself never had any prejudice against coloured people; in fact, I felt deeply for them because they were being treated like slaves in America. But I hated discrimination. The idea that sick people, white or coloured, should be robbed of their rations to feed healthy persons outraged my sense of justice, but I was powerless to do anything in the matter.

After my first clashes with this woman she left me severely alone. Once she became enraged because I refused to translate a Russian letter that had arrived for one of the prisoners. She had called me into her office to read the letter and tell her its contents. When I saw that the letter was not for me, I informed her that I was not employed by the prison as a translator. It was bad enough for the officials to pry into the personal mail of helpless human beings, but I would not do it. She said that it was stupid of me not to take advantage of her good-will. She could put me back in my cell, deprive me of my commutation time for good behaviour, and make the rest of my stay very hard. She could do as she pleased, I told her, but I would not read the private letters of my unfortunate sisters, much less translate them to her.

Then came the matter of the missing rations. The sick women began to suspect that they were not getting their full share and complained to the doctor. Confronted with a direct question from him, I had to tell the truth. I did not know what he said to the offending matron, but the full rations began to arrive again. Two days later I was called downstairs and locked up in the dungeon.

I had repeatedly seen the effect of a dungeon experience on

other women prisoners. One inmate had been kept there for twenty-eight days on bread and water, although the regulations prohibited a longer stay than forty-eight hours. She had to be carried out on a stretcher; her hands and legs were swollen, her body covered with a rash. The descriptions the poor creature and others had given me used to make me ill. But nothing I had heard compared with the reality. The cell was barren; one had to sit or lie down on the cold stone floor. The dampness of the walls made the dungeon a ghastly place. Worse yet was the complete shutting out of light and air, the impenetrable blackness, so thick that one could not see the hand before one's face. It gave me the sensation of sinking into a devouring pit. [. . .]

After the door shut behind me, I stood still, afraid to sit down or to lean against the wall. Then I groped for the door. Gradually the blackness paled. I caught a faint sound slowly approaching; I heard a key turn in the lock. A matron appeared. I recognized Miss Johnson, the one who had frightened me out of my sleep on my first night in the penitentiary. I had come to know and appreciate her as a beautiful personality. Her kindness to the prisoners was the one ray of light in their dreary existence. She had taken me to her bosom almost from the first, and in many indirect ways she had shown me her affection. Often at night, when all were asleep, and quiet had fallen on the prison, Miss Johnson would enter the hospital ward, put my head in her lap, and tenderly stroke my hair. She would tell me the news in the papers to distract me and try to cheer my depressed mood. I knew I had found a friend in the woman, who herself was a lonely soul, never having known the love of man or child.

She came into the dungeon carrying a camp-chair and a blanket. "You can sit on that," she said, "and wrap yourself up. I'll leave the door open a bit to let in some air. I'll bring you hot coffee later. It will help to pass the night." She told me how painful it was for her to see the prisoners locked up in the dreadful hole, but she could do nothing for them because most of them could not be trusted. It was different with me, she was sure.

At five in the morning my friend had to take back the chair and blanket and lock me in. I no longer was oppressed by the dungeon. The humanity of Miss Johnson had dissolved the blackness.

When I was taken out of the dungeon and sent back to the hospital, I saw that it was almost noon. I resumed my duties. Later I learned that Dr. White had asked for me, and upon being informed that I was in punishment he had categorically demanded my release. [. . .]

The nearer the day of my liberation approached, the more unbearable life in prison became. The days dragged and I grew restless and irritable with impatience. Even reading became impossible. I would sit for hours lost in reminiscences. [. . .]

Then Sasha, our life together, his act, his martyrdom—every moment of the five years since I had first met him I now relived with poignant reality. Why was it, I mused, that Sasha was still so deeply rooted in my being? Was not my love for Ed more ecstatic, more enriching? Perhaps it was his act that had bound me to him with such powerful cords. How insignificant was my own prison experience compared with what Sasha was suffering in the Allegheny purgatory! I now felt ashamed that, even for a moment, I could have found my incarceration hard. Not one friendly face in the court-room to be near Sasha and comfort him—solitary confinement and complete isolation, for no more visits had been allowed him. The Inspector had kept his promise; since my visit in November 1892, Sasha had not again been permitted to see anyone. How he must have craved the sight and touch of a kindred spirit, how he must be yearning for it!

My thoughts rushed on. Fedya, the lover of beauty, so fine and sensitive! And Ed. Ed—he had kissed to life so many mysterious longings, had opened such spiritual sources of wealth to me! I owed my development to Ed, and to the others, too, who had been in my life. And yet, more than all else, it was the prison that had proved the best school. A more painful, but a more vital, school. Here I had been brought close to the depths and complexities of the human soul; here I had found ugliness and beauty, meanness and generosity. Here, too, I had learned to see life through my own eyes and not through those of Sasha,

Most, or Ed. The prison had been the crucible that tested my faith. It had helped me to discover strength in my own being, the strength to stand alone, the strength to live my life and fight for my ideals, against the whole world if need be. The State of New York could have rendered me no greater service than by sending me to Blackwell's Island Penitentiary!

CHAPTER XIII

The days and weeks that followed my release were like a nightmare. I needed quiet, peace, and privacy after my prison experience, but I was surrounded by people, and there were meetings nearly every evening. I lived in a daze: everything around me seemed incongruous and unreal. My thoughts continued in captivity; my fellow convicts haunted my waking and sleeping hours, and the prison noises kept ringing in my ears. The command "Close!" followed by the crash of iron doors and the clank-clank of the chains, pursued me when I faced an audience.

The strangest experience I had was at the meeting arranged to welcome me on my release. It took place in the Thalia Theatre[1] and the house was crowded. Many well-known men and women of various social groups in New York had come to celebrate my liberation. I sat listless, in a stupor. [. . .]

I got to my feet, walked to the footlights, saw the audience rise to greet me. Then I tried to speak. My lips moved, but there was no sound. [. . .] Ed was near and he led me behind the stage into a dressing-room. I had never before lost control of myself or of my voice, and the occurrence frightened me. [. . .]

Presently the sound of a beautiful voice reached the dressing-room. Its speech was unfamiliar to me. "Who is speaking now?" I asked. "That is Maria Rodda, an Italian girl anarchist," Ed replied; "she is only sixteen years old and has just come to America." The voice electrified me and I was eager to see its owner. I stepped to the door leading to the platform. Maria Rodda was the most exquisite creature I had ever seen. [. . .] Maria proved a veritable ray of sunlight to me. My spooks vanished, the prison weights dropped off; I felt free and happy, among friends.

I spoke after Maria. The audience again rose, to a man, applauding. I sensed that the people were spontaneously responsive to my prison story, but I was not deceived; I knew intuitively that it was Maria Rodda's youth and charm that fascinated them and not my speech. Yet I, too, was still young— only twenty-five. I still had attraction, but compared with that lovely flower, I felt old. The sorrows of the world had matured me beyond my years; I felt old and sad. I wondered whether a high ideal, made more fervent by the test of fire, could stand out against youth and dazzling beauty. [. . .]

On the way to my room I spoke to Ed about Maria. To my surprise he did not share my enthusiasm. He admitted that she was ravishing, but he thought her beauty would not endure, much less her enthusiasm for our ideals. "Latin women mature young," he said; "they grow old with their first child, old in body and in spirit." "Well, then, Maria should guard against having children if she wants to devote herself to our movement," I remarked. "No woman should do that," Ed replied, emphatically. "Nature has made her for motherhood. All else is nonsense, artificial and unreal."

I had never before heard such sentiments expressed by Ed. His conservatism roused my anger. I demanded to know if he thought me also nonsensical because I preferred to work for an ideal instead of producing children. [. . .]

My life with Ed had been glorious and complete, without any rift. But now it came; my dream of love and true comradeship suffered a rude awakening. Ed had never stressed his longing, except when he had protested against my joining the movement of the unemployed. I thought then that it was only his concern for my health. How was I to know that it was something else, the interest of the male? Yes, that is what it was, the man's instinct of possession, which brooks no deity except himself. Well, it should not be, even if I had to give him up. All my senses cried out for him. Could I live without Ed, without the joy he gave me?

Weary and miserable, my thoughts dwelt on Ed, on Maria

Rodda, and on recollections of Santa Caserio.[2] The latter's image brought to my mind the revolutionary events in France of recent occurrence. A number of *Attentats* had taken place there. [. . .]

In the light of them my personal grief over my first serious quarrel with Ed now appeared like a mere speck on the social horizon of pain and blood. One by one the heroic names of those who had sacrificed their lives for their ideal or were still being martyred in prison came before me: my own Sasha and the others—all so finely attuned to the injustice of the world, so high-minded, driven by social forces to do the very thing they abhorred most, to destroy human life. Something deep in my consciousness rebelled against such tragic waste, yet I knew there was no escape. I had learned the fearful effects of organized violence: inevitably it begets more violence.

Sasha's spirit, fortunately, however, always hovered over me, helping me to forget everything personal. His letter of welcome on my release was the most beautiful I had so far received from him. It testified not only to his love and his faith in me, but also to his own valour and strength of character. Ed had kept the copies of the *Gefängniss-Blüthen*, the little underground magazine that Sasha, Nold, and Bauer were editing in prison. Sasha's will to life was apparent in every word, in his determination to fight on and not to permit the enemy to crush him. The spirit of the boy of twenty-three was extraordinary. It shamed me for my own faint heart. Yet I knew that the personal would always play a dominant part in my life. I was not hewn of one piece, like Sasha or other heroic figures. I had long realized that I was woven of many skeins, conflicting in shade and texture. To the end of my days I should be torn between the yearning for a personal life and the need of giving all to my ideal.

Ed came early the next day. He was his usual well-poised, outwardly calm self again. But I had looked into the turbulent waters of his soul too often to be misled by his reserve. He suggested that we take a trip. I had been out of prison about a fortnight and we had not yet had one complete day alone. We went to Manhattan Beach. The November air was sharp, the sea stormy; but the sun shone brightly. Ed was never much of a talker, but on this day he spoke a great deal about himself, his interest in the movement, his love for me. [. . .] He admitted that he would be happier if I would give up the platform and devote my time to study, to writing or a profession. That would not keep him in constant anxiety about my life and freedom. "You are so intense, so impetuous," he said, "I fear for your safety." He begged me not to be angry because he believed that woman was primarily a mother. He was sure that the strongest motive in my devotion to the movement was unsatisfied motherhood seeking an outlet. "You are a typical mother, my little Emma, by build, by feeling. Your tenderness is the greatest proof of it."

I was profoundly stirred. When I could find words, poor inadequate words, to convey what I felt, I could only tell him again of my love, of my need of him, of my longing to give him much of what he craved. My starved motherhood—was that the main reason for my idealism? He had roused the old yearning for a child. But I had silenced the voice of the child for the sake of the universal, the all-absorbing passion of my life. Men were consecrated to ideals and yet were fathers of children. But man's physical share in the child is only a moment's; woman's part is for years—years of absorption in one human being to the exclusion of the rest of humanity. I would never give up the one for the other. But I would give him my love and devotion. Surely it must be possible for a man and a woman to have a beautiful love-life and yet be devoted to a great cause. We must try. I proposed that we find a place where we could live together, no longer separated by silly conventions—a home of our own, even if poor. [. . .]

Nearly four weeks passed before we could carry out our plans. The papers had turned me into a celebrity, and I soon learned the German truism: *"Man kann nicht ungestraft unter Palmen wandeln."*[3] I knew of the American craze for celebrities, especially the American women's hunt for anyone in the limelight, be it prize-fighter, baseball-player, matinée idol, wife-killer, or decrepit European aristocrat. Thanks to my imprisonment and the space given to my name in the newspapers,

I also became a celebrity. Every day brought stacks of invitations to luncheons and dinners. Everyone seemed eager to "take me up."

Of the many invitations showered on me I welcomed most one from the Swintons.[4] They wrote asking me to come to dinner and to bring Ed and Justus [Schwab]. [. . .] They were charming hosts. John was especially gracious and full of warmth. He was a man of wide experience in people and affairs and he proved a veritable mint of information to me. I learned for the first time of his share in the campaign to save the Chicago anarchists from the gallows and of other public-spirited Americans who had valiantly defended my comrades. I became acquainted with Swinton's activities against the Russian-American Extradition Treaty, and the part he and his friends had played in the labour movement. The evening with the Swintons showed me a new angle of my adopted country. Until my imprisonment I had believed that except for Albert Parsons,[5] Dyer D. Lum,[6] Voltairine de Cleyre, and a few others America was barren of idealists. Her men and women cared only for material acquisitions, I had thought. Swinton's account of the liberty-loving people who had been and still were in every struggle against oppression changed my superficial judgment. John Swinton made me see that Americans, once aroused, were as capable of idealism and sacrifice as my Russian heroes and heroines. I left the Swintons with a new faith in the possibilities of America. On our way down town I talked with Ed and Justus, telling them that from now on I meant to devote myself to propaganda in English, among the American people. Propaganda in foreign circles was, of course, very necessary, but real social changes could be accomplished only by the natives. Their enlightenment was therefore much more vital, we all agreed. [. . .]

I had been out two months, but I did not forget the unfortunates in prison. I wanted to do something for them. I needed money for this purpose and I also wanted to earn my own living.

Much against Ed's wishes, I began to work as a practical nurse. Dr. Julius Hoffmann sent me his private patients after treating them in St. Mark's Hospital. Dr. White had told me before I left the prison that he would give me work in his office.

He could not recommend his patients to me, he had said. "They are mostly stupid, they would be afraid you'd poison them." The dear man kept his word: he employed me for several hours a day, and I also got work in the newly organized Beth-Israel Hospital on East Broadway. I loved my profession and I was able to earn more money than at any time previously. The joy of no longer having to grind at the machine, in or out of a shop, was great; greater still the satisfaction of having more time for reading and for public activity. [. . .]

I had realized at the very beginning of my nursing work that I should have to take up a regular course in a training-school. Practical nurses were paid and treated like servants, and without a diploma I could not hope to get employment as a trained nurse. Dr. Hoffmann urged me to enter St. Mark's Hospital, where he could get me credits for one year because of my experience. It was a great opportunity, but there was also another and a more alluring one. It was Europe.

Ed had always talked with glee of Vienna, of its beauty, charm, and possibilities. He wanted me to go there to study in the Allgemeines Krankenhaus. I could take up midwifery and other branches of nursing, he advised me. It would give me greater material independence later on and also enable us to be more together. It would be hard to endure another year's separation when I had barely been given back to him; but he was willing to let me go, knowing it was for my good. It seemed a fantastic idea for people as poor as we, but gradually Ed's enthusiasm infected me. I agreed to go to Vienna, but I would combine my trip abroad with a lecture tour in England and Scotland. Our British comrades had often asked me to come over. [. . .]

On the 15th of August 1895, exactly six years since my new life in New York had begun, I sailed for England. My departure was quite different from my arrival in New York in 1889. I was very poor then, poor in more than merely material things. I was a child, inexperienced and alone in the whirlpool of the American metropolis. Now I had experience, a name; I had been through the crucible; I had friends. Above all, I had the love of a beautiful personality. I was rich, yet I was sad. The Western Penitentiary lay heavily on my heart, with the thought of Sasha there.

I again travelled steerage, my means not permitting more than sixteen dollars for the passage. But there were only a few passengers, some of whom had been no longer in the States than I. They considered themselves Americans and they were treated accordingly, with more decency than the poor emigrants who had pilgrimed over as I did to the Promised Land in 1886.

CHAPTER XIV

Outdoor meetings in America are rare, their atmosphere always surcharged with impending clashes between the audience and the police. Not so in England. Here the right to assemble constantly in the open is an institution. It has become a British habit, like bacon for breakfast. The most opposing ideas and creeds find expression in the parks and squares of English cities. There is nothing to cause undue excitement and there is no display of armed force. The lone bobby on the outskirts of the crowd is there as a matter of form; it is not his duty to disperse meetings or club the people.

The social centre of the masses is the out-of-door meeting in the park. On Sundays they flock there as they do to music-halls on week-days. They cost nothing and they are much more entertaining. Crowds, often numbering thousands, drift from platform to platform as they would at a country fair, not so much to listen or learn as to be amused. The main performers at these gatherings are the hecklers, who hugely enjoy bombarding the speakers with questions. Pity him who fails to get the cue from these tormentors or who is not quick enough at repartee. He soon finds himself confused and the helpless butt for boisterous ridicule. All this I learned after I nearly came to grief at my first meeting in Hyde Park.

It was a novel experience to talk out of doors, with only a lone policeman placidly looking on. Alas, the crowd, too, was placid. It felt like climbing a steep mountain to speak against such inertia. I soon grew tired and my throat began to hurt, but I kept on. All at once the audience began to show signs of life. A volley of questions, like bullets, came flying at me from all directions. The unexpected attack, finding me quite unprepared, bewildered and irritated me. I felt my trend of thought slip from me, and my anger rise. Then a man in front called out: "Don't mind it, old girl, go right on. Heckling is a good old British custom." "Good, you call it?" I retorted; "I think it is rotten to interrupt a speaker like that. But all right, fire away, and don't blame me if you get the worst of the bargain." "That's right, old dear," the audience shouted; "go ahead, let's see what you can do."

I had been speaking on the futility of politics and its corrupting influence when the first shot was fired. "How about honest politicians—don't you believe there are such?" "If there are, I never heard of one," I hurled back; "Politicians promise you heaven before election and give you hell after." " 'Ear! 'Ear!" they screamed in approval. I had barely got back to my speech when the next bolt struck me. "I say, old girl, why do you speak of heaven?—Do you believe in such a place?" "Of course not," I replied; "I was only referring to the heaven you stupidly believe in." "Well, if there is no heaven, where else would the poor get their reward?" another heckler demanded. "Nowhere, unless they insist on their right here—take their reward by gaining possession of the earth." I continued that even if there were a heaven, the common people would not be tolerated there. "You see," I explained, "the masses have lived in hell so long they would not know how to behave in heaven. The angel at the gate would kick them out for disorderly conduct." This was followed by another half-hour of fencing, which kept the crowd in spasms. Finally they called for the hecklers to stop, admit defeat, and let me go on.

My fame travelled quickly; the crowds grew in size at every meeting. Our literature sold in large quantities, which delighted my comrades. They wanted me to remain in London because I could do so much good there. But I knew that out-of-door speaking was not for me. My throat would not hold out under the strain and I could not bear the disturbing noises of the street traffic so close at hand. Besides, I realized that people standing up for hours grew too restless and weary to be able to concentrate or to follow a serious talk. My work meant too much to me to turn it into a circus for the amusement of the British public. [. . .]

Anarchist activities in London were not limited to the natives. England was the haven for refugees from all lands, who carried on their work without hindrance. By comparison with the United States the political freedom in Great Britain seemed like the millennium come. But economically the country was far behind America.

I had myself experienced want and I knew of the poverty in the large industrial centres of the United States. But never had I seen such abject misery and squalor as I did in London, Leeds, and Glasgow. Its effects impressed me as not being the results of yesterday or even of years. They were century-old, passed on from generation to generation, apparently rooted in the very marrow of the British masses. One of the most appalling sights was that of able-bodied men running ahead of a cab for blocks to be on the spot in time to open the door for a "gentleman." For such services they would receive a penny, or tuppence at most. After a month's stay in England I understood the reason for so much political freedom. It was a safety-valve against the fearful destitution. The British Government no doubt felt that as long as it permitted its subjects to let off steam in unhampered talk, there was no danger of rebellion. I could find no other explanation for the inertia and the indifference of the people to their slavish conditions. [. . .]

After my return from Leeds and Glasgow, where I spoke at large meetings and became acquainted with many active and devoted workers, I found a letter from Kropotkin asking me to visit him. At last I was to realize my long-cherished dream, to meet my great teacher.

Peter Kropotkin was a lineal descendant of the Ruriks and in the direct succession to the Russian throne. But he gave up his title and wealth for the cause of humanity. He did more: since becoming an anarchist he had forgone a brilliant scientific career to be better able to devote himself to the development and interpretation of anarchist philosophy. He became the most outstanding exponent of anarchist communism, its clearest thinker and theoretician. He was recognized by friend and foe as one of the greatest minds and most unique personalities of the nineteenth century. On my way to Bromley, where the Kropotkins lived, I felt nervous. I feared I should find Peter difficult of approach, too absorbed in his work for ordinary social intercourse.

But five minutes in his presence put me at my ease. The family was away and Peter himself received me in such a gracious and kindly manner that I felt at home with him at once. He would have tea ready directly, he said. Meanwhile should I like to see his carpenter shop and the articles he had made with his own hands? He took me into his study and pointed with great pride to a table, a bench, and some shelves he had fashioned. They were very simple things, but he gloried in them; they represented labour and he had always stressed the need of combining mental activity with manual effort. Now he could demonstrate how well the two can be blended. No artisan ever looked more lovingly and with greater reverence upon the things created by his hands than did Peter Kropotkin, the scientist and philosopher. His wholesome joy in the products of his toil were symbolic of the burning faith he had in the masses, in their capacity to create and fashion life.

Over the tea which he himself prepared, Kropotkin asked me about conditions in America, about the movement, and about Sasha. He had followed the latter's case and he knew every phase of it, expressing great regard and concern for Sasha. I related to him my impressions of England, the contrasts between its poverty and extreme wealth alongside of political freedom. Was it not a bone thrown to the masses to pacify them, I asked. Peter agreed with my view. He said that England was a nation of shopkeepers engaged in buying and selling instead of producing the necessaries required to keep her people from starvation. "The British *bourgeoisie* has good reason to fear the spread of discontent, and political liberties are the best security against it. English statesmen are shrewd," he continued; "they have always seen to it that the political reins should not be pulled too tightly. The average Britisher loves to think he is free; it helps him to forget his misery. That is the irony and pathos of the English working classes. Yet England could feed every man, woman, and child of her population if she would but release the vast lands now held in monopoly by an old, decaying aristocracy." My visit with Peter Kropotkin convinced me that true greatness is always coupled with simplicity. He was the personification of both. The lucidity and brilliance of his mind combined with his warm-heartedness into the harmonious whole of a fascinating and gracious personality.

I was sorry to leave England; during my short visit I had met many people and made friends and I was enriched by personal contact with my great teachers. The days were indeed glorious. Never had I seen such a luscious green of trees and grass, such a profusion of gardens, parks, and flowers. At the same time I had never seen such dreary and dismal poverty. [. . .]

Vienna proved even more fascinating than Ed had described it. Ringstrasse, the principal street, with its array of splendid old mansions and gorgeous cafés, the spacious promenades lined with stately trees, and particularly the Prater, more forest than park, made the city one of the most beautiful I had ever seen. The whole was enhanced by the gaiety and light-heartedness of the Viennese people. London seemed a tomb by comparison. There was colour here, life and joy. I longed to become part of it, to throw myself into its generous arms, to sit in the cafés or in the Prater and watch the crowds. But I had come for another purpose; I could not afford to be distracted. [. . .]

In Vienna one could hear interesting lectures on modern German prose and poetry. One could read the works of the young iconoclasts in art and letters, the most daring among them being Nietzsche.[1] The magic of his language, the beauty of his vision, carried me to undreamed-of heights. [. . .]

I had to do my reading at the expense of much-needed sleep; but what was physical strain in view of my raptures over Nietzsche? The fire of his soul, the rhythm of his song, made life richer, fuller, and more wonderful for me. I wanted to share these treasures with my beloved, and I wrote him long letters depicting the new world I had discovered. His replies were evasive; Ed evidently did not share my fervour for the new art. He was more interested in my studies and in my health, and he urged me not to tax my energies with idle reading. I was disappointed, but

I consoled myself that he would appreciate the revolutionary spirit of the new literature when he had a chance to read it for himself. I must get money, I decided, to bring back a supply of books to Ed.

Through one of the students I learned of a lecture course given by an eminent young professor, Sigmund Freud.[2] I found, however, that it would be difficult to attend his series, only physicians and holders of special cards being admitted. My friend suggested that I enroll for the course of Professor Bruhl, who also was discussing sex problems. As one of his students I should have a better chance to secure admission to Freud.

Professor Bruhl was an old man with a feeble voice. The subjects he treated were mystifying to me. He talked of "Urnings," "Lesbians," and other strange topics. His hearers, too, were strange: feminine-looking men with coquettish manners and women distinctly masculine, with deep voices. They were certainly a peculiar assembly. Greater clarity in these matters came to me later on when I heard Sigmund Freud. His simplicity and earnestness and the brilliance of his mind combined to give one the feeling of being led out of a dark cellar into broad daylight. For the first time I grasped the full significance of sex repression and its effect on human thought and action. He helped me to understand myself, my own needs; and I also realized that only people of depraved minds could impugn the motives or find "impure" so great and fine a personality as Freud. [. . .]

When examinations drew near, I could no longer indulge in the temptations of the fascinating city on the Danube. Soon I was the proud holder of two diplomas, one for midwifery and one for nursing: I could return home. But I was loath to leave Vienna; it had given me so much. I lingered on for two more weeks. During that time I was a great deal with my comrades and learned much from them about the anarchist movement in Austria. At several small gatherings I lectured on America and our struggle in that country. [. . .]

Standing on the deck as the French liner steamed towards the New York dock, I spied Ed long before he saw me. He stood near the gang-plank holding a bunch of roses, but when I came down, he failed to recognize me. It was late afternoon of a rainy day, and I wondered whether it was because of the dusk, my large hat, or the fact that I had grown thin. For a moment I stood watching him scanning the passengers, but when I saw his anxiety growing, I tiptoed up from behind and put my hands over his eyes. He spun round quickly, pressed me tempestuously to his heart, and exclaimed in a trembling voice: "What is the matter with my *Schatz*? Are you ill?" "Nonsense!" I replied, "I have only grown more spiritual. Let's get home and I'll tell you all about it."

Ed had written me that he had changed our quarters for a more comfortable flat, which Fedya had helped to decorate. What I found far excelled my expectations. Our new home was an old-fashioned apartment in the German-inhabited part of Eleventh Street. The windows of the large kitchen overlooked a beautiful garden. The front room was spacious and high-ceilinged, simply but cosily furnished with lovely old mahogany. There were rare prints on the walls, and my books were arranged on shelves. The place had atmosphere and taste.

Ed played the host to me at an elaborate dinner he had prepared, with wine sent by Justus Schwab. He was rich now, he informed me; he was earning fifteen dollars a week! Then he related news of our friends: Fedya, Justus, Claus, and, most of all, Sasha. [. . .]

During my stay in Vienna several of our American friends had suggested an application to the Board of Pardons. Inwardly I rebelled against such a step on the part of an anarchist. I was certain that Sasha would not approve of it, and therefore I did not even write to him about the proposal. During my absence abroad he had been repeatedly put into the dungeon and kept in solitary confinement until his health gave way. I began to think that consistency, while admirable in oneself, was criminal if allowed to stand in the way of another. It led me to set aside all considerations and to implore Sasha to let us appeal to the Board of Pardons. His reply indicated that he felt indignant and hurt that I should want him to beg for pardon. His act bore its own justification, he wrote; it was a gesture of protest against the injustice of the capitalist system. The courts and the pardon boards were the bulwarks of that system. I must have grown less revolutionary, or perhaps it was only my concern for him that had decided me in favour of such a step. In any case he did not wish me to act against my principles in his behalf. [. . .]

I again wrote to Sasha, emphasizing that I considered his life and freedom too valuable to the movement to refuse to make an appeal. Some of the greatest revolutionists had, when serving long terms, appealed in order to gain their freedom. But if he still felt it inconsistent to take the step for his own sake, would he not permit our friends to do so for mine? I could no longer bear, I explained, the consciousness of his being in prison for an act in which I had been almost as much involved as he. My plea seemed to make some impression on Sasha. In his reply he reiterated that he had no faith whatever in the Board of Pardons; but his friends on the outside were in a better position to judge the step they intended to take and therefore he would offer no further objections. [. . .]

The campaign for the appeal was launched, the entire radical element supporting our efforts. A prominent Pittsburgh lawyer had become interested and consented to take the case to the Pennsylvania Board of Pardons.

We worked energetically, driven on by great expectations. Sasha's hopes, too, were reviving; life, pulsating life, now seemed to open before him. But our joy was short-lived. The Board refused to act on the appeal. Berkman would have to complete his first seven years' sentence before the "actual wrong" of his other sentences could be considered, the Board held. It was evident that nothing displeasing to Carnegie and Frick would be done.

The shock to me was crushing, and I dreaded its effect on Sasha. How should I write to him, what should I say to help him over the cruel blow? Ed's reassuring words that Sasha was brave enough to hold out until 1897 did not help me. I lost hope that a commutation would ever be granted him. The threat of Inspector Reed that Sasha would not be allowed out alive was ringing in my ears. Before I could bring myself to write him, a letter arrived from Sasha. He had not banked much on a favourable outcome, his letter read, and he was not much disappointed. The action of the Board merely proved once more the close alignment of the American Government and the plutocracy. It was what we anarchists had always claimed. The promise of the Board to reconsider the appeal in 1897 was merely a trick to hood-wink public opinion and to tire out the friends who had been working for him. He was sure the flunkeys of the steel interests would never act in his behalf. But it did not matter. He had survived the first four years and he meant to keep on fighting. "Our enemies shall never have the chance to say that they have broken me," he wrote. He knew he could always count on my support and on that of the new friends he had gained. I must not despair or relax in my zeal for our Cause. My Sasha, my wonderful Sasha—he was not only brave, as Ed had said; he was a tower of strength. As so often since that day when the steam monster at the Baltimore and Ohio Station had snatched him away from me, he stood out like a shining meteor on the dark horizon of petty interests, personal worries, and the enervating routine of everyday existence. He was like a white light that purged one's soul, inspiring even awe at his detachment from human frailties.

CHAPTER XV

A renaissance was now taking place in anarchist ranks; greater activity was being manifested than at any time since 1887, especially among American adherents. [. . .] In fact, all over the United States the spirit of the Chicago martyrs had been resurrected. The voice of Spies and his comrades was finding expression in the native tongue as well as in every foreign language of the peoples in America. [. . .]

The free-silver campaign was at its height. The proposition for the free coinage of silver at the ratio with gold of sixteen to one had become a national issue almost overnight. It gained in strength by the sudden ascendancy of William Jennings Bryan,[1] who had stampeded the Democratic Convention by an eloquent speech and the catch phrase: "You shall not press down upon the brow of labour the crown of thorns, you shall not crucify mankind upon the cross of gold." [. . .]

I could not share the enthusiasm for Bryan, partly because I did not believe in the political machine as a means of bringing about fundamental changes, and also because there was something weak and superficial about Bryan. I had a feeling that his main aim was to get into the White House rather than "strike off the chains" from the people. I resolved to steer clear of him. I sensed his lack of sincerity and I did not trust him. For this attitude I was assailed from two different sides on the same day. First it was Schilling[2] who urged me to join the free-silver campaign. "What are you Easterners going to do," he asked when I met him, "when the West marches in revolutionary ranks towards the East? Are you going to continue talking, or will you join forces with us?" He assured me that my name had travelled to the West and that I could be a valuable factor in the popular movement to free the masses from their despoilers. George was very optimistic in his ardour, but he failed to convince me. We parted as friends, George shaking his head over my lack of judgment about the impending revolution. [. . .]

My encounters with Schilling and McLuckie[3] made me aware of a large new field for activity. What I had done so far was only the first step of usefulness in our movement. I would go on a tour now, study the country and its people, come close to the pulse of American life. I would bring to the masses the message of a new social ideal. I was eager to start at once, but I determined first to become more proficient in English and to earn some money. I did not want to be dependent on the comrades or take pay for my lectures. Meanwhile I could continue my work in New York.

I was full of enthusiasm for the future, but in proportion as my spirits rose, Ed's interest in my aims waned. I had known for a long time that he begrudged every moment which took me away from him. I was also aware of our decided differences as far as the woman question was concerned. But outside of that, Ed had moved along with me, had always been helpful and ready to aid in my efforts. Now he became disgruntled, critical of everything I was doing. [. . .]

One evening Ed's reserve broke down. "You are drifting away from me!" he cried excitedly. "I can see that my hopes of a beautiful life with you must be given up. You have wasted a year in Vienna, you have acquired a profession only to throw it over for those stupid meetings. You have no concern about anything else; your love has no thought of me or my needs. Your interest in the movement, for which you are willing to break up our life, is nothing but vanity, nothing but your craving for applause and glory and the limelight. You are simply incapable of a deep feeling. You have never understood or appreciated the love I have given you. I have waited and waited for a change, but I see it is useless. I will not share you with anybody or anything. You will have to choose!" He paced the room like a caged lion, turning from time to time to fasten his eyes on me. All that had been accumulating in him for weeks now streamed out in accusation and reproaches.

I sat in consternation. The familiar old demand that I "choose" kept droning in my ears. Ed, who had been my ideal, was like the others. He would have me forswear my interests and the movement, sacrifice everything for love of him. Most had repeatedly given me the same ultimatum. I stared at him unable to speak or move, while he continued stalking about the room in uncontrolled anger. Finally he picked up his coat and hat and left.

For hours I sat as if paralysed; then a violent ring brought me to my feet. It was a call to a confinement case. I took the bag which I had been keeping ready for weeks and walked out with the man who had come for me.

In a two-room flat on Houston Street, on the sixth floor of a tenement-house, I found three children asleep and the woman writhing in labour pains. There was no gas-jet, only a kerosene lamp, over which I had to heat the water. The man looked blank when I asked him for a sheet. It was Friday. His wife had washed Monday, he told me, and all the bed-linen had got dirty since. But I might use the table-cloth; it had been put on that very evening for the Sabbath. "Diapers or anything else ready for the baby?" I asked. The man did not know. The woman pointed to a bundle which consisted of a few torn shirts, a bandage, and some rags. Incredible poverty oozed from every corner.

With the use of the table-cloth and an extra apron I had brought I prepared to receive the expected comer. It was my first private case, and the shock over Ed's outburst helped to increase my nervousness. But I steeled myself and worked on desperately. Late in the morning I helped to bring the new life into the world. A part of my own life had died the evening before. [. . .]

We took up our common life again, but I spent less time on my public interests. Partly it was due to the numerous calls on my professional services, but more to my determination to devote myself to Ed. As the weeks passed, however, the still small voice kept on whispering that the final rupture would only temporarily be deferred. I clung desperately to Ed and his love to ward off the impending end.

My profession of midwife was not very lucrative, only the poorest of the foreign element resorting to such services. [. . .] But while my work held out no hope of worldly riches, it furnished an excellent field for experience. It put me into intimate contact with the very people my ideal strove to help and emancipate. It brought me face to face with the living conditions of the workers, about which, until then, I had talked and written mostly from theory. Their squalid surroundings, the dull and inert submission to their lot, made me realize the colossal work yet to be done to bring about the change our movement was struggling to achieve.

Still more impressed was I by the fierce, blind struggle of the women of the poor against frequent pregnancies. Most of them lived in continual dread of conception; the great mass of the married women submitted helplessly, and when they found themselves pregnant, their alarm and worry would result in the determination to get rid of their expected offspring. It was incredible what fantastic methods despair could invent: jumping off tables, rolling on the floor, massaging the stomach, drinking nauseating concoctions, and using blunt instruments. These and similar methods were being tried, generally with great injury. It was harrowing, but it was understandable. Having a large brood of children, often many more than the weekly wage of the father could provide for, each additional child was a curse, "a curse of God," as orthodox Jewish women and Irish Catholics repeatedly told me. The men were generally more resigned, but the women cried out against Heaven for inflicting such cruelty upon them. During their labour pains some women would hurl anathema on God and man, especially on their husbands. "Take him away," one of my patients cried, "don't let the brute come near me—I'll kill him!" The tortured creature already had had eight children, four of whom had died in infancy. The remaining were sickly and undernourished, like most of the ill-born, ill-kept, and unwanted children who trailed at my feet when I was helping another poor creature into the world.

After such confinements I would return home sick and distressed, hating the men responsible for the frightful condition of their wives and children, hating myself most of all because I did not know how to help them. I could, of course, induce an abortion. Many women called me for that purpose, even going down on their knees and begging me to help them, "for the sake of the poor little ones already here." They knew that some doctors and midwives did such things, but the price was beyond their means. I was so sympathetic; wouldn't I do something for them? They would pay in weekly instalments. I tried to explain to them that it was not monetary considerations that held me back; it was concern for their life and health. I would relate the case of a woman killed by such an operation, and her children left motherless. But they preferred to die, they avowed; the city was then sure to take care of their orphans, and they would be better off.

I could not prevail upon myself to perform the much-coveted operation. I lacked faith in my skill and I remembered my Vienna professor who had often demonstrated to us the terrible results of abortion. He held that even when such practices prove successful, they undermine the health of the patient. I would not undertake the task. It was not any moral consideration for the sanctity of life; a life unwanted and forced into abject poverty did not seem sacred to me. But my interests embraced the entire social problem, not merely a single aspect of it, and I would not jeopardize my freedom for that one part of the human struggle. I refused to perform abortions and I knew no methods to prevent conception.

I spoke to some physicians about the matter. Dr. White, a conservative, said: "The poor have only themselves to blame; they indulge their appetites too much." Dr. Julius Hoffmann thought that children were the only joy the poor had. Dr. Solotaroff held out the hope of great changes in the near future when woman would become more intelligent and independent. "When she uses her brains more," he would tell me, "her procreative organs will function less." It seemed more convincing than the arguments of the other medicos, though no more comforting; nor was it of any practical help. Now that I had learned that women and children carried the heaviest burden of our ruthless economic system, I saw that it was mockery to expect them to wait until the social revolution arrives in order to right injustice. I sought some immediate solution for their purgatory, but I could find nothing of any use.

My home life was anything but harmonious, though externally all seemed smooth. Ed was apparently calm and contented again, but I felt cramped and nervous. If I attended a meeting and was detained later than expected, it would make me uneasy and I would hasten home in perturbation. Often I refused invitations to lecture because I sensed Ed's disapproval. Where I could not decline, I worked for weeks over my subject, my thoughts dwelling on Ed rather than on the matter in hand. I would wonder how this point or that argument might appeal to him and whether he would approve. Yet I never could get myself to read him my notes, and if he attended my meetings, his presence made me self-conscious, for I knew that he had no faith in my work. It served to weaken my faith in myself. I developed strange nervous attacks. Without preliminary warning I would fall to the ground as if knocked down by a heavy blow. I did not lose consciousness, being able to see and understand what was going on around me, but I was not able to utter a word. My chest felt convulsed, my throat compressed; I had an agonizing pain in my legs as if the muscles were being pulled asunder. This condition would last from ten minutes to an hour and leave me utterly exhausted. Solotaroff, failing to diagnose the trouble, took me to a specialist, who proved no wiser. Dr. White's examination also gave no results. Some physicians said it was hysteria, others an inverted womb. I knew the latter was the real cause, but I would not consent to an operation. More and more I had become convinced that my life would never know harmony in love for very long, that strife and not peace would be my lot. In such a life there was no room for a child.

From various parts of the country came requests for a series of lectures. I was very eager to go, but I lacked the courage to broach the matter to Ed. I knew he would not consent, and his refusal would most likely bring us nearer to a violent separation. My physicians had strongly advised a rest and change of scene, and now Ed surprised me by insisting that I ought to go away. [. . .]

I had spoken in Providence a number of times without the least trouble. Rhode Island was still one of the few States to maintain the old tradition of unabridged freedom of speech. Two of our open-air gatherings, attended by thousands, went

off well. But the police had evidently decided to suppress our
last meeting. Arriving with several friends at the square where
the assembly was to take place, we found a member of the Socialist Labor Party talking, and, not wishing to interfere with
him, we set up our box farther away. My good comrade John
H. Cook, a very active worker, opened the meeting, and I began
to speak. Just then a policeman came running towards us,
shouting: "Stop your jabbering! Stop it this minute or I'll pull
you off the box!" I went on talking. Someone called out:
"Don't mind the bully—go right on!" The policeman came up,
puffing heavily. When he got his breath he snarled, "Say, you,
are you deaf? Didn't I tell you to stop? What d'you mean not
obeying the law?" "Are you the law?" I retorted; "I thought it
is your duty to maintain the law, not to break it. Don't you
know the law in this State gives me the right of free speech?"
"The hell it does," he replied, "I'm the law." The audience began hooting and jeering. The officer started to pull me off the
improvised platform. The crowd looked threatening and began
closing in on him. He blew his whistle. A patrol wagon dashed
up to the square, and several policemen broke through the
crowd with their clubs swinging. The officer, still holding on to
me, shouted: "Drive those damn anarchists back so I can get
this woman. She's under arrest." I was led to the patrol wagon
and literally thrown into it.

At the police station I demanded to know by what right I had
been interfered with. "Because you're Emma Goldman," the
sergeant at the desk replied. "Anarchists have no rights in this
community, see?" He ordered me locked up for the night.

It was the first time since 1893 that I had been arrested, but,
constantly expecting to fall into the clutches of the law, I had
made it a practice to carry a book with me when going to meetings. I wrapped my skirts around me, climbed up on the board
placed for a bed in my cell, pressed close to the barred door,
through which shimmered a light, and started to read. [. . .]

The next morning I was taken, together with my neighbour
and other unfortunates, before a magistrate. I was held over
under bond, and as the amount could not be raised immediately I was returned to the station-house. At one o'clock in the

afternoon I was again called for, this time to see the Mayor. That individual, no less bulky and bloated than the policeman, informed me that if I would promise under oath never to return to Providence he would let me go. "That's nice of you, Mayor," I replied; "but inasmuch as you have no case against me, your offer isn't quite so generous as it appears, is it?" I told him that I would make no promises whatever, but that if it would relieve his mind, I could tell him that I was about to start on a lecture tour to California. "It may take three months or more, I don't know. But I do know that you and your city cannot do without me much longer than that, so I am determined to come back." The Mayor and his flunkies roared, and I was released. [. . .]

I had been away from Ed only two weeks, but my longing for him was more intense than it had been on my return from Europe. I could hardly contain myself until the train came to a stop in the Grand Central Station, where he met me. At home everything seemed new, more beautiful and enticing. Ed's endearing words sounded like music in my ears. Sheltered and protected from the strife and conflict outside, I clung to him and basked in the sunshine of our home. My eagerness to go on a long tour paled under the fascination of my lover. A month of joy and abandon followed, but my dream was soon to suffer a painful awakening.

It was caused by Nietzsche. Ever since my return from Vienna I had been hoping that Ed would read my books. I had asked him to do so and he promised he would when he had more time. It made me very sad to find Ed so indifferent to the new literary forces in the world. One evening we were gathered at Justus's place at a farewell party. James Huneker[4] was present and a young friend of ours, P. Yelineck, a talented painter. They began discussing Nietzsche. I took part, expressing my enthusiasm over the great poet-philosopher and dwelling on the impression of his works on me. Huneker was surprised. "I did not know you were interested in anything outside of propaganda," he remarked. "That is because you don't know anything about anarchism," I replied, "else you would understand that it embraces every phase of life and effort and that it undermines the old, outlived values." Yelineck asserted that he was an anarchist because he was an artist; all creative people must be anarchists, he held, because they need scope and freedom for their expression. Huneker insisted that art has nothing to do with any ism. "Nietzsche himself is the proof of it," he argued; "he is an aristocrat, his ideal is the superman because he has no sympathy with or faith in the common herd." I pointed out that Nietzsche was not a social theorist but a poet, a rebel and innovator. His aristocracy was neither of birth nor of purse; it was of the spirit. In that respect Nietzsche was an anarchist, and all true anarchists were aristocrats, I said.

Then Ed spoke. His voice sounded cold and constrained, and I sensed the tempest behind it. "Nietzsche is a fool," he said, "a man with a diseased mind. He was doomed from birth to the idiocy which finally overtook him. He will be forgotten in less than a decade, and so will all those other pseudo-moderns. They are contortionists in comparison with the truly great of the past."

"But you haven't read Nietzsche!" I objected heatedly; "how can you talk about him?" "Oh, yes, I have," he retorted, "I read long ago all the silly books you brought from abroad." I was dumb-founded. Huneker and Yelineck turned on Ed, but my hurt was too great to continue the discussion.

He had known how I had wanted him to share my books, how I had hoped and waited for him to recognize their value and significance. How could he have kept me in suspense, how could he have remained silent after he had read them? Of course, he had a right to his opinion; that I believed implicitly. It was not his differing from me that had stabbed me to the quick; it was his scorn and ridicule of what had come to mean so much to me. [. . .]

Late at night, when we returned home, he said to me: "Let's not spoil our beautiful three months; Nietzsche is not worth it." I felt wounded to the heart. "It isn't Nietzsche, it is you— you," I cried excitedly. "Under the pretext of a great love you have done your utmost to chain me to you, to rob me of all that is more precious to me than life. You are not content with binding my body, you want also to bind my spirit! First the movement and my friends—now it's the books I love. You want to tear me away from them. You're rooted in the old. Very well, remain there! But don't imagine you will hold me to it. You are not going to clip my wings, you shan't stop my flight. I'll free myself even if it means tearing you out of my heart." [. . .]

The last few days were outwardly calm, even friendly, Ed helping me to prepare for my departure. At the station he embraced me. I knew he wanted to say something, but he remained silent. I, too, could not speak.

When the train pulled out and Ed's form receded, I realized that our life would never be the same any more. My love had received too violent a shock. It was now like a cracked bell; never again would it ring the same clear, joyous song.

CHAPTER XVI

[. . .] On the way from Washington to Pittsburgh it poured incessantly. I was chilled to the bone and oppressed by the memory of Homestead and of Sasha. Always on my visits to the Steel City a heavy weight would settle on my heart. The sight of the belching fires from the huge furnaces scorched my soul. [. . .]

There were to be no lectures in Pittsburgh. Carl and Henry had begun a new move for Sasha's release, an appeal to the Board of Pardons to be backed exclusively by labour elements. I had no faith left in such steps, but I did not want to communicate my pessimism to my friends. Both of them were in a jovial mood. They had arranged a little dinner in a near-by restaurant, in a room all by ourselves where we would be undisturbed. We drank our first glass standing, in silence. It was to Sasha. His spirit hovered over us and brought us closer to each other in our common aims and work. Then Carl and Henry recounted to me their prison experience and the years they had spent under the same roof with Sasha. They had brought out a message for me which they feared to trust to the mails: Sasha was planning an escape.

His scheme was a masterly one; it fairly took my breath away. But even if he should succeed in getting out of prison, I reflected, where would he go? In America he would have to keep under cover for the rest of his life. He would be a haunted man, to be captured in the end. It would be different in Russia. Similar escapes had been repeatedly carried out there. But Russia had a revolutionary spirit and the political was a persecuted unfortunate in the eyes of the workers and the peasant; he could count on their sympathy and assistance. In the United States, on the other hand, nine-tenths of the workers themselves would immediately join in the hunt for Sasha. Nold and Bauer agreed with me, but they asked me not to communicate my fears to Sasha. He had reached the limit of endurance; his eyes were failing, his health was breaking down, and he had again been brooding on suicide. The hope of escape and the elaboration of his plan energized his fighting spirit. We must not discourage him, but perhaps we would induce him to wait until every legal means for his release had been tried. [. . .]

My correspondence with Ed after I left New York was of a friendly nature, though constrained. When I reached Detroit, I found a long letter from him in the old loving spirit. He made no reference to our last scene. He was anxiously waiting for me to return, he wrote, and he hoped to have me back for the holidays. "When one's sweet-heart is married to public life, one must learn to be *genügsam* [content with little]," his letter read. I could not imagine Ed being *genügsam,* but I understood that he was trying to meet my needs. I loved Ed and I wanted him, but I was determined to go on with my work. I greatly missed him, however, and his charm, which had not ceased to attract me. I wired him that I was on my way to visit sister Helena and that I should be home within a week.

Outside of a brief visit after my release from prison, I had not been in Rochester since 1894. It seemed ages, so much had happened in my life. Changes had also taken place in the fortunes of my beloved sister Helena. The Hochsteins now occupied more comfortable quarters in a little house with a touch of green in the back. Their steam-ship agency, though yielding small returns, had nevertheless improved their condition. Helena continued to shoulder the main burden; her children needed her even more than before, and so did the business. [. . .]

The day of my arrival offered no chance for communion with Helena. In the evening, when the children were asleep and the office closed, we could talk. She would not pry into my life; what I told her she accepted with understanding and affection. She herself spoke mostly about the children, hers and Lena's, and of the hard life of our parents. I knew well enough her reasons

for constantly dwelling on the difficulties of our father. She
strove to bring me closer to him and to help to a better understanding. She had suffered greatly because of our mutual antagonism, which in me had developed into hatred. She had been
horrified at the message I had sent her three years previously
when she had notified me that Father was near Death's door. He
had undergone a dangerous operation on his throat, and Helena
had called me to his bedside. "He should have died long ago,"
I had wired back. Since then she had tried repeatedly to change
my attitude towards the man whose harshness had marred the
childhood of all of us.

The memory of our sad past had made Helena more kind and
generous. It was her beautiful spirit and my own development
that gradually healed me of the bitterness I bore my father. I
came to understand that it is ignorance rather than cruelty that
makes parents do so many dreadful things to their helpless children. During my short stay in Rochester in 1894, I had seen my
father for the first time in five years. I still felt estranged, but no
longer so hostile. On that visit I found Father physically broken, a mere shadow of his former strong and energetic self. His
condition was constantly growing worse. Ten hours' work in
the shop on dry food were destructive to his weakened and nervous state of health, aggravated by the taunts and indignities he
had to endure. He was the only Jew, a man of nearly fifty, a for-
eigner not familiar with the language of the country. Most of
the youngsters who worked with him were of foreign parents,
but they had acquired the worst American traits without any of
the fine qualities. They were crude, coarse, and heartless. They
throve on the pranks and tricks they played on the "sheeny."
Repeatedly they had so molested and harassed him as to cause
him to faint. He would be brought home, only to compel himself to go back the next day. He could not afford to lose the job
that paid him ten dollars a week.

The sight of Father so ill and worn softened the last vestige of
my animosity towards him. I began to regard him as one of the
mass of the exploited and enslaved for whom I was living and
working.

In our talks Helena had always argued that Father's violence in his youth had been due to his exceptional energy, which found no adequate outlet in such a small place as Popelan. He had been ambitious for himself and his family, dreaming of the large city and the big things he could do there. The peasants eked out a poor existence on their land; but most of the Jews, with practically every profession closed to them, lived upon the peasants. Father was too honest for such methods, and his pride smarted under daily indignities from the officials he had to deal with. The failure of his life, the lack of opportunity to put his abilities to good use, had embittered him and made him ill-natured and hard towards his own. [. . .]

I saw a great deal of my sister Lena and her family on this visit. [. . .] The only joy Lena had was her children. The most radiant of the four was little Stella, who had always been my sunbeam in grey Rochester. [. . .] "I hate the people who are mean to my *Tante Emma*," Stella wrote when she was barely seven. "When I grow up, I will fight for her."

There was also my brother Yegor. Until the age of fourteen he was, like most American boys, crude and wild. He loved Helena because she had been so devoted to him. I had evidently not so impressed myself on his mind. I was just a sister, like Lena—nothing to be excited about. But on my visit in 1894 I seemed to awaken a deeper feeling in him. [. . .] "You have become my heroine," he wrote me; "you have been in prison, you are with the people and in touch with the aims of youth." I would understand his awakening, he added; his hopes were centred on me, for only I could induce our father to permit him to go to New York. He wanted to study. But, strange to say, instead of being glad, Father objected. He had lost faith in the fickle boy, he declared. Besides, the wages Yegor was earning were needed in the house now that his own health was failing and he could not continue much longer at work. It required days of pleading and my offer to take Yegor to my home in New York before Father yielded. Yegor had his wish and now saw his dream about to be fulfilled, and thus I won his lasting devotion.

My stay in Rochester this time proved to be my first un-clouded visit with my family. It was a novel experience to be accepted with warmth and affection by those who had always been strangers to me. My dear sister Helena and the two young lives that needed me helped me to closer communion with my parents.

On my way to New York I thought much about my frequent talks with Ed in regard to my taking up a course of medicine. It had been my aspiration when I was still in Königsberg, and my studies in Vienna had again awakened that desire. Ed had seized upon the idea with enthusiasm, assuring me he would soon be able to pay my way through college. My arrangements to have Yegor in New York with us and to assist him would, however, postpone the realization of my hope of becoming a doctor. I also feared Ed might resent the new obstacle and dislike having my brother in the house. I would certainly not force him on Ed. [. . .]

Yegor arrived after New Year's Day. Ed liked him from the first, and before long my brother was completely charmed by my beloved. I was soon to go on a new tour, and it was a great comfort to know that my two "children" would keep each other company in my absence.

CHAPTER XVII

[...] Chicago, city of our Black Friday, cause of my rebirth! Next to Pittsburgh it was the most ominous and depressing to me. But I no longer felt as friendless there as on previous occasions when the fury of 1887 was still active and the opposition from the followers of Most was blind and bitter against me. My imprisonment and succeeding activities had won me friends and turned the tide in my favour. [...]

The gatherings themselves were of the usual character, with no special incidents occurring. But several events lent significance to my stay in the city, proving a lasting factor in my life. Among them were my meeting Moses Harman[1] and Eugene V. Debs,[2] and my rediscovery of Max Baginski,[3] a young comrade from Germany. [...] The silent, depressed young man of my brief encounter in Philadelphia was very much alive and an interesting conversationalist, now intensely serious, again lighthearted as a boy. [...]

I felt I had found a kindred spirit in Max, one with understanding and appreciation of what had come to mean so much to me. The wealth of his mind and his sensitive personality held irresistible appeal. Our intellectual kinship was spontaneous and complete, finding also its emotional expression. We became inseparable, each day revealing to me new beauty and depth in his being. He was matured mentally far beyond his years, while psychically he was of the world of romance, of rare gentleness and refinement.

Another great event during my stay in Chicago was meeting Moses Harman, the courageous champion of free motherhood and woman's economic and sexual emancipation. His name had first become familiar to me through reading *Lucifer*, the weekly paper he was publishing. I knew of the persecution he had endured and of his imprisonment by the moral eunuchs of America, with Anthony[4] Comstock at their head. Accompanied by Max, I visited Harman at the office of *Lucifer*, which was also the home that he shared with his daughter Lillian.[5]

One's mental picture of great personalities usually proves false upon nearer contact. With Harman it was the contrary; I had not sufficiently visualized the charm of the man. His erect carriage (in spite of a lame leg, the result of a Civil War bullet), his striking head, with its flowing white hair and beard, together with his youthful eyes, combined to make the man a most impressive figure. There was nothing austere or forbidding about him; in fact, he was all kindliness. That characteristic explained his supreme faith in the country that had struck him so many blows. I was no stranger to him, he assured me. He had been outraged by the treatment I had received at the hands of the police, and he had protested against it. "We are comrades in more than one respect," he commented, with a pleasant smile. We spent the evening discussing problems affecting woman and her emancipation. During the talk I expressed doubt as to whether the approach to sex, so coarse and vulgar in America, was likely to change in the near future and Puritanism be banished from the land. Harman was sure it would. "I have seen such great changes since I began my work," he said, "that I am convinced we are not far now from a real revolution in the economic and sexual status of woman in the United States. A pure and ennobling feeling about sex and its vital rôle in human life is bound to develop." I called his attention to the growing power of Comstockism. "Where are the great men and women who can check that stifling force?" I asked; "outside of yourself and a handful of others the Americans are the most puritanical people in the world." "Not quite," he replied; "don't forget England, which has only recently suppressed Havelock Ellis's great work on sex."[6] He had faith in America and in the men and women that had been fighting for years, even suffering calumny and imprisonment for the idea of free motherhood.

During my stay in Chicago I attended a Labour convention in session in the city. I met a number of people there prominent in trade-union and revolutionary ranks, among them Mrs. Lucy Parsons,[7] widow of our martyred Albert Parsons, who took an active part in the proceedings. The most striking figure at the convention was Eugene V. Debs. Very tall and lean, he stood out above his comrades in more than a physical sense; but what struck me most about him was his naïve unawareness of the intrigues going on around him. Some of the delegates, non-political socialists, had asked me to speak and had the chairman put me on the list. By obvious trickery the Social Democratic politicians succeeded in preventing my getting the floor. At the conclusion of the session Debs came over to me to explain that there had been an unfortunate misunderstanding, but that he and his comrades would have me address the delegates in the evening.

In the evening neither Debs nor the committee was present. The audience consisted of the delegates that had extended the invitation to me and of our own comrades. Debs arrived, all out of breath, almost at the close. He had tried to get away from the various sessions in order to hear me, he said, but he had been detained. Would I forgive him and take lunch with him the next day? I had the feeling that possibly he had been a party to the petty conspiracy to suppress me. At the same time I could not reconcile his frank and open demeanour with mean actions. I consented. After spending some time with him I was convinced that Debs was in no way to blame. Whatever the politicians in his party might be doing, I was sure that he was decent and high-minded. His belief in the people was very genuine, and his vision of socialism quite unlike the State machine pictured in Marx's communist manifesto. Hearing his views, I could not help exclaiming: "Why, Mr. Debs, you're an anarchist!" "Not Mister, but Comrade," he corrected me; "won't you call me that?" Clasping my hand warmly, he assured me that he felt very close to the anarchists, that anarchism was the goal to strive for, and that all socialists should also be anarchists. Socialism to him was only a stepping-stone to the ultimate ideal, which was anarchism. "I know and love Kropotkin and his work," he said; "I admire him and I revere our murdered comrades who lie in Waldheim, as I do also all the other splendid fighters in your movement. You see, then, I am your comrade. I am with you in your struggle." I pointed out that we could not hope to achieve freedom by increasing the power of the State, which the socialists were aiming at. I stressed the fact that political action is the death-knell of the economic struggle. Debs did not dispute me, agreeing that the revolutionary spirit must be kept alive notwithstanding any political objects, but he thought the latter a necessary and practical means of reaching the masses.

We parted good friends. Debs was so genial and charming as a human being that one did not mind the lack of political clarity which made him reach out at one and the same time for opposite poles. [. . .]

My presence in Chicago gave me the opportunity to fulfil a wish of long standing: to do honour to our precious dead by placing a wreath upon their grave in Waldheim Cemetery. Before the monument erected to their memory we stood in silence, Max and I, our hands clasped. The inspired vision of the artist had transformed stone into a living presence. The figure of the woman on a high pedestal, and the fallen hero reclining at her feet, were expressive of defiance and revolt, mingled with pity and love. Her face, beautiful in its great humanity, was turned upon a world of pain and woe, one hand pointing to the dying rebel, the other held protectingly over his brow. There was intense feeling in her gesture, and infinite tenderness. The tablet on the back of the base was engraved with a significant passage from Governor Altgeld's reasons for pardoning the three surviving anarchists.[8] [. . .]

To see California for the first time in early spring, after twenty-four hours through drab Nevada, was like beholding a fairyland after a nightmare. Never before had I seen nature so lavish and resplendent. I was still under its spell when the scene changed to one of less exuberance, and the train pulled into Oakland.

My stay in San Francisco was most interesting and delightful. It enabled me to do the best work I had accomplished till then, and it brought me in contact with many free and rare spirits. The headquarters of anarchist activity on the Coast was *Free Society*, edited and published by the Isaak family. They were unusual people, Abe Isaak, Mary, his wife, and their three children.⁹ [. . .] In America the Isaaks had first settled in Portland, Oregon, where they came under the influence of anarchist ideas. Together with some native comrades, among whom were Henry Addis and H. J. Pope, the Isaaks founded an anarchist weekly called the *Firebrand*. Because of the appearance in the latter of Walt Whitman's poem, "A Woman Waits for Me," their paper was suppressed, its publishers arrested, and H. J. Pope imprisoned for obscenity. The Isaak family then started *Free Society*, later moving to San Francisco. Even the children co-operated in the undertaking, often working eighteen hours a day, writing, setting up type, and addressing wrappers. At the same time they did not neglect other propagandist activities.

The particular attraction of the Isaaks for me was the consistency of their lives, the harmony between the ideas they professed and their application. The comradeship between the parents and the complete freedom of every member of the household were novel things to me. In no other anarchist family had I seen children enjoy such liberty or so independently express themselves without the slightest hindrance from their elders. It was amusing to hear Abe and Pete, boys of sixteen and eighteen respectively, hold their father to account for some alleged infraction of principle, or criticize the propaganda value of his articles. Isaak would listen with patience and respect, even if the manner of the criticism were adolescently harsh and arrogant. Never once did I see the parents resort to the authority of superior age or wisdom. Their children were their equals; their right to disagree, to live their own lives and learn, was unquestioned.

"If you can't establish freedom in your own home," Isaak often said, "how can you expect to help the world to it?" To him and to Mary that was just what freedom meant: equality of the sexes in all their needs, physical, intellectual, and emotional.

The Isaaks maintained this attitude in the *Firebrand,* and now again in *Free Society*. For their insistence on sex equality they were severely censored by many anarchists in the East and abroad. I had welcomed the discussion of these problems in their paper, for I knew from my own experience that sex expression is as vital a factor in human life as food and air. Therefore it was not mere theory that had led me at an early stage of my development to discuss sex as frankly as I did other topics and to live my life without fear of the opinion of others. Among American radicals in the East I had met many men and women who shared my view on this subject and had the courage to practise their ideas in their sex life. But in my own immediate ranks I was very much alone. It was therefore a revelation to find that the Isaaks felt and lived as I did. It helped to establish a strong personal bond between us besides our common anarchist ideal.

Notwithstanding nightly lectures in San Francisco and adjoining towns, a mass meeting to celebrate the first of May, and a debate with a socialist, we still found time for frequent social gatherings jovial enough to be disapproved by the purists. But we did not mind it. Youth and freedom laughed at rules and strictures, and our circle consisted of people young in years and in spirit. In the company of the Isaak boys and the other young chaps I felt like a grandmother—I was twenty-nine—but in spirit I was the gayest, as my young admirers often assured me. We had the joy of life in us, and the California wines were cheap and stimulating. The propagandist of an unpopular cause needs, even more than other people, occasional light-hearted irresponsibility. How else could he survive the hardships and travail of existence? My San Francisco comrades could work strenuously; they took their tasks very seriously; but they could also love, drink, and play.

CHAPTER XVIII

[. . .] In New York Ed and my brother Yegor met me at the station. Yegor was overjoyed to have me back; Ed, always reserved in public, now appeared unusually so. I thought it was due to my brother's presence, but when he continued to keep aloof even when we were alone, I realized that some change had taken place in him. He was as attentive and considerate as usual, and our home as sweet as ever; but he had become different. [. . .]

Fortunately there was no time for brooding. The textile strike in Summit, New Jersey, was demanding my services. It presented the usual situation; meetings were either prohibited or broken up by police clubs. It required skilful manœuvring to meet in the woods outside of Summit. I was kept very much engaged, with hardly any time to see Ed. On the rare occasions when we were together, he would remain silent. Only his eyes spoke and they were full of reproach. [. . .]

In the midst of this work came an urgent request from the Alexander Berkman Defense Association in Pittsburgh for greater activity in behalf of his pardon. The case, which was to be heard in September, was now set for December 21. The attorneys advised that the decision of the Board of Pardons would largely depend on the stand of Andrew Carnegie in the matter and therefore they urged seeing the steel-magnate. It was an inane suggestion, which would certainly not be approved by Sasha. [. . .]

We now turned to Ernest Crosby,[1] a leading single-taxer and Tolstoyan, who was also a gifted poet and writer. [. . .] When we placed our case before Mr. Crosby, he agreed at once to see

Carnegie. There was only one thing that troubled him, he explained. If Carnegie should demand a guarantee that Alexander Berkman, when free, would not again commit an act of violence, what answer was he to give? He himself would never ask such a thing, aware that no one could say what he might do under pressure. But as the intermediary he felt it necessary to be informed by us on the matter. Of course, it was impossible for us to give such a guarantee, and I knew that Sasha would never make any pledges of "reform" or allow them to be made for him.

The matter finally ended with our decision not to apply to Carnegie at all. Sasha's case was not even brought before the Board of Pardons at the time intended. Its members were found to be too prejudiced against him, and it was hoped that the new Board, which was to take office in the following year, might prove more impartial. [. . .]

Three weeks later Ed fell ill with pneumonia. All my care and love were pitted against the great dread I felt at the possibility of losing the precious life. The big strong man, who used to make light of illness and who had often hinted "that such things were inherent only in the female species," now clung to me like an infant and would not have me out of sight even for a moment. [. . .]

At last the crisis was over. In the morning Ed opened his eyes. His hand groped for mine, and in a faint voice he asked: "Dear nurse, must I kick the bucket?" "Not this time," I comforted him, "but you must be very quiet." His face lit up with his old beautiful smile, and he dozed off again.

When Ed was already on his feet, though still very weak, I had to leave for a meeting I had promised to address long before his illness. Fedya remained with him. When I returned, late at night, Fedya was gone and Ed fast asleep. There was a note from Fedya saying that Ed was feeling fine and had urged him to go home.

In the morning Ed was still asleep. I took his pulse and noticed that he was breathing heavily. I became alarmed and sent for Doctor Hoffmann. The latter expressed concern over Ed's unusually protracted sleep. He asked to see the box of morphine he had left for Ed to take. Four powders were missing!

I had given Ed one before going away, and I had impressed upon Fedya that he was not to get any more. Ed had taken four times the ordinary dose—no doubt in an attempt to end his life! He wanted to die—now—after I had barely rescued him from the grave! Why? Why?

"We must get him on his feet and walk the floor with him," the doctor ordered; "he is alive, he is breathing; we must keep him alive." We supported his drooping body up and down the room, from time to time applying ice to his hands and face. Gradually his face began to lose its deathly pallor, and his lids responded to pressure. "Who would ever have thought that a reserved and quiet person like Ed would be capable of such a thing?" the doctor remarked. "He'll sleep on for many more hours, but no need to worry. He'll live."

I was shocked by Ed's attempted suicide and tried to fathom what particular cause had induced his action. On several occasions I was on the point of asking him for an explanation, but he was in such cheerful humour and recuperating so well that I was afraid to dig up the ghastly affair. He himself never referred to it.

Then one day he surprised me by mentioning that he had not intended to take his life at all. My leaving him to go to the meeting when he was still so ill had enraged him. He knew from past experience that he could stand a large dose of morphine, and he swallowed several powders, "just to scare you a little and cure you of your mania for meetings, which stops at nothing, not even at the illness of the man you pretend to love."

His words staggered me. I felt that the seven years of our life together had failed to make Ed grasp the pain and travail of my inner growth. A "mania for meetings"—that was all that it meant to him.

There followed days of conflict between my love for Ed and the realization that life had lost its content and meaning. At the end of my bitter struggle I knew that I must leave him. I told Ed that I should have to go, for good. [. . .]

I began preparations for my tour. The day of departure was approaching, and Ed pleaded with me to permit him to see me off. I declined; I was afraid I might give way at the last moment.

That day Ed came home at noon to have lunch with me. Both of us pretended to be cheerful. But at parting his face darkened for a moment. Before leaving he embraced me, saying: "This isn't the end, dearest—it cannot be! This is your home, now and for ever!" I could not speak; my heart was too full of grief. When the door had closed on Ed, I was unable to restrain my sobs. Every object about me assumed a strange fascination, speaking to me in many tongues. I realized that to linger meant to weaken my determination to leave Ed. With palpitating heart I walked out of the house I had loved and cherished as my home.

CHAPTER XIX

[. . .] It was not until I reached Chicago that I began to make my efforts count. As on my preceding tour, I was invited to speak by many labour organizations, including the conservative Woodworkers' Union, which had never before allowed an anarchist within its sacred portals. A number of lectures were also arranged for me by American anarchists. It was strenuous work and I should probably not have been able to carry it through but for the exhilarating companionship of Max Baginski. [. . .]

The Paris Exposition, which was being planned for 1900, suggested the idea to our European comrades of holding an anarchist congress at about the same time. There would be reduced fares, and many of our friends would be able to come from different countries. I had received an invitation; I spoke to Max about it and asked him to come with me. A trip to Europe together—the very thought of it transported us with ecstasy. My tour would last till August; then we could carry out our new plan. We might journey to England first; I was sure the comrades would want me to lecture there. Then to Paris. "Think of it, dearest—Paris!" "Wonderful, glorious!" he cried. "But the fare—have you thought of that, my romantic Emma?" "That's nothing. I will rob a church or a synagogue—I'll get the money somehow! We must go anyhow. We must go in quest of the moon!" "Two babes in the woods," Max commented; "two sane romantics in a crazy world!"

On my way to Denver I made a side trip to Caplinger Mills, an agricultural district in south-western Missouri. My only previous contact with farm life in the United States had been years before when I had canvassed Massachusetts farmers for orders to enlarge the pictures of their worthy ancestors. I had found them so dull, so rooted in old social traditions, that I did not even care to tell them what I stood for. I was sure they would think me possessed of the devil. It very much surprised me, therefore, to receive an invitation from Caplinger Mills to lecture there. The comrade who wrote that she had arranged my meetings was Kate Austen,[1] whose articles I had read in *Free Society* and other radical publications. Her writings showed her to be a logical thinker, well-informed, and of revolutionary fibre, while her letters to me indicated an affectionate, sensitive being.

At the station I was met by Sam Austen, Kate's husband, who announced that Caplinger Mills was twenty-two miles distant from the railroad. "The roads are very bad," he said; "I'm afraid I'll have to tie you to the seat of my wagon, else you may be shaken out." I soon found he had not been exaggerating. We had hardly covered half the way when there came a violent jolt and the cracking of wheels. Sam landed in a ditch, and when I attempted to get up, I felt sore all over. He lifted me out of the wagon and set me down by the wayside. Waiting and rubbing my aching joints, I tried to smile to encourage Sam. [. . .]

At last we arrived in Caplinger Mills at the Austen farm. "Put her to bed right away and give her a hot drink," Sam directed, "else she'll hate us for the rest of her life for having taken her over that road." After a hot bath and a good massage I felt much refreshed, though still aching in every joint.

My week with the Austens showed me new angles of the small American farmer's life. It made me see that we had been wrong to regard the farmer in the States as belonging to the *bourgeoisie*. Kate said it was true only of the very rich landowner who raised everything on a large scale; the vast mass of farmers in America were even more dependent than the city workers. They were at the mercy of the bankers and the railroads, not to speak of their natural enemies, storm and drought. To combat the latter and nourish the leeches who sap the farmer he must slave endless hours in every kind of weather and live almost on the edge of penury. It is his toilsome lot that makes him hard and close-fisted, Kate thought. She lamented especially the drab existence of the farmer's wife. "The womenfolk have nothing but cares, drudgery, and frequent child-bearing." [. . .]

The attendance at my three meetings testified to Kate's influence. From a radius of many miles the farmers came, on foot, in wagons, and on horseback. Two lectures I gave in the little country schoolhouse, the third in a large grove. It was a most picturesque gathering, with the faces of my listeners lit up by lanterns they had brought with them. From the questions some of the men asked, which centred mainly on the right to the land under anarchism, I could see that at least some of them had not come out of mere curiosity, and that Kate had awakened them to the realization that their own difficulties were part of the larger problems of society. [. . .]

CHAPTER XX

At the height of my California activities a letter came that shattered my visions of harmonious love: Max wrote me that he and his comrade "Puck" were about to go abroad together, financed by a friend. I laughed aloud at the folly of my hopes. After the failure with Ed how could I have dreamed of love and understanding with anyone else? Love and happiness—empty, meaningless words, vain reaching out for the unattainable. I felt robbed by life, defeated in my yearning for a beautiful relationship. I still had my ideal to live for, as I consoled myself, and the work I had set myself to do. Why expect more from life? But where get strength and inspiration to keep up the struggle? Men had been able to do the world's work without the sustaining power of love; why should not also women? Or is it that woman needs love more than man? A stupid, romantic notion, conceived to keep her for ever dependent on the male. Well, I would not have it; I would live and work without love. There is no permanency anywhere in nature or in life. I must drain the moment and then let the goblet fall to the ground. It is the sole protection against taking root, only to be painfully pulled up again. My young friends in San Francisco had been calling. The vision of life with Max had stood in the way. Now I could respond; I must respond in order to forget. [. . .]

During my previous visit in Detroit with Max I had met one of Robert Reitzel's[1] staunchest friends, Herman Miller, and another devotee of the *Armer Teufel*, Carl Stone. Miller was president of the Cleveland Brewing Company and a man of considerable means. [. . .]

Both Miller and Stone showed great interest in my struggle

and plans for the future. Asked about the latter, I informed them that I had none, except to work for my ideal. Didn't I wish to secure myself materially, by having some profession, for instance, Herman suggested. I had always wanted to study medicine, I told him, but had never had the means for it. I was completely taken off my feet by Herman's unexpectedly offering to finance my studies. Stone also wanted to share the expense, but the two friends thought it impracticable to turn the entire amount over to me. "I understand you always have a string of people needing help; you will be sure to give the money away," Herman said. They agreed to secure me for five years with an income of forty dollars a month. [. . .]

Before I took leave of my dear friends in Detroit, Herman shyly and unobtrusively put an envelope in my hand. "A love-letter," he said, "to be read on the train." The "love-letter" contained five hundred dollars, with a note: "For your passage, dear Emma, and to keep you from care until we meet in Paris."

The last hope of legal redress for Sasha was gone when the new Board of Pardons refused to hear our appeal. There was nothing left except the desperate venture Sasha had been planning for a considerable time—an escape. [. . .] With the possibility of release gone, I could do nothing but submit to Sasha's wishes, though with an anxious heart.

His letters, after I informed him that we would go ahead with his scheme, showed him to have undergone a wonderful transformation. He was buoyant again, full of hope and vigour. Soon he would send a friend to us, he wrote, a most trustworthy person, a fellow prisoner whom he called "Tony." The man would be released within a few weeks, and he would then bring us the necessary details of the plan. "It will not fail if my instructions are faithfully carried out," he wrote. He explained that two things would be required: dependable comrades of grit and endurance, and some money. He was sure I would find both.

Before long "Tony" was released, but certain preparatory work in Sasha's behalf kept him in Pittsburgh, and we could not get in personal touch with him. I learned, however, that Sasha's plan involved the digging of a tunnel from the outside into the prison, and that Sasha had entrusted "Tony" with all the necessary diagrams and measurements to enable us to do the work. The scheme seemed fantastic, the desperate design of one driven to stake everything, even his life, upon the throw of a card. Yet I was carried away by the project, so cleverly conceived, and worked out with utmost care. I reflected a long time upon whom to approach in regard to the undertaking. There were plenty of comrades who would be willing to risk their lives to rescue Sasha, but few who had the requisites for such a difficult and hazardous task. I finally decided upon our Norwegian friend Eric B. Morton, whom we had nicknamed "Ibsen." He was a veritable viking, in spirit and physique, a man of intelligence, daring, and will-power.

The plan appealed to him at once. Without hesitation he promised to do anything that would be required, and he was ready to start there and then. I explained that there would be an unavoidable delay; we had to wait for "Tony." Something was apparently detaining him much longer than he had expected. I was loath to leave for Europe without being sure that Sasha's plan was being carried out and I confessed to Eric that I felt uneasy about going at all. "It will be maddening to be three thousand miles away while Sasha's fate is hanging in the balance," I said. Eric understood my feelings in the matter, but he thought that as far as the proposed tunnel was concerned, I could do nothing. "In fact, your absence may prove of greater value," he argued, "than your presence in America. It will serve to ward off suspicion that something is being done for Sasha." He agreed with me that the question of Sasha's safety after the escape was of paramount importance. He feared, as I did, that Sasha could not remain very long in the country without being apprehended. "We'll have to get him away as quickly as possible to Canada or Mexico, and thence to Europe," he suggested. "The tunnel will require months of work, and that will give you time to prepare a place for him abroad. There he will be recognized as a political refugee, and as such he will not be extradited."

I knew Eric was a very level-headed man, entirely reliable. Still I hated to go away without seeing "Tony," learning the details of the plan, and finding out all he could tell us about Sasha.

Eric quieted my apprehensions by promising to take charge of the entire matter and to begin operations as soon as "Tony" arrived. He was a man of convincing manner and strong personality, and I had the fullest faith in his courage and ability to carry out successfully Sasha's directions. He was, moreover, splendid company, full of cheer, and with a fine sense of humour. At parting he jubilantly assured me that together with Sasha we should soon all meet in Paris to celebrate his escape.

Still "Tony" failed to appear and his absence filled me with misgivings. Involuntarily I thought of the unreliability of prisoners' promises. I remembered the great things several of the women in Blackwell's Island were going to do for me upon their release. They were all soon drawn into the whirlpool of life and personal interests, their best prison intentions slipping away from them. It is rare indeed that a released prisoner is willing and able to carry out the promises made to his fellow sufferers remaining behind the bars. "Tony" was probably like the majority, I thought. Still, I had several weeks yet before sailing— perhaps "Tony" would turn up in the meantime. [. . .]

Many friends came to the steamer to say adieu to me and to Mary Isaak, who was sailing with me. [. . .] It was hard also to part from my brother. I was glad to be able to leave him some money, and I would contribute to his needs from the monthly allowance my Detroit friends were to send me. I could manage on less; I had done it in Vienna. The boy had taken deep hold on my heart; he was so tender and considerate that his affection had become something very precious in my life. As the big liner steamed out, I remained on deck to watch the receding silhouettes of New York.

Our crossing was uneventful, except for a raging storm. We arrived in London two days too late for the eleventh-of-November meeting[2] and at the height of the Boer War.[3] In the house where Harry Kelly[4] and his family were living there was only one room vacant, and that was in the basement. Even in clear weather it had but little daylight, while on foggy days the gas-jet had to be kept going all the time. The fire-place warmed only one's side or back, never the entire body, and I constantly had to keep changing my position to balance, to some extent, the atmospheric difference between the fire and the cold room.

Having been in London during its best season, in late August and September, I used to think that people exaggerated when they spoke of the horrors of the London fogs, the dampness and greyness of its winter. But I realized this time that they had hardly done justice to the reality. The fog was like a monster, stealthily creeping up and enveloping the victim in its chilly embrace. Mornings I would awaken with a leaden feeling, my mouth parched. In vain the hope of enjoying a ray of light by opening the blinds; the blackness from the outside would soon creep into the room.

CHAPTER XXI

The war madness in England was so great, some of the comrades informed me, that it would be almost impossible to deliver my lectures as had been planned. Harry Kelly was of the same opinion. "Why not hold anti-war mass meetings?" I suggested. I referred to the splendid gatherings we had in America during the Spanish War. Now and then there had been attempts at interference, and several lectures had to be given up, but on the whole we had been able to carry through our campaign. Harry thought, however, that it would be impossible in England. His description of violent attacks on speakers (the jingo spirit being at its height) and of meetings being broken up by patriotic mobs sounded discouraging. [. . .]

At the invitation of the Kropotkins I went out with Mary Isaak to Bromley. This time Mrs. Kropotkin and her little daughter, Sasha, were at home. Both Peter and Sophia Grigorevna received us with affectionate cordiality. We discussed America, our movement there, and conditions in England. Peter had visited the States in 1898, but I was at the time on the Coast and unable to attend his lectures. I knew, however, that his tour had been very successful and that he had left a most gratifying impression. The proceeds of his meetings had helped to revive *Solidarity*[1] and inject new life into our movement. Peter was particularly interested in my tours through the Middle West and California. "It must be a splendid field," he remarked, "if you can cover the same ground three times in succession." I assured him that it was, and that much of the credit for my success in California had been due to *Free Society*. "The paper is doing splendid work," he warmly agreed, "but it would do more if it would not waste so much space discussing sex." I disagreed, and we became involved in a heated argument about the place of the sex problem in anarchist propaganda. Peter's view was that woman's equality with man had nothing to do with sex; it was a matter of brains. "When she is his equal intellectually and shares in his social ideals," he said, "she will be as free as he." We both got somewhat excited, and our voices must have sounded as if we were quarrelling. Sophia, quietly sewing a dress for her daughter, tried several times to direct our talk into less vociferous channels, but in vain. Peter and I paced the room in growing agitation, each strenuously upholding his side of the question. At last I paused with the remark: "All right, dear comrade, when I have reached your age, the sex question may no longer be of importance to me. But it is *now*, and it is a tremendous factor for thousands, millions even, of young people." Peter stopped short, an amused smile lighting up his kindly face. "Fancy, I didn't think of that," he replied. "Perhaps you are right, after all." He beamed affectionately upon me, with a humorous twinkle in his eye.

During dinner I broached the plan for the anti-war meetings. Peter was even more emphatic than Harry had been. It was out of the question, he thought; it would endanger my life; moreover, because I was a Russian, my stand on the war would unfavourably affect the status of the Russian refugees. "I'm not here as a Russian, but as an American," I protested. "Moreover, what do these considerations matter when such a vital issue as war is involved?" Peter pointed out that it mattered very much to people who had death or Siberia staring them in the face. He insisted, nevertheless, that England was still the only asylum in Europe for political refugees and that its hospitality should not be forfeited by meetings.

My first public appearance in London, in the Athenæum Hall, was a dismal failure. I had caught a severe cold that affected my throat so that my speaking was painful not only to myself but to the audience as well. I could hardly be heard. No less distressing was my nervousness when I learned that the most distinguished Russian refugees and some noted Englishmen had come to hear me. The names of those Russians had always symbolized to me all that was heroic in the struggle against the tsars. The thought of their presence filled me with awe. What could I say to such men, and how say it?

Harry Kelly acted as chairman, straightway proceeding to tell the audience that his comrade Emma Goldman, who had faced squadrons of police in America, had just confided to him that she was panicky before this assembly. The latter thought it a good joke and laughed heartily. Inwardly I raged at Harry, but the good humour of the audience and its evident desire to put me at my ease somewhat relieved my nervous tension. I plodded through my lecture, aware all the time that I was delivering a rotten speech. The questions that followed, however, gave me back my self-possession. I felt more in my element, and I did not care any more who was present. I regained my ordinary determined and aggressive manner.

My meetings in the East End offered no difficulties. There I was among my people; I knew their lives, hard and barren everywhere, but more so in London. I was able to find the right words to reach them; I was my own self in their midst. [. . .]

Before long, Harry Kelly came to inform me that some of the comrades had agreed to arrange an anti-war meeting and that steps would be taken to ensure security. Their plan was to bring a score of men from Canning Town, a suburb known for the fighting spirit and strength of its men. They would protect the platform and prevent a possible rush of the jingoes. [. . .]

On the appointed day, accompanied by my escort, I reached South Place Institute a few hours before the crowd began to gather. Very soon the hall was filled. When Tom Mann[2] stepped on to the platform, there was loud booing, which drowned the applause of our friends. For a time the situation looked hopeless, but Tom was an experienced speaker, skilled in the handling of crowds. The audience soon subsided. When I made my appearance, however, the patriots got out of leash again. Several tried to get on the platform, but the Canning Town men held them back. I stood silent for some moments, not knowing just how to approach the infuriated Britishers. I was certain I could achieve nothing by the direct and blunt manner that had invariably succeeded with my American audiences. Something different was needed, something that would touch their pride. My visit in 1895 and my experiences this time had taught me to know the pride of Englishmen in their traditions. "Men and women of England!" I shouted above the din, "I have come here in the firm belief that a people whose history is surcharged with the spirit of rebellion and whose genius in every field is a shining star upon the firmament of the world can be naught but liberty- and justive-loving. Nay, more, the immortal works of Shakespeare, Milton, Byron, Shelley, and Keats, to mention only the greatest in the galaxy of poets and dreamers of your country, must needs have enlarged your vision and quickened your appreciation of what is the most precious heritage of a truly cultivated people; I mean the grace of hospitality and a generous attitude towards the stranger in your midst."

Complete silence in the hall.

"Your behaviour tonight hardly sustains my belief in the superior culture and breeding of your country," I went on; "or is it that the fury of war has so easily destroyed what it has taken centuries to build up?" [. . .]

Silence continued, my hearers apparently bewildered by the unexpected turn of my speech, dumbfounded by the high-sounding words and compelling gestures. The audience became absorbed in my talk, carried to a pitch of enthusiasm which finally broke forth in loud applause. After that it was easy sailing. I delivered my lecture on War and Patriotism as I had given it all through the United States, merely changing the parts that had dealt with the causes of the Spanish-American hostilities to those behind the Anglo-Boer War. I concluded with the gist of Carlyle's idea of war as a quarrel between two thieves, themselves too cowardly to fight, compelling boys of one village and another into uniforms with guns in their hands and then letting them loose like ferocious beasts against each other.

The house went wild. Men and women waved their hats and shouted themselves hoarse in approval. Our resolution, a powerful protest against the war, was read by the Chair and adopted with only one dissenting voice. I bowed in the direction of the objector and said: "There is what I call a brave man who deserves our admiration. It requires great courage to stand alone, even if one is mistaken. Let us all join in hearty applause for our daring opponent."

Even our guard from Canning Town could no longer hold back the surging crowd. But there was no danger any more. The audience had turned from fierce antagonism to equally burning devotion, ready to protect me to the last drop of its blood. [. . .]

During my London stay I also spoke at a German meeting arranged by comrades of the *Autonomie* Club. In the discussion I was attacked by a young German. "What does Emma Goldman know about the life of the workers, anyway?" my opponent demanded; "she never worked in a factory and she's just like the other agitators, having a good time, travelling round and enjoying herself." [. . .]

After the meeting two men of about my own age came up to see me. They begged me not to hold all the comrades responsible for the stupid attack of the youth. [. . .] The two introduced themselves as Hippolyte Havel[3] and X, the former a Czech, the latter a German. X soon excused himself, and Havel asked me to take dinner with him.

My escort was of small stature, very dark, with large eyes gleaming in his pale face. He was dressed fastidiously, even to the point of gloves, which no men in our ranks wore. It struck me as dandyish, especially in a revolutionist. In the restaurant I noticed that Havel took off only one glove, keeping the other on all through the meal. I was on the point of asking him the reason, but he seemed so self-conscious that I did not wish to embarrass him. After a few glasses of wine he became more animated, talking in nervous staccato sentences. He had come to London from Zürich, he told me, and though not long in the city, he knew it well and would be happy to take me about. It would have to be Sunday afternoon, or late in the evening, his only free time.

Hippolyte Havel proved to be a veritable encyclopædia. He knew everybody and everything in the movement of the various European countries. I detected bitterness in his tone when he spoke of certain comrades in the *Autonomie* Club. It affected me unpleasantly, but on the whole he was exceedingly entertaining. It was already too late to catch a bus, and Havel hailed a cab to take me home. When I offered to pay the driver, he became incensed. "Just like an American, flaunting your money! I'm working, and I can afford to pay!" he protested. I ventured to suggest that for an anarchist he was strangely conventional to object to a woman's right to pay. Havel smiled for the first time during the whole evening, and I could not help noticing that he had beautiful white teeth. When I shook his hand, still encased in the glove, he gave a suppressed groan. "What is it?" I asked. "Oh, nothing," he replied, "but for a little lady you do have a strong grip."

There was something strange and exotic about the man. He was evidently very nervous and ungenerous in his estimate of people. Still, he was fascinating, even disturbing.

My Czech comrade came frequently, sometimes with his friend, but usually alone. He was far from gay company; in fact, he rather depressed me. Unless he had drunk a little, it was difficult to get him to converse; at other times he seemed tongue-tied. Gradually I learned that he had come into the movement when only eighteen and that he had been in prison several times, once for a term of eighteen months. On the last occasion he had been sent to the psychopathic ward, where he might have remained had he not aroused the interest of Professor Krafft-Ebing,[4] who declared him sane and helped him back to freedom. He had been active in Vienna and expelled from there, after which he had tramped through Germany, lecturing and writing for anarchist publications. He had visited Paris, but was not allowed to remain there long, being expelled. Finally he had gone to Zürich and thence to London. As he had no trade, he was compelled to accept any kind of job. At the time, he was working in an English boarding-house as an all-round man. His duties began at five in the morning and consisted in lighting the fires, cleaning the boots of the guests, washing dishes, and doing other kinds of "degrading and humiliating work." "But why degrading? Labour is never degrading," I protested. "Labour, as it is now, is always degrading!" he insisted vehemently; "in an English boarding-house it is even worse; it is an outrage on all human sensibilities, besides the drudgery it involves. Look at my hands!" With a nervous jerk he tore off his glove and the bandage underneath. His hand, red and swollen, was a mass of blisters. "How did it happen, and how can you keep on working?" I asked. "I got it from cleaning filthy boots in the early morning chill and carrying coals and wood to keep the fires going. What else can I do without a trade in a foreign country? I might starve, sink into the gutter, or end in the Thames," he added. "But I'm not just ready for it. Besides, I'm only one of the many thousands; why fuss about it? Let's talk about more cheerful things." He continued conversing, but I hardly heard what he said. I took his poor blistered hand, conscious of an irresistible desire to put it to my lips, in infinite sympathy and tenderness.

We went about together a good deal, visiting the poor quarters, Whitechapel and similar districts. On week-days the streets were littered with foul rubbish, and the smell of fried fish was nauseating. On Saturday nights the spectacle was even more harrowing. I had seen drunken women on the Bowery, old social dregs, their scraggy hair loose, their incongruous hats tilted to one side and skirts sweeping the sidewalk. "Bummerkes," the Jewish children called them. It used to make me furious to see the thoughtless youngsters taunt and chase those poor derelicts. But nothing compared in brutality and degradation with the sights I witnessed in the East End of London: drunken women lurching out of the public houses, using the vilest language and fighting until they would literally tear the clothes off one another. Small boys and girls hanging round the drinking-places in sleet and cold, infants in dilapidated carriages in a stupor from the whisky-soaked "suckers," the elder children keeping watch and greedily drinking the ale their parents would bring out to them from time to time. Too often I saw such pictures, more terrible than any conceived by Dante. Every time, filled with rage, disgust, and shame, I would promise myself never to go back to the East End, yet I would invariably return. When I broached the situation to some of my comrades, they thought me overwrought. Such conditions existed in every large city, they claimed; it was capitalism with its resultant sordidness. Why should I feel more disturbed in London than anywhere else?

Gradually I began to realize that the pleasure I found in

Havel's company was due to more than ordinary comradeship. Love was making its claims again, daily more insistent. I was afraid of it, afraid of the new pain, the new disappointments in store. Yet my need of it in the dismal surroundings was stronger than my apprehensions. Havel, too, cared for me. He had grown more timid, more restless and fidgety. He had been in the habit of coming to see me alone, but one evening he visited me with his friend, who remained for hours and showed no intention of leaving. I suspected that Havel had brought him because he did not trust himself to be alone with me, and that only increased my yearning. Finally, long after midnight, his friend left. No sooner was he gone than we found ourselves, hardly conscious how, in each other's embrace. London receded, the cry of the East End was far away. Only the call of love sounded in our hearts, and we listened and yielded to it.

I felt reborn with the new joy in my life. We would go together to Paris and later to Switzerland, we decided. [. . .] I departed from England for Paris, together with Hippolyte, arriving in that city on a drizzling January morning and stopping in a hotel on Boulevard Saint-Michel. Four years previously, in 1896, I had visited the city on my way from Vienna. That experience had been a great disappointment. The people I then stopped with, German anarchists, lived in a suburb, worked hard during the day, and were too tired to go out at night, and my French was not sufficient to enable me to go about alone. On the only free Sunday, friends had taken me to the Bois de Boulogne. Outside of that I had seen practically nothing of Paris, which I had longed so much to know, but I had promised myself that some day I would return to enjoy the delights of the wonderful city.

Now the opportunity was at hand at last, made more wonderful by the rebirth of love in my life. Hippolyte had been in Paris before and knew its charms; he made a perfect companion. For a month we were completely engrossed in the wonders of the city and in each other. [. . .]

Our cares and worries were forgotten in the world of beauty, in the treasures of architecture and art, created by the genius of man. The days were passing like a dream from which one feared to awaken. But I had come to Paris also for another purpose. It was time to begin the preparatory work for our congress.

France had been the cradle of anarchism, fathered for a long time by some of her most brilliant sons, of whom Proudhon was the greatest. The battle for their ideal had been strenuous, involving persecution, imprisonment, and often even the sacrifice of life. But it had not been in vain. Thanks to them anarchism and its exponents had come to be regarded in France as a social factor to be reckoned with. No doubt the French *bourgeoisie* continued to dread anarchism and to persecute it through the machinery of the State. I had occasion to witness the brutal manner in which the French police handled radical crowds, as well as proceedings in the French courts when dealing with social offenders. Still, there was a vast difference in the approach and methods used by the French in dealing with anarchists from the American way. It was the difference between a people seasoned in revolutionary traditions and one which had merely skimmed the surface of a struggle for independence. That difference was everywhere apparent, strikingly so in the anarchist movement itself. In the various groups I did not meet a single comrade who used the high-sounding term "philosophic" to mask his anarchism, as many did in America, because they thought it more respectable.

We were soon carried into the tide of the varied activities that went on in the anarchist ranks. The revolutionary-syndicalist movement, given new impetus by the fertile mind of Pelloutier,[5] was permeated with anarchist tendencies. Nearly all the leading men of the organization were outspoken anarchists. [. . .]

My studies of the movement, however, did not allay my personal interest in people, always stronger with me than theories. [. . .] Of the people I met I was most impressed by Victor Dave.[6] He was an old comrade who during forty years had participated in anarchist activities in various European countries. He had been a member of the first International, a co-worker of Michael Bakunin,[7] and the teacher of Johann Most. [. . .]

The most fascinating thing about Victor Dave was his innate feeling for life and ready enjoyment of fun. He was the freest and gayest among the many comrades I met in Paris, a companion after my own heart. But our good humour was often marred by Hippolyte's fits of extreme depression. From the very first he had taken a strong dislike to Victor. He would refuse to join us on our outings, yet peevishly resent having been left behind. Ordinarily his feeling would express itself in mute reproach, but the least quantity of liquor would incite him to abuse Victor. At first I took his outbreaks lightly, but gradually they began to affect me, making me uneasy when I was away from him. I loved the boy; I knew his unhappy past had left wounds in his soul that made him morbidly self-conscious and suspicious. I wanted to help him to a better understanding of himself and a broader approach to others. I hoped that my affection would soften his virulence. When sober, he regretted his attacks on Victor, and at such moments he would be all tenderness, clinging to our love. It led me to hope that he might out-grow his acrimonious moods. But the scenes kept recurring, and my apprehension increased.

In the course of time I realized that Hippolyte's resentment was directed not only against Victor, but against every man of my acquaintance. [. . .] Life with Hippolyte was growing more distressing, yet I could not think of parting.

CHAPTER XXII

A letter from Carl Stone unexpectedly changed my plans regarding the study of medicine. "I thought it was understood when you left for Europe," he wrote, "that you were to go to Switzerland to study medicine. It was solely for that purpose that Herman and I offered to give you an allowance. I now learn that you are at your old propaganda and with a new lover. Surely you do not expect us to support you with either. I am interested only in E. G. the woman—her ideas have no meaning whatever to me. Please choose." I wrote back at once: "E. G. the woman and her ideas are inseparable. She does not exist for the amusement of upstarts, nor will she permit anybody to dictate to her. Keep your money."

I could not believe that Herman Miller had had anything to do with the miserable letter. I was sure that I should hear from him in due time. Of the amount he had given me I still had enough money left for several months. The two hundred dollars from Stone I had turned over to Eric to be used in connexion with the tunnel. I experienced a sense of relief that the matter was closed. When the allowance stopped and no word reached me from Herman, I concluded that he also had changed his mind. It was rather disappointing, but I was happy that I should no longer be dependent on moneyed people. Tchaikovsky was right,[1] after all; one could not devote himself to an ideal and to a profession at the same time. I would return to America to take up my work.

One evening as I was about to go with Hippolyte to an important committee session, the hotel maid handed me a visiting-card. I was overjoyed to see on it the name of Oscar Panizza,

whose brilliant writings in the *Armer Teufel* had delighted me
for years. Presently a tall, dark man entered, introducing himself as Panizza. He had learned through Dr. Eugene Schmidt of
my presence in Paris and was anxious to "meet Cassandra, our
dear Robert's friend." He asked me to spend the evening with
him and Dr. Schmidt. "We are going up to see Oscar Wilde[2]
first," he said, "and we want you to come with us. Afterwards
we will have dinner."

What a marvellous event to meet Panizza and Wilde the same
evening! In a flurry of anticipation I knocked at Hippolyte's
door to tell him about it. I found him pacing his room, waiting
for me in great irritation. "You don't mean you are not going to
the session!" he cried angrily. "You have promised, you are expected, you have undertaken work to do! You can meet Oscar
Wilde some other time, and Panizza too. Why must it be tonight?" In my excitement I had forgotten all about the session.
Of course, I could not go back on it. With heavy heart I went
downstairs to tell Panizza that I was not able to come that evening. Could we not meet tomorrow or the next day? We agreed
on the following Saturday, at luncheon. He would invite Dr.
Schmidt again, but he could not promise as to Oscar Wilde.
The latter was in poor health and not always able to be about;
but he would try his best to arrange a meeting.

On Friday Dr. Schmidt called to say that Panizza had left unexpectedly, but he was to return to Paris before long, and he
would see me then. The doctor must have read disappointment
on my face. "It is lovely outside," he remarked, "come for a
walk." I was grateful, sick with regret for having given up the
rare opportunity of meeting Oscar Wilde and of spending an
evening with Panizza.

During our walk in the Luxembourg I told the doctor of the
indignation I had felt at the conviction of Oscar Wilde. I had
pleaded his case against the miserable hypocrites who had sent
him to his doom. "You!" the doctor exclaimed in astonishment,
"why, you must have been a mere youngster then. How did you
dare come out in public for Oscar Wilde in puritan America?"
"Nonsense!" I replied; "no daring is required to protest against

a great injustice." The doctor smiled dubiously. "Injustice?" he repeated; "it wasn't exactly that from the legal point of view, though it may have been from the psychological." The rest of the afternoon we were engaged in a battle royal about inversion, perversion, and the question of sex variation. He had given much thought to the matter, but he was not free in his approach, and I suspected that he was somewhat scandalized that I, a young woman, should speak without reservations on such tabooed subjects. [. . .]

Some of the documents I had received to be read at the congress treated of the importance of the discussion of sex problems in the anarchist press and lectures. Kate Austen's paper was particularly strong, giving the history of the American movement for freedom in love. Kate was no mincer of words; frankly and directly she set forth her views of sex as a vital factor in life. Victor assured me that certain French comrades would not consent to have Kate's paper read at the congress; surely not to discuss it. I could hardly believe it. The French, of all people! Victor explained that not being puritanical does not always mean being free. "The French have not the same serious attitude towards sex as the idealists in America," he said. "They are cynical about it and cannot see more than the mere physical side. Our older French comrades have always loathed such an attitude, and in protest against it they have outdone the Puritans. They now fear that any discussion of sex would serve only to increase the misconceptions of anarchism." I was not convinced, but a week later Victor informed me that one group had definitely decided not to have the American reports dealing with sex read at the congress. They might be taken up at private gatherings, but not at public meetings with the press representatives present.

I protested, and declared that I would immediately get in touch with the comrades in the United States and ask them to relieve me of the credentials and the instructions they had given me. While realizing that the matter in question was only one of the numerous issues involved in anarchism, yet I could not co-operate with a congress that attempted to silence opinion or suppress views that failed to meet the approval of certain elements. [. . .]

Shortly afterwards I learned through Victor that the Neo-Malthusian Congress[3] was soon to meet in Paris. Its sessions would have to be secret because the French Government proscribed any organized attempt to limit offspring. Dr. Drysdale, the pioneer of birth limitation, and his sister were already in Paris, and other delegates were arriving from various countries. [. . .]

The Neo-Malthusian conference, having to meet under cover, every session in a different place, had a very small attendance, of not more than a dozen delegates. But what it lacked in numbers it made up in vital interest. [. . .] I thought of my former patients on the East Side and the blessing it would have meant to them if they could have procured the contraceptives described at these sessions. The delegates were amused when I told them of my vain efforts, as midwife, to find some way of helping the poor women in the States. They thought that, with Anthony Comstock supervising American morals, it would take many years before methods to prevent conception could be discussed openly in that country. I pointed out to them, however, that even in France they had to meet in secret and I assured them that I knew many people in America brave enough to do good, even if prohibited, work. At any rate, I decided to take the matter up on my return to New York. I was complimented on my attitude by the delegates and supplied with literature and contraceptives for my future work. [. . .]

One morning I was awakened at an early hour by Hippolyte violently knocking on my door. He entered excitedly, a French newspaper in his hand. He started to say something; his lips moved, but he could not utter a word. "What is it?" I cried in instinctive apprehension. "Why don't you speak?" "The tunnel, the tunnel!" he whispered hoarsely; "it has been discovered. It is in the paper."

With fainting heart I thought of Sasha, his terrible disappointment at the failure of the project, the disastrous consequences, his desperate position. Sasha again thrust back into the black hopelessness of eleven more years in his inferno. What now? What now? I must go back to America at once. I should have never gone away! I had failed Sasha, I felt; I had left him when he needed me most. Yes, I must go back to America as quickly as possible.

But that very afternoon a cable from Eric B. Morton prevented my putting the plan into immediate action. "Sudden illness. Work suspended. Sailing for France," the message read. I should have to await his arrival.

The nervous tension of the days that followed would have been beyond my endurance were it not for the intensive work I had to do. Within a fortnight Eric appeared. I hardly recognized him; the change he had undergone since I saw him in Pittsburgh was appalling. The big, strong viking had grown very thin, his face ashen and covered with blisters full of pus.

As soon as Tony finally got in touch with him, Eric related, he went to Pittsburgh to attend to the preliminary arrangements. His first impression of Tony was not very favourable. Tony seemed obsessed by his self-importance over his part in Sasha's projects. Sasha had devised a special cipher for underground communications, and Tony, being the only person able to read it, exploited the situation by arbitrary behaviour and directions. Not a mechanic, Tony had little idea of the difficulties involved in the construction of the tunnel, and the danger attending the digging of it. The house they had rented on Sterling Street was almost directly opposite the main gate of the prison and about two hundred feet distant from it. From the cellar of the house the tunnel had to be dug in a slightly circular line in the direction of the southern gate, then underneath it and into the prison yard towards an outhouse indicated by Sasha on his diagram. Sasha was to manage somehow to leave the cell-block, reach the outhouse unobserved, tear up its wooden flooring, and, opening the tunnel, crawl through into the cellar of the house. There he would find citizen's clothes, money, and cipher directions where to meet his friends. But work on the tunnel was taking more time and money than had been expected. Eric and the other comrades working on the tunnel came upon unexpected difficulties in the rocky formation of the soil in the neighbourhood of the prison wall. It was found necessary to dig underneath its foundations, and there Eric and his co-workers were nearly asphyxiated by poisonous fumes leaking into the tunnel from some unknown source. This unforeseen trouble resulted in much delay and involved the installation of machinery to supply fresh air to the men toiling prostrate in the narrow passage deep in the bowels of the earth. The sounds of digging might attract the attention of the alert look-outs on the prison wall, and Eric hit upon the idea of hiring a piano and inviting a woman friend of his, Kinsella, a splendid musician, to come to his aid. Her singing and playing masked the noises from below, and the guards on the wall greatly enjoyed the fine performances of Kinsella.

The "invention" was a most ingenious undertaking, but also very dangerous, requiring great engineering skill and the utmost care in avoiding the least suspicion on the part of the prison guards and the passers-by on the street. At the first sign of danger the pianist would press an electric button near at hand to warn the diggers underground to cease operations immediately. Then all would remain quiet till she would again burst out into song. The staccato piano chords would be the signal that all was well. "Digging under such conditions was no snap," Eric continued. "To save time and expense we had decided to make the tunnel very narrow, just wide enough for a person to crawl through. Our work therefore could not be carried on even by kneeling. We had to lie flat on the stomach and do the drilling with one hand. It was so exhausting it was impossible to keep at it more than half an hour at a time. Naturally progress was slow. But what was more exasperating was that Tony constantly shifted from one idea to another. We wanted to keep strictly to Sasha's plans. The latter insisted on it all the time and we felt that he, being on the inside, knew best. But Tony was bent on carrying out his own notions. Sasha evidently considered it too dangerous to give us directions even in his underground letters; he did so only in his cipher, which no one except Tony could read. Therefore we were compelled to take our instructions from Tony. Well, at last the tunnel was finished."

"And then—and then?" I cried unable to contain myself any longer.

"Why, didn't anyone write you?" Eric asked in surprise. "When Sasha tried to make his escape through the hole in the prison yard where the tunnel terminated, according to Tony's directions, he found it covered with a pile of bricks and stone. They were putting up a new building in the penitentiary and they had emptied a wagon-load of rock just over the spot that Tony had selected as the terminal of the tunnel. You can imagine how Sasha must have felt about it, and the danger to which he had exposed himself by escaping from the cell-house only to have to return again. The most dreadful thing about it was that, as we learned later, Sasha had repeatedly warned Tony against ending the tunnel in the middle of the prison yard, as Tony had proposed to him. Sasha was absolutely against it, knowing that it was bound to prove a failure. His original plan called for the tunnel to terminate in a deserted outhouse, about twenty feet from that hole. Believing that we had dug the tunnel to the point desired by Sasha, and that our work was completed, we departed for New York, only Tony remaining in Pittsburgh. Sasha was desperate at Tony's arbitrary change from his instructions. He insisted that the digging be continued farther and up to the outhouse, according to his diagram. Tony finally realized the fatal results of his mad obstinacy. He notified Sasha that his wishes would be carried out and he immediately left for New York to see us with a view to raising more money to complete the tunnel. Our house opposite the prison was left vacant. During Tony's absence children playing in the street somehow got into the cellar, discovered the secret passage, and notified their parents, among whom was the agent of the house. Strange to say, he proved also to be a guard in the Western Penitentiary."

I sat silent, crushed by the thought of what Sasha must have gone through during the weeks and months of suspense and anxious waiting for the completion of the tunnel, only to have all his hopes blighted almost in sight of liberty.

"The most amazing thing is," Eric continued, "that to this day the prison officials have been unable to find out for whom the tunnel was intended. The police departments of Pittsburgh and Allegheny, as well as the State authorities, agreed that the tunnel was one of the cleverest pieces of engineering they had ever seen. The Warden and the Board of Prison Inspectors suspect Sasha, but they can find no proof to support their charges, while the police claim the tunnel was intended for a certain Boyd, a prominent forger serving a long term. No clues have been discovered; but at any rate they put Sasha in solitary."

"In solitary!" I screamed. "No wonder I haven't heard from him for so long!" "Yes, he's under very severe punishment," Eric admitted. The purgatory Sasha had already endured, the ghastly years still ahead of him, flitted through my mind. "They will kill him!" I groaned. I knew they were killing him inch by inch, and here I was away in Paris and unable to help him, to do anything, anything! "Better a thousand times for me to have been in prison than to sit by and helplessly see them murdering Sasha!" I cried. "That wouldn't do Sasha any good," Eric retorted; "in fact, it would make it harder for him, harder to bear his lot. You must realize that, so why eat your heart out?"

Why, why? Could I explain what those years had been to me, ever since that black day in July 1892. Life is inexorable; it does not let you pause at any point. My own life had been crowded with events, following each in quick succession. There had been little time to indulge in retrospection of the past, but it had eaten into my consciousness, and nothing could ever still its gnawing. Yet life kept on its course. There was no cessation. [. . .]

Our scheduled congress did not take place. At the last moment the authorities prohibited the public gathering of foreign anarchists. We held some sessions, nevertheless, in private homes, in the environs of Paris. Under the circumstances and in view of the necessary secrecy of our proceedings, we had time to discuss only the most urgent problems. [. . .]

The inspiring atmosphere of our movement in Paris and my other delightful experiences in the city made me wish to prolong my stay. But it was time to leave. Our money was almost entirely exhausted. Besides, detectives had already been at the hotel looking for information about Mme Brady.[4] It was a wonder the police had not yet ordered me out of the country. Victor Dave suggested that it was because of the Exposition; the authorities wanted to avoid unpleasant publicity about foreigners. On an early morning, dark and drizzling, Eric, Hippolyte, and I drove to the railroad station. We were followed by several secret-service men in a cab and one on a bicycle. They waved good-bye to us as the train pulled out, but one of them we found in the compartment next to our coupé. He followed us to Boulogne, leaving only when we boarded the boat. [. . .]

My precious "baby" brother, tall and handsome, was at the dock to greet me. He was considerably surprised to see me return with a body-guard of two. We went immediately to a pawnshop to hock my clam-shell watch, for which I received ten whole dollars, enough to pay for a week's rent in a Clinton Street room and treat the company to dinner.

CHAPTER XXIII

[. . .] The most urgent necessity on my arrival in America was to secure employment. I had left my visiting-card with several of my medical friends, but weeks passed and not a single call came. [. . .]

At last on Christmas Eve Dr. Hoffmann sent for me. "The patient is a morphine addict," he informed me, "a very difficult and trying case. The night nurse had to be given a week off; she could not stand the strain. You have been called to substitute for a week." The prospect was not enticing, but I needed work.

It was almost midnight when I arrived with the doctor at the patient's house. In a large room on the second floor a woman was lying half dressed on the bed, in a stupor. Her face, framed in a mass of black hair, was white and she was breathing heavily. Looking about, I noticed on the wall the portrait of a heavy man peering at me out of small, hard eyes. I recognized the likeness as that of a person I had seen before, but I could not recollect where or under what circumstances. Dr. Hoffmann began giving me directions. The patient's name was Mrs. Spenser, he said. [. . .]

At the end of the third week Mrs. Spenser was able to go downstairs to her parlour. In the process of putting the sick-room in order I came across peculiar slips of paper marked: "Jeannette, 20 times; Marion, 16; Henriette, 12." There were about forty names of women, each checked off by a number. What a strange record! I thought. When about to join my patient in the sitting-room, I was arrested by a voice that I recognized as that of Mrs. Spenser's visitor. "MacIntyre was at the house again last night," I heard her say, "but none of the girls wanted him. Jeannette said she preferred twenty others to that filthy creature." Mrs. Spenser must have heard my step, for the conversation suddenly broke off, and she called through the door, "Is that you, Miss Goldman? Please come in." As I entered, the tea-tray I carried crashed to the ground, and I stood staring at a man sitting next to my patient on the sofa. It was the original of the portrait and I immediately recognized him as the detective-sergeant who had been instrumental in sending me to the penitentiary in 1893.

The slips of paper, the report I had just overheard—I understood it all in a flash. Spenser was the keeper of a "house," and the detective her paramour. I fled to the second storey, filled with the one idea of getting out and away from the house. Hastening downstairs with my suit-case, I saw Mrs. Spenser at the bottom of the stairs, hardly able to stand, her hands nervously gripping the banister. I realized that I could not leave her in that state; I was responsible to Dr. Hoffmann, for whom I must wait. I led Mrs. Spenser to her room and put her to bed.

She burst into hysterical sobbing, begging me not to go away and assuring me that I should never have to see the man again; she would even have his portrait removed. She admitted being the keeper of a house. "I dreaded to have you find it out," she said, "but I did think that Emma Goldman, the anarchist, would not condemn me for being a cog in a machine I did not create." Prostitution was not of her making, she argued; and since it existed, it did not matter who was "in charge." If not she, it would be someone else. She did not think keeping girls was any worse than underpaying them in factories; at least she had always been kind to them. I could inquire of them myself if I wished. She talked incessantly, weeping herself into exhaustion. I remained.

Mrs. Spenser's "reasons" did not influence me. I knew that everyone offered the same excuse for vile deeds, the policeman as well as the judge, the soldier as well as the highest war-lord; everybody who lives off the labour and degradation of others. I felt, however, that in my capacity as nurse I could not concern myself with the particular trade or occupation of my patients. I had to minister to their physical needs. Besides, I was not only a nurse, I was also an anarchist who knew the social factors behind human action. As such, even more than as a nurse I could not refuse her my services. [. . .]

While nursing Mrs. Spenser I became engaged in work preparatory to the projected visit of Peter Kropotkin. He had notified us that he was coming to America to deliver a series of lectures at the Lowell Institute on Ideals in Russian Literature, and that he would also be able to talk on anarchism if we wished it. [. . .]

From all parts of the city people came streaming in to Grand Central Palace to hear Peter Kropotkin on the first Sunday afternoon in May. For once even the papers were decent: they could not gainsay the man's charm, the power of his intellect, the simplicity and logic of his delivery and argumentation. In the audience was also Mrs. Spenser, completely carried away by the speaker.

A social evening was being prepared for Kropotkin, an unofficial affair, to enable him to meet the comrades and others in sympathy with our ideas. Mrs. Spenser inquired whether she would be admitted. "What if your friends find out who I am?" she asked anxiously. I assured her that my friends were in no way akin to Anthony Comstock and that no one would by word or deed make her feel out of place. She looked wonderingly at me out of her luminous eyes.

The evening before the social gathering several of the more intimate comrades dined with our beloved teacher. I related the story of Mrs. Spenser. Peter was much interested; she was a real human document, he thought. Indeed, he would meet my patient, and autograph a copy of his *Memoirs* for her, as she had requested. Before I left, Peter embraced me. "You are giving a convincing example of the beauty and humanity of our ideals," he remarked. I knew that he, so rich in compassion, understood why I had remained to care for the social pariah.

At last my patient was far enough advanced in her cure to dispense with me. I was eager to go on tour. The comrades in a number of cities had been urging me to come for lectures. [. . .]

Hippolyte had left for Chicago to work on the *Arbeiter Zeitung*. The offer of employment had come at a period when life had become insupportable to him, and he in turn had added much to my unhappiness. The thought that he would now have the soothing companionship of Max, as well as work he was fitted to do, gave me much consolation. I was planning to meet him in Chicago.

Ed came often to visit me or to invite me to dinner. He was charming and there was no sign of the storm that had tossed us about for seven years. It had given way to a calm friendship. He did not bring his little daughter[1] and I suspected that the mother must have objected to my seeing the child. Whether she also resented our companionship I had no way of knowing. Ed never mentioned her. When he learned that I was about to begin a lecture tour, he asked me again to act as the representative of his firm.[2] [. . .]

The subject of my lecture in Cleveland, early in May of that year, was Anarchism, delivered before the Franklin Liberal Club, a radical organization. During the intermission before the discussion I noticed a man looking over the titles of the pamphlets and books on sale near the platform. Presently he came over to me with the question: "Will you suggest something for me to read?" He was working in Akron, he explained, and he would have to leave before the close of the meeting. He was very young, a mere youth, of medium height, well built, and carrying himself very erect. But it was his face that held me, a most sensitive face, with a delicate pink complexion; a handsome face, made doubly so by his curly golden hair. Strength showed in his large blue eyes. I made a selection of some books for him, remarking that I hoped he would find in them what he was seeking. I returned to the platform to open the discussion and I did not see the young man again that evening, but his striking face remained in my memory.

The Isaaks had moved *Free Society* to Chicago, where they occupied a large house, which was the centre of the anarchist activities in that city. On my arrival there, I went to their home and immediately plunged into intense work that lasted eleven weeks. The summer heat became so oppressive that the rest of my tour had to be postponed until September. I was completely exhausted and badly in need of rest. Sister Helena had repeatedly asked me to come to her for a month, but I had not been able to spare the time before. Now was my opportunity. I would have a few weeks with Helena, the children of my two sisters, and Yegor, who was spending his vacation in Rochester. He had two college chums with him, he had written me; to make the circle of young people complete I invited Mary, the fourteen-year-old daughter of the Isaaks, to come with me for a holiday. I had earned some money on orders for Ed's firm and I could afford to play Lady Bountiful to the young people and grow younger with them.

On the day of our departure the Isaaks gave me a farewell luncheon. Afterwards, while I was busy packing my things, someone rang the bell. Mary Isaak came in to tell me that a young man, who gave his name as Nieman, was urgently asking to see me. I knew nobody by that name and I was in a hurry, about to leave for the station. Rather impatiently I requested Mary to inform the caller that I had no time at the moment, but that he could talk to me on my way to the station. As I left the house, I saw the visitor, recognizing him as the handsome chap of the golden hair who had asked me to recommend him reading-matter at the Cleveland meeting.

Hanging on to the straps on the elevated train, Nieman told me that he had belonged to a Socialist local in Cleveland, that he had found its members dull, lacking in vision and enthusiasm. He could not bear to be with them and he had left Cleveland and was now working in Chicago and eager to get in touch with anarchists.

At the station I found my friends awaiting me, among them Max. I wanted to spend a few minutes with him and I begged Hippolyte to take care of Nieman and introduce him to the comrades.

The Rochester youngsters took me to their hearts. My two sisters' children, my brother Yegor and his chums, and young Mary, all combined to fill the days with the loveliness only young ardent souls can give. It was a new and exhilarating experience, to which I completely abandoned myself. The roof of Helena's house became our garden and the gathering-place where my youthful friends confided to me their dreams and aspirations. [...]

My holiday in Rochester was somewhat marred by a notice in *Free Society* containing a warning against Nieman. It was written by A. Isaak, editor of the paper, and it stated that news had been received from Cleveland that the man had been asking questions that aroused suspicion, and that he was trying to get into the anarchist circles. The comrades in Cleveland had concluded that he must be a spy.

I was very angry. To make such a charge, on such flimsy grounds! I wrote Isaak at once, demanding more convincing proofs. He replied that, while he had no other evidence, he still felt that Nieman was untrustworthy because he constantly talked about acts of violence. I wrote another protest. The next issue of *Free Society* contained a retraction.

The Pan-American Exposition, held at Buffalo, interested me and I had long wanted also to see the Niagara Falls. But I could not leave my precious youngsters behind and I did not have enough money to take them with me. Dr. Kaplan, a Buffalo friend, who knew that I was holidaying with my family, solved our difficulties. He had asked me before to pay him a visit and bring my friends along. When I wrote him that my means would not allow such a luxury, he called me up on the long-distance telephone and offered to contribute forty dollars towards expenses and be our host for a week. In merry anticipation of the adventure, I took the older children to Buffalo. We were treated to a round of festivities, "did" the Falls, saw the Exposition, and enjoyed music and parties, as well as gatherings with comrades, at which the young generation participated in the discussions on a footing of equality.

On our return to Rochester I found two letters from Sasha. The first, *sub rosa,* dated July 10, had evidently been delayed in transmission. Its contents threw me into despair. It read:

> From the hospital. Just out of the strait jacket, after eight days.
> For over a year I was in the strictest solitary; for a long time mail and reading-matter were denied me. . . . I have passed through a great crisis. Two of my best friends died in a frightful manner. The death of Russell, especially, affected me. He was

very young, and my dearest and most devoted friend, and he died
a terrible death. The doctor charged the boy with shamming, but
now he says it was spinal meningitis. I cannot tell you the awful
truth—it was nothing short of murder, and my poor friend rotted
away by inches. When he died, they found his back one mass of
bedsores. If you could read the pitiful letters he wrote, begging to
see me and to be nursed by me! But the Warden wouldn't permit
it. In some manner his agony seemed to communicate itself to me,
and I began to experience the pains and symptoms that Russell
described in his notes. I knew it was my sick fancy; I strove
against it, but presently my legs showed signs of paralysis, and I
suffered excruciating pain in the spinal column, just like Russell.
I was afraid that I would be done to death like my poor friend. . . .
I was on the verge of suicide. I demanded to be relieved from the
cell, and the Warden ordered me punished. I was put in the strait
jacket. They bound my body in canvas, strapped my arms to the
bed, and chained my feet to the posts. I was kept that way eight
days, unable to move, rotting in my own excrement. Released
prisoners called the attention of our new Inspector to my case. He
refused to believe that such things were being done in the penitentiary. Reports spread that I was going blind and insane. Then the
Inspector visited the hospital and had me released from the jacket.

I am in pretty bad shape, but they have put me in the general
ward now, and I am glad of the chance to send you this note.

The fiends! It would have been a convenient way to send
Sasha into the madhouse or to make him take his own life. I
was sick with the thought that I had been living in a world of
dreams, youthful fancies and gaiety, while Sasha was undergoing hellish tortures. My heart cried out: "It isn't fair that he
alone should go on paying the price—it isn't fair!" My young
friends clustered around me in compassion. Stella's large eyes
were filled with tears. Yegor held out the other letter, saying:
"This is of a later date. It may have better news." I was almost
afraid to open it. I had barely read the first paragraph when I
cried in joy: "Children—Stella—Yegor! Sasha's term has been
commuted! Only five years more and he will be free! Think of

it, only five more years!" Breathlessly I went on reading. "I can visit him again!" I exclaimed. "The new Warden has restored his privileges—he can see his friends!" I ran about the room laughing and crying.

Helena rushed up the stairs, followed by Jacob. "What is it? What has happened?" I could only cry: "Sasha! My Sasha!" Gently my sister drew me down on the sofa, took the letter from my hand, and read it aloud in a trembling voice:

> *Direct to Box A 7.*
> *Allegheny City, Pa.*
> *July 25, 1901.*

DEAR FRIEND,—

I cannot tell you how happy I am to be allowed to write to you again. My privileges have been restored by our new Inspector, a very kindly man. He has relieved me from the cell, and now I am again on the range. The Inspector requested me to deny to my friends the reports which have recently appeared in the papers concerning my condition. I have not been well of late, but now I hope to improve. My eyes are very poor. The Inspector has given me permission to have a specialist examine them. Please arrange for it through our local comrades.

There is another piece of very good news, dear friend. A new commutation law has been passed, which reduces my sentence by 2½ years. It still leaves me a long time, of course; almost four years here, and another year in the workhouse. However, it is a considerable gain, and if I should not get into solitary again, I may—I am almost afraid to utter the thought—I may live to come out. I feel as if I am being resurrected. [. . .]

I was interrupted in this writing by being called out for a visit. I could hardly credit it: the first comrade I have been allowed to see in nine years! It was Harry Gordon, and I was so overcome by the sight of the dear friend, I could barely speak. He must have prevailed upon the new Inspector to issue a permit. The latter is now Acting War-

den, owing to the serious illness of Captain Wright. Perhaps
he will allow me to see my sister. Will you kindly communicate with her at once? Meantime I shall try to secure a
pass. With renewed hope, and always with green memory
of you,

                                                              ALEX

"At last, at last the miracle!" Helena exclaimed amid tears.
She had always admired Sasha. Since his imprisonment she had
taken a keen interest in his condition and in every bit of news
that had come out of his living grave. She had shared my grief,
and now she rejoiced with me over the wonderful news.

Once more I stood within the prison walls of the Western Penitentiary, with fast-beating heart straining to catch the sound of
Sasha's step. Nine years had passed since that November day in
1892 when for a fleeting moment I had been brought face to
face with him, only again to be wrenched away—nine years replete with the torment of endless time.

"Sasha!" I rushed forward with outstretched arms. I saw the
guard, beside him a man in a grey suit, the same greyness in his
face. Could it really be Sasha, so changed, so thin and wan? He
sat mute at my side, fumbling with the fob of my watch-chain. I
waited tensely, listening for a word. Sasha made no sound. Only
his eyes stared at me, sinking into my very soul. They were
Sasha's eyes, startled, tortured eyes. They made me want to
weep. I, too, was mute.

"Time's up!" The sound almost froze my blood. With heavy
steps I turned to the corridor, out of the enclosure, through the
iron gate into the street.

The same day I left Allegheny City for St. Louis, where I was
met by Carl Nold, whom I had not seen for three years. He was
the same kind Carl, eager for news of Sasha. He had already
learned of the unexpected change in his status and he was
highly elated over it. "So you have seen him!" he cried. "Tell
me quickly all about him."

I told him what I could of the ghastly visit. When I had finished
he said: "I am afraid your visit to the prison came too soon af-

ter his year in solitary. A whole year of enforced isolation, never a chance to exchange a word with another human being, or to hear a kindly voice. You grow numb and incapable of giving expression to your longing for human contact." I understood Sasha's fearful silence.

The following day, September 6, I canvassed every important stationery and novelty store in St. Louis for orders for Ed's firm, but I failed to interest anyone in my samples. Only in one store was I told to call the next day to see the boss. As I stood at a street-corner wearily waiting for a car, I heard a newsboy cry: "Extra! Extra! President McKinley shot!" I bought a paper, but the car was so jammed that it was impossible to read. Around me people were talking about the shooting of the President.

Carl had arrived at the house before me. He had already read the account. The President had been shot at the Exposition grounds in Buffalo by a young man by the name of Leon Czolgosz.[3] "I never heard the name," Carl said; "have you?" "No, never," I replied. "It is fortunate that you are here and not in Buffalo," he continued. "As usual, the papers will connect you with this act." "Nonsense!" I said, "the American press is fantastic enough, but it would hardly concoct such a crazy story."

The next morning I went to the stationery store to see the owner. After considerable persuasion I succeeded in getting an order amounting to a thousand dollars, the largest I had ever secured. Naturally I was very happy over it. While I was waiting for the man to fill out his order, I caught the headline of the newspaper lying on his desk: "ASSASSIN OF PRESIDENT McKINLEY AN ANARCHIST. CONFESSES TO HAVING BEEN INCITED BY EMMA GOLDMAN. WOMAN ANARCHIST WANTED."

By great effort I strove to preserve my composure, completed the business, and walked out of the store. At the next corner I bought several papers and went to a restaurant to read them. They were filled with the details of the tragedy, reporting also the police raid of the Isaak house in Chicago and the arrest of everyone found there. The authorities were going to hold the prisoners until Emma Goldman was found, the papers stated. Already two hundred detectives had been sent out throughout the country to track down Emma Goldman.

On the inside page of one of the papers was a picture of McKinley's slayer. "Why, that's Nieman!" I gasped.

When I was through with the papers, it became clear to me that I must immediately go to Chicago. The Isaak family, Hippolyte, our old comrade Jay Fox,[4] a most active man in the labour movement, and a number of others were being held without bail until I should be found. It was plainly my duty to surrender myself. I knew there was neither reason nor the least proof to connect me with the shooting. I would go to Chicago.

Stepping into the street, I bumped into "V.," the "rich man from New Mexico" who had managed my lecture in Los Angeles some years before. The moment he saw me he turned white with fear. "For God's sake, Emma, what are you doing here?" he cried in a quavering voice; "don't you know the police of the whole country are looking for you?" While he was speaking, his eyes roved uneasily over the street. It was evident he was panicky. I had to make sure that he would not disclose my presence in the city. Familiarly I took his arm and whispered: "Let's go to some quiet place."

Sitting in a corner, away from the other guests, I said to him: "Once you assured me of your undying love. You even made me an offer of marriage. It was only four years ago. Is anything left of that affection? If so, will you give me your word of honour that you will not breathe to anybody that you have seen me here? I do not want to be arrested in St. Louis—I intend to give Chicago that honour. Tell me quickly if I can depend on you to keep silent." He promised solemnly.

When we reached the street, he walked away in great haste. I was sure he would keep his word, but I knew that my former devotee was no hero.

When I told Carl I was going to Chicago, he said that I must be out of my senses. He pleaded with me to give up the idea, but I remained adamant. He left me to gather up a few trusted friends, whose opinion he knew I valued, hoping they would be able to persuade me not to surrender myself. They argued with me for hours, but they failed to change my decision. I told them jokingly that they had better give me a good send-off, as we probably should never again have an opportunity for a jolly evening together. They engaged a private dining-room at a restaurant, where we were treated to a Lucullan meal, and then they accompanied me to the Wabash Station, Carl having secured a sleeper for me.

In the morning the car was agog with the Buffalo tragedy, Czolgosz and Emma Goldman. "A beast, a bloodthirsty monster!" I heard someone say; "she should have been locked up long ago." "Locked up nothing!" another retorted; "she should be strung up to the first lamp-post."

I listened to the good Christians while resting in my berth. I chuckled to myself at the thought of how they would look if I were to step out and announce: "Here, ladies and gentlemen, true followers of the gentle Jesus, here is Emma Goldman!" But I did not have the heart to cause them such a shock and I remained behind my curtain.

Half an hour before the train pulled into the station I got dressed. I wore a small sailor hat with a bright blue veil, much in style then. I left my glasses off and pulled the veil over my face. The platform was jammed with people, among them several men who looked like detectives. I asked a fellow-passenger to be kind enough to keep an eye on my two suit-cases while I went in search of a porter. I finally got one, walking the whole length of the platform to my luggage, then back again with the porter to the check-room. Securing my receipt, I left the station.

The only person who knew of my coming was Max, to whom I had sent a cautious wire. I caught sight of him before he saw me. Passing him slowly, I whispered: "Walk towards the next street. I'll do the same." No one seemed to follow me. After some zigzagging with Max and changing half a dozen street-cars we reached the apartment where he and Millie ("Puck") lived. Both of them expressed the greatest anxiety about my safety, Max insisting that it was insanity to have come to Chicago. The situation, he said, was a repetition of 1887; the press and the police were thirsty for blood. "It's *your* blood they want," he repeated, while he and Millie implored me to leave the country.

I was determined to remain in Chicago. I realized that I could not stay at their home, nor with any other foreign comrades. I

had, however, American friends who were not known as anarchists. Max notified Mr. and Mrs. N., who I knew were very
fond of me, of my presence and they came at once. They also
were worried about me, but they thought I would be safe with
them. It was to be only for two days, as I was planning to give
myself up to the police as quickly as possible.

Mr. N., the son of a wealthy preacher, lived in a fashionable
neighbourhood. "Imagine anybody believing I would shelter
Emma Goldman," he said when we had arrived in his house.
Late in the afternoon, on Monday, when Mr. N. returned from
his office, he informed me that there was a chance to get five
thousand dollars from the Chicago *Tribune* for a scoop on an
interview. "Fine!" I replied; "we shall need money to fight my
case." We agreed that Mr. N. should bring the newspaper representative to his apartment the next morning, and then the
three of us would ride down to police headquarters together. In
the evening Max and Millie arrived. I had never before seen my
friends in such a state of nervous excitement. Max reiterated
that I must get away, else I was putting my head in the noose.
"If you go to the police, you will never come out alive," he
warned me. "It will be the same as with Albert Parsons. You
must let us get you over to Canada."

Millie took me aside. "Since Friday," she said, "Max has
not slept or taken food. He walks the floor all night and keeps
on saying: 'Emma is lost; they will kill her.'" She begged me to
soothe Max by promising him that I would escape to Canada,
even if I did not intend doing so. I consented and asked Max
to make the necessary arrangements to get me away. Overjoyed, he clasped me in his arms. We arranged for Max and
Millie to come the next morning with an outfit of clothes to
disguise me.

I spent the greater part of the night tearing up letters and papers and destroying what was likely to involve my friends. All
preparations completed, I went to sleep. In the morning Mrs. N.
left for her office, while her husband went to the Chicago *Tribune*. We agreed that if anyone called, I was to pretend to be
the maid.

About nine o'clock, while taking a bath, I heard a sound as if

someone was scratching on the window-sill. I paid no attention
to it at first. I finished my bath leisurely and began to dress.
Then came a crash of glass. I threw my kimono over me and
went into the dining-room to investigate. A man was clutching
the window-sill with one hand while holding a gun in the other.
We were on the third floor and there was no fire-escape. I called
out: "Look out, you'll break your neck!" "Why the hell don't
you open the door? Are you deaf?" He swung through the window and was in the room. I walked over to the entrance and
unlocked it. Twelve men, led by a giant, crowded into the
apartment. The leader grabbed me by the arm, bellowing:
"Who are you?" "I not speak English—Swedish servant-girl."
He released his hold and ordered his men to search the place.
Turning to me, he yelled: "Stand back! We're looking for
Emma Goldman." Then he held up a photo to me. "See this?
We want this woman. Where is she?" I pointed my finger at the
picture and said: "This woman I not see here. This woman
big—you look in those small boxes will not find her—she too
big." "Oh, shut up!" he bawled; "you can't tell what them an-
archists will do."

After they had searched the house, turning everything upside
down, the giant walked over to the book-shelves. "Hell, this is a
reg'lar preacher's house," he remarked: "look at them books. I
don't think Emma Goldman would be here." They were about
to leave when one of the detectives suddenly called: "Here,
Captain Schuettler, what about this?" It was my fountain-pen,
a gift from a friend, with my name on it. I had overlooked it.
"By golly, that's a find!" cried the Captain. "She must have been
here and she may come back." He ordered two of his men to remain behind.

I saw that the game was up. There was no sign of Mr. N. or
the *Tribune* man, and it could serve no purpose to keep the
farce up longer. "I am Emma Goldman," I announced.

For a moment Schuettler and his men stood there as if petrified. Then the Captain roared: "Well, I'll be damned! You're the
shrewdest crook I ever met! Take her, quick!"

When I stepped into the cab waiting at the curb, I saw N.
approaching in the company of the *Tribune* man. It was too late

for the scoop, and I did not want my host recognized. I pretended not to see them.

I had often heard of the third degree used by the police in various American cities to extort confessions, but I myself had never been subjected to it. I had been arrested a number of times since 1893; no violence, however, had ever been practised on me. On the day of my arrest, which was September 10, I was kept at police headquarters in a stifling room and grilled to exhaustion from 10.30 a.m. till 7 p.m. At least fifty detectives passed me, each shaking his fist in my face and threatening me with the direst things. One yelled: "You was with Czolgosz in Buffalo! I saw you myself, right in front of Convention Hall. Better confess, d'you hear?" Another: "Look here, Goldman, I seen you with that son of a bitch at the fair! Don't you lie now—I seen you, I tell you!" Again: "You've faked enough— you keep this up and sure's you're born you'll get the chair. Your lover has confessed. He said it was your speech made him shoot the President." I knew they were lying; I knew I had not been with Czolgosz except for a few minutes in Cleveland on May 5, and for half an hour in Chicago on July 12. Schuettler was most ferocious. His massive bulk towered above me, bellowing: "If you don't confess, you'll go the way of those bastard Haymarket anarchists."

I reiterated the story I had told them when first brought to police headquarters, explaining where I had been and with whom. But they would not believe me and kept on bullying and abusing me. My head throbbed, my throat and lips felt parched. A large pitcher of water stood on the table before me, but every time I stretched out my hand for it, a detective would say: "You can drink all you want, but first answer me. Where were you with Czolgosz the day he shot the President?" The torture continued for hours. Finally I was taken to the Harrison Street Police Station and locked in a barred enclosure, exposed to view from every side.

Presently the matron came to inquire if I wanted supper. "No, but water," I said, "and something for my head." She returned with a tin pitcher of tepid water, which I gulped down. She could give me nothing for my head except a cold compress. It proved very soothing, and I soon fell asleep.

I woke up with a burning sensation. A plain-clothes man held a reflector in front of me, close to my eyes. I leaped up and pushed him away with all my strength, crying: "You're burning my eyes!" "We'll burn more before we get through with you!" he retorted. With short intermissions this was repeated during three nights. On the third night several detectives entered my cell. "We've got the right dope on you now," they announced; "it was you who financed Czolgosz and you got the money from Dr. Kaplan in Buffalo. We have him all right, and he's confessed everything. Now what you got to say?" "Nothing more than I have already said," I repeated; "I know nothing about the act."

Since my arrest I had had no word from my friends, nor had anyone come to see me. I realized that I was being kept *incommunicado*. I did get letters, however, most of them unsigned. "You damn bitch of an anarchist," one of them read, "I wish I could get at you. I would tear your heart out and feed it to my dog." "Murderous Emma Goldman," another wrote, "you will burn in hell-fire for your treachery to our country." A third cheerfully promised: "We will cut your tongue out, soak your carcass in oil, and burn you alive." The description by some of the anonymous writers of what they would do to me sexually offered studies in perversion that would have astounded authorities on the subject. The authors of the letters nevertheless seemed to me less contemptible than the police officials. Daily I was handed stacks of letters that had been opened and read by the guardians of American decency and morality. At the same time messages from my friends were withheld from me. It was evident that my spirit was to be broken by such methods. I decided to put a stop to it. The next time I was given one of the opened envelopes, I tore it up and threw the pieces into the detective's face.

On the fifth day after my arrest I received a wire. It was from Ed, promising the backing of his firm. "Do not hesitate to use our name. We stand by you to the last." I was glad of the assurance, because it relieved me of the need of keeping silent about my movements on business for Ed's house.

The same evening Chief of Police O'Neill of Chicago came to my cell.[5] He informed me that he would like to have a quiet talk with me. "I have no wish to bully or coerce you," he said; "perhaps I can help you." "It would indeed be a strange experience to have help from a chief of police," I replied; "but I am quite willing to answer your questions." He asked me to give him a detailed account of my movements from May 5, when I had first met Czolgosz, until the day of my arrest in Chicago. I gave him the requested information, but without mentioning my visit to Sasha or the names of the comrades who had been my hosts. As there was no longer any need of shielding Dr. Kaplan, the Isaaks, or Hippolyte, I was in a position to give practically a complete account. When I concluded—what I said being taken down in shorthand—Chief O'Neill remarked: "Unless you're a very clever actress, you are certainly innocent. I think you are innocent, and I am going to do my part to help you out." I was too amazed to thank him; I had never before heard such a tone from a police officer. At the same time I was sceptical of the success of his efforts, even if he should try to do something for me.

Immediately following my conference with the Chief I became aware of a decided change in my treatment. My cell door was left unlocked day and night, and I was told by the matron that I could stay in the large room, use the rocking-chair and the table there, order my own food and papers, receive and send out mail. I began at once to lead the life of a society lady, receiving callers all day long, mostly newspaper people who came not so much for interviews as to talk, smoke, and relate funny stories. Others, again, came out of curiosity. Some women reporters brought gifts of books and toilet articles. Most attentive was Katherine Leckie, of the Hearst papers. She possessed a better intellect than Nelly Bly,[6] who used to visit me in the Tombs in 1893, and had a much finer social feeling. A strong and ardent feminist, she was at the same time devoted to the cause of labour. Katherine Leckie was the first to take my story of the third degree. She became so outraged at hearing it that she undertook to canvass the various women's organizations in order to induce them to take the matter up. [. . .]

Another visitor was a lawyer from Clarence Darrow's office.[7] He had come to warn me that I was hurting my case by my persistent defence of Czolgosz; the man was crazy and I should admit it. "No prominent attorney will accept your defence if you ally yourself with the assassin of the President," he assured me; "in fact, you stand in imminent danger of being held as an accessory to the crime." I demanded to know why Mr. Darrow himself did not come if he was so concerned, but his representative was evasive. He continued to paint my case in sinister colours. My chances of escape were few at best, it seemed, too few for me to allow any sentimentality to aggravate it. Czolgosz was insane, the man insisted; everybody could see it, and, besides, he was a bad sort to have involved me, a coward hiding behind a woman's skirts.

His talk was repugnant to me. I informed him that I was not willing to swear away the reason, character, or life of a defenceless human being and that I wanted no assistance from his chief. I had never met Darrow, but I had long known of him as a brilliant lawyer, a man of broad social views, an able writer and lecturer. According to the papers he had interested himself in the anarchists arrested in the raid, especially the Isaaks. It seemed strange that he should send me such reprehensible advice, that he should expect me to join the mad chorus howling for the life of Czolgosz.

The country was in a panic. Judging by the press, I was sure that it was the people of the United States and not Czolgosz that had gone mad. Not since 1887 had there been evidenced such lust for blood, such savagery of vengeance. "Anarchists must be exterminated!" the papers raved; "they should be dumped into the sea; there is no place for the vultures under our flag. Emma Goldman has been allowed to ply her trade of murder too long. She should be forced to share the fate of her dupes."

It was a repetition of the dark Chicago days. Fourteen years, years of painful growth, yet fascinating and fruitful years. And now the end! The end? I was only thirty-two and there was yet so much, so very much, undone. And the boy in Buffalo—his life had scarce begun. What was his life, I wondered; what the forces that drove him to this doom? "I did it for the working people," he was reported to have said. The people! Sasha also had done something for the people; and our brave Chicago martyrs, and the others in every land and time. But the people are asleep; they remain indifferent. They forge their own chains and do the bidding of their masters to crucify their Christs.

CHAPTER XXIV

Buffalo was pressing for my extradition, but Chicago asked for authentic data on the case. I had already been given several hearings in court, and on each occasion the District Attorney from Buffalo had presented much circumstantial evidence to induce the State of Illinois to surrender me. But Illinois demanded direct proofs. There was a hitch somewhere that helped to cause more delays. I thought it likely that Chief of Police O'Neill was behind the matter.

The Chief's attitude towards me had changed the behaviour of every officer in the Harrison Street Police Station. The matron and the two policemen assigned to watch my cell began to lavish attentions on me. The officer on night duty now often appeared with his arms full of parcels, containing fruit, candy, and drinks stronger than grape-juice. [. . .]

Even some of the reporters did not seem to be losing sleep over the case. One of them was quite amazed when I assured him that in my professional capacity I would take care of McKinley if I were called upon to nurse him, though my sympathies were with Czolgosz. [. . . .]

"I don't get you, you're beyond me," he reiterated. The next day there appeared these headlines in one of the papers: "EMMA GOLDMAN WANTS TO NURSE PRESIDENT; SYMPATHIES ARE WITH SLAYER."

Buffalo failed to produce evidence to justify my extradition. Chicago was getting weary of the game of hide-and-seek. The authorities would not turn me over to Buffalo, yet at the same time they did not feel like letting me go entirely free. By way of compromise I was put under twenty-thousand-dollar bail. The

Isaak group had been put under fifteen-thousand-dollar bail. I knew that it would be almost impossible for our people to raise a total of thirty-five thousand dollars within a few days. I insisted on the others being bailed out first. Thereupon I was transferred to the Cook County Jail. [. . .]

Monday morning, flanked by a heavily armed guard, I was led out of the station-house. [. . .] Ahead of me were two handcuffed prisoners roughly hustled about by the officers. When we reached the patrol wagon, surrounded by more police, their guns ready for action, I found myself close to the two men. Their features could not be distinguished: their heads were bound up in bandages, leaving only their eyes free. As they stepped to the patrol wagon, a policeman hit one of them on the head with his club, at the same time pushing the other prisoner violently into the wagon. They fell over each other, one of them shrieking with pain. I got in next, then turned to the officer. "You brute," I said, "how dare you beat that helpless fellow?" The next thing I knew, I was sent reeling to the floor. He had landed his fist on my jaw, knocking out a tooth and covering my face with blood. Then he pulled me up, shoved me into the seat, and yelled: "Another word from you, you damned anarchist, and I'll break every bone in your body!"

I arrived at the office of the county jail with my waist and skirt covered with blood, my face aching fearfully. No one showed the slightest interest or bothered to ask how I came to be in such a battered condition. They did not even give me water to wash up. For two hours I was kept in a room in the middle of which stood a long table. Finally a woman arrived who informed me that I would have to be searched. "All right, go ahead," I said. "Strip and get on the table," she ordered. I had been repeatedly searched, but I had never before been offered such an insult. "You'll have to kill me first, or get your keepers to put me on the table by force," I declared; "you'll never get me to do it otherwise." She hurried out, and I remained alone. After a long wait another woman came in and led me upstairs, where the matron of the tier took charge of me. She was the first to inquire what was the matter with me. After assigning me to a cell she brought a hot-water bottle and suggested that I lie down and get some rest.

The following afternoon Katherine Leckie visited me. I was taken into a room provided with a double wire screen. It was semi-dark, but as soon as Katherine saw me, she cried: "What on God's earth has happened to you? Your face is all twisted!" No mirror, not even of the smallest size, being allowed in the jail, I was not aware how I looked, though my eyes and lips felt queer to the touch. I told Katherine of my encounter with the policeman's fist. She left swearing vengeance and promising to return after seeing Chief O'Neill. Towards evening she came back to let me know that the Chief had assured her the officer would be punished if I would identify him among the guards of the transport. I refused. I had hardly looked at the man's face and I was not sure I could recognize him. Moreover, I told Katherine, much to her disappointment, that the dismissal of the officer would not restore my tooth; neither would it do away with police brutality. "It is the system I am fighting, my dear Katherine, not the particular offender," I said. But she was not convinced; she wanted something done to arouse popular indignation against such savagery. "Dismissing wouldn't be enough," she persisted; "he should be tried for assault." [. . .]

One evening, while engrossed in a book, I was surprised by several detectives and reporters. "The President has just died," they announced. "How do you feel about it? Aren't you sorry?" "Is it possible," I asked, "that in the entire United States only the President passed away on this day? Surely many others have also died at the same time, perhaps in poverty and destitution, leaving helpless dependents behind. Why do you expect me to feel more regret over the death of McKinley than of the rest?"

The pencils went flying. "My compassion has always been with the living," I continued; "the dead no longer need it. No doubt that is the reason why you all feel so sympathetic to the dead. You know that you'll never be called upon to make good your protestations." "Damned good copy," a young reporter exclaimed, "but I think you're crazy."

I was glad when they left. My thoughts were with the boy in Buffalo, whose fate was now sealed. What tortures of mind and body were still to be his before he would be allowed to breathe his last! How would he meet the supreme moment? There was something strong and determined about his eyes, emphasized by his very sensitive face. I had been struck by his eyes on first seeing him at my lecture in Cleveland. Was the idea of his act already with him then or had some particular thing happened since that compelled his deed? What could it have been? "I did it for the people," he had said. I paced my cell trying to analyse the probable motives that had decided the youth in his purpose.

Suddenly a thought flitted through my mind—that notice by Isaak in *Free Society*!—the charge of "spy" against Nieman because he had "asked suspicious questions and tried to get into the anarchist ranks." I had written Isaak at the time, demanding proofs for the outrageous accusation. As a result of my protest *Free Society* had contained a retraction to the effect that a mistake had been made. It had relieved me and I had given the matter no further thought. Now the whole situation appeared in a new light, clear and terrible. Czolgosz must have read the charge; it must have hurt him to the quick to be so cruelly misjudged by the very people to whom he had come for inspiration. I recalled his eagerness to secure the right kind of books. It was apparent that he had sought in anarchism a solution of the wrongs he saw everywhere about him. No doubt it was that which had induced him to call on me and later on the Isaaks. Instead of finding help the poor youth saw himself attacked. Was it that experience, fearfully wounding his spirit, that had led to his act? There must also have been other causes, but perhaps his great urge had been to prove that he was sincere, that he felt with the oppressed, that he was no spy.

But why had he chosen the President rather than some more direct representative of the system of economic oppression and misery? Was it because he saw in McKinley the willing tool of Wall Street and of the new American imperialism that flowered under his administration? One of its first steps had been the annexation of the Philippines, an act of treachery to the people whom America had pledged to set free during the Spanish War. McKinley also typified a hostile and reactionary attitude to labour: he had repeatedly sided with the masters by sending troops into strike regions. All these circumstances, I felt, must have exerted a decisive influence upon the impressionable Leon, finally crystallizing in his act of violence.

Throughout the night thoughts of the unfortunate boy kept crowding in my mind. In vain I sought to divest myself of the harassing reflections by reading. The dawning day still found me pacing my cell, Leon's beautiful face, pale and haunted, before me.

Again I was taken to court for a hearing and again the Buffalo authorities failed to produce evidence to connect me with Czolgosz's act. The Buffalo representative and the Chicago judge sitting on the case kept up a verbal fight for two hours, at the end of which Buffalo was robbed of its prey. I was set free. [. . .]

Upon my release I was met by Max, Hippolyte, and other friends, with whom I went to the Isaak home. The charges against the comrades arrested in the Chicago raids had also been dismissed. Everyone was in high spirits over my escape from what they had all believed to be a fatal situation. "We can be grateful to whatever gods watch over you, Emma," said Isaak, "that you were arrested here and not in New York." "The gods in this case must have been Chief of Police O'Neill," I said laughingly. "Chief O'Neill!" my friends exclaimed; "what did he have to do with it?" I told them about my interview with him and his promise of help. Jonathan Crane, a journalist friend of ours present, broke out into uproarious laughter. "You are more naïve than I should have expected, Emma Goldman," he said; "it wasn't you O'Neill cared a damn about! it was his own schemes. Being on the *Tribune,* I happen to know the inside story of the feud in the police department." Crane then related the efforts of Chief O'Neill to put several captains in the penitentiary for perjury and bribery. "Nothing could have come more opportunely for those blackguards than the cry of anarchy," he explained; "they seized upon it as the police did in 1887; it was their chance to pose as saviours of the country and incidentally to whitewash themselves. But it wasn't to O'Neill's interest to let those birds pose as heroes and get back into the department. That's why he worked for you. He's a shrewd Irishman. Just the same, we may be glad that the quarrel brought us back our Emma."

I asked my friends their opinion as to how the idea of connecting my name with Czolgosz had originated. "I refuse to believe that the boy made any kind of a confession or involved me in any way," I stated; "I cannot think that he was capable of inventing something which he must have known might mean my death. I'm convinced that no one with such a frank face could be so craven. It must have come from some other source."

"It did!" Hippolyte declared emphatically. "The whole dastardly story was started by a *Daily News* reporter who used to hang round here pretending to sympathize with our ideas. Late in the afternoon of September 6 he came to the house. He wanted to know all about a certain Czolgosz or Nieman. Had we associated with him? Was he an anarchist? And so forth. Well, you know what I think of reporters—I wouldn't give him any information. But unfortunately Isaak did."

"What was there to hide?" Isaak interrupted. "Everybody about here knew that we had met the man through Emma, and that he used to visit us. Besides, how was I to know that the reporter was going to fabricate such a lying story?"

I urged the Chicago comrades to consider what could be done for the boy in the Buffalo jail. We could not save his life, but we could at least try to explain his act to the world. [. . .]

"Leon Czolgosz and other men of his type," I wrote in my article [in *Free Society*], entitled: "The Tragedy of Buffalo," "far from being depraved creatures of low instincts are in reality supersensitive beings unable to bear up under too great social stress. They are driven to some violent expression, even at the sacrifice of their own lives, because they cannot supinely witness the misery and suffering of their fellows. The blame for such acts must be laid at the door of those who are responsible for the injustice and inhumanity which dominate the world." [. . .]

The police and the press were continuing their hunt for anarchists throughout the country. Meetings were broken up and innocent people arrested. In various places persons suspected of being anarchists were subjected to violence. In Pittsburgh our good friend Harry Gordon[1] was dragged out into the street and

nearly lynched. A rope already around his neck, he was saved at
the last moment by some bystanders who were touched by the
pleading of Mrs. Gordon and her two children. In New York the
office of the *Freie Arbeiter Stimme* was attacked by a mob,
the furniture demolished, and the type destroyed. In no case did
the police interfere with the doings of the patriotic ruffians. Johann Most was arrested for an article in the *Freiheit* reproducing an essay on political violence by Karl Heinzen,[2] the famous
'48 revolutionist, then dead many years. Most was out on bail
awaiting his trial. The German comrades in Chicago arranged
an affair to raise funds for his defence and invited me to speak.
Our feud of 1892 was a matter of the past to me. Most was
again in the clutches of the police, in danger of being sent to
Blackwell's Island, and I gladly consented to do all I could for
him. [. . .]

On my way back to New York I stopped off in Rochester.
Arriving in the evening, I walked to Helena's place in order to
avoid recognition. A policeman was stationed at the house, but
he did not know me. Everyone gasped when I made my appearance. "How did you get by?" Helena cried; "didn't you see the
officer at the door?" "Indeed I saw him, but he evidently didn't
see me," I laughed. "Don't you folks worry about any policeman; better give me a bath," I cried lightly. My nonchalance
dispelled the family's nervous tension. Everybody laughed and
Helena clung to me in unchanged love.

All through my incarceration my family had been very devoted to me. They had sent me telegrams and letters, offering
money for my defence and any other help I might need. Not a
word had they written about the persecution they had been subjected to on my account. They had been pestered to distraction
by reporters and kept under surveillance by the authorities. My
father had been ostracized by his neighbours and had lost many
customers at his little furniture store. At the same time he had
also been excommunicated from the synagogue. My sister Lena,
though in poor health, had also been given no peace. She had
been terrorized by the police ordering Stella to appear at headquarters, where they had kept the child the whole day, plying
her with questions about her aunt Emma Goldman. Stella had

bravely refused to answer, defiantly proclaiming her pride and faith in her *Tante* Emma. Her courage, combined with her youth and beauty, had won general admiration, Helena said. [. . .]

The encouraging telegram I had received in Chicago from Ed had been followed by a number of letters assuring me that I could count on him for whatever I might need: money, help and advice, and, above all, his friendship. It was good to know that Ed remained so staunch. When we met upon my return to New York, he offered me the use of his apartment while he and his family would be staying with friends. "You won't find much changed in my place," he remarked; "all your things are intact in the room that is my sanctum, where I often dream of our life together." I thanked him, but I could not accept his generous proposal. He was too tactful to press the matter, except to inform me that his firm owed me several hundred dollars in commissions.

"I need the money badly," I confided to Ed, "to send somebody to Buffalo to see Czolgosz. Possibly something can be done for him. We also ought to organize a mass meeting at once." He stared at me in bewilderment. "My dear," he said, shaking his head, "you are evidently not aware of the panic in the city. No hall in New York can be had and no one except yourself would be willing to speak for Czolgosz." "But no one is expected to eulogize his act!" [. . .]

A trusted person was dispatched to Buffalo, but he soon returned without having been able to visit Czolgosz. He reported that no one was permitted to see him. A sympathetic guard had disclosed to our messenger that Leon had repeatedly been beaten into unconsciousness. His physical appearance was such that no outsider was admitted, and for the same reason he could not be taken to court. My friend further reported that, notwithstanding all the torture, Czolgosz had made no confession whatever and had involved no one in his act. A note had been sent in to Leon through the friendly guard.

I learned that an effort had been made in Buffalo to secure an attorney for Czolgosz, but no one would accept his defence. That made me even more determined to raise my voice in behalf of the poor unfortunate, denied and forsaken by everyone. Before long, however, I became convinced that Ed had been right. No one among the English-speaking radical groups could be induced to participate in a meeting to discuss the act of Leon Czolgosz. Many were willing to protest against my arrest, to condemn the third degree and the treatment I had received. But they would have nothing to do with the Buffalo case. Czolgosz was not an anarchist, his deed had done the movement an irreparable injury, our American comrades insisted. [. . .]

In desperation I clung to the hope that by perseverance and appeals I should be able to rally some public-spirited Americans to express ordinary human sympathy for Leon Czolgosz, even if they felt that they must repudiate his act. Every day brought more disappointment and heart-ache. I was compelled to face the fact that I had been fighting against an epidemic of abject fear that could not be overcome.

The tragedy in Buffalo was nearing its end. Leon Czolgosz, still ill from the maltreatment he had endured, his face disfigured and head bandaged, was supported in court by two policemen. In its all-embracing justice and mercy the Buffalo court had assigned two lawyers to his defence. What if they did declare publicly that they were sorry to have to plead the case of such a depraved criminal as the assassin of "our beloved" President! They would do their duty just the same! They would see to it that the rights of the defendant were protected in court.

The last act was staged in Auburn Prison. It was early dawn, October 29, 1901. The condemned man sat strapped to the electric chair. The executioner stood with his hand on the switch, awaiting the signal. A warden, impelled by Christian mercy, makes a last effort to save the sinner's soul, to induce him to confess. Tenderly he says: "Leon, my boy, why do you shield that bad woman, Emma Goldman? She is not your friend. She has denounced you as a loafer, too lazy to work. She said you had always begged money from her. Emma Goldman has betrayed you, Leon. Why should you shield her?"

Breathless silence, seconds of endless time. It fills the death

chamber, creeps into the hearts of the spectators. At last a muf-
fled sound, an almost inaudible voice from under the black mask.

"It doesn't matter what Emma Goldman has said about me.
She had nothing to do with my act. I did it alone. I did it for the
American people."

A silence more terrible than the first. A sizzling sound—the
smell of burnt flesh—a final agonized twitch of life.

CHAPTER XXV

It was bitter hard to face life anew. In the stress of the past weeks I had forgotten that I should again have to take up the struggle for existence. It was doubly imperative; I needed forgetfulness. Our movement had lost its appeal for me; many of its adherents filled me with loathing. They had been flaunting anarchism like a red cloth before a bull, but they ran to cover at his first charge. I could no longer work with them. Still more harrowing was the gnawing doubt of the values I had so fervently believed in. No, I could not continue in the movement. I must first take stock of my own self. Intensive work in my profession, I felt, was the only refuge. It would fill the void and make me forget.

I had lost my identity; I had assumed a fictitious name, for no landlord was willing to lodge me, and most of my erstwhile comrades and friends proved equally brave. [. . .] The struggle and disappointment of the past twelve years had taught me that consistency is only skin-deep in most people. As if it mattered what name you took, as long as you kept your integrity. Indeed, I would take another name, the most common and inoffensive I could think of. I became Miss E. G. Smith.

I met with no further objections from landlords. I rented a flat on First Street; Yegor and his chum Dan moved in with me, our furniture purchased on the instalment plan. Thereupon I went out to call on my physicians, to apprise them of the fact that henceforth they could recommend me as E. G. Smith. [. . .]

It was evident my prospects were not very bright. I knew it involved a desperate struggle to win new ground, but I was determined to start all over again. I would not submit passively to the forces that were trying to crush me. "I must, I will, go on, for the sake of Sasha and of my brother, who need me," I told myself.

Sasha! I had not heard from him for nearly two months, and I also had been unable to write him. While under arrest, I could not express myself freely, and the last month had been too dreary and depressing. I was sure that of all people my dear Sasha would understand the social meaning of the Buffalo shot, and that he would appreciate the boy's integrity. Dear Sasha! Since the unexpected commutation of his prison term his spirit had grown buoyant. "Only five years more," he had written in his last letter; "just think, dear friend, only five years more!" To see him free at last, resurrected; what were all my hardships compared with that moment? In that hope I plodded on. Occasionally I was called to a case; at other times I had orders for dresses. I seldom went out. We could not afford music or theatres, and I dreaded to appear at public meetings. [. . .]

I was again compelled to take piece-work from the factory. I had advanced in the trade; I was sewing gaudy silk morning gowns now. The many ruffles, ribbons, and laces required painstaking effort, affecting my lacerated nerves until I felt like screaming. [. . .]

The thought of a lecture or meeting had become repugnant to me. Even concerts and theatres had lost their attraction because of my fear, grown almost to an obsession, of meeting people or being recognized. Dejection was upon me, the feeling that my existence had lost its meaning and was bereft of content.

Life dragged on with its daily cares and worries. By far the greatest of them was Sasha's reported condition. Friends in Pittsburgh had written that he was again being persecuted by the prison authorities, and that his health was breaking down. At last, on December 31, a letter arrived from him. No greater New Year's gift could have come to me. Yegor knew that I liked to be alone on such occasions, and he thoughtfully tiptoed out of the room.

I pressed my lips to the precious envelope, opening it with trembling fingers. It was a long *sub rosa* letter, dated December

20 and written on several slips of paper in the very small script Sasha had acquired, each word standing out clear and distinct.

"I know how your visit and my strange behaviour must have affected you," he wrote. "The sight of your face after all these years completely unnerved me. I could not think, I could not speak. It was as if all my dreams of freedom, the whole world of the living, were concentrated in the shiny little trinket that was dangling from your watch-chain. I couldn't take my eyes off it, I couldn't keep my hand from playing with it. It absorbed my whole being. And all the time I felt how nervous you were at my silence, and I couldn't utter a word."

The frightful months since my visit to Sasha had obscured the poignancy of my disappointment at that time. His lines again revived it. But his letter showed how closely he had followed the events. "If the press mirrored the sentiments of the people," he continued, "the nation must have suddenly relapsed into cannibalism. There were moments when I was in mortal dread for your very life, and for the safety of the other arrested comrades. . . . Your attitude of proud self-respect and your admirable self-control contributed much to the fortunate outcome. I was especially moved by your remark that you would faithfully nurse the wounded man, if he required your services, but that the poor boy, condemned and deserted by all, needed and deserved your sympathy and aid more than the President. More strikingly than your letters, that remark discovered to me the great change wrought in us by the ripening years. Yes, in us, in both, for my heart echoed your beautiful sentiment. How impossible such a thought would have been to us in the days of a decade ago! We should have considered it treason to the spirit of revolution; it would have outraged all our traditions even to admit the humanity of an official representative of capitalism. Is it not significant that we two—you living in the very heart of anarchist thought and activity, and I in the atmosphere of absolute suppression and isolation— should have arrived at the same evolutionary point after ten years of divergent paths?"

The dear, faithful pal—how big and brave it was of him so frankly to admit the change! As I read on I grew even more astounded at the amount of knowledge Sasha had acquired since his imprisonment. Works of science, philosophy, economics, even metaphysics—he had evidently read a great many of them, critically studied and digested them. His letter stirred a hundred memories of the past, of our common life, our love, our work. I was lost in recollections; time and space disappeared; the intervening years became blotted out, and I relived the past. My hands caressed the letter, my eyes dreamily wandering over the lines. Then the word "Leon" fastened my gaze, and I continued to read:

"I have read of the beautiful personality of the youth, of his inability to adapt himself to brutal conditions, and of the rebellion of his soul. It throws a significant light upon the causes of the *Attentat*. Indeed, it is at once the greatest tragedy of martyrdom and the most terrible indictment of society that it forces the noblest men and women to shed human blood, though their souls shrink from it. The more imperative it is that drastic methods of this character be resorted to only as a last extremity. To prove of value they must be motived by social rather than individual necessity and be aimed against a direct and immediate enemy of the people. The significance of such a deed is understood by the popular mind, and in that alone lies the propagandistic, educational import of an *Attentat*, except if it is exclusively an act of terrorism."

The letter dropped from my hand. What could Sasha mean? Did he imply that McKinley was not "an immediate enemy of the people"? Not a subject for an *Attentat* of "propagandistic, educational import"? I was bewildered. Had I read right? There was still another passage: "I do not believe that Leon's deed was terroristic, and I doubt whether it was educational, because the social necessity for its performance was not manifest. That you may not misunderstand, I repeat: as an expression of personal revolt it was inevitable, and in itself an indictment of existing conditions. But the background of social necessity was lacking, and therefore the value of the act was to a great extent nullified."

The letter fell to the floor, leaving me in a daze. A strange, dry voice screamed out: "Yegor! Yegor!"

My brother ran in. "What has happened, dear? You're all trembling. What's the matter?" he cried in alarm. "The letter!" I whispered hoarsely. "Read it; tell me if I've gone mad."

"A beautiful letter," I heard him say, "a human document, though Sasha does not see social necessity in Czolgosz's act."

"But how can Sasha," I cried in desperation, "he of all people in the world—himself misunderstood and repudiated by the very workers he had wanted to help—how can *he* misunderstand so?"

Yegor tried to soothe me, to explain what Sasha had meant by "the necessary social background." Picking up another slip of the letter, he began reading to me:

"The scheme of political subjection is subtle in America. Though McKinley was the chief representative of our modern slavery, he could not be considered in the light of a direct and immediate enemy of the people. In an absolutism the autocrat is visible and tangible. The real despotism of republican institutions is far deeper, more insidious, because it rests on the popular delusion of self-government and independence. That is the source of democratic tyranny, and as such it cannot be reached with a bullet. In modern capitalism economic exploitation rather than political oppression is the real enemy of the people. Politics is but its handmaid. Hence the battle is to be waged in the economic rather than the political field. It is therefore that I regard my own act as far more significant and educational than Leon's. It was directed against a tangible, real oppressor, visualized as such by the people."

Suddenly a thought struck me. Why, Sasha is using the same arguments against Leon that Johann Most had urged against Sasha. Most had proclaimed the futility of individual acts of violence in a country devoid of proletarian consciousness and he had pointed out that the American worker did not understand the motives of such deeds. No less than I had Sasha then considered Most a traitor to our cause as well as towards himself. I had fought Most bitterly for it—Most, who had been my teacher, my great inspiration. And now Sasha, still believing in acts of violence, was denying "social necessity" to Leon's deed.

The farce of it—the cruel, senseless farce! I felt as if I had lost Sasha—I broke down in uncontrollable sobbing. [. . .]

I wrote Sasha several times pointing out that anarchism does not direct its forces against economic injustices only, but that it includes the political as well. His replies only emphasized the wide difference in our view-points. They increased my misery and made me realize the futility of continuing the discussion. In despair I stopped writing.

After the death of McKinley the campaign against anarchism and its adherents continued with increased venom. The press, the pulpit, and other public mouthpieces were frantically vying with each other in their fury against the common enemy. Most ferocious was Theodore Roosevelt, the new-fledged President of the United States. As Vice-President he succeeded McKinley to the presidential throne. The irony of fate had, by the hand of Czolgosz, paved the way to power for the hero of San Juan. In gratitude for that involuntary service Roosevelt turned savage. His message to Congress, intended largely to strike at anarchism, was in reality a death-blow to social and political freedom in the United States.

Anti-anarchist bills followed each other in quick succession, their congressional sponsors busy inventing new methods for the extermination of anarchists. Senator Hawley[1] evidently did not consider his professional wisdom sufficient to slay the anarchist dragon. He declared publicly that he would give a thousand dollars to get a shot at an anarchist. It was a cheap offer considering the price Czolgosz had paid for his shot.

In my bitterness I felt that the American radicals who had shown the white feather when courage and daring were so needed were mainly responsible for the developments. No wonder the reactionaries so brazenly clamoured for despotic measures. They saw themselves complete masters of the situation in the country, with hardly any organized opposition. The Criminal Anarchy law, rushed through the New York legislature, and a similar statute in New Jersey, helped to strengthen my conviction that our movement in the United States was paying dearly for its inconsistencies.

Signs of an awakening in our ranks gradually began to manifest themselves; voices were being raised against the impending danger to American liberties. But I had the feeling that the psychological moment had been neglected; nothing could be done to stem the tide of reaction. At the same time I could not reconcile myself to the fearful situation. My indignation was roused by the mad pack howling for our lives. Yet I remained benumbed and inert, unable to do anything except torment myself with everlasting whys and wherefors. [....]

With the advent of warm weather the number of my patients decreased. I did not regret it; I was very tired and needed a rest. I wanted more time for reading and leisure to be with Dan, Yegor, and Ed. A sweet and harmonious *camaraderie* with the latter had replaced our turbulent emotions of the past. Our separation had had a profound effect on Ed, made him more tolerant and mellow, more understanding. In his little girl and in much reading he found solace. Our intellectual companionship had never before been so stimulating and enjoyable.

I had everything a human being could wish, yet there was chaos in my mind, an ever-growing craving in my heart. I longed to take up the old struggle, to make my life count for more than a mere round of personal interests. But how get back—where begin again? It seemed to me that I had burned the bridges behind me, that I could never again span the gap that had grown so wide since the dreadful Buffalo days. [...]

"Will the Czolgosz tragedy haunt me to the end of my days?" I kept asking myself. The answer came sooner than I anticipated.

"BLOODY RIOTS—WORKERS AND PEASANTS KILLED— STUDENTS WHIPPED BY COSSACKS. ..." The press was filled with the events that were happening in Russia. Once more the struggle against tsarist autocracy was being brought to the attention of the world. The appalling brutality on one side, the glorious courage and heroism on the other, tore me out of the lethargy that had paralysed my will since the Buffalo days. With accusing clarity I realized that I had left the movement at its most critical moment, had turned my back on our work when I was most needed, that I had even begun to doubt my life's faith and ideal. And all because of a handful that had proved to be base and cowardly.

I tried to excuse my faint-heartedness by the deep concern

I felt in the forsaken boy. My indignation against the weaklings had sprung, I argued with myself, from my sympathy with Czolgosz. No doubt that had been the impelling motive for my stand—so impelling, indeed, that it had even turned me against Sasha because he had failed to see in Czolgosz's act what had been so clear to me. My bitterness had extended to that dear friend and had made me forget that he was in prison and still needed me.

Now, however, another thought hammered in my brain, the thought that there might have been other motives, motives not quite so selfless as I had made myself and others believe. My own inability to face the first great issue in my life now made me see that the self-assurance with which I had always proclaimed that I could stand alone had deserted me the moment I was called upon to make good. I had not been able to bear being repudiated and shunned; I could not brave defeat. But, instead of admitting it to myself at least, I had kept on beating my wings in blind fury. I had become embittered and had drawn back within myself.

The qualities I had most admired in the heroes of the past, and also in Czolgosz, the strength to stand and die alone, had been lacking in me. Perhaps one needs more courage to live than to die. Dying is of a moment, but the claims of life are endless—a thousand small and petty things which tax one's strength and leave one too spent to meet the testing hour.

I emerged from my tortuous introspection as from a long illness, not yet in possession of my former vigour, but with a determination to try once more to steel my will to meet the exigencies of life, whatever they might be.

My first faltering step after the months of spiritual death was a letter to Sasha.

The news from Russia stirred the East Side radicals into intense activity. Trade-unionists, socialists, and anarchists set aside their political differences, the better to be able to help the victims of the Russian régime. Large meetings were held and funds raised for the sufferers in prison and exile. I took up the work with new-born strength. I stopped nursing in order to devote myself entirely to the needs of Russia. At the same time there was also enough happening in America to tax our utmost energies.

The coal-miners were on strike. Conditions in the coal districts were appalling and aid was urgently needed. [. . .] President Roosevelt suddenly evinced an interest in the miners. He would help the strikers, he announced, if their representatives would be reasonable and give him a chance to go after the mine-owners. That was manna for the politicians in the unions. They immediately transferred the burden of responsibility to the presidential shoulders of Teddy. No need to worry any more; his official wisdom would find the right solution of vexing problems. Meanwhile the miners and their families were starving and the police browbeating those who came to the coal region to encourage the strikers.

The radical elements refused to be duped by the President's interest, nor did they have greater faith in the sudden change of heart of the employers. They worked steadily to raise funds and keep up the spirit of the men. The heat had grown too oppressive for public meetings, which meant a lull in our efforts. Still we were able to canvass unions, hold picnics, and arrange other affairs to raise money. My return to public activity rejuvenated me and gave me a new interest in life. I was asked to undertake a lecture tour for the purpose of raising funds for the miners and the victims in Russia. [. . .]

My tour was trying and strenuous, made more so by the necessity of speaking surrounded by watch-dogs ready to spring on me at any moment, as well as by being compelled to change halls at a moment's notice. But I welcomed the difficulties. They helped to rekindle my fighting spirit and to convince me that those in power never learn to what extent persecution is the leaven of revolutionary zeal. [. . .]

CHAPTER XXVI

The Anti-Anarchist Immigration Law was at last smuggled through Congress, and thereafter no person disbelieving in organized government was to be permitted to enter the United States. Under its provisions men like Tolstoy, Kropotkin, Spencer,[1] or Edward Carpenter[2] could be excluded from the hospitable shores of America. Too late did the lukewarm liberals realize the peril of this law to advanced thought. Had they opposed in a concerted manner the activities of the reactionary element, the statute might not have been passed. The immediate result of this new assault on American liberties, however, was a very decided change of attitude towards anarchists. I myself now ceased to be considered anathema; on the contrary, the very people who had been hostile to me began to seek me out. Various lecture forums, like the Manhattan Liberal Club, the Brooklyn Philosophical Society, and other American organizations invited me to speak. I accepted gladly because of the opportunity I had been wanting for years to reach the native intelligentsia, to enlighten it as to what anarchism really means. [. . .]

My public life grew colourful. Nursing became less strenuous when several of my "charges" moved out of my apartment and thus reduced my expenses. I could afford to take longer rests between cases. It gave me the opportunity to do much reading that had been neglected for some time. I enjoyed my new experience of living alone. I could go and come without considering others and I did not always find a crowd at home upon my return from a lecture. I knew myself well enough to realize that I was not easy to live with. [. . .] I enjoyed the boon of retirement and the companionship of a few chosen friends, the dearest among them Ed—no longer jealously watching, possessively demanding every thought and every breath, but giving and receiving free and spontaneous joy.

Often he would visit me weary and depressed. I knew it was the growing friction in his home; not that he had ever spoken about it, but now and then a chance remark disclosed to me that he was not happy. [. . .] To cheer him I would turn the talk into other channels, or ask about his daughter. At once his face would light up and his depression lift. One day he brought me a picture of the little one. I had never seen such a striking resemblance. I was so moved by the beautiful face of the child that unthinkingly I cried out: "Why don't you ever bring her to see me?" "Why?" he replied, vehemently; "the mother! The mother! If you only knew the mother!" "Please, please!" I remonstrated; "don't say anything more; I don't want to know about her!" He began excitedly to pace the floor, breaking out into a torrent of words. "You must; you must let me speak!" he cried. "You must let me tell you all I have suppressed so long." I tried to stop him, but he paid no attention. "Rage and bitterness against you drove me to that woman," he continued, tempestuously; "yes, and to drink. For weeks after our last break-up I kept drinking. Then I met the woman. I had seen her at radical affairs before, but she had never meant anything to me. Now she excited me; I was maddened by the loss of you and by drink. So I took her home. I quit working and gave myself up to a wild debauch, hoping to blot out the resentment I felt against you for going away. [. . .]

"The break has come, though, at last," he went on. "It had to, anyway, even if you and I had not become good friends again. It was bound to come as soon as I began to realize the effect those quarrels were having on the child." He added that for a long time he had wanted to go to Europe to see his mother again, but he had lacked the means. Now he was in a position to do so. He would take his child to Vienna with him, and he asked me to accompany him.

"How do you mean, take the child?" I cried. "The mother, what about her? It's her child, too, isn't it? It must mean everything to her. How can you rob her of it?" Ed got on his feet and raised me up also. His face close to mine, he said: "Love! Love! Haven't you always insisted that the love of the average mother either smothers the child with kisses or kills it with blows? Why this sudden sentimentality for the poor mother?" "I know, I know, my dear," I answered; "I haven't changed my views. Just the same, the woman endures the agony of birth and she nourishes the infant with her own substance. The man does almost nothing, and yet he claims the child. Can't you see how unjust it is, Ed? Go to Europe with you? I'd do it at once. But I cannot have a mother robbed of her child on my account." He charged me with not being free; I was like all feminists who rail against man for the wrongs he supposedly does to woman, without seeing the injustices that the man suffers, and also the child. He would go anyway and take his little girl along. Never would he allow his child to grow up in an atmosphere of strife. [. . .]

After much thought I concluded that my feeling in regard to the mother of Ed's child was deeply embedded in my sentiments for motherhood in general, that blind, dumb force that brings forth life in travail, wasting woman's youth and strength, and leaving her in old age a burden to herself and to those to whom she has given birth. It was this helplessness of motherhood that had made me recoil from adding to its pain. [. . .]

One morning, very early, I was roused out of bed by persistent and violent ringing. It was Timmermann, whom I had not seen for more than a year. "Claus!" I cried; "what brings you at such an hour?" [. . .]

"It's about Ed," he began. "Ed!" I cried, suddenly alarmed; "is anything the matter with him? Is he ill? Have you a message for me?"

"Ed—Ed—" he stammered—"Ed has no more messages." I held out my hand as if to ward off a blow. "Ed died last night," I heard Claus say in a shaken voice. I stood staring at him. "You're drunk!" I cried; "it can't be!" Claus took my hand and gently pulled me down beside him. [. . .]

Finally Claus spoke. He had gone to Ed's house to meet him for supper; he had waited until nine o'clock, but Ed did not return, so he decided to leave. At that moment a cab drove up to the house. The driver inquired for Brady's apartment, saying that Mr. Brady was in the cab, sick. Would someone help to carry him up? Neighbours came out and surrounded the cab. Ed was inside, sunk back in the seat, unconscious and breathing heavily. People carried him upstairs, while Claus ran for a doctor. When he came back the cabman was gone. All he had been able to tell was that he had been called to a saloon near the Long Island station, where he had found the gentleman hunched up in a chair, bleeding from a cut on his face. He was conscious, but able only to give his address. The saloon-keeper explained that the gentleman had asked for a drink and had taken it standing at the bar. Then he had paid and started towards the toilet. On the way he had suddenly fallen down in a heap, striking his forehead against the bar. That was all any of them knew.

The doctor had worked frantically to revive Ed; but it was in vain. He died without regaining consciousness. [. . .]

Funerals had always been abhorrent to me; I felt that they expressed grief turned inside out. My loss was too deep for it. I went to the crematory and found the ceremony over, the coffin already closed. The friends who knew of my bond with Ed lifted the cover again for me. I approached to look at the dear face, so beautifully serene in sleep. The silence about me made death less gruesome.

Suddenly a shriek echoed through the place, followed by another and another. A female voice, hysterically crying: "My husband! My husband! He is mine!" The shrieking woman, her black widow's veil resembling a crow's wings, threw herself between me and the coffin, pushing me back and falling over the dead. A little blond girl with frightened eyes, suffocating with sobs, was clutching at the woman's dress.

For a moment I stood petrified with horror. Then I slowly moved towards the exit, out into the open, away from the revolting scene. My mind was full of the child, the replica of its father, its life now to be so different from what he had intended.

CHAPTER XXVII

Memories of my former life with Ed filled me with longing for what had again been just within my reach, only to be snatched away. Recollections of the past compelled me to look into the most hidden crevices of my being; their strange contradictions tore me between my hunger for love and my inability to have it for long. It was not only the finality of death, as in the case of Ed, nor the circumstances that had robbed me of Sasha in the springtime of our lives, that always came between. There were other forces at work to deny me permanency in love. Were they part of some passionate yearning in me that no man could completely fulfil or were they inherent in those who for ever reach out for the heights, for some ideal or exalted aim that excludes aught else? Was not the price they exacted conditioned in the very nature of the thing I wished to achieve? The stars could not be climbed by one rooted in a clod of earth. If one soared high, could he hope to dwell for long in the absorbing depths of passion and love? Like all who had paid for their faith, I too would have to face the inevitable. Occasional snatches of love; nothing permanent in my life except my ideal. [. . .]

Sasha's letters breathed a zest in life that carried me along and filled me with increased admiration for him. I, too, began to dream and plan for the great moment when my heroic boy would be free again and united with me in life and work. Only thirty-three months more and his martyrdom would be at an end!

Meanwhile John Turner[1] had announced his coming to the States. He had been in America in 1896 and had lectured extensively during seven months. He was planning a new tour and wished especially to study the conditions of the men and women employed as clerks and sales-people in the United States. [. . .]

His opening address was on "Trade Unionism and the General Strike." Murray Hill Lyceum was filled to the doors with people from every walk of life. The police were present in large numbers. I introduced our British comrade to the audience and then went to the rear of the hall to look after our literature. When John had finished speaking, I noticed several plain-clothes men approach the platform. Sensing trouble, I hastened over to John. The strangers proved immigration officials who declared Turner was under arrest. Before the audience had time to realize what was happening, he was rushed out of the hall. Turner was given the honour of being the first to fall under the ban of the Federal Anti-Anarchist Law passed by Congress on March 3, 1903. [. . .] When I announced to the audience that John Turner had been arrested and would be deported, the meeting unanimously resolved that if our friend had to go, it should not be without a fight. . . .

The Free Speech League had asked me to visit a number of cities in behalf of the John Turner fight, and I had also received two other invitations: one from the garment-workers in Rochester, and the other from miners in Pennsylvania. The Rochester tailors had had trouble with some clothing firms, among them that of Garson and Meyer. It was strangely significant that I should be called to speak to the wage-slaves of the man who had once exploited my labour for two dollars and fifty cents a week. I welcomed the opportunity, which would also enable me to see my family.

Within the last few years I had felt more drawn to my people, Helena remaining nearest to me. I always stayed with her on my visits to Rochester, and my folks had learned to take it as a matter of course. My arrival this time was the occasion for a general family reunion. It gave me a chance to get in closer touch with my brother Herman and his charming young wife, Rachel. I learned that the boy who could not memorize his lessons at school had become a great mechanical expert, his specific line the construction of intricate machinery. When it grew late and the other members of the family retired, I remained with my dear Helena. We always had much to say to each other, and it was nearly morning when we separated. Sister consoled me by saying I could sleep late.

I had hardly dozed off when I was awakened by a messenger bringing a letter. Glancing at the signature first, in a half-drowsy state, I saw with surprise that it was signed "Garson." I read it several times to make sure that I was not dreaming. He felt proud that a daughter of his race and city had achieved nation-wide fame, he wrote; he was glad of her presence in Rochester and he would consider it an honour to welcome me at his office soon.

I handed the letter to Helena. "Read it," I said, "and see how important your little sister has become." When she got through, she asked: "Well, what are you going to do?" I wrote on the back of the letter: "Mr. Garson, when I needed you, I came to you. Now that you seem to need me, you will have to come to me." My anxious sister was worried about the outcome. What could he want and what would I say or do? I assured her that it was not difficult to guess what Mr. Garson wanted, but I intended, nevertheless, to have him tell it to me in person and in her presence. I would receive him in her store and treat him "as a lady should."

In the afternoon Mr. Garson drove up in his carriage. I had not seen my former employer for eighteen years, and during that time I had hardly given him a thought. Yet the moment he entered, every detail of the dreadful months in his shop stood out as clearly as if it had happened but yesterday. I saw the shop again and his luxurious office, American Beauties on the table, the blue smoke of his cigar swelling in fantastic curves, and myself standing trembling, waiting until Mr. Garson would deign to notice me. I visioned it all again and I heard him saying harshly: "What can I do for you?" Everything to the minutest detail I recalled as I looked at the old man standing before me, silk hat in hand. The thought of the injustice and humiliation his workers were suffering, their driven and drained existence, agitated me. I could barely suppress the impulse to show him the door. If my life depended on it, I could not have asked Mr. Garson to sit down. It was Helena who offered him a chair—more than he had done for me eighteen years before.

He sat down and looked at me, evidently expecting me to speak first. "Well, Mr. Garson, what can I do for you?" I finally asked. The expression must have recalled something to his mind; it seemed to confuse him. "Why, nothing at all, dear Miss Goldman," he presently replied; "I just wanted to have a pleasant talk with you." "Very well," I said, and waited. He had worked hard all his life, he related, "just like your father, Miss Goldman." He had saved penny by penny and in that way had accumulated a little money. "You may not know how difficult it is to save," he went on, "but ask your father. He works hard, he is an honest man, and he is known in the whole city as such. There isn't another man in Rochester more respected and who has so much credit as your father."

"Just a moment, Mr. Garson," I interrupted; "you forgot something. You forgot to mention that you had saved by the assistance of others. You were able to put aside penny by penny because you had men and women working for you."

"Yes, of course," he said apologetically, "we had 'hands' in our factory, but they all made good livings."

"And were they all able to open factories from their savings of penny by penny?"

He admitted that they were not, but it was because they were ignorant and spendthrift. "You mean they were honest workingmen like my father, don't you?" I continued. "You've spoken in such high terms of my father, you certainly will not accuse him of being a spendthrift. But though he has worked like a galley-slave all his life, he has accumulated nothing and he has not been able to start a factory. Why do you suppose my father and others remained poor, while you succeeded? It is because they lacked the forethought to add to their shears the shears of ten others, or of a hundred or several hundred, as you have done. It isn't the saving of pennies that makes people rich; it is the labour of your 'hands' and their ruthless exploitation that has created your wealth. Eighteen years ago there was an excuse for my ignorance of it, when I stood like a beggar before you, asking for a rise of a dollar and a half in pay. There is no excuse for you, Mr. Garson—not now, when the truth of the relation between labour and capital is being cried from the house-tops."

He sat looking at me. "Who would have thought that the little girl in my shop would become such a grand speaker?" he said at last. "Certainly not you!" I replied, "nor could she have if you had had your way. But let's come down to your request that I visit your office. What is it you want?"

He began talking about labour's having its rights; he had acknowledged the union and its demands (whenever reasonable) and had introduced many improvements in his shop for the benefit of his workers. But times were hard and he had sustained heavy losses. If only the grumblers among his employees would listen to reason, be patient awhile, and meet him halfway, everything could be amicably adjusted. "Couldn't you put this before the men in your speech," he suggested, "and make them see my side a little? Your father and I are great friends, Miss Goldman; I would do anything for him if he should be in trouble—lend him money or help in any way. As to his brilliant daughter, I have already written you how proud I am that you come from my race. I should like to prove it by some little gift. Now, Miss Goldman, you are a woman, you must love beautiful things. Tell me what you'd like best."

His words did not rouse my anger. Perhaps it was because I had expected some such offer from his letter. My poor sister was regarding me with her sad, anxious eyes. I rose quietly from my chair; Garson did the same and we stood facing each other, a senile smile on his withered face.

"You've come to the wrong person, Mr. Garson," I said; "you cannot buy Emma Goldman."

"Who speaks of buying?" he exclaimed. "You're wrong; let me explain."

"No need of it," I interrupted him. "Whatever explanation is necessary I will make tonight before your workers who have invited me to speak. I have nothing more to say to you. Please go."

He edged out of the room, silk hat in hand, followed by Helena, who saw him to the door. [. . .]

During my brief stay in Rochester I had another caller, much more interesting than Mr. Garson: a newspaper woman who introduced herself as Miss T. She came to interview me, but she stayed to tell a remarkable story. It was about Leon Czolgosz. [. . .]

What Miss T. told me bore out all that I had guessed and

what I had learned about Leon in 1902 when I visited Cleveland. I had hunted up his parents; they were dark people, the father hardened by toil, the stepmother with a dull, vacant look. His own mother had died when he was a baby; at the age of six he had been forced into the street to shine shoes and sell papers; if he did not bring enough money home, he was punished and deprived of meals. His wretched childhood had made him timid and shy. At the age of twelve he began his factory life. He grew into a silent youth, absorbed in books and aloof. At home he was called "daft"; in the shop he was looked upon as queer and "stuck-up." The only one to be kind to him was his sister, a timid, hard-working drudge. When I saw her, she told me that she had been once to Buffalo to see Leon in jail, but he had asked her not to come again. "He knew I was poor," she said; "our family was pestered by the neighbours, and father was fired from his job. So I didn't go again," she repeated, weeping.

Perhaps it was just as well, for what could the poor creature give to the boy who had read queer books, had dreamed queer dreams, had committed a queer act, and had even been queer in the face of death. People out of the ordinary, those with a vision, have ever been considered queer; yet they have often been the sanest in a crazy world.

In Pennsylvania I found the condition of the miners since the "settlement" of the strike worse than in 1897 when I had gone through the region. The men were more subdued and helpless. Only our own comrades were alert, and even more determined since the shameful defeat of the strike, brought about by the treachery of the union leaders. They were working part time, barely earning enough to live on, yet somehow they managed to contribute to the propaganda. It was inspiring to see such consecration to our cause.

Two experiences stood out on my trip. One happened down in a mine, the other in the home of a worker. As on my previous visits, I was taken to the pit to talk to the men in one of the shafts during lunch-hour. The foreman was away, and the miners eager to hear me. I sat surrounded by a group of black faces. During my talk I caught sight of two figures huddled together—a man withered with age and a child. I inquired who they were. "That's

Grandpa Jones," I was told; "he's ninety and he has worked in the mines for seventy years. The kid is his great-grandchild. He says he's fourteen, but we know he's only eight." My comrade spoke in a matter-of-fact manner. A man of ninety and a child of eight working ten hours a day in a black pit!

After the first meeting I was invited by a miner to his home for the night. The small room assigned me had already three occupants: two children on a narrow cot, and a young girl in a folding bed. I was to share the bed with her. The parents and their infant girl slept in the next room. My throat felt parched; the stifling air in the room made me cough. The woman offered me a glass of hot milk. I was tired and sleepy; the night was heavy with the breathing of the man, the pitiful wailing of the infant, and the monotonous tramp of the mother trying to quiet her baby.

In the morning I asked about the child. Was it ill or hungry that it cried so much? Her milk was too poor and not enough, the mother said; the baby was bottle-fed. A horrible suspicion assailed me. "You gave me the baby's milk!" I cried. The woman attempted to deny it, but I could see in her eyes that I had guessed correctly. "How could you do such a thing?" I upbraided her. "Baby had one bottle in the evening, and you looked tired and you coughed; what else could I do?" she said. I was hot with shame and overcome with wonder at the great heart beneath that poverty and those rags.

Back in New York from my short tour, I found a message from Dr. Hoffmann calling me again to nurse Mrs. Spenser. I could undertake only day duty, my evenings being taken up with the Turner campaign. The patient consented to the arrangement, but after a few weeks she urged me to take care of her during the night. She had become more to me than merely a professional case, but her present surroundings were repugnant. It was one thing to know that she lived from the proceeds of a brothel, quite different to have to work in such a house. To be sure, my patient's business now went by the respectable name of a Raines hotel.[2] Like all legislation for the elimination of vice, the Raines Law only multiplied the very thing it claimed to abolish. It relieved the keepers of responsibility towards the inmates and increased their revenue from prostitution. The customers no longer had to come to Mrs. Spenser. The girls were now compelled to solicit on the street. In rain or cold, well or ill, the unfortunates had to hustle for business, glad to take anyone who consented to come, no matter how decrepit or hideous he might be. They had, furthermore, to endure persecution from the police and pay graft to the department for the right to "work" in certain localities. Each district had its price, according to the amount the girls were able to get from the men. Broadway, for instance, paid more in graft than the Bowery. The policeman on the beat took care that there should be no unauthorized competition. Any girl who dared trespass on another's beat was arrested and often sent to the workhouse. Naturally the girls clung to their territory and fought the intrusion of any colleague who did not "belong" there. [. . .]

To see those poor slaves and their males going in and out of Mrs. Spenser's hotel all through the night, tired, harassed, and generally drunk, to be compelled to overhear what went on, was more than I could bear. Moreover, Dr. Hoffmann had told me that there was no hope of permanent cure for our patient. Her persistent use of drugs had broken her will and weakened her power of resistance. No matter how well we should succeed in weaning her, she would always go back to them. I informed my patient that I must resign. She flew into a rage, berating me bitterly and concluding by saying that if she could not have me when she wanted me, she preferred that I leave altogether.

I needed all my strength for public work, of which the John Turner campaign was the most important. [. . .] Henceforth I gave more time to English propaganda, not only because I wanted to bring anarchist thought to the American public, but also to call attention to certain great issues in Europe. Of these the struggle for freedom in Russia was among the least understood.

CHAPTER XXVIII

For a number of years the Friends of Russian Freedom, an American group, had been doing admirable work in enlightening the country about the nature of Russian absolutism. Now that society was inactive and the splendid efforts of the radical Yiddish press were confined entirely to the East Side. The sinister propaganda carried on in America by the representatives of the Tsar through the Russian Church, the Consulate, and the New York *Herald,* under the ownership of James Gordon Bennett, was widespread. These forces combined to picture the autocrat as a kind-hearted dreamer not responsible for the evils in his land, while the Russian revolutionists were denounced as the worst of criminals. Now that I had greater access to the American mind, I determined to use whatever ability I possessed to plead the heroic cause of revolutionary Russia. [. . .]

Our spirits were greatly raised by the news of the approaching visit of Catherine Breshkovskaya,[1] affectionately called Babushka, the Grandmother of the Russian Revolution. Those familiar with Russia knew of Breshkovskaya as one of the most heroic figures in that country. Her visit would therefore be an event of exceptional interest. We had no anxiety about her success with the Yiddish population—her fame guaranteed it. But the American audiences knew nothing about her, and it might be difficult to get them interested. [. . .]

When Catherine Breshkovskaya arrived, she was immediately surrounded by scores of people, many of them moved more by curiosity than by genuine interest in Russia. I did not wish to swell the number, and so I waited. [. . .]

I was greatly excited and awed when I reached the house

where Breshkovskaya was staying. I found her in a barren flat, badly lighted and inadequately heated. Dressed in black, she was wrapped in a thick shawl, a black kerchief over her head, leaving the ends of her waving grey hair exposed. She gave the impression of a Russian peasant woman, except for her large grey eyes, expressive of wisdom and understanding, eyes remarkably youthful for a woman of sixty-two. Ten minutes in her presence made me feel as if I had known her all my life; her simplicity, the tenderness of her voice, and her gestures, all affected me like the balm of a spring day.

Her first appearance in New York was at Cooper Union and proved the most inspiring manifestation I had seen for years. Babushka, who had never before had a chance to face such a vast gathering, was somewhat nervous at first. But when she got her bearings, she delivered a speech that swept her audience off its feet. The next day the papers were practically unanimous in their tributes to the grand old lady. They could afford to be generous to one whose attack was levelled against far-off Russia instead of their own country. But we welcomed the attitude of the press because we knew that publicity would arouse interest in the cause Babushka had come to plead. Subsequently she spoke in French at the Sunrise Club before the largest assembly in the history of that body. I acted as interpreter, as I did also at most of the private gatherings arranged for her. [....]

Often after the late gatherings Babushka would come with me to my flat to spend the night. It was amazing to see her run up the five flights with an energy and vivacity that put me to shame. "Dear Babushka," I once said to her, "how have you been able to keep your youth after so many years of prison and exile?" "And how did you manage to retain yours, living in this soul-destroying, materialistic country?" she returned. Her long exile had never been stagnant; it was always rejuvenated by the stream of politicals passing through. "I had much to inspire and sustain me," she said; "but what have you in a country where idealism is considered a crime, a rebel an outcast, and money the only god?" I had no answer except that it was the example of those who had gone before, herself included, and the ideal we had chosen that gave us courage to persevere. The hours with Babushka were among the richest and most precious experiences of my propaganda life.

Our strenuous work for Russia at this time received additional significance by the news of the appalling tragedy of January 22 in St. Petersburg. Thousands of people, led by Father Gapon, assembled before the Winter Palace to appeal to the Tsar for relief, had been brutally mowed down, massacred in cold blood by the autocrat's henchmen. Many advanced Americans had held aloof from Babushka's work. They were willing enough to pay homage to her personality, her courage and fortitude; they were sceptical, however, about her description of conditions in Russia. Things could not be quite so harrowing, they claimed. The butchery on "Bloody Sunday" gave tragic significance and incontestable proof to the picture Babushka had painted. Even the lukewarm liberals could no longer close their eyes to the situation in Russia.

At the Russian New Year's ball we greeted the advent of 1905 standing in a circle, Babushka dancing the *kazatchok* with one of the boys. It was a feast for the eyes to see the woman of sixty-two, her spirit young, cheeks ruddy, and eyes flashing, whirling about in the popular Russian dance.

In January Babushka went on a lecture tour, and I could turn to other interests and activities. My dear Stella had come from Rochester in the late fall to live with me. It had been her great dream to do so since early childhood. My narrow escape during the McKinley hysteria had changed the attitude of my sister Lena, Stella's mother, making her more kindly and affectionate towards me. She no longer begrudged me Stella's love, having learned to understand how deep was my concern for her child. Stella's parents realized that their daughter would have better opportunity for development in New York, and that she would be safe with me. I was happy in the anticipation of having with me my little niece, whose birth had brightened my dark youth. Yet when the long-awaited moment arrived, I was too busy with Babushka to give much time to Stella. The old revolutionist was captivated by my niece, and she in turn completely fell under Babushka's charm. Still we both longed to have more of each other, and now, with the departure of the revolutionary "Grandmother," we could at last come closer together. [. . .]

Not until Babushka left the country did I realize how strenuous the month had been. I was utterly exhausted and unable to face the ordeal of nursing. I had realized for some time past that I could not keep up much longer the hard work, responsibility, and anxiety my profession involved while continuing my platform activities. [. . .]

During the hot summer months many of my patients left for the country. Stella and I decided that we also needed a vacation. In our search for a suitable place we came upon Hunter Island, in Pelham Bay, near New York, as ideal a spot as we could wish for. [. . .]

A friend of mine, Clara Felberg, together with her sister and brother, joined us. We were just beginning to settle down on our island and enjoy its peace and beauty when Clara brought back from New York the announcement that the Paul Orleneff troupe was stranded in the city. Its members had been thrown out of their apartment for failure to pay the rent, and they were without means of livelihood.

Pavel Nikolayevitch Orleneff[2] and Mme Nazimova[3] had come to America in the early part of 1905, taking the East Side by storm with their wonderful production of Tchirikov's *The Chosen People*. It was said that Orleneff had been prevailed upon by a group of writers and dramatists in Russia to take the play abroad as a protest against the wave of pogroms then sweeping Russia. The Orleneff troupe arrived at the very height of our activities for Babushka, which had prevented my getting in touch with the Russian players. But I had attended every performance. [. . .] Nothing like its ensemble acting had ever been seen on the American stage before. It was therefore a shock to learn that Orleneff's troupe, who had given us so much, should find themselves stranded, without friends or funds. We might pitch a tent for Orleneff on our island, I thought, but how help his ten men? Clara promised to borrow some money, and within a week the entire troupe was on the island with us. It was a motley crowd and a motley life, and our hopes for a restful summer soon went by the board. During the day, when Stella and I had to return to the heat of the city, we regretted that Hunter Island had ceased to be a secluded spot. But at night, sitting around our huge bonfire, with Orleneff in the centre, guitar in hand, softly strumming an accompaniment to his own singing, the whole troupe joining in on the chorus, the strains echoing far over the bay as the large *samovar* buzzed, our regrets of the day were forgotten. Russia filled our souls with the plaint of her woe.

The spiritual proximity of Russia brought Sasha poignantly near. I knew how profoundly he would enjoy our inspiring nights; how he would be stirred and soothed by the songs of the native land he had always passionately loved. It was the month of July 1905. Just thirteen years before, he had left me to stake his life for our cause. His Calvary was soon to end, but only to continue in another place; he still had to serve another year in the workhouse. The judge who had added the extra year to the inhuman sentence of twenty-one now appeared more barbarous than on that trial day in September 1892. But for that, Sasha would be free now, out of the power of his jailers.

It somewhat lessened my misery to think that Sasha would have to spend only seven months in the workhouse, the Pennsylvania law granting five months' commutation on his final year. But even that consolation was soon destroyed. A letter from Sasha informed me that, though he was legally entitled to a five months' reduction, he had learned that the workhouse authorities had decided to regard him as a "new" prisoner and to allow him only two months' time off, provided his behaviour was "good." Sasha was to be forced to drain the bitter cup to the last drop.

Several months previously Sasha had sent to me a friend whom he called "Chum." His name was John Martin, I learned, and he was socialistically inclined. [. . .] John Martin broached a new appeal to the Pardon Board, to get the year in the workhouse set aside. He could not bear to think that Alex, as he called Sasha, after so many years in one hell should have to go to another. I was deeply touched by Martin's beautiful spirit, but we had failed in our previous attempts to rescue Sasha and I was sure that we could expect no better success now. Moreover, I knew that he himself would not want it tried. He had endured thirteen years and I was certain he would prefer to stand the additional ten months rather than have to go begging again. My attitude was justified by a letter from Sasha. He wanted nothing from the enemy, he wrote.

The sickening anxiety of the days preceding his transfer was finally over. Two days later I received his last note from the penitentiary. It read:

DEAREST GIRL:

It's Wednesday morning, the 19th, at last!

> *Geh stiller, meines Herzens Schlag*
> *Und schliesst euch alle meine alten Wunden,*
> *Denn dieses ist mein letzter Tag,*
> *Und dies sind seine letzten Stunden!**

My last thoughts within these walls are of you, dear friend, the Immutable.

SASHA

Only ten months more to the 18th of May, the glorious day of liberation—the day of your triumph, Sasha, and mine! [. . .]

---

*"Go slower, beating heart of mine—and close, ye bleeding wounds—this is my final day—and these its waning hours."

CHAPTER XXIX

The news of the Russian revolution of October 1905 was electrifying and carried us to ecstatic heights. The many tremendous events that had happened since the massacre in front of the Winter Palace had kept us in far-away America in constant tension. Kalayev and Balmashov, members of the Fighting Organization of the Social Revolutionary Party, had taken the lives of Grand Duke Sergius and Shipiaghin in retaliation for the butchery of January 22. Those acts had been followed by a general strike throughout the length and breadth of Russia, participated in by large sections from every stratum in society. Even the most insulted and degraded human beings, the prostitutes, had made common cause with the masses and had joined the general strike. The ferment in the Tsar-ridden land had finally come to a head; the subdued social forces and the pent-up suffering of the people had broken and had at last found expression in the revolutionary tide that swept our beloved *Matushka Rossiya*.[1] The radical East Side lived in a delirium, spending almost all of its time at monster meetings and discussing these matters in cafés, forgetting political differences and brought into close comradeship by the glorious events happening in the fatherland.

It was at the very height of those events that Orleneff and his troupe made their first appearance in the little theatre on Third Street. Who cared if the place was ugly, the acoustics unspeakably bad, the stage too small to move about on, the scenery atrociously painted, the incongruous properties borrowed from a dozen different friends? We were too full of new-born Russia, too inspired by the thought of the great artists that were to depict for us the dreams of life. When the curtain rose for the first time, triumphant joy rolled like thunder from the audience to the people on the stage. It raised them to heights of artistic expression that surpassed anything they had done before. [. . .]

The Russian Revolution had barely begun to flower when it was thrust back into the depths and stifled in the blood of the heroic people. Cossack terror stalked through the land, torture, prison, and the gallows doing their deadly work. Our bright hopes turned to blackest despair. The whole East Side profoundly felt the tragedy of the crushed masses.

The renewed massacres of Jews in Russia brought tears and sorrow to numerous Jewish homes in America. In their disappointment and bitterness, even advanced Russians and Jews turned against everything Russian, and as a result the audience at the little theatre began to dwindle. And then, out of the darkness of some slimy corner, came hideous whispers that Orleneff had members of the Black Hundred,[2] the organized Russian Jew-baiters, in his troupe. A veritable boycott followed. No Jewish store, restaurant, or café would accept posters or advertisements of the Russian plays. The radical press protested vehemently against these utterly unfounded rumours, but without effect. Orleneff was heart-broken over the malicious charges. He had put his very soul into Nachman, the hero of *The Chosen People,* and had pleaded for the Russian cause. Ruin was staring him in the face, with creditors pressing on every side, and the performances barely paying for rent.

Orleneff had once told me of a testimonial performance that had been arranged for him and Mme Nazimova in London by Beerbohm Tree.[3] It had been a brilliant affair, attended by the most distinguished men and women of the British stage. It occurred to me that we might try a similar plan in New York. It would help raise the desperately needed money and perhaps also calm the troubled waters of the East Side, for I knew from years of experience the effect of American opinion upon the immigrant members of my race. I accompanied Orleneff to Arthur Hornblow, editor of the *Theatre Magazine,* who had repeatedly expressed his admiration for the Russian troupe. [. . .]

More help and encouragement came from other quarters.

Four matinées in the Criterion Theatre and two out-of-town engagements—Boston for a week, and Chicago for a fortnight—
put new life into the Russian troupe. [. . .]

The social groups of the city [Chicago] backing the venture,
including the Jewish and Russian radicals, combined to fill the
Studebaker Theatre night after night. Notwithstanding the numerous social affairs, I repeatedly managed to steal away to deliver lectures arranged by my comrades. My "double" life would
have shocked many a Puritan, but I led it quite bravely. I had
got used to shedding the skin of Miss Smith[4] and wearing my
own, but on several occasions the process failed to work.

The first time was when Orleneff and his leading lady were
invited to the home of Baron von Schlippenbach, the Russian
consul. I told Orleneff that not even for his sake could Emma
Goldman be comfortable, in any guise, under the roof of a person that represented the Russian imperial butcher. Another occasion was in connexion with the Hull House.[5] I had met Jane
Addams as E. G. Smith at the office of the Studebaker Theatre
when she had come to order seats. It had been a business transaction, on neutral ground, calling for no enlightenment as to
my identity. But to come to her sanctum under an assumed name,
when she herself was supposed to stand for advanced social
ideas, seemed an unfair advantage and was distasteful to me. I
therefore called up Miss Addams to tell her that Miss Smith
could not attend her Orleneff party, but that Emma Goldman
would, if welcome. I could hear by the catch in her breath that
the disclosure had been made somewhat too suddenly.

When I related the incident to Orleneff, he got very angry. He
knew that Jane Addams had made a great fuss over Kropotkin
during his visit in Chicago, that she had hung her place with
Russian peasant work, and that she and her helpers had worn
Russian peasant costumes. How could she, then, object to me,
he wondered. I explained that Peter, who hated display of any
kind, certainly had had nothing to do with the Russianization
of Hull House; furthermore, I did not happen to be known to
Miss Addams as a princess. [. . .]

Orleneff had once asked me what I would like to do most if

I had money, and I had replied that I should want to publish a magazine that would combine my social ideas with the young strivings in the various art forms in America. Max and I had often discussed such a venture, greatly needed. It had been our cherished dream for a long time, though apparently hopeless. Now Orleneff broached the matter again, and I submitted my plan to him. He offered to give a special performance for the purpose and promised to see Nazimova about playing Strindberg's *Countess Julia,* a drama she had always wanted to present with him. He did not care particularly for the part of Jean, he said, but "You have done so much for me," he added, "I will stage the piece."

Before long, Orleneff had set a definite date for the performance. We rented the Berkeley Theatre, printed announcements and tickets, and, with the help of Stella and a few young comrades, set to work to fill the house. At the same time we arranged a gathering at 210 East Thirteenth Street,[6] to which we invited a number of people we knew would be interested in the magazine venture we had in mind. [. . .] When our friends left that night, the expected child had a name, *The Open Road,* as well as foster-parents and a host of others anxious to help in its care.

I walked on air. At last my preparatory work of years was about to take complete form! The spoken word, fleeting at best, was no longer to be my only medium of expression, the platform not the only place where I could feel at home. There would be the printed thought, more lasting in its effect, and a place of expression for the young idealists in art and letters. In *The Open Road* they should speak without fear of the censor. Everybody who longed to escape rigid moulds, political and social prejudices, and petty moral demands should have a chance to travel with us in *The Open Road.* [. . .]

We had enough for the first number, which we decided to issue in the historic revolutionary month of March.[7] What other free-lance publication had ever started with more? Meanwhile we sent out a general appeal to our friends. Among the responses we received one from Colorado bearing the heading: *The Open Road.*[8] It threatened to set the law on us for infringement of copyright! Poor Walt Whitman would have surely turned in his grave if he knew that someone had dared to legalize the title of his great poem. But there was nothing for us to do except to christen the child differently. Friends sent in new names, but we did not find one expressing our meaning.

While visiting the little farm one Sunday, Max and I went for a buggy ride.[9] It was early in February, but already the air was perfumed by the balm of spring. The soil was beginning to break free from the grip of winter, a few specks of green already showing and indicating life germinating in the womb of Mother Earth. "Mother Earth," I thought; "why, that's the name of our child! The nourisher of man, man freed and unhindered in his access to the free earth!" The title rang in my ears like an old forgotten strain. The next day we returned to New York and prepared the copy for the initial number of the magazine. It appeared on the first of March 1906, in sixty-four pages. Its name was *Mother Earth*. [. . .]

With *Mother Earth* off the press and mailed to our subscribers, I left a substitute in my office and, together with Max, started on tour. We had large audiences in Toronto, Cleveland, and Buffalo. It was my first visit to the last-named city since 1901. The police were still haunted by the shades of Czolgosz; they were in force and commanded that no language but English be spoken. That prevented Max from delivering his address, but I did not permit the opportunity to pass without paying my respects to the police. The second meeting, the next evening, was stopped before we could get into the hall.

While still in Buffalo, we received the news of the death of Johann Most. He had been on a lecture tour and had died in Cincinnati, fighting for his ideal to the very last. Max had loved Most devotedly and he was quite unnerved by the blow. And I—all my early feeling for Hannes now perturbed me as if there had never been the bitter clash that separated us. Everything he had given me in the years when he had inspired and taught me stood before me now and made me realize the senselessness of that feud. My own long struggle to find my bearings, the disillusionments and disappointments I had experienced, had made me less dogmatic in my demands on people than I had been. They had helped me to understand the hard and lonely life of the rebel who had fought for an unpopular cause. Whatever bitterness I had felt against my old teacher had given way to deep sympathy long before his death. [. . .]

CHAPTER XXX

[. . .] May 1906 came at last. Only two more weeks remained till Sasha's resurrection. I had become restless, assailed by perturbing thoughts. What would it be like to stand face to face with Sasha again, his hand in mine, with no guard between us? Fourteen years are a long time, and our lives had flowed in different channels. What if they had moved too far apart to enable them to converge again into the life and comradeship that had been ours when we had parted? The thought of such a possibility sickened me with fear. I busied myself to still my fluttering heart: *Mother Earth,* arrangements for a short tour, preparations for lectures. I had planned to be the first at the prison gate when Sasha would step out into freedom, but a letter from him requested that we meet in Detroit. He could not bear to see me in the presence of detectives, reporters, and a curious mob, he wrote. It was a bitter disappointment to have to wait longer than I had planned, but I knew his objection was justified.

Carl Nold now lived with a woman friend in Detroit. They occupied a small house, surrounded by a garden, away from the noise and confusion of the city. Sasha could rest quietly there. Carl had shared Sasha's lot under the same prison roof and had remained one of his staunchest friends. It was only fair that he should participate in the great moment with me.

Buffalo, Toronto, Montreal, meetings, crowds—I went through them in a daze, conscious only of one thought—*the 18th of May,* the date of Sasha's release. I reached Detroit on the early morning of that day, with the vision of Sasha impatiently pacing his cell before his final liberation. Carl met me at the station. He had arranged a public reception for Sasha and a meeting, he informed me. I listened confused, constantly watching the clock striking off the last prison minutes of my boy. At noon a telegram arrived from friends in Pittsburgh: "Free and on the way to Detroit." Carl snatched up the wire, waved it frantically, and shouted: "He is free! Free!" I could not share his joy; I was oppressed by doubts. If only the evening would come and I could see Sasha with my own eyes!

Tense I stood at the railroad station, leaning against a post. Carl and his friend were near, talking. Their voices sounded afar, their bodies were blurred and faint. Out of my depths suddenly rose the past. It was July 10, 1892, and I saw myself at the Baltimore and Ohio Station in New York, standing on the steps of a moving train, clinging to Sasha. The train began moving faster; I jumped off and ran after it, with outstretched hands, crying frantically: "Sasha! Sasha!"

Someone was tugging at my sleeve, voices were calling: "Emma! Emma! The train is in. Quick—to the gate!" Carl and his girl ran ahead, and I too wanted to run, but my legs felt numb. I remained riveted to the ground, clutching at the post, my heart throbbing violently.

My friends returned, a stranger walking between them, with swaying step. "Here is Sasha!" Carl cried. That strange-looking man—was that Sasha, I wondered. His face deathly white, eyes covered with large, ungainly glasses; his hat too big for him, too deep over his head—he looked pathetic, forlorn. I felt his gaze upon me and saw his outstretched hand. I was seized by terror and pity, an irresistible desire upon me to strain him to my heart. I put the roses I had brought into his hand, threw my arms around him, and pressed my lips to his. Words of love and longing burned in my brain and remained unsaid. I clung to his arm as we walked in silence.

On reaching the restaurant Carl ordered food and wine. We drank to Sasha. He sat with his hat on, silent, a haunted look in his eyes. Once or twice he smiled, a painful, joyless grin. I took off his hat. He shrank back embarrassed, looked about furtively, and silently put his hat on again. His head was shaved! Tears welled up into my eyes; they had added a last insult to the years of cruelty; they had shaved his head and dressed him in hideous clothes to make him smart at the gaping of the outside world. I choked back my tears and forced a merry tone, pressing his pale, transparent hand.

At last Sasha and I were alone in the one spare room of Carl's home. We looked at each other like children left in the dark. We sat close, our hands clasped, and I talked of unessential things, unable to pour out what was overflowing in my heart. Utterly exhausted, I wearily dragged myself to bed. Sasha, shrinking into himself, lay down on the couch. The room was dark, only the gleam of Sasha's cigarette now and then piercing the blackness. I felt stifled and chilled at the same time. Then I heard Sasha groping about, come closer, touch me with trembling hands.

We lay pressed together, yet separated by our thoughts, our hearts beating in the silence of the night. He tried to say something, checked himself, breathed heavily, and finally broke out in fierce sobs that he vainly tried to suppress. I left him alone, hoping that his tortured spirit might find relief in the storm that was shaking him to the roots. Gradually he grew calm and said he wanted to go out for a walk, the walls were crushing him. I heard him close the door, and I was alone in my grief. I knew with a terrible certainty that the struggle for Sasha's liberation had only begun.

I woke up with the feeling that Sasha needed to go away somewhere, alone, to a quiet place. But meetings and receptions had been arranged in Detroit, Chicago, Milwaukee, and New York; the comrades wanted to meet him, to see him again. The young people especially were clamouring to behold the man who had been kept buried alive for fourteen years for his *Attentat*. I was beset with anxiety about him, but there would be no escape for him, I felt, until all the scheduled affairs were over. He would then be able to go to the little farm and perhaps find his way slowly back to life.

The Detroit papers were full of our visit with Carl, and before we left the city, they even had me married to Alexander Berkman and on our honeymoon. In Chicago the reporters were constantly on our trail, the meetings under heavy police guard. The reception in Grand Central Palace, New York, because of its size and the intense enthusiasm of the audience, depressed

Sasha even more than the others. But now the misery was at an end and we went out to the little Ossining farm. Sasha was pleased with it; he loved its wildness, seclusion, and quiet. And I was filled with new hope for him and for his release from the grip of the prison shadows.

Having been starved for so many years, he now ate ravenously. It was extraordinary what an amount of food he could absorb, especially of his favourite Jewish dishes, of which he had been deprived so long. It was nothing at all for him to follow up a substantial meal with a dozen *blintzes* (a kind of Yiddish pancake containing cheese or meat) or a huge apple pie. I cooked and baked, happy in his enjoyment of the food. Most of my friends were in the habit of paying court to my culinary art, but no one ever did so much justice to it as my poor, famished Sasha.

Our country idyll was short-lived. The black phantoms of the past were again pursuing their victim, driving him out of the house and robbing him of peace. Sasha roamed the woods or lay for hours stretched on the ground, silent and listless.

The quiet of the country increased his inner turmoil, he told me. He could not endure it; he must go back to town. He must find work to occupy his mind or he would go mad. And he must make a living; he would not be supported by public collections. He had already declined to accept the five hundred dollars the comrades had raised for him, and had distributed the money among several anarchist publications. There was another thing that tormented him: the thought of his unfortunate comrades of so many years. How could he enjoy peace and comfort, knowing that they were deprived of both? He had pledged himself to voice their cause and to cry out against the horrors within prison walls. Yet he was doing nothing but eating, sleeping, and drifting. He could not go on that way, he said.

I understood his suffering, and my heart bled for my dear one, so bound by the past. We returned to 210 East Thirteenth Street, and there the struggle grew more intense, the struggle for adjustment to living. In his depleted physical condition Sasha could find no work to do, and the atmosphere surrounding me appeared strange and alien to him. With the passing weeks and months his misery increased. When we were alone in the flat, or in the company of Max, he breathed a little freer, and he was not unhappy with Becky Edelson, a young comrade who often came to visit us. All my other friends irritated and disturbed him; he could not bear their presence and he always looked for some excuse to leave. Generally it was dawn before he returned. I would hear his weary steps as he went to his room, hear him fling himself dressed upon his bed and fall into restless sleep, always disturbed by frightful nightmares of his prison life. Repeatedly he would awaken with fearful shrieks that chilled my blood with terror. Entire nights I would pace the floor in anguish of heart, racking my brain for some means to help Sasha find his way back to life.

It occurred to me that a lecture tour might prove a wedge to it. It would enable him to unburden himself of what lay so heavily on his mind—prison and its brutality—and it would help him perhaps to readjust himself to life away from the work he considered mine. It might bring back his old faith in himself. I prevailed upon Sasha to get in touch with our people in a few cities. Soon he had numerous applications for lectures. Almost immediately it brought about a change; he became less restless and depressed, somewhat more communicative with the friends who came to see me, and he even showed an interest in the preparations for the October issue of Mother Earth.

That number was to contain articles on Leon Czolgosz, in memory of the fifth anniversary of his death. Sasha and Max strongly favoured the idea of a memorial issue, but other comrades fought against it on the ground that anything about Czolgosz would hurt the cause as well as the magazine. They even threatened to withdraw their material support. I had promised myself when I started Mother Earth never to permit anyone, whether group or individual, to dictate its policy; opposition now made me the more determined to go through with my plan of dedicating the October number to Czolgosz.

As soon as the magazine was off the press, Sasha began his tour. His first stops were Albany, Syracuse, and Pittsburgh. I hated the idea of his going back to the dreadful city so soon, particularly because I knew that according to the provisions of the Pennsylvania commutation law Sasha remained at the mercy of the authorities of that State for eight years, during which period they had the legal right to arrest him at any time for the slightest offence and send him back to the penitentiary to complete his full term of twenty-two years. Sasha was set, however, on lecturing in Pittsburgh, and I clung to the faint hope that speaking in that city might free him from his prison nightmare. I felt relieved when a telegram came from him saying that the Pittsburgh gathering had been a success, and that all was well.

His next stop was Cleveland. On the day after his first meeting in that city I received a wire informing me that Sasha had left the house of the comrade with whom he had spent the night and had not yet returned. It did not disturb me very much, knowing how the poor boy dreaded contact with people. He had probably decided to go to a hotel, I thought, to be by himself, and he would undoubtedly appear for the lecture in the evening. But at midnight another wire notified me that he had not attended the meeting, and that the comrades were worried. I, too, became alarmed and telegraphed Carl in Detroit, the next city Sasha was expected in. There could be no answer the same day, and the night, full of black forebodings, seemed to stand still. The morning newspapers carried large headlines about the "disappearance of Alexander Berkman, the recently freed anarchist."

The shock completely unnerved me. I was too paralysed at first to form any idea of what might have happened to him. Finally two possibilities presented themselves: that he had been kidnapped by the authorities in Pittsburgh, or—more likely and terrible—that he might have ended his life. I was frantic that I had failed to plead with him not to go to Pittsburgh. Yet, though fearful of his danger, the more dreadful thought persisted in my brain, the thought of suicide. Sasha had been in the throes of such depression that he had said repeatedly he did not care to live, that prison had unfitted him for life. My heart rebelled in passionate protest against the cruel forces that could drive him to leave me just when he had come back. I was tormented by bitter regrets that I had suggested the idea of the lecture tour.

For three days and three nights we in New York and our people in every city searched police stations, hospitals, and morgues for Sasha, but without result. Cables came from Kropotkin and other European anarchists inquiring about him, and streams of people besieged my flat. I was nearly mad with uncertainty, yet dreaded to make up my mind that Sasha had taken the fatal step.

I had to go to Elizabeth, New Jersey, to address a meeting. Long public life had taught me not to expose joy or sorrow to the idle gaze of the market-place. But how hide what now was obsessing my every thought? I had promised weeks previously, and I was compelled to go. Max accompanied me. He had already bought our tickets and we were almost at the railroad gate. Suddenly I was seized by a feeling of some impending calamity. I stopped short. "Max! Max!" I cried, "I can't go! Something is pulling me back to the flat!" He understood and urged me to return. It would be all right, he assured me; he would explain my absence and speak in my stead. Hastily pressing his hand, I dashed off to catch the first ferry-boat back to New York.

On Thirteenth Street near Third Avenue I saw Becky running towards me, excitedly waving a yellow slip of paper. "I've been looking for you everywhere!" she cried. "Sasha is alive! He is waiting for you at the telegraph office on Fourteenth Street!" My heart leaped to my throat. I snatched the paper from her. It read: "Come. I am waiting for you here." I ran full speed towards Fourteenth Street. When I got to the office, I came face to face with Sasha. He was leaning against the wall, a small hand-bag at his side.

"Sasha!" I cried; "oh, my dear—at last!" At the sound of my voice he pulled himself together, as if out of a harrowing dream. His lips moved, but he remained silent. His eyes alone told of his suffering and despair. I took his arm and steadied him, his body shaking as in a chill. We had almost reached 210 East Thirteenth Street when he suddenly cried: "Not here! Not here! I can't see anybody in your flat!" For a moment I did not know what to do; then I hailed a cab and told the driver to go to the Park Avenue Hotel.

It was dinner-hour, and the lobby filled with guests. Everybody was in evening dress; conversation and laughter blended with the strains of music from the dining-hall. When we were alone in a room, Sasha grew dizzy and had to be helped to the couch, where he fell down in a heap. I ran to the telephone and ordered whisky and hot broth. He drank eagerly, indicating that it refreshed him. He had not eaten in three days, nor taken off his clothes. I prepared a bath for him, and while helping him to undress, my hand suddenly came in contact with a steel object. It was a revolver he was trying to hide in his hip pocket.

After the bath and another hot drink Sasha spoke to me. He had hated the idea of the tour the moment he got out of New York, he said. The approach of each lecture would throw him into a panic and fill him with an irresistible desire to escape. The meetings had been badly attended and lacked spirit. The homes of the comrades he had stopped with were congested, with no separate corner for him. More terrible even had been the constant stream of people, the incessant questions. Still he had kept on. Pittsburgh had somewhat relieved his depression; the presence of a horde of police, detectives, and prison officials had roused his fighting spirit and had lifted him out of himself. But Cleveland was a ghastly experience from the moment he arrived. There was no one to meet him at the station, and he spent the day in an exhausting search to locate comrades. The audience in the evening was small and inert; after the lecture came an endless ride to the farm of the comrade whose guest he was to be. Worn and sick unto death, he fell into a heavy sleep. He awoke in the middle of the night and was horrified to find a strange man snoring at his side. His years of solitude in prison had made close human proximity a torture to him. He rushed out of the house, into the country road, to look for some hiding-place where he could be alone. But peace would not come, nor relief from the feeling that he was unfit for life. He determined to end it.

In the morning he walked to the city and bought a revolver. He decided to go to Buffalo. No one knew him there, no one would discover him in life or claim him in death. He roamed through the city all day and night, but New York drew him with irresistible force. Finally he went there and spent two days and nights circling around 210 East Thirteenth Street. He was in constant terror of meeting anyone, yet he could not keep away. Each time on returning to his squalid little room on the Bowery he would take up the revolver for the final gesture. He went to the park nearby, determined to make an end. The sight of little children playing turned his mind to the past and the "sailor girl." "And then I knew that I could not die without seeing you again," he concluded. [...]

I held out my hand to him and begged him to come home with me. "Only Stella is there, my dearest," I pleaded, "and I will see that no one intrudes upon you." At the flat I found Stella, Max, and Becky waiting anxiously for our return. I took Sasha through the corridor into my room and put him to bed. He went off to sleep like a weary child.

Sasha remained in bed for several days, asleep most of the time and only half-aware of his surroundings during his waking hours. [...] Gradually I came to see that it was not so much the question of earning a living that harassed Sasha as something deeper and more bitter to face: the contrast between his dream-world of 1892 and my reality of 1906. The world of ideals he had taken with him to prison at twenty-one had defied the passage of time. Perhaps it was fortunate that it was so; it had been his spiritual support through all the terrible fourteen years, a star to illumine the blackness of his prison existence. It had even coloured his mind's-eye view of the outside world—of the movement, his friends, and especially myself. During that time life had kicked me about, forced me into the current of events, to sink or to swim—I had ceased to be the little "sailor girl" whose image had remained with Sasha from former days. I was a woman of thirty-seven who had undergone profound changes. I no longer fitted into the old mould, as he had expected me to. Sasha saw and felt it almost immediately upon his release. He had tried to understand the mature personality which had burst forth from the shell of the inexperienced girl, and, failing, he became resentful, critical, and often condemnatory of my life, my views, and my friends. He charged me with intellectual aloofness and revolutionary inconsistency. Every thrust from him cut me to the quick and made me cry out my grief. Often I wanted to run away, never to see him again, but I was held by something greater than the pain: the memory of his act, for which he alone had paid the price. More and more I realized that to my last breath it would remain the strongest link in the chain that bound me to him. The memory of our youth and of our love might fade, but his fourteen years' Calvary would never be eradicated from my heart.

A way out of the distressing situation suggested itself in the imperative need of my going on tour for *Mother Earth*. Sasha could remain in charge as editor of the magazine; it would help to release him from his cramped feeling and enable him to find freer expression. [. . .]

CHAPTER XXXI

[...] After my coast-to-coast lecture tour I returned to New York at the end of June with a net result of a considerable number of subscribers to *Mother Earth* and a substantial surplus from the sale of literature to sustain the magazine during the inactive summer months.

In the early spring our European comrades had issued a call for an anarchist congress to be held in Amsterdam, Holland, in August. Some of the groups in the cities I had visited had requested me to attend the gathering as their delegate. It was gratifying to have the confidence of my comrades, and Europe always had its lure for me. But there was Sasha, only one year out of prison, and I had already been away from him for months. I longed to see him again and to try to bridge the gap which his imprisonment had created between us.

Sasha had done splendidly on *Mother Earth* while I was away. He had surprised everybody by the vigour of his style and the clarity of his thoughts. It was an amazing achievement for a man who had gone into prison ignorant of the English language and who had never written for publication before. His letters to me during my four months on tour were free from depression, and he showed much interest in the magazine and my work. I was proud of Sasha and his efforts, and I was full of hope that we might yet dispel the clouds that had been hanging in our sky since he had re-entered the outside world. These considerations made me hesitate to go to Amsterdam. I would decide when I reached New York, I told my comrades.

On my return I found Sasha as I had left him—in the same mental turmoil, in torturing conflict between the vision that had inspired his deed and the reality that confronted him now. He continued to dwell in the past, in the mirage he had created for himself during his living death. Everything in the present was alien to him, made him wince and avoid it. It was bitter irony that I, of all Sasha's friends, should cause him the deepest disappointment and pain—I who had never had him out of my mind in all the cruel years, or out of my heart, no matter who else had been there, not even Ed, whom I had loved more deeply and intensely than anyone else. Yet it was I who most roused Sasha's impatience and resentment; not in a personal sense, but because of the changes I had undergone in my attitude to life, to people, and to our movement. We did not seem to have a single thought in common. Yet I felt bound to Sasha, bound for ever by the tears and blood of fourteen years.

Often, when I could no longer bear up under his censure and condemnation, I would fight back with harsh and bitter words, then run to my room and cry out in pain against the differences that were tearing us apart. Yet I would always come back to Sasha, feeling that whatever he had said or done was nothing in the light of what he had endured. I knew *that* would ever weigh heaviest in the balance with me and bring me to his side at every moment of his need. Just now it seemed that I was of little help. Sasha appeared to feel more at ease when I was away.

I decided to comply with the request of my Western comrades to represent them at the anarchist congress. Sasha said he would continue on the magazine until my return, but that his heart was not in *Mother Earth*. He wanted a weekly propaganda paper that would reach the workers. He had already discussed the project with Voltairine de Cleyre, Harry Kelly, and other friends. They had agreed with him that such a paper was needed and had promised to sign an appeal for the necessary funds. They had been worried, however, that I might misunderstand, that I might consider the new publication a competitor of *Mother Earth*. "What a ridiculous notion," I protested; "I claim no monopoly of the movement. By all means try to get out a weekly paper. I will add my name to the call." Sasha was quite moved, embraced me tenderly, and sat down to write the appeal. My poor boy! If only I could have had the assurance that his project would bring him peace, help him back to life and to the work his mastery of language and his pen should enable him to do!

More and more I was beginning to see that there was an inner resentment in Sasha, perhaps not even conscious, against being part of the activities I had created for myself. He longed for something of his own making, something that would express his own self. I hoped fervently that the weekly paper would prove the means of his release and that it might succeed.

I was getting ready for my trip abroad. Max was going too, representing some German groups at the Amsterdam conference. ... In the middle of August 1907 Max and I waved our friends good-bye from the Holland-America pier. Besides our mission at the congress, we both looked upon our trip as a quest for something to fill our inner void. The calm sea and the ever-soothing companionship of Max helped me to relax from the tension of the months preceding and following Sasha's liberation. [...]

It was certainly a commentary on democratic America and republican France that an international anarchist congress, prohibited in both countries, should have the right to meet quite openly in monarchical Holland. Eighty men and women, most of them hounded and persecuted in their own countries, were here able to address large meetings, gather in daily session, and discuss openly such vital problems as revolution, syndicalism, mass insurrection, and individual acts of violence, without any interference from the authorities. We went about the city singly or in groups, had social gatherings in restaurants or cafés, talked, and sang revolutionary songs until early morning hours, yet we were not shadowed, spied upon, or in any way molested.

More remarkable still was the attitude of the Amsterdam press. Even the most conservative newspapers treated us, not as criminals or lunatics, but as a group of serious people who had come together for a serious purpose. Those papers were opposed to anarchism, yet they did not misrepresent us or distort anything said at our sessions.

One of the vital subjects discussed at length by the congress was the problem of organization. Some delegates deprecated Ibsen's[1] idea, as presented by Dr. Stockmann in *An Enemy of the People*, to the effect that the strongest is he who stands alone.

They preferred Peter Kropotkin's view, so brilliantly elucidated in all his books, that it is mutual aid and co-operation that secure the best results. Max and I, however, stressed the need of both. We held that anarchism does not involve a choice between Kropotkin and Ibsen; it embraces both. While Kropotkin had thoroughly analysed the social conditions that lead to revolution, Ibsen had portrayed the psychologic struggle that culminates in the revolution of the human soul, the revolt of individuality. Nothing would prove more disastrous to our ideas, we contended, than to neglect the effect of the internal upon the external, of the psychologic motives and needs upon existing institutions.

There is a mistaken notion in some quarters, we argued, that organization does not foster individual freedom; that, on the contrary, it means the decay of individuality. In reality, however, the true function of organization is to aid the development and growth of personality. Just as the animal cells, by mutual co-operation, express their latent powers in the formation of the complete organism, so does the individuality, by co-operative effort with other individualities, attain its highest form of development. An organization, in the true sense, cannot result from the combination of mere nonentities. It must be composed of self-conscious, intelligent individualities. Indeed, the total of the possibilities and activities of an organization is represented in the expression of individual energies. Anarchism asserts the possibility of an organization without discipline, fear, or punishment and without the pressure of poverty: a new social organism, which will make an end to the struggle for the means of existence—the savage struggle which undermines the finest qualities in man and ever widens the social abyss. In short, anarchism strives towards a social organization which will establish well-being for all. [. . .]

While we were yet in Holland, news had come that Peter Kropotkin had at last been readmitted to France. Peter loved the country and its people. To him France signified the cradle of liberty, the French Revolution the symbol of all that the world had of social idealism. To be sure, France was very short of the glory my great teacher had invested her with; his own eighteen months' incarceration in a French prison and subsequent expulsion had demonstrated it. Yet by some peculiar partiality Peter hailed France as the banner-bearer of freedom and the most cultured country in the world. We knew that nothing he had personally suffered had changed his feeling about the French people, and we rejoiced that he was now able to satisfy his longing to return.

Peter was already in Paris when we arrived, living but a few doors from my hotel, on Boulevard Saint-Michel. I found him in higher spirits than I had ever seen him before; he looked more vigorous and vivacious. Pretending not to know the reason, I inquired what had brought about the happy change. "Paris, Paris, my dear!" he cried. "Is there any other city in the world that gets into one's blood like Paris?" [. . . .]

Amid brilliant sunshine Max and I left Paris. It was bleak and penetrating when we reached London, with no change in the weather during our stay of two weeks. The first thing to greet us on our arrival were press dispatches from America reporting that the Federal authorities were planning to keep me out of the country under the provisions of the Anti-Anarchist Law. I paid no attention to the matter at first, believing it to be a newspaper fabrication. I was a citizen by my marriage to Kershner. Before long, letters from several attorney friends in the United States confirmed the rumours. They informed me that Washington was determined to refuse me readmission, and they urged me to sail back as quickly and quietly as possible. [. . . .] Max and I left for Liverpool, sailing from there to New York via Montreal.

The Canadian immigration authorities proved less inquisitive than the American and we experienced no trouble whatever getting into Canada. On the way from Montreal to New York the Pullman porter took our tickets, together with a generous tip, and he did not show up again until we were safely in New York. It was two weeks later, at my first public appearance, that the newspapers learned of my being back in the States. They tried frantically to find out how I had managed to get in and I suggested that they inquire of the immigration authorities.

On my return I found *Mother Earth* in a deplorable condition financially. Very little had come in during my absence, and the monthly expenses had far exceeded the amount I had left for the maintenance of the magazine. Something had to be done at once, and, being the only one who could raise funds, I lost no time in arranging various affairs to secure aid for the publication and also decided upon an immediate tour.

Sasha's critical attitude to me had not changed; if anything, it had become more pronounced. At the same time his interest in young Becky had grown. I became aware that they were very close to each other, and it hurt me that Sasha did not feel the need of confiding in me. I knew that he was not communicative by nature, yet something within me felt both offended and injured at his apparent lack of trust. I had realized even before I left for Europe that my physical attraction for Sasha had died with his prison years. I had clung to the hope that when he learned to understand my life, to know that my having loved others had not changed my love for him, his old passion would flame up again. It was painful to see that the new love that had come to Sasha completely excluded me. My heart rebelled against the cruel thing, but I knew that I had no right to complain. While I had experienced life in all its heights and depths, Sasha had been denied it. For fourteen years he had been starved for what youth and love could give. Now it had come to him from Becky, ardent and worshipful as only an eager girl of fifteen can be. Sasha was two years younger than I, thirty-six, but he had not lived for fourteen years, and in regard to women he had remained as young and naïve as he had been at twenty-one. It was natural that he should be attracted to Becky rather than to a woman of thirty-eight who had lived more intensely and variedly than other women double her age. I saw it all clearly enough, yet at the same time I felt sad that he should seek in a child what maturity and experience could give a hundredfold. [. . .]

CHAPTER XXXII

All through the winter of 1907 and 1908 the country was in the grip of financial depression. Thousands of workers in every large city were idle, in poverty and misery. The authorities, instead of devising ways and means to feed the starving, aggravated the appalling conditions by interfering with every attempt to discuss the causes of the crisis. [. . .]

In Chicago the police had dispersed a large demonstration of the unemployed. [. . .] Similar outrages had happened throughout the country. Touring under such conditions was a great strain and yielded barely enough to pay expenses; my situation was aggravated by a very severe cold I had caught, which racked me with a fearful cough. But I kept on in the hope of a favourable change by the time I should reach Chicago. . . .

Two days before my arrival a Russian youth who had been clubbed by the police during the unemployment demonstration called at the house of the Chief of Police, with the intention of taking his life, as the papers reported.[1] I did not know the boy, yet my meetings were immediately suppressed and my name was connected with the matter. [. . .]

When I had almost given up hope of being able to speak in Chicago, Becky Yampolsky[2] brought word that Dr. Ben L. Reitman had offered us a vacant store he was using for gatherings of unemployed and hobos.[3] We could hold our meetings there, he had said, and he had also asked to see me to discuss the matter. In the press accounts of the unemployed parade in Chicago, Reitman had been mentioned as the man who had led the march and who had been among those beaten by the police. I was curious to meet him.

He arrived in the afternoon, an exotic, picturesque figure with a large black cowboy hat, flowing silk tie, and huge cane. "So this is the little lady, Emma Goldman," he greeted me; "I have always wanted to know you." His voice was deep, soft, and ingratiating. I replied that I also wanted to meet the curiosity who believed enough in free speech to help Emma Goldman.

My visitor was a tall man with a finely shaped head, covered with a mass of black curly hair, which evidently had not been washed for some time. His eyes were brown, large, and dreamy. His lips, disclosing beautiful teeth when he smiled, were full and passionate. He looked a handsome brute. His hands, narrow and white, exerted a peculiar fascination. His finger-nails, like his hair, seemed to be on strike against soap and brush. I could not take my eyes off his hands. A strange charm seemed to emanate from them, caressing and stirring.

We discussed the meeting. Dr. Reitman said that the authorities had assured him that they did not object to my speaking in Chicago. "It is up to her to find a place," they had told him. He was glad to help me put them to a test. His place could seat over two hundred people; it was filthy, but his hobos would help him clean it up. Once I had carried through the venture in his hall, it would be easy to get any place I wanted. With much enthusiasm and energy my visitor elaborated on the plan to defeat the police by our gathering at the headquarters of the Brotherhood Welfare Association, as he called his place. He stayed several hours, and when he went away, I remained restless and disturbed, under the spell of the man's hands.

With the help of his hobos Reitman cleaned his store, built a platform, and arranged benches to seat two hundred and fifty people. Our girls prepared little curtains to make the place attractive and to shut out the curious gaze. All was ready for the event, the press carrying sensational stories about Reitman and Emma Goldman, who were conspiring against police orders. On the afternoon of the scheduled gathering the store was visited by officials from the building and fire departments. They questioned the doctor as to how many he expected to seat. Sensing trouble, he said fifty. "Nine," decided the building-department.

"The place is not safe for more," echoed the fire department. With one stroke our meeting was condemned, and the police scored another victory. [. . .]

Meeting-places being closed, I suggested to the comrades that we arrange a social and concert at the Workmen's Hall, my name not to appear in the public announcements. I would try to elude the watch-dogs and get into the hall at the appointed time. Only a few members of our group were apprised of the plan, the others being left under the impression that the sole purpose of the social was to raise funds for our fight.

One outsider was drawn into our secret, and that was Ben Reitman. Some comrades objected on the ground that the doctor was a new-comer and as such not to be trusted. I argued that the man had shown a large spirit in offering his place, and that he had been of great help in securing publicity for our efforts. There could be no doubt about his interest. I did not convince the objectors, but the other comrades agreed that Reitman should be told.

That night I could not sleep. I tossed about in a disturbed state of mind, questioning myself why I had pleaded so warmly for a person I really knew almost nothing about. I had always opposed ready confidence in strangers. What was there in this man that had made me trust him? I had to admit to myself that it was his intense attraction to me. From the moment he had first entered Yampolsky's office, I had been profoundly stirred by him. Our being much together since had strengthened his physical appeal for me. I was aware that he also had been aroused; he had shown it in every look, and one day he had suddenly seized me in an effort to embrace me. I had resented his presumption, though his touch had thrilled me. In the quiet of the night, alone with my thoughts, I became aware of a growing passion for the wild-looking handsome creature, whose hands exerted such fascination.

On the evening of our social gathering, March 17, I succeeded in slipping away through the back entrance of Yampolsky's house while the detectives were waiting for me out in front. I got safely through the police lines near the hall. The audience was large and many officers were inside, stationed against the walls. The concert had begun and someone was playing a violin solo. In the half-light I walked to the front of the platform. When the music was over, Ben Reitman ascended the platform to announce that a friend they all knew would address the gathering. I quickly got up and began to speak. The first tones of my voice and the ovation by the crowd brought the police to the platform. The Captain in charge pulled me off by force, almost ripping open my dress. At once confusion broke out. Fearing that some of our young people might be moved to a rash act, I called out: "The police are here to cause another Haymarket riot. Don't give them a chance. Walk out quietly and you will help our cause a thousand times more." The audience applauded and intoned a revolutionary song, filing out in perfect order. The Captain, infuriated because he had failed to gag me altogether, pushed me towards the exit, cursing and swearing. When we got to the stairs, I refused to budge until my coat and hat, which remained in the hall, were brought to me. I was standing with my back against the wall, waiting for my wraps, when I saw Ben Reitman dragged out by two officers, pushed down the stairs and into the street. He passed me without a look or a word. It affected me disagreeably, but I thought that he had pretended not to know me in order to dupe the officers. He would surely come to Yampolsky's when he had shaken off the police, I reassured myself. I was led out, followed by policemen, detectives, newspaper men, and a large crowd to the door of Becky Yampolsky's home.

I found our comrades already in her office, discussing in what manner the authorities and reporters had learned that I would be present at the gathering. I sensed that they were suspecting Reitman. I felt indignant, but said nothing; I expected he would soon come and speak for himself. But the night wore on and the doctor failed to appear. The suspicion of my comrades grew stronger and communicated itself to me. "He must have been detained by the police," I tried to explain. Faithful Becky and Nathanson agreed that that must be the reason, but the others doubted it. I spent a wretched night, clinging to my faith in the man, yet fearing that he might be at fault.

Reitman called early next morning. He had not been arrested, he said, but for certain important reasons he could not come to Becky's after the meeting. He had no idea who had notified the press and the authorities. I looked searchingly at him, trying to fathom his soul. Whatever doubts I had had the night before melted like ice at the first rays of the sun. It seemed impossible that anyone with such a frank face could be capable of treachery or deliberate lies. [. . .]

The suppression of my meetings in Chicago advertised me through the length and breadth of the country as I had not been since the Buffalo tragedy. I had repeatedly visited Milwaukee before, but I had not been able to attract much attention. Now the attendance was far beyond the capacity of our halls, and great numbers had to be turned away. [. . .]

I had every reason to be satisfied with the Milwaukee response and to be happy in the circle of my good comrades, yet I was restless and discontented. A great longing possessed me, an irresistible craving for the touch of the man who had so attracted me in Chicago. I wired for him to come, but once he was there, I fought desperately against an inner barrier I could neither explain nor overcome. After my scheduled meetings I returned with Reitman to Chicago. The police were no longer on my trail, and for the first time in weeks I was able to enjoy some privacy, to move about freely, and to talk with friends without fear of being under surveillance. To celebrate my release from the everlasting presence of detectives the doctor took me out to dinner. He spoke of himself and his youth, telling me of his wealthy father, who had divorced his mother and left her in poverty to shift for herself and her two children. The boy's *Wanderlust* had asserted itself at the age of five, always luring him to the railroad tracks. He ran away at the age of eleven, tramped over the United States and Europe, always close to the depths of human existence, to vice and crime. He had worked as janitor in the Chicago Polytechnic, where the professors took an interest in him. He had married at the age of twenty-three and was divorced soon after a child had come from the short union. He spoke of his passion for his mother, the influence of a Baptist preacher on him, and of many adventures, some colourful and some bleak, all of which had gone into the making of his life.

I was enthralled by this living embodiment of the types I had only known through books, the types portrayed by Dostoyevsky and Gorki. The misery of my personal life, the hardships I had endured through the weeks in Chicago, seemed to vanish. I was care-free and young again. I craved life and love, I yearned to be in the arms of the man who came from a world so unlike mine.

That night at Yampolsky's I was caught in the torrent of an elemental passion I had never dreamed any man could rouse in me. I responded shamelessly to its primitive call, its naked beauty, its ecstatic joy.

The day brought me back to earth and to the work for my ideal, which brooked no other god. On the eve of my departure from Minneapolis for Winnipeg some friends invited me to a restaurant for dinner. Ben was to meet us there later. We were a gay party, making merry in the last hours of my strenuous Chicago stay. Soon Ben arrived, and with him came a heightened mood.

Not far from us sat a group of men, one of whom I recognized as Captain Schuettler, whose presence seemed to me to pollute the very air. Suddenly I saw him motion towards our table. To my amazement, Ben rose and walked over to Schuettler. The latter greeted him with a jovial: "Hello, Ben," familiarly pulling him down to his side. The others, evidently police officials, all seemed to know Ben and be on friendly terms with him. Anger, disgust, and horror all mingled together, beat against my temples, and made me feel ill. My friends sat staring at each other and at me, which increased my misery.

Ben Reitman, whose embrace had filled me with mad delight, chumming with detectives! The hands that had burned my flesh were now close to the brute who had almost strangled Louis Lingg, near the man who had threatened and bullied me in 1901. Ben Reitman, the champion of freedom, hob-nobbing with the very sort of people who had suppressed free speech, who had clubbed the unemployed, who had killed poor

Overbuch.[4] How could he have anything to do with them? The terrible thought struck me that he might be a detective himself. For some moments I was utterly dazed. I tried to eliminate the dreadful idea, but it kept growing more insistent. I recalled our social on March 17 and the treachery that had brought the police and the reporters to that gathering. Was it Reitman who had informed them? Was it possible? And I had given myself to that man! I, who had been fighting the enemies of freedom and justice for nineteen years, had exulted in the arms of a man who was one of them.

I strove to control myself and suggested to my friends that we leave. The comrades who accompanied me to the train were kind and understanding. They talked of the good work I had done and their plans for my return. I was grateful for their tact, but I longed for the train to take me away. At last it pulled out and I was alone, alone with my thoughts and the storm in my heart.

The night was endless. I tossed about between nerve-racking doubts and shame that I could still reach out for Ben. In Milwaukee I found a wire from him asking why I had rushed away. I did not reply. Another telegram in the afternoon said: "I love you, I want you. Please let me come." I replied: "Do not want love from Schuettler's friends." In Winnipeg a letter awaited me, a mad outpouring of passion, and a piteous pleading to let him explain.

My days were busy with work for the meetings, which made it less difficult to be brave and resist my desire for Ben. But the nights were a raging conflict. My reason repudiated the man, but my heart cried out for him. I fought frantically against his lure, trying to stifle my craving by throwing myself completely into my lectures. [. . .]

Returning to Minneapolis, I again found letters from Ben beseeching me to let him come. I struggled against it for a time, but in the end a strange dream decided the issue. I dreamed that Ben was bending over me, his face close to mine, his hands on my chest. Flames were shooting from his finger-tips and slowly enveloping my body. I made no attempt to escape them. I strained towards them, craving to be consumed by their fire.

When I awoke, my heart kept whispering to my rebellious brain that a great passion often inspired high thoughts and fine deeds. Why should I not be able to inspire Ben, to carry him with me to the world of my social ideals?

I wired: "Come," and spent twelve hours between sickening doubt and mad desire to believe in the man. It could not be that my instinct should be so misleading, I reiterated to myself—that anyone worthless could so irresistibly appeal to me.

Ben's explanation of the Schuettler scene swept my doubts away. It was not friendship for the man or connexion with the police department that had made him known to them, he said. It was his work among tramps, hobos, and prostitutes, which often brought him in contact with the authorities. The outcasts always came to him when in trouble. They knew and trusted him and he understood them much better than the so-called respectable people. He had been part of the underworld himself, and his sympathies were with the derelicts of society. They had made him their spokesman, and as such he frequently called on the police to plead in their behalf. "It never was anything else," Ben pleaded; "please believe me and let me prove it to you." Whatever might have been at stake, I had to believe in him with an all-embracing faith.

CHAPTER XXXIII

[. . .] Before I started out for California, Ben asked to let him come with me on the tour. He had enough money to pay his own way, he assured me. He would help with the work, arrange meetings, sell literature, or do anything else to be near me. The suggestion made me happy with anticipation. It would be wonderful to have someone with me on the long and weary tramps through the country, someone who was lover, companion, and manager. Yet I hesitated. My lectures, deducting my own expenses, left only small margins for *Mother Earth*. They could hardly bring enough to cover an additional burden, and I was not willing to accept Ben's co-operation without his sharing in the results. There was also another consideration—my comrades. They had helped faithfully, if not always efficiently; they were sure to see in Ben an interloper. He was from another world; moreover, he was impetuous and not always tactful. Clashes would surely follow, and I already had had to face far too many. I found it difficult to decide, but my need of Ben, of what his primitive nature could yield, was compelling. I resolved to have him; let the rest take care of itself.

Sitting beside Ben in the rushing train, his hot breath almost touching my cheek, I listened to him reciting one of his favourite Kipling[1] stanzas:

> I sits and looks across the sea
> Until it seems that no one's left but you and me.

"You and me, my blue-eyed Mommy," he whispered. [. . .] The meetings in San Francisco were being looked after by my friend Alexander Horr; not expecting any trouble where I had never been interfered with before, I felt at ease.

I had reckoned, however, without the ambitious Chief of Police of San Francisco. Envious, perhaps, of the laurels carried off by his colleagues in the East, Chief Biggey seemed anxious to gain similar glory. [. . .]

My meetings were veritable battle encampments. For blocks the streets were lined with police in autos, on horseback, and on foot. Inside the hall were heavy police guards, the platform surrounded by officers. Naturally this array of uniformed men advertised our meetings far beyond our expectations. Our hall had a seating capacity of five thousand, and it proved too small for the crowds that clamoured for admittance. Lines formed hours before the time set for the opening of my lectures. Never in all the years since I had first gone on tour, with the exception of the Union Square demonstration in 1893, had I seen masses so eager and enthusiastic. It was all due to the stupendous farce staged by the authorities at huge expense to San Francisco taxpayers.

The most interesting meeting took place one Sunday afternoon when I spoke on "Patriotism." The crowds struggling to get in were so large that the doors of the hall had to be closed very early to prevent a panic. The atmosphere was charged with indignation against the police, who were flaunting themselves importantly before the assembled people. [. . .]

The subject I had selected for the meeting was particularly timely because of the patriotic stuff which had been filling the San Francisco papers for days past. The presence of so vast an audience testified that I had chosen well. The people were certainly eager to hear some other version of the nationalist myth. [. . .]

I proceeded with an analysis of the origin, nature, and meaning of patriotism, and its terrific cost to every country. At the close of my speech of an hour, delivered amid tense silence, a storm rolled over me and I felt myself surrounded by men and women clamouring to shake my hand. [. . .]

In Portland, Oregon, we learned the cheerful news that the two halls rented for my lectures, the Arion, belonging to a German society, and the Y.M.C.A., had been refused at the last moment. Fortunately the city had a number of people to whom the right of free speech was not merely a theory. [. . .]

The audiences at my meetings kept increasing, the crowds representing every social stratum; lawyers, judges, doctors, men of letters, society women, and factory girls came to learn the truth about the ideas they had been taught to fear and to hate.

We had started for Butte, Montana, after successful meetings in Seattle and Spokane. The trip gave me opportunity to observe the Western farmer and the Indians on the reservations. The Montana farmer differed very little from his New England brother. I found him just as inhospitable and close-fisted as the farmers Sasha and I had canvassed for crayon portraits in 1891. Montana is among the most beautiful States, its soil rich and fertile far beyond the unyielding New England sod. Yet those farmers were unkind, greedy, and suspicious of the stranger. The Indian reservation revealed to me the blessings of the white man's rule. The true natives of America, once masters of the length and breadth of the land, a simple and sturdy race possessing its own art and conception of life, had dwindled to mere shadows of what they had once been. They were infected with venereal disease; their lungs were eaten by the white plague. In return for their lost vigour they had received the gift of the Bible. The kindly and helpful spirit of the Indians was very cheering after the forbidding attitude of their white neighbours.

My tour, more eventful than any previous one, was at an end, and I was on my way to New York. Ben remained in Chicago for a visit with his mother and would join me in the autumn. It was a painful wrench to separate after the intimacy of four months. Only four months since that strange being had come so unexpectedly into my life, and already I felt him in every pore, consumed by longing for his presence!

I had tried all through the months to explain to myself the appeal Ben had for me. With all my absorption in him, I was not deceived about the difference that existed between us. I knew from the first that we had intellectually very little in common, that our outlook on life, our habits, our tastes, were far apart. In spite of his degree of M.D. and his work for the outcast, I had felt Ben to be intellectually crude and socially naïve.

He had profound sympathy for society's derelicts, he understood them, and he was their generous friend, but he had no real social consciousness or grasp of the great human struggle. Like many liberal Americans, he was a reformer of surface evils, without any idea of the sources from which they spring. That alone should have been enough to keep us apart, and there were still other and graver differentiations.

Ben was typically American in his love of publicity and of show. [. . .] Moreover, Ben had the American swagger, which he would display with particular gusto at our meetings and in the homes of comrades. The antagonism his manner aroused caused me great distress and I lived in constant fear of what he might do next. Indeed, there were many elements in my lover to jar my nerves, outrage my taste, and sometimes even make me suspicious of him. Yet it all did not weigh in the scale against the magic that bound me to him and filled my soul with new warmth and colour.

I could find but two explanations of the riddle: First, Ben's child-like nature, unspoiled, untrained, and utterly lacking in artifice. Whatever he said or did came spontaneously, dictated by his intensely emotional nature. It was a rare and refreshing trait, though not always pleasant in its effects. The second was my great hunger for someone who would love the woman in me and yet who would also be able to share my work. I had never had anyone who could do both.

Sasha had been but a short time in my life, and he had been too obsessed by the Cause to see much of the woman who craved expression. Hannes and Ed, who had loved me profoundly, had wanted merely the woman in me; all the others had been attracted by the public personality only. Fedya belonged to the past. He had married, had a child, and disappeared from my ken. My friendship with Max, still as fragrant as it had always been, was less of the senses than of the understanding. Ben had come when I had greatest need of him; our four months together had proved that in him were combined the emotions I had yearned for so long.

Already he had greatly enriched my life. As helpmate in my work he had shown his interest and his worth. With complete absorption and abundance of energy Ben had achieved wonders in the size of our meetings and the increased sales of literature. As travelling companion he had made my trip a new, delightful experience. He was touchingly tender and solicitous, most comforting in releasing me from the petty annoyances and details involved in travelling. As lover he had unleashed elements in me that made all differences between us disappear as so much chaff in a storm. Nothing mattered now except the realization that Ben had become an essential part of myself. I would have him in my life and in my work, whatever the cost.

That the cost would not be small I already knew by the opposition to him which was growing in our ranks. Some of my comrades sensed Ben's possibilities and his value to the movement. Others, however, were antagonistic to him. Of course, Ben did not feel at ease under those circumstances. He could not understand why people standing for freedom should object to anyone's behaving naturally. He was particularly nervous about my New York friends. How would they act towards him and our love? Sasha—what would he say? My account of Sasha's act, his imprisonment and suffering, had stirred Ben profoundly. "I can see Berkman is your greatest obsession," he had once said to me; "no one will ever have a chance alongside of him." "Not an obsession, but a fact," I had told him; "Sasha has been in my life so long that I feel we have grown together like the Siamese twins. But you need fear no rivalry from him. Sasha loves me with his head, not with his heart."

He was not convinced and I could see he was worried. I myself was apprehensive because of the difference in their personalities. Yet I hoped that Sasha, who had touched the depths of life, would understand Ben better than the rest. [. . .]

My hopes proved vain. Not that Sasha or the other friends were unkind to Ben, but the atmosphere was strained, and no one seemed to find the right word. The situation acted on Ben as on a child expected to be on its good behaviour. He began to show off and brag, boast of his exploits, and talk nonsense, which made matters worse. I felt ashamed of Ben, bitterly resentful of my friends, and angry with myself for having brought him into their midst.

My deepest grief was Sasha. He said nothing to Ben, but he said plenty of cutting things to me. He scoffed at the idea that I could love such a man. It was nothing but a temporary infatuation, he felt sure. Ben lacked social feeling, he had no rebel spirit, and he did not belong in our movement, he insisted. Moreover, he was too ignorant to have passed through college or to have earned a degree. He would write to the university to find out. This, coming from Sasha, completely unnerved me. "You are a zealot," I cried; "you judge human quality by your criterion of one's value to the Cause, as the Christians do from the standpoint of the Church. That has been your attitude towards me since your release. The years of struggle and travail I suffered for my growth mean nothing to you, because you are bound in the confines of your creed. With all your talk of the movement, you thrust back the outstretched hand of a man who comes to learn about your ideals. You and the other intellectuals prate about human nature, yet when someone out of the ordinary appears, you don't even try to understand him. But all that can have no bearing on my feeling for Ben. I love him, and I will fight for him to the death!"

I left the farm with Ben. I was sick from the scene with Sasha, the harsh words I had hurled in his face; and I was tortured by my own doubts. I had to admit to myself that much that Sasha had said about Ben was true. I could see his defects much better than anyone else and I knew how lacking he was. But I could not help loving him.

It had been my plan to devote the winter to New York. I was tired out from trains, strange places, and other people's "atmosphere." Here I had my home, limited and crowded though it was. *Mother Earth* also needed my presence. I was certain that if I lectured through the winter, I should attract large Yiddish and English audiences. I had talked it over with Ben and he had decided to move to New York and devote himself to my task.

But now Ben hated the city and hated 210 East Thirteenth Street. He could never do any good there, he felt. With me on the road he would be able to put his energies into the work and he would grow, develop, and become a force. I, too, wanted to get away from the disharmony and the censure of the people nearest to me. I was anxious to give Ben a better chance, to help him to an understanding of himself, to bring out what was finest in him.

The previous year I had received an invitation from Australia. J. W. Fleming,[2] our most active comrade there, had even raised enough money for my fare. At that time I could not decide to go away so far and make the long journey alone. With Ben at my side the voyage would be turned into a joy and give me a much needed rest, free from strife. [. . .]

Everything was ready for my departure. Ben was to precede me to do advance work. A few days before leaving he sent me a letter thirty pages long, a rambling, incoherent account of things he had done since we first met. He had been reading *The Power of a Lie,* by the Norwegian author Boyer,[3] he wrote; it had struck deep into him, and he felt impelled to confess to me the falsehoods he had told and the mean things he had done while on tour with me. It was giving him no rest. He could keep silent no longer.

He had lied when he had told me that it was not he who had disclosed the plan of my speaking at the social in Chicago last March. He had not informed the police, but he had confided it to a reporter, who had promised to keep it to himself. He had lied when he had given "important matters" as the reason for not calling on me that evening to explain about the presence of the police. He had gone straight from the hall to a girl he cared about. He had lied when he had assured me that he had money to pay his way on the trip with me. He had borrowed the money, gradually paying it back from the sales of our literature. He had also taken money from the receipts to send to his mother. He loved her passionately, and he had always looked after her. He had not dared to tell me that his mother depended on him, because he feared I would send him away. Every time I had expressed surprise that money was apparently missing from our accounts, he had lied. The excuses he had given for so often vanishing after my meetings or for staying away during the day were all false. He had gone with other women, women he had met at the lectures or somewhere else. In nearly every city he had gone with women. He did not love them, but they attracted him physically to the point of obsession. He had always had such obsessions and probably always would have. These women had never meant anything more than a moment's distraction. He always forgot them afterwards; often he did not even know their names. Yes, he had gone with other women during the four months; yet he loved only me. He had loved me from the first, and each day his passion for me had increased. I was the greatest force in his life, my work his deepest concern. He would prove it if I only would not send him away, if I would forgive him his lies and his betrayal, if only I would again have confidence in him. But even if I should send him away after I had read the letter, he would still feel relieved that he had confessed to me. He realized now how disintegrating and crushing is the power of a lie.

I had the feeling of sinking into a swamp. In desperation I clutched the table in front of me and tried to cry out, but no sound came from my throat. I sat numb, the terrible letter seeming to creep over me, word by word, and drawing me into its slime.

I was brought back to myself by Sasha's arrival. Sasha—at this moment—of all people! How he would feel justified by this letter in all he had said about Ben! I broke out in uncontrollable laughter.

"Emma, your laugh is terrible. It cuts like a knife. What is it?"

"Nothing, nothing, only I must get out on the street or I shall choke."

I snatched up my coat and hat and ran down the five flights. I walked for hours, the letter burning in my head.

This was the man whom I had taken into my heart, my life, my work! Fool, lovesick fool that I was, blinded by passion not to see what everyone else saw. I, Emma Goldman, to be carried away like any ordinary woman of forty by a mad attraction for a young man, a stranger picked up at a chance meeting, an alien to my every thought and feeling, the reverse of the ideal of man I had always cherished. [. . .]

Days of anguish followed, tortured by attempts to explain and excuse Ben's acts, attempts irritating and vain. Over and again I repeated to myself: "Ben comes from a world where lies prevail in all human relations. He does not know that free spirits in their love and tasks honestly and frankly share everything life brings; that among people with ideals no one need cheat, steal, or lie. He is of another world. What right have I to condemn, I who claim to teach new values of life?" "But his obsessions? His going with every woman?" My heart cried out in protest. "Women he does not love, does not even respect. Can you justify that, too? No, no!" came from the depths of my woman's soul. "Yes," replied my brain, "if it is his nature, his dominant need, how can I object? I have propagated freedom in sex. I have had many men myself. But I loved them; I have never been able to go indiscriminately with men. It will be painful, lacerating, to feel myself one of many in Ben's life. It will be a fearful price to pay for my love. But nothing worth while is gained except at heavy cost. I've paid dearly for the right to myself, for my social ideal, for everything I have achieved. Is my love for Ben so weak that I shall not be able to pay the price his freedom of action demands?" There was no answer. In vain did I strive to harmonize the conflicting elements that were warring in my soul.

Dazed and hardly aware of my surroundings, I jumped out of bed. It was still dark. Like a sleep-walker I got into my clothes, felt my way to Sasha's room, and shook him out of sleep.

"I must go to Ben," I said. "Will you take me to him?"

Sasha was startled. He switched on the light and searchingly looked at me. But he asked no questions and said nothing. He hurriedly dressed and accompanied me.

We walked in silence. My head swam, my feet were unsteady. Sasha put my arm in his. In my purse was a key to the house where Ben was rooming. I let myself in, then turned to Sasha for a moment. Without a word I closed the door and ran up the two flights, bursting into Ben's room.

He jumped up with a cry. "Mommy, you've come at last! You have forgiven, you have understood." We clung to each other, everything else wiped out.

CHAPTER XXXIV

In planning our tour to take place during the presidential campaign we had overlooked the interest of the American masses in the political circus. The result was failure of the initial part of our trip. In Indianapolis, the first city to bring out a large attendance, my lecture was suppressed in the usual manner. The Mayor expressed regret that the police had overstepped their powers, but of course he could not act against the department. The Chief said that stopping the meeting might have been bad law, but that it was good common sense. [. . .]

San Francisco held a special attraction. The ex-soldier William Buwalda,[1] as a result of our agitation in his behalf, had been pardoned by President Roosevelt. He was released after ten months' imprisonment, two weeks before our arrival in the city. [. . .]

Among the sensational reports in the San Francisco press regarding the raid of our meeting and our arrest was one enlarging upon "Emma Goldman's lack of sentiment and feeling."[2] While in jail, she had been given a telegram announcing her father's death, the paper stated, which she received without the least sign of emotion. As a matter of fact, my father's end, though not unexpected, had affected me deeply and had recalled to me the details of his wasted life. An invalid for over thirty years, he had of late been more frequently ill than usually. When I had seen him on my last visit to Rochester, in October, I had been shocked to find him so near death. The giant he had once been was now shattered by the storms of life.

With the passing years had come to me better understanding

of Father, and mutual sympathy had drawn us gradually closer. My beloved Helena had had much to do with my change towards him. It was helped also by my awakening to the complexities of sex as a force dominating our feelings. I had learned to understand better my own turbulent nature, and my experiences had made me see what had been obscure to me so long in the character of my father. His violence and hardness had only been symptoms of an intensely sexual nature that had failed to find adequate expression.

My parents had been brought together in the traditional Jewish orthodox fashion, without love. They were mismated from the first. Mother had been left a widow at twenty-three, with two children, a little store her only earthly possession. Whatever love she had had died with the young man to whom she had been married at the age of fifteen. Father had brought into the match a fire of passionate youth. His wife was only one year his senior and radiantly beautiful. The impelling need of his nature drove him to her and made him more insistent in proportion as Mother fought back his insatiable hunger. My coming had marked her fourth childbirth, each one nearly bringing her to the grave. I recalled some remarks I had heard her make when I was too young to understand their meaning. They illuminated much that had been dark to me and caused me to realize what a purgatory my parents' intimacy must have been for them both. No doubt they would have been shocked had anyone called to their attention the true source of the struggle between them and of Father's uncontrollable temper. With the decline of health came also a lessening of his erotic vitality and a resultant psychic change. Father grew more mellow, patient, and kindly. The affection he had rarely shown his own children he now lavished on those of my two sisters. When I once referred to the harsh methods he had used towards us, he assured me that it could not be true. The tenderness that had come into his nature blotted out even the remembrance of past severity. The best in him, formerly hidden by emotional stress, by the struggle for existence and years of physical suffering, came into its own at last. He now felt and gave us a newly born affection, which in its turn awakened our love for him. [...]

Our departure for Australia had been set for January. The arrest and subsequent free-speech fight in San Francisco forced us to postpone it until April. At last we were ready, our trunks packed, a grand farewell party arranged for us. We were about to secure passage when a telegram from Rochester demolished our plans. "Washington revoked Kershner's citizenship papers," it read; "dangerous to leave country."

My sister had written me months before that two suspicious-looking individuals had been snooping about to secure data on Kershner. He had left the city years previously and nothing had been heard from him since then. Not finding Kershner, the men had pestered his parents and tried to get information from them. I had dismissed the matter from my mind at the time as of no consequence. But now the blow came. I was deprived of my citizenship without even an opportunity to contest the action of the Federal authorities. I knew that if I should leave the country, I should not be permitted to re-enter it. My Australian tour had to be abandoned at a great financial loss, not to mention the expenditures invested by our Australian friends in preparing for my activities there. It was a bitter disappointment, much mitigated, fortunately, by the undaunted optimism of my hobo manager. His zeal merely increased with the obstacles we encountered. His energy was dynamic and tireless. [...]

CHAPTER XXXV

I needed a rest badly, but, our tour this time having brought us more glory than cash, I could not afford to take it. In fact, we were so short of funds that we were compelled to reduce the size of *Mother Earth* from sixty-four to thirty-two pages. Our financial condition made it necessary for me to start lecturing again. Ben joined me in New York in the latter part of March, and by the 15th of April he had succeeded in organizing for me a series of lectures on the drama. All went well at first, but May proved to be a record-breaker. During that month I was stopped by the police in eleven different places. [. . .]

In September I went with Ben on a short tour through Massachusetts and Vermont. We were stopped, stopped, and stopped, either by direct police interference or by the intimidation of the hall-owners. [. . .]

The most important event of our Worcester visit was an address given by Sigmund Freud on the twentieth anniversary of Clark University. I was deeply impressed by the lucidity of his mind and the simplicity of his delivery. Among the array of professors, looking stiff and important in their university caps and gowns, Sigmund Freud, in ordinary attire, unassuming, almost shrinking, stood out like a giant among pygmies. He had aged somewhat since I had heard him in Vienna in 1896. He had been reviled then as a Jew and irresponsible innovator; now he was a world figure; but neither obloquy nor fame had influenced the great man. [. . .]

CHAPTER XXXVI

In the latter part of 1909 New York again experienced a vice crusade. The reformers had discovered the white-slave traffic! They got busy, though they were without the slightest notion regarding the sources of the evil they were trying to eradicate. [. . .]

I prepared a lecture on the white-slave traffic, dealing with its causes, effects, and possible elimination. It became the strongest drawing card in my new course and also aroused the most heated criticism and discussion. The lecture was published in the January issue of *Mother Earth* and subsequently in pamphlet form.

Shortly afterwards Ben and I went on our annual tour. Everywhere we met with complaints from our subscribers that they had not received the January number of the magazine. I wired Sasha about it and he went after the postal authorities. He was informed that some copies had been held up on the complaint of Anthony Comstock. While we felt flattered that we were at last given a place among other victims of Comstockery, we nevertheless demanded to know the reason for the unexpected honour.

After several calls Sasha succeeded in getting into the august presence of the keeper of American morals. Comstock admitted that *Mother Earth* had been held up, but denied that it had been done on his complaint.

"The matter is now in my hands," he told Sasha; "the reason for it is Miss Goldman's article on the white-slave traffic." At Comstock's request Sasha accompanied him to the office of the District Attorney, where St. Anthony held a secret conference lasting two hours. After that came a prolonged consultation with the Chief Post Office Inspector. Finally the censor declared that nothing objectionable had been found in the article.

The next day the New York *Times* contained an interview with Comstock in which he entirely denied the whole matter. It was "a scheme of Emma Goldman to attract attention to her publication," he stated. He had made no complaint against the magazine, he said, nor had it been held up by the Post Office. It required another week of energetic work by Sasha, canvassing various postal departments and repeatedly wiring to Washington, before the January issue was finally released.

If Comstock had been decent enough at least to inform us of his intention in advance, we should have printed fifty thousand copies of the proscribed number. Even as it was, his interference helped to advertise our publication. The demand for *Mother Earth* greatly increased, but unfortunately we had only our usual edition on hand.

For the first time since the free-speech fight in Chicago in 1908 I could go back to that city. The police, perhaps mindful of the publicity they had given anarchism at that time by their treatment of me, actually assured Ben that I should not be molested any more. [. . .]

Chicago had been significant in my life. I owed my spiritual birth to the martyrs of 1887. Ten years later I found Max there, whose understanding and tender companionship had not ceased to inspire and sustain me through the years. It was also in Chicago, in 1901, that I had been brought close to death because of my attitude towards Leon Czolgosz, and was it not Chicago that had given me Ben? Ben, with all his faults, irresponsibility, and obsessions—the man who had already caused me greater agony of spirit than anyone else in my life, and who had brought me deeper devotion and a complete consecration to my work. Only two years we had been together, and during that period he had tested my soul a hundred times, my brain always in rebellion against the strange boy whose nearness was yet a vital need to me.

I had been lecturing in the city on Lake Michigan since 1892, but it was only on this visit that I realized its possibilities. Within ten days I addressed six English and three Yiddish meetings, attended by large crowds that were sufficiently interested to pay admission and to purchase large quantities of our literature. [. . .]

In my travels through the United States I had always found university towns the most indifferent to the social struggle. American student bodies were ignorant of the great issues in their native land and lacked sympathy with the masses. I was therefore not enthusiastic when Ben suggested our invading Madison, Wisconsin.

Great was my surprise when I discovered an entirely new note in the University of Wisconsin. I found the professors and pupils vitally interested in social ideas, and a library containing the best selection of books, papers, and magazines. [. . .]

A group of students invited us to lecture in the Y.M.C.A. hall on the campus. Ben spoke on the relation between education and agitation, and I discussed the difference between Russian and American college men. [. . .]

My second appearance was at the Artists' Guild, a society composed of "respectable" Bohemians. [. . .] The majority of the Guilders impressed me as people to whom "bohemianism" was a sort of narcotic to help them endure the boredom of their lives. Of course there were others, those who knew the struggle that is the lot of every sincere and free person, whether he aspires to an ideal in life or in art. To them I addressed my talk on "Art in Life," pointing out, among other things, that life in all its variety and fullness is art, the highest art. The man who is not part of the stream of life is not an artist, no matter how well he paints sunsets or composes nocturnes. It certainly does not mean that the artist must hold a definite creed, join an anarchist group or a socialist local. It does signify, however, that he must be able to feel the tragedy of the millions condemned to a lack of joy and beauty. The inspiration of the true artist has never been the drawing-room. Great art has always gone to the masses, to their hopes and dreams, for the spark that kindled their souls. The rest, "the many, all too many," as Nietzsche called mediocrity, have been mere commodities that can be bought with money, cheap glory, or social position. [. . .]

Michigan State University is only ten hours removed from the University of Wisconsin, but in spirit it was fifty years behind. Instead of broad-minded professors and keen students, I was confronted with five hundred university rowdies in our hall, whistling, howling, and acting like lunatics. I had addressed difficult crowds in my day—long-shoremen, sailors, steel-workers, miners, men aroused by war hysteria. They resembled boarding-school girls compared with the tough gang that had come this time, evidently intent upon breaking up the meeting. [. . .]

Several students who had entertained us at a fraternity dinner grew anxious about my safety and offered to call the police. I felt that such a step would only aggravate the situation and perhaps cause a riot. I informed them that I would face the music myself and take the consequences.

My appearance on the platform was greeted with shouts, bells, stamping of feet, and cries of "Here she is, the anarchist bomb-thrower; here's the free lover! You can't speak in our town, Emma! Get out—you'd better get out!"

I saw clearly that if the situation was to be met, I must not show nervousness or lose patience. I folded my arms and stood there facing the young savages while the deafening noises continued. During a slight lull I said: "Gentlemen, I can see you are in a sporting mood, you want a contest. Very well, you shall have it. Just go on with the noise. I will wait until you are through."

There was an amazed silence for a moment, and then they again broke loose. I continued to stand, my arms folded, all my will-power concentrated in my stare. Gradually the yelling subsided and then someone cried: "All right, Emma, let's hear about your anarchism!" The cry was taken up by others, and after a while comparative quiet prevailed. Then I began to speak.

I talked for an hour amid repeated interruptions, but before long, silence settled over the assembly. Their behaviour, I told them, was the best proof of the effects of authority and of its system of education. "You are the result of it," I said; "how can you know the meaning of freedom of thought and speech? How can you feel respect for others or be kind and hospitable to a stranger in your midst? Authority at home, in the school, and in the body politic destroys those qualities. It turns the individual into a parrot repeating time-worn slogans, until he becomes incapable of thinking for himself or of feeling social wrongs. But I believe in the possibilities of youth," I continued, "and you are young, gentlemen, very, very young. That is fortunate, because you are still uncorrupted and impressionable. The energy you have so ably demonstrated this afternoon could be put to better use." [. . .]

As soon as I had finished, they broke out with the college yell. It was the highest tribute, I was told later, that I could receive. Towards the evening a committee of students came to my hotel to offer apologies for the behaviour of their comrades and to pay the damage for the literature and vase. "You won, Emma Goldman," they said, "you have made us ashamed. Next time you visit our city, we will give you a different welcome." [. . .]

In San Francisco I learned that Jack London[1] lived in the neighbourhood. I had met him with other young socialist students at the Strunskys' on my first visit to California, in 1897. I had since read most of his works and I was naturally eager to renew our acquaintance. There was also another reason: the Modern School the Ferrer Association[2] was planning to establish in New York. [. . .] I wanted to interest Jack London in our project. I wrote requesting him to attend my lecture on Francisco Ferrer.

His reply was characteristic. "Dear Emma Goldman," it read, "I have your note. I would not go to a meeting even if God Almighty were to speak there. The only time I attend lectures is when I am to do the talking. But we want you *here*. Will you not come to Glen Ellen and bring whomever you have with you?" Who could resist such an amiable invitation? . . .

How different was the real Jack London from the mechanical, bell-button socialist of the *Kempton-Wace Letters*![3] Here was youth, exuberance, throbbing life. Here was the good comrade, all concern and affection. He exerted himself to make our visit a glorious holiday. We argued about our political differences, of course, but there was in Jack nothing of the rancour I had so often found in the socialists I had debated with. But, then, Jack London was the artist first, the creative spirit to whom freedom is the breath of life. As the artist he did not fail to see the beauties of anarchism, even if he did insist that society would have to pass through socialism before reaching the higher stage of anarchism. In any case it was not Jack London's politics that mattered to me. It was his humanity, his understanding of and his feeling with the complexities of the human heart. [. . .]

For fifteen years before this my lectures had been made possible by my comrades, who had always given me their best assistance. But they had never been able to reach a large American public. Some of them had been too centred in their own language-group activities to trouble about interesting the native element. The results during those years were scant and unsatisfactory. Now with Ben as my manager my work was lifted out of its former narrow confines. On this tour I visited thirty-seven cities in twenty-five States, among them many places where anarchism had never been discussed before. I lectured one hundred and twenty times to vast audiences, of which twenty-five thousand paid admission, besides the great number of poor students or unemployed admitted without charge. The most gratifying part of the enlarged scope of my work was that ten thousand pieces of literature were sold and five thousand distributed free. Not least important were the various free-speech fights, with the entire expense for them raised at our own gatherings. [. . .]

I took heart in the certainty that during the past two years I had done better work and that I had made anarchism more widely known than in the previous years. And it had been the skill and devotion of Ben that had brought it about.

CHAPTER XXXVII

May 18, the day of Sasha's resurrection, remained graven on my heart, although my yearly tours had always prevented my being with him on the anniversary of his release. In a spiritual sense, however, neither space nor time could separate me from Sasha or make me forget the day I had longed and worked for throughout the years of his imprisonment. On May 18 this year a telegram from him found me in Los Angeles. It filled me with great joy, for it brought the news that he had determined to begin his prison memoirs. I had often urged him to write them, believing that if he could re-create his prison life on paper, it might help him to get rid of the phantoms that were making his readjustment to life so difficult. Now he had decided it at last, on Our Day, the day that represented the most significant moment in both our lives. I immediately notified him that I would soon return to relieve him in the *Mother Earth* office, and that I would devote myself for the rest of the summer to his needs. [. . .]

Sasha and I went out to the little farm. We loved the beauty and restfulness of the place. He pitched a tent on one of the highest hills, which gave him a gorgeous view over the Hudson. I was occupied in setting the house in order. Meanwhile Sasha began to write.

Notwithstanding the many police raids I had suffered since Sasha had gone to Pittsburgh in 1892, I had managed to rescue some copies of "The Prison Blossoms," which he had published *sub rosa* in the penitentiary. Carl Nold, Henry Bauer, and several other friends also had kept copies. They were helpful to Sasha, but they were insignificant in comparison with the memory of what he had lived through in that house of the living dead. All the horrors he had known, the agony of body and soul, the suffering of his fellow-prisoners, all this he had now to dig out from the depths of his being and re-create. The black spectre of fourteen years again began to haunt his waking and sleeping hours.

Day after day he would sit at his desk staring into vacancy, or he would write as if driven by furies. What he had written he often wanted to destroy, and I would wrestle with him to save it, as I had fought through all the years to save him from his grave. Then would come days when Sasha would vanish into the woods to escape human contact, to escape me, and above all to escape himself and the ghosts that had come to life since he had begun to write. I would torment myself to find the right way and the right word with which to soothe his harassed spirit. It was not only because of my affection for him that I took up this struggle each day; it was also because I perceived in the very first chapter of his writing that Sasha was in the birth-throes of a great work. No price on my part seemed too high to help it to life. [. . .]

In January 1911 Ben and I again started on our annual tour. Before we left, my selected lectures, *Anarchism and Other Essays*, came off the press. The book also contained a biographic sketch of the author by Hippolyte Havel, comprising the most significant events of my public career. Some of the lectures in the volume had been repeatedly suppressed by the police. Even when I had been able to deliver them, it had never been without anxiety and travail. They represented a mental and spiritual struggle of twenty years, the conclusions arrived at after much reflection and growth. I owed the inspiration to write the book to Ben, but the main assistance, including the revision and the reading of proofs, was due to Sasha. It was hard to say which of us was the happier at seeing my first literary effort in print. [. . .]

During the summer Sasha and I again went out to our retreat on the Hudson and he resumed work on his book. [. . .] I could devote my time to Sasha and look after his comfort. I sought to encourage him in his work: with him I had lived through the agony of his prison years, and now the turmoil of his spirit re-echoed in my heart.

The end of the summer saw his *Prison Memoirs* completed. It was a document profoundly moving, a brilliant study of criminal psychology. I was filled with wonder to see Sasha emerge from his Calvary an artist with a rare gift of music in his words.

"Now for New York and the publishers!" I cried; "surely there will be many who will appreciate the dramatic appeal of your work, the understanding and sympathy for those you have left behind."

We hastened back to the city and I began to canvass the publishers. The more conservative houses refused even to read the manuscript the moment they learned the author's name. "Alexander Berkman, the man who shot Frick!" the representative of a large firm exclaimed; "no, we can't have him on our shelves." "It is a vital literary work," I urged; "aren't you interested in that and in his interpretation of prisons and crime?" They were looking for such a book, he said, but they could not afford to risk the name of the author.

Some publishers asked whether Alexander Berkman would be willing to use a pseudonym. I resented the suggestion and pointed out that *Prison Memoirs* was a personal story, the product of years of suffering and pain. Could the writer be expected to hide his identity concerning something that was flesh of his flesh and blood of his blood?

I turned to some of the "advanced" publishers and they promised to read the manuscript. I waited anxiously for weeks, and when they at last requested me to come, I found them enthusiastic. "It is a remarkable work," one said, "but would Mr. Berkman leave out the anarchist part?" Another insisted on eliminating the chapters relating to homosexuality in prison. A third suggested other changes. Thus it went on for months. I clung to the hope that someone of literary and human judgment would accept the manuscript. I still believed that we could discover in America what Dostoyevsky had found in tsarist Russia—a publisher courageous enough to issue the first great American study of a "House of the Dead."[1] In vain. Finally we decided to publish the book ourselves. [. . .]

When I informed Gilbert [Roe][2] that Sasha's manuscript had
been turned down by many publishers, and that we wanted the
Mother Earth Publishing Association to have the honour of giving the book to the American public, my good friend said simply: "All right. We will arrange an evening in our apartment
and invite some people to hear you read parts of the manuscript. Then we will make an appeal for subscriptions." "Read
Sasha's work?" I cried in alarm; "I'll never be able to do it. It is
too vital a part of my own life. I shall be sure to break down."
Gilbert scoffed at the idea of my being nervous at a small private gathering, considering that I had so often faced thousands
in my public work.

When I arrived with the manuscript, the guests were already
at Roe's. I felt myself growing faint and covered with a cold
sweat. Gilbert took me to the dining-room and handed me a
stiff drink. "To give strength to your weak knees," he teased.
We returned to a darkened room, with only one light for me at
the desk. I began to read. Soon the assembled people seemed to
vanish, and Sasha emerged. Sasha at the Baltimore and Ohio
Station, Sasha as I saw him in convict clothes in prison, and
then Sasha resurrected at the railroad station in Detroit. All the
agony, all the hope and despair I had shared with him, leaped
up in my throat as I read.

"Whether it is the manuscript or your reading," Gilbert
presently remarked, "it is a tremendous piece of work." [. . .]

CHAPTER XXXVIII

[. . .] The next job was already at hand, the Lawrence strike. Twenty-five thousand textile workers, men, women, and children, were involved in the struggle for a fifteen-per-cent increase in their wage. For years they had toiled fifty-six hours a week for an average weekly pay of eight dollars. Out of the strength of these people the mill-owners had grown immensely rich. Poverty and misery had at last driven the Lawrence textile workers to strike. The struggle was hardly under way when the mill lords began to show their teeth. In this they had the support of the State, and even of the college authorities. The Governor of Massachusetts, himself a mill-owner, sent the militia to protect his interests and those of his mill-owning colleagues. The president of Harvard was, as one of the stockholders, equally interested in dividends from the Lawrence mills. The result of this unity between State, capitalism, and seats of learning in Massachusetts was a horde of police, detectives, soldiers, and collegiate ruffians let loose on the helpless strikers. The first victims of the reign of military terror were Anna Lapezo and John Ramo. During a skirmish the girl was shot and the young man bayoneted to death by a soldier. Instead of apprehending the perpetrators of the crime, the State and local authorities arrested among others, Joseph Ettor and Arturo Giovannitti, the two foremost strike leaders. These men were conscious rebels, backed by the Industrial Workers of the World and by the other revolutionary elements in the country. Labour in the East rallied with particular generosity to the support of the Lawrence strikers and to the defence of the two men. The gap left by the arrest of Ettor and Giovannitti was immediately filled by Bill

Haywood[1] and Elizabeth Gurley Flynn.[2] Haywood's years of experience in the labour struggle, his determination and tact, made him a distinctive power in the Lawrence situation. On the other hand, Elizabeth's youth, charm, and eloquence easily won everybody's heart. The names of the two and their reputation gained for the strike country-wide publicity and support.

I had known and admired Elizabeth since I had first heard her, years before, at an open-air gathering. She could not have been more than fourteen years of age at the time, with a beautiful face and figure and a voice vibrant with earnestness. She made a strong impression on me. Later I used to see her in the company of her father at my lectures. She was a fascinating picture with her black hair, large blue eyes, and lovely complexion. I often found it hard to take my eyes off her, sitting in the front row at my meetings.

The splendid free-speech fight she had made in Spokane with other members of the I.W.W., and the persecution she had endured, brought Elizabeth Gurley Flynn very near to me. And when I heard she was ill, after the birth of her child, I felt great sympathy for this young rebel, one of the first American women revolutionists of proletarian background. My interest in her had served to increase my efforts in raising funds, not only for the Spokane fight, but for Elizabeth's own use during her first months of young motherhood.

Since she had returned to New York we were often thrown together, in meetings and in more intimate ways. Elizabeth was not an anarchist, but neither was she fanatical or antagonistic, as were some of her comrades who had emerged from the Socialist Labor Party. She was accepted in our circles as one of our own, and I loved her as a friend.

Bill Haywood had but recently come to live in New York. We had met almost immediately and became very friendly. Bill also was not an anarchist, but, like Elizabeth, he was free from narrow sectarianism. He frankly admitted that he felt much more at home with the anarchists, and especially with the *Mother Earth* group, than with the zealots in his own ranks.

The most notable characteristic of Bill was his extraordinary sensitiveness. This giant, outwardly so hard, would wince at a coarse word and tremble at the sight of pain. On one occasion, when he addressed our eleventh-of-November commemoration, he related to me the effect the crime of 1887 had had on him. He was but a youngster at the time, already working in the mines. "Since then," he told me, "our Chicago martyrs have been my greatest inspiration, their courage my guiding star." The apartment at 210 East Thirteenth Street became Bill's retreat. Frequently he spent his free evenings at our place. There he could read and rest to his heart's content, or drink coffee "black as the night, strong as the revolutionary ideal, sweet as love." [. . .]

San Diego, California, had always enjoyed considerable freedom of speech. Anarchists, socialists, I.W.W. men, as well as religious sects, had been in the habit of speaking out of doors to large crowds. Then the city fathers of San Diego passed an ordinance doing away with the old custom. The anarchists and I.W.W.'s initiated a free-speech fight, with the result that eighty-four men and women were thrown into jail. [. . .]

When I arrived with Ben in Los Angeles in April, San Diego was in the grip of a veritable civil war. The patriots, known as Vigilantes, had converted the city into a battle-field. They beat, clubbed, and killed men and women who still believed in their constitutional rights. Hundreds of them had come to San Diego from every part of the United States to participate in the campaign. They travelled in box cars, on the bumpers, on the roofs of trains, every moment in danger of their lives, yet sustained by the holy quest for freedom of speech, for which their comrades were already filling the jails.

The Vigilantes raided the I.W.W. headquarters, broke up the furniture, and arrested a large number of men found there. They were taken out to Sorrento to a spot where a flag-pole had been erected. There the I.W.W.'s were forced to kneel, kiss the flag, and sing the national anthem. As an incentive to quicker action one of the Vigilantes would slap them on the back, which was the signal for a general beating. After these proceedings the men were loaded into automobiles and sent to San Onofre, near the county line, placed in a cattle-pen with armed guards over them, and kept without food or drink for eighteen hours. The following morning they were taken out in groups of five and compelled to run the gauntlet. As they passed between the double line of Vigilantes, they were belaboured with clubs and blackjacks. Then the flag-kissing episode was repeated, after which they were told to "hike" up the track and never come back. They reached Los Angeles after a tramp of several days, sore, hungry, penniless, and in deplorable physical condition. [. . .]

Some comrades in San Diego had undertaken to arrange a meeting, and I chose a subject which seemed to express the situation best—Henrik Ibsen's *An Enemy of the People*.[3]

On our arrival we found a dense crowd at the station. It did not occur to me that the reception was intended for us; I thought that some State official was being expected. We were to be met by our friends Mr. and Mrs. E. E. Kirk, but they were nowhere to be seen, and Ben suggested that we go to the U. S. Grant Hotel. We passed unobserved and got into the hotel autobus. It was hot and stuffy inside and we climbed up on top. We had barely taken our seats when someone shouted: "Here she is, here's the Goldman woman!" At once the cry was taken up by the crowd. Fashionably dressed women stood up in their cars screaming: "We want that anarchist murderess!" In an instant there was a rush for the autobus, hands reaching up to pull me down. With unusual presence of mind, the chauffeur started the car at full speed, scattering the crowd in all directions.

At the hotel we met with no objections. We registered and were shown to our rooms. Everything seemed normal. Mr. and Mrs. Kirk called to see us, and we quietly discussed final arrangements for our meeting. In the afternoon the head clerk came to announce that the Vigilantes had insisted on looking over the hotel register to secure the number of our rooms; he would therefore have to transfer us to another part of the house. We were taken to the top floor and assigned to a large suite. Later on, Mr. Holmes, the hotel manager, paid us a visit. We were perfectly safe under his roof, he assured us, but he could not permit us to go down for our meals or leave our rooms. He would have to keep us locked in. I protested that the U. S. Grant Hotel was not a prison. He replied that he could not keep us incarcerated against our will, but that, as long as we remained the

guests of the house, we should have to submit to his arrangement for our safety. "The Vigilantes are in an ugly mood," he
warned us; "they are determined not to let you speak and to
drive you both out of town." He urged us to leave of our own
account and volunteered to escort us. He was a kindly man and
we appreciated his offer, but we had to refuse it.

Mr. Holmes had barely left when I was called on the telephone. The speaker said that his name was Edwards, that he
was at the head of the local Conservatory of Music, and that he
had just read in the papers that our hall-keeper had backed out.
He offered us the recital hall of the conservatory. "San Diego
still seems to have some brave men," I said to the mysterious
person at the other end of the telephone, and I invited him to
come to see me to talk over his plan. Before long a fine-looking
man of about twenty-seven called. In the course of our conversation I pointed out to him that I might cause him trouble by
speaking in his place. He replied that he did not mind; he was an
anarchist in art and he believed in free speech. If I were willing
to take a chance, so was he. We decided to await developments.

Towards evening a bedlam of auto horns and whistles filled
the street. "The Vigilantes!" Ben cried. There was a knock at
the door, and Mr. Holmes came in, accompanied by two other
men. I was wanted downstairs by the city authorities, they informed me. Ben sensed danger and insisted that I ask them to
send the visitors up. It seemed timid to me. It was early evening
and we were in the principal hotel of the city. What could happen
to us? I went with Mr. Holmes, Ben accompanying us. Downstairs we were ushered into a room where we found seven men
standing in a semicircle. We were asked to sit down and wait for
the Chief of Police, who arrived before long. "Please come with
me," he addressed me; "the Mayor and other officials are awaiting you next door." We got up to follow, but, turning to Ben, the
Chief said: "You are not wanted, doctor. Better wait here."

I entered a room filled with men. The window-blinds were
partly drawn, but the large electric street light in front disclosed
an agitated mass below. The Mayor approached me. "You hear
that mob," he said, indicating the street; "they mean business.
They want to get you and Reitman out of the hotel, even if they

have to take you by force. We cannot guarantee anything. If you consent to leave, we will give you protection and get you safely out of town."

"That's very nice of you," I replied, "but why don't you disperse the crowd? Why don't you use the same measures against these people that you have against the free-speech fighters? Your ordinance makes it a crime to gather in the business districts. Hundreds of I.W.W.'s, anarchists, socialists, and trade-union men have been clubbed and arrested, and some even killed, for this offence. Yet you allow the Vigilante mob to congregate in the busiest part of the town and obstruct traffic. All you have to do is to disperse these law-breakers."

"We can't do it," he said abruptly; "these people are in a dangerous mood, and your presence makes things worse."

"Very well, then, let me speak to the crowd," I suggested. "I could do it from a window here. I have faced infuriated men before and I have always been able to pacify them."

The Mayor refused.

"I have never accepted protection from the police," I then said, "and I do not intend to do so now. I charge all of you men here with being in league with the Vigilantes."

Thereupon the officials declared that matters would have to take their course, and that I should have only myself to blame if anything happened.

The interview at an end, I went to call Ben. The room I had left him in was locked. I became alarmed and pounded on the door. There was no answer. The noise I made brought a hotel clerk. He unlocked the door, but no one was there. I ran back to the other room and met the Chief, who was just coming out.

"Where is Reitman?" I demanded. "What have you done with him? If any harm comes to him, you will pay for it if I have to do it with my own hands."

"How should I know?" he replied gruffly.

Mr. Holmes was not in his office, and no one would tell me what had become of Ben Reitman. In consternation I returned to my room. Ben did not appear. In dismay I paced the floor, unable to decide what steps to take or whom to approach to help me find Ben. [. . .]

I felt helpless. Time dragged on, and at midnight I dozed off from sheer fatigue. I dreamed of Ben, bound and gagged, his hands groping for me. I struggled to reach him and woke up with a scream, bathed in sweat. There were voices and loud knocking at my door. When I opened, the house detective and another man stepped in. Reitman was safe, they told me. I looked at them in a daze, hardly grasping their meaning. Ben had been taken out by the Vigilantes, they explained, but no harm had come to him. They had only put him on a train for Los Angeles. I did not believe the detective, but the other man looked honest. He reiterated that he had been given absolute assurance that Reitman was safe. [. . .]

Mr. Holmes seemed genuinely concerned. I knew there was no chance of holding a meeting. Now that Ben was safe, there was no sense in harassing Mr. Holmes any further. I consented to leave, planning to take the Owl, the 2:45 A.M. train, for Los Angeles. I called for a taxi and drove to the station. The town was asleep, the streets deserted.

I had just purchased my ticket and was walking towards the Pullman car when I caught the sound of approaching autos— the fearful sound I had first heard at the station and later at the hotel. The Vigilantes, of course.

"Hurry, hurry!" someone cried; "get in quick!"

Before I had time to make another step, I was picked up, carried to the train, and literally thrown into the compartment. The blinds were pulled down and I was locked in. The Vigilantes had arrived and were rushing up and down the platform, shouting and trying to board the train. The crew was on guard, refusing to let them on. There was mad yelling and cursing— hideous and terrifying moments till at last the train pulled out.

We stopped at innumerable stations. Each time I peered out eagerly in the hope that Ben might be waiting to join me. But there was no sign of him. When I reached my apartment in Los Angeles, he was not there. The U. S. Grant Hotel men had lied in order to get me out of town!

"He's dead! He's dead!" I cried in anguish. "They've killed my boy!" In vain I strove to drive the terrible thought away. [. . .]

At ten o'clock I was called on the long-distance phone. A strange voice informed me that Dr. Reitman was boarding the train for Los Angeles and that he would arrive in the late afternoon. "His friends should bring a stretcher to the station." "Is he alive?" I shouted into the receiver. "Are you telling the truth? Is he alive?" I listened breathlessly, but there was no response.

The hours dragged on as if the day would never pass. The wait at the station was more excruciating still. At last the train pulled in. Ben lay in a rear car, all huddled up. He was in blue overalls, his face deathly pale, a terrified look in his eyes. His hat was gone, and his hair was sticky with tar. At the sight of me he cried: "Oh, Mommy, I'm with you at last! Take me away, take me home!"

The newspaper men besieged him with questions, but he was too exhausted to speak. I begged them to leave him alone and to call later at my apartment.

While helping him to undress, I was horrified to see that his body was a mass of bruises covered with blotches of tar. The letters I.W.W. were burned into his flesh. Ben could not speak; only his eyes tried to convey what he had passed through. After partaking of some nourishment and sleeping several hours, he regained a little strength. In the presence of a number of friends and reporters he told us what had happened to him.

"When Emma and the hotel manager left the office to go into another room," Ben related, "I remained alone with seven men. As soon as the door was closed, they drew out revolvers. 'If you utter a sound or make a move, we'll kill you,' they threatened. Then they gathered around me. One man grabbed my right arm, another the left; a third took hold of the front of my coat, another of the back, and I was led out into the corridor, down the elevator to the ground floor of the hotel, and out into the street past a uniformed policeman, and then thrown into an automobile. When the mob saw me, they set up a howl. The auto went slowly down the main street and was joined by another one containing several persons who looked like business men. This was about half past ten in the evening. The twenty-mile ride was frightful. As soon as we got out of town, they began kicking and beating me. They took turns at pulling my long hair and they stuck their fingers into my eyes and nose. 'We could tear your guts out,' they said, 'but we promised the Chief of Police not to kill you. We are responsible men, property-owners, and the police are on our side.' When we reached the county line, the auto stopped at a deserted spot. The men formed a ring and told me to undress. They tore my clothes off. They knocked me down, and when I lay naked on the ground, they kicked and beat me until I was almost insensible. With a lighted cigar they burned the letters I.W.W. on my buttocks; then they poured a can of tar over my head and, in the absence of feathers, rubbed sage-brush on my body. One of them attempted to push a cane into my rectum. Another twisted my testicles. They forced me to kiss the flag and sing 'The Star Spangled Banner.' When they tired of the fun, they gave me my underwear for fear we should meet any women. They also gave me back my vest, in order that I might carry my money, railroad ticket, and watch. The rest of my clothes they kept. I was ordered to make a speech, and then they commanded me to run the gauntlet. The Vigilantes lined up, and as I ran past them, each one gave me a blow or a kick. Then they let me go."

Ben's case was but one out of many since the struggle in San Diego had begun, but it helped to focus greater attention on the scene of savagery. [. . .]

In Los Angeles the tide of sympathy rose very high and we drew unusually large crowds. On the evening of our protest meeting we had to address our audience in two halls. We could have filled several more if we had had them and enough speakers to go round.

San Francisco, fruitful for years, turned out an enormous crowd this time. Our comrades were spared the labour and expense of advertising; the Vigilantes had done that for us. [. . .]

Our friends in Portland begged us not to proceed to Seattle. Our comrades in Seattle, anxious for our safety, offered to call off the meetings. But I insisted on going through with our program. [. . .]

On the Sunday of my first lecture a sealed note was left at my hotel for me. The anonymous writer warned me of a plot against my life: I was going to be shot when about to enter the hall, he assured me. Somehow I could give no credence to the story. [. . .]

I was never more calm than as I walked leisurely from the hotel to the meeting-place. When within half a block of it I instinctively raised to my face the large bag I always carried. I got safely into the hall and walked towards the platform still holding the bag in front of my face. All through the lecture the thought persisted in my brain: "If I could only protect my face!" In the evening I repeated the same performance, holding my bag to my face all the way to the hall. The meetings went off well, without any sign of the plotters.

For days after, I tried to find some plausible explanation for my silly action with the bag. Why had I been more concerned about my face than about my chest or any other part of my body? Surely no man would think of his face under such circumstances. Yet I, in the presence of probable death, had been afraid to have my face disfigured! It was a shock to discover in myself such ordinary female vanity.

CHAPTER XXXIX

[. . .] The year 1912, rich with varied experiences, closed with three important events: the appearance of Sasha's book, the twenty-fifth anniversary of the eleventh of November, and the seventieth birthday of Peter Kropotkin.

Sasha was reading the final proofs of his *Prison Memoirs*. In renewed agony he was living through again every detail of the fourteen years, and experiencing harrowing doubt as to whether he had succeeded in making them real in his work. He kept revising until our bill for author's corrections mounted to four hundred and fifty dollars. He was worried and exhausted, yet he hung on, going over his proofs again and again. The final chapters had to be taken from him almost by force to save him from the curse of his tormenting anxiety.

And now the book was ready at last. Verily, not a book, but a life suffered in the solitude of interminable prison days and nights, with all their pain and grief, their disillusionments, despair, and hope. Tears of joy sprang to my eyes as I held the precious volume in my hands. I felt it my triumph as well as Sasha's—*our* fulfilment of twenty years, giving the promise of Sasha's real resurrection from his prison nightmare, and my own release from the gnawing regret of not having shared his fate.

Prison Memoirs of an Anarchist was widely reviewed and acclaimed a work of art and a deeply moving human document. "A story of prison life by an author who spent fourteen years behind the bars gathering his material ought to have value as a human document," commented the New York *Tribune*. "When the writer, furthermore, wields his pen in the manner of the Slavic realists and is compared by critics with such men as Dostoyevsky and Andreieff, his work must possess a tremendous fascination as well as a social value."

The literary critic of the New York *Globe* stated that "nothing could exceed the uncanny spell exercised by this story. Berkman has succeeded in making you live his prison experiences with him, and his book is probably as complete a self-revelation as is humanly possible."

Such praise from the capitalist press helped to accentuate my disappointment over Jack London's attitude towards Sasha's book. Having been requested to write a preface for it, Jack had asked to see the manuscript. After he had read it, he wrote us in his impetuous way how tremendously he was impressed by it. But his preface turned out to be a lame apology for the fact that he, a socialist, was writing an introduction to the work of an anarchist. [. . .]

Jack London was not the only one who condemned while praising. There were others, even in our own ranks, among them S. Yanofsky,[1] the editor of the *Freie Arbeiter Stimme*. He was one of the speakers at the banquet given to celebrate the appearance of Sasha's book. He was the only one of the five hundred guests who interjected a discordant note into the otherwise beautifully harmonious evening. Yanofsky paid high tribute to Sasha's *Memoirs* as the "mature product of a mature mind," but he "regretted the useless and futile act of a silly boy." I felt outraged by the man's denouncing the *Attentat* on the occasion of the birth of Sasha's book, a work conceived in that heroic moment of July 1892 and nourished by tears and blood throughout the dark and terrible years that followed. When I was called upon to speak, I turned upon the man who presumed to represent a great ideal and yet who was lacking in the least understanding of one so truly the idealist.

"To you the impressionable youth of Alexander Berkman appears silly," I said, "and his *Attentat* futile. [. . .] His act was the protest of a sensitive spirit that would rather perish for his ideal than continue for a lifetime as a smug inhabitant of a complaisant and callous world. If our comrade did not perish, it was certainly not due to the mercy of those who had openly declared he should not survive his living grave. It was due entirely

to the same traits that inspired Alexander Berkman's act: his
unwavering purpose, his indomitable will, and his faith in the
ultimate triumph of his ideal. These elements have gone into the
making of the 'silly' youth, into his act and into his martyrdom
of fourteen years. It is these same elements that have inspired
the creation of *Prison Memoirs*. Whatever greatness and humanity the book possesses, they are woven of these elements.
There is no gap between the silly youth and the mature man.
There is a continuous flow, a red thread that winds like a leit-
motif throughout the entire life of Alexander Berkman."

November 11, 1887—November 11, 1912! Twenty-five years,
an infinitesimal fraction of time in the upward march of the
race, but an eternity for him who dies many deaths in the
course of his life. The twenty-fifth anniversary of the Chicago
martyrdom intensified my feeling for the men I had never personally known, but who by their death had become the most
decisive influence in my existence. [. . .]

I was one of the many speakers eager to pay tribute to our
precious dead and to recall once more the valour and heroism
of their lives. I awaited my turn, stirred to the roots by the historic occasion, its great social significance and personal meaning to me. Memories of the distant past flitted through my
mind—Rochester and a woman's voice ringing like music in my
ears: "You will love our men when you learn to know them, and
you will make their cause your own!" In times of ascent to
heights, in days of faint-heartedness and doubt, in hours of
prison isolation, of antagonism and censure from one's own
kind, in failure of love, in friendships broken and betrayed—
always their cause was mine, their sacrifice my support. [. . .]

The effect on Ben of his San Diego experience proved to be
stronger and more lasting than any of us had expected. He remained in the throes of those harrowing days and he became a
victim of the *idée fixe* that he must return there. He followed
his activities with even more than his wonted energy, working
as if driven by furies and driving everybody else in turn. I became to him a means rather than an end, the end being meetings,

meetings, meetings, and plans for more meetings. But I saw that he did not really live in his work, or in our love. His whole being was centred on San Diego, and it became almost a hallucination with him. He taxed my powers of endurance, and often my affection, by his constant insistence on starting for the Coast. His restlessness kept increasing and he was not content until we were finally on our way.

Our Los Angeles friends were strongly opposed to our returning to San Diego. They said that Ben's obsession was nothing but bravado, and that I was weak in giving in to his irrational scheme. They even brought the matter to the attention of the audience at our last meeting, urging a unanimous vote against our going.

I knew that our friends were concerned only for our safety, but I could not agree with them. I did not feel about San Diego as Ben did; to me it was but one of the many towns in the United States where free speech had been gagged and its defenders maltreated. To such places I always kept returning until the right of free speech was again established there. That was one of the motives for my wanting to go back to San Diego, but it was by no means the strongest motive. I was certain that Ben would not be freed from the hold of that city unless he returned to the scene of the May outrage. My love for him had grown more intense with the years. I could not permit him to go to San Diego alone. I therefore informed my comrades that I would go with Ben, no matter what might be awaiting us there. [. . .]

An active worker in our ranks volunteered to precede us to San Diego, secure a hall, and advertise my lecture, which was again to be on *An Enemy of the People*. Before long he notified us that all was well and promising.

After our last meeting in Los Angeles we were taken by our friends Dr. and Mrs. Percival T. Gerson to the railroad station. On the way Ben's excitement reached such a pitch that the doctor suggested a sanatorium instead of San Diego. But Ben insisted that nothing would cure him except to go back. In the train he became deathly pale, and large drops of perspiration poured over his face. His body shook with nervousness and fear. All night he tossed about sleeplessly in his berth. [. . .]

It was early dawn, and only a few passengers got off the train. The platform was deserted as we made our way towards the exit. But before we had proceeded far, five men suddenly confronted us. Four of them exposed detective badges and informed us that we were under arrest. I demanded the reason for our detention, but they gruffly ordered us to come with them.

San Diego was asleep as we walked to the police station. Something in the appearance of the man accompanying the officers seemed familiar to me. I strove to remember where I had seen him before. Then it dawned on me that it was he who had come to my room in the U. S. Grant Hotel to tell me that I was wanted by the authorities. I recognized him as the reporter who had caused our former difficulties there. He was a leader of the Vigilantes!

Ben and I were locked up. There was nothing to be done but await developments. I again took up my book. Weary, I put my head on the little cell table and dozed off.

"You must have been very tired to sleep like that," the matron said as she woke me. "Didn't you hear the racket?" She looked fixedly at me. "Better have some coffee," she added, not unkindly. "You may need your strength before the day is over."

Noises and yelling came from the street. "The Vigilantes," the matron said in a low voice. There were loud cries outside and I could hear voices calling: "Reitman! We want Reitman!" Then came the tooting of automobile horns and the shriek of the riot signal. And again cries of "Reitman!" My heart sank.

The riot call boomed and howled. The noises beat like tom-toms on my brain. Why had I ever let Ben come, I thought; it was madness, madness! They could not forgive him for returning. They wanted his life!

In a frenzy I rapped on my cell door. The matron arrived and with her the Chief of Police and several detectives.

"I want to see Dr. Reitman!" I demanded.

"That's what we've come for," the Chief replied. "He wants you to consent to being taken out of town, and your other comrade too."

"What other comrade?"

"The chap who arranged your meeting. He's in the jail, and lucky for him he is."

"You're playing the benefactor again," I retorted; "but you won't dupe me this time. Take those two out of town. *I* will not go under your protection."

"All right," he growled. "Come and talk to Reitman yourself."

The pale horror staring at me out of Ben's eyes made me realize the meaning of fear as I had never seen it before. "Let's get out of town," he whispered, trembling. "We can't hold the meeting anyway. Chief Wilson[2] promises to get us away safe. Please say yes."

I had completely forgotten our meeting. It was my objection to leaving under police protection that made me urge Ben to go himself.

"It is your life that is in danger," I said; "they don't want me. No harm will come to me. But in any case I can't run away."

"All right, I'll stay too," he replied determinedly.

I struggled with myself for a moment. I knew that if I let him stay, I should jeopardize his life and possibly also the safety of the other comrade. There was no other way out; I should have to consent.

No play was ever staged with greater melodrama than our rescue from the San Diego jail and our ride to the railroad station. At the head of the procession marched a dozen policemen, each carrying a shot-gun, with revolvers sticking in their belts. Then came the Chief of Police and the Chief of Detectives, heavily armed, Ben between them. I followed with two officers on each side. Behind me was our young comrade. And behind him more police.

Our appearance was greeted with savage howls. As far as the eye could reach, there was a swaying, jostling human pack. The shrill cries of women mingled with the voices of the men, drunk with the lust of blood. The more venturesome of them tried to make a rush for Ben.

"Back, back!" shouted the Chief. "The prisoners are under the protection of the law. I demand respect for the law. Get back!"

Some applauded him, others jeered. He proudly led the procession through the phalanxes of police, accompanied by the yelling of the frenzied crowd.

Automobiles were waiting us, gaily bedecked with American flags. One of them had rifles posted at every corner. Police and plain-clothes men stood on the running-board. I recognized the reporter among them. We were piled into this armed citadel, Chief Wilson standing over us like a stage hero, with a shotgun pointed at the mob. Cameras from houses and tree-tops began to click, the sirens screamed, the riot call boomed again, and off we dashed, followed by the other cars and the angry bellowing of the mob.

At the railroad station we were pushed into a Pullman, six policemen crowding around Ben. Just as the train was about to start, a man ran in, shoved the officers aside, and spat full in Ben's face. Then he rushed out again.

"That's Porter," Ben cried, "the leader of last year's attack on me!"

I thought of the savagery of the mob, terrifying yet fascinating at the same time. I realized why Ben's previous experience had so obsessed him until it had driven him back to San Diego. I felt the overwhelming power of the crowd's concentrated passion. I knew I should find no peace until I had returned to it, to subdue it or to be destroyed.

I would go back, I promised myself, but not with Ben. There was no relying on him in a critical moment. I knew he had imaginative flights, but strength of will he had not. He was impulsive, but he lacked stamina and a sense of responsibility. These traits of his character had repeatedly clouded our lives and made me tremble for our love. I grieved to realize that Ben was not of heroic stuff. He was not of the texture of Sasha, who had courage enough for a dozen men and extraordinary coolness and presence of mind in moments of danger. [. . .]

The train sped on. Ben's face was close to mine, his voice whispering endearments, his eyes gazing pleadingly into mine. As so often before, all my doubts and all my pain dissolved in my love for my impossible boy. [. . .]

Upon our return to New York Ben urged a larger house to give us better living-quarters and also enough room for a combination office and book-shop. He was sure he could build up a good trade to help make *Mother Earth* independent of tours. Ben was anxious to have his mother under the same roof with him, especially now that she was not well.

We found a place at 74 East One Hundred and Nineteenth Street, a ten-room house in good condition. The parlour, conveniently seating a hundred people, was the very thing we needed for small sessions and social gatherings; the basement was light and spacious enough for an office and book-shop; the upper floors would afford privacy for each of us. I had never dreamed of such comfort, yet the cost of the rent and heating was lower than our previous expenditures for these items. The large house would need someone to look after it, because I should be busy revising my drama lectures for publication.

I decided to invite my friend Rhoda Smith as housekeeper. [. . .] We needed a secretary for our office work, and Ben suggested a friend of his, Miss M. Eleanor Fitzgerald.[3] I had first met her in Chicago, during our free-speech campaign. She was a striking girl with red hair, delicate skin, and blue-green eyes. Very fond of Ben, she had no inkling of his ways with women. She did not know of my relationship with Ben and she was considerably shocked when I told her that we were very much more to each other than merely manager and lecturer. Miss Fitzgerald (or "Lioness," as Ben called her, because of her red mane of hair) was a most likable person, with something very fine and large about her. [. . .]

Our new quarters were ready and we began breaking up our old home. When I had first moved into 210 East Thirteenth Street, in 1903, to share the flat with the Horrs, we were the first tenants in the recently built house. [. . .]

There were no facilities for heating at 210, except the kitchen stove, and my room was farthest from it. It faced the yard and looked right into the windows of a large printing house. The nerve-racking buzz of its linotypes and presses never let up. My room was the living-room, dining-room, and *Mother Earth* office, all in one. I slept in a little alcove behind my bookcase. There was always someone sleeping in front, some-one who had stayed too late and lived too far away or who was too shaky on his feet and needing cold compresses or who had no home to go to.

All the other tenants of the house were in the habit of applying to us when ill or in trouble. Our most frequent callers, usually in the wee hours of the morning, were the gamblers. Expecting a raid, they would run up the fire-escape to ask us to hide their paraphernalia. "In your place," they once told me, "the police may look for bombs, but never for chips." Everyone in distress came to us in 210 as to an oasis in the desert of their lives. It was flattering, but at the same time wearying, never to have any privacy by day or at night.

Our little flat had grown very dear to me; a good deal of my life had been spent in it. It had witnessed a decade of the most varied activities, and men and women famous in the annals of life had laughed and cried there. The Russian campaigns of Catherine Breshkovskaya and of Tchaikovsky, the Orleneff work, free-speech fights and revolutionary propaganda, not to speak of the many personal dramas, with all their griefs and joys, had flowed through the historic place. The entire kaleidoscope of human tragedy and comedy had been reflected in colourful variegation within the walls of 210. [. . .]

Ten years had streamed by in a rushing current, with little leisure to reflect on how dear the place had grown to me. Only when the time came to leave it did I realize how rooted I had become at 210. Taking a last look at the empty rooms, I walked out with a feeling of deep loss. Ten most interesting years of my life left behind!

CHAPTER XL

At last we were installed in our new quarters. Ben and Miss Fitzgerald were in charge of the office, Rhoda of the house, while Sasha and I took care of the magazine. With each one busy in his own sphere, the differences in character and attitude had more scope for expression without mutual invasiveness. We all found "Fitzi," as we called our new co-worker, a most charming woman, and Rhoda also liked her, though she often took delight in shocking our romantic friend by her peppery jokes and stories.

Ben was happy to have his mother with him. She had two sons, but her entire world was centred in Ben. Her mental horizon was very narrow; she was unable even to read or write and felt no interest in anything except the little home Ben had made for her. In Chicago she had lived among her pots and kettles, untouched by the stream outside. She loved her son and she was always most patient with his moods, no matter how irrational they were. He was her idol who could do no wrong. As to his numerous affairs with women, she was sure it was they who led her child astray. She had hoped her son would become a successful doctor, honoured, respected, and rich. Instead he had dropped his practice when he had barely begun it, "took up" with a woman nine years his senior, and got himself involved with a dangerous lot of anarchists. Ben's mother was always respectful when she met me, but I could sense her keen dislike. [. . .]

She was given the best room in the house, supplied with her own furniture, so as to make her feel more at home. Ben always took his breakfast alone with her, with no one near to disturb their idyll. At our common meals she was given the seat of honour and treated by everybody with utmost consideration. But she felt ill at ease, out of her environment. She longed for her old Chicago place and she became dissatisfied and unhappy. Then, one unfortunate day, Ben began to read *Sons and Lovers* by D. H. Lawrence.[1] From the very first page he lived in the book with his mother. He saw in it the story of himself and of her. The office, our work, and our life were blotted out. He could think of nothing but the story and his mother, and he began to imagine that I—and everyone else—was treating her badly. He would have to take her away, he decided; he must give up everything and live only for his mother.

I was in the midst of my drama manuscript. There were lectures on hand, a large undertaking for *Mother Earth*. [. . .] I reasoned, I argued, I pleaded with Ben not to permit Lawrence's book to rob him of his senses. But to no avail. Scenes with Ben became more frequent and violent. Our life was daily growing more impossible. A way out had to be found. I could not share my misery with anyone, least of all with Sasha, who had from the beginning been opposed to the scheme of the house and a life with Ben and his mother under the same roof.

The break came. Ben had started again the old plaint about his mother. I listened in silence for a while, and then something snapped in me. The desire seized me to make an end of Ben as far as I was concerned, to do something that would shut out for ever every thought and every memory of this creature who had possessed me all these years. In blind fury I picked up a chair and hurled it at him. It whirled through space and came crashing down at his feet.

He made a step towards me, then stopped and stared at me in wonder and fright.

"Enough!" I cried, beside myself with pain and anger. "I've had enough of you and your mother. Go, take her away—today, this very hour!"

He walked out without a word.

Ben rented a small flat for his mother and went to live with her. He began again attending to the office. We still had that much in common, but the rest seemed dead. [. . .]

The close of the year was at hand, and we had not yet held a
house-warming in our new place. New Year's was decided
upon as the right moment for our party of friends and active
supporters of *Mother Earth* to help kick out the Old with all
its trouble and pain and gaily meet the New no matter what it
might bring. Rhoda was all excitement and she worked hard
and late to make ready for the festive occasion. New Year's Eve
brought the procession of friends, among them poets, writers,
rebels, and Bohemians of various attitude, behaviour, and
habit. They argued about philosophy, social theories, art, and
sex. They ate the delicious things Rhoda had prepared and drank
the wines our generous Italian comrades had supplied. Everybody danced and grew gay. But my thoughts were with Ben,
whose birthday it was. He was thirty-five and I nearing forty-
four. That was a tragic difference in age. I felt lonely and unutterably sad.

Still young was the new year when the country began to echo
with new outrages against labour. The horrors in West Virginia
were followed by cruelties in the hop-fields of Wheatfield, California, in the mines of Trinidad, Colorado, and in Calumet,
Michigan. The police, the militia, and gangs of armed citizens
were carrying on a reign of despotism. [. . .]

The latest victim of these American Black Hundreds was
Mother Jones, a famous native agitator.[2] In truly tsarist manner she
was deported from Trinidad at the order of General Chase, who
threatened to imprison her *incommunicado* if she dared to return.
[. . .]

My relation with Ben, which had grown more strained, finally became unbearable. Ben was no less unhappy than I. He
decided to return with his mother to Chicago and take up the
practice of medicine again. I did not try to detain him.

For the first time I was to give a full course of lectures on
"The Social Significance of the Modern Drama" in New York,
both in English and in Yiddish. The Berkeley Theatre on Forty-
fourth Street was rented for the purpose. It was disheartening to
start out on an important venture without Ben, for the first time
in six years. [. . .] No man I had loved had ever so paralysed

my will before. I fought against it with all my strength, but my heart wildly called for Ben.

I could see from his letters that he was going through the same purgatory as I, and that he also could not free himself. He yearned to return to me. [. . .]

His letters were like a narcotic. They put my brain to sleep, but they made my heart beat faster. I clung to the assurance of his love.

Again, in the winter, the country was in the throes of unemployment. Over a quarter of a million persons were out of work in New York, and other cities were stricken in no lesser degree. The suffering was augmented by the extraordinarily severe weather. The papers minimized the appalling state of affairs; the politicians and reformers remained lukewarm. A few palliatives and the threadbare suggestion of an investigation were all they could offer to meet the widespread misery.

The militant elements resolved upon action. The anarchists and the I.W.W.'s organized the unemployed and secured considerable relief for them. At my Berkeley Theatre lectures and other meetings appeals for the jobless met with generous response. But it was a mere drop in the ocean of need. [. . .]

The Socialist Party and some prominent I.W.W. leaders tried to paralyse the activities of the jobless. This only helped to increase the zeal of the Conference of the Unemployed, which consisted of various labour and radical organizations. A mass meeting at Union Square was decided upon and the date fixed for March 21. Neither the Socialists nor the I.W.W.'s would participate. It was Sasha who was the active spirit of the movement. He had a double share to perform, as I was hard at work finishing my manuscript, lecturing frequently, and supervising our office.

The mass meeting was large and spirited; it reminded me of a similar event in the same place and for the same purpose, the demonstration of August 1893. Apparently nothing had changed since then. Now as then capitalism was relentless, the State crushing every individual and social right, and the Church in league with them. Now as then those daring to give voice to the suffering of the dumb multitude were persecuted and jailed, and the masses too seemed to have remained as ever in their submissive helplessness. The thought was depressing and made me want to run away from the square. But I stayed. I stayed because deep down in me there was the certainty that there is no sameness in nature. Eternal change, I knew, is for ever at work, life always is in flux, new currents flowing from the dried-up springs of the old. I stayed, and I spoke to the huge crowd as I could speak only when really lifted out of myself.

I left the square after my speech, while Sasha remained at the meeting. When he came home, I learned that the demonstration had ended in a parade up Fifth Avenue, the vast assembly marching and carrying a large black flag as a symbol of their revolt. It must have been a menacing sight to the dwellers on Fifth Avenue no less than to the police, for the latter did not interfere. The unemployed marched all the way to the Ferrer Center, from Fourteenth to One Hundred and Seventh Street, where they were treated to a substantial meal, given tobacco and cigarettes, and provided with temporary lodgings.

This demonstration was the beginning of a city-wide campaign for the unemployed. Sasha, whose valour had endeared him to everyone who knew about his life, was its organizing and directing influence. In his tireless efforts he had the support of a large number of our young rebels, who vigorously worked with him.

My Berkeley Theatre series brought some interesting and amusing experiences. [. . .] The last Sunday at the Berkeley Theatre was turned into a gala night. Leonard D. Abbott[3] presided, and among the speakers were the noted actress Mary Shaw,[4] the first to defy American purists with her performances of *Ghosts* and of *Mrs. Warren's Profession;* Fola La Follette, gifted and frankly outspoken; and George Middleton, who had a volume of one-act plays to his credit.[5] They dwelt on what the drama meant to them, and what a powerful factor it was in awakening social consciousness in people who might not be reached in any other way. They were very appreciative of my work, and I was grateful to them for making me feel that my efforts had brought some of the American intelligentsia into closer rapport with the struggle of the masses. [. . .] A young man named Paul Munter [. . .] attended my entire series, for six weeks, and at the end presented me with my course in perfectly typewritten sheets.

Paul's gift proved to be of great value in the preparation of my manuscript of *The Social Significance of the Modern Drama*.[6] Thanks to it the work was less difficult than the writing of my essays, though I had been in a more tranquil state of mind then; I still had hopes of a harmonious life with Ben. Little was left of that hope now. Perhaps therefore I clung more tenaciously to its remaining shreds. Ben's pleading letters from Chicago added fuel to the smouldering fires of my longing. After two months I began to realize the wisdom of the Russian peasant saying: "If you drink, you'll die, and if you don't drink, you'll die. Better drink and die."

To be away from Ben meant sleepless nights, restless days, sickening yearning. To be near him involved conflict and strife, daily denial of my pride. But it also meant ecstasy and renewed vigour for my work. I would have Ben and go with him on tour again, I decided. If the price was high, I would pay it; but I would drink, I would drink! [. . .]

My drama book was off the press, looking quite attractive in its simple attire. It was the first English volume of its kind to point out the social meaning of thirty-two plays by eighteen authors of different countries. My only regret was that my own adopted land had to be left out. I had tried diligently to find some American dramatist who could be placed alongside the great Europeans, but I could discover no one. [. . .] The dramatic master [. . .] was not yet in sight. He would no doubt appear some day, but meanwhile I had to be content with calling the attention of America to the works of the foremost playwrights of Europe and the social significance of modern dramatic art. [. . .]

CHAPTER XLI

[. . .] While Ben and I were busy with our meetings in the West, Sasha was engaged in strenuous activities in New York. With Fitzi, Leonard D. Abbott, the comrades of anarchist groups, and the young members of the Ferrer School he was conducting the unemployed movement and the anti-militarist campaign. Their persistency in fighting for free speech in New York had resulted in the repeated breaking up of their gatherings by mounted police, involving incredible brutality and violence. [. . .]

I eagerly scanned the papers from New York. I had no anxiety about Sasha, for I knew how dependable and cool he was in times of danger. But I longed to be at his side, in my beloved city, to take part with him in those stirring activities. My engagements, however, kept me in the West. Then came the news of an explosion in a tenement-house on Lexington Avenue which cost the lives of three men—Arthur Carron, Charles Berg, and Karl Hanson—and of an unknown woman. The names were unfamiliar to me. The press was filled with the wildest rumours. The bomb, it was reported, had been intended for Rockefeller, whom the speakers at the New York meetings had charged with direct responsibility for the Ludlow massacres.[1] The premature explosion had probably saved his life, the papers declared. Sasha's name was dragged into the case, and the police were looking for him and the owner of the Lexington apartment, our comrade Louise Berger. Word came from Sasha that the three men who had lost their lives in the explosion were comrades who had worked with him in the Tarrytown campaign.[2] They had been badly beaten up by the police at one of the Union Square demonstrations. The bomb might have been intended for Rockefeller, Sasha wrote, but in any case the men had kept their intentions to themselves, for neither he nor anyone else knew how the explosion had occurred.

Comrades, idealists, manufacturing a bomb in a congested tenement-house! I was aghast at such irresponsibility. But the next moment I remembered a similiar event in my own life. It came back with paralysing horror. In my mind I saw my little room in Peppi's flat, on Fifth Street, its window-blinds drawn, Sasha experimenting with a bomb, and me watching. I had silenced my fear for the tenants, in case of an accident, by repeating to myself that the end justified the means. With accusing clarity I now relived that nerve-racking week in July 1892. In the zeal of fanaticism I had believed that the end justifies the means! It took years of experience and suffering to emancipate myself from the mad idea. Acts of violence committed as a protest against unbearable social wrongs—I still believed them inevitable. I understood the spiritual forces culminating in such *Attentats* as Sasha's, Bresci's, Angiolillo's,[3] Czolgosz's, and those of others whose lives I had studied. They had been urged on by their great love for humanity and their acute sensitiveness to injustice. I had always taken my place with them as against every form of organized oppression. But though my sympathies were with the man who protested against social crimes by a resort to extreme measures, I nevertheless felt now that I could never again participate in or approve of methods that jeopardized innocent lives.

I was worried about Sasha. He was the spirit of the tremendous campaign in the East, and I feared the police would involve him in their dragnet. I wanted to return to New York, but his letters held me back. He was perfectly safe, he wrote, and there were plenty of people to help him in the work. He had succeeded in obtaining the bodies of the dead comrades for cremation, and he was planning a monster demonstration at Union Square. [. . .]

Now the remains of the dead comrades, Sasha wrote me, were deposited in a specially designed urn in the form of a clenched fist rising from the depths. The urn was exposed in the office of *Mother Earth*, which had been decorated with wreaths and red and black banners. Thousands passed through our quarters to pay the last tribute to Carron, Berg, and Hanson.

I was happy to learn that the perilous situation in New York had ended so favourably. But when I received copies of the July issue of *Mother Earth*, I was dismayed at its contents. The Union Square speeches were published there in full; with the exception of Sasha's own address and those of Leonard D. Abbott and Elizabeth Gurley Flynn, the harangues were of a most violent character. I had tried always to keep our magazine free from such language, and now the whole number was filled with prattle about force and dynamite. I was so furious that I wanted the entire issue thrown into the fire. But it was too late; the magazine had gone out to the subscribers. [. . .]

When I arrived in New York I was confronted with a serious financial situation. Sasha's activities among the unemployed, together with the anti-militarist and Ludlow campaigns, had swallowed up most of the funds I had sent to our office from my tour. We could not meet the obligations of *Mother Earth,* much less the expense of the house, which in my absence had been turned into a free-for-all lodging- and feeding-place. We were in debt to our printer and to the mailing-house, and money was owed to every store-keeper in the neighbourhood. The strain of the agitation he had carried on, the danger and the responsibility he had faced, had left Sasha in a high-strung and irritable state. He was sensitive to my criticism, and hurt that I should even mention money matters. I had hoped for rest, harmony, and peace after six months of constant lecturing and the struggle involved in my tour. Instead I was swamped with new cares.

I was dazed by the situation and I felt very indignant with Sasha. Entirely absorbed in his own propaganda, he had given me no thought. He was the revolutionist of old, with the same fanatical belief in the Cause. His sole concern was the movement, and I was to him but a means for it. He was nothing more to himself than that; how could I expect to be any more to him?

Sasha did not understand my resentment. He grew impatient at my mentioning money matters. He had spent our funds for the movement; the latter was more important than my drama lectures, he said. I spoke bitterly to him, telling him that without my drama lectures he would have had no means to finance his activities. The clash made us both unhappy. Sasha withdrew into himself.

The only ones I could turn to in my misery were my dear nephew Saxe and my old friend Max.[4] Both were very understanding, but neither of them was worldly enough to be of much assistance to me. I should have to face the situation alone.

I decided to give up our house and to declare myself bankrupt. My friend Gilbert E. Roe, to whom I confided my troubles, laughed at my strange notion. "Bankruptcy is resorted to by those who want to get out of paying debts," he said; "it will involve you in year-long litigation, and your creditors will attach every penny you make to the end of your days." He offered to lend me money, but I could not accept his generosity.

Then a new idea struck me. I would tell the printer exactly how I stood. The frank and open way is always the best, I decided. My creditors proved to be very accommodating. They lost no sleep over the money I owed them, they said; I could be depended on to make good. It was finally arranged that I pay my indebtedness in monthly instalments. Our mailing-house even declined my promissory notes. "Pay what you can and when you can," the manager said; "your word is good enough for us."

I resolved to start from the bottom up again; to rent a small place—one room for an office, the other for my living-quarters—and to accept every lecture engagement I could secure, and practise the strictest economy in order to keep up *Mother Earth* and my work. I wired Ben dates for my dramatic course in Chicago, and then I went out to look for a new home. It was a discouraging task; the Lexington Avenue explosion and the publicity given to Sasha's activities were fresh in the public mind, and the landlords were timid. But at last I found a two-room loft on One Hundred and Twenty-fifth Street, and I set to work to make it fit for my use.

Sasha and Fitzi came to help me get my new place in order, but our relations were strained. Yet Sasha was too deeply rooted in my being to permit me to remain angry with him very long. There was also something else to change my resentful attitude. The realization had come to me that it was not Sasha, but I who was at fault. Not only since my return from the last tour, but all through the eight years since his release from prison, it was I who had been responsible for the breaks that came between us. I had committed a great wrong against him. Instead of giving him a chance to find his way back to life, after his resurrection, I had brought him into my atmosphere, into an environment that could only be galling to him. I had done this in the mistaken belief, usual with mothers, that they know best what is good for their children; fearing the latter will be crushed in the world outside, they desperately try to shield them from the experiences so essential to their growth. I had committed the same mistake in regard to Sasha. Not only had I not urged him to launch out for himself, but I had trembled at every step he made, because I could not see him exposed to new suffering and hardships. Yet I had saved him from nothing; I had only awakened his resentment. Perhaps he was not even aware of it, yet it was always there, breaking out in one form or another. Sasha had always wanted his own work and his own place. I had offered him everything one human being can give to another, but I had not helped him to what he wanted and needed most. There was no blinking the hard fact. But now that Sasha had found a woman who could give him both love and understanding, it was my opportunity to repair the wrong I had done him.

I would enable them to go on a cross-country tour, I decided. Once Sasha reached California, he could carry out his dream of a paper of his own.

Fitzi and Sasha eagerly responded to my suggestion for a tour. I arranged with my young friend Anna Baron, who used to do part-time typing for us, to take care of the business side of the Mother Earth office. Max and Saxe were to look after the editorial work of the magazine. There were also Hippolyte and other friends to help. Sasha felt rejuvenated, and there was no further friction between us. [. . .]

I was busy preparing the new drama course I had promised

to deliver in Chicago and a series of lectures on the war. Three months had passed since its outbreak in Europe. Outside of *Mother Earth* and our anti-militarist campaign in New York I had not been able to raise my voice in the West against the slaughter, except on one occasion, in Butte, when I had spoken from an automobile to a large crowd and denounced the criminal stupidity of war. I felt that but for the socialist betrayal of their ideals, the great catastrophe would have been impossible. In Germany the party counted twelve million adherents. What a power to prevent the declaration of hostilities! But for a quarter of a century the Marxists had trained the workers in obedience and patriotism, trained them to rely on parliamentary activity and, particularly, to trust their socialist leaders blindly. And now most of those leaders had joined hands with the Kaiser!⁵ Instead of making common cause with the international proletariat, they had called upon the German workers to rise to the defence of "their" fatherland, the fatherland of the disinherited and degraded. Instead of declaring the general strike and thus paralysing war preparations, they had voted the Government money for slaughter. The socialists of the other countries, with certain notable exceptions, had followed their example. No wonder, for the German social democracy had for decades been the pride and inspiration of the socialists throughout the world.

My drama course under the auspices of my two wealthy patrons proved to be a most disagreeable experience. Mr. L., the advertising genius, had taken it upon himself to "edit" the announcements I had sent. Indeed, he had changed their entire character, handling the subjects of my lectures as if they had been chewing-gum ads.

Then happened something to shock the tender sensibilities of my patrons. My first drama talk fell on November 10, a day of momentous importance to me. It had been the last day on earth of my comrades martyred in Chicago twenty-seven years before. I introduced my lecture by contrasting the changes in the public attitude towards anarchism between 1887 and 1914. The vision of our precious dead was before me, bearing witness to the last prophecy of August Spies: "Our silence will be more powerful than the voices you strangle today." In 1887 Chicago's sole answer to anarchism was the gallows; in 1914 it was eagerly listening to the ideas for which Parsons and his comrades had died. During my brief introduction I saw one of my backers and his family, in the first row, uncomfortably fidgeting in their seats; some people in the rear ostentatiously left the hall. Unconcernedly I went on with the subject of the evening, "The American Drama."

Subsequently my backers informed Ben that I had "missed the opportunity of a lifetime." They had induced the "wealth and influence of Chicago" to attend my lectures, "the rich Rosenwalds among them." They would have helped to secure my drama work for the rest of my life, and then "Emma Goldman had to spoil in ten minutes all that we had worked weeks to achieve."

I felt as if I had been put up on the block for sale. The incident had a most depressing effect on me. Try as I would, I could not get my usual intensity into my further drama talks. It was different when I discussed the war. In my own hall, under no obligations to anyone, I could freely express my abhorrence of slaughter and frankly discuss whatever phase of the social question I took up. At the close of my drama course we reimbursed my "patrons" for their outlay. I did not regret the experience; it taught me that patronage is paralysing to one's integrity and independence. [. . .]

CHAPTER XLII

Helena and our young folks in Rochester always brought me back to that city even when I did not have to lecture there. This year there were additional reasons for visiting my home town: an opportunity to speak on the war, and the great family event of David Hochstein's first concert with the local symphony orchestra. [. . .]

On my arrival in Rochester I found my people in anxious suspense over David's forthcoming concert. Well I knew how my sister Helena yearned for the dreams and aspirations of her own frustrated life to be realized in her youngest son. At the first signs of his talent my timid sister had developed determination and strength to defy every difficulty that beset the beloved child's artistic career. She drudged and saved to enable her children, particularly David, to have the opportunities she herself had been deprived of in life, and she was consumed by a great longing to give herself to the uttermost. On my visits she would sometimes pour out her heart to me, never complaining, but only regretting that she was able to do "so little" for her dear ones.

Now the crowning moment of her struggle had arrived. David had returned from Europe the finished artist she had slaved to help him become. Her heart trembled for his triumph. The cold critics, the unappreciative audience—what would her darling's playing mean to them? Would they understand his genius? She refused seats in a box. "It might disturb him to see me," she said. She would feel more comfortable with Jacob in the gallery.

I had heard David in New York and I knew how his playing had impressed everyone. He was truly an artist. Handsome and of good appearance, he made a striking figure on the platform.

I felt no anxiety about his Rochester engagement. My sister's excitement, however, had communicated itself to me, and all during the concert my thoughts were with her whose fierce love and hope were now being fulfilled. David's violin charmed the audience and he was acclaimed with an enthusiasm seldom accorded a young artist in his native town. [. . .]

The tenth anniversary of *Mother Earth* was approaching. It seemed nothing short of a miracle for our magazine to have survived a whole decade. It had faced the condemnation of enemies and the unfriendly criticism of well-wishers and had had a hard struggle to keep alive. Even most of those who had helped at its birth had expressed misgivings about its continued existence. Their fears were not groundless, in view of the reckless founding of the magazine. Blissful ignorance of the publishing business, combined with the ridiculous nest-egg of two hundred and fifty dollars—how could anyone hope to succeed with such a start? But my friends had overlooked the most important factors in the heritage of *Mother Earth*, a Yiddish perseverance and a boundless enthusiasm. These had proved to be stronger than gilt-edged securities, large income, or even popular support. From the very beginning I had outlined for it a twofold purpose: to voice without fear every unpopular progressive cause, and to aim for unity between revolutionary effort and artistic expression. To achieve these ends I had to keep *Mother Earth* untrammelled by party policies, even by anarchist policies, free from sectarian favouritism and from every outside influence, however well-intentioned. For this I was charged even by some of my comrades with using the magazine for my personal ends, and by socialists with being in the employ of capitalism and of the Catholic Church.

Its survival was due in no little measure to the devotion of a small band of comrades and friends who helped to realize my dream of an independent radical spokesman in the United States. [. . .]

After my return from the Neo-Malthusian Conference, held in Paris in 1900, I had added to my lecture series the subject of birth-control. I did not discuss methods, because the question of limiting offspring represented in my estimation only one aspect of the social struggle and I did not care to risk arrest for it. Moreover, I was so continually on the brink of prison because of my general activities that it seemed unjustifiable to court extra trouble. Information on methods I gave only when privately requested for it. Margaret Sanger's[1] difficulties with the postal authorities over her publication of *The Woman Rebel,* and the arrest of William Sanger for giving his wife's pamphlet on methods of birth-control to a Comstock agent, made me aware that the time had come when I must either stop lecturing on the subject or do it practical justice. I felt that I must share with them the consequences of the birth-control issue. [. . .]

E. C. Walker, president of the Sunrise Club, had invited me to speak at one of its fortnightly dinners. His organization was among the few libertarian forums in New York open to free expression. I had often lectured there on various social topics. On this occasion I chose birth-control as my theme, intending openly to discuss methods of contraception. I faced one of the largest audiences in the history of the club, numbering about six hundred persons, among them physicians, lawyers, artists, and men and women of liberal views. Most of them were earnest people who had come together to lend moral support to the test case that this first public discussion represented. Everyone felt certain that my arrest would follow, and some friends had come prepared to go bail for me. I carried a book with me in case I should have to spend the night in the station-house. That possibility did not disturb me, but I did feel uneasy because I knew that some of the diners had come out of curiosity, for the sex thrills they expected to experience on this evening.

I introduced my subject by reviewing the historical and social aspects of birth-control and then continued with a discussion of a number of contraceptives, their application and effects. I spoke in the direct and frank manner that I should use in dealing with ordinary disinfection and prophylaxis. The questions and the discussion that followed showed that I had taken the right approach. Several physicians complimented me on having presented so difficult and delicate a subject in a "clean and natural manner."

No arrest followed. Some friends feared I might be picked up on my way home, and insisted on seeing me to my door. Days passed and the authorities had taken no steps in the matter. It was the more surprising in view of the arrest of William Sanger for something he had not said nor written himself. People wondered why I, who had been so frequently arrested when I had not broken the law, should be allowed to go unpunished when I had done so deliberately. Perhaps Comstock's failure to act was due to the fact that he knew that those who were in the habit of attending the Sunrise Club gatherings were probably already in possession of contraceptives. I must therefore deliver the lecture at my own Sunday meetings, I decided.

Our hall was packed, mostly with young people, among them students from Columbia University. The interest evinced by my audience was even greater than at the Sunrise dinner, the questions put by the young folks of a more direct and personal nature. I did not mince matters, yet there was no arrest. Evidently I should have to make another test—on the East Side. [. . .]

My tour this year met with no police interference until we reached Portland, Oregon, although the subjects I treated were anything but tame: anti-war topics, the fight for Caplan and Schmidt,[2] freedom in love, birth-control, and the problem most tabooed in polite society, homosexuality. Nor did Comstock and his purists try to suppress me, although I openly discussed methods of contraception before various audiences.

Censorship came from some of my own comrades because I was treating such "unnatural" themes as homosexuality. Anarchism was already enough misunderstood, and anarchists considered depraved; it was inadvisable to add to the misconceptions by taking up perverted sex-forms, they argued. Believing in freedom of opinion, even if it went against me, I minded the censors in my own ranks as little as I did those in the enemy's camp. In fact, censorship from comrades had the same effect on me as police persecution; it made me surer of myself, more determined to plead for every victim, be it one of social wrong or of moral prejudice.

The men and women who used to come to see me after my

lectures on homosexuality, and who confided to me their anguish and their isolation, were often of finer grain than those who had cast them out. Most of them had reached an adequate understanding of their differentiation only after years of struggle to stifle what they had considered a disease and a shameful affliction. One young woman confessed to me that in the twenty-five years of her life she had never known a day when the nearness of a man, her own father and brothers even, did not make her ill. The more she had tried to respond to sexual approach, the more repugnant men became to her. She had hated herself, she said, because she could not love her father and her brothers as she loved her mother. She suffered excruciating remorse, but her revulsion only increased. At the age of eighteen she had accepted an offer of marriage in the hope that a long engagement might help her grow accustomed to a man and cure her of her "disease." It turned out a ghastly failure and nearly drove her insane. She could not face marriage and she dared not confide in her fiancé or friends. She had never met anyone, she told me, who suffered from a similar affliction, nor had she ever read books dealing with the subject. My lecture had set her free; I had given her back her self-respect.

This woman was only one of the many who sought me out. Their pitiful stories made the social ostracism of the invert seem more dreadful than I had ever realized before. To me anarchism was not a mere theory for a distant future; it was a living influence to free us from inhibitions, internal no less than external, and from the destructive barriers that separate man from man.

Los Angeles, San Diego, and San Francisco were record-breaking in the size of our meetings and the interest shown. In Los Angeles I was invited by the Women's City Club. Five hundred members of my sex, from the deepest red to the dullest grey, came to hear me speak on "Feminism." They could not excuse my critical attitude towards the bombastic and impossible claims of the suffragists as to the wonderful things they would do when they got political power. They branded me as an enemy of woman's freedom, and club-members stood up and denounced me.

The incident reminded me of a similar occasion when I had

lectured on woman's inhumanity to man. Always on the side of the under dog, I resented my sex's placing every evil at the door of the male. I pointed out that if he were really as great a sinner as he was being painted by the ladies, woman shared the responsibility with him. The mother is the first influence in his life, the first to cultivate his conceit and self-importance. Sisters and wives follow in the mother's footsteps, not to mention mistresses, who complete the work begun by the mother. Woman is naturally perverse, I argued; from the very birth of her male child until he reaches a ripe age, the mother leaves nothing undone to keep him tied to her. Yet she hates to see him weak and she craves the manly man. She idolizes in him the very traits that help to enslave her—his strength, his egotism, and his exaggerated vanity. The inconsistencies of my sex keep the poor male dangling between the idol and the brute, the darling and the beast, the helpless child and the conqueror of worlds. It is really woman's inhumanity to man that makes him what he is. When she has learned to be as self-centred and as determined as he, when she gains the courage to delve into life as he does and pay the price for it, she will achieve her liberation, and incidentally also help him become free. Whereupon my women hearers would rise up against me and cry: "You're a man's woman and not one of us."

Our experience in San Diego two years previously, in 1913, had exerted the same effect on me as the night ride in 1912 had on Ben. I was set on returning to deliver my suppressed lecture. In 1914 one of our friends had gone to San Diego to try to secure a hall. The socialists, who had their own place, refused to have anything to do with me. Other radical groups were equally brave, so that my plan had to be abandoned. Only temporarily, I had promised myself, however. [. . .]

I had long before decided that I would return to San Diego without Ben. I had planned to go alone, but fortunately Sasha was in Los Angeles at the time. I knew I could count on his poise in a difficult situation and on his utter fearlessness in the face of the gravest danger. Sasha and my romantic admirer Leon Bass[3] left for San Diego two days ahead of me to look over the field. Accompanied by Fitzi and Ben Capes,[4] I departed quietly from Los Angeles in an auto. Nearing the Vigilante city, the picture of Ben surrounded by fourteen thugs rose before me. They had covered the same route, with Ben at the mercy of savages who were beating and humiliating him. I thought of him writhing in pain, with no one to succour him or alleviate his terror. Barely three years had passed. I was free, with dear friends at my side, securely riding through the balmy night. I could enjoy the beauty around me, the golden Pacific on one side, majestic mountains on the other, their fantastic formations towering above us. The very glory of this magnificent country-side must have been mockery to Ben, a mockery in league with his torturers. May 14, 1912—June 20, 1915—what an incredible change! Yet what might be awaiting us in San Diego? [. . .]

When our meeting opened, at eleven in the morning, we became aware that a number of Vigilantes were present. The situation was tense, the atmosphere charged with suppressed excitement. It furnished a fitting background for my subject, which was Ibsen's *Enemy of the People*. Our men were on the alert, and no untoward incident took place, the Vigilantes evidently not daring to start any hostile demonstration. [. . . .]

Ben insisted on visiting San Diego again, and he returned there later on, not in any public capacity, but just to convince himself that he was not afraid. He went to the exposition in the company of his mother and several friends. No one paid any attention to them. The Vigilante conspiracy had been broken.

Among my numerous friends in Los Angeles none was more helpful in my work and welfare than Dr. Percival T. Gerson, together with his wife. They interested scores of people in my lectures, gave me the opportunity to address gatherings in their home, and entertained me lavishly. It was also Dr. Gerson who procured for me an invitation to speak before the Severance Club, named in honour of Caroline M. Severance, co-worker of Susan B. Anthony, Julia Howe, and the group of militants of the preceding generation.[5]

Before I began my lecture, I was introduced to a man who, in the absence of the president, had been asked to preside. There was nothing striking about him as he sat buried in my volume of *Anarchism and Other Essays*. In his opening remarks this chairman, whose name was Tracy Becker, astonished the audience by the announcement that he had been connected with the District Attorney's office in Buffalo when President McKinley was killed. Until very recently he had considered Emma Goldman a criminal, he said—not one who had courage to do murder herself, but one who unscrupulously played on weak minds and induced them to commit crimes. During the trial of Leon Czolgosz he felt certain, he continued, that it was I who had instigated the assassination of the President and he had thought that I ought to be made to pay the extreme penalty. Since he had read my books and had talked to some of my friends, he realized his mistake and he now hoped that I would forgive him the injustice he had done me.

Dead silence followed his remarks, and everybody's eyes were turned on me. I felt frozen by the sudden resurrection of the Buffalo tragedy, and in an unsteady voice, at first, I declared that since we are all links in the social chain, no one can avoid responsibility for such deeds as that of Leon Czolgosz; not even the chairman. He who remains indifferent to the conditions that result in violent acts of protest cannot escape his share of blame for them. Even those of us who see clearly and work for fundamental changes are not entirely exempt from guilt. Too absorbed in efforts for the future, we often turn a deaf ear to those who reach out for sympathetic understanding and who hunger for the fellowship of kindred spirits. Leon Czolgosz had been one of such.

I talked with growing feeling as I proceeded to describe the bleak background of the boy, his early environment and life. I related the impressions of the Buffalo newspaper woman who had sought me out to tell me what she had experienced during Czolgosz's trial, and I pointed out the motives of Leon's act and martyrdom. I felt no resentment against the man who had confessed his eagerness to send me to the electric chair. Indeed, I rather admired him for frankly admitting his error. But he had revived in my memory the fury of that period, and I was in no mood to meet him or to listen to his idle pleasantries. [. . .]

CHAPTER XLIII

[. . .] The conflagration in Europe was spreading; already six countries had been swept by it. America was also beginning to catch fire. The jingo and military cliques were growing restive. "Sixteen months of war," they cried, "and our country is still keeping aloof!" The clamour for "preparedness" began, people joining in who but yesterday waxed hot against the atrocities of organized slaughter. The situation called for more energetic anti-war agitation. It became doubly necessary when we learned of the attitude of Peter Kropotkin.

Rumours had been filtering through from England that Peter had declared himself in favour of the war. We ridiculed the idea, certain that it was a newspaper fabrication to charge our Grand Old Man with pro-war sentiments. Kropotkin, the anarchist, humanitarian, and gentlest of beings—it was preposterous to believe that he could favour the European holocaust. But presently we were informed that Kropotkin had taken sides with the Allies, defending them with the same vehemence that the Haeckels and the Hauptmanns were championing "their" fatherland. He was justifying all measures to crush the "Prussian menace," as those in the opposite camp were urging the destruction of the Allies. It was a staggering blow to our movement, and especially to those of us who knew and loved Peter. But our devotion to our teacher and our affection for him could not alter our convictions nor change our attitude to the war as a struggle of financial and economic interests foreign to the worker and as the most destructive factor of what is vital and worth while in the world.

We determined to repudiate Peter's stand, and fortunately

we were not alone in this. Many others felt as we did, distressing as it was to turn against the man who had so long been our inspiration. [. . .]

Our first step was the publication in *Mother Earth* of Peter Kropotkin's pamphlet on "Capitalism and War," embodying a logical and convincing refutation of his new position. In numerous meetings and protests we pointed out the character, significance, and effects of war, my lecture on "Preparedness" showing that "readiness," far far from assuring peace, has at all times and in all countries been instrumental in precipitating armed conflicts. The lecture was repeatedly delivered before large and representative audiences, and it was among the first warnings in America against the military conspiracy behind the protestations of peace.

Our people in the States were awakening to the growing danger, and demands for speakers and for literature began pouring into our office from every part of the country. We were not rich in good English agitators, but the situation was urgent, and I was continually busy filling the gap.

I went about the country, speaking almost every evening, my days occupied with numerous calls on my time and energy. At last even my unusual powers of endurance gave way. Returning to New York after a lecture in Cleveland, I was taken ill with the grippe. I was too ill to be transferred to a hospital. After I had spent two weeks in bed, the physician in charge ordered me taken to a decent hotel room, my own quarters lacking all comforts. On my arrival at the hotel I was too weak to register, and Stella, my niece, wrote my name in the guest book. The clerk looked at it and then retired to an inner office. He returned to say that a mistake had been made; there was no vacant room for me in the place. It was a cold and grey day, the rain coming down in torrents, but I was compelled to return to my old quarters. [. . .]

My lectures in New York that winter included the subject of birth-control. I had definitely decided some time previously to make public the knowledge of contraceptives, particularly at my Yiddish meetings, because the women on the East Side needed that information most. Even if I were not vitally interested in the matter, the conviction of William Sanger and his condemnation to prison would have impelled me to take up the question. [. . .]

My lectures and attempts at lecturing on birth-control finally resulted in my arrest, whereupon a public protest was arranged in Carnegie Hall. It was an impressive gathering, with our friend and ardent co-worker Leonard D. Abbott presiding. [. . .] In court, I pleaded my own case. [. . .]

I spoke for an hour, closing with the declaration that if it was a crime to work for healthy motherhood and happy child-life, I was proud to be considered a criminal. Judge O'Keefe, reluctantly I thought, pronounced me guilty and sentenced me to pay a fine of one hundred dollars or serve fifteen days in the workhouse. On principle I refused to pay the fine, stating that I preferred to go to jail. It called forth an approving demonstration, and the court attendants cleared the room. I was hurried off to the Tombs, whence I was taken to the Queens County Jail.

Our following Sunday meeting, which I could not attend, since my forum was now a cell, was turned into a protest against my conviction. Among the speakers was Ben, who announced that pamphlets containing information about contraceptives were on the literature table and could be taken free of charge. Before he had got off the platform, the last of the pamphlets had been snatched up. Ben was arrested on the spot and held for trial.

In Queens County Jail, as on Blackwell's Island years previously, I saw it demonstrated that the average social offender is made, not born. One must have the consolation of an ideal to survive the forces designed to crush the prisoner. Having such an ideal, the fifteen days were a lark to me. I read more than I had for months outside, prepared material for six lectures on American literature, and still had time for my fellow prisoners.

Little did the New York authorities foresee the results of the arrests of Ben and me. The Carnegie Hall meeting had awakened interest throughout the country in the idea of birth-control. Protests and public demands for the right to contraceptive information were reported from numerous cities. In San Francisco forty leading women signed a declaration to the effect that they would get out pamphlets and be ready to go to prison. Some proceeded to carry out the plan and they were arrested, but their cases were discharged by the judge, who stated that there was no ordinance in the city to prohibit the propagation of birth-control information. [. . .]

In the excitement of the birth-control campaign I did not forget other important issues. The European slaughter was continuing, and the American militarists were growing bloodthirsty at the smell of the red stream. Our numbers were few, our means limited, but we concentrated our best energies to stem the tide of war. [. . .]

Ben was meanwhile serving his sentence in the Queens County Jail. His letters breathed a serenity I had never known him to feel before. I was due to leave on my tour. There were many friends to look after Ben in my absence, and we planned to have him join me in California upon his release. There was no reason for anxiety about him, and he himself urged me to go, yet I was loath to leave him in prison. For eight years he had shared the pain and joy of my struggle. How would it be, I wondered, to tour again without Ben, without his elemental activity, which had helped so much to make my meetings a success? And how should I bear the strain of the struggle without Ben's affection and the comfort of his presence? The thought chilled me, yet the larger purpose, which was my life, was too vital to be affected by personal needs. I left alone.

CHAPTER XLIV

[. . .] My lectures in Los Angeles were organized by Sasha, who had specially come for the purpose from San Francisco, where he was publishing the *Blast*. He had worked energetically, and my meetings proved to be successful in every way. Yet I missed Ben, Ben with all his weaknesses, his irresponsibility and ways that were so often harsh. [. . .]

In San Francisco Sasha and Fitzi had prepared everything to make my month's stay in the city pleasant and useful. My first lectures were most satisfactory, and they held out much promise for the rest of my series. I had my own apartment, as I was expecting Ben to join me in July. But I spent a great deal of my free time with Sasha and Fitzi in their place.

On Saturday, July 22, 1916, I was lunching with them. It was a golden California day, and the three of us were in a bright mood. We were a long time over our luncheon, Sasha regaling us with a humorous account of Fitzi's culinary exploits. The telephone rang, and he stepped into his office to answer it. When he returned, I noticed the extremely serious expression on his face, and I intuitively felt that something had happened.

"A bomb exploded in the Preparedness Parade this afternoon," he said; "there are killed and wounded." "I hope they aren't going to hold the anarchists responsible for it," I cried out. "How could they?" Fitzi retorted. "How could they not?" Sasha answered; "they always have."

My lecture on "Preparedness" had originally been scheduled for the 20th. But we learned that the liberal and progressive labour elements had arranged an anti-preparedness mass meeting for the same evening, and, not wishing to conflict with the occasion, postponed my talk for the 22nd. It struck me now that we had barely escaped being involved in the explosion; had my meeting taken place as scheduled, prior to the tragedy, everyone connected with my work would have undoubtedly been held responsible for the bomb. The telephone call had come from a newspaper man who wanted to know what we had to say about the explosion—the usual question of reporters and detectives on such occasions.

On the way to my apartment I heard news-boys calling out extra editions. I bought the papers and found what I had expected—glaring headlines about an "Anarchist Bomb" all over the front pages. The papers demanded the immediate arrest of the speakers at the anti-preparedness meeting of July 20. Hearst's *Examiner*[1] was especially bloodthirsty. The panic that followed on the heels of the explosion exposed strikingly the lack of courage, not only of the average person, but of the radicals and liberals as well. Before the 22nd of July they had filled our hall every evening for two weeks, waxing enthusiastic over my lectures. Now at the first sign of danger they ran to cover like a pack of sheep at the approach of a storm.

On the evening following the explosion there were just fifty people at my meeting, the rest of the audience consisting of detectives. The atmosphere was very tense, everybody fidgeting about, apparently in terror of another bomb. In my lecture I dealt with the tragedy of the afternoon as proving more convincingly than theoretic dissertations that violence begets violence. Labour on the Coast had been opposed to the preparedness parade, and union members had been asked not to participate. It was an open secret in San Francisco that the police and the newspapers had been warned that something violent might happen if the Chamber of Commerce kept insisting on the public demonstration of its mailed fist. Yet the "patriots" had permitted the parade to take place, deliberately exposing the participants to danger. The indifference to human life on the part of those who had staged the spectacle gave a foretaste of how cheaply life would be considered should America enter the war.

A reign of official terror followed the explosion. Revolutionary workers and anarchists were, as always, the first victims.

Four labour men and one woman were immediately arrested. They were Thomas J. Mooney and his wife, Rena, Warren K. Billings, Edward D. Nolan, and Israel Weinberg.[2] [. . .]

To charge these men with responsibility for the preparedness-parade explosion was a deliberate attempt to strike Labour a deadly blow through its most energetic and uncompromising representatives. We expected a concerted response in behalf of the accused from the liberal and radical elements, regardless of political differences. Instead we were confronted by complete silence on the part of the very people who had for years known and collaborated with Mooney, Nolan, and their fellow-prisoners. [. . .]

It was a desperate situation. Only Sasha and I dared speak up for the prisoners. But we were known as anarchists and it was a question whether the accused, of whom only Israel was an anarchist, would wish to have us affiliated with their defence; they might feel that our names would hurt their case rather than do them good. I myself knew them but slightly, and Warren K. Billings I had never met. But we could not sit by idly and be a party to the conspiracy of silence. We should have come to their assistance even if we had thought them guilty of the charges, but Sasha knew all of the accused well and he was absolutely certain of their innocence. He considered none of them capable of throwing a bomb into a crowd of people. His assurance was sufficient guarantee for me that they had had no connexion whatever with the preparedness-parade explosion. [. . .]

Ben, who had arrived from New York upon the completion of his prison term, was violently opposed to my remaining in San Francisco to finish my lecture series. My meetings were under police surveillance, the hall filled with hordes of detectives, whose presence kept my audiences away. He could not stand defeat; the mere handful of faithful friends in our hall, holding a thousand, was too much for him. Something else also seemed to be on his mind. He was more than usually restless and he besought me to discontinue my lectures and leave the city. But I could not go back on my engagements and I stayed on. I succeeded in raising at my meetings a hundred dollars and in borrowing a considerable sum for the defence of the arrested labour men. But so terrified was San Francisco that no attorney of standing would accept the case of the prisoners, who had already been condemned by every paper in the city. [. . .]

The sublime and the ridiculous often overlap each other. At the height of all the worry and anxiety about the San Francisco situation, while on my way to Portland with Ben, he was seized with one of his periodic fits to "nurse his soul, tabulate his ideas, and get acquainted with himself." His plaint was again that he could not continue for ever a "mere office boy," carrying bundles and selling literature; he had other ambitions; he wanted to write. He had wanted to write all along, he said, but I had never given him the chance. Sasha, he declared, was my god, Sasha's life and work my religion. In every difficulty that had arisen between him and Sasha I had always sided with the latter, he said. Ben had never been permitted his way in anything; I had even denied him his longing for a child. He insisted he had not forgotten that I had told him I had made my choice and that I could not allow a child to handicap my work in the movement. My attitude had hung over him like a pall, he declared, and it had made him afraid to confess that he had been living with another girl. His yearning for a child, always very strong, had become more compelling since he had met that girl. During his imprisonment in the Queens County Jail he had determined to allow nothing to stand in the way of the fulfilment of his great wish.

"But you have a child," I said, "your little Helen! Have you ever shown paternal love for her, or even the least interest, except on Valentine's Day, when I would pick out your cards for her?"

He was only a mere youth when the child was born, he replied; and the whole thing had been an accident. Now he was thirty-eight, with a "conscious feeling for fatherhood."

I knew there was no use in arguing. Unlike his confession in the first year of our love, which had struck me like a bolt of lightning out of a clear sky, this new disclosure hardly shocked or wounded me. The other had left scars too deep to heal or ever to allow me freedom from doubt. I had always guessed his deceptions; so accurately, indeed, that he called me a Sherlock Holmes "from whose eyes nothing is hidden."

Peculiar irony of circumstances! In New York Ben had started a "Sunday-school class," which exposed me to the ridicule of my comrades. "A Sunday-school in an anarchist office!" they laughed; "Jesus in the sanctum of the atheist." I sided with Ben. Free speech included his right to Jesus, I said. I knew that Ben was no more a Christian than the millions of others who proclaim themselves followers of the Nazarene. It was rather the personality of the "Son of Man" that appealed to Ben, as it had ever since his early youth. His religious sentimentalism would do no thinking person any harm, I thought. Most of his Sunday-school pupils were girls who were much more attracted to their teacher than to his Lord. I felt that Ben's religious emotionalism was stronger than his anarchistic convictions, and I could not deny him his right of expression.

To maintain consistency in a world of crass contradictions is not easy, and I had frequently been anything but consistent in regard to Ben. His love-affairs with all sorts of women had caused me too many emotional upheavals to allow me to act always in consonance with my ideas. Time, however, is a great leveller of feeling. I no longer cared about Ben's erotic adventures, and his newest confession did not affect me deeply. But it was indeed the height of tragicomedy that my stand in favour of Ben's Sunday-school in the *Mother Earth* office should result in an affair with one of his girl pupils. And then my anxiety about leaving Ben in the jail and going on tour without him at the very time he was absorbed in his new obsession! It was all so absurd and grotesque—I felt unutterably weary and possessed only of a desire to get away somewhere and forget the failure of my personal life, to forget even the cruel urge to struggle for an ideal.

I decided to go to Provincetown for a month, to visit with Stella and her baby. With them I would rest and perhaps find peace, peace.

Stella a mother! It seemed such a short while since she herself had been a little baby, the one ray of sunshine in my bleak Rochester days. When she was about to give birth to her child, I longed to be with her in that supreme moment. Instead I had

been obliged to lecture in Philadelphia, while my heart palpi-
tated with anxiety for my dear Stella in the throes of bringing
forth new life. Time had passed with giant strides, and now I
beheld Stella radiant in her young motherhood, and her little
one, six months old, a striking replica of what my niece had
looked at that age.

The charm of Provincetown, Stella's care, and the baby's
loveliness filled my visit with a delight I had not known in years.
[. . .] Variegated in mind and heart was that Provincetown
group,[3] and its company stimulating, but no one exerted such a
restful effect on me as did Max, who had come at my invitation
to spend a few weeks with me. He had remained unchanged, his
fine spirit and intuitive understanding even more mellowed with
the years. Kind and wise, he always found the right word to
soothe distress. An hour with him was like a spring day, and I
found solace and peace at his side. A month spent with him, in
the circle of Stella's little family, would make me strong to con-
quer the world.

Alas, there was no month and no conquest! The eternal
struggle for liberty was calling. Letters and telegrams from
Sasha cried for help to save the five lives endangered in San
Francisco. Could I think of rest, he indignantly demanded,
while Tom Mooney and his comrades were facing death? Had I
forgotten San Francisco, the terrorized prejudice against the
victims in jail there, the cowardice of the labour leaders, the
lack of funds for the defence of the prisoners, and the impossibility of securing a good lawyer for them? A note of desperation, unusual with Sasha, sounded in his letters, and he
besought me to return to New York to secure for the defence a
man prominent in the legal profession. That failing, I should go
to Kansas City and try to prevail upon Frank P. Walsh[4] to take
the case.

My peace was gone; the forces of reaction had broken in on
my golden freedom and had robbed me of the rest I needed so
much. I even resented Sasha's strange impatience, but somehow I felt guilty. I was tormented by the feeling that I had broken faith with the victims of a social system which I had fought
for twenty-seven years. Days of inner conflict and of galling

indecision followed. Then came Sasha's telegram informing me that Billings had been convicted and sentenced to prison for life. There was no more hesitancy on my part. I prepared to leave for New York.

On the last day of my Provincetown stay I went for a walk with Max across the dunes. The tide was out. The sun hung like a golden disk, no ripple on the transparent blue of the ocean in the distance. The sand seemed a sheet of white stretched far out and disappearing into the coloured crystal of the waters. Nature breathed repose and wondrous peace. My mind, too, was at rest; peace had come with my resolve. Max was frolicsome, and I felt in tune with his mood. We slowly made our way across the vast expanse towards the sea. Oblivious of the world of strife outside, we were held rapt by the spell of the enchantment around us. Fishermen returning laden with their spoils recalled us to the lateness of the day. With light step we started on our way back, our gay song ringing in the air.

We were barely half-way across to the beach when we caught the sound of gurgling water rising from somewhere. Sudden apprehension silenced our song. We turned to look back, and then Max gripped my hand and we ran for the shore. The tide was welling in with a fast sweep. It rose from a cove that emptied into the sea at that point. It was already close behind us, the waves rushing over the sand with increasing speed and volume. The terror of being caught drove us on. Now and then our feet would sink in the soft sand, but the foaming peril at our back kept steeling the instinctive will to live.

Terrified, we reached the bottom of a hill. With a last effort we scrambled up and fell exhausted on the green soil. We were safe at last!

On our way to New York we stopped off in Concord. I had always wanted to visit the home of America's past cultural epoch. The museum, the historic houses, and the cemetery were the only remaining witnesses of its days of glory. [....]

We visited Frank B. Sanborn, the biographer of Henry David Thoreau, the last of the great Concord circle.[5] [. . .] He talked with reverence of Thoreau, the great lover of man and of beast, the rebel against the encroachments of the State on the rights of the individual, the supporter of John Brown when even his own friends had denied him. [. . .]

Sanborn's estimate of Thoreau bore out my conception of the latter as the precursor of anarchism in the United States. To my surprise, Thoreau's biographer was scandalized at my remark. "No, indeed!" he cried; "anarchism means violence and revolution. It means Czolgosz. Thoreau was an extreme non-resistant." We spent several hours trying to enlighten this contemporary of the most anarchistic period of American thought about the meaning of anarchism.

From Provincetown I had written Frank P. Walsh about the San Francisco situation, telling him that I would go to Kansas City to talk the matter over further if there was any chance of his taking charge of the Mooney defence. His reply awaited me in New York. He could not accept my suggestion, Walsh wrote; he was involved in an important criminal case in his own city, and he had also undertaken to line up the liberal elements in the East for the Woodrow Wilson campaign.[6] He was of course interested in the San Francisco labour cases, his letter continued; he would soon be in New York and take the question up with me; perhaps he would be able to make some useful suggestions. [. . .]

At the Wilson campaign headquarters in New York, presided over by Frank P. Walsh, George West, and other intellectuals, I had a long talk with Walsh about the Mooney case. He seemed much impressed and he assured me that he would like to step in and do something for the prisoners. It was a serious situation, he said, but a far graver issue was facing the country—the war. The militarist elements were anxious for Wilson to get out of office so they could have their own man as President. It was up to all liberal-minded and peace-loving persons to re-elect Woodrow Wilson, Walsh emphasized. [. . .]

I left Walsh with a feeling of impatience at the credulity of this radically minded man and his co-workers in the Wilson campaign. It was an additional proof to me of the political blindness and social muddle-headedness of American liberals. [. . .]

Persecution of birth-control advocates went merrily on. Margaret Sanger, her sister Ethel Byrne, a trained nurse, and their assistant, Fanya Mandell, were rounded up in a raid on Mrs. Sanger's clinic in Brooklyn. [. . .]

The various hearings and trials in connexion with this matter proved that at least the judges were being educated. One of them declared that he distinguished between persons who gave out birth-control information free because of personal conviction and those who sold it. Certainly no such differentiation had been made previously, in William Sanger's case, in Ben's, or in mine. Even more striking proof that the agitation for family limitation was beginning to have an effect was given by Judge Wadhams during the trial of a woman charged with theft. Her husband, tubercular and out of work for a long time, was unable to support his large family. In summing up the causes that had led the prisoner to crime Judge Wadhams remarked that many nations in Europe had adopted birth-regulation with seemingly excellent results. "I believe we are living in an age of ignorance," he continued, "which at some future time will be looked upon aghast as we now look back on the dark ages. We have before us the case of a family increasing in numbers, with a tubercular husband, the woman with a child at her breast and with other small children at her skirts, in poverty and want."

We had reason to feel that it was worth going to jail if the urgency of limiting offspring was getting to be admitted even by the bench. Direct action, and not parlour discussion, was responsible for these results. [. . .]

At my lecture in Cleveland on "Family Limitation" Ben conceived the idea of calling for volunteers to distribute birth-control pamphlets. A number of people responded. At the end of the meeting Ben was arrested. A hundred persons, each carrying the forbidden pamphlet, followed him to the jail, but only Ben was held for trial. We immediately organized a Free Speech League, which combined with the local birth-control organization to fight the case. [. . .]

Similar experiences attended my lectures in various cities, as well as those of other advocates of family limitation. Sometimes it was Ben who was arrested, at other times I and the friends who were actively co-operating with us, or other lecturers who were trying to enlighten the people on the proscribed issue. In San Francisco the *Blast* was held up by the post-office on account of an article on birth-control and because of *lèse-majesté* against Woodrow Wilson. Birth-control had become a burning issue, and the authorities exerted every effort to silence its advocates. Nor did they shrink from foul means to accomplish their ends. [...]

While still on tour, I received a telegram from Harry Weinberger, my New York attorney, informing me that I had been denied a jury trial. On January 8 my case came up before three judges. Presiding Judge Cullen warned me severely that he would not permit any theories of the defendant to be aired in court. But he might have saved himself the trouble, because my case collapsed before either my lawyer or I had a chance to say anything. The evidence given by the detectives to the effect that I had distributed birth-control pamphlets on Union Square in May was so obviously contradictory that even the Court refused to take it seriously. I was acquitted.

Ben was not so fortunate, however, in regard to the Cleveland charge against him. [...] The Judge was a Roman Catholic and rigidly opposed to any form of sex hygiene. He talked at length about the carnal sins of the flesh and denounced birth-control and anarchism. Of the twelve jurymen five were Catholics. The others were apparently loath to convict, for they held out for thirteen hours without coming to an agreement. The Court sent them back, however, with instructions to remain out until they could bring in a verdict. Long hours in a stuffy room will cause most juries to grow unanimous. Ben was found guilty and sentenced to six months in the workhouse and to pay a thousand dollars' fine. It was the heaviest penalty imposed for a birth-control offence. Ben made a frank avowal of his belief in family limitation, and on the advice of counsel he appealed the case.

The result of the trial was due mainly to the absence of proper publicity. Margaret Sanger had lectured in the city a short time previously, and it had been expected that she would take note of the situation and urge her hearers to rally to Ben's support. Her refusal to do so had incensed our friends at the inexcusable breach of solidarity, but unfortunately no time had been left to arouse public sentiment in regard to Ben's case.

It was not the first occasion on which Mrs. Sanger had failed to aid birth-control advocates caught in the meshes of the law. [. . .] From numerous places friends wrote me that Mrs. Sanger had given the impression that she considered the issue as her own private concern. Subsequently Mr. and Mrs. Sanger publicly repudiated birth-control leagues organized by us, as well as our entire campaign for family limitation. [. . .]

We felt that we had reason for some satisfaction with our share in the campaign. We had presented the ideas of family limitation throughout the length and breadth of the country, bringing the knowledge of methods into the lives of the people who needed them most. We were ready now to leave the field to those who were proclaiming birth-control as the only panacea for all social ills. I myself had never considered it in that light; it was unquestionably an important issue, but by no means the most vital one.

In San Francisco the *Blast* had been suppressed and its office raided twice because of the paper's anti-war work and its efforts in behalf of Mooney. During the last raid Fitzi was brutally handled and her arm almost broken by an official ruffian. It became impossible to continue the publication on the Coast, and Fitzi brought it to New York, where she joined Sasha in his activities for the California defence. [. . .]

Tom Mooney had been convicted and sentenced to death. . . . The bosses who had declared themselves for the "open shop" had determined to hang Tom Mooney, as a warning to other labour organizers, and Mooney's doom was sealed.

Nor was the State of California the only section of the country where law and order had centred all their might to crush the workers and effectively stifle further protest on the part of the disinherited and humiliated. In Everett, Washington, seventy-four I.W.W. boys were fighting for their lives, and in every other State of the Union the jails and prisons were filled with men convicted for their ideals.

The political sky in the United States was darkening with heavy clouds, and the portents were daily growing more disquieting, yet the masses at large remained inert. Then, unexpectedly, the light of hope broke in the east. It came from Russia, the land tsar-ridden for centuries. The day so long yearned for had arrived at last—the Revolution had come!

CHAPTER XLV

The hated Romanovs were at last hurled from their throne, the Tsar and his cohorts shorn of power. It was not the result of a political *coup d'état;* the great achievement was accomplished by the rebellion of the entire people. Only yesterday inarticulate, crushed, as they had been for centuries, under the heel of a ruthless absolutism, insulted and degraded, the Russian masses had risen to demand their heritage and to proclaim to the whole world that autocracy and tyranny were for ever at an end in their country. The glorious tidings were the first sign of life in the vast European cemetery of war and destruction. They inspired all liberty-loving people with new hope and enthusiasm, yet no one felt the spirit of the Revolution as did the natives of Russia scattered all over the globe. They saw their beloved *Matushka Rossiya* now extend to them the promise of manhood and aspiration.

Russia was free; yet not truly so. Political independence was but the first step on the road to the new life. Of what use are "rights," I thought, if the economic conditions remain unchanged. I had known the blessings of democracy too long to have faith in political scene-shifting. Far more abiding was my faith in the people themselves, in the Russian masses now awakened to the consciousness of their power and to the realization of their opportunities. The imprisoned and exiled martyrs who had struggled to free Russia were now being resurrected, and some of their dreams realized. They were returning from the icy wastes of Siberia, from dungeons and banishment. They were coming back to unite with the people and to help them build a new Russia, economically and socially.

America also was contributing its quota. At the first news of the Tsar's overthrow thousands of exiles hastened back to their native country, now the Land of Promise. Many had lived in the United States for decades and acquired families and homes. But their hearts dwelt more in Russia than in the country they were enriching by their labour, which nevertheless scorned them as "foreigners." Russia was welcoming them, her doors wide open to receive her sons and daughters. Like swallows at the first sign of spring they began to fly back, orthodox and revolutionists for once on common ground—their love and longing for their native soil.

Our own old yearning, Sasha's and mine, began to stir again in our hearts. All through the years we had been close to the pulse of Russia, close to her spirit and her superhuman struggle for liberation. But our lives were rooted in our adopted land. We had learned to love her physical grandeur and her beauty and to admire the men and women who were fighting for freedom, the Americans of the best calibre. I felt myself one of them, an American in the truest sense, spiritually rather than by the grace of a mere scrap of paper. For twenty-eight years I had lived, dreamed, and worked for that America. Sasha, too, was torn between the urge to return to Russia and the necessity of continuing his campaign to save the life of Mooney, whose fatal hour was fast approaching. Could he forsake the doomed man and the others whose fate hung in the balance?

Then came Wilson's decision that the United States must join the European slaughter to make the world safe for democracy. Russia had great need of her revolutionary exiles, but Sasha and I now felt that America needed us more. We decided to remain.

The declaration of war by the United States dismayed and over-awed most of the middle-class pacifists. Some even suggested that we terminate our anti-militarist activities. [...] With the collapse of the pseudo-radicals the entire burden of anti-war activity fell upon the more courageous militant elements. Our group in particular redoubled its efforts, and I was kept feverishly busy travelling between New York and nearby cities, speaking and organizing the campaign. [...]

I had known for some time of the presence in New York of

Mme Alexandra Kollontay[1] and Leon Trotsky.[2] From the former I had received several letters and a copy of her book on woman's share in the world's work. She had asked me to meet her, but I had been unable to spare the time. Later on I had invited her to dinner, but she was prevented by illness from coming. Leon Trotsky I had also never met before, but I happened to be in the city when an announcement was made of a farewell meeting which he was to address before leaving for Russia. I attended the gathering. After several rather dull speakers Trotsky was introduced. A man of medium height, with haggard cheeks, reddish hair, and straggling red beard stepped briskly forward. His speech, first in Russian and then in German, was powerful and electrifying. I did not agree with his political attitude; he was a Menshevik (Social Democrat), and as such far removed from us. But his analysis of the causes of the war was brilliant, his denunciation of the ineffective Provisional Government in Russia scathing, and his presentation of the conditions that led up to the Revolution illuminating. He closed his two hours' talk with an eloquent tribute to the working masses of his native land. The audience was roused to a high pitch of enthusiasm, and Sasha and I heartily joined in the ovation given the speaker. We fully shared his profound faith in the future of Russia.

After the meeting we met Trotsky to bid him good-bye. He knew about us and he inquired when we meant to come to Russia to help in the work of reconstruction. "We will surely meet there," he remarked. [. . .]

In the spirit of her military preparations America was rivalling the most despotic countries of the Old World. Conscription, resorted to by Great Britain only after eighteen months of war, was decided upon by Wilson within one month after the United States had decided to enter the European conflict. Washington was not so squeamish about the rights of its citizens as the British Parliament had been. The academic author of *The New Freedom* did not hesitate to destroy every democratic principle at one blow.[3] He had assured the world that America was moved by the highest humanitarian motives, her aim being to democratize Germany. What if he had to Prussianize the United States in order to achieve it? Free-born Americans had to be forcibly pressed into the military mould, herded like cattle, and shipped across the waters to fertilize the fields of France. Their sacrifice would earn them the glory of having demonstrated the superiority of "My Country, 'Tis of Thee" over "Die Wacht am Rhein."[4] No American president had ever before succeeded in so humbugging the people as Woodrow Wilson, who wrote and talked democracy, acted despotically, privately and officially, and yet managed to keep up the myth that he was championing humanity and freedom.

We had no illusions about the outcome of the conscription bill pending before Congress. We regarded the measure as a complete denial of every human right, the death-knell to liberty of conscience, and we determined to fight it unconditionally. We did not expect to be able to stem the tidal wave of hatred and violence which compulsory service was bound to bring, but we felt that we had at least to make known at large that there were some in the United States who owned their souls and who meant to preserve their integrity, no matter what the cost.

We decided to call a conference in the *Mother Earth* office to broach the organization of a No-Conscription League and draw up a manifesto to clarify to the people of America the menace of conscription. We also planned a large mass meeting as a protest against compelling American men to sign their own death-warrants in the form of forced military registration. [. . .]

Almost ten thousand people filled the place [the Harlem River Casino], among them many newly rigged-out soldiers and their woman friends, a very boisterous lot indeed. Several hundred policemen and detectives were scattered through the hall. When the session opened, a few young "patriots" tried to rush the stage entrance. Their attempt was foiled, because we had prepared for such a contingency. [. . .]

The future heroes were noisy all through the speeches, but when I stepped on the platform, pandemonium broke loose. They jeered and hooted, intoned "The Star-Spangled Banner," and frantically waved small American flags. Above the din the voice of a recruit shouted: "I want the floor!" The patience of the audience had been sorely tried all evening by the interrupters. Now men rose from every part of the house and called to the disturber to shut up or be kicked out. I knew what such a thing would lead to, with the police waiting for a chance to aid the patriotic ruffians. Moreover, I did not want to deny free speech even to the soldier. Raising my voice, I appealed to the assembly to permit the man to speak. "We who have come here to protest against coercion and to demand the right to think and act in accordance with our consciences," I urged, "should recognize the right of an opponent to speak and we should listen quietly and grant him the respect we demand for ourselves. The young man no doubt believes in the justice of his cause as we do in ours, and he has pledged his life for it. I suggest therefore that we all rise in appreciation of his evident sincerity and that we hear him out in silence." The audience rose to a man.

The soldier had probably never before faced such a large assembly. He looked frightened and he began in a quavering voice that barely carried to the platform, although he was sitting near it. He stammered something about "German money" and "traitors," got confused, and came to a sudden stop. Then, turning to his comrades, he cried: "Oh, hell! Let's get out of here!" Out the whole gang slunk, waving their little flags and followed by laughter and applause.

Returning from the meeting home we heard news-boys shouting extra night editions—the conscription bill had become a law! Registration day was set for June 4. The thought struck me that on that day American democracy would be carried to its grave.

We felt that May 18 was the beginning of a period of historic importance. To Sasha and myself the day had also a profound personal meaning. It was the twelfth anniversary of his resurrection from the Western Penitentiary of Pennsylvania, the first time in years that he and I were together in the same city and on the same platform.

Streams of callers besieged our office from morning till late at night; young men, mostly, seeking advice on whether they should register. We knew, of course, that among them were also decoys sent to trick us into saying that they should not. The majority, however, were frightened youths, fearfully wrought up

and at sea as to what to do. They were helpless creatures about
to be sacrificed to Moloch. Our sympathies were with them,
but we felt that we had no right to decide the vital issue for
them. There were also distracted mothers, imploring us to save
their boys. By the hundreds they came, wrote, or telephoned.
All day long our telephone rang; our offices were filled with
people, and stacks of mail arrived from every part of the country asking for information about the No-Conscription League,
pledging support and urging us to go on with the work. In this
bedlam we had to prepare copy for the current issues of *Mother
Earth* and the *Blast*, write our manifesto, and send out circulars
announcing our forthcoming meeting. At night, when trying to
get some sleep, we would be rung out of bed by reporters wanting to know our next step. [. . .]

The June issue of *Mother Earth* appeared draped in black,
its cover representing a tomb bearing the inscription: "IN
MEMORIAM—AMERICAN DEMOCRACY." The sombre attire of
the magazine was striking and effective. No words could express more eloquently the tragedy that turned America, the
erstwhile torch-bearer of freedom, into a grave-digger of her
former ideals.

We strained our capital to the last penny to issue an extra
large edition. We wanted to mail copies to every Federal officer,
to every editor, in the country and to distribute the magazine
among young workers and college students. Our twenty thousand copies barely sufficed to supply our own needs. It made us
feel our poverty more than ever before. Fortunately an unexpected ally came to our assistance: the New York newspapers!
They had reprinted whole passages from our anti-conscription
manifesto, some even reproducing the entire text and thus
bringing it to the attention of millions of readers. Now they co-
piously quoted from our June issue and editorially commented
at length on its contents.

The press throughout the country raved at our defiance of
law and presidential orders. We duly appreciated their help in
making our voices resound through the land, our voices that
but yesterday had called in vain. Incidentally the papers also
gave wide publicity to our meeting scheduled for June 4. [. . .]

When we got within half a dozen blocks of Hunt's Point Palace, our taxi had to come to a stop. Before us was a human dam, as far as the eye could see, a densely packed, swaying mass, counting tens of thousands. On the outskirts were police on horse and on foot, and great numbers of soldiers in khaki. They were shouting orders, swearing, and pushing the crowd from the sidewalks to the street and back again. The taxi could not proceed, and it was hopeless to try to get Sasha to the hall on his crutches.[5] We had to make a detour around vacant lots until we reached the back entrance of the Palace. There we came upon a score of patrol wagons armed with search-lights and machine-guns. The officers stationed at the stage door, failing to recognize us, refused to let us pass. A reporter who knew us whispered to the police sergeant in charge. "Oh, all right," he shouted, "but nobody else will be admitted. The place is overcrowded."

The sergeant had lied; the house was only half filled. The police were keeping the people from getting in, and at seven o'clock they had ordered the doors locked. While they were denying the right of entry to workers, they permitted scores of half-drunken sailors and soldiers to enter the hall. The balcony and the front seats were filled with them. They talked loudly, made vulgar remarks, jeered, hooted, and otherwise behaved as befits men who are preparing to make the world safe for democracy.

In the room behind the stage were officials from the Department of Justice, members of the Federal attorney's office, United States marshals, detectives from the "Anarchist Squad," and reporters. The scene looked as if set for bloodshed. The representatives of law and order were obviously keyed up for trouble. [. . .]

When the meeting was opened and Leonard D. Abbott took the chair, he was greeted by the soldiers and sailors with catcalls, whistles, and stamping of feet. This failing of the desired effect, the uniformed men in the gallery began throwing on the platform electric lamps which they had unscrewed from the fixtures. Several bulbs struck a vase holding a bunch of red carnations, sending vase and flowers crashing to the floor. Confusion followed, the audience rising in indignant protest and demanding that the police put the ruffians out. John Reed, who was with us, called on the police captain to order the disturbers removed, but that official declined to intervene.

After repeated appeals from the chairman, supported by some women in the audience, comparative quiet was restored. But not for long. Every speaker had to go through the same ordeal. Even the mothers of prospective soldiers, who poured out their anguish and wrath, were jeered by the savages in Uncle Sam's uniform.

Stella was one of the mothers to address the audience. It was the first time she had to face such an assembly and endure insults. Her own son was still too young to be subject to conscription, but she shared the woe and grief of other, less fortunate, parents, and she could articulate the protest of those who had no opportunity to speak. She held her own against the interruptions and carried the audience with her by the earnestness and fervour of her talk.

Sasha was the next speaker; others were to follow him, and I was to speak last. [. . .] Renewed shouts, whistles, stamping, and hysterical cries of the women accompanying the soldiers greeted Sasha. Above the clamour a hoarse voice cried: "No more! We've had enough!" But Sasha would not be daunted. He began to speak, louder and louder, berating the hoodlums, now reasoning with them, now holding them up to scorn. His words seemed to impress them. They became quiet. Then, suddenly, a husky brute in front shouted: "Let's charge the platform! Let's get the slacker!" In an instant the audience were on their feet. Some ran up to grab the soldier. I rushed to Sasha's side. In my highest pitch I cried: "Friends, friends—wait, wait!" The suddenness of my appearance attracted everyone's attention. "The soldiers and sailors have been sent here to cause trouble," I admonished the people, "and the police are in league with them. If we lose our heads there will be bloodshed, and it will be our blood they will shed!" There were cries of "She's right!" "It's true!" I took advantage of the momentous pause. "Your presence here," I continued, "and the presence of the multitude outside shouting their approval of every word they can catch, are convincing proof that you do not believe in violence, and it equally proves that you understand that war is the most fiendish violence. War kills deliberately, ruthlessly, and destroys innocent lives. No, it is not we who have come to create a riot here. We must refuse to be provoked to it. Intelligence and a passionate faith are more convincing than armed police, machine-guns, and rowdies in soldiers' coats. We have demonstrated it tonight. We still have many speakers, some of them with illustrious American names. But nothing they or I could say will add to the splendid example you have given. Therefore I declare the meeting closed. File out orderly, intone our inspiring revolutionary songs, and leave the soldiers to their tragic fate, which at present they are too ignorant to realize."

The strains of the "Internationale" rose above the approval shouted by the audience, and the song was taken up by the many-throated mass outside. Patiently they had waited for five hours and every word that had reached them through the open windows had found a strong echo in their hearts. All through the meeting their applause had thundered back to us, and now their jubilant song. [. . .]

We scheduled a mass meeting for June 14. It was not necessary for us to print announcements. We merely called up the newspapers, and they did the rest. They denounced our impudence in continuing anti-war activities, and they sharply criticized the authorities for failing to stop us. As a matter of fact, the police were working overtime waylaying draft-evaders. They arrested thousands, but many more had refused to register. The press did not report the actual state of affairs; it did not care to make it known that large numbers of Americans had the manhood to defy the government. We knew through our own channels that thousands had determined not to shoulder a gun against people who were as innocent as themselves in causing the world slaughter. [. . .]

The day of our Forward Hall meeting arrived. In the late afternoon I was called on the telephone, and a strange voice warned me against attending the gathering. The man had overheard a plot to kill me, he informed me. I asked for his name, but he declined to give it; nor would he consent to see me. I thanked him for his interest in my welfare and hung up the receiver. Jocularly I told Sasha and Fitzi that I must prepare my will. [. . .]

The meeting was very spirited and our program was carried out without a hitch. But at the close every man in the hall who appeared subject to the draft was detained by the officers, and those who could not show a registration card were placed under arrest. It was apparently the intention of the Federal authorities to use our meeting as a trap. We therefore resolved to hold no more public gatherings unless we could make sure that those who had not complied with the registration law would keep away. We decided to concentrate more on the printed word.

On the following afternoon we were all busy in our offices. Sasha and Fitzi were on the upper floor, preparing the next issue of the *Blast*. [. . .] Above the hum of conversation and the clicking of the typewriter we suddenly heard the heavy stamping of feet on the stairway, and before any one of us had a chance to see what was the matter, a dozen men burst into my office. The leader of the party excitedly cried: "Emma Goldman, you're under arrest! And so is Berkman; where is he?" It was United States Marshal Thomas D. McCarthy. I knew him by sight; of late he had always stationed himself near the platform at our No-Conscription meetings, his whole attitude one of impatient readiness to spring upon the speakers. The newspapers had reported him as saying that he had repeatedly wired Washington for orders to arrest us.

"I hope you will get the medal you crave," I said to him. "Just the same, you might let me see your warrant." Instead he held out a copy of the June *Mother Earth* and demanded whether I was the author of the No-Conscription article it contained. "Obviously," I answered, "since my name is signed to it. Furthermore, I take the responsibility for everything else in the magazine. But where is your warrant?"

McCarthy declared that no warrant was necessary for us; *Mother Earth* contained enough treasonable matter to land us in jail for years. He had come to get us and we had better hurry up.

Leisurely I walked towards the stairs and called: "Sasha, Fitzi—some visitors are here to arrest us." McCarthy and several of his men roughly pushed me aside and dashed up to the *Blast* office. The deputy marshals took possession of my desk and began examining the books and pamphlets on our shelves, throwing them in a pile on the floor. [. . .]

I started for my room to change my dress, aware that a night's free lodging was in store for me. One of the men rushed up to detain me, taking hold of my arm. I wrenched myself loose. "If your chief didn't have the guts to come up here without a body-guard of thugs," I said to him, "he should at least have instructed you not to act like one. I'm not going to run away. I only want to dress for the reception awaiting us, and I don't propose to let you act as my maid." The men ransacking my desk laughed coarsely. "She's a caution," one remarked, "but it's all right, officer, let her go to her room." When I emerged with my book and small toilet outfit, I found that Fitzi and Sasha, who was still on crutches, were already down. McCarthy was with them.

"I want the membership list of the No-Conscription League," he demanded.

"We ourselves are always ready to receive our friends the police," I retorted; "but we are careful not to take chances with the names and addresses of those who cannot afford the honour of an arrest. We don't keep the No-Conscription list in our office, and you can't find out where it is." [. . .]

In the Federal Building we were joined by Harry Weinberger, our pugnacious lawyer and unfailing friend. He asked for immediate arraignment and release on bail, but our arrest had purposely been staged for the late afternoon after the official closing hour. We were ordered to the Tombs prison.

The following morning we were taken before United States Commissioner Hitchcock. The prosecutor, Federal Attorney for the District of New York, Harold A. Content, charged us with "conspiracy against the draft" and demanded that our bail be set high. The commissioner fixed the bonds at twenty-five thousand dollars each. Mr. Weinberger protested, but in vain. [. . .]

I wanted Sasha bailed out first because of his injured leg,

which still needed treatment; I did not mind remaining in the Tombs, for I was resting and enjoying an absorbing book Margaret Anderson[6] had sent me. It was *A Portrait of the Artist As a Young Man*, by James Joyce.[7] I had not read that author before and I was fascinated by his power and originality.

The Federal authorities were not anxious to let us out of prison. The three hundred thousand dollars' worth of real estate offered as our bond was refused on a flimsy technicality by Assistant Federal Attorney Content, who declared that nothing but cash would be accepted. There was enough on hand to bail out one of us. Sasha, always gallant, refused to come out first, and therefore the bond was given for me and I was released. [. . .]

At last we succeeded in procuring the twenty-five-thousand-dollar cash bond demanded for Sasha, and on June 25 he was released from the Tombs. We were entirely at one regarding our trial. We did not believe in the law and its machinery, and we knew that we could expect no justice. We would therefore completely ignore what was to us a mere farce; we would refuse to participate in the court proceedings. Should this method prove impractical, we would plead our own case, not in order to defend ourselves, but to give public utterance to our ideas. We decided to go into court without an attorney. [. . .]

It was Tuesday, June 27, at 10 a.m., when, together with Sasha, still on crutches, I walked through the crowded court-room in the Federal Building to face the prosecution. [. . .]

June 27 happened to be my forty-eighth birthday. It marked twenty-eight years of my life spent in an active struggle against compulsion and injustice. The United States now symbolizing concentrated coercion, I could not have wished for a more appropriate celebration than to meet its challenge. It gave me much joy to feel that my friends had, in the excitement of the moment, not forgotten the event. On my return to court they presented me with flowers and gifts. The demonstration of their love and esteem on this special occasion moved me profoundly.

Active participation in our trial having been thrust upon us, Sasha and I determined to use it to best advantage. We decided to wring from our enemies every chance to propagate our ideas.

Should we succeed, it would be the first time since 1887 that anarchism had raised its voice in an American court. Nothing else was worth considering in comparison with such an achieve-ment.

I had known Sasha twenty-eight years. As far as one human being can foretell how another will act under stress or when confronted with the unexpected, I had always believed that I could in reference to him. But Sasha as a brilliant lawyer was a revelation even to me, his oldest friend. At the end of the first day I almost pitied the unfortunate talesmen whom he had been catechizing for hours. Like bullets Sasha fired his ques-tions at the prospective jurymen, examining them on social, political, and religious matters, making them writhe at the ex-posure of their ignorance and prejudice, and almost convincing the victims themselves that they were not fit to try intelligent men. His flashes of humour and charming manners captivated the spectators.

When Sasha had finished quizzing the jurymen, they could hardly restrain their expression of relief. I followed to question them on marriage, divorce, sex enlightenment of the young, and birth-control. Would my radical views on these matters prevent their rendering an unbiased verdict? It was with the greatest difficulty that I was able to get my questions across. I was often interrupted by the Federal Attorney, became involved in verbal clashes with him, and was repeatedly admonished by the Judge to confine myself to "relevant" matters.

We knew very well that the twelve men we had finally se-lected could not and would not render an unbiased verdict. But by our examination of the talesmen we had succeeded in un-covering the social issues involved in the trial, had created a lib-ertarian atmosphere, and had broached problems never before mentioned in a New York court.

Attorney Content opened his case by stating that he would prove that in our writings and speeches we had urged men not to register. As evidence he produced copies of *Mother Earth*, the *Blast*, and our No-Conscription manifesto. Cheerfully we admitted our authorship of every word, insisting, however, that the prosecution quote page and line where advice not to register was given. Unable to do so, Content called Fitzi to the witness-stand and tried to make her say that we had worked for profit. Though utterly irrelevant to the crime charged against us, the Court permitted the procedure. In her quiet, unruffled manner Fitzi very soon punctured this bubble. [. . .]

Every day increased the tension in court. The atmosphere grew more antagonistic, the official attendants more insulting. Our friends were either kept out or treated roughly when they succeeded in gaining admittance. On the street below, a re-cruiting station had been erected, and patriotic harangues min-gled with the music of a military band. Each time the national anthem was struck up, everybody in court was commanded to rise, the soldiers present standing at attention. One of our girls refused to get up and she was dragged out of the room by force. A boy was literally kicked out. Sasha and I remained seated throughout the display of patriotism by the mailed fist. What could the officials do? They could not very well order us removed from this Punch and Judy show; we at least had that advantage.

After endlessly repetitious "evidence" of our crime, which in reality proved nothing, the prosecution closed its case. The last round in the contest between ideas and organized stupidity was set for July 9. [. . .]

Prosecutor Content could in no way compare in ability and forcefulness with his colleague who had prosecuted me in 1893; he had been drab and colourless all through the trial and stereotyped in his address to the jury. At one moment he had at-tempted to climb to oratorical heights. "You think this woman before you is the real Emma Goldman," he declared, "this well-bred lady, courteous, and with a pleasant smile on her face? No! The real Emma Goldman can be seen only on the platform. There she is in her true element, sweeping all caution to the winds! There she inflames the young and drives them to violent deeds. If you could see Emma Goldman at her meetings, you would realize that she is a menace to our well-ordered institu-tions." It was therefore the jury's duty to save the country from *that* Emma Goldman by bringing in a verdict of guilty.

Sasha followed the prosecutor. He held the close attention of the men in the box, as well as of the entire court-room, for two hours. That was no small feat in an atmosphere oozing with prejudice and hate. His playful and witty handling of the so-called evidence to prove our "crime" caused much merriment and often loud laughter. [. . .]

I spoke after Sasha, for an hour. I discussed the farce of a government undertaking to carry democracy abroad by suppressing the last vestiges of it at home. I took up the contention of Judge Mayer that only such ideas are permissible as are "within the law." Thus he had instructed the jurymen when he had asked them if they were prejudiced against those who propagate unpopular ideas. I pointed out that there had never been an ideal, however humane and peaceful, which in its time had been considered "within the law." I named Jesus, Socrates, Galileo, Giordano Bruno. "Were they 'within the law'?" I asked. "And the men who set America free from British rule, the Jeffersons and the Patrick Henrys? The William Lloyd Garrisons, the John Browns, the David Thoreaus and Wendell Phillipses— were they within the law?"[8]

At that moment the strains of the "Marseillaise" floated through the window, and the Russian Mission marched past on its way to the City Hall. I seized upon the occasion. "Gentlemen of the jury," I said, "do you hear the stirring melody? It was born in the greatest of all revolutions, and it was most emphatically not within the law! And that delegation your government is now honouring as the representatives of new Russia. Only five months ago every one of them was considered what you have been told we are: criminals—not within the law!" [. . .]

Judge Mayer fully rose to our expectations. In his charge to the jury he declared with much solemnity: "In the conduct of this case, the defendants have shown remarkable ability. An ability which might have been utilized for the great benefit of this country, had they seen fit to employ themselves in behalf of it rather than against it. In this country of ours we regard as enemies those who advocate the abolition of our government and those who counsel disobedience to our laws by those of minds less strong. American liberty was won by the forefathers, it was maintained by the Civil War, and today there are the thousands who have already gone, or are getting ready to go, to foreign lands to represent their country in the battle for liberty." He then instructed that jury that "whether the defendants are right or wrong can have no bearing on the verdict. The duty of the jury is merely to weigh the evidence presented as to the innocence or guilt of the defendants of the crime as charged."

The jury filed out. The sun had set. The electric lights looked yellow in the dusk. Flies buzzed, their swirl mingling with the whisperings in the room. The minutes crept on, clammy with the day's heat. The jury returned; its deliberation had lasted just thirty-nine minutes.

"What is your verdict?" the foreman was asked.

"Guilty," he answered. [. . .]

"In the United States, law is an imperishable thing," the Court declared in imposing sentence, "and for such people as would nullify our laws we have no place in our country. In a case such as this I can but inflict the maximum sentence which is permitted by our laws."

Two years in prison with a fine of ten thousand dollars each. The Judge also instructed the Federal Attorney to send the records of the trial to the immigration authorities in Washington with his recommendation to deport us at the expiration of our prison terms.

His Honour had done his duty. He had served his country well and merited a rest. He declared court adjourned and turned to leave the bench.

But I was not through. "One moment, please," I called out. Judge Mayer turned to face me. "Are we to be spirited away at such neck-breaking speed? If so, we want to know it now. We want everybody here to know it."

"You have ninety days in which to file an appeal."

"Never mind the ninety days," I retorted. "How about the next hour or two? Can we have that to gather up a few necessary things?"

"The prisoners are in the custody of the United States Marshal," was the curt answer.

The Judge again turned to leave. Again I brought him to a stop. "One more word!" He stared at me, his heavy-set face flushed. I stared back. I bowed and said: "I want to thank you for your leniency and kindness in refusing us a stay of two days, a stay you would have accorded the most heinous criminal. I thank you once more."

His Honour grew white, anger spreading over his face. Nervously he fumbled with the papers on his desk. He moved his lips as if to speak, then abruptly turned and left the bench.

CHAPTER XLVI

The automobile sped on. It was filled with deputy marshals, with me in their midst. Twenty minutes later we reached the Baltimore and Ohio Station. The hand of time seemed set back twenty-five years. I visioned myself at the same station a quarter of a century ago, straining towards the disappearing train which was bearing Sasha away, leaving me desolate and alone. A gruff voice startled me. "Are you seeing ghosts?" it demanded.

I was in a compartment, a big man and a woman at my side, the deputy marshal and his wife. Then I was left with the woman.

The day's heat, the excitement, and three hours' wait in the Federal Building had exhausted me. I felt worn and sticky in my sweaty clothes. I started for the wash-room, and the woman followed me. I objected. She regretted she could not let me go unattended; her instructions were not to permit me out of sight. She had a rather kindly face. I assured her that I would not try to escape, and she consented to close the door half-way. Having cleaned up, I crawled into my berth and immediately fell asleep.

I was awakened by the loud voices of my keepers. The man's coat was already off and he was proceeding to undress. "You don't mean you're going to sleep here?" I demanded.

"Sure," he answered, "what's wrong? My wife is here. You've got nothing to fear."

What more could morality wish for than the presence of the deputy's wife? It wasn't fear, I told him; it was disgust.

The watchful eyes of the law were closed in sleep, but its mouth was wide open, emitting a rattle of snores. The air was putrid. Anxious thoughts about Sasha beset me. A quarter of a century had passed, crammed with events and rich in the inter-play of light and shade. The painful frustration with Ben—friendships shattered—others that had never lost their bloom. The earth-spirit often in conflict with the impelling aspirations of the ideal, and Sasha ever dependable all through the long span of time and always my comrade in the struggle. The thought was soothing, and the strain of weeks found relief in blessed sleep. [. . .]

Arriving in Jefferson City,[1] my escorts offered to take me to the penitentiary in a taxi. I requested that we walk. It might be my last chance for a long while, I thought. They readily con-sented, no doubt because they could pocket the price and charge it to their expense accounts. [. . .]

With the exception of my two weeks in Queens County Jail, I had somehow managed to steer clear of prisons since my "rest-cure" on Blackwell's Island. There had been numerous ar-rests and several trials, but no other convictions. A disgusting record for one who could boast of the never-failing attention of every police department in the country.

"Any disease?" the head matron demanded abruptly.

I was somewhat taken aback at the unexpected concern over my health. I answered her that I had nothing to complain of ex-cept that I needed a bath and a cold drink.

"Don't be impudent and pretend you don't know what I mean," she sternly reproved me. "I mean the disease immoral women have. Most of those delivered here have it."

"Venereal disease is not particular whom it strikes," I told her; "the most respectable people have been known to be vic-tims of it. I don't happen to have it, which is due perhaps much more to luck than to virtue."

She looked scandalized. She was so self-righteous and prim, she needed to be shocked, and I was catty enough to enjoy watching the effect.

After having been subjected to the routine search for dope and cigarettes, I was given a bath and informed that I could keep my own underwear, shoes, and stockings.

My cell contained a cot with stiff but clean sheets and blan-kets, a table and a chair, a stationary wash-stand with running water, and, blessing of blessings, a toilet built in a little alcove, hidden from view by a curtain. So far my new home was a decided improvement over Blackwell's Island. Two things marred my pleasant discovery. My cell faced a wall that shut off the air and light, and all through the night the clock in the prison yard struck every fifteen minutes, whereupon stentorian voices would call out: "All's well." I tossed about, wondering how long it would take to get used to this new torture.

Twenty-four hours in the prison gave me an approximate idea of its routine. The institution had a number of progressive features: more frequent visits, the opportunity to order foodstuffs, the privilege of writing letters three times a week, according to the grade one had reached, recreation in the yard daily and twice on Sunday, a bucketful of hot water every evening, and permission to receive packages and printed matter. These were great advantages over conditions in Blackwell's Island. The recreation was especially gratifying. The yard was small and had but little protection from the sun, but the prisoners were free to walk about, talk, play, and sing, without interference from the matron who presided in the yard. On the other hand, the prevailing labour system required definite tasks. The latter were so difficult to accomplish that they kept the inmates in constant trepidation. I was informed that I would be excused from making the complete task, but that was small comfort. With a woman serving a life sentence on one side of me, and another doomed to fifteen years, both forced to do the full amount of work, I did not care to take advantage of my exemption. At the same time I feared that I might never be able to accomplish the task. The subject was the main topic of discussion and the greatest worry of the inmates.

After a week spent in the shop I began suffering excruciating pain in the back of my neck. My condition was aggravated by the first news from New York. Fitzi's letter conveyed what I already knew, that Sasha had been taken to Atlanta. It was far away, she wrote, and it would prevent our friends from visiting him. She had many worries and hardships to face. The Federal authorities, in co-operation with the New York police, had terrorized the proprietor of our office. He had ordered Fitzi to remove *Mother Earth* and the *Blast,* without even giving her a week's notice. [. . .]

Two weeks after I had been delivered to the prison, the same deputy marshal and his wife arrived to take me back to New York. Irrepressible Harry Weinberger had succeeded in getting Supreme Court Justice Louis D. Brandeis[2] to sign the application for our appeal, which admitted Sasha and me to bail and temporary freedom. [. . .] I was sure that our liberty would be of short duration; still, it was good to return to our friends and resume the work where it had been interrupted by our arrest.

It was with emotions quite different from those I had felt on my way to prison that I boarded the train for New York. [. . .]

The return journey had many pleasant features, the main one being the absence of the deputy. His wife also did not intrude, both remaining outside my compartment. The door was left ajar, more to afford me air than to keep me in view. It was an unusually close day, and I had a foretaste of what was to be meted out to such a godless creature when I should have joined the departed.

In the Tombs the keepers received the prodigal daughter with glad acclaim. It was late and the prison had closed for the day, but I was permitted a bath. The head matron was an old friend of mine, of the birth-control fight days. She believed in family limitation, she had confided to me, and she had been kind and solicitous, once even attending our Carnegie Hall meeting as my guest. When the other matrons left, she engaged me in conversation and remarked that she saw no reason to be excited about what the Germans had done to the Belgians. England had treated Ireland no better during hundreds of years and recently again during the Easter uprising.[3] She was Irish, and she had no use for the Allies. I explained that my sympathies were not with any of the warring countries, but with the people of every land, because they alone have to pay the terrible price. She looked rather disappointed, but she gave me clean sheets for my bunk, and I liked her as a good Irish soul.

In the morning friends came to see me, among them Harry Weinberger, Stella, and Fitzi. I inquired about Sasha. Had he been brought back, and how was his leg? Fitzi averted her face.

"What is it?" I asked anxiously.

"Sasha is in the Tombs," she replied in a dead voice; "he will be safer there for a while."

Her tone and manner filled me with apprehension. Urged to tell me the worst, she informed me that Sasha was wanted in San Francisco. He had been indicted for murder in connexion with the Mooney case.

The Chamber of Commerce and the District Attorney had carried out their threat to "get" Sasha. They were going to have revenge for the splendid work he had done to expose the frame-up against five lives. Billings had already been put out of the way, immured for life, and Tom Mooney was facing death. Their next prey was Sasha. I knew they meant to murder him. Instinctively I raised my hand as if to ward off a blow.

I fully realized only when I was bailed out what Fitzi had meant by saying that Sasha would be safer in the Tombs. Released on bail, he would be in danger of being kidnapped and spirited away to California. [. . .] We immediately set to work, Fitzi, the "Swede,"[4] and I. We called a group of people together to organize a publicity committee. [. . .]

Sasha himself was in gay spirits. To see his visitors he had to be taken from the Tombs to the Federal Building and back again, which afforded him a walk in the fresh air. He had not yet been able to discard his crutches, and hobbling along was rather uncomfortable. But when one faces the possible loss of one's life, promenading even on crutches is a great boon. [. . .]

Uncertain how long I should remain at liberty, I had not taken an apartment. I shared with Fitzi her flat and spent an occasional weekend with Stella in Darien. [. . .]

In the midst of those trying days there came another and far greater shock. I learned that my nephew David Hochstein had waived exemption and volunteered for the army. His mother, all unconscious of the blow awaiting her, was on her way to New York to meet him. My sister had only recently lost her husband after a short illness. I could not bear to think how the news about David would affect her. David, her beloved son, in whom she had concentrated all her hopes—a soldier! His young life to be given for something Helena had always hated as the crime of crimes! [. . .]

I visited Helena at Darien. Her appearance told me more than words. The frightened expression in her eyes made me fear that she would not survive the blow of the vain sacrifice of her boy. I found David also there, and I longed to talk to him. But I remained dumb. Notwithstanding his family affection for me and my love for him, we had remained distant. How could I now hope to reach his mind? I had proclaimed that the choice of military service must be left to the conscience of every man. How could I attempt to impose my views on David, even if I could hope to persuade him, which I did not? [. . .]

Our activities for Sasha and the San Francisco cases received unexpected and far-reaching impetus through news from Russia: demonstrations in their behalf had taken place in Petrograd and Kronstadt.[5] It was the answer to the message we had sent to the councils of workers, soldiers, and sailors by the refugees that had departed in May and June. [. . .]

Shortly afterwards came further news from Russia of still greater moment. A resolution proposed by the sailors of Kronstadt and adopted at a monster meeting called for the arrest of Mr. Francis, the American Ambassador in Russia, who was to be held as hostage until the San Francisco victims and Sasha should be free. A delegation of armed sailors had marched to the American Embassy in Petrograd to carry out the decision. Our old comrade Louise Berger, who with other Russian refugees had returned to her native land after the outbreak of the Revolution, served as their interpreter. Mr. Francis had solemnly assured the delegation that it was all a mistake, and that the lives of Mooney, Billings, and Berkman were in no danger. But the sailors were insistent, and Mr. Francis in their presence cabled to Washington and promised to exert himself further with the American Government to secure the release of the San Francisco prisoners.

The threat of the sailors evidently had an effect on the Ambassador, with the result that President Wilson was moved to prompt action. Whatever the message of the President to Governor

Whitman, our delegation found the latter in a very receptive mood. Moreover, quantity is always appreciated by aspiring politicians, and the labour delegation consisted of a hundred men, representing nearly a million organized workers of New York. With them were Morris Hillquit[6] and Harry Weinberger, who impressed upon the Governor that Alexander Berkman did not stand alone, and that his extradition would be resented by labour all through the United States. Mr. Whitman thereupon decided to telegraph District Attorney Fickert for the records of the case and promised to postpone final action until he had thoroughly acquainted himself with the indictment against Sasha.

It was a victory indeed, though it did only temporarily delay proceedings. But instead of sending the requested documents, the San Francisco prosecutor wired Albany that "the Berkman extradition would not be pressed for the present." We had known all along that Fickert could not afford to produce the records, since they did not contain a scintilla of evidence to connect Sasha with the explosion. [. . .]

America, only seven months in the war, had already outstripped in brutality every European land with three years' experience in the business of slaughter. Non-combatants and conscientious objectors from every social stratum were filling the jails and prisons. The new Espionage Law[7] turned the country into a lunatic asylum, with every State and Federal official, as well as a large part of the civilian population, running amuck. They spread terror and destruction. Disruption of public meetings and wholesale arrests, sentences of incredible severity, suppression of radical publications and indictments of their staffs, beating of workers—even murder—became the chief patriotic pastime.

In Bisbee, Arizona, twelve hundred I.W.W.'s were manhandled and driven across the border. In Tulsa, Oklahoma, seventeen of their comrades were tarred and feathered and in a half-dead condition left in the sage-brush. [. . .] Through the length and breadth of the country stalked the madness of jingoism. One hundred and sixty I.W.W.'s were arrested in Chicago and held for trial on charges of treason. [. . .] There was hardly a city or town in the wide United States where the jails did not contain some men and women who would not be terrorized into patriotic slaughter. [. . .]

The assaults on life and on free speech were supplemented by the suppression of the printed word. Under the Espionage Law and similar statutes passed in the war fever the Postmaster General had been constituted absolute dictator over the press. Even private distribution had become impossible for any paper opposed to the war. *Mother Earth* became the first victim, soon followed by the *Blast*, the *Masses*, and other publications, and by indictments against their editorial staffs.

The reactionaries were not the only element responsible for the patriotic orgy. Sam Gompers[8] handed over the American Federation of Labor to the war baiters. The liberal intelligentsia [. . .] all shared in the glory. The Socialist war phobia, the resolutions of their Minneapolis Conference, their patriotic special train, draped in red, white, and blue, their urging of every worker to support the war, all helped to destroy reason and justice in the United States.

On the other hand, the Industrial Workers of the World and those socialists who had not gone back on their ideals had by their blind self-sufficiency in the past also helped to sow the seeds of the crop they were now reaping. As long as persecution had been directed only against anarchists, they had refused to take notice or even to comment on the matter in their press. Not one of the I.W.W. papers had protested against our arrest and conviction. [. . .] Now the American Huns no longer discriminated between one radical group and another: liberals, I.W.W.'s, socialists, preachers, and college professors were being made to pay for their former short-sightedness.

In comparison with the patriotic crime wave the suppression of *Mother Earth* was a matter of insignificance. But to me it proved a greater blow than the prospect of spending two years in prison. No offspring of flesh and blood could absorb its mother as this child of mine had drained me. A struggle of over a decade, exhausting tours for its support, much worry and grief, had gone into the maintenance of *Mother Earth*, and now with one blow its life had been snuffed out! We decided to continue it in another form. The circular letter I had sent out to our subscribers and friends, informing them of the suppression of the magazine and of the new publication I was contemplating, brought many promises of help. Some, however, declined to have anything to do with the matter. It was reckless to defy the war sentiment of the country, they wrote. They could not give their support to such a purpose—they could not afford to get into trouble. Too well I knew that consistency and courage, like genius, are the rarest of gifts. Ben, of my own intimate circle, was sadly lacking in both. Having endured him for a decade, how could I condemn others for running to cover in danger?

A new project was sure to make Ben enthusiastic. The idea of a *Mother Earth Bulletin* caught his fancy, and his usual energy was put into motion at once to bring the publication about. But we had drifted apart too far. He wanted the *Bulletin* kept free from the war; there were so many other matters to discuss, he argued, and continued opposition to the Government was sure to ruin what we had built up during so many years. We must be more cautious, more practical, he insisted. Such an attitude seemed incredible in one who had been quite reckless in his anti-war talks. It was strange and ludicrous to see Ben in that rôle. His change, like everything else about him, was without reason or consistency.

Our strained relations could not last. One day the storm burst, and Ben left. For good. Listless and dry-eyed, I sank into a chair. Fitzi was near me, soothingly stroking my head.

CHAPTER XLVII

The *Mother Earth Bulletin* looked small compared with our previous publication, but it was the best we could do in those harassing days. The political sky was daily growing darker, the atmosphere charged with hate and violence, and no sign of relief anywhere in the wide United States. And again it was Russia to shed the first ray of hope upon an otherwise hopeless world.

The October Revolution[1] suddenly rent the clouds, its flames spreading to the remotest corners of the earth, carrying the message of fulfilment of the supreme promise the February Revolution had held out.

The Lvovs and the Miliukovs had pitted their feeble strength against the great giant, a people risen in rebellion, and had been crushed in their turn, like the Tsar before them.[2] Even Kerensky and his party had also failed to learn the great lesson; they forgot their pledges to the peasants and workers as soon as they had ascended to power. For decades the Social Revolutionists—next to the anarchists, although far more numerous and better organized—had been the most potent leaven in Russia. Their lofty ideal and aims, their heroism and martyrdom, had been the luminous beacon to draw thousands to their banner. For a brief period their party and its leaders, Kerensky, Tchernov,[3] and others, had remained attuned to the spirit of the February days. They had abolished the death-penalty, thrown open the prisons of the living dead, and brought hope to every peasant's hut and worker's hovel, to every man and woman in bondage. They had proclaimed freedom of speech, press, and assembly for the first time in the history of Russia, grand gestures that met with the acclaim of all liberty-loving people in the world.

To the masses, however, the political changes had represented only the outward symbol of the real liberty to come—cessation of war, access to the land, and reorganization of the economic life. These were to them the fundamental and essential values of the Revolution. But Kerensky and his party had failed to rise to the situation. They had ignored the popular need, and the onrushing tide swept them away. The October Revolution was the culmination of passionate dreams and longings, the bursting of the people's wrath against the party that it had trusted and that had failed.

The American press, never able to see beneath the surface, denounced the October upheaval as German propaganda, and its protagonists, Lenin, Trotsky, and their co-workers, as the Kaiser's hirelings. For months the scribes fabricated fantastic inventions about Bolshevik Russia. Their ignorance of the forces that had led up to the October Revolution was as appalling as their puerile attempts to interpret the movement headed by Lenin. Hardly a single newspaper evidenced the least understanding of bolshevism as a social conception entertained by men of brilliant minds, with the zeal and courage of martyrs.

Unfortunately the American press did not stand alone in the misrepresentation of the Bolsheviki. Most of the liberals and socialists were with them. It was the more urgent for the anarchists and other real revolutionists to take up cudgels for the vilified men and their part in hastening events in Russia. In the columns of the *Mother Earth Bulletin*, from the platform, and by every other means we defended the Bolsheviki against calumny and slander. Though they were Marxists and therefore governmentalists, I sided with them because they had repudiated war and had the wisdom to stress the fact that political freedom without corresponding economic equality is an empty boast. I quoted from Lenin's pamphlet *Political Parties and the Problems of the Proletariat* to prove that his demands were essentially what the Social Revolutionists had wanted, but had been too timid to carry out. Lenin strove for a democratic republic managed by soviets of workers, soldiers, and peasant deputies. He demanded the immediate convocation of the Constituent Assembly, speedy general peace, no indemnities and no annexations, and the abolition of secret treaties. His program included the return of the land to the peasant population according to need and actual working ability, control of industries by the proletariat, the formation of an International in every land for the complete abolition of the existing governments and capitalism, and the establishment of human solidarity and brotherhood.

Most of these demands were entirely in keeping with anarchist ideas and were therefore entitled to our support. But while I hailed and honoured the Bolsheviki as comrades in a common fight, I refused to credit them with what had been accomplished by the efforts of the entire Russian people. The October Revolution, like the February overthrow, was the achievement of the masses, their own glorious work.

Again I longed to return to Russia and to participate in the task of re-creating her new life. Yet once more I was detained by my adopted country, firmly held by two years' prison sentence. However, I still had two months at my disposal before the decision of the United States Supreme Court should be handed down, and I could accomplish something in the meantime. [. . .]

Our stand against conscription and our condemnation to prison had gained us many new friends, among them Helen Keller.[4] I had long wanted to meet this remarkable woman who had overcome the most appalling physical disabilities. I had attended one of her lectures, which was to me an affecting experience. Helen Keller's phenomenal conquest had strengthened my faith in the almost illimitable power of the human will.

When we had begun our campaign, I wrote to her asking her support. Not receiving a reply for a long time, I concluded that her own life was too difficult to permit interest in the tragedies of the world. Weeks later came a message from her that filled me with shame for having doubted her. Far from being self-absorbed, Helen Keller proved herself capable of an all-embracing love for humanity and profound feeling for its woe and despair. She had been absent with her teacher-companion in the country, she wrote, where she had heard of our arrest.

"My heart was troubled," the letter continued, "and I wanted to do something and I was trying to make up my mind what to do when your letter came. Believe me, my very heart-pulse is in the revolution that is to inaugurate a freer, happier society. Can you imagine what it is to sit idling these days of fierce action, of revolution and daring possibilities? I am so full of longing to serve, to love and be loved, to help things along, and to give happiness. It seems as if the very intensity of my desire must bring fulfilment, but, alas, nothing happens. Why have I this passionate desire to be a part of a noble struggle when fate has sentenced me to days of ineffectual waiting? There is no answer. It is tantalizing almost to the point of frenzy. But one thing is sure—you can always count upon my love and support. Those who are blinded in eye because they refuse to see tell us that in times like these wise men hold their tongues. But you are not holding your tongue, nor are the I.W.W. comrades holding their tongues—blessings upon you and them. No, Comrade, you must not hold your tongue, your work must go on, although all the earthly powers combine against it. Never were courage and fortitude so terribly needed as now. ...."

This letter was soon followed by our meeting, which took place at a ball given by *The Masses*. [....] I was glad to learn that Helen Keller was present. The marvellous woman, bereft of the most vital human senses, could nevertheless, by her psychic strength, see and hear and articulate. The electric current of her vibrant fingers on my lips and her sensitized hand over mine spoke more than mere tongue. It eliminated physical barriers and held one in the spell of the beauty of her inner world.

1917 had been a year of most intense activity, and it deserved to receive a fitting farewell. Our New Year's party in Stella's and Teddy's quarters appropriately performed the pagan rites. For once we forgot the present and ignored what tomorrow might bring. The bottles popped, the glasses clinked, and hearts grew young in play and dance. [...]

The end of January terminated the hopes many of our friends had naïvely entertained. The Supreme Court declined to grant us a rehearing or to delay the course of legal justice further. February 5 was set for our recommitment to prison. Seven more days of freedom, the nearness of loved ones, the association of faithful friends—we poured ourselves into every second. [. . .]

It was late, or rather early February 4, when our friends bade us hail and farewell. There were still the proofs to be read of my brochure *The Truth about the Bolsheviki*, but Fitzi considerately undertook to see the pamphlet safely through.

A few hours later we proceeded to the Federal Building to surrender. I offered to make the trip to the prison by myself and pay my own fare, but my suggestion met with the incredulous smiles of the officials. The deputy marshal and his lady again shared my compartment on our way to the Jefferson City penitentiary.

My fellow-prisoners greeted me as a long-lost sister. They were very sorry that the Supreme Court had decided against me, but since I had to serve my sentence, they had hoped that I would be returned to Jefferson City. I might help to bring about some improvements, they thought, if I could manage to get at Mr. Painter, the Warden. He was considered "a good man," but they rarely saw him, and they were sure he did not know what was going on in the female wing.

Already during my first stay of two weeks I had realized that the inmates in the Missouri penitentiary, like those at Blackwell's Island, were recruited from the lowest social strata. With the exception of my cell neighbour, who was a woman above the average, the ninety-odd prisoners were poor wretches of the world of poverty and drabness. Coloured or white, most of them had been driven to crime by conditions that had greeted them at birth. My first impression was strengthened by daily contact with the inmates during a period of twenty-one months. The contentions of criminal psychologists notwithstanding, I found no criminals among them, but only unfortunates, broken, hapless, and hopeless human beings.

The Jefferson City prison was a model in many respects. The cells were double the size of the pest holes of 1893, though they were not light enough, except on very sunny days, unless one was so fortunate as to have a cell directly facing a window. Most of them had neither light nor ventilation. Perhaps Southern people do not care for much fresh air; the precious element certainly seemed tabooed in my new boarding-house. Only in extremely hot weather were the corridor windows opened. Our life was very democratic in the sense that we all received the same treatment, were made to inhale the same vitiated air and bathe in the same tub. The great advantage, however, was that one was not compelled to share one's cell with anyone else. This blessing could be appreciated by those only who had endured the ordeal of the continuous proximity of another human being.

The contract labour system had been officially abolished in the penitentiary, I was told. The State was now the employer, but the obligatory task the new boss imposed was not much lighter than the toil the private contractor had exacted. Two months were allowed to learn the trade, which consisted in sewing jackets, overalls, auto coats, and suspenders. The tasks varied from forty-five to a hundred and twenty-one jackets a day, or from nine to eighteen dozen suspenders. While the actual machine work on the different tasks was the same, some of them required double physical exertion. The full complement of work was demanded without regard to age or physical condition. Even illness, unless of a very serious nature, was not considered sufficient cause for relieving the worker. Unless one had previous experience in sewing, or a special aptitude for it, the achievement of the task was a source of constant trouble and worry. There was no consideration for human variations, no allowance for physical limitations, except for a few favourites of the officials, who were usually the most worthless.

The shop was dreaded by all the inmates, particularly on account of the foreman. He was a boy of twenty-one who had been in charge of the treadmill since he was sixteen. An ambitious young man, he was very clever in pressing the tasks out of the women. If insults failed, the threat of punishment brought results. The women were so terrorized by him that they rarely dared to speak up. If anyone did, she became his special target for persecution. He was not even averse to robbing them of a part of their work and then reporting them for impudence, thus increasing their punishment for being short of the task. Four unfavourable marks a month meant a drop in the grade, which in return brought a loss of "good time."

The Missouri penitentiary was run on the merit system, of which Grade A was the highest. To attain that goal meant to have one's sentence reduced almost by half, at least so far as the State prisoners were concerned. We Federals might work ourselves to death without benefiting by our efforts. The only reduction of time we were allowed was the usual two months off each year. The dread of failing to reach Class A whipped the non-Federals beyond their strength in an attempt to accomplish the task.

The foreman was of course but a cog in the prison machine, the centre of which was the State of Missouri. It was doing business with private firms, drawing its customers from every part of the United States, as I soon discovered by the labels we had to sew on the things we manufactured. Even poor old Abe had been turned into a sweater of convict labour: the Lincoln Jobbing House of Milwaukee had the picture of the Liberator on its label, bearing the legend: "True to his country, true to our trade." The firms bought our labour for a song and they were therefore in a position to undersell those employing union labour. In other words, the State of Missouri was slave-driving and tormenting us, and in addition also acting as scab on the organized workers. In this commendable enterprise the official bully in our shop was very useful. Captain Gilvan, the acting warden, and Lilah Smith, the head matron, made up the triple alliance in control of the prison régime.

Gilvan used to administer flogging when that method of reformation was in vogue in Missouri. Other forms of punishment had since taken its place: deprivation of recreation, being locked up for forty-eight hours, usually from Saturday to Monday, on a diet of bread and water, and the "blind" cell. The latter measured about four feet by eight and was entirely dark; only one blanket was permitted and the daily food-allowance consisted of two slices of bread and two cups of water. In that cell prisoners were kept from three to twenty-two days. There were also bullrings, which, however, were not used on white women during my stay.

Captain Gilvan loved to punish the inmates in the blind cell and to hang them up by the wrists. "You must make the task," he would bellow; "no such thing as 'can't.' I punish cheerfully, mark you that!" He forbade us to leave our work without permission, even to go to the toilet. Once in the shop, after a more than usually brutal outbreak on his part, I approached him. "I must tell you that the task is sheer torture, especially for the older women," I said; "the insufficient food and constant punishment make things even worse." The Captain turned livid. "Look here, Goldman," he growled; "you're up to mischief. I have suspected it since your arrival. The convicts have never complained before, and they have always made the task. It's you who's putting notions into their heads. You had better look out. We have been kind to you, but if you do not stop your agitation, we will punish you like the rest, do you hear?"

"That's all right, Captain," I replied, "but I repeat that the task is barbarous and no one can make it regularly without breaking down."

He walked away, followed by Miss Smith, and I returned to my machine.

The shop matron, Miss Anna Gunther, was a very decent sort. She would patiently listen to the complaints of the women, often excuse them from work if they were ill, and even overlook a shortage in the task. She had been exceedingly kind to me, and I felt guilty over having left my place without permission. She did not reproach me, but said that I had been rash to talk to the Captain as I had. Miss Anna was a dear soul, the only moral prop the inmates had. Alas, she was only a subordinate.

The reigning queen was Lilah Smith. A woman in the forties, she had been employed in penal institutions since her teens. Of small stature, but compactly built, in appearance she suggested rigidity and coldness. She had an ingratiating manner, but underneath were the hardness and severity of the Puritan, hating implacably every emotion that had dried up in her own being. Neither pity nor compassion dwelt in Lilah's breast, and she was ruthless when she sensed them in anyone else. The fact that my fellow-prisoners liked and trusted me was enough to damn me in her eyes. Aware that I was in the good graces of the Warden, she never showed her antagonism openly. Hers was the insidious way.

The nerve-racking noises in the shop and the furious drive of the work laid me low the first month. My old stomach complaint became aggravated, and I suffered great pain in my neck and spine. The prison physician had anything but a good reputation among the inmates. He knew nothing, they claimed, and was too afraid of Miss Smith to excuse a prisoner from the shop, however ill she might be. I had seen inmates barely able to keep on their feet sent back to work by the doctor. The female department had no dispensary where patients could be examined. Even the seriously ill were kept in their cells. I hated to go to the doctor, but my agony became so unbearable that I had to see him. His gentle manner surprised me. He had been told that I was feeling bad, he said; why hadn't I come sooner? I must have a rest and not resume work until permitted by him, he ordered. His unexpected interest was certainly a far cry from the treatment other prisoners were receiving from him. I wondered whether his kindness to me was not due to the intercession of Warden Painter.

The doctor came to my cell every day, massaged my neck, entertained me with amusing stories, and even ordered a special broth. My improvement was slow, particularly because of the depressing effect of my cell. Its dirty grey walls, the lack of light and ventilation, and my inability to read or do anything else to while away the time made the day oppressively long. Former occupants of the cell had made pitiful attempts to beautify their prison house by family photos and newspaper pictures of their matinée idols. Black-and-yellow patches had been left on the wall, their fantastic outlines adding to my nervous restlessness. Another factor in my misery was the sudden stoppage of my mail; not a word came from anybody for ten days.

Two weeks in the cell made me realize why prisoners preferred the torture of the task. Some sort of occupation is the only escape from despair. None of the inmates enjoyed being idle. The shop, terrible as it was, was better than being locked up in the cells. I returned to work. It was a bitter struggle between physical pain, which drove me to my cot, and mental torment, which forced me back to the shop.

At last I was handed a large package of mail with a note from Mr. Painter saying that he had had to submit my incoming and outgoing correspondence to a Federal inspector in Kansas City, by orders from Washington. It made me feel very important to be considered dangerous even while in prison. Just the same, I wished that Washington were less attentive now, when every line I sent out or received was being read by the head matron and the Warden. [. . .]

Ben Capes came to see me, a veritable beam of sunshine, his joyous nature shedding balm. [. . .] He sent in an enormous box of delicacies from the most expensive Jefferson City grocery, and my fellow-prisoners expressed the hope that my other visitors might prove equally extravagant. [. . .] The food was never wholesome or sufficient for hard-working people. [. . .]

Prison life tends to make one wondrously resourceful. Some of the women had devised an original dumb-waiter, consisting of a bag attached by strings to a broomstick. The contraption would be passed through the bars of an upper-tier cell, and I, directly underneath, would fish the bag in, fill it with sandwiches and goodies, then push it out far enough to enable my upper neighbour to pull the bag up again. The same procedure would be repeated with my neighbour below. Then the things would be passed from cell to cell along each gallery. The orderlies shared in the bounty, and by their help I was able also to feed the occupants of the rear tiers.

Various friends kept me supplied with eatables, especially St. Louis comrades. They even ordered a spring mattress for my cot and arranged with a Jefferson City grocer to send me anything I ordered. It was this helpful solidarity that enabled me to share with my prison companions.

The visit of Benny Capes increased my disappointment in "Big Ben." The grief he had caused me, especially in the course of the last two years of our life, undermined my faith in him and filled my cup with bitterness. [. . .] His approaching fatherhood added fuel to my emotional stress. His minute description of the feelings engendered in him, and his delight in the little garments prepared for the expected child, afforded me a glimpse into an unsuspected aspect of Ben's character. Whether it was the defeat of my own motherhood or the pain that another should have given Ben what I would not, his rhapsodies increased my resentment against him and everyone connected with him. The announcement of the birth of his son also contained the information that the Appellate Court in Cleveland had sustained the verdict against him. He was leaving for that city, Ben wrote, to serve his sentence of six months in the workhouse. He was to be torn away from what he had looked forward to so eagerly and go to prison. Once more an inner voice spoke for him, submerging everything else in my heart.

At last I was assigned to a cell facing a window, which permitted the sun to look in upon me occasionally. The Warden had also instructed the head matron to allow me to take three baths a week. These privileges soon changed my condition for the better. He had furthermore promised to have my cell whitewashed, but he could not keep his word. The whole prison badly needed a new coat of paint, but Mr. Painter had failed to secure an appropriation for it. He could not make an exception of me, and I agreed with him. I devised something else to cover up the hideous patches on the walls—*crêpe* paper of a lovely green which Stella had sent me. With it I panelled the entire cell, and presently it began to look quite attractive, its cosiness enhanced by beautiful Japanese prints I had received from Teddy and a shelf of books I had accumulated.

There was no library in the female department, nor were we allowed to take out books from the men's wing. Once I asked Miss Smith why we could not get reading-matter from the male library. "Because I can't trust the girls to go there alone," she said, "and I have no time to accompany them. They would be sure to start flirtations." "What harm would that do?" I remarked naïvely, and Lilah was scandalized.

I requested Stella to see some publishers and also to induce our friends to send me books and magazines. Before long, four leading New York houses supplied me with many volumes. Most of them were above the understanding of my fellow inmates, but they soon learned to appreciate good novels. [. . .]

Among the books sent me was one from my friend Alice Stone Blackwell,[5] containing the letters of Catherine Breshkovskaya and a biographic sketch of her. It was symbolic of the eternal recurrence of the struggle for freedom that I should be able to read the account of our Little Grandmother's exile under the tsars while I myself was a prisoner. [. . .]

The news of Breshkovskaya's arrival in America filled me with hope that an authentic word would at last be said for Soviet Russia and an effective protest voiced against conditions in America. [. . .]

The reports of her first public appearance in Carnegie Hall and her bitter denunciation of the Bolsheviki came as a fearful shock. Catherine Breshkovskaya, one of those whose revolutionary work for the past fifty years had paved the way for the October upheaval, was now surrounded by the worst enemies of Russia, working hand in glove with White[6] generals and Jew-baiters, as well as with the reactionary element in the United States. It seemed incredible. I wrote Stella for accurate information, meanwhile continuing to cling to my faith in her who had been my inspiration and guiding star. Her simple grandeur, the charm and beauty of her personality, which I had learned to love during our common work in 1904 and 1905, had too deeply impressed me for me to give Babushka up so easily. I would write her. I would tell her of my own stand regarding Soviet Russia; I would assure her that I believed in her right of criticism, but I would plead with her not to lend herself as an unwitting tool to those who were trying to crush the Revolution. Stella was coming to visit me and I would have her smuggle out my letter to Babushka, type it, and deliver it to her in person.

I had attained to the highest ambition of my fellow sufferers in the penitentiary: I was placed in Grade A. Not entirely through my own efforts, though, for I was still unable to make the full task. I was indebted for it to the kindness of several coloured girls in the shop. Whether it was due to greater physical strength, or because they had been longer at the tasks, most of the Negro inmates succeeded better than the white women. Some of them had acquired such dexterity that they were often able to finish their tasks by three o'clock in the afternoon. Poor and friendless and desperately in need of a little money, they would help out those who fell behind. For this service they were entitled to five cents per jacket. Unfortunately, most of the whites were too poor to pay. I was considered the millionaire; my exchequer was often called upon to extend "loans," and I gladly complied. But the girls helping me with my work would not accept remuneration. They even felt hurt at the very suggestion of it. I was sharing my food and books with them, they protested; how could they take money from me? They agreed with my little Italian friend, Jennie de Lucia, who had constituted herself my maid. "No take money from you," she had declared, and the other women all echoed her sentiment. Thanks to those kind souls, I reached Grade A, which entitled me to send out three letters a week—really four, including the extra letter I had been writing regularly to my counsellor.

On the eve of June 27 my coloured friends presented me with a full task of jackets for the following day. They had remembered my birthday. "It would be so nice if Miss Emma could keep out of the shop on that day," they had said. The next morning my table was covered with letters, telegrams, and flowers from my own kin and comrades, as well as with innumerable packages from friends in different parts of the country. I was proud to have so much love and attention, but nothing touched me so deeply as the gift of my fellow-sufferers in prison. [. . .]

A three days' visit from my dear Stella proved a more real holiday for me than the Fourth of July. I was able to hand her my letter for Babushka, several notes my cell neighbours wanted smuggled out, and samples of the fake shop labels. They were three days of freedom from the shop, spent with my beloved child in our own world, a visit long awaited and quickly passed, to be followed by the reaction of the prison routine.

In my letter to Babushka I had begged her not to think that I denied her the right of criticism of Soviet Russia, or that I wished her to gloss over the faults of the Bolsheviki. I pointed out that I differed with them in ideas and that my stand against every form of dictatorship was irrevocable. But that was not important, I insisted, while every government was at the throat of the Bolsheviki. I pleaded with her to bethink herself, not to go back on her glorious past and the high hopes of Russia's present generation.

Babushka had grown feebler and whiter, Stella told me, but she had remained the old rebel and fighter, her heart aflame for the people as of yore. Still, it was true that she was permitting reactionary elements to make use of her. It was impossible to doubt Babushka's integrity or to think her capable of conscious betrayal, but I could not approve her attitude towards the Soviets. [. . .]

CHAPTER XLVIII

[. . .] The influenza epidemic raging through the country had reached our prison, and thirty-five inmates were stricken down. In the absence of any hospital facilities, the patients were kept in their cells, exposing the other inmates to infection. At the first sign of the disease I had offered my services to the physician. He knew I was a trained nurse and he welcomed my aid. He promised to see Miss Smith about letting me take care of the sick, but days passed without bringing results. Later I learned that the head matron had refused to take me out of the shop. I was already enjoying too many privileges, she had said, and she would not stand for more.

Not being officially permitted to nurse, I sought means to aid the sick unofficially. Since the influenza invasion our cells were being left unlocked at night. The two girls assigned to nursing were so hard-worked that they would sleep all through the night, and the orderlies were my friends. That offered me a chance to make hurried calls from cell to cell and do what little was possible to make the patients more comfortable.

On November 11, at ten in the morning, the electric power in our shop was switched off, the machines stopped, and we were informed that there would be no further work that day. We were sent to our cells, and after lunch we were marched to the yard for recreation. It was an unheard-of event in the prison and everyone wondered what it could mean. My thoughts dwelt in the days of 1887. I had intended to strike against work on the anniversary that marked the birth of my social consciousness. But there were so few women able to go to the shop that I did not want to add to the number of absentees. The unexpected

holiday gave me the opportunity to be alone for spiritual communion with my martyred Chicago comrades. [. . .]

Late in the evening the prison silence was torn by deafening
noises coming from the male wing. The men were banging on
bars, whistling, and shouting. The women grew nervous, and the
block matron hastened over to reassure them. The declaration
of armistice was being celebrated she said. "What armistice?" I
asked. "It's Armistice Day," she replied; "that's why you have
been given a holiday." At first I hardly grasped the full significance of the information, and then I, too, became possessed of
a desire to scream and shout, to do something to give vent to
my agitation. "Miss Anna, Miss Anna!" I called the matron
back. "Come here, please, come here!" She approached again.
"You mean that hostilities have been stopped, that the war has
come to an end and the prisons will be opened for those who refused to take part in the slaughter? Tell me, tell me!" She put
her hand soothingly on mine. "I have never seen you so excited
before," she said; "a woman of your age, working yourself up
to such a pitch over such a thing!" She was a kindly soul, but
she knew nothing outside her prison duties. [. . .]

A ray of light came with the commutation of Tom Mooney's
death-sentence to life imprisonment. It was a travesty on justice
to immure a man for life who had been proved innocent by the
State's own witnesses. Nevertheless, the commutation was an
achievement, due mostly, I felt, to the effective work our people
had done. [. . .]

Christmas was approaching and my companions were in nervous wonderment as to what the day of days would bring them.
Nowhere is Christianity so utterly devoid of meaning as in
prison, nowhere its precepts so systematically defied, but myths
are more potent than facts. Fearfully strong is their hold on the
suffering and despairing. Few of the women could expect anything from the outside; some had not even a single human being
to give them a thought. Yet they clung to the hope that the day
of their Saviour's birth would bring them some kindness. The
majority of the convicts, of infantile mentality, talked of Santa
Claus and the stocking with naïve faith. It served to help them

over their degradation and misery. Forsaken by God, by man forgot, it was their only refuge.

Long before Christmas, gifts began to arrive for me. Members of my family, comrades, and friends fairly deluged me with presents. Soon my cell began to look like a department store, and every day brought additional packages. As usual, our dear Benny Capes, in response to my request for trinkets for the inmates, sent a huge consignment. Bracelets, ear-rings, necklaces, rings, and brooches, enough to make the Woolworth stock feel ashamed, and lace collars, handkerchiefs, stockings, and other things sufficient to compete with any store on Fourteenth Street. [. . .]

It was a problem to divide the gifts so as to give each what she might like best, without arousing envy or suspicion of preference and favouritism. I called to my aid three of my neighbours, and with their expert advice and help I played Santa Claus. On Christmas Eve, while our fellow-prisoners were attending the movies, a matron accompanied us to unlock the doors, our aprons piled high with gifts. With gleeful secrecy we flitted along the tiers, visiting each cell in turn. When the women returned from the cinema, the cell-block resounded with exclamations of happy astonishment. "Santa Claus's been here! He's brung me something grand!" "Me, too! Me, too!" re-echoed from cell to cell. My Christmas in the Missouri penitentiary brought me greater joy than many previous ones outside. I was thankful to the friends who had enabled me to bring a gleam of sunshine into the dark lives of my fellow-sufferers.

On New Year's again the prison was filled with noisy hilarity. Fortunate indeed are they whom each year brings nearer to the passionately longed-for hour of release. Not so the poor creatures sent up for life. No hope or cheer for them in the new day or new year. [. . .]

With the New Year came the shock of David's death. For months rumours of the boy's end had hung like a pall over his family. Helena's appeals to Washington for news of her son had brought no results. The United States Government had done its duty; it had

shipped David with thousands of others to the fields of France.
It could not be bothered by the anguish of those left behind. It
was from an officer returned from France that Stella had learned
of Dave's tragic fate.

The boy had preferred a responsible position, though dangerous, to the safety of the military orchestra to which he had
been assigned, his comrade reported to Stella. He lost his life on
October 15, 1918, in the Bois de Rappe, in the Argonne forest,
killed one month before Armistice Day, in the prime and glory
of his youth. My poor sister was still ignorant of the blow awaiting her. She would be informed as soon as official confirmation
was received, Stella's letter said. I foresaw the effect of the terrible news on Helena and I felt sickening apprehension for her
sake. [. . .]

The hardest thing to bear in prison is one's utter powerlessness
to do aught for one's loved ones in distress. My sister Helena
had given me more affection and care than my parents. Without her my childhood would have been even more barren. She
had saved me many blows and had soothed my youth's sorrows
and pains. Yet in her own greatest need I could do nothing to
help her. [. . .]

With Easter came spring's awakening, flooding my cell with
warmth and filling it with the perfume of flowers. Life was
gaining new meaning—only six more months to liberty!

April added another political, Mrs. Kate Richards O'Hare,[1]
to our company. I had met her once before, when she had called
at the prison on her visit to Jefferson City to see Governor
Gardner. She had been convicted under the Espionage Law, but
she was emphatic that the Supreme Court would reverse the
verdict, and that in any event she would not serve time in our
place. [. . .]

Soon we politicals—Kate, Ella,[2] and I—were nicknamed "the
trinity." We spent much time together and became very neigh-
bourly. Kate had the cell on my right, and Ella was next to her.
We did not ignore our fellow-prisoners or deny ourselves to them,
but intellectually Kate and Ella created a new world for me, and
I basked in its interests, its friendship and affection. [. . .]

Meanwhile Kate was bringing about changes in the Missouri penitentiary which I had in vain been trying for fourteen months to accomplish. She had an advantage in the presence of her husband nearby, in St. Louis, and access to the press, and we often banteringly discussed which of the two was of more value. Her letters to O'Hare, criticizing the lack of a library for the women, and her condemnation of our food, standing for two hours before being served, had appeared in the *Post Dispatch* and brought immediate improvement. The head matron announced that books could henceforth be had from the men's department, and the food was served hot, "for the first time in the ten years I've been here," as Aggie[3] commented.

In the interim an unusual feature was introduced by the Warden independently of Kate's influence. It was announced that we were to have picnics every second Saturday in the city park. So extraordinary was the innovation that we felt inclined to consider it a joke, too good to be true. But when we were assured that the first outing would actually take place the following Saturday, that we could spend the whole afternoon in the park, where the male band would play dance music, the women lost their heads and forgot all about the prison rules. They laughed and wept, shouted, and acted generally as if they had gone mad. The week was tense with excitement, everyone working to exhaustion to make the task, so as not to be left behind when the great day should arrive. During recreation the sole talk was of the picnic, and in the evenings the cell block was filled with whispered conversation about the impending event—how to fix up to look nice, how it would feel to walk about in the park. And would the band boys be near enough to talk to? No débutante was ever more wrought up over her first ball than the poor creatures, most of whom had not stepped out of the prison walls for a decade.

The picnic did take place, but to us—to Kate, Ella, and me—it was a ghastly experience. There were heavily armed guards behind and in front of us, and not a step was permitted outside the prescribed area. Guards surrounded the prison orchestra, while the matrons let no woman out of sight the moment dancing began. The supper was most depressing. The whole thing was a farce and an insult to human dignity. But to our unfortunate fellow-convicts it was like manna to the Jews in the desert.

In my next letter to Stella I quoted Tennyson's "Light Brigade." In the course of the week the Warden sent for me to ask what I had meant by my reference. I told him that I should prefer to remain in my cell Saturday afternoon rather than picnic by the grace of an armed force. There was no danger of any woman's escaping, with the open country-side offering no place to hide. "Don't you see, Mr. Painter," I appealed to him, "it is not the park which will prove an influence for good? It will be your trust in the women, their feeling that at least once in two weeks they are given a chance to eliminate the prison from their consciousness. That sense of freedom and release will create a new morale among the inmates."

The following Saturday there were fewer guards and they did not flaunt their weapons in our faces. Limit restrictions were abolished, and the entire park was ours. The band boys were permitted to meet the girls at the soda-water stand and to treat them to pop and ginger ale. Our suppers in the park were gradually discarded, having proved too hard a task for the two matrons to supervise. But none of us minded it, since we were given another two hours of recreation in the prison yard after supper. The inmates had now something to look forward to and live for. Their state of mind changed; they worked with more zest, and their former distress and irritableness decreased. [. . .]

CHAPTER XLIX

[. . .] My fiftieth birthday I spent in the Missouri penitentiary. What more fitting place for the rebel to celebrate such an occasion? Fifty years! I felt as if I had five hundred on my back, so replete with events had been my life. While at liberty I had hardly noticed age creeping up, perhaps because I had counted my real birth from 1889, when, as a girl of twenty, I had first come to New York. Like our Sasha, who would jestingly give his age minus his fourteen years in the Western Penitentiary, I used to say that my first twenty years should not be held against me, for I had merely existed then. The prison, however, and still more the misery abroad in every land, the savage persecution of radicals in America, the tortures social protestants were enduring everywhere, had an ageing effect on me. The mirror lies only to those who want to be deceived.

Fifty years—thirty of them in the firing line—had they borne fruit or had I merely been repeating Don Quixote's idle chase? Had my efforts served only to fill my inner void, to find an outlet for the turbulence of my being? Or was it really the ideal that had dictated my conscious course? Such thoughts and queries swirled through my brain as I pedalled my sewing-machine on June 27, 1919. [. . .]

My own family's affection for me had grown with the years. Sister Lena had blossomed out like a flower in her love for me. Her life, filled with hardships and pain, might have corroded the heart of many another woman. But Lena had become more gentle and understanding, even humble. "I do not presume to compare my love for you with Helena's," she once wrote me, "but I love you just the same." It made me remorseful to think of the poor affection I had given her in the past. My old mother had also come very close to me of late years. She kept sending me gifts, things made by her own trembling hands. Her birthday letter, written in Yiddish, was filled with affection for her most wayward child.

The thought of Helena was the only cloud on my birthday sky. Her daughter Minnie had come all the way from Manila to help her mother over their great loss. But my sister was wrapped in her precious dead, and the living could do nothing to loosen its hold. Helena alone had failed me on the day she had always filled with her love before. But I understood. [. . .]

On August 28, 1919, Sasha and I had completed twenty months of our two-year sentence. Wicked anarchists though we were, we had earned four months each for good behaviour. We had done our bit much longer than many of the boys in the dugouts. We should have been honourably discharged from service and allowed to return from the prison front. But Judge Julius Mayer had willed it otherwise by placing a high valuation on our heads. Twenty thousand dollars' fine! A United States commissioner was sent to the penitentiary to question me about my financial standing. He looked incredulous when I told him that anarchist propaganda is a pleasure and not a paying business. He grew still more dubious when I explained that the Kaiser, having been unseemly hurried in his departure from Germany, had neglected to make provision for our welfare. The commissioner decided to "look into the matter." Meanwhile Berkman and I would have to serve an extra month in payment of our fine, he declared. Two months for twenty thousand dollars! When did Sasha and I ever expect to earn so much money in so short a time?

Only thirty days. Then release from the hateful shop, the control, the surveillance, the thousand humiliations prison involves. Back to life and work again—with Sasha. Back to my family, comrades, and friends. An alluring fantasy, soon dispelled by the immigration authorities. Ellis Island was waiting for the two distinguished guests. I wondered who would compete for my favours next. Would it be Russia, the long-awaited, or America, my old flame? In our uncertain fortunes only one thing was certain: Sasha and I would meet the future as we had always met it in the past. [. . .]

Saturday, September 28, 1919, I left the Missouri penitentiary, accompanied by my faithful Stella, who had come from New York for the occasion. Only technically free, I was taken to the Federal Building to make an affidavit that I possessed no real estate or cash. The Federal agent looked me up and down. "You're dressed so swell, funny you claim to be poor," he commented. "I am a multimillionaire in friends," I replied.

The fifteen-thousand-dollar bond demanded by the Government pending inquiries by the Immigration Bureau was secured, and I was at last at liberty.

CHAPTER L

In St. Louis we were almost mobbed by friends, reporters, and camera-men who had come to meet us at the station. I could not bear to see many people and I was eager to be left alone.

Stella grew uneasy on hearing that on our way east I intended to stop off in Chicago, where Ben was living. She implored me to give up the idea. "You will only lose the peace you have gained through months of struggle to free yourself from Ben," she pleaded. There was no need for anxiety, I assured her. In the isolation and loneliness of the cell one finds the courage to face the nakedness of one's soul. If one survives the ordeal, one is less hurt by the nakedness of other souls. I had worked my way through much anguish and travail to a better understanding of my relation with Ben. [. . .] Erotically Ben and I were of the same earth, but in a cultural sense we were separated by centuries of time. With him social impulses, sympathy with mankind, ideas, and ideals were moods of the moment, and as fleeting. He had no means of sensing basic verities or inner need to convert them into his own.

My life was linked with that of the race. Its spiritual heritage was mine, and its values were transmuted into my being. The eternal struggle of man was rooted within me. That made the abyss between us. [. . .]

In Chicago he called, bringing a large bouquet of flowers. It was the same old Ben, instinctively reaching out and his eyes opening wide in wonder at meeting no response. No change in him nor understanding for mine. He wanted to give me a party at his home. Would I come, he asked. "Of course," I said, "I will come to meet your wife and your child." I went. The dead had buried their dead, and I felt serene. [. . .]

On our way to Rochester Stella had described Helena's condition and had cautioned me to be prepared. But my worst mental picture was not so horrible as the sight my dear sister presented. Emaciated to the bone, she was a bent old woman, moving with lifeless steps. Her face was shrunken and ashy, unutterable despair in her hollow eyes. I held her close to me, her poor little body convulsed with sobs. She had done nothing but weep since the news of David's death, my people told me; her life was ebbing out in tears.

"Take me away, let me live with you in New York," she pleaded. It had been her dream in our youth to be always near me. Now the moment had come to realize it, she reiterated. I was filled with pity and fear. [. . .] I told her I would rent an apartment in New York at once, and soon Minnie could bring her to me. She sighed deeply and seemed somewhat consoled.

With Helena's collapse the care of two families had fallen upon my sister Lena. She worked for everybody without complaint. [. . .] Mother had, since Father's death, become a veritable autocrat. No statesman or diplomat excelled her in wit, shrewdness, and force of character. Whenever I visited Rochester, Mother had new conquests to report. For years the orthodox Jews of the city had discussed the need of an orphanage and a home for the indigent aged. Mother did not waste words; she located two sites, purchased them on the spot, and for months canvassed the Jewish neighbourhood for contributions to pay off the mortgage and build the institutions the others had only talked about. There was no prouder queen than Mother on the opening day of the new orphanage. She invited me to "come and speak a piece" on the great occasion. I had once told her that my aim was to enable the workers to reap the fruit of their labours, and every child to enjoy our social wealth. A mischievous twinkle had come into her still sparkling eyes as she replied: "Yes, my daughter, that is all very good for the future; but what is to become of our orphans now, and the old and decrepit who are alone in the world? Tell me that." And I had no answer to give. [. . .]

Many anecdotes circulated about my mother, characteristic of her vitality and broad sympathies, but none amused me so much as the story of how Mrs. Taube Goldman had put the chairlady of a powerful lodge "in her place." At one of the meetings Mother had talked rather too long. Another member asked for the floor, and the chairlady timidly suggested that Mrs. Goldman had already exceeded her time. Drawing herself up to full stature, my mother defiantly announced: "The whole United States Government could not stop my daughter Emma Goldman from speaking, and a fine chance you have to make her mother shut up!" [. . .]

Harry Weinberger had gone to Atlanta to meet Sasha on his release. The fates had never been kind to him in prison; this time they robbed him of three days. Instead of September 28, Sasha was released on October 1. [. . .] He looked haggard and pale, but otherwise apparently his usual stoical and humorous self. But soon we realized that it was only the flush of his release and the joy of being free, for Sasha was very ill. Uncle Sam's prison had succeeded in accomplishing in twenty-one months what the Western Penitentiary of Pennsylvania had failed to do in fourteen years. Atlanta had broken his health and had sent him back a physical wreck, with the horrors of his experience burned into his soul.

Sasha had been kept in an underground dungeon for protesting against the brutalities practised on the other inmates. The cell was too small to move about in and fetid with the bucket of excrement that was emptied only once in twenty-four hours. He was allowed only two small slices of bread and one cup of water a day. Later on, for interceding for a coloured prisoner, he was again punished by the "hole," which measured two and a half feet by four and a half, and where he could not even stand up straight. The "hole" was provided with double doors, one iron-barred, the other "blind," thus entirely excluding all light and air. In that cell, known as "the tomb," one is subjected to gradual suffocation. It is the worst punishment known in the Atlanta penitentiary, and it is designed to break the prisoner's spirit and force him to beg for mercy. Sasha refused to do so. To keep from suffocating he had to lie flat on the floor with his mouth close to the groove where the double doors fit into the stone casing. Only thus could he keep alive. Released from "the tomb," he was for three months deprived of his mail privileges, allowed no books or other reading-matter, and not permitted any exercise whatever. After that he remained continuously in solitary and isolation for seven-and-a-half months, from February 21 to the day of his discharge, October 1. [. . .]

On my return from Jefferson City I found destroyed what we had slowly built up through a long period of years. The literature confiscated in the raid had not been returned to us, and *Mother Earth*, the *Blast*, Sasha's *Prison Memoirs*, and my essays were under the ban. The large sums of money raised while we were in prison, including the three thousand dollars contributed by our old Swedish comrade, had gone for appeals in cases of conscientious objectors, in the political-amnesty activities, and in other work. We had nothing left, neither literature, money, nor even a home. The war tornado had swept the field clean, and we had to begin everything anew.

Among my first callers was Mollie Steimer,[1] who came accompanied by another comrade. [. . .] Mollie and her escort informed me that they had come as delegates of their group to ask me to write for their *Bulletin*, which they were publishing underground. Unfortunately I could not comply with their request. Even if I were not already overburdened with too much work, I could not ally myself with secret activities. I told them that I had thought of continuing *Mother Earth sub rosa*, but had discarded the plan because of the hazard it involved for others. I was not afraid of danger if I could meet it in the open, but I did not want to be trapped by spies and informers, who are always found in secret revolutionary bodies. [. . .]

An additional disagreement between us was due to my attitude to Soviet Russia. My young comrades thought that the Bolsheviki, representing a government, should be treated by anarchists like other governments. I insisted that Soviet Russia, the object of attack by the combined reactionists of the world, was not at all to be considered as an ordinary government. I did not object to criticism of the Bolsheviki, but I could not approve active opposition to them, anyway not until they should be in a less dangerous situation. [...]

I found a cozy apartment, and soon Minnie arrived with her mother, and the three of us moved in. For a while it seemed as if Helena would get herself in hand. She was busy attending to the *ménage,* sewing and mending. To afford her more work, I used to invite many friends to dinner. Dutifully my sister would prepare the food, serve it attractively, and charm everybody with her personality. But soon the novelty wore off and the old woe was again upon her. It was no use—her life was crushed, she kept on saying; it had lost meaning and purpose. Everything in her was dead, dead as David in the Bois de Rappe. She could not continue, she insisted, she must make an end of it, and I must help her out of her purgatory. Day after day she would repeat her piteous appeal, and call me cruel and inconsistent for my refusal. I had always claimed that everyone had a right to do with his life what he willed, and that persons suffering from incurable disease should not be compelled to live. And yet I was refusing her the relief I would give even a sick animal.

It was madness, and yet I felt that Helena was right. I was inconsistent. I saw her dying by inches with a desperate determination to escape from life. It would be an act of humanity to help her do so. I had no doubt as to the justification of making an end to one's misery or aiding another in it when there is no hope of recovery. Moved by Helena's plea, I would decide to comply with her wishes; and yet I could not bring myself to cut short her life—the life of one who had been mother, sister, friend to me, everything I had had in my childhood. I continued to struggle with her in the silent hours of the night. In the daytime, when I had to leave her, I would go through sickening terror lest on my return home I should find her dashed on the sidewalk. I could not absent myself unless I knew that someone was staying with her when Minnie and I were out.

My deportation hearing, twice postponed, was finally set for October 27. Sasha had already made his statement prior to leaving Atlanta. He had refused to answer the questions of the

Federal immigration agent, who had called on him in the prison to give him "a hearing" in the matter of deportation. [. . .]

Sasha, not being a citizen and not caring about that side of the issue, nevertheless joined me in my fight against deportation because he considered such governmental methods as the worst form of autocracy. I also had an additional reason for contesting the Washington scheme to drive me out of the country. The United States Government still owed me an explanation for the shady methods it had employed in 1909 to rob me of my citizenship. And I was determined to have them disclosed.

I had always longed to revisit Russia, and after the February-October Revolution I had definitely decided to return to my native land to help in its reconstruction. But I wanted to go of my own free will, at my own expense, and I denied the right of the government to force me. I was aware of its brutal strength, but I did not propose to submit without a fight. [. . .]

At my hearing before the immigration officials I found the inquisitors sitting at a desk piled high with my dossier. The documents, classified, tabulated, and numbered, were passed on to me for inspection. They consisted of anarchist publications in different languages, most of them long out of print, and of reports of speeches I had delivered a decade previously. No objection had been made to them at the time by the police or the Federal authorities. Now they were being offered as proof of my criminal past and as justification for banishing me from the country. It was a farce I could not participate in, and I consequently refused to answer any questions. I remained silent throughout the "hearing," at the end of which I handed to my examiners a statement, reading in part:

[. . .] The free expression of the hopes and aspirations of a people is the greatest and only safety in a sane society. In truth, it is such free expression and discussion alone that can point the most beneficial path for human progress and development. But the object of deportations and of the Anti-Anarchist Law, as of all similar repressive measures, is the very opposite. It is to stifle the voice of the people, to muzzle every aspiration of labour. That is the real and terrible menace of the star-chamber proceedings and of the tendency of exiling those who do not fit into the scheme of things our industrial lords are so eager to perpetuate.

With all the power and intensity of my being I protest against the conspiracy of imperialist capitalism against the life and the liberty of the American people.

EMMA GOLDMAN

[. . .] A year had passed since the Armistice, and political amnesty had been granted in every European country. America alone failed to open her prison doors. Instead, official raids and arrests increased. There was hardly a city where workers known as Russians or suspected of sympathy with radical ideas were not being picked up, taken at their work-benches or on the street. Behind these raids stood Attorney General Mitchell Palmer,[2] panicky at the thought of radicals. Many of the arrests were accompanied by brutal manhandling of the victims. New York, Chicago, Pittsburgh, Detroit, Seattle, and other industrial centres had their detention houses and jails filled with these "criminals." I was besieged by requests for lectures. The Federal deportation mania[3] was terrorizing the foreign workers of the country, and there were many calls upon me to speak on the matter and enlighten the people on the subject. [. . .]

From New York to Detroit and thence to Chicago we made a whirlwind tour, our movements watched by local and Federal agents, every utterance noted down and attempts made to silence us. Unperturbed we continued. It was our last supreme effort and we felt our die had been cast. [. . .]

During the farewell dinner given us by our friends in Chicago, on December 2, reporters dashed in with the news of Henry Clay Frick's death. We had not heard of it before, but the newspaper men suspected that the banquet was to celebrate the event. "Mr. Frick has just died," a blustering young reporter addressed Sasha. "What have you got to say?" "Deported by God," Sasha answered dryly. I added that Mr. Frick had collected his debt in full from Alexander Berkman, but he had died without making good his own obligations. "What do you mean?" the reporters demanded. "Just this: Henry Clay Frick was a man of the passing hour. Neither in life nor in death would he have been remembered long. It was Alexander Berkman who made him known, and Frick will live only in connexion with Berkman's name. His entire fortune could not pay for such glory."

The next morning brought a telegram from Harry Weinberger informing us that the Federal Department of Labor had ordered our deportation, and that we must surrender on December 5. We had two more days of freedom and another lecture on hand. There was much to attend to in New York, and Sasha left to arrange our affairs there. I remained for the last meeting. However the storm might rage and the waves mount high, I was determined to face it to the end. [. . .]

At the Grand Central terminal in New York friends awaited us, including Sasha, Fitzi, Stella, Harry, and other intimates. There was no time left even to go to my apartment to bid my dear Helena good-bye. We piled into taxis and drove straight to Ellis Island. There Sasha and I surrendered, while Harry Weinberger prepared to demand the return of the thirty thousand dollars deposited as our bond.

"That is the end, Emma Goldman, isn't it?" a reporter remarked. "It may only be the beginning," I flashed back.

CHAPTER LI

The room I was assigned to on the island already contained two occupants, Ethel Bernstein and Dora Lipkin, who had been rounded up at the raid of the Union of Russian Workers. The documents discovered there consisted of English grammars and text-books on arithmetic. The raiders had beaten up and arrested those found on the premises for possessing such inflammatory literature. [...]

Sasha and I had long before decided to write a pamphlet on deportation. We knew that the Ellis Island authorities would confiscate such a manuscript, and it therefore became necessary to prepare and send it out secretly. We wrote at night, our room-mates keeping watch. In the morning, during our joint walks, we would discuss what we had written and exchange suggestions. Sasha made the final revision and gave it to friends to smuggle out.

Each day brought scores of new candidates for deportation. From various States they came, most of them without clothes or money. They had been kept in jails for months and were then shipped to New York just as they were at the time of their unexpected arrest. In that condition they were facing a long voyage in the winter. We bombarded our people with requests for clothing, blankets, shoes, and other wearing-apparel. Soon supplies began to arrive, and great was the rejoicing among the prospective deportees.

The condition of the emigrants on Ellis Island was nothing short of frightful. Their quarters were congested, the food was abominable, and they were treated like felons. These unfortunates had cut their moorings in the homeland and had pilgrimed to the United States as the land of promise, liberty, and opportunity. Instead they found themselves locked up, ill-treated, and kept in uncertainty for months. I marvelled that things had changed so little since my Castle Garden days of 1886. The emigrants were not permitted to mingle with us, but we managed to get from them notes that strained all our linguistic acquirements, almost every European language being represented. It was little enough we were in a position to do for them. We interested our American friends and did the best we could to show the forsaken strangers that not all of the United States was represented by official barbarians. We were loaded with work, and neither Sasha nor I could complain of ennui. [. . .]

Harry Weinberger was meeting with unexpected difficulties in Washington, due to bureaucratic pettiness and red tape. The Clerk of the Court refused to accept his papers because they were not in printed form. Harry successfully appealed to Chief Justice White. On December 11 he was permitted to argue his motion, but the Court denied us the writ of error. A stay of deportation for Sasha was also refused. The documents in my case were ordered printed and returned within one week.

I decided that if Sasha was to be driven out of the country, I would go with him. He had come into my life with my spiritual awakening, he had grown into my very being, and his long Golgotha would for ever remain our common bond. He had been my comrade, friend, and co-worker through a period of thirty years; it was unthinkable that he should join the Revolution and I remain behind.

"You are staying to make the fight, aren't you?" Sasha asked me at recreation that day. I could do much for the deportees, he added, as well as for Russia, if I should establish my right to remain in the United States. The same old Sasha, I thought; always considering propaganda values first. I could hardly restrain the pang I felt over his detachment even at such a moment. Yet I knew the real Sasha; I knew that although he would not admit it even to himself, there was a great deal of the all-too-human underneath his rigid revolutionary exterior. "It's no use, old scout," I said; "you can't get rid of me so easily. I have made my decision, and I am going with you." He gripped hard my hand, but he said not a word. [...]

Saturday, December 20, was a hectic day, with vague indications that it might be our last. We had been assured by the Ellis Island authorities that we were not likely to be sent away before Christmas, certainly not for several days to come. Meanwhile we were photographed, finger-printed, and tabulated like convicted criminals. The day was filled with visits from numerous friends who came individually and in groups. Self-evidently, reporters also did not fail to honour us. Did we know when we were going, and where? And what were my plans about Russia? "I will organize a Society of Russian Friends of American Freedom," I told them. "The American Friends of Russia have done much to help liberate that country. It is now the turn of free Russia to come to the aid of America."

Harry Weinberger was still very hopeful and full of fight. He would soon get me back to America, he insisted, and I should keep myself ready for it. Bob Minor[1] smiled incredulously. He was greatly moved by our approaching departure; we had fought together in many battles and he was fond of me. Sasha he literally idolized and he felt his deportation as a severe personal loss. The pain of separation from Fitzi was somewhat mitigated by her decision to join us in Soviet Russia at the first opportunity. Our visitors were about to leave when Weinberger was officially notified that we were to remain on the island for several more days. We were glad of it and we arranged with our friends to come again, perhaps for the last time, on Monday, no callers being allowed on the island on the Lord's day.

I returned to the pen I was sharing with my two girl comrades. [...] I had not met either of the girls before, but our two weeks on Ellis Island had established a strong bond between us. This evening my room-mates again kept watch while I was hurriedly answering important mail and penning my last farewell to our people. It was almost midnight when suddenly I caught the sound of approaching footsteps. "Look out, someone's coming!" Ethel whispered. I snatched up my papers and letters and hid them under my pillow. Then we threw ourselves on our beds, covered up, and pretended to be asleep.

The steps halted at our room. There came the rattling of keys; the door was unlocked and noisily thrown open. Two guards and a matron entered. "Get up now," they commanded, "get your things ready!" The girls grew nervous. Ethel was shaking as in fever and helplessly rummaging among her bags. The guards became impatient. "Hurry, there! Hurry!" they ordered roughly. I could not restrain my indignation. "Leave us so we can get dressed!" I demanded. They walked out, the door remaining ajar. I was anxious about my letters. I did not want them to fall into the hands of the authorities, nor did I care to destroy them. Maybe I should find someone to entrust them to, I thought. I stuck them into the bosom of my dress and wrapped myself in a large shawl.

In a long corridor, dimly lit and unheated, we found the men deportees assembled, little Morris Becker[2] among them. He had been delivered to the island only that afternoon with a number of other Russian boys. One of them was on crutches; another, suffering from an ulcerated stomach, had been carried from his bed in the island hospital. Sasha was busy helping the sick men pack their parcels and bundles. They had been hurried out of their cells without being allowed even time to gather up all their things. Routed from sleep at midnight, they were driven bag and baggage into the corridor. Some were still half-asleep, unable to realize what was happening.

I felt tired and cold. No chairs or benches were about, and we stood shivering in the barn-like place. The suddenness of the attack took the men by surprise and they filled the corridor with a hubbub of exclamations and questions and excited expostulations. Some had been promised a review of their cases, others were waiting to be bailed out pending final decision. They had received no notice of the nearness of their deportation and they were overwhelmed by the midnight assault. They stood helplessly about, at a loss what to do. Sasha gathered them in groups and suggested that an attempt be made to reach their relatives in the city. The men grasped desperately at that last hope and appointed him their representative and spokesman.

He succeeded in prevailing upon the island commissioner to permit the men to telegraph, at their own expense, to their friends in New York for money and necessaries. [. . .]

Hardly had the last wire been sent when the corridor filled with State and Federal detectives, officers of the Immigration Bureau and Coast Guards. [. . .] The uniformed men stationed themselves along the walls, and then came the command: "Line up!" A sudden hush fell upon the room. "March!" It echoed through the corridor.

Deep snow lay on the ground; the air was cut by a biting wind. A row of armed civilians and soldiers stood along the road to the bank. Dimly the outlines of a barge were visible through the morning mist. One by one the deportees marched, flanked on each side by the uniformed men, curses and threats accompanying the thud of their feet on the frozen ground. When the last man had crossed the gang-plank, the girls and I were ordered to follow, officers in front and in back of us.

We were led to a cabin. A large fire roared in the iron stove, filling the air with heat and fumes. We felt suffocating. There was no air nor water. Then came a violent lurch; we were on our way.

I looked at my watch. It was 4:20 A.M. on the day of our Lord, December 21, 1919. On the deck above us I could hear the men tramping up and down in the wintry blast. I felt dizzy, visioning a transport of politicals doomed to Siberia, the *étape* of former Russian days. Russia of the past rose before me and I saw the revolutionary martyrs being driven into exile. But no, it was New York, it was America, the land of liberty! Through the port-hole I could see the great city receding into the distance, its sky-line of buildings traceable by their rearing heads. It was my beloved city, the metropolis of the New World. It was America, indeed, America repeating the terrible scenes of tsarist Russia! I glanced up—the Statue of Liberty!

Dawn was breaking when our barge pulled up alongside of the large ship. We were quickly transferred and assigned to a cabin. It was six o'clock. Exhausted, I crawled into my bunk and immediately fell asleep.

I was awakened by someone pulling at my covers. A white

figure stood at my berth, probably the stewardess. Was I ill, she asked, to remain in bed so long. It was already six o'clock in the evening. I had shut out the hideous sights in twelve hours of blessed sleep. Stepping into the corridor, I was startled by someone roughly grabbing me by the shoulder. "Where are you going?" a soldier demanded. "To the toilet, if you must know it. Any objection?" He loosed his hold and followed me; he waited till I emerged again, and accompanied me back to the cabin. My girl companions informed me that guards had been stationed at our door since our arrival, and that they had also been escorted to the place of pressing needs every time they left the cabin.

At noon the next day we were conducted by the sentry to the officers' dining-room. At a large table sat the captain and his retinue, civilian and military. A separate table was assigned to us.

After lunch I requested to see the Federal official in charge of the deportees. He proved to be F. W. Berkshire, an immigration inspector detailed to manage the *Buford* expedition. Did we like our cabin and was the food good, he inquired solicitously. We had no complaints to make, I told him, but how about our men comrades? Could we take our meals with them and meet them on deck? "Impossible," Berkshire said. I then demanded to see Alexander Berkman. Also impossible. Thereupon I informed the inspector that I had no desire to cause trouble, but that I would give him twenty-four hours to change his mind about allowing me to talk to my friend. If my demand should be refused, at the expiration of that time I would go on a hunger-strike.

In the morning Sasha was brought under escort to see me. It seemed weeks since I had beheld his dear face. He told me that the conditions of the men were harrowing. They were cooped up in the hold of the ship, forty-nine in a place barely large enough for half that number. The rest of them were in two other compartments. The bunks, three tiers high, were old and worn out; those in the lower ones bumped their heads against the wire netting of the uppers every time they turned around. The boat, built at the end of the last century, had been used as a transport in the Spanish-American War and later discarded as unsafe. The floor of the steerage was wet all the time, the beds and blankets damp. Only salt water was to be had for washing, and no soap. The food was abominable, especially the bread, half-baked and uneatable. And, worst of all, there were only two toilets for the two hundred and forty-six men. [. . .]

Sasha advised against pressing our request to eat with the men. It would be better to save what we could from our food for the sick boys who could not stomach the rations given them. Meanwhile he was trying to see what improvements he could secure. He was negotiating with Berkshire a list of demands he had submitted. I was happy to see Sasha full of vital energy again. He had forgotten his own physical troubles the moment he saw that the others were depending on him. [. . .]

We were in rough waters, and many of the deportees fell ill. The coarse and badly cooked food was causing general stomach-complaints, and the dampness of the bunks laid many of the men low with rheumatism. The ship's doctor, too busy to attend the increasing number of patients, called upon Sasha to aid him. My offer to serve as nurse had been refused, but my hands were fully occupied with my two girl companions, who had to keep to their beds almost all the time. It was a very strained atmosphere those Christmas days, with forebodings of impending strife.

Our guards were extremely antagonistic, but with the passing of time I seemed to detect a gradual change. [. . .] The sentry who had so roughly grabbed me the first day was holding out longest against us. One evening I kept watching him as he paced up and down in front of our cabin. He looked exhausted with the endless walking and I suggested that he sit down for a while. When I placed a camp-chair before him, his reserve broke down. "I daren't," he whispered, "the sergeant may be along." I offered to change rôles with him: I would remain on the look-out. "My God!" he exclaimed, unable to restrain himself any longer, "they told us you were a desperado, that you had killed McKinley and are always plotting against someone." From that moment he became very friendly, ready to do us any service. He had apparently spoken of the incident to his buddies, and they began to hang around our door, eager to show us some kindness. Our cabin had also a special attraction for them: my good-looking young companion Ethel. The soldiers were wild about her, discussed anarchism every free moment at their disposal, and became greatly interested in our fate. They hated their superiors. They would like to drop them into the sea, they said, because they were treated as chattel slaves and punished on every pretext.

One of the lieutenants also was very courteous and humane. He borrowed from me some books, and when he returned them, I found a note containing the news that Kalinin[3] had become President of Soviet Russia and hinting that we were not to be taken to any parts occupied by the Whites. Uncertainty as to our exact destination had all the time been a source of great anxiety and worry among the deportees. The information of the friendly officer proved a great relief in allaying our worst fears. [. . .]

Sasha had become chummy with the assistant steward, and by means of him we organized a mail service. Copious notes passed every day between us, and we kept each other informed of happenings. Our friend, whom we had christened "Mac," became so devoted that he began to take a personal interest in our fate. He was very clever and ingenious, and he managed to appear at the most unexpected moments, just when he was needed. He seemed suddenly to develop the habit of walking with his hands under his apron, and he never came to us without some little gift hidden about his person. Delicacies from the pantry, sweet morsels from the captain's table, even fried chicken and pastry, we would find stuck away under our beds or in Sasha's bunk. And then one day he brought to Sasha several soldiers who confided to him that they had come as delegates of their comrades in arms. They had a serious mission. It was an offer to supply the deportees with guns and ammunition, to arrest all those in charge, turn the command of the *Buford* over to Sasha, and sail with all aboard to Soviet Russia.

It was January 5, 1920, when we reached the English Channel. The mail-bag carried away by the pilot contained our first letters to the United States. For the sake of safety they were addressed to Frank Harris, Alexander Harvey,[4] and other American friends whose correspondence was subject to less scrutiny than that of our own people. Mr. Berkshire had also consented to let us send a cable to America. The favour was rather costly, amounting to eight dollars, but it was worth the relief our friends would feel at the message that we were alive and still safe.

When we left the English Channel, we were followed by an Allied destroyer. Twofold fear on the part of the *Buford* authorities was responsible for the presence of the warship. Our men had repeatedly complained about the quality of the bread rationed to them. Their protest ignored, they had threatened to strike. Mr. Berkshire brought Sasha "strict orders from the Colonel" for the deportees to submit. The men laughed in his face. "Berkman is the only 'Colonel' *we* recognize," they shouted. The military chief sent for Sasha. He stormed about the disorganization of the ship's discipline, raved about the deportees fraternizing with the soldiers, and threatened to have the men searched for hidden weapons. Sasha boldly declared that his comrades would resist. The Colonel did not press the matter, and it was evident that he felt he could not rely on the force under his command. Sasha offered to solve the difficulty by putting two of the deportees, who were cooks, in charge of the bakery, without pay. The Colonel was loath to accept what he considered a reflection upon his supreme authority, but Sasha insisted and he won Berkshire to his side. Sasha's plan was finally adopted, and henceforth everyone enjoyed bread of the best quality. What might have proved serious trouble had thus been averted, but the talk of a strike, and the organized stand of our comrades, had had its effect on the commanding officers. Confidence in their exclusive power shaken, an Allied destroyer was a useful thing to have near. With a crowd on the *Buford* that had no respect for epaulets and gold braid, with two hundred and forty-nine radicals on hand who believed in strikes and direct action, the warship was a veritable godsend.

Another reason was the *Buford* itself. The battered old tub had been unseaworthy at the start, and the long journey had not improved her condition. The United States Government had been fully aware that the boat was unsafe, yet it had entrusted five hundred or more lives to it. We were heading for German waters and the Baltic Sea, the latter still thickly dotted with mines. The British destroyer was sadly needed in such a hazardous situation. The captain realized the imminent peril. He ordered the life-boats held in readiness and authorized Sasha to take charge of twelve of them and organize the men for quick action in case of alarm. [. . .]

After nineteen days of dangerous cruising we at last reached the Kiel Canal. Badly battered, the *Buford* had to remain for twenty-four hours for repair. The men were locked below deck, and special guards stationed on watch. German barges came alongside of our ship. They were in front of our cabin, and I threw them a note through the port-hole, telling them who we were. They consented to forward a letter, and I covered two sheets in the smallest German script I could write, describing our deportation, the reaction we left behind, and the treatment of the revolutionists imprisoned without benefit of amnesty. I addressed the letter to the *Republik,* organ of the Independent Socialists, and I added an appeal to the German workers to make their revolution as fundamental as that of Russia.

The men locked in the steerage and almost suffocating in the vile air made vigorous protests, demanding the daily exercise they had won after the first days of the journey. Meanwhile they were bombarding the German workers on the dock with missiles in which messages had been secreted. Presently the repair men, their work done and my letter safe in their hands, pulled away, shouting cheers for the political deportees from America and *die soziale Revolution.* It was a stirring demonstration of comradely solidarity which even war could not destroy.

We learned that our destination was Libau, in western Latvia, but two days later a radiogram notified the captain that fighting was continuing on the Baltic front, and the course of the *Buford* was changed. Again we were at sea in more senses than one. Deportees and crew became impatient and irritable with the drawn-out, perilous voyage. Longing filled me for those I had left behind and sickening uncertainty of the things ahead. Roots embedded in the soil of one's entire life are not easily transplanted. I felt uneasy and restless, between hope and doubt. My spirit was still in the United States.

The ghastly trip was over at last. We had reached Hango, a Finnish port. Supplied with three days' rations, we were turned over to the local authorities. America's obligation was at an end and so were her fears. [. . .]

All was ready. It was the twenty-eighth day of our journey, and at last we were on the threshold of Soviet Russia. My heart trembled with anticipation and fervent hope.

CHAPTER LII

Soviet Russia! Sacred ground, magic people! You have come to symbolize humanity's hope, you alone are destined to redeem mankind. I have come to serve you, beloved *matushka*. Take me to your bosom, let me pour myself into you, mingle my blood with yours, find my place in your heroic struggle, and give to the uttermost to your needs!

At the border, on our way to Petrograd, and at the station there, we were received like dear comrades. We who had been driven out of America as felons were welcomed on Soviet soil as brothers by her sons and daughters who had helped to set her free. Workers, soldiers, and peasants surrounded us, took us by the hand, and made us feel akin to them. Pale-faced and hollow-cheeked they were, a light burning in their sunken eyes, and determination breathing from their ragged bodies. Danger and suffering had steeled their wills and made them stern. But underneath beat the old childlike, generous Russian heart, and it went out to us without stint. [. . .]

In Petrograd, after a third reception, *Tovarishtch* Zorin,[1] in whose company we had made the trip, invited Sasha and me to come with him to a waiting automobile. Darkness covered the big city, fantastic shadows over the glistening snow on the ground. The streets were entirely deserted, the grave-like silence disturbed only by the rattling of our car. We sped on, several times halted by human forms suddenly emerging from the blackness of the night. Soldiers they were, heavily armed, their flashlights searchingly on us. "*Propusk, tovarishtch!* (Pass-card, comrade!)," was their curt demand. "Military precautions," our escort explained; "Petrograd has only recently escaped the menace of Yudenich. Too many counter-revolutionists are still lurking about for us to take any chances." [. . .]

Liza, Zorin's wife, bade us a hearty welcome, her greeting as kindly as Zorin's attitude had been throughout the day. She felt sure we were hungry. She had not much to offer us, but we should partake of everything she had, which proved to be herring, *kasha*, and tea. The Zorins looked none too well fed themselves, and I promised myself to replenish their scanty larder when our trunks were unpacked. Our American friends had provided us with a huge trunkful of supplies and we had also rescued some of the rations given us on leaving the *Buford*. I chuckled inwardly at the thought of the United States Government unwittingly feeding the Russian Bolsheviks. [. . .]

The Zorins had much to relate to us and they could do it in English. They told us of the Revolution, its achievements and hopes, and many other things we wanted to learn about. Their story of the events leading up to October and the developments since, though more detailed, was somewhat repetitious of what we had already heard at our receptions. It concerned the blockade and its fearful toll; the iron ring that surrounded Russia and the devastating sabotage of the interventionists; the armed attacks by Denikin, Kolchak, and Yudenich;[2] the havoc wrought by them and the revolutionary spirit that kept at its height against terrible odds, fighting on numerous fronts and routing its enemies. Fighting also on the industrial front, building the new Russia out of the ruins of the old. Already much constructive work had been achieved, they informed us; we should have the opportunity to see it with our own eyes. Schools, workers' colleges, social protection of mother and child, care of the aged and the sick, and much more were made possible by the dictatorship of the proletariat. Of course, Russia was very far yet from perfection, with every hand raised against her. The blockade, the intervention, the counter-revolutionary plotters—foremost amongst them the Russian intelligentsia—they were the greatest menace. It was they who were responsible for the fearful obstacles the Revolution encountered and for the ills the country was suffering. [. . .]

In the hotel corridor we ran into a young woman who told us

that she was on her way to the Zorins' to call us. A friend from America was waiting, eager to see us. We followed her to an apartment on the fourth floor, and when the door was opened, I found myself in the embrace of our old comrade Bill Shatoff.[3] "Bill, you here!" I cried in surprise; "why, Zorin told me you had left for Siberia!" [. . .]

Bill had put on considerable weight since the farewell send-off we had given him in New York. His military uniform accentuated his bulging lines and made his face look rather hard. But he was the same old Bill, impulsive, affectionate, and jovial. He pelted us with a volley of questions about America, the San Francisco labour cases, our imprisonment and deportation. "Never mind all that for the present," we parried; "better tell us first about yourself. How do you happen still to be in Petrograd? And why were you not on the reception committee for the American deportees?" Bill looked somewhat embarrassed and sought to dodge our questions, but we were insistent. I could not bear the uncertainty about Zorin and I was not willing to suspect him of deliberate deception. "I see you have not changed," Bill teased; "you are the same old persistent pest." He tried to explain that in the strenuous life of Russia people had no time for mere sociability. He and Zorin, having different duties, rarely met. [. . .] "And why could you not have come on your own account?" "The dictatorship of the proletariat," Bill replied, patting me on the back indulgently; "but of that some other time. Now I just want to tell you," he continued earnestly, "that the Communist State in action is exactly what we anarchists have always claimed it would be—a tightly centralized power, still more strengthened by the dangers to the Revolution. Under such conditions one cannot do as one wills. One does not just hop on a train and go, or even ride the bumpers, as I used to in the United States. One needs permission. But don't get the idea that I miss my American 'blessings.' Me for Russia, the Revolution, and its glorious future!"

Bill was certain we would come to feel just as he did about things in Russia. No need to worry about trifles like *propusks* during our first hours together. "*Propusks!* I have a whole trunkful of them, and so will you soon," he concluded, a mischievous twinkle in his eye. I caught his mood and dismissed my questions. I was dazed by the impressions that had crowded the day. Was it really only one day, I wondered. I seemed to have lived years since our arrival.

Bill Shatoff did not leave for another fortnight, and we spent together most of our time, often into the wee hours of the morning. The revolutionary canvas he unrolled before us was of far larger scope than had been painted before by anyone else. It was no longer a few individual figures thrown on the picture, their rôle and importance accentuated by the vast background. Great and small, high and low, stood out in bold relief, imbued with a collective will to hasten the complete triumph of the Revolution. Lenin, Trotsky, Zinoviev,[4] with their small band of inspired comrades, had a tremendous part to play, Bill declared with enthusiastic conviction; but the real power behind them was the awakened revolutionary consciousness of the masses. The peasants had expropriated the masters' land all through the summer of 1917 . . . workers had taken possession of the factories and shops . . . the soldiers had flocked back by the hundred thousands from the warring fronts . . . the Kronstadt sailors had translated their anarchist motto of direct action into the everyday life of the Revolution . . . the Left Socialist Revolutionists, as also the anarchists, had encouraged the peasantry in socializing the land. . . . All these forces had helped to energize the storm that broke over Russia, finding full expression and release in the terrific sweep of October.

Such was the epic of dazzling beauty and overwhelming power, infused with palpitating life by the ardour and eloquence of our friend. Presently Bill himself broke the spell. He had shown us the transformation in the soul of Russia, he continued; he would have to let us see her ills of the body as well. "Not to prejudice you," he emphasized, "as has been feared by people whose criterion of revolutionary integrity is a membership card." Before long we would ourselves meet the appalling afflictions that were sapping the country's strength, he said. His object was merely to prepare us—to help us diagnose the source of the disease, to point out the danger of its spreading and enable us to see that only the most drastic measures could effect a cure. The Russian experience had taught him that we anarchists had been the romanticists of revolution, forgetful of the cost it would entail, the frightful price the enemies of the Revolution would exact, the fiendish methods they would resort to in order to destroy its gains. One cannot fight fire and sword with only the logic and justice of one's ideal. The counter-revolutionists had combined to isolate and starve Russia, and the blockade was taking frightful toll of human life. The intervention and the destruction in its wake, the numerous White attacks, costing oceans of blood, the hordes of Denikin, Kolchak, and Yudenich; their pogroms, bestial revenge, and the general havoc wrought had imposed on the Revolution a warfare that its most far-sighted exponents had never dreamed about. A warfare not always in keeping [with our] romantic ideas of revolutionary ethics, indispensable none the less to drive off the hungry wolves ready to tear the Revolution limb from limb. He had not ceased to be an anarchist, Bill assured us; he had not become indifferent to the menace of a Marxian State machine. That danger was no longer a subject for theoretic discussion, but an actual reality because of the existing bureaucracy, inefficiency, and corruption. He loathed the dictatorship and its handmaiden, the Cheka,[5] with their ruthless suppression of thought, speech, and initiative. But it was an unavoidable evil. The anarchists had been the first to respond to Lenin's essentially anarchistic call to revolution. They had the right to demand an accounting. "And we will! Never doubt that," Bill fairly shouted, "we will! But not now, not now! Not while every nerve must be strained to save Russia from the reactionary elements which are desperately fighting to come back to power." [. . .]

Our comrade was the enthusiastic bard of old, his song the saga of the Revolution, the most stupendous event of our time. Its miracles were many, its horrors and woe the martyrdom of a people nailed to the cross.

Bill was entirely right, we thought. Nothing was of moment compared with the supreme need of giving one's all to safeguard the Revolution and its gains. The faith and fervour of our comrade swept me along to ecstatic heights. Yet I could not entirely free myself from an undercurrent of uneasiness one often feels when left alone in the dark. Resolutely I strove to drive it back, moving like a sleep-walker through enchanted space. Sometimes I would stumble back to earth only half-aroused by a harsh voice or an ugly sight. The gagging of free speech at the session of the Petro-Soviet that we had attended, the discovery that better and more plentiful food was served Party members at the Smolny dining-room and many similar injustices and evils had attracted my attention. Model schools where the children were stuffed with sweets and candies, and side by side with them schools dismal, poorly equipped, unheated, and filthy, where the little ones, hungry all the time, were herded together like cattle. A special hospital for Communists, with every modern comfort, while other institutions lacked the barest medical and surgical necessities. Thirty-four different grades of rations—under alleged *Communism*!—while some markets and privileged stores were doing a lively business in butter, eggs, cheese, and meat. The workers and their womenfolk standing long hours in endless queues for their ration of frozen potatoes, wormy cereals, and decayed fish. Groups of women, their faces bloated and blue, accompanied by Red soldiers and bargaining with them for their pitiful wares. [. . .]

Zinoviev did not look the formidable leader his reputation would have led one to assume. He impressed me as flabby and weak. His voice was adolescent, high-pitched and lacking in appeal. But he had faithfully helped the Revolution to its birth and he was indefatigably working for its further development, we had been told. He certainly deserved confidence and respect. "The blockade," he reiterated, "Kolchak, Denikin, Yudenich, the counter-revolutionist Savinkov,[6] as well as the Menshevik[7] traitors and the Socialist Revolutionists of the Right, are a constant menace. They are eternally plotting vengeance and the death of the Revolution." Zinoviev's plaint added tragic momentum to the general chorus. I joined in with the rest.

Soon, however, other voices rose from the depths, harsh, accusing voices that greatly disturbed me. I had been asked to attend a conference of anarchists in Petrograd, and I was amazed to find that my comrades were compelled to gather in secret in an obscure hiding-place. Bill Shatoff had spoken with great pride of the courage shown by our comrades in the Revolution and on the military fronts, and he had extolled the heroic part they had played. Why should people with such a record, I wondered, be driven under cover.

Presently came the answer—from workers in the Putilov Iron-works, from factories and mills, from the Kronstadt sailors, from Red Army men, and from an old comrade who had escaped while under sentence of death. The very brawn of the revolutionary struggle was crying out in anguish and bitterness against the people they had helped place in power. They spoke of the Bolshevik betrayal of the Revolution, of the slavery forced upon the toilers, the emasculation of the soviets, the suppression of speech and thought, the filling of prisons with recalcitrant peasants, workers, soldiers, sailors, and rebels of every kind. They told of the raid with machine-guns upon the Moscow headquarters of the anarchists by the order of Trotsky; of the Cheka and the wholesale executions without hearing or trial. These charges and denunciations beat upon me like hammers and left me stunned. I listened tense in every nerve, hardly able clearly to understand what I heard, and failing to grasp its full meaning. It couldn't be true—this monster indictment! Had not Zorin pointed the jail out to us and assured us that it was almost empty? Capital punishment, he had said, had been abolished. And had not Bill Shatoff paid glowing tribute to Lenin and his co-workers, glorifying their vision and valour? Bill had not covered up the dark spots on the Soviet horizon; he had explained the reason for them and the methods they had forced upon the Bolsheviki, and indeed upon all rebels serving the Revolution.

The men in that dismal hall must be mad, I thought, to tell such impossible and preposterous stories, wicked to condemn the Communists for the crimes they must know were due to the counter-revolutionary gang, to the blockade and the White generals attacking the Revolution. I proclaimed my conviction to the gathering, but my voice was drowned in the laughter of derision and jeers. I was roundly denounced for my wilful blindness. "That's the gag they have given you!" my comrades shouted at me. "You and Berkman have fallen for it and swallowed it whole. And Zorin, the bigot who hates anarchists and would shoot them all in cold blood! Bill Shatoff, too, the renegade!" they shouted; "you believe them and not us. Wait, wait until you have seen things with your own eyes. You will sing another song then." [. . .]

Sasha had been laid up with a severe cold and was too ill to attend the conference of the anarchist group. But I had kept him informed, and now I burst into his room in great mental turmoil to tell him of this last dreadful day. He dismissed the charges as the irresponsible prattle of ineffective and disgruntled men. The Petrograd anarchists were like so many in our ranks in America who used to do least and criticize most, he said. Perhaps they had been naïve enough to expect anarchism to emerge overnight from the ruins of autocracy, from the war and blunders of the Provisional Government. It was absurd to denounce the Bolsheviki for the drastic measures they were using, Sasha urged. How else were they to free Russia from the strangle-hold of counter-revolution and sabotage? [. . .]

Sasha's illness had driven back the phantoms of my sleepless nights. Physicians were few, medicine scarce, and disease rampant in Petrograd. Zorin had immediately sent out for a doctor, but the patient's fever was too alarming for a long wait. My old professional experience never served a better purpose. With the help of my small, well-equipped medicine chest which the kindly doctor of the *Buford* had given me, I succeeded in breaking Sasha's fever. Two weeks of careful nursing brought him out of bed, looking thin and pale, but on the road to complete recovery. About this time two men were sent up to see us: George Lansbury,[8] editor of the London *Daily Herald*, and Mr. Barry, an American correspondent. They had not been expected and no provision had been made for an English-speaking person to meet them. They did not understand a word of Russian and they wanted to get to Moscow. We communicated their plight to Mme Ravich, head of the Interior Department and chief of the Foreign Office in Petrograd. She requested Sasha to accompany the English visitors to Moscow, and he consented.

His departure left me free to go about again. The Zorins were always willing to take me to places of interest, but I was beginning to pick up my Russian and I preferred to go alone. The anarchist conference having been held under cover, I had not been in a position to talk to the Zorins about it, much less tell them what I had heard. It made me feel somewhat guilty in their presence. Added to it was my impression that Zorin was purposely keeping me away from certain things. I had asked him whether I could visit some factories. He had promised to secure a *propusk* for me, but he had failed to do so. He had also shown impatience with Liza [Zorin] when she had asked me to address the girls of a shop-collective. Not that I had consented; my Russian was still too halting. Moreover, I had come to Russia to learn and not to teach. Zorin seemed greatly relieved at my refusal. I had paid no attention to his peculiar attitude at the time, but when he also broke his promise to take me to the mills, I began to wonder whether there was not something wrong there. I did not believe that conditions were as bad as described at the conference; why, then, should Zorin refuse to let me see them? However, my relations with the Zorins continued very friendly. [. . .]

One thing Bill Shatoff had told us about was certainly not overdrawn: the matter of *propusks*. They played a greater rôle in Soviet Russia than passports had under the tsars. One could not even get in or out of our hotel without a permit, not to speak of visiting any Soviet institution or important official. Almost everyone carried portfolios stocked with *propusks* and *oodostoverenyas* (identification papers). Zorin had told me that they constituted a necessary precaution against counter-revolutionary plotters, but the longer I stayed in Russia, the less I saw their value. Paper was at a high premium, yet reams upon reams of it were used for "permits," and much time was wasted in securing them. On the other hand, the very quantity of them defeated any real control. What sane counter-revolutionist, I argued, would expose himself to discovery by standing for hours in line waiting for a *propusk*? He could more easily secure it in other ways. But it was useless; every Communist I met seemed to suffer from counter-revolutionary fixation, no doubt due to the attacks already endured. How could I take issue with them? My stay in Russia had been too short for me to advise them on the most practical method of coping with the enemies of the Revolution. And what did the pesky pieces of paper matter in view of the great things already achieved? Everywhere I witnessed sublime courage, selfless devotion, and simple grandeur on the part of those holding the revolutionary fort against the entire inimical world. Thus I reasoned with myself, determinedly refusing to see the reverse side of Russia's face. But its scarred and twisted countenance would not be ignored. It kept calling me back, urging me to look, forcing me to view its suffering. I wanted to see only its beauty and radiance, longed passionately to believe in its strength and power, yet the very hideousness of the other side compelled with an irresistible appeal. "Look, look!" it grinned, "within reach of Petrograd are vast stretches of forest, enough to heat every home and make every factory wheel turn. Yet the city is perishing from cold, and the machines are frozen. The *razverstka* (forcible collection of food) drains the peasantry to feed Petrograd, they are told; fertile Ukraine is forced to ship carloads of provisions northward, yet the population of the cities is starving. A goodly half of the provisions somehow vanishes along the route, the rest reaching, in the main, the markets rather than the hungry masses; and the constant shootings on the Gorokhovaya (Cheka headquarters), have you been deaf to those? And the planned prison for morally defective children—has your indignation not been aroused by this, you who have for thirty-five years hurled anathema at the traducers of child-life? What about all these ghastly blotches so skilfully hidden by Communist rouge?" [. . .]

I dispatched a note to [Maxim] Gorki,[9] requesting him to see me. I felt lost in the labyrinth of Soviet Russia, stumbling constantly over the many obstacles, vainly groping for the revolutionary light. I needed his friendly, guiding hand, I wrote him. Meanwhile I turned to Zinoviev. "Forests within easy reach of Petrograd," I said; "why must the city freeze?" "Any amount of fuel," Zinoviev replied; "but of what avail? Our enemies have destroyed our means of transportation; the blockade has killed off our horses as well as our men. How are we to get at the woodland?" "What about the population of Petrograd?" I persisted. "Could it not be appealed to for co-operation? Could it not be induced to go *en masse* with pick and ax and ropes to haul wood for its own use? Would not such a concerted effort alleviate much suffering and at the same time decrease the antagonism against your party?" It might help to diminish the misery from cold, Zinoviev replied, but it would interfere with the carrying out of the main political policies. What were they? "Concentration of all power in the hands of the proletarian *avant-garde,*" Zinoviev explained, "the *avant-garde* of the Revolution, which is the Communist Party." "Rather a dear price to pay," I objected. "Unfortunately," he agreed; "but the dictatorship of the proletariat is the only workable program during a revolutionary period. Anarchist groups, free initiative of communes, as your great teachers have suggested, may be feasible in centuries to come, but not now in Russia, with the Denikins and Kolchaks ready to crush us. They have doomed the whole of Russia, yet your comrades fret about the fate of one city." One city, with a million and a half inhabitants reduced to four hundred thousand! A mere bagatelle in the eyes of the Communist political program! Disheartened, I left the man so cock-sure of his party's wisdom, so ensconced in the heavenly Marxian constellation and self-conscious of being one of its major stars.

John Reed[10] had burst into my room like a sudden ray of light, the old buoyant, adventurous Jack that I used to know in the States. He was about to return to America, by way of Latvia. Rather a hazardous journey, he said, but he would take even greater risks to bring the inspiring message of Soviet Russia to his native land. "Wonderful, marvellous, isn't it, E.G.?" he exclaimed. "Your dream of years now realized in Russia, your dream scorned and persecuted in my country, but made real by the magic wand of Lenin and his band of despised Bolsheviks. Did you ever expect such a thing to happen in the country ruled by the tsars for centuries?"

"Not by Lenin and his comrades, dear Jack," I corrected, "though I do not deny their great part. But by the whole Russian people, preceded by a glorious revolutionary past. No other land of our days has been so literally nurtured by the blood of her martyrs, a long procession of pioneers who went to their death that new life may spring from their graves."

Jack insisted that the young generation cannot for ever be tied to the apron-strings of the old, particularly when those strings are tightly drawn around its throat. "Look at your old pioneers, the Breshkovskayas and Tchaikovskys, the Chernovs and Kerenskys and the rest of them," he cried heatedly; "see where they are now! With the Black Hundreds, the Jew-baiters, and the ducal clique, aiding them to crush the Revolution. I don't give a damn for their past. I am concerned only in what the treacherous gang has been doing during the past three years. To the wall with them! I say. I have learned one mighty expressive Russian word, 'razstrellyat'!" (execute by shooting).

"Stop, Jack! Stop!" I cried; "this word is terrible enough in the mouth of a Russian. In your hard American accent it freezes my blood. Since when do revolutionists see in wholesale execution the only solution of their difficulties? In time of active counter-revolution it is no doubt inevitable to give shot for shot. But cold-bloodedly and merely for opinion's sake, do you justify standing people against the wall under such circumstances?" I went on to point out to him that the Soviet Government must have realized the futility of such methods, not to speak of their barbarity, because it had abolished capital punishment. Zorin had told me that. Was the decree revoked, that Jack spoke so glibly of standing men against the wall? I mentioned the frequent shooting I heard in the city at night. Zorin had said that it was target practice of *kursanty* (Communist students at the military training-school for officers). "Do you know anything about it, Jack?" I questioned. "Tell me the truth."

He did know, he said, that five hundred prisoners, considered counter-revolutionists, had been shot on the eve the decree was to go into force. It had been a stupid blunder on the part of over-zealous Chekists and they had been severely reprimanded for it. He had not heard of any other shootings since, but he had always thought me a revolutionist of the purest dye, one who would not shirk any measure in defence of the Revolution.

He was surprised to see me so worked up over the death of a few plotters. As if that mattered in the scales of the world revolution!

"I must be crazy, Jack," I said, "or else I never understood the meaning of revolution. I certainly never believed that it would signify callous indifference to human life and suffering, or that it would have no other method of solving its problems than by wholesale slaughter. Five hundred lives snuffed out on the eve of a decree abolishing the death-penalty! You call it a stupid blunder. I call it a dastardly crime, the worst counter-revolutionary outrage committed in the name of the Revolution."

"That's all right," said Jack, trying to calm me; "you are a little confused by the Revolution in action because you have dealt with it only in theory. You'll get over that, clear-sighted rebel that you are, and you'll come to see in its true light everything that seems so puzzling now. Cheer up, and make me a cup of the good old American coffee you have brought with you. Not much to give you in return for all my country has taken from you, but greatly appreciated in starving Russia by her native son."

I marvelled at his capacity to change so quickly to a light tone. It was the same old Jack, with his zest for the adventures of life. I longed to join in his gay mood, but my heart was heavy. Jack's appearance had brought back memories of my recent life, my people, Helena and those dear to me. Not a word from anyone had reached me in two months. Uncertainty about them added to my depression and restlessness. Sasha's letter, suggesting that I come to Moscow, put new energy into me. Moscow was much more alive than Petrograd, he wrote, and there were interesting people to meet. A few weeks in the capital might help to clarify the revolutionary situation to me. I wanted to go immediately. I had already learned, however, that in Soviet Russia one does not just buy a ticket and board a train. I had seen people standing in queues for days and nights to obtain a permit for their journey and then again wait in long lines to purchase their tickets. Even with the helpful co-operation of Zorin it required ten days before I could leave. He had arranged for me to be in the party of Soviet officials going to Moscow, he informed me. Demyan Bedny, the official poet, would be there and he would place me in the Hotel National. Zorin was as obliging as ever, though somewhat distant.

Arrived at the station, I found myself in distinguished company. Karl Radek, who had escaped the fate of Liebknecht, Rosa Luxemburg, and Landauer, was there.[11] Chiperovich, head of the Petrograd labour unions, Maxim Gorki, and several lesser lights were also in the same car with me.

Gorki had previously replied to my letter and had asked me to call for a talk. I did, but there was no talk. I found him suffering from a heavy cold and constantly coughing, while four women were fluttering about him, ministering to his needs. When he saw me in the car, he said we could have our postponed talk *en route;* he would come to my compartment later. I waited eagerly the largest part of the day. Gorki did not appear, nor anyone else except the porter with sandwiches and tea for the Soviet party. Radek, in the next compartment, was evidently holding court. In true Russian fashion everybody talked at once. But the little, nervous Radek managed to outstrip the others. For hours he rattled on. My brain grew weary and I dozed off.

I was roused from my sleep by a gaunt and lanky figure towering above me. Maxim Gorki stood before me, his peasant face deeply lined with pain. I asked him to sit down beside me and he crumpled into the seat, a tired and languid man, much older than his fifty years.

I had looked forward with much anticipation to the chance of talking to Gorki, yet now I did not know how to begin. "Gorki knows nothing about me," I was saying to myself. . . . "He may think me merely a reformer, opposed to the Revolution as such. Or he may even get the impression that I am just fault-finding on account of personal grievances or because I could not have 'buttered toast and grape-fruit for breakfast' or other material American blessings." [. . .]

At last I began by saying that I should first have to introduce myself before I could talk to him about the things that were distressing me. "Hardly necessary," Gorki interrupted; "I know a good deal about your activities in the United States. But even if

I knew nothing about you, the fact that you were deported for your ideas would be proof enough of your revolutionary integrity. I need nothing more." "That is most kind of you," I replied, "yet I must insist on a little preliminary." Gorki nodded, and I proceeded to tell him of my faith in the Bolsheviki from the very beginning of the October Revolution, and my defence of them and of Soviet Russia at a time when even very few radicals dared speak up for Lenin and his comrades. I had even turned from Catherine Breshkovskaya, who had been our torch for a generation. It had been no easy task to cry in the wilderness of fury and hate in defence of people who in point of theory had always been my political opponents. But who could think of such differences when the life of the Revolution was at stake? Lenin and his co-workers personified that life to me and to my nearest comrades and friends. Therefore we had fought for them and we would have cheerfully given our lives for the men who were holding the revolutionary fort. "I hope you will not consider me boastful or think that I have exaggerated the difficulties and dangers of our struggle in America for Soviet Russia," I said. Gorki shook his head and I continued: "I also hope you will believe me when I say that, though an anarchist, I had not been naïve enough to think that anarchism could rise overnight, as it were, from the debris of old Russia."

He stopped me with a gesture of his hand. "If that is so, and I do not doubt you, how can you be so perplexed at the imperfections you find in Soviet Russia? As an old revolutionist you must know that revolution is a grim and relentless task. Our poor Russia, backward and crude, her masses, steeped in centuries of ignorance and darkness, brutal and lazy beyond any other people in the world!" I gasped at his sweeping indictment of the entire Russian people. His charge was terrible, if true, I told him. It was also rather novel. No Russian writer had ever spoken in such terms before. He, Maxim Gorki, was the first to advance such a peculiar view, and the first not to put all the blame upon the blockade, the Denikins and Kolchaks. Somewhat irritated, he replied that the "romantic conception of our great literary genuises" had entirely misrepresented the Russian and had wrought no end of evil. The Revolution had dispelled the bubble of the goodness and naïveté of the peasantry. It had proved them shrewd, avaricious, and lazy, even savage in their joy of causing pain. The rôle played by the counter-revolutionary Yudeniches, he added, was too obvious to need special emphasis. That is why he had not considered it necessary even to mention them, nor the intelligentsia, which had been talking revolution for over fifty years and then was the first to stab it in the back with sabotage and conspiracies. But all these were contributory factors, not the main cause. The roots were inherent in Russia's brutal and uncivilized masses, he said. They have no cultural traditions, no social values, no respect for human rights and life. They cannot be moved by anything except coercion and force. All through the ages the Russians had known nothing else.

I protested vehemently against these charges. I argued that in spite of his evident faith in the superior qualities of other nations, it was the ignorant and crude Russian people that had risen first in revolt. They had shaken Russia by three successive revolutions within twelve years, and it was they and their will that gave life to "October."

"Very eloquent," Gorki retorted, "but not quite accurate." He admitted the share of the peasantry in the October uprising, though even that, he thought, was not conscious social feeling, but mere wrath accumulated for decades. If not checked by Lenin's guiding hand, it would have surely destroyed rather than advanced the great revolutionary aims. Lenin, Gorki insisted, was the real parent of the October Revolution. It had been conceived by his genius, nurtured by his vision and faith, and brought to maturity by his far-sighted and patient care. Others had helped to deliver the lusty child, particularly the small band of Bolsheviki, aided by the Petrograd workers, together with the sailors and soldiers of Kronstadt. Since the birth of October it was again Lenin who was steering its development and growth.

"Miracle-worker, your Lenin," I cried; "but I seem to remember that you have not always thought him a god or his comrades infallible." I reminded Gorki of his scathing arraignment of the Bolsheviki in the journal *Zhizn*, edited by him in the days of Kerensky. What had caused his change? He had attacked the Bolsheviki, Gorki acknowledged, but the march of events had convinced him that a revolution in a primitive country with a barbarous people could not survive without resort to drastic methods of self-defence. [. . .]

Maxim Gorki had been my idol, and I would not see his feet of clay. I became convinced, however, of one thing: neither he nor anyone else could solve my problems. Only time and patient seeking could do it, aided by sympathetic understanding of cause and effect in the revolutionary struggle of Russia.

The occupants of the car had retired, and all was quiet. The train sped on. I tried to gain some sleep, but found myself thinking of Lenin. What was this man and what the power that drew everyone to him, even those who disagreed with his course? Trotsky, Zinoviev, Bukharin,[12] and the other prominent men I had come across, all differed on many problems, yet were unanimous in their appraisal of Lenin. His was the clearest mind in Russia, everyone assured me, of iron will and dogged perseverance in pursuit of his aims, no matter what the cost. It was peculiar, though, that no one ever referred to any generous impulses of the man. [. . .] Now I was on my way perhaps to meet the man once hounded as a criminal and exile and who was now holding the fate and future of Russia in his hands.

Half asleep I heard the porter call out "Moscow!" When I reached the platform, I found that my fellow-passengers had already departed, including Demyan Bedny. I had had no means of notifying Sasha of my arrival, and no one else in the capital knew of my coming. I felt quite lost in the noise and bustle of the station and helpless with my bags and bundles. I had been warned that things had a way of vanishing in Russia under one's very eyes. I could not go in search of an *izvostchik*[13] and I stood irresolutely wondering what to do. Presently a familiar voice struck my ears. It was Karl Radek talking to some friends. He had not come near me during the entire journey, nor did he show any sign that he knew my identity. I felt awkward about turning to him for help. Suddenly he wheeled round and approached me. Was I waiting for anyone, he inquired, or could he be of aid? I could have hugged the dear little man for his kindly interest, but I was afraid of scandalizing him by such a display of "*bourgeois* sentimentality." I had frequently heard the expression used with great derision. I assured Radek that he was more chivalrous than the chaperon Zorin had given me. He had faithfully promised to see me safely to Moscow and secure a room for me there, and he had basely run away. "Chivalry, nonsense!" laughed Radek; "we are comrades, aren't we, even if you are not a member of my party?" "But how do you know who I am?" "News travels quickly in Russia," he replied. "You're an anarchist, you are Emma Goldman, and you were driven out of plutocratic America. That's three good reasons to entitle you to my comradeship and assistance."

He invited me to accompany him and to give the "comrade chauffeur" directions where to let me off. I explained that I had only the name and number of the street where my comrade Alexander Berkman was stopping. He was not expecting me and he would probably not be in. Moreover, he had no room of his own. [. . .] It was certainly not going to be easy to secure a room for me in Moscow, he remarked; the city was overcrowded and few quarters were available. But I should not worry; he'd take me to his apartment in the Kremlin and then we should see.

After the desolation of Petrograd, Moscow appeared a veritable cauldron of activity. Crowds everywhere, almost everyone lugging bundles or pulling loaded sleighs, rushing about and jostling, pushing and swearing as only Russians can. Very conspicuous was the number of soldiers and hard-faced men in leather jackets, with guns in their belts. [. . .]

Radek and his car were evidently well known to the sentries along our route. We were not halted, not even when the auto dashed through the portals of the Kremlin. The sight of its stone walls brought back to me memories of the tsarist régime. Through the centuries its rulers had dwelt in the magnificence of the huge palaces, their drunken orgies and black deeds echoing through the vast halls. [. . .] The builders of the new Russia in the seats of the mighty of old seemed incongruous in the extreme. How could they feel comfortable or at ease in the creeping shadows of the gruesome past, I wondered. A few hours in the Kremlin were enough to give me the uncanny feeling of the dead trying to come to life again. [. . .]

The repeated telephoning of Radek to the commandant of the National about a room for me finally brought results. At ten in the evening he sent me off in his car to the hotel, bundles and all. He was most cordial, assuring me that I could call on him in any emergency. [. . .]

It was a novel sensation to be with Sasha in the same city and not be able to reach him. Radek had tried all through the day to get hold of him, but he was not in. Seeing my anxiety, Radek had assured me that Berkman would surely be at his lodgings before midnight. He could remain nowhere else, it being strictly prohibited as a protectionary measure against counter-revolution. [. . .]

Radek proved right. At one o'clock I reached Sasha. Not having expected me, he had left for the day. He could not come to me then, because his *propusk* was good only till midnight, but he would call in the morning.

Sasha's voice over the telephone was already a great comfort. It helped to take the edge from the loneliness I felt in the great, strange city. My dear old pal arrived bright and early "to drink a cup of coffee with you," he said. He had had nothing like it since he had left Petrograd, he told me, nor much of anything else. [. . .]

The food at the Kharitonensky[14] was not bad, but entirely insufficient for adults. The other guests at the house somehow managed to supply themselves with extra morsels, which they would bring to the common dinner-table, but Sasha did not care to do this. His main difficulty, however, was the black bread, which was causing him serious stomach trouble. In fact, he had been compelled to stop eating it altogether. But now he would pick up lost weight quickly, he joked; now that I was in Moscow, he was sure I would manage to prepare good meals out of scraps, as I had always done. My dear Sasha! What amazing capacity for adaptation and what splendid sense for the comic sides of life!

The main attraction of the place where he lived, Sasha related, was the interesting types of humanity domiciled there. Chinese,

Koreans, Japanese, and Hindu delegates, come to study the achievements of "October" and to enlist aid for the work of liberation in their native countries.

Our comrades in Moscow, Sasha informed me, seemed to enjoy considerable freedom. The Anarcho-Syndicalists of the group Golos Truda were publishing anarchist literature and selling it openly at their book-shop on the Tverskaya. The Universalist Anarchists had club-rooms with a co-operative restaurant and held open weekly gatherings at which revolutionary problems were freely discussed. A little anarchist sheet was also published by our old Georgian comrade Attabekian, a close friend of Peter Kropotkin, who had his own print-shop. "What an extraordinary situation," I remarked, "to grant anarchists in Moscow so much freedom, and none at all to the Petrograd circle! Most of the dreadful charges I heard there against the Bolsheviki must have been mere fabrication, but one thing was obvious: they were compelled to meet in secret." Sasha explained that he had come upon quite a number of strange contradictions. Thus, many of our comrades were in prison, for no cause apparently, while others were not molested in their activities. But I would have ample opportunity to learn everything at first hand, he added; the Universalist group had invited us to a special conference where the anarchist angle of the Revolution and current events would be presented by three able speakers.

I could hardly wait for the approaching meeting, which held out the hope of better understanding of Russian reality. In the meantime I tramped Moscow many hours a day, sometimes with, but more often without, Sasha. He lived too far away, a full hour's walk from the National, and there were no streetcars and but few *izvostchiky*. But I urged Sasha to have at least one meal a day with me. He needed building up, and I had brought with me part of our groceries from Petrograd. The markets in Moscow were wide open, doing a rushing business. I saw no betrayal of the Revolution in buying necessaries there. Zorin had indeed told me that trading of any kind was the worst counter-revolution and was strictly prohibited. When I had called his attention to the open markets, he had assured me that only speculators were to be found there. I thought it was sheer nonsense to expect people to starve to death in sight of food. There was no heroism in that, nor could the Revolution profit by it. Starving people could not produce, and without production revolution is doomed to failure. Zorin had insisted that the blockade, the Allied intervention, and the White generals were responsible for the lack of food. [. . .]

The Soukharevka[15] made more flagrant the discrimination against smaller places of barter. The little market near the National was being constantly raided. Yet there were but the poorest of the poor desperately trying to keep alive: old women, children in tatters, derelict men, their wares as wretched as themselves. Ill-smelling *tshchi* (vegetable soup), frozen potatoes, biscuits black and hard, or a few boxes of matches—they held them out to the passers-by with trembling hands, in trembling voices pleading: "Buy, *barinya* (lady), buy, for the love of Christ, buy!" In the raids their measly wares would be seized, their soup and kvass poured out on the square, and the unfortunates dragged off to prison as speculators. Those lucky enough to escape the raiders would soon crawl back, gather up the matches and cigarettes strewn about, and begin their wretched trade again.

The Bolsheviki, in common with other social rebels, had always stressed the potency of hunger as the cause of most of the evils in capitalist society. They never grew tired of condemning the system that punished the effects while leaving their sources intact. How could they now pursue the same stupid and incredible course, I wondered. True, the appalling hunger was not of their making. The blockade and the interventionists *were* chiefly responsible for that. More reason, then, it seemed to me, why the victims should not be hounded and punished. [. . .]

The National, almost exclusively occupied by Communists, was manned by a large kitchen force that was wasting time and precious foodstuffs in preparing uneatable meals. Next to it was another kitchen with private servants cooking all day for their masters, prominent Soviet officials. They and their friends were permitted special privileges, often receiving three and even more rations, while the ordinary mortals were wearing out their depleted strength to attain their meagre due.

The housing arrangements disclosed similar favouritism and injustice. Large and well-furnished apartments were easily obtainable for a monetary consideration, but it required weeks of humiliation before petty officials to secure one room in a dismal flat without water, heat, or light. Lucky indeed the person if, after all his exhausting efforts, he did not find someone else occupying the same room. [. . .]

The hideous sores on revolutionary Russia could not for long be ignored. The facts presented at the gathering of the Moscow anarchists, the analysis of the situation by leading Left Socialist Revolutionists, and my talks with simple people who claimed no political affiliations enabled me to look behind the scenes of the revolutionary drama and to behold the dictatorship without its stage make-up. Its rôle was somewhat different from the one proclaimed in public. It was forcible tax-collection at the point of guns, with its devastating effect on villages and towns. It was the elimination from responsible positions of everyone who dared think aloud, and the spiritual death of the most militant elements whose intelligence, faith, and courage had really enabled the Bolsheviki to achieve their power. The anarchists and Left Socialist Revolutionists had been used as pawns by Lenin in the October days and were now doomed to extinction by his creed and policies. It was the system of taking hostages for political refugees, not exempting even old parents and children of tender age. The nightly *oblavas* (street and house raids) by the Cheka, the population frightened out of sleep, their few belongings turned upside down and ripped open for secret documents, the dragnet of soldiers left behind to haul in the crop of unsuspecting callers at the besieged house. The penalties for flimsy charges often amounted to long prison terms, exile to desolate parts of the country, and even execution. [. . .]

Even the Moscow Anarchist Conference had not gone so far in its indictment. The Soviet State was different from capitalist and *bourgeois* governments, they had told us when we objected to their absurdly illogical resolution asking for the legalisation of their work and the release of our comrades from prison. "In no country have the anarchists ever begged favours from the government," we argued, "nor do they believe in loyalty to the State.

Why do it here, if the Bolsheviki have broken faith?" The Bolshevik government was revolutionary in spite of its offences; it was proletarian in its nature and purposes, the Russian comrades insisted. Whereupon we had signed the petition and agreed to present it to the proper authorities.

Both Sasha and I held on to the firm belief that the Bolsheviki were our brothers in a common fight. Our very lives and all our revolutionary hopes were staked upon it. Lenin, Trotsky, and their co-workers were the soul of the Revolution, we were sure, and its keenest defenders. We would go to them, to Lunacharsky,[16] Kollontay, Balabanoff.[17] Jack Reed had spoken of them with deepest admiration and affection. They were capable of other criteria than a membership card in estimating people and events, Jack had said. They would help me see things in their proper light. I would seek them out. And our old teacher, Peter Kropotkin—we had drifted apart over our stand on the World War, but our love and esteem for his great personality and acute mind had not changed. I was certain that his feeling for us had also remained the same. We had been eager to see our dear comrade immediately upon our arrival in Russia. He was living in the village of Dmitrov, we had been informed, about sixty versts from Moscow, in his own little house, and he was well supplied with all necessaries by the Soviet Government. Travel was impossible then, but our trip would be arranged in the spring, Zorin had assured us. [. . .]

Alexandra Kollontay and Angelica Balabanoff were within easy reach, as they were living in the National. I sought out the former first. Mme Kollontay looked remarkably young and radiant, considering her fifty years and the severe operation she had recently undergone. A tall and stately woman, every inch the *grande dame* rather than the fiery revolutionist. Her attire and suite of two rooms bespoke good taste, the roses on her desk rather startling in the Russian greyness. They were the first I had seen since our deportation. [. . .] She leaned back in her arm-chair and I began speaking of the harrowing things that had come to my knowledge. She listened attentively without interrupting me, but there was not the slightest indication in her cold, handsome face of any perturbation on account of my recital. "We do have some dull grey spots in our vivid revolutionary picture," she said when I had concluded. "They are unavoidable in a country so backward, with a people so dark and a social experiment of such magnitude, opposed by the entire world as it is. They will disappear when we have liquidated our military fronts and when we shall have raised the mental level of our masses." I could help in that, she continued. I could work among the women; they were ignorant of the simplest principles of life, physical and otherwise, ignorant of their own functions as mothers and citizens. I had done such fine work of that kind in America, and she could assure me of a much more fertile field in Russia. "Why not join me and stop your brooding over a few dull grey spots?" she said in conclusion; "they are nothing more, dear comrade, really nothing more."

People raided, imprisoned, and shot for their *ideas*! The old and the young held as hostages, every protest gagged, iniquity and favouritism rampant, the best human values betrayed, the very spirit of revolution daily crucified—were all these nothing but "grey, dull spots," I wondered! I felt chilled to the marrow of my bones.

Two days later I went to see Anatol Lunacharsky. His quarters were in the Kremlin, the impenetrable citadel of authority in the popular mind of Russia. I bore several credentials, and my escort was a "Sovietsky" anarchist held in high esteem by the Communists. Nevertheless we made very slow progress in reaching the seat of the People's Commissar for Education. Repeatedly the sentries scrutinized our *propusks* and asked questions regarding the purpose of our coming. At last we found ourselves in a reception room, a large salon filled with many objects of art and a crowd of people. They were artists, writers, and teachers awaiting an audience, my companion explained. A sorry and undernourished lot they were, their gaze steadily riveted on the door leading to the Commissar's private office. Hope and fear burned in their eyes. I too was anxious, though my rations did not depend on the man who presided over the cultural positions. Lunacharsky's greeting was warmer and more cordial than Kollontay's. He also inquired whether I had already found suitable work. If not, he could suggest a number of occupations in his department. The American system of education was being introduced in Soviet Russia, he said, and I, coming from that country, would undoubtedly be able to make valuable suggestions in regard to its proletarian application. I gasped. I forgot all about the purpose of my visit. The educational system found wanting and rejected by the best pedagogues in the United States now accepted as a model in revolutionary Russia? Lunacharsky looked much astonished. Was the system really being opposed in America, he inquired, and by whom? What changes had they suggested? I should explain the whole matter to him and his teachers, and he would call a special conference for the purpose. I could do much good, he urged, and I could be of great help to him in his struggle with the reactionary elements among the teachers who were clamouring for the old methods in dealing with the child and who even favoured prison for the mental defectives. [. . .]

Lunacharsky continued to talk of his difficulties with the conservative instructors and of the controversy raging in the Soviet press about defective children and their treatment. He and Maxim Gorki were standing out against prison as a reformative influence; he himself was even opposed to milder forms, in fact to any form, of coercion in dealing with the young. "You are more in tune with the modern approach to the child than Maxim Gorki," I said. In part, however, he agreed with Gorki, he replied, for most of Russia's young generation were tainted with bad heredity, which the years of war and civic strife had accentuated. But rejuvenation could not be brought about by punishment or terror, he emphasized. "That is splendid," I remarked; "but are not terror and punishment the methods of dictatorship? And do you not approve of the latter?" He did, but only as a transitory factor, while Russia was being bled by the blockade and attacked on numerous fronts. "Once these have been liquidated, we will begin in earnest to build the real Socialist Republic, and the dictatorship will then go, of course." [. . .]

On my way back to the National I learned from my escort that the People's Commissar for Education was considered not only sentimental, but also a scatter-brain and a wastrel. He was doing very little for the *proletcult* (proletarian culture), spending huge sums instead to protect *bourgeois* art. Worst of all, he was devoting most of his time to saving the last remnants of the counter-revolutionary intelligentsia. With the co-operation of Maxim Gorki he had succeeded in reinstating the old professors and teachers in the Dom Utcheniy (Home of the Learned). There they could keep warm while at work and get their rations without standing in line. He had also committed a grave offence in establishing the so-called academic ration for the more noted writers, thinkers, and scientists of Russia, irrespective of party affiliation. The academic ration was far from luxury and by no means too plentiful; many of the responsible Communists received even better provisions, but they were bitter against Lunacharsky for "favouring" the intelligentsia, my informant declared. [. . .]

The two leading Communist women of Russia proved the greatest contrast. Angelica Balabanoff lacked what Kollontay possessed in abundance: the latter's fine figure, good looks, and youthful litheness, as well as her worldly polish and sophistication. But Angelica had something that far outweighed the external attributes of her handsome comrade. In her large sad eyes there shone profundity, compassion, and tenderness. The tribulations of her people, the birth-pangs of her native land, the suffering of the downtrodden she had served her whole life were deeply graven on her pallid face. I found her ill, crumpled up on the couch of her small room, but she immediately became all interest and concern for me. Why had I not let her know that I was her neighbour, she asked. She would have come to me at once. And why had I waited so long before seeking her out? Did I need anything? She would see to it that my wants should be looked after. Coming from the States, I must find it very hard to adjust myself to Russia's poverty. It was different with the native masses, who had never known anything except hunger and want. Ah, the Russian masses, their power of endurance, their capacity for suffering, their heroism in the face of such fearful odds! Children in their weakness, giants in their strength! She had come to know them better since "October" than in all her previous years in Russia. She had grown to believe in them with a more abiding faith and to feel with them an all-embracing love.

It was dusk; the city's noises did not penetrate the cell-like room. Yet it was vibrant with stirring sounds. The face before me, shrunken and ashy, was beauteous now in the glow of its inner light. Without a word from me Angelica Balabanoff had guessed my doubts and travail. I sensed that her tribute to the Russian masses was her unique way of making me feel that nothing mattered so much to the ultimate triumph of the Revolution as the spiritual resources of the people themselves. I inquired whether that was her meaning, and she nodded assent. She knew from her own struggle that mine must be very hard and she wanted me never to lose sight of the peaks of the "October" ascendancy.

I walked to her couch and stroked her thick braided black hair, already streaked with grey. I must call her Angelica, she said, drawing me to her heart. She asked me to ring for a comrade on the same floor to bring the samovar. She had some *varenya* (fruit jelly), and Swedish comrades had given her some biscuits and butter. She felt very guilty to enjoy such luxuries when the people did not have enough bread. But her stomach was bad; she could digest nothing, and so perhaps she was not so inconsistent as it might appear. Such selflessness amidst the callous indifference I had found everywhere moved me deeply. I broke down and wept as I had not since I had held my dear Helena in my arms at our final parting. Angelica became frightened. Had she said anything to cause me pain, or was I ill or in trouble? I opened my heart to her and poured out everything, my shocks, disillusionments, and nightmares, all the dreadful things and thoughts that had been oppressing me since my arrival. What was the answer, what the explanation, and where the responsibility?

Life itself is behind all frustration, Angelica replied, in an individual as well as in a social sense. Life was hard and cruel, and those who would live must also grow cruel and hard. Life is replete with eddies and whirlpools; its currents are violent and destructive. The sensitive, those shrinking from hurt, cannot hold their own against it. As with man, so with his ideas and ideals. The finer they are, the more humane, the sooner their death from the impact of Life. "But this is fatalism with a vengeance," I protested; "how can you harmonize such an attitude with your socialistic views and materialistic conception of history and human development?" Angelica explained that Russian reality had convinced her that life, and not theories, dictates the course of human events. "Life! Life!" I cried impatiently, "what is it but what the genius of man imparts to it? And what is the use of human striving if some mysterious power called Life can turn it to naught?" Angelica replied that there really was no particular sense in our efforts, except that living meant striving, reaching out for something better. But I should not mind her, she hastened to add. She was probably all wrong, and those others right who could pay the full measure life exacts. "You must go to see 'Ilich,'" she advised; only he, Lenin, could help me, for he knew how to meet the demands of Life. She would arrange an interview for me.

I left the dear little woman with mixed feelings. Soothed and comforted by her rich fount of love, I at the same time disapproved of her acquiescence in the evils and abuses about her. I had known of her as a fighter, always firm and unflinching in her stand. What had made her so passive now, I wondered. Communists enjoyed the right of criticism, as I had learned from the Bolshevik press. Why, then, did Angelica not use her pen and voice in and out of the party? It kept worrying me and I sought an opportunity to speak to her woman comrade who had served us tea. From her I learned that Angelica had been secretary of the Third International. In that capacity she had fought determinedly against the growing bureaucracy of the clique led by Zinoviev, Radek, and Bukharin. As a result she was most unceremoniously kicked out and denied all responsible work. [. . .] Her mental state was due to the methods employed by her party, including the wide-spread suffering, the terror, and the cheapness of human life. Angelica could not face them. [. . .]

When Angelica had suggested that I go to see Lenin, I decided to work out a memorandum of the most salient contradictions in Soviet life, but, not having heard anything more about the proposed interview, I had not done anything about

the matter. Angelica's telephone message one morning, informing me that "Ilich" was waiting to see Sasha and me, and that
his auto had come for us, was therefore most disconcerting. We
knew Lenin was so crowded with work that he was almost in-
accessible. The exception in our favour was a chance we could
not miss. We felt that even without our memorandum we
should find the right approach to our discussion; moreover, we
should have the opportunity to present to him the resolutions
our Moscow comrades had entrusted to us.

Lenin's auto rushed at furious speed along the congested
streets and into the Kremlin, past every sentry without being
halted for *propusks*. At the entrance of one of the ancient buildings that stood apart from the rest, we were asked to alight. An
armed guard was at the elevator, evidently already apprised of
our coming. Without a word, he unlocked the door and motioned us within, then locked it and put the key into his pocket.
We heard our names shouted to the soldier on the first floor,
the call repeated in the same loud voice at the next and the next.
A chorus was announcing our coming as the elevator slowly ascended. At the top a guard repeated the process of unlocking
and locking the elevator, then ushered us into a vast reception
hall with the announcement: "*Tovarishtchy* Goldman and
Berkman." We were asked to wait a moment, but almost an
hour passed before the ceremony of leading us to the seat of the
highest was resumed. A young man motioned us to follow him.
We passed through a number of offices teeming with activity,
the click of typewriters, and busy couriers. We were halted before a massive door ornamented with beautifully carved work.
Excusing himself for just a minute, our attendant disappeared
behind it. Presently the heavy door opened from within, and
our guide invited us to step in, himself vanishing and closing
the door behind us. We stood on the threshold awaiting the
next cue in the strange proceedings. Two slanting eyes were
fixed upon us with piercing penetration. Their owner sat behind a huge desk, everything on it arranged with the strictest
precision, the rest of the room giving the impression of the same
exactitude. A board with numerous telephone switches and a
map of the world covered the entire wall behind the man; glass

cases filled with heavy tomes lined the sides. A large oblong table hung with red; twelve straight-backed chairs, and several arm-chairs at the windows. Nothing else to relieve the orderly monot-ony, except the bit of flaming red.

The background seemed most fitting for one reputed for his rigid habits of life and matter-of-factness. Lenin, the man most idolized in the world and equally hated and feared, would have been out of place in surroundings of less severe simplicity.

"Ilich wastes no time on preliminaries. He goes straight to his objective," Zorin had once said to me with evident pride. In-deed, every step Lenin had made since 1917 testified to this. But if we had been in doubt, the manner of our reception and the mode of our interview would have quickly convinced us of the emotional economy of Ilich. His quick perception of its supply in others and his skill in making the utmost use of it for his pur-pose were extraordinary. No less amazing was his glee over any-thing he considered funny in himself or his visitors. Especially if he could put one at a disadvantage, the great Lenin would shake with laughter so as to compel one to laugh with him.

His sharp scrutiny having bared us to the bone, we were treated to a volley of questions, one following the other like ar-rows from his flint-like brain. America, her political and eco-nomic conditions—what were the chances of revolution there in the near future? The American Federation of Labor—was it all honeycombed with *bourgeois* ideology or was it only Gom-pers and his clique, and was the rank and file a fertile soil for boring from within? The I.W.W.—what was its strength, and were the anarchists actually as effective as our recent trial would seem to indicate? He had just finished reading our speeches in court. "Great stuff! Clear-cut analysis of the capi-talist system, splendid propaganda!" Too bad we could not have remained in the United States, no matter at what price. We were most welcome in Soviet Russia, of course, but such fight-ers were badly needed in America to help in the approaching revolution, "as many of your best comrades had been in ours." "And you, *Tovarishtch* Berkman, what an organizer you must be, like Shatoff. True metal, your comrade Shatoff; shrinks from nothing and can work like a dozen men. In Siberia now, commissar of railroads in the Far Eastern Republic. Many other anarchists hold important positions with us. Everything is open to them if they are willing to co-operate with us as true *ideiny* anarchists. You, *Tovarishtch* Berkman, will soon find your place. A pity, though, that you were torn away from America at this portentous time. And you, *Tovarishtch* Goldman? What a field you had! You could have remained. Why didn't you, even if *Tovarishtch* Berkman was shoved out? Well, you're here. Have you thought of the work you want to do? You are *ideiny* anarchists, I can see that by your stand on the war, your defence of 'October,' and your fight for us, your faith in the soviets. Just like your great comrade Malatesta,[18] who is entirely with Soviet Russia. What is it you prefer to do?"

Sasha was the first to get his breath. He began in English, but Lenin at once stopped him with a mirthful laugh. "Do you think I understand English? Not a word. Nor any other foreign languages. I am no good at them, though I have lived abroad for many years. Funny, isn't it?" And off he went in peals of laughter. Sasha continued in Russian. He was proud to hear his comrades praised so highly, he said; but why were anarchists in Soviet prisons? "Anarchists?" Ilich interrupted; "nonsense! Who told you such yarns, and how could you believe them? We do have bandits in prison, and Makhnovtsy,[19] but no *ideiny* anarchists."

"Imagine," I broke in, "capitalist America also divides the anarchists into two categories, philosophic and criminal. The first are accepted in the highest circles; one of them is even high in the councils of the Wilson Administration. The second category, to which we have the honour of belonging, is persecuted and often imprisoned. Yours also seems to be a distinction without a difference. Don't you think so?" Bad reasoning on my part, Lenin replied, sheer muddle-headedness to draw similar conclusions from different premises. Free speech is a *bourgeois* prejudice, a soothing plaster for social ills. In the Workers' Republic economic well-being talks louder than speech, and its freedom is far more secure. The proletarian dictatorship is steering that course. Just now it faces very grave obstacles, the greatest of them the opposition of the peasants. They need nails, salt, textiles, tractors, electrification. When we can give them these, they will be with us, and no counter-revolutionary power will be able to swerve them back. In the present state of Russia all prattle of freedom is merely food for the reaction trying to down Russia. Only bandits are guilty of that, and they must be kept under lock and key.

Sasha handed Lenin the resolutions of the anarchist conference and emphasized the assurance of the Moscow comrades that the imprisoned comrades were *ideiny* and not bandits. "The fact that our people ask to be legalized is proof that they are with the Revolution and the Soviets," we argued. Lenin took the document and promised to submit it to the next session of the Party Executive. We would be notified of its decision, he said, but in any event it was a mere trifle, nothing to disturb any true revolutionist. Was there anything else? We had fought in America for the political rights even of our opponents, we told him; the denial of them to our own comrades was therefore no trifle to us. I, for one, felt, I informed him, that I could not co-operate with a régime that persecuted anarchists or others for the sake of mere opinion. Moreover, there were even more appalling evils. How were we to reconcile them with the high goal he was aiming at? I mentioned some of them. His reply was that my attitude was *bourgeois* sentimentality. The proletarian dictatorship was engaged in a life-and-death struggle, and small considerations could not be permitted to weigh in the scale. Russia was making giant strides at home and abroad. It was igniting the world revolution, and here I was lamenting over a little blood-letting. It was absurd, and I must get over it. "Do something," he advised; "that will be the best way of regaining your revolutionary balance."

Lenin might be right, I thought. I would take his advice. I would start at once, I said. Not with any work within Russia, but with something of propaganda value for the United States. I should like to organize a society of Russian Friends of American Freedom, an active body to give support to America's struggle for liberty, as the American Friends of Russian Freedom had done in aid of Russia against the tsarist régime.

Lenin had not moved in his seat during the entire time, but

now he almost leaped out of it. He swung round and stood facing us. "That's a brilliant idea!" he exclaimed, chuckling and rubbing his hands. "A fine practical proposal. You must proceed to carry it out at once. And you, *Tovarishtch* Berkman, will you co-operate in it?" Sasha replied that we had talked the matter over and had already worked out the details of the plan. We could start immediately if we had the necessary equipment. No difficulty in that, Lenin assured us; we would be supplied with everything—an office, a printing outfit, couriers, and whatever funds would be needed. We must send him our prospectus of work and the itemized expenses involved in the project. The Third International[20] would take care of the matter. It was the proper channel for our venture, and it would afford us every help.

In blank astonishment we looked at each other and at Lenin. Simultaneously we began to explain that our efforts could prove effective only if free from any affiliation with known Bolshevik organizations. It must be carried out in our own way; we knew the American psychology and how best to conduct the work. But before we could proceed further, our guide suddenly appeared, as unobtrusively as he had left, and Lenin held out his hand to us in good-bye. "Don't forget to send me the prospectus," he called after us.

[. . .] We agreed with Lenin in one thing, the need of getting to work. Not, however, in any political capacity or in a Soviet bureau. We must find something that would bring us in direct touch with the masses and enable us to serve them. Moscow was the seat of the Government with more State functionaries than workers, bureaucratic to the last degree. Sasha had visited a number of factories, all of them in a palpably neglected and deserted condition. In most of them the Soviet officials and members of the Communist *yacheika* (cell) far outnumbered the actual producers. He had talked with the workers and found them embittered by the arrogance and arbitrary methods of the industrial bureaucracy. Sasha's impressions only served to strengthen my conviction that Moscow was no place for us. If at least Lunacharsky had kept his promise! But he was swamped with work, he wrote, and unable just then to call the teachers' conference. It might take weeks before it could be done. He understood how difficult it was for people used to doing things in their own independent manner to fit themselves into a groove. But it was the only effective place in Russia and I would have to reconcile myself to that. Meanwhile I must keep in touch with him, his letter concluded.

It was a subtle hint that the dictatorship was all-pervading and that it would brook no independent effort. Not in Moscow, at any rate. After all, every seat of government inevitably breeds the martinet and the flunkey, the courtier and the spy, a herd of hangers-on fed by the official hand. Moscow was evidently no exception. We could not find our place there, nor come close to the toiling masses. One more thing we would attempt—get to see our comrade Kropotkin and then back to Petrograd, we decided.

We learned that George Lansbury and Mr. Barry were about to go to Dmitrov in a special train. We decided to ask permission to join them, though we were not elated over the prospect of seeing Peter in the presence of two newspaper men. [. . .]

The train crawled snail-like, stopping at every water-tank. It was late evening when we at last reached the house. We found Peter ill and worn-looking. He appeared a mere shadow of the sturdy man I had known in Paris and London in 1907. Since my coming to Russia I had been repeatedly assured by the most prominent Communists that Kropotkin lived in very comfortable circumstances and that he lacked neither food nor fuel; and here were Peter, his wife, Sophie, and their daughter, Alexandra, actually living in one room by no means sufficiently heated. The temperature in the other rooms was below zero, so that they could not be inhabited. Their rations, sufficient to exist on, had until recently been supplied by the Dmitrov co-operative society. That organization had since been liquidated, like so many other similar institutions, and most of its members arrested and taken to the Butirky prison in Moscow. How did they manage to exist, we inquired. Sophie explained that they had a cow and enough produce from her garden for the winter. The comrades from the Ukraine, particularly Makhno, had contrived to supply them with extra provisions. They would have managed to better advantage had not Peter been ailing of late and in need of more nourishing food. [. . .]

Peter would accept nothing from the Bolsheviki, Sophie told us. Only a short time previously, when the rouble still stood well, he had refused the offer of 250,000 roubles from the Government Publication Department for the right to issue his literary work. Since the Bolsheviki had expropriated others, they might as well help themselves to his books, he had said. But it would not be done with his consent. He had never willingly dealt with any government and he had no intention of doing so with the one that in the name of socialism had abrogated every revolutionary and ethical value. [. . .]

Sasha was speaking to Peter of the maze of revolutionary contradictions we had found in Russia, the varied interpretations we had heard of the causes of the crying evils, and our interview with Lenin. We were eager to hear Peter's view-point and get his reactions to the situation. He replied that it was what it had always been to Marxism and its theories. He had foreseen its dangers and he had always warned against them. All anarchists had done so, and he himself had dealt with them in nearly every one of his writings. True, none of us had fully realized to what proportions the Marxian menace would grow. Perhaps it was not so much Marxism as the Jesuitical spirit of its dogmas. The Bolsheviki were poisoned by it, their dictatorship surpassing the autocracy of the Inquisition. Their power was strengthened by the blustering statesmen of Europe. The blockade, the Allied support of the counter-revolutionary elements, the intervention, and all the other attempts to crush the Revolution had resulted in silencing every protest against Bolshevik tyranny within Russia itself. "Is there no one to speak out against it?" I demanded, "no one whose voice would carry weight? Yours, for instance, dear comrade?" Peter smiled sadly. I would know better, he said, after I had been awhile longer in the country. The gag was the most complete in the world. He had protested, of course, and so had others, among them the venerable Vera Figner,[21] as well as Maxim Gorki on several occasions. It had no effect whatever, nor was it possible to do any

writing with the Cheka constantly at one's door. One could not
keep "incriminating" things in one's house nor expose others to
the peril of discovery. It was not fear; it was the realization of
the futility and impossibility of reaching the world from the inner prisons of the Cheka. The main drawback, however, was
the enemies surrounding Russia. Anything said or written
against the Bolsheviki was bound to be interpreted by the outside world as an attack upon the Revolution and as alignment
with the reactionary forces. The anarchists in particular were
between two fires. They could not make peace with the formidable power of the Kremlin, nor could they join hands with the
enemies of Russia. Their only alternative at present, it seemed
to Peter, was to find some work of direct benefit to the masses.
He was glad that we had decided on that. "Ridiculous of Lenin
to want to bind you to the apron-strings of the party," he declared. "It shows how far mere shrewdness is from wisdom. No
one can deny Lenin's shrewdness, but neither in his attitude to
the peasants nor in his appraisal of those within or outside the
reach of corruption has he shown real judgment or sagacity."

It was growing late and Sophie had been trying to prevail
upon Peter to retire. But he persistently declined. [. . .] Gentle
and gallant was our Peter even in his fatigue. Nothing would do
but he must see us to the exit and once more clasp us lovingly to
his heart.

Our train was not to start till two a.m., and it was only eleven.
The woman porter was fast asleep. She had forgotten to look
after the fire, and the car was bitterly cold. The boys set to
work over the stove, but it would yield nothing except smoke.
Meanwhile Lansbury, wrapped up to his ears in his great fur
coat, held forth on what a pity it was that Peter Kropotkin's age
disqualified him from taking an active part in Soviet affairs.
Living away from the centre, Kropotkin was not in a position
to do justice to the grandiose achievements of the Bolsheviki, he
reiterated. I was almost frozen and too miserable over Peter's
condition to argue. But the boys did it for the three of us. At the
Moscow station Sasha had another tilt with the London editor.
Starved and half-naked children besieged us for a piece of

bread. I had sandwiches on hand and we gave them to the kids, who devoured them ravenously. "A terrible sight," Sasha remarked. "Look here, Berkman, you are too sentimental," Lansbury retorted; "I could show you any number of poverty-stricken children in the East End of London." "I am sure you could," Sasha replied, "but you forget that the Revolution *has* taken place in Russia, not in England." [. . .]

I could not bear Moscow any longer. It had grown into a veritable monster that I had to escape lest it destroy me. Petrograd held out the hope of relief in useful labour. And there was also my gnawing longing for news from my old home. Five months had passed without a word from anyone. The address we had left with our friends in America was Petrograd. My yearning was mingled with some unaccountable apprehension, both combining into the *idée fixe* that I must hasten back to the northern city.

Mail was actually awaiting us there, received four weeks previously. Why had it not been forwarded, we asked Liza Zorin. "What was the use?" she replied; "I did not think anything from America so important and interesting as what you must have seen and heard in Moscow." The letters were from Fitzi and Stella. Not "so important"—only news of the death of my beloved Helena. What could personal sorrow mean to people who had become cogs in the wheel that was crushing so many at every turn? I myself seemed to have turned into one of the cogs. I could find no tears for the loss of my darling sister, no tears or regrets. Only paralysing numbness and a larger void.

My deportation, Stella wrote, had proved the last blow to Helena's shattered condition. She had grown steadily worse from the moment she had heard about it. Death was more kind to her than life: it came quickly through a stroke. [. . .]

On our return to Petrograd we found our fellow-passengers of the *Buford* considerably diminished in numbers. Some of them had succeeded in getting sent to their native places. Others, who in America had been bitter opponents of our defence of the Bolsheviki, became reconciled to the Soviet régime. In Rome now, they argued, they would howl with the Romans. The eleven Communists among the deportees were entirely in clover. They found the flesh-pots prepared for them, and the tables laden. They had but to grab the best place and morsels.

The remaining group was in a deplorable condition. Their attempts to secure useful work, for which years of labour in the United States had qualified them, brought no results. They were being sent from one institution to another, from commissar to commissar, without anyone able to decide whether their efforts were needed and where.

Here was Russia, famished for what these men could and longed to give, yet their productive capacities were compelled to lie fallow, and everything was being done to turn their devotion to hatred. Was this to be the lot of other workers to be deported from the United States and of those who would flock to Soviet Russia to aid the Revolution, we wondered. We could not sit by without at least essaying some effort to prevent the repetition of such criminal stupidity. Sasha proposed a clearinghouse for the American deportees, those already in Russia and the others that were being expected. [. . .] His project included the classification of the refugees by trade and occupation and assignment to useful and needed work. "Think of the gain to the Revolution if American training and experience were sensibly directed into productive channels," Sasha commented. His plan also provided an immediate opening for our own usefulness and that of other deportees in the city. [. . .]

Now they achieved in a fortnight what Ravich and Kaplan admitted would have ordinarily taken months to accomplish. Three old germ-eaten buildings were renovated and equipped for the use of the expected deportees; the distribution of their rations organized so as to save their standing in queues, medical attention prepared in case of need, and employment secured for the "swimming" contingent.

Sasha and Ethel[22] had in the meantime taken charge of the welcome to be given the deportees on the Latvian border. They were awaiting them there, with two trains held in readiness to bring the expected thousand refugees to Petrograd. They spent two weeks in vain waiting, only to find out that another blunder had been added to the chaos and confusion of the Soviet situation. The wireless announcing returning war prisoners had been misread by the Foreign Office to mean American deportees. [. . .]

We proposed to use the buildings we had prepared for the benefit of the war prisoners, and Mme Ravich favoured the suggestion. But the men were under the jurisdiction of the War Department, and she felt she must first get permission. Nothing further was heard of the matter. The quarters renovated with so much effort and time were sealed up and three able-bodied militiamen stationed on guard. All our labour was wasted, and Sasha's plan of organizing the deportees or the war prisoners for useful work was allowed to go by the board.

The same disheartening results met our other attempts to do practical work outside of the State machine. We would not be daunted, however.

The palatial residences of the former rich in the part of Petrograd known as Kammenny Ostrov (Island) were to be turned into rest-homes for toilers. "Marvellous idea, isn't it?" Zorin remarked to us; "we must complete it within six weeks." Only American speed and efficiency could accomplish the job on time. Would we help? We took the work in hand and became absorbed in it, until again we struck the impassable wall of Soviet bureaucracy.

From the start we had insisted that at least one warm meal a day should be provided for the workers employed in the preparation of rest-homes for their brothers. I had undertaken to supervise the cooking and the equitable distribution of the rations. For a while all went well; the men were satisfied with the arrangements, and their labours were making unusual progress—unusual for Russians, at any rate. But presently the Bolshevik staffs and their favourites began to increase and the rations of the workers to diminish. The latter were not long in perceiving that they were being robbed of their share for the sake of unnecessary office-holders and hangers-on. Their interest in the work showed signs of waning and presently the effects became apparent. We protested to Zorin against the farce of ill-treating one set of workers to enable another set to enjoy leisure and a rest. Equally we objected to the peremptory eviction from their homes of people whose only offence was a university degree. Old teachers and professors had been occupying some houses on the island ever since October, and no one had troubled them in any way. Now they and their families were to be deprived of home without any possibility of securing another roof over their heads. Zorin had requested Sasha to have the eviction orders carried out. But Sasha emphatically refused to act as the bully of the Communist State. Zorin felt indignant at our "rank sentimentality." A man with Berkman's revolutionary record, he said, should not shrink from any task; it made no difference whether the *bourgeois* parasites ended in the gutter or threw themselves into the Neva. [. . .] Before long, however, we found others in our places, persons more pliable in the hands of the political machine. We understood.

The rest-homes were inaugurated with much éclat. To us the rows of rusty iron bedsteads in the vast salons, with their furniture of faded silk and plush, looked tawdry, cold, and uninviting. No worker with any self-respect could feel at ease or enjoy a rest in such surroundings. Many shared our views, and some even felt convinced that none but those within the party or hanging on to its coat-tails would ever see the inside of the Rest Homes for Workers on the Kammenny Ostrov. [. . .]

The Sovietsky soup-kitchens were an abomination, Zorin had repeatedly told us. Could we suggest some improvement, he asked. Sasha again became all interest, completely immersing himself in his new project of reorganizing the nauseating dining-rooms. In a few days he had outlined a complete project, every item provided for in his usual painstaking manner. [. . .]

But again the bureaucracy blocked every move initiated without them. Difficulties began to appear in the most unexpected quarters. Officials were too busy to aid Sasha's work, and, after all, wholesome eating-places were not so important in the scale of the world revolution that was expected to break out momentarily. It was absurd to lay stress on immediate amelioration in the face of the general situation. At best it could have no vital effect on the course of the Revolution. And Berkman could do more important work. He should not busy himself as a reformer. It was most disappointing, for everyone had thought him to be a revolutionist of steel and iron. It was naïve of Berkman to claim that feeding the masses was the first concern of the Revolution, the care of the people, their contentment and joy, its main hope and safety, and indeed its only *raison d'être* and moral meaning. Such sentimentality was the purest *bourgeois* ideology. The Red Army and the Cheka were the strength of the Revolution, and its best defence. The capitalist world knew it and was trembling before the might of armed Russia.

One more hope perished, like the preceding ones. [. . .] Sasha's determination and strength had never been greater. My Yiddish perseverance also refused to surrender. All Soviet streams do not lead to the same muddy pools, we thought. [. . .]

I talked to the wife of Lashevich, Zinoviev's friend, high in the Bolshevik councils, about the condition of the hospitals. I was a trained nurse and I should be happy to give my services in improving them. She volunteered to call the matter to the attention of Comrade Pervoukhin, the Petrograd Board of Health Commissar. Weeks passed before I received word to call on him. I hastened to the Board of Health.

A trained nurse, months in Russia already and yet not assigned to him for service, Pervoukhin exclaimed. I should have known that he was desperately in need of just such aid. The hospitals were in a wretched condition; there was great scarcity of dispensaries and a lack of trained help, not to speak of the dearth of medical facilities and surgical instruments. [. . .] He would take me for the first tour of inspection as soon as I was ready to start. Could I report to him in the morning?

[. . .] I would do my utmost, of course, I could promise him that. He would expect nothing else from a *tovarishtch,* he replied, from an old revolutionist and Communist, as he had been informed. I was indeed a Communist, I assented, but of the anarchist school. Oh yes, he understood that, but there was really no difference. Many anarchists had realized this and they were entirely with the party, working with the Bolsheviki and doing finely. "I also am with you," I said, "in the defence of the Revolution, even to my last breath." Not with the Communism of the dictatorship, however, I explained. I had not been able to reconcile myself to that, for I could not see the remotest relationship between the coerced and forced form of State communism and that of the free and voluntary co-operation of anarchist communism.

I had so often seen Communists on such occasions instantly alter their tone and manner that I was not surprised at the sudden change in Commissar Pervoukhin. The kindly physician so deeply concerned in the people's health, the humanitarian who had a moment previously so lamented his lack of nurses to minister to the ill and afflicted, immediately became the political fanatic fairly oozing antagonism and resentment. Did my differing view-point matter in the care of the sick, or did he think it would affect my usefulness as a nurse, I inquired. He forced a sickly smile, replying that in Soviet Russia everyone who wants to work is welcome. His ideas are not questioned, provided he is a true revolutionist willing to set all political considerations aside. Would I do so? I could make no pledges except one, I replied. I would help him to the best of my ability.

I called the next day and every day for a week. Pervoukhin did not take me on the planned tour of inspection. [. . .]

With the help of my Astoria Hotel neighbour, young Kibalchich, I succeeded in visiting a few hospitals. Their condition was appalling. The true cause of it was not so much poor equipment or the lack of nurses. It was the omnipresent machine, the Communist "cell," the commissars, the eternal suspicion and surveillance. Physicians and surgeons with splendid records in their profession, touchingly devoted to their work, were hampered at every turn and paralysed in the atmosphere of dread, hatred, and fear. Even the Communists among them were helpless. Some of them had not yet been entirely divested of human feeling by the régime. Being of the intelligentsia, they were considered doubtful characters and were kept in leash. I understood why Pervoukhin could not have me on his staff.

These rude awakenings in the Soviet Arcadia of dictatorship were followed by repeated and more forcible jolts. They helped still further to uproot my cherished belief in the Bolsheviki as the clarion voice of "October."

The militarization of labour, rushed through the ninth Party Congress with typical Tammany Hall steam-roller methods, definitely turned every worker into a galley-slave. The substitution of one-man power in the shops and mills in place of co-operative management placed the masses again under the thumb of the very elements they had for three years been taught to hate as the worst menace. The "specialists" and professional men of the intelligentsia, formerly denounced as vampires and enemies guilty of sabotaging the Revolution, were now installed in high positions and clothed with almost supreme power over the men in the factories. It was a step that with one stroke destroyed the principal achievements of "October," the right of the workers to industrial control. Insult was added to injury by the introduction of the labour book, which virtually stamped everyone a felon, robbed him of the last vestiges of freedom, deprived him of the choice of place and occupation, and fastened him to a given district without the right of straying too far, on pain of severest penalties. True, these reactionary and anti-revolutionary measures were determinedly fought by a substantial minority within the party, as well as denounced by the people at large. We were among them, Sasha even more vigorously than I, although his faith in the Bolsheviki was still very strong. [. . .]

For hours he would argue against my "impatience" and deficient judgment of far-reaching issues, my kid-glove approach to the Revolution. [. . .] The continued danger from the outside, the natural indolence of the Russian worker and his failure to increase production, the peasants' lack of the most necessary implements, and their resultant refusal to feed the cities had compelled the Bolsheviki to pass those desperate measures. Of course he regarded such methods as counter-revolutionary and bound to defeat their purpose. Still, it was preposterous to suspect men like Lenin or Trotsky of deliberate treachery to the Revolution. [. . .]

I assured Sasha that nothing was further from my thought than to charge the Bolsheviki with treachery. Indeed, I considered them quite consistent, truer to their aims than those of our own comrades who were working with them. Especially did I feel Lenin as a man hewn out of one piece. To be sure, his policies had undergone extraordinary changes; there was no denying his great agility as a political acrobat. But he had never deviated from his objective. His bitterest enemies would not accuse him of that. But his objective was the very crux of Russia's tragedy, I insisted. It was the Communist State, its absolute supremacy and exclusive power. [. . .] In point of clarity of vision, concentration of will, and unflagging determination Lenin had my respect. But as to the effect of his purposes and methods upon the Revolution, I considered him the greatest menace, more pernicious than the combined interventionists, because his objective was more elusive, his methods more deceptive.

Sasha did not gainsay this. [. . .] He himself had come to see that revolution in action is a quite different thing from revolution in the realm of theory mouthed by parlour radicals. It meant blood and iron, and it was unavoidable.

The dear companionship of my old pal and our intellectual harmony had mitigated much of the lacerating process of finding my way through the Soviet labyrinth. Sasha was all that had been left me from the tornado that had swept over my life. [. . .] I was certain my friend would in time realize the falsity of his position. I knew that his desperate attempt to defend Bolshevik methods was his last stand in a lost battle, the battle we had been the first to wage in the United States in behalf of the October Revolution.

Among our many callers during our Moscow stay had been an interesting young woman, Alexandra Timofeyevna Shakol. [. . .] An expedition was being planned, she explained, that was to cover the length and breadth of the country in search of documents bearing on the Revolution and the revolutionary movement of Russia since its inception. The collected material would ultimately serve as archives for the study of the great upheaval. Would we join such a venture?

For a moment we had been carried away by the plan and by the opportunity it offered to see Russia in her Revolutionary everyday life, to learn at first hand what the Revolution had done for the masses and how it affected their existence. We might never have such another chance. But on second thought we felt it bitter irony that would condemn us to collect dead material amidst the raging life of Russia. Thirty years long we had stood in the very thick of the social battle, always on the firing line. Could we now be content with anything less in our reborn native land? [. . .]

Since our return to Petrograd we had been so busy chasing

Soviet windmills, so eagerly reaching out for a new hold, that we had hardly thought of our comrade Shakol and her proposal. But with every hope of useful work gone, her offer once more came to our minds. It might afford an escape from our meaningless existence. [. . .] We finally decided to try it, since nothing else was open to us. "If only the new project will also not turn out a bubble," I said to Sasha on our way to the Winter Palace, where the Museum of the Revolution was located. [. . .]

We were received by the secretary, M. B. Kaplan, a man in the middle thirties, of pleasant and intelligent appearance. [. . .] Though it was the latter part of May, the vast chambers of the Winter Palace were breathing a penetrating chill. We were warmly clad, yet we quickly felt benumbed with the cold. We marvelled at the men and women working in the fearful dampness all through the severe months of the Petrograd winter. They had been employed there for almost three years now. Their faces were streaked with blue blotches, their hands frostbitten. Some had contracted severe cases of rheumatism and tubercular [afflictions]. His own health had become undermined, the secretary admitted. But it was revolutionary Russia, and he and his co-workers were happy to be privileged to help in building its future. Most of them, like himself, were non-partisan. He was all eagerness to be able to count on our aid. His enthusiasm was too infectious to resist, and we agreed. [. . .]

We left the genial secretary and his collaborators in a more cheerful frame of mind. We did not yet feel about the work before us as did the other members of the museum. We knew we could not for long be content with merely collecting parchments when more important work was so urgently needed which we might do. But the devotion and fortitude of those people had lifted the weight of despair from our hearts. [. . .] These great souls redeemed for us much that was hateful in the Bolshevik régime.

Preparations for the expedition were progressing rather slowly, leaving us time to visit museums, art galleries, and similar places of interest, as well as to attend to other things. A report had reached us of the arrest of two anarchist girls, aged fifteen and seventeen, charged with the circulation of a protest against the degrading aspects of the labour book and also against the unbearable conditions of the politicals in the Shpalerny and Gorokhovaya jails in the city. Several Petrograd comrades called on us in the matter and we immediately addressed ourselves to the leading Bolsheviki. [. . .]

On this occasion a wink from Zinoviev and Mme Ravich had immediate effect upon Bakayev.[23] He also lived at the Astoria and he phoned me to call on him. He would release the arrested anarchist girls, he informed me, provided we were willing to vouch for it that that would stop their "bandit activities." [. . .] I assured the Cheka chief that it would be grist to the American prison mills to learn that the jails in Soviet Russia were no better than those in the States. This seemed to reach Bakayev in the right spot. He would give the girls another chance, he declared, for, after all, they were proletarians even if they had not yet realized that they must not injure their own class by criticizing the dictatorship. He would also see what improvement the jails required, though conditions had been greatly exaggerated.

Getting people out of jail had been among our various activities in America. But we had never dreamed that we should find the same necessity in revolutionary Russia. [. . .]

My long-awaited opportunity to visit factories and possibly to talk to the workers at the bench came when Mme Ravich requested me to act as guide to a certain American journalist who had suddenly appeared in Petrograd.[24] [. . .]

The function of an official cicerone was not exactly to my liking. But I did not care to refuse Ravich who had always been responsive to my intercession for unfortunates. Moreover, I felt that the Russian situation was too great and vital and that I had not yet grasped it fully, though I had reached a definite decision not to work within Bolshevik political confines. Most important to me was it not to be quoted by any American paper against Soviet Russia, not while the latter was still forced to fight for life itself on so many fronts. I was therefore in the predicament of not wanting Clayton to secure information by my aid and I did not cherish the prospect of having to tell him deliberate lies. I reasoned that Mme Ravich knew what she was about when she had given Clayton permission to visit factories. They were probably not so bad as had been reported to me. Or she may have thought that with me as guide things would be made to appear less harsh. Fortunately Sasha was accompanying us. That would give one of us a chance to lag behind and talk to the workers while the other would interpret to Clayton the official version of conditions.

The Putilov works proved to be in a forlorn state, most of the machines deserted, others out of repair, the place filthy and neglected. While Sasha was explaining to Clayton what the superintendent of the shop was relating, I lingered behind. I found the men very unwilling to talk until I mentioned that I was a *tovarishtch* from America and not a Bolshevik. That made a big difference. They could tell me a great deal, they said, but even the walls had ears. Not a day passed but what some of their fellows failed to return to work. Sick? No, but they had protested a little too loud. I urged that, as the authorities had informed me, the workers in the Putilovsky, being engaged in one of the vital industries, received considerably better rations than other toilers—two pounds of bread a day and special shares of other products. The men stared at me in amazement. I might try their bread, one of them suggested, holding out a black chunk to me. "Bite hard," he said ironically. I tried, but knowing I could ill afford a dentist's bill, I had to return the leathery piece, much to the amusement of the group clustered about me. I suggested that the Communists could not be blamed for the bad bread and the scarcity of it. If the Putilov workers and their brothers in other industries would increase production, the peasants would be able to raise more grain. Yes, they replied, that was the yarn given them every day in explanation of the militarization of labour. It had been hard enough to work on empty stomachs when they were not being driven. Now it was altogether impossible. The new decree had only added to the general misery and bitterness. It was taking the workers too far away from their villages, which formerly had helped them out with provisions. Besides, the number of officials and overseers had been increased and they too had to be fed. "Of the seven thousand employed here, only two thousand are actual producers," an old worker near me remarked. Hadn't I seen the markets, another man demanded in a whisper. Had I noticed much scarcity there for those who had the price to pay? There was no time for a reply. At a warning from their neighbours the men hastened back to their benches and I joined my companions.

Our next objective looked like a military camp, with armed sentinels stationed all around the huge warehouse and about the mill inside. "Why so many guards?" Sasha asked the Commissar in charge. The flour had of late been disappearing by the carload, came the reply, and the soldiers were there to cope with the evil. They had not succeeded in stopping the thefts, but some offenders had been apprehended. They had proved to be workers misled by a gang of speculators. Somehow the official explanation did not sound plausible. I slackened my pace in the hope of getting close to some of the millmen. I knew the right password: "From America, bringing you the solidaric greetings of the militant proletariat and their gift of cigarettes." A young chap with a firm jaw and intelligent eyes attracted my attention as he passed me with a sack of flour on his shoulders. When he returned to pick up another, I tried my magic key. It worked. Would he tell me why armed soldiers were there? Didn't I know of the new decree *militarizing* labour, he demanded. The workers had resented it as an insult to their revolutionary manhood. As a result their brother soldiers, who had helped them during the October days, were now installed over them as watch-dogs. I asked about the theft of flour and whether the guards were not there to prevent it. The man smiled sadly. No one knew better than the commissars, he said, who was stealing the flour, for they themselves passed it through the gates. "And the Revolution? Has it given you workers nothing?" I questioned. "Oh, yes," he replied, "but it has been checked long ago. Now it is a stagnant pool. It will break out again, though, never fear."

In the evening, when Sasha and I compared notes, we agreed that we had seen all we wanted to know of Soviet factory conditions. We could leave the doubtful honour to the official guides, who were less squeamish about turning black into white, and grey into crimson hues. Sasha emphatically refused to act again as cicerone and I completed my unsolicited job by taking Clayton the next morning to the Laferm Tobacco Works. We found them in good condition, because the former owner and manager himself was still in charge.

Before long, Clayton departed, declaring that he would soon return for a longer stay and a more thorough study of conditions. His wife was Russian, he said, and she would serve as his guide, which would make it unnecessary for him to impose on our time and good will. He would guard against making misleading statements concerning Russia, he faithfully promised.

"Misleading," I mused. The poor chap could not know that every day of my Russian existence was misleading, misleading others as well as myself. Would the time ever come when I should once more stand firmly in my own boots, I wondered.

Preparations for the expedition were progressing very slowly, while my nervous tension almost reached breaking-point. Whatever poise I had of late gained had been destroyed by my recent impressions of the appalling conditions under which the masses were living and toiling. The arrival of Angelica Balabanoff somewhat helped to lighten my frame of mind. She had been sent from Moscow to complete arrangements for the reception of the expected British Labour Mission. [. . .]

The mission at last arrived, most of its members of the usual Anglo-Saxon better-than-thou attitude. They were against intervention, of course, and they boasted of having repudiated the attacks on Soviet Russia, but as to revolution or communism, no, thank you, none of that for them. Their reception was calculated to speak to the larger audience of the British labouring masses and to the workers of the entire world. No effort was to be spared to make the occasion propagandistically effective. The grand military display on the square of the Uritsky Palace was but the initial part of the program. Other functions were to prove even more persuasive. The dinners at the Narishkin Palace, its tables laden with the best starving Russia could command, the personally conducted tours through the model schools, selected factories, and rest-homes, theatrical performances, ballets, concerts, and opera, with the members of the mission in the former Tsar's loge, composed some of the festivities. British reserve could not resist such hospitality. Most members of the mission fell for the show and became the more pliable the longer they stayed.

Some of them exerted their best logic to persuade me that the dictatorship and the Cheka were inevitable in a country as backward as Russia, with her people for centuries used to despotic rule. [. . .]

I walked away to the rear of the box to watch the rest of the ballet undisturbed by British complacent superiority. Presently the door opened and a man in military uniform entered. When the lights went on again, I recognized him as Leon Trotsky. What a change in his appearance and bearing within three years! He was no longer the pale, lean, and narrow-chested exile I had seen in New York in the spring of 1917. The man in the box seemed to have grown in breadth and height, though he showed no superfluous flesh. His pale face was bronze now, his reddish hair and beard considerably streaked with grey. He had tasted power and he looked conscious of his authority. He carried himself with proud mien, and there was disdain in his eyes, even contempt, as he glanced at the British guests. He spoke to no one and soon left. He did not recognize me, nor did I make myself known to him. The gulf between our worlds had widened too far to be reached across.

There were certain members of the British Mission, however, not entirely inclined to look in open-mouthed wonder at the things about them, with their mental eyes shut. These were not of the labouring element. One of them was Mr. Bertrand Russell.[25] Very politely but decisively he had from the very first refused to be officially chaperoned. He preferred to go about himself. He also showed no elation over the honour of being quartered in a palace and fed on special morsels. Suspicious person, that Russell, the Bolsheviki whispered. But then, what can you expect of a *bourgeois*? [. . .]

Sasha had in the meantime succeeded in securing a car for the Museum Expedition. It was an old dilapidated Pullman containing six compartments, but soon he had it cleaned up, painted, and disinfected for our use. Having proved so successful where others had failed, the museum appointed Sasha general manager of the expedition. Shakol was nominated secretary, while I was entrusted with three jobs, besides the work of collecting historical material, in which we all shared. I was chosen treasurer, housekeeper, and cook. A Russian couple on our staff were supposed to be experts on revolutionary documents. The sixth in our group was a young Jewish Communist, whose special work was to visit local party institutions. As the only Communist in our circle he felt at first quite lost, being among three anarchists and two non-partisans.

Our car needed mattresses, blankets, dishes, and similar utensils, for which I received an order from Yatmanov on the supplies of the Winter Palace. Equipped with this "order," I went down to the basements of the palace, where the Tsar's household goods were stored. The transitoriness of station and power had never before struck me so forcibly as when looking at the wealth that had but recently been used by the reigning family on its State occasions. The toil of every country and clime was gathered there in priceless porcelain, rare silver, copper, glass, and damask. Room after room was stacked to the ceiling with utensils and plate, thickly covered with dust, mute witnesses to the glory that was no more. And there I was, rummaging in all that magnificence for dishes for our expedition! Could any legend be more fantastic, more significant of the ephemeral nature of human destiny?

It took a whole day to select what was suitable for our use, and even at that the things were more fit for a museum. I could not get excited over the fact that we should eat our herring and potatoes, and if lucky also *borscht*, from the plate that had fed the Lord of all the Russias and his family. It amused me to think, however, how the newspapers in America would play up such an incident. Berkman and Goldman, arch-anarchists, using the crested linen and china of the Romanovs! And the freeborn Americans, such as the Daughters of the Revolution, dying for the sight of royalty, dead or alive, or even for some souvenir of an old boot that had squeezed a royal foot!

On June 30, 1920, just seven months after we had landed on Soviet soil, our renovated car was hitched to a night train, known as "Maxim Gorki," and headed for Moscow. It being the "centre," we had to stop off there for additional credentials from various departments. [. . .]

There was great excitement in the city, due to the arrival of a number of foreign delegates for the Second Congress of the Red Trade-Union International. Among them we were delighted to find some Anarcho-Syndicalists from Spain, France, Italy, Germany, and Scandinavia. There were also labour men from England, more militant and less comfortable than their countrymen on the British Mission. Learning of our presence in Moscow, they sought us out and we had many conferences together. [. . .]

Our foreign comrades were accredited representatives of militant labour bodies. They were not likely to use anything I might tell them to the detriment of the Revolution, as newspaper reporters might do. I had no intention of biasing them, but neither did I think that I should keep the facts from them. I wanted at least our own comrades in Europe and America to behold the reverse side of the shiny Soviet medal. [. . .]

Europe and America seemed removed from me by decades. It was gratifying to have them brought closer by our foreign visitors and to learn from them about the anarchist and revolutionary labour activities outside of Russia. To the request of the delegates that I send a message to the workers abroad, I replied: "May they emulate the spirit of their Russian brothers in the coming revolution, but not their naïve faith in political leaders, no matter how fervent their protestations and how red their slogans! That alone can safe-guard future revolutions from being harnessed to the State and enslaved again by its bureaucratic whip." [. . .]

Our red-painted car on a side track at the Moscow railroad station attracted many visitors, among them Henry G. Alsberg and Albert Boni,[26] who had come to Russia. Both were envious of our trip and eager to come with us. Of the two men, Sasha and I liked Alsberg the best. We told him we would prevail on the members of our expedition to allow him to come with us if he would get the necessary credentials from the Soviet authorities.

On the day of our departure he arrived with written permission from Zinoviev, the Foreign Office, and the Cheka. The representative of the Cheka in the Foreign Office insisted, however, Alsberg would have to secure an additional visa from the local Moscow Cheka. Karakhan's secretary (Foreign Office), under whose jurisdiction he was, definitely informed him that he did not need this extra visa and the Foreign Office "guaranteed" he would not be molested if he went on the expedition. Alsberg hesitated but we urged him to take a chance without the *proposk* of the Moscow Cheka. His American passport and the fact that he represented two pro-Soviet newspapers should save him from serious difficulties. Our secretary consented that he should join us, and there was an extra bunk in Sasha's compartment. Thereupon he decided to become the seventh member of our company. [. . .]

Our first important stop was at Kharkov. It looked prosperous after Petrograd and Moscow. The people, fine physical types of humanity, appeared well fed and carefree in spite of the numerous invasions, changes of government, and the ravages the city had experienced. There was evident a scarcity only of wearing-apparel, particularly of shoes, hats, and hosiery. Men, women, and children were bare-legged, some wearing queer-shaped sandals of wood and straw. The women were especially incongruously attired in dresses of the finest linen and batiste, wearing hand-made lace and multi-coloured kerchiefs. The brightly embroidered native costumes predominated, presenting a pleasant sight after the monotony of the Moscow streets. [. . .]

The markets were the main gathering-places and centres of attraction. The stalls spread for blocks, piled high with fruit, vegetables, butter, and other provisions. One had no longer believed such profusion existed in Russia. Some of the tables were laden with toys in carved and painted wood, mountains of them of curious shape and design. My heart ached for the children of Petrograd and Moscow, with their broken and mis-shaped dolls and the battered wooden monstrosities they called Cossack

steeds. For two dollars in Kerensky paper money I carried off
an armful of wonderful toys. I knew that the joy they would
give to my Petrograd youngsters would transcend any monetary
value.

Bringing anything into another city without special permission was considered speculation and treated as a counter-
revolutionary offence, often subject to the "supreme penalty,"
which meant death. Neither Sasha nor I could see the wisdom or
justice, let alone the revolutionary necessity, of such a prohibition. We agreed that speculation in food-stuff was indeed criminal. But it was absurd to decry everyone as a speculator who
tried to bring in half a sack of potatoes or a pound of bacon for
his family use. Far from deserving punishment, we argued, one
should be glad that the Russian masses still possessed such indomitable will to live. Therein alone was the hope of Russia,
rather than in mute submission to a slow death by starvation.

Long before we had started on our expedition, we had
agreed that if it was right to import dusty documents for future
historians, it could not be wrong to bring back some provisions
for the relief of present want, particularly for the sick and
needy among our friends. The abundance of food on the
Kharkov markets made us more determined to lay in a supply
on our return trip. We only regretted that we could not take
with us enough to feed every man, woman, and child in the
stricken cities.

Moscow had been hot, but Kharkov was ablaze, with the
railroad station miles from the town. It was physically impossible to spend the day in collecting material and then return to
our car for meals. Comrades in the city helped me to secure a
room where I could also prepare meals for our secretary,
Alexandra Shakol, Henry Alsberg, Sasha, and myself. As a pro-
Soviet American correspondent Henry had no difficulty in getting a room, which he invited Sasha to share with him. Shakol
preferred to sleep in the car. The Russian couple shifted for
themselves, having friends in the city, and our Communist
member was taken care of by his party comrades. These arrangements completed, we set out on our labours, each member being assigned to cover certain Soviet institutions. Sasha's task

was to visit labour, revolutionary, and co-operative organizations; mine included the departments of education and social welfare.

Our reception at those institutions was anything but cordial. Not that the officials were openly disagreeable, but one could sense the frigidity of their manner. I wondered what could be the reason until Sasha reminded me of the resentment the Ukrainian Communists felt against Moscow for depriving them of self-determination in their local affairs. They saw in our mission a new imposition of the centre. [. . .]

A Russian engineer who had just returned from the Don basin and whom we met in Kharkov threw considerable light on the Ukrainian situation. It was silly to put the entire blame for conditions on Moscow, he said. The Communists in the south in no way differed from the followers of Lenin in the north in their methods of dictatorship. If anything, their despotism was even more irresponsible in the Ukraine than anywhere else in Russia. His experience in the mines had convinced him of their ruthless persecution of those of the intelligentsia who were unwilling to co-operate with them. As to their inefficiency and inhumanity, a visit to the prisons and concentration camps would convince us as it did him. Only in one thing they differed from their comrades in the north: they took no stock in the imminence of the world revolution and they were not interested in it or in the international proletariat. All they wanted was to have their own independent Communist State and to command in the Ukrainian instead of in the Russian language. That was their main reason for dissatisfaction with Moscow, he thought.

I inquired about the feeling of anti-Semitism in the Ukraine. The engineer admitted that it was widespread, though it was not true that all Ukrainian Communists were against the Jews. He knew many Bolsheviki who were free from that racial prejudice. In any event, it was unjust of the northern Communists to charge their Ukrainian brothers with anti-Semitism, for they knew very well how prevalent the feeling was among themselves. There was a great deal of it in the Red Army. Moscow was trying to keep it down by iron force, though it did not entirely succeed in preventing anti-Jewish outbreaks on a small scale. In the Ukraine the Whites had so far been the only ones responsible for pogroms. Whether the Ukrainian Red forces would be willing and able to cope with the evil was yet to be seen.

We decided to visit the local prison and detention camp. [. . .] Both penal institutions bore out the statement of our engineering acquaintance as regards Ukrainian Communist management and despotism. The camp, called *kantslager*, occupied an old building without any provisions for sanitation and not half large enough for its thousand inmates. The dormitories, overcrowded and smelly, were barren except for wide boards that served as beds and had to be shared by two and sometimes three persons. During the day they had to squat on the floor and even eat their meals in that position. For an hour they were taken out in sections to the yard, the rest of the time being kept indoors without anything to occupy their time and minds. Their offences ranged from sabotage to speculation, and they were all counter-revolutionists, as our stern guide impressed upon us. [. . .]

The occupants of locked cells were dangerous criminals, she assured us, one, a woman, was a member of the counter-revolutionary bandit army of Makhno,[27] and the man occupying the adjoining cell had been caught in a counter-revolutionary plot. Both deserved severest treatment and the supreme penalty. Nevertheless she had ordered their cell opened for several hours a day and she had given permission to the other prisoners to talk to them in the presence of a guard.

The Makhnovka, an old peasant woman, was crouching in the corner of her cell like a frightened hare. She blinked stupidly when the door was opened. Suddenly she threw herself headlong before me and shrieked: "*Barinya,* let me out, I know nothing, I know nothing!" I tried to quiet her and get her to tell me about her case. Maybe I could help her, I urged. But she was frantic, whining piteously that she knew nothing about Makhno. In the corridor I told our guide that it seemed absurd to consider that stupefied old creature dangerous to the Revolution. She was half-crazed with the solitary and the fear of execution, and if kept locked up much longer, she would surely go stark mad. "It is mere sentimentality on your part," the guide upbraided me; "we live in a revolutionary period, with enemies on all sides."

The man in the next cell was sitting on a low stool, his head bent. With a sudden jerk he turned his eyes on the door, a terrorized and hunted look in their anticipation. Just as quickly he pulled himself together, his body stiffened, and his look fastened on our guide with concentrated contempt. Two words, no more audible than a sigh, yet petrifying in their effect, broke the silence. "Scoundrels! Murderers!" A horrible feeling overcame me that he believed us to be officials. I took a step towards him to explain, but he turned his back upon us and was standing erect and forbidding beyond my reach. With heavy heart I followed my companions out of the corridor.

Sasha had said nothing, but I felt that he was affected no less than I. With seeming nonchalance he sauntered along the corridors, his object being to find a young anarchist imprisoned in the place, as we had been confidentially informed. I was kept back by the superintendent, enlarging on my *bourgeois* sympathies. [. . .]

When alone with Sasha, I learned what our imprisoned comrade had communicated to him. The head of the Workers' and Peasants' Inspection was a former Chekist and she attempted to run the prison in the usual Cheka manner. She had introduced most severe restrictions, including solitary confinement for the politicals. The inmates sought to effect a change without resorting to drastic methods. But when the half-witted peasant woman and the man doomed to die were isolated from the rest and kept under lock, the entire prison protested. A hunger-strike followed. Though it failed of the desired results, it succeeded in opening the cells part of the day for their two fellow inmates. Another hunger-strike was being planned in the near future to compel a change in the despotic régime.

I understood the terrorized expression on the face of the man and the hate in his cry: "Scoundrels! Murderers!" He was being kept in isolation previous to execution, all the time in uncertainty as to when the fatal shot would silence his palpitating heart. Could any "revolutionary necessity" explain such refined cruelty? If only I had come to Russia in the October days,

I thought, I might have found the answer or a fitting end to my past. Now I felt caught in a coil that was growing more strangling every day.

The people who least understood my travail were my own comrades in Kharkov. Most of them were from America and had been affiliated with my work there. [. . .] Our coming to Russia had been a great impetus to them, they told us. They had been sure that we would continue on Soviet soil the work we had so energetically carried on in the United States. They knew, of course, that we would not give up our faith in the Bolsheviki until we became convinced that they had gone back on their revolutionary slogans. [. . .]

Our Kharkov people were willing to concede that they had been too hasty in their expectations. But now, they argued, after eight months in Soviet Russia, with all the opportunities we had enjoyed of learning conditions at first hand, why did we still hesitate? Our movement needed us. The field was large and promising. We could easily organize the anarchists of the Ukraine into a strong, federated body that would reach the workers and the peasantry by its propaganda. The latter in particular, through the aid of Nestor Makhno. He knew the peasants and they trusted him. He had repeatedly urged the anarchists throughout the country to take advantage of the propaganda possibilities the south offered. He would put everything necessary at our disposal, including funds, a printing-press, paper, and couriers, our comrades urged, pleading for our speedy decision.

If I should make up my mind to become active in Russia, I explained to them, the support of Makhno would lure me no more than Lenin's offer of aid through the Third International. I was not denying Makhno's services to the Revolution in the struggle against the White forces, nor the fact that his *povstantsy*[28] army was a spontaneous mass movement of the toilers. I did not think, however, that anarchism had anything to gain from military activity or that our propaganda should depend on military or political spoils. But that was beside the point. I was not in a position to join their work, nor was it a question of the Bolsheviki any more. I was ready to admit frankly that I had erred grievously when I had defended Lenin and his party as the true champions of the Revolution. But I would not engage in active opposition to them so long as Russia was still being attacked by outside enemies. I was no longer deceived by their mask, but my real problem lay much deeper. It was the Revolution itself. Its manifestations were so completely at variance with what I had conceived and propagated as revolution that I did not know any more which was right. My old values had been shipwrecked and I myself thrown over-board to sink or swim. All I could do was to try to keep my head above water and trust to time to bring me to safe shores. [. . .]

Our stay in Kharkov came to a sudden end. Our secretary learned that our material was in danger of being held up by the Party Executive and not permitted to leave the Ukraine. We needed no further hint. The same night we managed to get our car hitched to a train going to Poltava, and off we lurched.

We speed-spoiled Americans could scoff and make fun of such slow travel, but to the congested humanity at every railroad station in Russia, waiting for days and even weeks to get on a train, the creeping pace was of great advantage. An appalling sight they were—these rag-covered, bundle-loaded, exhausted people, shouting, cursing, and falling over each other in the mad skirmish to swing on. Pushed off, often by the butt of a soldier's gun, not once but many times, doggedly they would try again and again until they succeeded in clinging to the railing or steps. It was an Inferno awaiting the master hand of a Russian Dante. [. . .]

Everything in life is relative, looming in value according to one's necessity. The platforms of our car were coveted more than palaces. They offered to a few creatures a night's security against wind and hot soot and preserved them from falling off the roof of the car, a thing that was a common occurrence on the road. Life was cheap and people too preoccupied with their own little share of it to get excited over such matters. No one knew whether he might not come next and no one cared. Once squeezed past the soldiers to the tiniest spot on the train, they looked neither behind nor ahead. The present moment alone was theirs and they snatched at it greedily. Quickly they forgot their tears, their cursing and shrieking. They felt sociable again

and capable of fun and frolic. Once more they could give vent
to their rich imagery and song. What a people! What kaleidoscopic changes of spirit!

Our credentials from the centre found greater favour in Poltava
than in Kharkov. The secretary of the *Revkom* (revolutionary
committee acting as the local government) received us pleasantly
and gave us *carte blanche* to every Soviet department. [. . .]

Curiously enough, Poltava showed but few physical traces of
the numerous invaders. Hardly any damage had been done to
buildings and parks. Her stately trees were in their appointed
places, looking contemptuously down from their great height
upon the puny thing called man. Flowers were profuse, vegetable
patches at their side, with no armed guards or even a fence to
protect them from despoilers. After the distressing scenes of our
journey from Kharkov the sight of nature's bounty and a walk
along the shady alleys were heaven indeed.

The Soviet institutions presented little interest. They were
running true to type, managed in conformity with the established one-track idea and according to the Moscow formula.
The official interviews added no new note. It gave us time to
look for the tabooed part of the population. Inadvertently we
came upon two of that class and by their aid met a larger group
held together by their common fate, though widely separated in
ideas. Our discovery was two women, one of them the daughter
of Vladimir Korolenko,[29] the last of the old school of Russian
writers. The other was the head of the "Save the Children" organization, founded in 1914 and continued through all the vicissitudes of the intervening years. They invited us to their
home, where we came in contact with others of their circle.
They were of the old radical intelligentsia that had always been
dedicated to the enlightenment and succour of the Russian
masses. They were not able to reconcile themselves to the dictatorship, they frankly admitted; nor were they actively engaged
against it. In fact, they were co-operating economically with the
Bolsheviki and working in the social welfare departments. Nevertheless they were being persecuted as *sabotazhniky* and the
"Save the Children" society had been repeatedly raided by
the local authorities as a counter-revolutionary body. This in

spite of Lunacharsky's express permission to continue their work.

Henry remarked to our hosts that, no matter what might be said against the Bolsheviki, they could not be charged with neglecting the children. They were doing more in that direction than any other country. Why, then, the need of private welfare associations? Our hostesses smiled sadly. They had no intention whatever, they said, to deprecate the sincerity of the Bolsheviki in relation to the child. They had done much for it and would no doubt do still more. That referred, however, only to a privileged class of children. The destitute ones had alarmingly increased in numbers, and thousands were constantly added. Prostitution, venereal diseases, and every form of crime were rampant among the children of even tender age, and pregnancies frequent among girls of ten and eight. The more thoughtful Communists were aware that the scourge could not be cured by political decrees or the Cheka. [. . .]

Vladimir Korolenko was convalescing after a severe illness and not accessible to visitors. His daughter promised, however, to see her father about us and invited us to come to the home of her parents the next day.

In the evening I called on Mme X, chairman of the Political Red Cross. In the past the organization had been aiding the political victims of the Romanovs. I was interested to learn what they were being permitted to do by the new régime. Mme X was a beautiful woman with snowy white hair and large, tender blue eyes. She was the best type of the old Russian idealist, rarely met with nowadays. Warmth, kindliness, and utmost hospitality had been their characteristics, and my hostess had lost none of these qualities, although she had lived through every phase of misery since 1914. It was a hot evening and we sat out on the little balcony, with the puffing *samovar* between us. The bright moon and the glowing coal in the large tea-urn lent romance to the scene. But our conversation was of Russian reality, of the unfortunates who had filled the Tsar's dungeons and places of exile. The activities of her group were more limited now, the old lady informed me. They were becoming more circumscribed all the time and harassed by many difficulties for reasons that had not existed in the past. The dictatorship and the persecution of everyone even remotely suspected of disagreement with the régime robbed the politicals of their former ethical status and the high regard they had enjoyed in all but the most reactionary circles. Now they were denounced as bandits, counter-revolutionists, and enemies of the people. [. . .]

I related to her my great shock on first learning of the Jesuitical methods resorted to by the Bolsheviki to slay their opponents, and my long struggle against crediting such things. I told her of my interview with Lenin and his contention that only bandits and counter-revolutionists were in prison. It seemed unbelievable that a man of his mental stature should stoop to such despicable falsehoods to justify his methods. Mme X shook her head. It was apparent, she said, that I was not conversant with Lenin's habitual ways. In his early writings I would find that he had for years advocated and defended such methods of attack against his political opponents, methods to "cause them to be loathed and hated as the vilest of creatures." He had used such tactics when his victims could defend themselves; why should he now not add insult to injury when he had the whole of Russia as his forum? "Yes, and the rest of the radical world," I added, "for in Lenin it sees the revolutionary Messiah. I had believed him that myself, as did also my comrade Alexander Berkman. We had been among the earliest crusaders in America in his behalf. Even now we find it bitter hard to free ourselves from the Bolshevik myth and its principal spook."

It was growing late and I was anxious to hear from the old lady about Korolenko. I knew that like Tolstoy he had for decades been a great moral force in Russia. I wondered what influence he had been able to exert since 1917. I had been informed that Mme X was Korolenko's sister-in-law and very close to the great writer. I begged her to tell me about him.

The prophet of Yasnaya Polyana,[30] she said, had fortunately been spared the spectacle of the old autocracy surviving the Revolution in a new dress. He was saved the agony of writing letters of protest to the new Tsar. Not so her brother-in-law. Though almost seventy and in poor health, Vladimir Korolenko had to spend most of his time in the Cheka pleading for some innocent life or penning entreating letters to Lenin, Lunacharsky, and Maxim Gorki to put a stop to the wholesale executions. Maxim Gorki, she continued, had proved a great disappointment. No, Maxim found the company of Lenin a safer haven, and the Kremlin a pleasanter abode, than exile in a desolate village. Maxim Gorki had not even the courage, she added, to live up to the honoured tradition among Russian authors of encouraging and helping members of the profession and standing by them in distress.

My own experience with Maxim Gorki came to my mind. I recalled his lame apology for Bolshevik autocracy. [. . .] Still I stressed the point that Maxim Gorki might really believe in the righteousness of Lenin's policies. He was a poet, not a politician; it was probably the glamour about Lenin's name that made him worship. I preferred to think so rather than to believe Gorki capable of selling his birthright for a mess of pottage.

I expressed my surprise that Korolenko was still permitted to be at large, in view of his repeated offences of *lèse-majesté*. Mme X did not consider it strange. Lenin was a very clever man, she explained. He knew his trump cards: Peter Kropotkin, Vera Figner, Vladimir Korolenko were names to reckon with. Lenin realized that if he could point to them as remaining at liberty, he could effectively disprove the charge that only the gun and the gag were applied under his dictatorship. [. . .]

I felt too stifled to return to the narrow quarters of my compartment. It was past two in the morning, the break of day already near. I suggested to the friend who accompanied me that we take a walk. The air outside was balmy, the streets deserted. Poltava was soothing in her sleeping peace. Silently we walked on, each absorbed in the impressions of the evening. I was trying to see beyond the immediate and reaching upward to a point that might hold out the hope of a renaissance in the life of Russia. Approaching steps, their thud falling regularly on the granite walk, startled me. A detachment of soldiers marched by, rifles slung over their shoulders, a group of huddled people in their midst. "And shooting is being kept up as a matter of course," flitted through my mind.

In the morning, still in the throes of the preceding evening,

I went, together with Henry Alsberg, to the Korolenko home. It was a little green gem, entirely hidden from view by trees and vines—an enchanting place, with its old native furniture, ornate copper, brass, and colourful Ukrainian peasant handiwork.

Vladimir Korolenko, white of hair and beard, in girdled peasant tunic, suggested amid the surroundings of his home a world removed by centuries. [. . .] He was aware of the danger still facing Russia, he said, but "great as it may be, it is not anything nearly so grave as the inner menace threatening the Revolution." It was the Bolshevik claim that every form of terror, including wholesale execution and the taking of hostages, is justifiable as a revolutionary necessity. To Korolenko it was the worst travesty on the basic idea of revolution and on all ethical values.

"It has always been my conception," he added, "that revolution means the highest expression of humanity and justice. The dictatorship has denuded it of both. At home the Communist State daily divests the Revolution of its essence, substituting for it deeds that far exceed in arbitrariness and barbarity those of the Tsar. His *gendarmes*, for instance, had the authority to arrest me. The Communist Cheka has the power to shoot me, as well. At the same time the Bolsheviki have the temerity to proclaim the world revolution. In reality their experiment upon Russia must retard social changes abroad for a long period. What better excuse needs the European *bourgeoisie* for its reactionary methods than the ferocious dictatorship in Russia?" [. . .]

I should have loved to remain awhile longer in beautiful Poltava and to spend some more time with the wonderful spirits I met there. But our expedition had finished its labours and we had to proceed. Our next destination was to be Kiev, but the contrariness of Russian engines compelled us to stop at Fastov.

We did not regret the delay. We had heard and read of ghastly anti-Jewish pogroms, but we had never before come face to face with their ravages. On our way to the town we met neither human being nor beast until we reached the market square. A dozen stands displayed a miserable assortment of cabbages, potatoes, herring, and cereals. Their owners were mostly women. Instead of showing some animation at the sudden avalanche of so many customers, they hurriedly pulled their handkerchiefs over their foreheads and shrank back in fright. But their eyes remained riveted in terror on the men with us, consisting of Sasha, Henry, and our young Communist collaborator. We were completely nonplussed. Being the best-versed in Yiddish, I addressed an old Jewess near by. Except for our woman companion, I told her, we were the children of *Yehudim,* and we had come from America. Would she not tell me why the women acted so strangely? She pointed to the men. "Send them away," she begged. The men withdrew. I remained with our secretary, Shakol, and the women approached nearer. Soon the whole group surrounded us, each competing with the rest in their eagerness to tell us the story of their *tsores* (troubles).

The news of the arrival of Americans spread quickly, and presently the whole village was on its feet. Men came running from the synagogue, women and children hurried towards us to behold the strangers from afar. We must come to the house of prayer, a man declared, to hear the story of the Fastov *goles* (servitude). The march began, and on the way we were met by the rabbi, the *khasin* (singer), and the *magid* (preacher) as honoured guests. Everybody was fearfully excited, gesticulating and talking, most of the women laughing and crying, as if Messiah had indeed come at last.

Our three male companions joined us in the synagogue. The whole assembly tried to tell us the tragic story of their town, all at once. We suggested that they choose a committee of three, each in his turn to relate to us what had happened. In that way we were able to get a coherent account of one of the worst pogroms that had taken place in the Ukraine. Fastov had repeatedly been the scene of Jewish massacres, perpetrated by the hordes of every White general who had invaded the district. They had suffered from Denikin, from Petlura and the other enemy forces. But the pogrom organized in 1919 by Denikin had been the most fiendish one. It had lasted a whole week and had taken the lives of four thousand persons outright and of several thousand more that had perished while escaping to Kiev. But death had not been the worst infliction, the rabbi said in a broken voice. Far more harrowing had been the violation of the women, regardless of age, the young among them repeatedly and in the presence of their male kin, whom the soldiers held pinioned. Old Jews were trapped in the synagogue, tortured, and killed, while their sons were driven to the market square to meet similar fates.

The old rabbi being too shaken to continue, the narrative was taken up by another of the committee. Fastov had been, he said, one of the most prosperous cities in the south. When the Denikin hordes tired of their blood orgy, they pilfered every home, demolished the things they could not carry away, and set the houses on fire. The larger part of the town was destroyed. The survivors, a mere handful, most of them old women and small children, were now doomed to slow extinction unless help quickly came from somewhere. God had heard their prayers and had sent us at the moment when they had almost despaired of the Jewish world's learning of their great calamity. "*Borukh Adonai!*" he cried solemnly, "blessed be Thy name." And everyone repeated after him: "*Borukh Adonai!*"

Their religious fervour was all these people had rescued from their hideous experiences, and, in spite of all certainty that there was no Jehovah to hear them, I was strangely stirred by the tragic scene in the poverty-stricken synagogue in outraged and devastated Fastov. The Jews of America were more likely to answer their prayers, and, alas, neither Sasha nor I had access to them. All we could do was to write about the dreadful pogroms. Excepting the anarchist press, however, we had no assurance that any paper would publish our account. It would have been too cruel to tell these people that in America we were considered *Ahasverus*.[31] We could make known their great tragedy only to the radical labour world and to our own comrades. But there was Henry. He could do a great deal for these unfortunates, and I was sure he would. [...]

In the whole gruesome picture of Fastov two redeeming features stood out. The Gentiles of the town had had no share in the massacres. And no pogroms had taken place since the Bolshevik forces had entered the district. Our informants admitted that the Red soldiers were not free from anti-Semitism, but the establishment of Soviet authority in Fastov had lifted the dread of new massacres, and the villagers had been praying for Lenin ever since. "Why only for Lenin?" we asked; "why not also for Trotsky and Zinoviev?" "Well, you see, Trotsky and Zinoviev are *Yehudim*," an old Jew explained with Talmudic intonation; "do they deserve praise for helping their own? But Lenin is a *goi* (Gentile). So you can understand why we bless him." We too felt grateful that the *goi* had at least one saving grace in his régime. [...]

The nightmare of travel we had experienced between Kharkov and Fastov was again repeated during the six days that it required to reach Kiev. It left us bruised and battered and made us realize anew the incredible persistency of the Slav in overcoming the greatest hardships. The masses of desperate human beings fighting at every station to get on the train were increased by the village poor, the destitute and ragged children presenting the most awful sight. [...]

The crowds at the stations, Sasha and Henry reported, were as nothing compared with the swarms at the village markets. There they were thick as ants and as determined in their attacks. They were the torment of hucksters and of the militiamen ordered to drive them off the streets. No sooner were the markets cleared of them than they would flock back, apparently in even larger numbers. "Drive them away—what solution is that?" I remarked to Henry. "With the blockade starving Russia, there seems no other way," he replied. I wished I could still believe that it was only the blockade and not general inefficiency and the bureaucratic Frankenstein monster which were mainly responsible for the situation. No governmental machinery can cope with great social issues, I said to Henry. Even the United States, with its vast resources and powerful organization, had to enlist the co-operation of the social forces in the war. Trained and efficient men and women outside the Government limits won the World War for Woodrow Wilson rather than his generals. The dictatorship would have none of the social elements to help, and their energy and abilities were compelled to lie fallow. Thousands of Russia's public-spirited men and women were eager to render service to their country, but were refused participation because they could not swallow the twenty-one points of the Third International. How, then, could one hope that the Communist State would ever succeed in solving difficult social problems?

Henry insisted that my impatience with the Bolshevik régime was due to my belief that a revolution *à la Bakunin* would have brought more constructive results, if not immediate anarchism. Yet as a matter of fact the Russian Revolution had been *à la Bakunin,* but it had since been transformed *à la Karl Marx.* That seemed to be the real trouble. I had not been naïve enough to expect anarchism to rise phœnix-like from the ashes of the old. But I did hope that the masses, who had made the Revolution, would also have the chance to direct its course. Henry did not believe that the Russian people would have been capable of accomplishing constructive work even if the dictatorship had not monopolized all power. He was certain, however, that the Bolsheviki would do better, once the blockade had been lifted and the military fronts liquidated. How I wished I could share his hope! But I could not see the slightest sign of the reins being loosened. On the contrary, there was an unmistakable tightening up until all the life was pressed out of the original Revolution. [. . .]

Our need for a thorough scrub and a real night's rest was compelling. Not less so was our eager anticipation of the rich material, particularly counter-revolutionary data, to be found in Kiev. The city on the Dnieper had been the pivot of all the battles in the Ukraine between the Red and the White forces. Only recently the Poles had invaded Kiev.

While still in Petrograd, Sasha and I had shared the indignation of the Soviet press over the vandalism of the Polish occupation. They had demolished all the art treasures of the city, Lunacharsky and Chicherin[32] declared. The ancient cathedrals, the Sophia and the Vladimir, famous for their architectural beauty, had been wrecked. We feared that on our arrival we should find the greater part of the old Russ capital in ruins. But we had failed to take into account the Soviet methods of propaganda, of turning a mole-hill into a mountain. The Poles may have indeed intended much damage to Kiev, but they had evidently not succeeded in accomplishing their purpose. Several small bridges and some railroad tracks were all that had been destroyed. No other ruins were awaiting our arrival. On the other hand, we were assured that the enemy had left behind a wealth of material, but to get possession of it proved a most difficult task. The native Communists fairly oozed antagonism to Moscow, disdainfully ignoring our credentials from "the centre." [. . .]

Dispirited, our secretary returned from her interview with *Tovarishtch* Vetoshkin, chairman of the all-powerful *Ispolkom* [Executive Committee]. She was almost in tears. The official was adamant and absolutely refused to aid our efforts. It were better to continue our journey without further loss of time. In spite of her pessimism we decided to try our American sesame. It had worked in seemingly hopeless situations before. Why not in Kiev? We had a real, honest-to-goodness native American son with us, and a full-fledged correspondent at that. [. . .]

Henry's press card worked like a charm. Not only did Vetoshkin come out in person to greet us, but we were invited into his sanctum and treated to a lengthy and interesting account of Petlura, Denikin, and other adventurers who had been driven out of the Ukraine by Red forces. [. . .]

The Whites had also left very little valuable material. Fourteen different times Kiev had changed hands, and only in one thing the various governments had agreed and co-operated—in pogroms against the Jews.

In the Jewish hospital, now known as the Soviet Clinic, we came upon the victims of the Denikin outrages in Fastov. Though considerable time had elapsed since the last pogrom in that city, many of the women and girls were still very ill, some of them crippled for life as a result of their injuries. The most fearful cases were those of children suffering from the shock of having been forced to witness the torture and violent death of their parents. From Dr. Mandelstamm, the surgeon of the institution, we learned of his gruesome experiences during the pogroms, whose battle-field had been the hospital. He also spoke of the Denikin fury as the worst of all the attacks. Not a patient would have been left alive, he related, nor the building intact, but for the heroic resistance of his staff, most of whom were Gentiles.

Bravely they had remained at their posts, rescuing many of their charges. "Fortunately the Bolsheviki came back, bringing with them security from further atrocities," he said.

One of the startling finds I made in Kiev consisted of copies of *Mother Earth*. They were given to me by a man we had called to see in reference to data on pogroms. [. . .] Why had I not explained who Berkman and I were, he chided me; he would not have given us such an indifferent reception. He had received the copies only the previous evening from a friend whom he had told about the visit of "the Americans." [. . .] Now that he knew of our identity, he declared, we must come to his house for tea, and he would also invite the local Jewish intelligentsia to meet us. They would never forgive him when they learned that we had been in Kiev and they were not apprised of our presence. Before leaving, the man informed me that he was Latzke, former Minister for Jewish Affairs in the Rada (Ukrainian National Assembly).

In the Russian cataclysm my former life in America had receded into pale memory, becoming a dream bereft of living fibre and I myself a mere shadow without firm hold, all my values turned to vapour. The sudden appearance of the *Mother Earth* copies revived the poignancy of my aimless and useless existence. Yearning, sickening yearning, possessed me, chilling the very marrow of my being. I was pulled back to reality by the arrival of Sonya Avrutskaya, a very sympathetic local comrade. With her was a stranger, a young woman in peasant costume, who was introduced to me as Gallina, the wife of Nestor Makhno. I forgot my distress at the peril that threatened her, Sonya, and all of us. I knew that the Bolsheviki had set a price on Makhno's head, dead or alive. They had already killed his brother and several members of his wife's family in vengeance for their failure to capture Makhno. Anyone even distantly suspected of having any relationship with him was in imminent jeopardy of his life. Discovery would mean certain death for Gallina. How could she risk coming to our place, well known to the authorities as it was and open to every caller, including Bolsheviki? She had faced danger too often to care, Gallina replied. The purpose of her visit was too important to be entrusted to anyone else. She was bringing a message from Nestor to Sasha and me, asking us to consent to a *coup* he was planning. He was not far from Kiev, with a detachment of his forces. His plan was to hold up our train on its journey south, to take us prisoners, as it were. The rest of our expedition could proceed on its way. He wanted to explain to us his position and aims and he would give us safe conduct back to Soviet territory. Such a manœuvre would clear us of suspicion of deliberate dealing with him. It was a desperate scheme, he was aware, but so was also his situation. Bolshevik lies and denunciations had blackened him and the revolutionary integrity of his *povstantsy* army and misrepresented his motives as an anarchist and internationalist. We were his only opportunity to give his side of the situation to the proletarian world outside Russia, to explain that he was neither bandit nor *pogromshtchik*,[33] that he had in fact punished with his own hands individual *povstantsy* guilty of offences against the Jews. He was with the Revolution to the last breath and he hoped and urged that we would render him this vital and solidaric service, to let him talk to us and present his aims. Would we consent to his plan?

It was an ingenious scheme, recklessly daring, its adventurous quality enhanced by the beauty and youth of Makhno's messenger. Presently Sasha and Henry arrived and we were all held spellbound by the passionate pleading of Gallina. Sasha's conspiratory imagination caught fire and he was almost ready to consent. I also felt strongly tempted to accept. But there were others to consider, our companions of the expedition. We could not lead them blindly into something that was undoubtedly fraught with grave consequences. There was also something else that acted as a restraining influence. I had not yet been able to cut the last threads that bound me to the Bolsheviki as a revolutionary body. I felt I could not be guilty of deliberate deception towards those whom I was still trying to exonerate emotionally, though intellectually I could no longer accept them.

In the entire city there was no hiding-place for Makhno's wife. My room offered scant security, but it was her only cover for the night. Tense and moving were the hours spent with

Gallina. We sat in darkness, except for the pale moonlight that lit up now and then her lovely face. She seemed completely oblivious of the danger of her presence in my quarters. She was vital, and hungry for information about the life and work of her sisters abroad, particularly in America. What were the women doing there, she questioned, and what have they accomplished in independence and recognition? What was the relationship of the sexes, woman's right to the child and to birth-control? Amazing was the thirst for knowledge and information in a girl born and bred in primitive surroundings. Her passionate eagerness was infectious and revived my own mainsprings for a while. The break of morning compelled us to part. Gallina walked out into the dawning day with brave and sure gait. I stood behind the portières, watching her receding figure.

After Gallina's visit I no longer felt at ease in accepting aid even for our official mission. Not that I was conscious of any breach of confidence so far as the Bolsheviki were concerned. Makhno's wife was in my estimation no counter-revolutionist; and even if I had thought her one, I should not have turned her over to certain death at the hands of the Cheka. Just the same, I realized that I had no business with the *Revkom* and I decided not to visit it any more. [. . .]

On the way to Odessa we lost our good friend Henry Alsberg. Inadvertently he had caused his own arrest. Henry had joined the expedition without having secured the consent of the Moscow Cheka and he could have continued till the end of our journey without the eagle eye of the Soviet being able to discover his whereabouts. But he had added his signature to the telegram we had sent to Lenin in behalf of the arrested Albert Boni. As a result the All-Russian Cheka in the capital had at once sent orders to apprehend the criminal who had dared absent himself without its permission. Things moving at a snail's pace in Russia, the command failed to reach Kiev while we were there. It was wired to every station along our route and overtook us in Zhmerinka. [. . .]

Alsberg's arrest proved the beginning of a chain of adversities that pursued us for the rest of our journey. Barely out of

Zhmerinka we received the news of the defeat of the Twelfth Army and the advance of the Poles on Kiev. The line was clogged with military trains on their retreat, and at the stations everything was in the wildest confusion. Our car was repeatedly attached to trains ordered south and as many times detached again to be sent in the opposite way. At last we were lucky enough to get into an echelon actually going in the direction of our next destination, the great city on the Black Sea. From there we planned to reach the Caucasus, but the movements of General Wrangel[34] decided otherwise. His forces had just invested Alexandrovsk, a suburb of Rostov, thus shutting off the route we were to take to the Crimea. [. . .]

At last we reached the great city on the Black Sea, only to find that a devastating fire had laid the main telegraph office and the electric station in ashes the previous day, leaving the city in utter darkness. The holocaust was declared to be the work of White incendiaries, and the city was placed under martial law. The general nervousness was increased by the report that the Poles had taken Kiev and that Wrangel was advancing north. The public had no means of learning the truth of the situation, which only increased their trepidation.

An atmosphere of suspicion and fear dominated the Soviet institutions. All eyes were turned on us as Shakol, Sasha, and I entered the *Ispolkom*. Our credentials were carefully scrutinized and we were examined as to our identity and purpose before we were permitted to come into the august presence of the *predsedatel*.[35] [. . .] All he could do, he told us finally, was to supply us with a pass to the other Soviet departments and with written permission to be out on the streets "after permitted hours." He could aid us no more and he was not interested in museums, anyhow. It was a sinecure for the intelligentsia, but the workers had more important things to do to defend the Revolution. Everything else was a waste of time, he declared. [. . .]

As we were walking down the stairs, several young people approached us. They stared at us a moment and then shouted: "Hello, Sasha! Emma! You here?" The unexpected encounter with our comrades from America was a pleasant surprise after the sight of the Bolshevik martinet. [. . .] Our comrades suggested that we might be aided in our efforts for the museum by our American comrade Orodovsky, who held a responsible position in the city, and there were several others who might also assist us. The Mensheviki, too, could supply us with information and material. They had recently been cleared out of the unions; still, some of them were so influential with the rank and file that the Bolsheviki had not dared to arrest them.

Orodovsky was a first-class printer and a man of a practical turn of mind. He had managed to get into the Government publishing house and he organized it in a manner to astonish the authorities. From the confiscated and neglected materials he formed the best printing shop in the city, and great was his pride in showing us through the place. It was a model of cleanliness, order, and efficient production. His efforts were hampered at every turn; he was not considered one of their "own" and therefore he was under suspicion. He loved the work and he felt he was doing something for the Revolution, but it made him sad to foresee the inevitable approaching. "Ah, the Revolution," he sighed, "what has become of it?"

Through Orodovsky we were enabled to meet several other anarchists active in the economic department. All of them felt themselves, like Orodovsky, only temporarily tolerated and in constant danger of getting into trouble as men who were "not entirely" with the established standards of opinion. The most interesting of them was Shakhvorostov, of proletarian origin, whose whole life had been spent among the workers. [. . .]

Shakhvorostov substantiated the charges of widespread sabotage made by our young comrades. He added that, while most Soviet officials were simply inefficient, others were downright *sabotazhniky,* purposely hampering every effort for the welfare of the people. [. . .]

A week's canvass of the Soviet institutions convinced us that, far from exaggerating, our comrades had not painted half the picture of Odessa sabotage. The local officials proved the worst shirkers we had ever come across in Russia. From the highest commissar to the last *barishnya* (young woman) typist they made it a habit of coming to work two hours late and quitting an hour earlier than closing time. Often the clerk's window would be shut right in the face of an applicant who had spent hours waiting his turn, only to be told that it was "too late" and to come tomorrow. We received almost no assistance in our work from the Soviet authorities. "Too busy, without a minute to spare," they would assure us. Yet most of them stood about smoking cigarettes and talking by the hour, while the "young ladies" were engaged in polishing their nails and rouging their lips. It was the most open and shameless official parasitism.

The Workers' and Peasants' Inspection, created specially to fight this kind of sabotage, seemed to take little interest in the purpose of their existence. Most of them were notorious speculators, and if anyone wanted tsarist or Kerensky money changed, though the practice was strictly forbidden, he would be advised to go to some well-known official to have the transaction attended to. "Ordinary citizens are shot for such speculation," a well-known Bundist* commented to us, "but who can touch these officials? They all work hand in glove." The corruption and autocracy of the highest Soviet circles were an open secret in the city, the man related. The Cheka in particular was nothing more than a gang of cut-throats. Extortion, bribery, and indiscriminate shooting of victims who could not pay were its common practices. It was a frequent occurrence that big speculators, sentenced to die, were set free by the Cheka for the payment of exorbitant ransom. Another practice was to notify the relatives of some prominent prisoner that he had been executed. While the family would be plunged in grief, a Cheka emissary would arrive to inform them that it had been a mistake. The condemned man was still alive, but only a certain sum, invariably very large, could save his life. Family and friends would divest themselves of everything to secure the necessary amount, and the money was always accepted. There would come no more emissaries to explain that the alleged mistake had been no mistake at all. If anyone dared show signs of protest, he would be arrested and shot for "attempting to corrupt" the Cheka. Almost every morning at dawn a truckload of those that were to die would clatter down "Cheka Street" at a

---

*Member of the *Bund,* Jewish Social Democratic organization.

furious pace towards the outskirts of the city. The doomed ones
were forced to lie in the wagon face down, their hands and feet
tied, armed guards standing over them. Chekists on horseback
accompanied the truck, shooting at anyone who showed himself at an open window along their route. A narrow strip of red
in the path of the returning truck would be all that was left to
tell the story of those taken on their last ride to be *razmenyat*
(destroyed).

The Bundist called again a few days later in the company of a
friend whom he introduced as Dr. Landesman, a Zionist and
member of a circle that included the famous Jewish poet Byalek
and other public-spirited men.[36] No doubt we knew, the doctor
said, that Rosh Hashona was at hand, and he would be happy
to have us celebrate the great day together in the company of
his family. We confessed that we had not been aware of the approach of the Jewish New Year, but we were Jews enough to
want to spend the holiday with him.

The home of the Landesman family, adjoining his former
private clinic, now turned into a Soviet sanatorium, was beautifully situated. Perched on a high elevation, it was buried
amidst a profusion of trees and shrubbery on one side, while
the other faced the Black Sea, its waters beating against the
foot of the hill. [. . .]

We were sitting on the terrace, the *samovar* before us, the
sky streaked with blue and amethyst, the sun a ball of fire
slowly sinking into the Black Sea. The city with all its terror
and suffering seemed far off, and the green bowered nook an
idyll. If it would last awhile longer, I mused . . . but one lived in
seconds only.

New guests arrived, Byalek among them, square-set and
broad-shouldered, looking more like a prosperous merchant
than a poet. A slender man with vibrantly sensitive features was
introduced as a famous authority on Jewish persecution and
pogroms. Sasha immediately engaged him in conversation on
the subject, but in the midst of it, during the meal, he suddenly
grew deathly pale and begged to be excused. Together with
Doctor Landesman, I reached Sasha just in time to save him
from falling in a faint. He was writhing in pain and gasping for

breath, and presently he became unconscious. After a half-hour that seemed an eternity the good doctor had him somewhat restored. Packed in hot water bottles, he felt relieved, but still very weak. I told Landesman that my friend had been very ill when he left the United States, and that he had never been quite well since. The black bread in particular seemed to affect his condition, and he had showed considerable improvement since we had been able to procure white bread in the south. Our hosts insisted that we remain overnight with them in view of the possibility of Sasha's suffering another attack. "What good will it do?" the patient suddenly piped up. "The expedition must proceed to Moscow." The doctor suggested that the expedition proceed, but that Sasha and his nurse remain in Odessa until he could find out the cause of the trouble. Presently Sasha fell quietly asleep and I sat watching his thin, pale face intently. It had lost nothing of its endearment to me since we had met so many, many years ago. What would it mean to lose him, and in Russia? I shuddered at the thought, my mind unable to follow up the cruel possibility. My pal lay peacefully resting, and I went back to the dining-room, my thoughts upon my life and the struggle I had gone through together with my friend and comrade.

The dishes were about to be cleared away when Sasha suddenly entered as if nothing had happened. Did they think he would be so easily done out of his share of the meal, he demanded with a broad grin. His appetite was great, he announced, and he would not think of allowing a little indisposition to stand between him and Mme Landesman's culinary art. The company roared with laughter. The doctor, however, vetoed heavy dishes, but Sasha read him the riot act about attempting to keep an anarchist from eating what he likes. I stared at him in wonder. It was the same boy who had called for extra steak and coffee in Sachs's restaurant in New York just thirty-one years before. The patient of an hour ago not only ate heartily, but became the spirit of the company. He had found the man for whom he had been looking for a long time, he declared, and he held on to the expert investigator of pogroms for the rest of the evening.

The man proved a walking encyclopædia on the subject. He had visited seventy-two cities where pogroms had taken place, and he had collected a wealth of data. Jew-baiting during the various Ukrainian régimes, he stated, had been of more fiendish character than the worst massacres under the tsars. He admitted that no pogroms had taken place since the Bolsheviki had come to power, but he agreed with the younger element of the Kiev writers that Bolshevism had intensified anti-Semitic feeling among the masses. Some day it would break out, he was certain, in the wholesale slaughter of vengeance.

Sasha argued heatedly with him. Speculations about future possibilities aside, he emphasized, it remained a generally recognized fact that the Bolsheviki had put the lid down on pogroms. Did that not point to a sincere and determined purpose to eradicate every violent manifestation of the old disease, if not the disease itself? The investigator denied it, asserting that the Bolsheviki had deprived the Jews of their right of self-defence, forbidding them to organize for the purpose. They were even suspected of plotting against the Soviet Government because they had applied for permission to arm themselves against future attacks. Doctor Landesman added that the local authorities had refused to allow him to form a Yiddish boy-scout unit. He had intended such a group to serve not only as a defence for the Jews, but also for the protection of the citizens generally against the notorious ruffian bands from whom no one was safe in Odessa.

On closer examination the doctor found Sasha suffering from an ulcerated stomach and offered to place him in his sanatorium for treatment. "Give a doctor a chance at your insides and he is sure to find something radically wrong there," Sasha joked, waving aside the good physician's offer. The expedition had to proceed, he insisted, and he with it.

We heartily thanked the Landesmans for their generous hospitality. In social ideas we were far removed from each other, but they were among the most human and friendly beings that it had been our good fortune to meet in Russia. We had exhausted the historical possibilities of Odessa and we had to leave. The Crimea was definitely out of the question, the entire

route being in the line of the Wrangel advance. We were promised connexion with a train that was to depart for Kiev within
forty-eight hours. [. . .]

On our journey back to Kiev we did as the Romans. The markets still displayed quantities of foodstuffs, but the prices had
risen enormously since our previous visit. We were sure that in
Petrograd they were even more prohibitive, if anything could be
procured at all. We therefore felt it imperative not to return
with empty hands to our friends. Of course, there was the risk
of arrest as speculators. What other motive could induce anyone to expose himself to such danger and obloquy? Sympathy,
the desire to share with others, the need of alleviating misery
and suffering? These terms no longer existed in the dictionary
of the dictatorship. We knew too well that we should be pillo-
ried not only in Russia, but also abroad. We should have no
means of making ourselves heard, in our own defence, either on
the charge of speculation or on our present attitude to the Bolsheviki. Notwithstanding all this, it was impossible to forgo the
opportunity of securing food for starving friends in the north.
Most decisive, however, was my concern about Sasha and his
health. We had not gone very far out of Odessa when he again
collapsed. This time his attack lasted longer and was more serious. The black bread and the wormy cereals would have been
poison to him in his condition. I knew no law of the Communist State for which I would jeopardize his life, least of all the
absurd order that made it a counter-revolutionary offence to
bring provisions to a hungry population. I would therefore lay
in a supply of food and take the consequences, I decided. No
one would accept Soviet roubles as payment. "What can we do
with these scraps?" the peasants and shop-keepers would ask.
"They are of no use even as wrapping-paper, and for cigarettes
we already have sacks of them." Tsarist money or even that of
Kerensky they would accept, although they preferred woollens,
shoes, or other apparel. [. . .]

Early in the morning Shakol and I were torn out of sleep by
someone knocking on our door. Still dazed, we heard Sasha's
voice demanding to know why we had played such a fool hoax

on him. On opening the door of our compartment I saw him standing there wrapped in his blanket. "Where are my clothes?" he asked; "you girls have hidden them from me!" The secretary roared at the sight of him and we assured him that we were quite innocent of the prank. Thereupon he returned to his compartment. Presently he announced that excepting his portfolio of documents and some Sovietsky money, everything was gone. The robbers had made a clean haul, not leaving him a thing to put on. Even the valuable Browning which the secretary of Mme Ravich had lent Sasha for the journey, and a little gold watch, a gift from Fitzi, were missing. They had hung over Sasha's bed directly above his head, and the thief must have been very skilful not to have awakened him or anyone else in the car. Borrowing the most necessary things from the other men, Sasha rigged himself out and prepared to report his loss. In the midst of it he began chuckling to himself. "The fellow that swiped my pants will be fooled, though," he laughed, "for my money is in a secret pocket there that he'll never find." For a moment I did not grasp what he meant; then it struck me that Sasha had also been robbed of our entire fortune of sixteen hundred dollars. Six hundred of it I had turned over to him only the previous evening while my petticoat, in which I had kept it, was drying. "Our independence!" I screamed; "it's gone!"

Through all the bitter disappointments in Russia and our struggle to find ourselves and our work I had been sustained by one thought—our material independence. We did not have to beg or cringe like so many others who were driven by hunger. We had been able to keep our self-respect and to refuse any truck with the dictatorship because we had been made secure by our American friends. Now all was gone! "What now, Sasha?" I cried. "What is going to become of us?" Impatiently he replied: "You seem more concerned about the damned money than about our lives. Don't you realize that if I had stirred, or anyone else in the car, the burglars would have shot us dead?" He had never known me to cling to material things, he added; it was funny I should have thought of the money first of all. "Not so funny when one is compelled to forswear all one holds high in order to exist," I replied. I simply could not face the possibility of eating out of the hand of the Bolshevik State. For myself I should have preferred to be finished by our night callers. [. . .]

In Bryansk we were greeted with the joyful news of the complete rout of Wrangel. Strange to say, Nestor Makhno was being proclaimed a hero who had materially helped to bring about the great victory. But yesterday denounced as a counter-revolutionary, a bandit, the aid of Wrangel, with a large price on his head—what had brought the sudden change of front on the part of the Bolsheviki, we wondered. And how long would the love-feast last? For Trotsky had in turn eulogized the leader of the rebel peasant army and in turn condemned him to death.

Sad news clouded our joy. In a Soviet paper we read of the death of John Reed. Both Sasha and I had been very fond of Jack and we felt his demise as a personal loss. I had last seen him the previous year when he returned from Finland, a very sick man indeed. I had learned that he was put up at the Hotel International in Petrograd, alone and without anyone to take care of him. I had found him in a deplorable condition, his arms and legs swollen, his body covered with ulcers, and his gums badly affected as a result of scurvy acquired in prison. The poor boy suffered even more spiritually, because he had been betrayed to the Finnish authorities by a Russian Communist, a sailor whom Zinoviev had sent with him as a companion. The valuable documents and the large sum of money Jack was taking to his comrades in America all fell into the hands of his captors. It was Jack's second failure of the kind and he took it much to heart. Two weeks' nursing helped put him on his feet again, but he remained fearfully distressed over the methods of Zinoviev and others in jeopardizing the lives of their comrades. "Needlessly and recklessly," he kept saying. He himself had twice been sent on a wild goose chase without any trouble having been taken to find out whether there was any possibility of the venture's succeeding. But at least he could take care of himself and he went into it with open eyes. Moreover, as an American he did not run the same grave risks as the Russian comrades. Communists, mere youngsters, were being sacrificed by the score for the glory of the Third International, he had complained. "Perhaps revolutionary necessity," I had suggested; "at least your comrades always say so." He had believed it also, he had admitted, but his experience and that of others had made him doubt it. His faith in the dictatorship was still fervent, but he was beginning to doubt some of the methods used, particularly by men who themselves always remained in safety.

In Moscow we learned of the presence in the city of Louise Bryant, Reed's wife. Ordinarily I should not have looked her up. I had known Louise for years, even before she was with Jack. An attractive, vivid creature, one had to like her even when not taking her social protestations seriously. On two occasions I had realized her lack of depth. During our trial in New York, when Jack had bravely come to our assistance, Louise had studiously avoided us. They were planning to go to Russia and she was evidently afraid of having her name connected with ours during that dangerous war period, though she had always protested her great friendship in times of peace. I considered it of no great importance, however.

A much graver offence, and one that had angered me considerably, was her misrepresentation of anarchism in her book on Russia. My niece Stella had sent me the volume at the Missouri prison and I was indignant to find repeated in it the stupid story of Russia's nationalizing women that had made its rounds in the American press. Louise charged the anarchists with having been the first to issue the decree. She had taken no trouble to adduce any evidence for her wild assertions, nor had she done so in reply to my letter demanding it. I considered it on a par with the cheap journalistic libelling of the Bolsheviki and I decided to have nothing more to do with Louise.

That seemed ages ago now. Louise had suffered the loss of Jack and she was all broken up over it, I was told by common friends. I went to her without any mental reservations, too deeply moved by her tragedy to remember the past. I found her a wreck, completely shattered. She broke down in convulsive weeping that no words could allay. I took her in my arms, holding her quivering body in a silent embrace. She quieted down after a while and began relating to me the sad story of Jack's death. She had made her way to Russia disguised as a sailor and under great difficulties, only to find on landing in Petrograd that Jack had been ordered to Baku to attend the Congress of Eastern Races. He had begged Zinoviev not to insist on his going, because he had not yet fully recovered from his experience in Finland. But the chief of the Third International was relentless. Reed was to represent the American Communist Party at the Congress, he had declared. In Baku Jack was stricken with typhus and he was brought back to Moscow shortly after Louise had arrived.

I sought to console her by the assurance that all possible care must have been given Jack after his return to Moscow, but she protested that nothing had been done for the boy. A whole week had been lost before the physicians agreed in their diagnosis, and after that Jack had been turned over to an incompetent doctor. No one in the hospital knew anything about nursing, and only after a protracted argument had Louise succeeded in getting permission to take care of Jack. But he had been delirious in his last days and he had probably not even been aware of the presence of his beloved. "Didn't he speak at all?" I inquired. "I could not understand what he meant," Louise replied, "but he kept on repeating all the time: 'Caught in a trap, caught in a trap.' Just that." "Did Jack really use that term?" I cried in amazement. "Why do you ask?" Louise demanded, gripping my hand. "Because that is exactly how I have been feeling since I looked beneath the surface. Caught in a trap. Exactly that."

Had Jack also come to see that all was not well with his idol, I wondered, or had it only been the approach of death that had for a moment illumined his mind? Death strips to the naked truth—it knows no deception. [. . .]

A grey sky overhanging Moscow, rain steadily drizzling its melancholy tune, and artificial wreaths that had served at other funerals were Jack Reed's farewell in the Red Square. No beauty for the man who had loved it so, no colour for his artist-soul. No spark of the red-white flame of the fighter to inspire those who in bombastic speeches claimed him as their comrade. Alexandra Kollontay alone came close to the spirit of John Reed and found the words that would have pleased him most. During her simple and beautiful tribute to Jack, Louise crumpled to the ground in a dead faint just as the coffin was being lowered into the grave. Sasha had almost to carry her to the automobile Nuorteva had put at our disposal. Our old American friend Dr. W. Wovschin, a recent arrival, accompanied us to aid the desolate Louise.

In the Museum of the Revolution, in Petrograd, we were hailed as heroes come back from the front. It was a considerable achievement to return alive after four months of such a journey as we had made, they said, and to have also rescued a whole carload of material of historical value. The future, they assured us, would reward us according to our deserts. All the museum could do now was to give us a month's rest. We were henceforth on the permanent staff of the museum, Yatmanov and Kaplan[37] informed us, and we need not look for other activities. Within a month we should start on a new journey. [. . .]

We should have liked to remain in our car, but there was the problem of heating and of reaching the city. Mme Ravich suggested that we take up our abode at the Hotel International. [. . .] Its main attraction was cleanliness and an opportunity to take a bath. It was the first place of its kind in Russia for other mortals than Communists and we were relieved at the chance to be quartered there.

The museum material, not considered contraband, was easily transferred from our car. Not so the food we had brought with us. Entitled to pass freely through the railroad gates, we aroused no suspicion, though it required a week and four persons to remove the stuff. In the apartment of a friend everything was made up in parcels and sent to sick friends and to those who had children needing fats and sweets. Quite selfishly I had intended to keep enough white flour for the winter to safeguard Sasha from black bread. Now that we were soon to start on another journey, the unpleasant task became unnecessary. It was no small satisfaction to be able to relieve the need of a few more persons, if only for a little while.

In spite of all planning we went neither to the Crimea nor to the Far Eastern Republic. Instead we journeyed to Archangel, "to round out the year," as Yatmanov said. That district having been the centre of the interventionist operations, in which my erstwhile country had played such a disgraceful part, I was glad we were given the opportunity to explore it. [. . .]

Archangel, at the mouth of the northern Dvina, was separated from the railroad terminus by the frozen river. On arriving we found a temperature of fifty below zero, but the brilliant sun and the dry, crisp air made the cold far less penetrating than in Petrograd. [. . .] In fact, the city presented numerous surprises. Our credentials, scorned in the south, here proved a veritable magic wand, opening wide the doors of every Soviet institution. The chairman of the *Ispolkom* and all other officials went out of their way to aid the efforts of our mission. They exerted themselves to make our stay a memorable experience, as indeed it proved to be. Their fraternal attitude to the population, their equitable efforts to supply them with food and clothing so far as was in their power, made us feel that here principles different from those of "the centre" were operating. The men and women at the helm of affairs in Archangel had grasped the great truth that discrimination, brutality, and hounding were not calculated to convince the people of the beauty or desirability of communism or to cause them to love the Soviet régime. They sought more effective methods. They abolished speculation in food by organizing a more just distribution of rations. They did away with the humiliating and exhausting standing in line by instituting co-operative stores where the inhabitants received due attention and courteous treatment. They introduced a friendly tone and atmosphere in every Soviet institution. While this had not converted the whole community into disciples of Marx or Lenin, it had helped to eliminate the dissatisfaction and antagonism widespread in other parts of the country. People said that the Communists had acquired organization, efficiency, and order from the example of the Americans quartered in the city. If so, they certainly proved apt pupils. For the usual characteristics of Soviet life, including sabotage, waste, and confusion, were almost entirely missing in Archangel.

Those sturdy sons of the north apparently had something that was very unsovietsky—respect for human life and recognition of its sanctity. Former nuns, monks, White officers, and members of the *bourgeoisie* put to useful work instead of against the wall were an extraordinary revelation. The mere suggestion of such a thing elsewhere in Russia would have marked us as very suspicious characters if not out and out counter-revolutionists. Here the new method had rescued hundreds of lives and had gained for the régime additional workers. Not that the Cheka was absent or capital punishment abolished. A dictatorship could hardly exist without these. But in Archangel the Cheka had not attained the unlimited powers it enjoyed in other places. It did not constitute a State within the State whose sole function was terror and vengeance. If these measures were really dictated by revolutionary necessity, the barbarous methods of the Whites in northern Russia would have certainly justified their use. Not only Communists, but even those remotely sympathetic with them had been subjected to torture and death. Entire families had been ruthlessly exterminated by the Whites. Kulakov, chairman of the *Ispolkom,* for instance, had lost every member of his family. Even his youngest sister, a mere child of twelve, had not escaped the fiendishness of the enemy, and there was hardly a radical or liberal home that had not felt the cruel hand of those that had come to crush the Revolution.

"Naturally we could not meet such fury with gloved hands," the chairman of the educational department said to us. "We fought back desperately, but when the enemy had been driven to flight, we saw no need of retaliation or terror. We felt that vengeance would serve no other purpose than to antagonize the population against us. We set to work to bring order out of the chaos left by the Whites and to reclaim as many lives as we could among our captives."

"Did all your comrades agree with such 'sentimental' methods?" I asked in astonishment. "Of course not," he replied; "there were many who insisted on drastic measures, and there are those who still insist that we shall yet have to pay dearly for what they call our reformist attitude to those who had conspired against the Revolution." However, the chairman continued, the more level-headed comrades had prevailed, and experience proved that even former White officers could be utilized in various walks of life. A number of them were employed as teachers and they were doing faithful and useful work. The same held good of several other departments. Moreover, even such dark and bigoted elements as nuns and monks had responded to humane treatment. It was not at all sentimentality, but good common sense that taught him, he added, that the will to life was not dictated by creeds. Nuns and monks were as subject to that law of nature as any average person. After they had been dispossessed from the cloisters and monasteries and faced death if they continued plotting, or starvation if they refused to work, they proved themselves only too eager to make themselves useful in some way. We could convince ourselves of it, he said, by visiting the schools, nurseries, and arts and crafts studios. [. . .]

Archangel proved so absorbing that we overstayed our time by two weeks. We still had Murmansk to visit, while our credentials were good only till the end of the year. With regret we left the friends we had made and the splendid people we had met in the city.

Within three days' distance from our objective we had to turn back. Heavy snow-storms blocked our route, and our progress resembled that of a snail. It would have required weeks to reach our destination, the road having first to be cleared of mountain-high snow. Fifty miles from Petrograd we were again stalled, this time by a blinding blizzard. Luckily we had fuel and provisions for several days. We settled down for a patient wait, for there was nothing else we could do under the circumstances.

On Christmas Eve, still held up on the road, Shakol and Sasha gave me a surprise. A wee pine-tree, decorated for the occasion and studded with coloured candles, gaily lit up our compartment. America contributed the gifts, or rather my women friends who had sent presents before we sailed. A good hot grog, brewed from the rum supplied us in Archangel, helped to make the festivity complete.

I thought of our Christmas of a year ago—of 1919. Sasha and I, together with many other undesirable rebels on the *Buford*, torn away from our work, our comrades, and our loved ones, cruising to an unknown destination. In enemy hands, under rigid military discipline, our male companions herded below deck like cattle and fed on wretched food, all of us exposed to imminent danger from war mines. Yet we did not care. Soviet Russia was beckoning us, liberated and reborn, the fulfilment of the heroic struggle of a hundred years. Our hopes ran high, our faith flamed red-white, all our thoughts centred on our *Matushka Rossiya*.

Now it was Christmas 1920. We were in Russia, her soil serene after the raging storms, her attire of white and green under a jewelled sky. Our house on wheels was warm and cozy. My old pal was at my side and a new dear friend. They were in a holiday mood and I longed to join in their merriment. But in vain. My thoughts were in 1919. Only a year had passed, and nothing was left but the ashes of my fervent dreams, my burning faith, my joyous song. [. . .]

Our expedition was being reorganized and arrangements made for our third tour, which was definitely decided upon as a journey to the Crimea. But at the eleventh hour our plans were blocked by an order of the *Ispart*, the newly created Communist body for the purpose of collecting data on the history of the Communist Party. The Museum of the Revolution was curtly notified that henceforth the new organization would take charge of all expeditions, the *Ispart* claiming precedence, by virtue of its Communist character, in all such undertakings. [. . .]

Our efforts in behalf of the Petrograd Museum were being blocked on every hand by the concentrated authority of Communist machinery and were proving fruitless. Petrograd urged a personal report and we decided to return there. We had already bought our tickets when word came from Dmitrov that our old comrade Peter Kropotkin had been stricken with pneumonia. The shock was the greater because we had visited Peter in July and had found him in good health and buoyant spirits. He seemed then younger and better than when we had seen him the previous March. The sparkle in his eyes and his vivacity had impressed us with his splendid condition. The Kropotkin place had looked lovely in the summer sunshine, with the flowers and Sophie's vegetable garden in full bloom. With much pride Peter had spoken of his companion and her skill as a gardener. Taking Sasha and me by the hand, he had led us in boyish exuberance to the patch where Sophie had planted a special kind of lettuce. She had succeeded in raising heads as large as cabbages, their leaves crispy and luscious. He himself had also been digging in the soil, but it was Sophie, he had reiterated, who was the real expert. Her potato crop of the previous winter had been so large that there was enough left over to exchange for fodder for their cow and even to share with their Dmitrov neighbours, who had few vegetables. Our dear Peter had been frolicking in his garden and talking about these matters as if they were world events. Infectious had been the youthful spirit of our comrade, carrying us along by its freshness and charm.

In the afternoon, assembled in his study, he had again become the scientist and thinker, clear and penetrating in his judgment of persons and events. We had discussed the dictatorship, the methods forced upon the Revolution by necessity and those inherent in the nature of the party. I wanted Peter to help me to a better understanding of the situation which was threatening to bankrupt my faith in the Revolution and in the masses. Patiently and with the tenderness one uses towards a sick child he had sought to soothe me. There was no reason to despair, he had urged. He understood my inner conflict, he had assured me, but he was certain that in time I should learn to distinguish between the Revolution and the régime. The two were worlds apart, the abyss between them bound to grow wider as time went on. The Russian Revolution was far greater than the French and of more potent world-wide significance. It had struck deep into the lives of the masses everywhere, and no one could foresee the rich harvest humanity would reap from it. The Communists, irrevocably adhering to the idea of a centralized State, were doomed to misdirect the course of the Revolution. Their end being political supremacy, they had inevitably become the Jesuits of socialism, justifying all means to attain their purpose. Their methods, however, paralysed the energies of the masses and terrorized the people. Yet without the people, without the direct participation of the toilers in the reconstruction of the country, nothing creative and essential could be accomplished.

Our own comrades, Kropotkin had continued, had in the past failed to give sufficient consideration to the fundamental elements of the social revolution. The basic factor in such an upheaval is the organization of the economic life of the country. The Russian Revolution proved that we must prepare for that. He had come to the conclusion that syndicalism was likely to furnish what Russia lacked most: the channel through which the industrial and economic upbuilding of the country could flow. He was referring to anarcho-syndicalism, indicating that such a system, by aid of the co-operatives, would save future revolutions the fatal blunders and fearful suffering Russia was passing through. [. . .]

The Petrograd Museum was waiting for Sasha's report on his conferences with the *Ispart*, necessitating his immediate departure for the north, while I remained in Moscow ready for a call from Dmitrov. Several days passed without my receiving word from Alexandra, which led me to conclude that Peter was improving and that my services were not needed. I thereupon left for Petrograd.

I had hardly been in the city an hour when Mme Ravich telephoned to inform me that my presence was urgently called for from Dmitrov. She had received a message from Moscow on the long-distance wire urging my immediate coming. Peter had grown worse and the family had begged for me to be notified to come at once.

My train ran into a raging storm and we arrived in Moscow ten hours behind schedule. [. . .] I hastened to the Kropotkin cottage. Alas, too late! Peter had ceased breathing an hour before. He died at four a.m., February 8, 1921.

The distracted widow told me that Peter had repeatedly inquired whether I was already on my way and how soon I would arrive. Sophie was near collapse, and in the need of looking after her I forgot the cruel combination of circumstances that had prevented my rendering even the least service to him who had been such a potent inspiration in my life and work.

We learned from Sophie that Lenin, when informed of Peter's illness, had sent the best Moscow physicians to Dmitrov, together with provisions and delicacies for the patient. He had also ordered that frequent bulletins of Peter's condition should be sent him as well as published in the press. It was a sad commentary that so much attention should have been given on his death-bed to the man who had twice been raided by the Cheka and who had thereby been compelled to go into undesired retirement. [. . .]

Peter had never sought or accepted favours from any government nor tolerated pomp and display. We therefore determined there should be no intrusion from the State at his funeral, and that it should not be vulgarized by the participation of official-dom. Peter's last days upon earth should rest in the hands of his comrades only. [. . .]

I had known Peter for over a quarter of a century, was familiar with his life, his works and colourful personality. But only his death disclosed his cherished secret that he had also been an artist of unusual quality. I found, hidden away in a box, a number of drawings Peter had made in his all too few leisure moments. Their exquisite line and form proved that he might have achieved as much with his brush as he had with his pen had he cared to devote himself to it. In music also Peter would have excelled. He loved the piano and he could find expression and release in his fine interpretation of the masters. [. . .]

Richly endowed with creative ability, Peter had been still richer in his vision of a noble social ideal and in his humanity, which embraced all mankind. For that more than for anything else he had laboured during the conscious part of his almost fourscore years. In fact, until the very day when he had to take to his bed, Peter had continued working, under most distressing conditions, on his volume on *Ethics*, which he had hoped to make the supreme effort of his life. His deepest regret in his last hours was that he had not been given a little longer to complete what he had begun years before. [. . .]

In Moscow the expressions of esteem and affection for Peter Kropotkin became a tremendous demonstration. From the moment the body arrived in the capital and was placed in the Trade Union House, and all during the two days that the dead lay in state in the Marble Hall, there began an outpouring of the people such as had not been manifested since the days of "October."

The Funeral Commission had sent a request to Lenin to release temporarily the anarchists imprisoned in Moscow to enable them to take part in the last honours paid their dead teacher and friend. Lenin had promised and the Executive Committee of the Communist Party had directed the Veh-Cheka (the All-Russian Cheka) to free "according to its judgment" the imprisoned anarchists for participation in the obsequies. But the Veh-Cheka apparently was not disposed to obey even Lenin or the supreme authority of its own party. Would the Funeral Commission guarantee the return of the prisoners to jail, it demanded. The commission pledged itself collectively. Whereupon the Veh-Cheka declared that there were "no anarchists in the Moscow prisons." The truth, however, was that the Butirky and the inner jail of the Cheka were filled with our comrades arrested in the raid of the Kharkov Conference, though the latter had been officially permitted according to the Soviet agreement with Nestor Makhno. Moreover, Sasha had gained admission to the Butirky and there talked with more than a score of our imprisoned comrades. Accompanied by the Russian anarchist Yarchook, he had also visited the inner prison of the Moscow Cheka and there conversed with Aaron Baron, who represented on the occasion a number of other imprisoned anarchists. Still the Cheka insisted that there were "no anarchists imprisoned in Moscow."

Once again the Funeral Commission was compelled to resort to direct action. On the morning of the funeral it instructed Alexandra Kropotkin to telephone to the Moscow Soviet that a public announcement of its breach of faith would be made and that the wreaths laid on the bier of Kropotkin by Soviet and Communist organizations would be removed forthwith if the promise given by Lenin was not kept. [. . .]

The funeral was held up for an hour. The great masses of bereaved outside kept shivering in the bitter Moscow frost, all waiting for the arrival of the imprisoned pupils of the great dead. At last they came, but only seven of them, from the Cheka jail. There were none of the Butirky comrades, but at the last moment the Cheka assured the commission that they had been released and were on their way to the hall.

The prisoners on leave acted as the honorary pall-bearers. In proud sadness they carried the last remains of their beloved teacher and comrade out of the hall. In the street they were received in impressive silence by the vast assembly. Soldiers without arms, sailors, students, and children, labour organizations of every trade, and groups of men and women representing the learned professions, peasants, and numerous anarchist bodies, all with their banners of red or black, a multitudinous mass united without coercion, orderly without force, stretched along the long march of two hours to the Devichy Cemetery, on the outskirts of the city.

At the Tolstoy Museum the strains of Chopin's *Funeral March* greeted the *cortège*, and a chorus by the followers of the seer of Yasnaya Polyana. In appreciation our comrades lowered their flags as a fitting tribute of one great son of Russia to another.

Passing the Butirky prison, the procession came to a second halt, and our flags were lowered in token of Peter Kropotkin's last greeting to his courageous comrades who were waving their adieu to him from their barred windows.

Spontaneous expressions of deep-felt sorrow characterized the speeches made by representative men of various political tendencies at the grave of our departed comrade. The dominant note was that the death of Peter Kropotkin was a loss of a great moral force, the equal of which was well-nigh extinct in their native land.

For the first time since my coming to Petrograd my own voice rang out in public. It sounded to me strangely hard and inadequate to express all that Peter had meant to me. My grief over his passing away was bound up with my despair over the defeat of the Revolution, which none of us had been able to avert.

The sun, slowly disappearing below the horizon, and the sky, bathed in dark red, made a fitting canopy over the fresh soil that was now Peter Kropotkin's eternal resting-place. [. . .]

Sophie Kropotkin, whose whole life had been wrapped up in Peter and his work, was completely shattered by her loss. She could not bear to go on without him, she told me, unless she could devote the rest of her days to the perpetuation of his memory and efforts. A Peter Kropotkin museum was her idea as a fitting testimonial, and she pleaded with me to remain in Moscow to help her realize the project. [. . .]

She felt that, with Sasha and me on the museum committee, the main support would come from America and very little would therefore have to be asked from the soviets. The members of the Kropotkin Funeral Commission favoured Sophie's plan. Whatever the nature of the dictatorship, they held, the fact remained that the great Revolution had taken place in Russia, and that country was therefore the proper home for a Kropotkin museum.

The Peter Kropotkin Funeral Commission reorganized itself into a Memorial Committee, with Sophie Kropotkin as its chairman, Sasha as general secretary, and me as manager. In addition I was also to substitute for Sophie during her absence in Dmitrov. [. . .]

Together with Sasha I returned to Petrograd to sever our connexions with the Museum of the Revolution. [. . .] Our presence in Moscow was urgent and we should have to live there. Alexandra Kropotkin was leaving for Europe, and Sophie had promised that we could have the two small rooms they had occupied in an apartment on the Leontevsky Pereulok. At last we should be able to live like the rest of the non-official population.

In my early Russian period the question of strikes had puzzled me a great deal. People had told me that the least attempt of that kind was crushed and the participants sent to prison. I had not believed it, and, as in all similar things, I had turned to Zorin for information. "Strikes under the dictatorship of the proletariat!" he had exclaimed; "there's no such thing." He had even upbraided me for crediting such wild and impossible tales. Against whom, indeed, should the workers strike in Soviet Russia, he had argued. Against themselves? They were the masters of the country, politically as well as industrially. To be sure, there were some among the toilers who were not yet fully class-conscious and aware of their own true interests. These were sometimes disgruntled, but they were elements incited by the *shkurniky*,[38] by self-seekers and enemies of the Revolution. Skinners, parasites, they were, who were purposely misleading the dark people. They were the worst kind of *sabotazhniky*, no better than out and out counter-revolutionists, and of course the Soviet authorities had to protect the country against their kind. Most of them were in prison.

Since then I had learned by personal observation and experience that the real *sabotazhniky*, counter-revolutionists, and bandits in Soviet penal institutions were a negligible minority. The bulk of the prison population consisted of social heretics who were guilty of the cardinal sin against the Communist Church. [. . .]

Within less than twenty-four hours of our return to Petrograd we learned that the city was seething with discontent and strike talk. [. . .] We decided of course to remain in the city. Not that we hoped to avert impending trouble, but we wanted to be on hand in case we could be of help to the people.

The storm broke out even before anyone expected it. It began with the strike of the millmen at the Troubetskoy works. Their demands were modest enough: an increase in their food rations, as had long ago been promised them, and also the distribution of the foot-gear on hand. The Petro-Soviet refused to parley with the strikers until they returned to work. Companies of armed *kursanty*, consisting of young Communists in military training, were sent to disperse the workers gathered about the mills. The cadets sought to incite the crowd by firing into the air, but fortunately the workers had come unarmed and there was no bloodshed. The strikers resorted to a more powerful weapon, the solidarity of their fellow-toilers, with the result that the employees of five more factories laid down their tools and joined the strike movement. To a man, they streamed from the Galernaya docks, the Admiralty shops, the Patronny mills, the Baltiysky and Laferm factories. Their street demonstration was promptly broken up by soldiers. [. . .]

The plea of the workers for more bread and some fuel soon flared into decided political demands, thanks to the arbitrariness and ruthlessness of the authorities. A manifesto, pasted on the walls no one knew by whom, called for "a complete change in the policies of the Government." It declared that, "first of all, the workers and peasants need freedom. They don't want to live by the decrees of the Bolsheviki; they want to control their own destinies." Every day the situation grew more tense and new demands were being voiced by means of proclamations on the walls and buildings. At last appeared a call for the *Uchredilka*, the Constituent Assembly so hated and denounced by the ruling party.

Martial law was declared and the workers were ordered to return to the shops on pain of being deprived of their rations. This entirely failed of any effect, whereupon a number of unions were liquidated, their officials and the more recalcitrant strikers placed in prison. [. . .]

The strike kept spreading, all extreme measures notwithstanding. Arrests followed upon arrests, but the very stupidity with which the authorities dealt with the situation served to encourage the dark elements. Anti-revolutionary and Jew-baiting proclamations began to appear, and the wild rumours of military suppression and Cheka brutality against the strikers filled the city.

The workers were determined, but it was apparent that they would soon be starved into submission. There was no means by which the public could aid the strikers even if they had anything to give. All avenues of approach to the industrial districts of the city were cut off by massed troops. Moreover, the population itself was in dreadful want. The little we could gather in foodstuffs and clothing was a mere drop in the ocean. We all realized that the odds between the dictatorship and the workers were too uneven to permit the strikers to hold out much longer.

Into this tense and desperate situation there was presently introduced a new factor that held out the hope of some settlement. It was the sailors of Kronstadt. True to their revolutionary traditions and solidarity with the workers, so loyally demonstrated in the revolution of 1905, and later in the March and October upheavals of 1917, they now again took up the cudgels in behalf of the harassed proletarians in Petrograd. By no means blindly so. Quietly and without outsiders knowing about it, they had sent a committee to investigate the claims of the strikers. Its report roused the sailors of the warships *Petropavlovsk* and *Sevastopol* to adopt a resolution in favour of the demands of their brother workers on strike. They declared themselves devoted to the Revolution and the soviets, as well as loyal to the Communist Party. They protested, however, against the arbitrary attitude of certain commissars and stressed the need of greater self-determination for the organized bodies of workers. They further demanded freedom of assembly for labour unions and peasant organizations and the release of all labour and political prisoners from Soviet prisons and concentration camps.

The example of these brigades was taken up by the First and Second Squadrons of the Baltic Fleet stationed at Kronstadt. At an open-air meeting on March 1, attended by sixteen thousand sailors, Red Army men, and workers of Kronstadt, similar resolutions were adopted unanimously with the exception of only three votes. The dissenters included Vassiliev, president of the Kronstadt Soviet, who was chairman of the mass meeting; Kuzmin, the Commissar of the Baltic Fleet; and Kalinin, President of the Federated Socialist Soviet Republics.

Two anarchists who had attended the gathering returned to tell us of the order, enthusiasm, and fine spirit that had prevailed there. Not since the early days of October had they seen such spontaneous demonstration of solidarity and fervent comradeship. If only we had been there, they lamented. The presence of Sasha, for whom the Kronstadt sailors had made such a valiant stand when he was in danger of extradition to California, in 1917, and of me, whom the sailors knew by reputation, would have added weight to the resolution, they declared. We agreed that it would have been a wonderful experience to participate in the first great mass meeting on Soviet soil that was not machine-made. Gorki had assured me long ago that the men of the Baltic Fleet were born anarchists and that my place was with them. I had often longed to go to Kronstadt to meet the crews and talk to them, but I had felt that in my disturbed and confused state of mind I could give them nothing constructive. But now I would go to take my place with them, though I knew that the Bolsheviki would raise the cry that I was inciting the sailors against the régime. Sasha said he did not care what the Communists would say. He would join the sailors in their protest in behalf of the striking Petrograd workers. [. . .]

We felt elated over the splendid solidarity of the Kronstadt sailors and soldiers with their striking brothers in Petrograd and we hoped that a speedy termination of the trouble would soon result, thanks to the mediation of the sailors.

Alas, our hopes proved vain within an hour after we had received news of the Kronstadt proceedings. An order signed by Lenin and Trotsky spread like wildfire through Petrograd. It declared that Kronstadt had mutinied against the Soviet Government, and denounced the sailors as "tools of former tsarist generals who together with Socialist-Revolutionist traitors staged a counter-revolutionary conspiracy against the proletarian Republic."

"Preposterous! It's nothing short of madness!" Sasha cried as he read the copy of the order. "Lenin and Trotsky must be misinformed by someone. They could not possibly believe the sailors guilty of counter-revolution. Why, the crews of the *Petropavlovsk* and *Sevastopol* in particular had been the staunchest supporters of the Bolsheviki in October and ever since. And did not Trotsky himself greet them as 'the pride and flower of the Revolution'!" [. . .]

Extraordinary martial law was declared over the entire Petrograd Province, and none but specially authorized officials could leave the city. The Bolshevik press opened a campaign of calumny and vituperation against Kronstadt, proclaiming that the sailors and soldiers had made common cause with the "tsarist general Kozlovsky," and declaring the Kronstadt people outlawed. Sasha began to realize that the situation involved a good deal more than mere misinformation on the part of Lenin and Trotsky. The latter was to attend the special session of the Petro-Soviet where the fate of Kronstadt was to be decided. We resolved to be present.

It was my first opportunity in Russia to hear Trotsky. We

might remind him of his parting words in New York, I thought; the hope he had expressed that we should come to Russia soon to assist in the great work made possible by the overthrow of tsarism. We would plead with him to let us help settle the Kronstadt difficulty in a comradely spirit, to dispose of our time and energies, even of our lives, in the supreme test to which the Revolution was putting the Communist Party.

Unfortunately Trotsky's train was delayed and he failed to appear at the session. The men who addressed the gathering were beyond reason or appeal. Fanaticism run mad was in their words, and blind fear in their hearts. [. . .]

Above the din of the howling and stamping mob a single voice strove to be heard—the tense, earnest voice of a man in the front rows. He was a delegate of the striking employees at the arsenal works. He was moved to protest, he declared, against the misrepresentations uttered from the platform against the brave and loyal men of Kronstadt. Facing Zinoviev and pointing his finger directly at him, the man thundered: "It's the cruel indifference of yourself and of your party that drove us to strike and that roused the sympathy of our brother sailors, who had fought side by side with us in the Revolution. They are guilty of no other crime, and you know it. Consciously you malign them and call for their destruction." Cries of "Counter-revolutionist! Traitor! *Shkurnik!* Menshevik bandit!" turned the assembly into a bedlam. [. . .]

A tall man in a sailor's uniform stood up in the back. Nothing had changed in the revolutionary spirit of his brothers of the sea, he declared. To the last man they were ready to defend the Revolution with their every drop of blood. Then he proceeded to read the Kronstadt resolution adopted at the mass meeting on March 1. The uproar his daring evoked made it impossible for any but those nearest to hear him. But he stood his ground and kept on reading to the end.

The only reply to these two sturdy sons of the Revolution was Zinoviev's resolution demanding the complete and immediate surrender of Kronstadt on pain of extermination. It was rushed through the session amidst a pandemonium of confusion, with every opposing voice gagged.

The atmosphere, surcharged with the hysteria of passion and hate, crept into my being and held me by the throat. All evening I wanted to cry out against the mockery of men stooping to the lowest political trickery in the name of a great ideal. My voice seemed to have left me, for I could not utter a sound. My thoughts reverted to another occasion where the spirit of vengeance and hate had run amuck—the eve of registration, June 4, 1917, at Hunts Point Palace, New York. I had been able to speak out then, entirely oblivious of danger from the war-drunk patriots. Why could I not now? Why did I not brand the impending fratricide by the Bolsheviki, as I had Woodrow Wilson's crime that had dedicated the young manhood of America to the Moloch of war? Had I lost the grit that had sustained me all through the years of fighting against every injustice and every wrong? Or was it helplessness which paralysed my will, the despair that had settled on my heart with the growing realization that I had mistaken a phantom for a life-giving force? Nothing could alter that crushing consciousness or make any protest worth while.

Yet silence in the face of the threatened slaughter was also intolerable. I had to make myself heard. But not by the obsessed, who would choke back my voice as they had done with the others. I would make known my stand in a statement to the supreme power of the Soviet Defence, that very night.

When we were alone and I spoke to Sasha about the matter, I was glad to learn that my old pal had conceived the same plan. He suggested that our letter should be a joint protest and deal exclusively with the murderous resolution passed by the Petro-Soviet. Two comrades who had been with us at the session shared his view and offered to sign their names to our joint appeal to the authorities.

I had no hope that our message would exert any sobering or restraining influence on the events decreed against the sailors. But I was determined to have my attitude registered in a manner to bear future witness that I had not remained a silent party to the blackest betrayal of the Revolution by the Communist Party.

At two o'clock in the morning Sasha got in touch by telephone with Zinoviev, to inform him that he had something important to communicate to him regarding Kronstadt. Perhaps Zinoviev assumed that it was something that might aid the conspiracy against Kronstadt. Otherwise he would have hardly troubled to rush Mme Ravich over at that hour of the night, ten minutes after Sasha had talked to him. She could be trusted absolutely, Zinoviev's note said, and she was to be given the message. We handed her our communication, which read:

> To the Petrograd Soviet of Labour and Defence,
> Chairman Zinoviev:

To remain silent now is impossible, even criminal. Recent events impel us anarchists to speak out and to declare our attitude in the present situation.

The spirit of ferment and dissatisfaction manifest among the workers and sailors is the result of causes that demand our serious attention. Cold and hunger have produced dissatisfaction, and the absence of any opportunity for discussion and criticism is forcing the workers and sailors to air their grievances in the open.

White-guardist bands wish and may try to exploit this dissatisfaction in their own class interests. Hiding behind the workers and the sailors, they throw out slogans of the Constituent Assembly, of free trade, and similar demands.

We anarchists have long since exposed the fiction of these slogans, and we declare to the whole world that we will fight with arms against any counter-revolutionary attempt, in co-operation with all friends of the Social Revolution and hand in hand with the Bolsheviki.

Concerning the conflict between the Soviet Government and the workers and sailors, we hold that it must be settled, not by force of arms, but by means of comradely, fraternal revolutionary agreement. Resort to bloodshed on the part of the Soviet Government will not—in the given situation—intimidate or quiet the workers. On the contrary, it will serve only to aggravate matters, and will strengthen the hands of the Entente and of internal counter-revolution.

More important still, the use of force by the Workers' and Peasants' Government against the workers and sailors will have a reactionary effect upon the international revolutionary movement and will everywhere result in incalculable harm to the Social Revolution.

Comrades Bolsheviki, bethink yourselves before it is too late. Do not play with fire; you are about to make a most serious and decisive step.

We hereby submit to you the following proposition: Let a commission be selected, to consist of five persons, inclusive of two anarchists. The commission is to go to Kronstadt to settle the dispute by peaceful means. In the given situation it is the most radical method. It will be of international revolutionary significance.

Petrograd	ALEXANDER BERKMAN
March 5, 1921	EMMA GOLDMAN
	PERKUS
	PETROVSKY

Proof that our appeal had fallen on deaf ears came to us the very same day on the arrival of Trotsky and his ultimatum to Kronstadt. By order of the Workers' and Peasants' Government, he declared to the Kronstadt sailors and soldiers, he would "shoot like pheasants" all those who had dared to "raise their hand against the Socialist fatherland." The rebellious ships and crews were commanded to submit immediately to the orders of the Soviet Government or be subdued by force of arms. Only those surrendering unconditionally might count on the mercy of the Soviet Republic.

The final warning was signed by Trotsky, as Chairman of the Revolutionary Military Soviet, and by Kamenev, the Commander-in-Chief of the Red Army. Daring to question the divine right of rulers was again to be punished by death.

Trotsky kept his word. [. . .] From my room window in the Hotel International I saw them led by in small groups, surrounded by strong detachments of Cheka troops. Their step had lost its spring, their hands hung at their sides, and their heads were bowed in grief.

The Petrograd strikers were no longer feared by the authorities.

They were weakened by slow starvation and their energy sapped. They were demoralized by the lies spread against them and their Kronstadt brothers, their spirit broken by the poison of doubt instilled by Bolshevik propaganda. They had no more fight nor faith left to come to the aid of their Kronstadt comrades who had so selflessly taken up their cause and who were about to give up their lives for them.

Kronstadt was forsaken by Petrograd and cut off from the rest of Russia. It stood alone. It could offer almost no resistance. "It will go down at the first shot," the Soviet press proclaimed. They were mistaken. Kronstadt had thought of nothing less than of mutiny or resistance to the Soviet Government. To the very last moment it was determined to shed no blood. It appealed all the time for understanding and amicable settlement. But, forced to defend itself against unprovoked military attack, it fought like a lion. During ten harrowing days and nights the sailors and workers of the besieged city held out against a continuous artillery fire from three sides and bombs hurled from aeroplanes upon the non-combatant community. Heroically they repulsed the repeated attempts of the Bolsheviki to storm the fortresses by special troops from Moscow. Trotsky and Tukhachevsky had every advantage over the men of Kronstadt.[39] The entire machinery of the Communist State backed them, and the centralized press continued to spread venom against the alleged "mutineers and counter-revolutionists." They had unlimited supplies and men whom they had masked in white shrouds to blend with the snow of the frozen Finnish Gulf in order to camouflage the night attack against the unsuspecting men of Kronstadt. The latter had nothing but their unflinching courage and abiding faith in the justice of their cause and in the free soviets they championed as the saviour of Russia from the dictatorship. They lacked even an ice-breaker to halt the onrush of the Communist enemy. They were exhausted by hunger and cold and sleepless nights of vigil. Yet they held their own, desperately fighting against overwhelming odds.

During the fearful suspense, the days and nights filled with the rumbling of heavy artillery, there sounded not a single voice amid the roar of guns to cry out against or call a halt to the terrible blood bath. Gorki, Maxim Gorki, where was he? His voice would be heard. "Let us go to him," I pleaded with some of the intelligentsia. He had never made the slightest protest in grave individual cases, neither in those concerning members of his own profession nor even when he knew of the innocence of doomed men. He would not protest now. It was hopeless.

The intelligentsia, the men and women that had once been revolutionary torch-bearers, leaders of thought, writers and poets, were as helpless as we and paralysed by the futility of individual effort. Most of their comrades and friends were already in prison or exile; some had been executed. They felt too broken by the collapse of all human values.

I turned to the Communists of our acquaintance, imploring them to do something. Some of them realized the monstrous crime their party was committing against Kronstadt. They admitted that the charge of counter-revolution was a downright fabrication. [. . .]

These Communist friends spent nights with us—talking, talking—but none of them dared raise his voice in open protest. We did not realize, they said, the consequences it would involve. They would be excluded from the party, they and their families deprived of work and rations and literally condemned to death by starvation. Or they would simply vanish and no one would ever know what had become of them. Yet it was not fear that numbed their will, they assured us. It was the utter uselessness of protest or appeal. Nothing, nothing could stop the chariot-wheel of the Communist State. It had rolled them flat and they had no vitality left, even to cry out against it.

I was beset by the terrible apprehension that we also—Sasha and I—might reach the same state and become as spinelessly acquiescent as these people. Anything else would be preferable to that. Prison, exile, even death. Or escape! Escape from the horrible revolutionary sham and pretence.

The idea that I might want to leave Russia had never before entered my mind. I was startled and shocked by the mere thought of it. I to leave Russia to her Calvary! Yet I felt that

I would take even that step rather than become a cog in the machinery, an inanimate thing to be manipulated at will.

The cannonade of Kronstadt continued without let-up for ten days and nights and then came to a sudden stop on the morning of March 17. The stillness that fell over Petrograd was more fearful than the ceaseless firing of the night before. It held everyone in agonized suspense, and it was impossible to learn what had happened and why the bombardment had ceased. In the late afternoon the tension gave way to mute horror. Kronstadt had been subdued—tens of thousands slain—the city drenched in blood. The Neva a grave for masses of men, *kursanty* and young Communists whose heavy artillery had broken through the ice. The heroic sailors and soldiers had defended their position to the last breath. Those not fortunate enough to die fighting had fallen into the hands of the enemy to be executed or sent to slow torture in the frozen regions of northernmost Russia.

We were stunned. Sasha, the last thread of his faith in the Bolsheviki broken, desperately roamed the streets. Lead was in my limbs, unutterable weariness in every nerve. I sat limp, peering into the night. Petrograd was hung in a black pall, a ghastly corpse. The street-lamps flickered yellow, like candles at its head and feet.

The following morning, March 18, still heavy with sleep after the lack of it during seventeen anxious days, I was roused by the tramp of many feet. Communists were marching by, bands playing military tunes and singing the "Internationale." Its strains, once jubilant to my ear, now sounded like a funeral dirge for humanity's flaming hope.

March 18—the anniversary of the Paris Commune of 1871, crushed two months later by Thiers and Gallifet, the butchers of thirty thousand Communards. Emulated in Kronstadt on March 18, 1921.

The full significance of the "liquidation" of Kronstadt was disclosed by Lenin himself three days after the frightfulness. At the Tenth Congress of the Communist Party, staged in Moscow while the siege of Kronstadt was in progress, Lenin unexpectedly changed his inspired Communist song to an equally inspired

pæan to the New Economic Policy. Free trade, concessions to
the capitalists, private employment of farm and factory labour,
all damned for over three years as rank counter-revolution and
punished by prison and even death, were now written by Lenin
on the glorious banner of the dictatorship. Brazenly as ever he
admitted what sincere and thoughtful persons in and out of the
party had known for seventeen days: that "the Kronstadt men
did not really want the counter-revolutionists. But neither did
they want us." The naïve sailors had taken seriously the slogan of
the Revolution: "All power to the Soviets," by which Lenin and
his party had solemnly promised to abide. That had been their
unforgivable offence. For that they had to die. They had to be
martyred to fertilize the soil for Lenin's new crop of slogans,
which completely reversed the old. Their *chef d'œuvre* the New
Economic Policy, the NEP.

Lenin's public confession in regard to Kronstadt did not stop
the hunt for the sailors, soldiers, and workers of the defeated
city. They were arrested by the hundreds, and the Cheka was
again busy "target-shooting."

Strangely enough, the anarchists had not been mentioned in
connexion with the Kronstadt "mutiny." But at the Tenth Congress Lenin had declared that the most merciless war must be
waged against the "petty *bourgeoisie*," including the anarchist
elements. The anarcho-syndicalist leanings of the labour opposition proved that these tendencies had developed in the Communist Party itself, he had said. Lenin's call to arms against the
anarchists met with immediate response. The Petrograd groups
were raided and scores of their members arrested. In addition
the Cheka closed the printing and publishing offices of the *Golos Truda,* belonging to the anarcho-syndicalist branch of our
ranks. We had purchased our ticket to Moscow before this happened. When we learned about the wholesale arrests, we decided to stay a little longer in case we too should be wanted. We
were not molested, however, perhaps because it was necessary
to have a few anarchist celebrities at large to show that only
"bandits" were in Soviet prisons.

In Moscow we found all except half a dozen anarchists arrested and the *Golos Truda* book-store closed. In neither city

had any charges been made against our comrades, nor had they been given a hearing or brought to trial. Nevertheless, a number of them had already been sent away to the penitentiary of Samara. Those still in the Butirky and the Taganka prisons were being subjected to the worst persecution and even physical violence. Thus one of our boys, young Kashirin, had been beaten by a Chekist in the presence of the prison warden. Maximov and other anarchists who had fought on the revolutionary fronts, and who were known and respected by many Communists, had been forced to declare a hunger-strike against the terrible conditions.

The first thing we were asked to do on our return to Moscow was to sign a manifesto to the Soviet authorities denouncing the concerted tactics to exterminate our people.

We did so of course, Sasha now as emphatic as I that protests from within Russia by the handful of politicals still out of prison were entirely futile. On the other hand, no effective action could be expected from the Russian masses, even if we could reach them. Years of war, civil strife, and suffering had sapped their vitality, and terror had silenced them into submission. Our recourse, Sasha declared, was Europe and the United States. The time had come when the workers abroad must learn about the shameful betrayal of "October." The awakened conscience of the proletariat and of other liberal and radical elements in every country must be crystallized into a mighty outcry against the ruthless persecution for opinion's sake. Only that might stay the hand of the dictatorship. Nothing else could.

This much the martyrdom of Kronstadt had already done for my pal. It had demolished the last vestiges of his belief in the Bolshevik myth. Not only Sasha, but also the other comrades who had formerly defended the Communist methods as inevitable in a revolutionary period, had at last been forced to see the abyss between "October" and the dictatorship.

If only the cost for the profound lesson taught them had not been so terrific, I should have taken comfort in the knowledge that Sasha and I were again united in our stand, and that my Russian comrades hitherto antagonistic to my attitude to the

Bolsheviki had now come closer to me. It would be a relief not to have to grope further in distressing isolation and not to feel so alien in the midst of people whom I had known in the past as the ablest among the anarchists, not to have to choke back my thoughts and emotions before the one human being who had shared my life, my ideals, and my labours through our common lot of thirty-two years. But there was the black cross erected in Kronstadt and the blood of the modern Christs trickling from their hearts. How could one cherish personal comfort and relief? [. . .]

One solace was left us. We did not have to eat out of the slayer's hand. My dear old mother and our friend Henry Alsberg[40] had saved us from that degradation. Through a friend my mother had sent me three hundred dollars, and Henry had left Sasha some clothing to exchange for food. In our new mode of living these would go a long way to keep us above water.

We had not yet adapted ourselves to the process of existence that the bulk of the non-privileged were forced to undergo. Waylaying peasants at dawn for a supply of wood, pulling it home on a sleigh, chopping it with frozen hands, carrying it up three flights of stairs; then fetching water several times a day from a long distance and up to our quarters; cooking, washing, and sleeping in a little hall bedroom, Sasha's smaller even than mine and never quite warm—this was bitter hard, at first, and terribly exhausting. My hands were chapped and swollen, and my spine, never very strong, was full of aches. My dear friend also suffered a great deal, especially from the return of his old trouble with his legs, the ligaments of which he had stretched by his fall in New York and which had crippled him for a year.

However, physical pain and weariness were as nothing to our inner liberation—the spiritual release we felt that we no longer had to ask or accept anything from the powers that had dealt the final blow to "October" by the slaughter of Kronstadt. [. . .]

In the first weeks of Sasha's anguish that followed the massacre of Kronstadt I had not dared to mention the idea of definitely leaving Russia that had come to me during the siege. I feared it might add to his agony. Later, when he had bravely pulled himself together, I broached the subject to him, not at all sure that he would want to go, but certain that I could not leave him behind under the murderous régime. I was therefore immensely relieved to find that Sasha had spent many sleepless nights brooding over the same idea. After we had discussed every possibility for making our lives count for more than mere existences in Russia, we had come to the conclusion that no word nor act of ours would be of value to the Revolution or to our movement or of the least help to our persecuted comrades. We might proclaim from the market-place the anti-revolutionary nature of Bolshevism, or we might hurl our lives against Lenin, Trotsky, and Zinoviev and go down with them. Far from serving our cause or the interest of the masses by such an act, we should be merely aiding the dictatorship. Its skilful propaganda would drag our names through the mire and brand us before the world as traitors, counter-revolutionists, and bandits. Nor could we continue gagged and chained. Therefore we decided to go. Once Sasha was clear that there was nothing vital for us to do in Russia, with the Revolution crushed by the iron hand of dictatorship, he insisted on our leaving soon and illegally. We should not be given passports, he said. Why, then, keep up the torture? Leave Russia like thieves in the night, I protested, Russia that had promised the fulfilment of our hopes? I could not do that, not until we had tried other means. I pleaded that we should get in touch with our comrades abroad to find out what country would admit us. Syndicalist delegates were sure to attend the Congress of the Red Trade Union International to be held in July in Moscow. We might entrust a message to them, or still better to Henry Alsberg, who was about to leave Russia. He would not be like the others who had promised to deliver our message to our people in America and to tell them frankly of the situation. Most of them either had not done so or had misquoted us. No wonder Stella and Fitzi still kept writing enthusiastically about our wonderful opportunity for activity in Russia. Henry was absolutely dependable; we must wait until he saw our comrades in Germany. Sasha agreed, though reluctantly. He would find no more peace with Kronstadt on his mind, he said.

I shared his grief, as indeed did all our people and nearly

everyone else who still had revolutionary fibre left. Our place in Moscow became the oasis for our comrades, as well as for others outside of our ranks. They came at all hours of the day and even late at night, hungry, spiritless, in black despair. The meals intended for ourselves and perhaps for one or two invited guests had to perform the miracle of Christ's loaves for the many who would drift in by the time we sat down to eat. To assure them that there was enough to go round I had to invent all kinds of reasons for my poor appetite: headaches, stomach trouble, and the vice of cooks who always have their pick of the best before the meal is served. I minded the faintness that would sometimes overcome me much less than the lack of privacy. But these people had no other place to go, nowhere where they might feel at home or free to communicate their troubled spirit. It was the only service we could render and we did so out of the fullness of our hearts. [....]

The Nep spread.[41] The hour of the new *bourgeoisie* had arrived. No further need to worry about Sovietsky soup or rations with such an assortment of delicacies on hand. No further anxiety to hide the loot taken from the predecessors of the new privileged class. I could hardly trust my eyes when at the Stanislavsky First Studio I met a number of women dressed in velvet and silks, wearing costly shawls, and bedecked with jewelry. Why not? The Sovietsky ladies knew how to appreciate fine clothes, even if they were somewhat crumpled from their hiding-places and not exactly in keeping with the latest Parisian fashions!

The grey and drab continued, however, among the masses, wearing out their already depleted strength in the long wait for an order for a hole to live in, a bit of calico or medicine for their sick family or even a coffin for their dead. This was no hallucination of my exhausted brain. It was one of the many ghastly realities. One such case was related to me by Angelica Balabanoff. She had been sent back to a little room in the National and completely divested of her Soviet functions. Ill, disillusioned, and broken, she suffered more than most of her comrades from the latest somersault of her idol Ilich. To see constantly the hungry crowds around the bakeries and pastry-shops was torture to one who, like Angelica, felt guilty to accept the gift of even a few biscuits from her Swedish friends. It was a purgatory which only we, who knew her well, could appreciate. [. . .]

The Nep flourished, and the inspired, flocking to the holy grail, were assured that the proletariat was in full control and that money was no more needed in Soviet Russia because the workers had free access to the best the land produced. A large contingent of the devout believers from America had confidingly turned over to the reception committee on the border all their possessions. In Moscow they were packed like sardines in common quarters, given a small ration of bread and soup, and left to their fate. Within a month two children of the group died of undernourishment and infection. The men became despondent, the women ill, one of them going insane from anxiety about her children and the shock of the conditions she had found in Russia. [. . .]

Over and above this crazy pattern of Soviet life, the famine suddenly loomed across the land; want and death spread through the Volga region and threatened the rest of the country. The Soviet Government had known for two months that millions were likely to perish unless immediate steps for relief were taken. Agricultural specialists and economists had warned the authorities of the impending calamity. They had frankly declared that the main cause of the situation was inefficiency, mismanagement, and bureaucratic corruption. Instead of setting the Soviet machinery to work to relieve the calamity, to acquaint the public with the situation and rouse it to the danger, the report of the specialists had been suppressed.

The few non-Communists who knew of it were powerless to do anything. We were among the latter. [. . .] The actual workers of the relief, however, were the foreign bodies that had meantime organized their aid. The workers of Russia and the majority of the non-Communist population were performing superhuman labour to succour the famine-stricken districts. The intelligentsia accomplished miracles. In their capacity as physicians, nurses, and distributors of supplies scores of them sacrificed themselves. Many died of exposure and infection, and a number were even killed by the dark and crazed people whom they had come to help. With millions of lives devoured by the famine, the loss of a few hundred *bourgeois* was hardly worth noticing by the Government. It was more important for the world revolution that the Soviet régime suddenly discovered the wealth contained in the churches. It could have been confiscated before without much protest from the peasantry. But now the expropriation of the Church treasures added fuel to the fires of hate which the dictatorship had engendered in all classes of the people. Another demonstration of the continued revolutionary zeal of the Communist State was to order its own members to deliver forthwith all the valuables they had in their possession, even to the last trinket. It was a shock to learn that Communists should be suspected by their own party of hoarding jewelry or other valuables. But apparently there actually were such members. [. . .]

The famine continued its devastating march. But Moscow was far from the stricken region, and great events were being prepared for within its gates. Three international congresses were to take place: those of the Communist International, of the Women's Organizations, and of the Red Trade Unions. A number of buildings adjoining the Hotel de Luxe were being renovated and the city cleaned up and decorated for the occasion. The blue and gold of the cupolas on the forty times forty churches intermingled with the scarlet hues of the bunting and flags. All was ready for the reception of the foreign delegates and visitors from every part of the world.

Among the early arrivals were two I.W.W. delegates from America, Williams and Cascaden. Others also soon came, among them Ella Reeves Bloor, William Z. Foster,[42] and William D. Haywood. How could "Big Bill" come, we wondered, for we knew that he was out on twenty-thousand-dollar bail and under sentence of twenty years' imprisonment. Was it possible that he had jumped his bond? Sasha was inclined to believe it; he had lost faith in Bill since 1914, when the latter had shown himself weak-kneed during the free-speech fights that Sasha had conducted in New York. I defended Bill hotly, pointing out that our actions are not always to be judged so easily. "Not even your own, old man," I said. But Sasha refused to come with me to the hotel where Haywood was lodged. "He will come to us if he is really anxious to see us," he declared. I laughed at such ceremony with Bill.

Bill Haywood had often been under our roof, by day and by night, always our welcome guest, our comrade in many battles, though not sharing the same ideas. I hastened to the Hotel de Luxe, where the most favoured delegates were quartered, to find the old war-horse, of whom I had always been very fond. Bill received me in the same warm and genial manner that had captured all his friends. In fact, he immediately embraced me, before the whole crowd. A roar went up from the boys, who began teasing Bill for keeping it secret that E.G. was among his many lady-loves. He laughed good-naturedly and drew me down to a seat at his side. I had come only for a moment, I told him, just to welcome him and to tell him where and when he could find us. I still could give him a cup of coffee "as black as night, as sweet as love, as strong as revolutionary zeal." Bill smiled in remembrance. "I'll come tomorrow," he said. [. . .]

Sasha was out when Bill arrived in the late afternoon the following day. My visitor transferred me back to America, my old arena of so many years' effort. I plied him with questions about my friends, about Stella and Fitzi, Elizabeth Gurley Flynn, and many others whom I still had in my heart. I wanted to hear about the general situation, the labour movement, and the I.W.W., which had since been all but demolished by the war phobia, as well as about my own comrades. Bill stopped my volley of questions. Before we proceeded, he said, he would first have to make his own position clear to me. I noticed that he was under the nervous tension that used to come over him when he stood before a large audience, his big frame shaking with suppressed feeling. He had jumped his bail, he said suddenly; he had run away. Not because of the twenty years of prison that faced him, though that was no small matter at his age. "Ridiculous, Bill," I interrupted; "you would never have to serve the whole sentence. Gene Debs was pardoned and Kate Richard O'Hare also." "Listen first," he interrupted; "the prison

was not the deciding factor. It was Russia, Russia, which fulfilled what we had dreamed about and propagated all our lives,
I as well as you. Russia, the home of the liberated proletariat,
was calling me." He had also been urged by Moscow to come, he
added. He was told he was needed in Russia. From here he would
be able to revolutionize the American masses and to prepare
them for the dictatorship of the proletariat. It had not been easy
to decide to leave his comrades to face their long terms in prison
alone. But the Revolution was more important and its ends justified all means. Of course, the twenty-thousand-dollar bail
would be paid by the Communist Party. He had been given a
solemn pledge for that. He hoped, he said, that I would understand his motives and not think him a shirker.

I did not ask any more about America, nor did I satisfy his request to tell him my impressions of Russia. With a shock I realized that Bill was as blindfolded as we had been on our arrival
in the country. Would he also undergo the excruciating operation that would remove the scales from his eyes? And what
would become of Bill when his house of cards had tumbled over
him, and all his hopes were buried like ours? [. . .]

Sasha ridiculed the motives Bill had given for running away.
Russia and all the other reasons were not convincing to him.
They were no doubt contributory factors, but the main reason
was that Bill quaked before the twenty years in Leavenworth.
In late years he had repeatedly shown the white feather. I need
have no anxiety about Bill's future, Sasha assured me. He
would fit in, even when he came to see the stupendous delusion
foisted on the world by Moscow. There was no reason why he
shouldn't. Bill had always stood for a strong State and centralization. What was his One Big Union but a dictatorship? "Bill
will be in clover here," Sasha concluded; "just wait and see."

Two days later William Z. Foster telephoned to ask whether
he could come up. It was my wash-day and I was too busy, but
Sasha offered to receive Foster in his room until I should be
through with my work. It occurred to me that Foster might like
to meet Schapiro and other comrades still free. But when I
asked him about it, he said he was not interested in Russian
syndicalists. He only wanted to talk to Sasha and me. Foster

had been among the first in America to advocate revolutionary labour tactics in the economic struggle, which the Russian Anarcho-Syndicalists had applied. It seemed strange that he should decline to meet these rebels and to hear from them what place, if any, syndicalism had in the Communist régime.

He arrived in the company of Jim Browder,[43] a Kansas boy, whom we used to know as an active I.W.W. Sasha took them in charge. At noon, when my work was finished and lunch prepared, I invited our guests to share it with us. Vegetables and fruit were plentiful on the market and much cheaper than meat and fish. We lived almost entirely on this diet. The boys had evidently not lost their American appetite. They ate with relish and expressed appreciation of E.G.'s skill in preparing such dishes. Foster said nothing during the meal except to inform us that he was in Russia in the capacity of a reporter for the Federated Labor Press. Browder talked a great deal about the marvels of the Communist State and the wonderful things the party had achieved. I inquired how long he had been in the country. "About a week," he replied. "And you have already discovered that all is wonderful?" "Indeed," he said, "it can be seen at a glance." I congratulated him on his extraordinary vision and turned our conversation into less turbulent waters. Our callers soon left, which I did not regret.

Two other Americans came to see us, Agnes Smedley and her Hindu friend Chato.[44] I had heard a good deal about Agnes in the States in connexion with her Hindu activities, but I had never met her personally. She was a striking girl, an earnest and true rebel, who seemed to have no other interest in life except the cause of the oppressed people in India. Chato was intellectual and witty, but he impressed me as a somewhat crafty individual. He called himself an anarchist, though it was evident that it was Hindu nationalism to which he had devoted himself entirely. [. . .]

The other delegates kept aloof from us, including my erstwhile devoted Ella Reeves Bloor. Bill Haywood also did not return. They had all been warded off by their "interpreters." [. . .] The Latin delegates had also been given a gentle hint in regard to us, we learned. But they were of different mettle from the

Anglo-Saxons. They informed their "guides" that they did not propose to deny their comrades or to be dictated to about whom they should associate with. The French, Italian, Spanish, German, and Scandinavian Anarcho-Syndicalists lost no time in seeking us out. In fact, they made our place their headquarters. They spent with us every free hour they had, eager to know our impressions and views. They had heard of the alleged persecution of the Left-wing elements by the Communists, but they had taken it as a capitalist fabrication. Their French Communist friends, who had made the journey with them, were also sincerely desirous to learn the facts. Among them Boris Souvarine was the most intelligent and alert inquirer. [...]

The Communists in France were co-operating on many occasions with their anarchist comrades, Souvarine argued. Why could not the same conditions be brought about in Russia? The reason was not far to see, we explained. The French Communists had not yet attained political power in their country. They had not yet achieved a dictatorship there, but when that hour arrived, their comradeship with the French anarchists would be at an end, we assured Souvarine. He thought it impossible and he insisted that he should discuss the subject with the leading Bolsheviki. He wanted to bring about an amicable relationship between his Russian comrades and ours.

Just at that moment Olya Maximova called. Pale and trembling, she told us that Maximov and twelve other comrades in the Taganka prison had declared a hunger-strike to the death. They had repeatedly demanded the reason for their imprisonment since March. Information was refused them, nor had any charges been brought against them. Having failed to receive a reply to their protests, they had decided to call the attention of the foreign delegates to their intolerable situation by means of a desperate hunger-strike.

The syndicalists present jumped to their feet in great excitement. They would have never believed such a state of affairs possible in Soviet Russia, they declared, and they would immediately demand an accounting. They would raise the question at the opening of the Red Trade Union Congress the following morning. Souvarine implored them to wait and first to see the trade-union leaders, among them Tomsky, the labour head, Losovsky, and others.[45] An open discussion at the public sessions would be working into the enemy's hand, he argued; the capitalist press and the *bourgeoisie* in France and other countries would make the most of it. The matter must be settled quietly and in a friendly way, Souvarine pleaded. The delegates left, assuring us that they would not rest until justice was done to our suffering comrades. They returned late at night to inform us that the trade-union leaders had begged them not to make the scandal public and had promised to do their utmost to get redress for the imprisoned anarchists. They had suggested a committee of one delegate from each country, including Russia, to confer with Lenin and Trotsky. Our comrades from Europe were only too glad to avoid a breach and they had willingly accepted the proposal. [. . .]

The committee was at last organized and ready to call on Lenin. None of them was a match for the shrewd Grand Mogul. He knew better how to divert their attention than they to compel his. [. . .] But the Labour Syndicalists refused to be side-tracked by the solicitous inquiries of Ilich about the conditions of labour abroad, the strength of the Syndicalists and their prospects. They insisted on knowing what he had to say about the revolutionary hunger-strikers in Russia. Lenin stopped short. He did not care if all the politicals perished in prison, he declared. He and his party would brook no opposition from any side, Left or Right. He would consent, however, to have the imprisoned anarchists deported from the country, on pain of being shot if they should return to Soviet soil. Lenin's ears had become attuned for nearly four years to shooting and he had grown infatuated with the sound of it. [. . .]

On the tenth day of the hunger-strike the joint committee finally met in the Kremlin. Sasha and Schapiro[46] had been asked by the Taganka prisoners to represent their demands. [. . .] A letter signed by the joint committee, but not concurred in by Alexander Berkman, was forwarded [. . .] to the Taganka men. [. . .]

I was glad Sasha had refused to concur in the outrageous decision that established the precedent of deportation of revolutionists from Soviet Russia, of men who had valiantly defended the Revolution, had fought on its fronts, and had suffered untold danger and hardships. What a commentary on the Communist State outdoing Uncle Sam! He, poor boob, went only as far as deporting his foreign-born opponents. Lenin and Company, themselves political refugees from their native land only a short time ago, were now ordering the deportation of Russia's native sons, the best flower of her revolutionary past. [. . .]

The Red Trade Union Congress was over. Its most pathetic harlequin proved to be Bill Haywood. The founder of the I.W.W. in America and its dominant figure for twenty years, he allowed himself to be persuaded to vote at the Congress for the Communist plan to "liquidate" the militant minority labour organizations, including the I.W.W., and force their members to join the American Federation of Labor, which Haywood had for years denounced as "capitalistic and reactionary." [. . .]

Soviet Russia had become the modern socialist Lourdes, to which the blind and the lame, the deaf and the dumb were flocking for miraculous cures. I was filled with pity for these deluded ones, but I felt only contempt for those others who had come, had seen with open eyes and understood, and had yet been conquered. Of these was William Z. Foster, once the champion of revolutionary syndicalism in America. He was keen-eyed and he had come as a press correspondent. He went back to do Moscow's bidding.

No word had arrived from our comrades in Germany in reply to the letter sent them about securing visas. Sasha was chafing under the delay of getting out of Russia. He could stand the fearful tragi-comedy no longer, he said. A German Syndicalist delegate, member of the Seamen's and Transport Workers' Union, had also taken a letter from us and had promised to see our people in Berlin. There was no news yet. As in his early days after his coming out of the Western Penitentiary, Sasha became very restless. He could not endure being indoors or seeing people. He would roam the streets of Moscow most of the day and late into the night, and my anxiety about him grew. [. . .]

Sasha returned from one of his long tramps in the city looking unusually pale and distressed. When he made sure that I was alone, he said in a whisper: "Fanya Baron[47] is in Moscow.

She has just escaped from the Ryazan prison and she is in great danger; without money or papers and no place to go."

I was struck dumb with horror of the fate awaiting Fanya if discovered. Fanya in the very fortress of the Cheka! "Oh, Sasha, why did she come here, of all places?" I cried. "That isn't the question now," he returned; "better let us think quickly how we can help her."

Our own place would be a trap for her. She would be discovered within twenty-four hours. The other comrades were also being watched. To give her shelter would mean death for them as for her. Of course, we would supply her with money, clothing, and food. But how about a roof over her head? She was safe for the night, Sasha said, but on the morrow something would have to be devised. There was no more sleep for me that night—Fanya weighed heavily on my mind.

Early next morning Sasha left the house with money and things for Fanya, and I remained in sickening suspense until the late afternoon, beset by fears for both. My friend had a less anxious look when he returned. Fanya had found shelter with a brother of Aaron Baron. [. . .]

Fanya's mission in Moscow, Sasha confided to me, was to prepare the escape of Aaron Baron. She had learned of the persecution he was undergoing in prison and she had determined to rescue her lover from his living death. Her own escape was made for that very purpose. Brave, wonderful Fanya, dedicated to Aaron as few wives are, yet not tied by law! My heart went out to our splendid comrade in trembling fear for her mission, her sweetheart, and herself. [. . .]

Then the blow came and left us stunned. Two of our comrades fell into the Cheka net—Lev Tchorny, gifted poet and writer, and Fanya Baron! She had been arrested in the home of her Communist brother-in-law. At the same time eight other men had been shot at on the street by Chekists and taken prisoners. They were *existy* (expropriators), the Cheka declared.

Sasha had seen Fanya the preceding evening. She had been in a hopeful mood: the preparations for Aaron's escape were progressing satisfactorily, she had told him, and she felt almost gay, all unconscious of the sword that was to fall upon her head the following morning. "And now she is in their clutches and we are powerless to help," Sasha groaned.

He could not go on any longer in the dreadful country, he declared. Why would I persist in my objection to illegal channels? We were not running away from the Revolution. It was dead long ago; yes, to be resurrected, but not for a good while to come. That we, two such well-known anarchists, who had given our entire lives to revolutionary effort, should leave Russia illegally would be the worst slap in the face of the Bolsheviki, he emphasized. Why, then, should I hesitate? [. . .]

We agreed to leave immediately for Moscow. On reaching the capital we learned that Vassily, arrested when he had called on us during our absence, had already been liberated. So were also ten of the thirteen Taganka hunger-strikers. [. . .]

Our Taganka comrades found themselves "free," weak and ill as a result of their long hunger-strike. They were in tatters, without money or means of existence. We did what we could to alleviate their need and to cheer them, although we ourselves felt anything but cheerful. Meanwhile Sasha had somehow succeeded in communicating with Fanya in the inner Cheka prison. She informed him that she had been transferred the previous evening to another wing. The note did not indicate whether she realized the significance of it. She asked that a few toilet things be sent her. But neither she nor Lev Tchorny needed them any more. They were beyond human kindness, beyond man's savagery. Fanya was shot in the cellar of the Cheka prison, together with eight other victims, on the following day, September 30, 1921. The life of the Communist brother of Aaron Baron was spared. Lev Tchorny had cheated the executioner. His old mother, calling daily at the prison, was receiving the assurance that her son would not be executed and that within a few days she would see him at liberty. Tchorny indeed was not executed. His mother kept bringing parcels of food for her beloved boy, but Tchorny had for days been under the ground, having died as the result of the tortures inflicted on him to force a confession of guilt. [. . .]

And our dear, splendid Fanya, radiant with life and love, unswerving in her consecration to her ideals, touchingly feminine, yet resolute as a lioness in defence of her young, of indomitable will, she had fought to the last breath. She would not go submissively to her doom. She resisted and had to be carried bodily to the place of execution by the knights of the Communist State. Rebel to the last, Fanya had pitted her enfeebled strength against the monster for a moment and then was dragged into eternity as the hideous silence in the Cheka cellar was rent once more by her shrieks above the sudden pistol-shots.

I had reached the end. I could bear it no longer. In the dark I groped my way to Sasha to beg him to leave Russia, by whatever means. "I am ready, my dear, to go with you, in any way," I whispered, "only far away from the woe, the blood, the tears, the stalking death."

Sasha was planning to go to the Polish frontier, to arrange for our leaving by that route. I was afraid to let him go alone in his present condition, his nerves shattered by the fearful shock of recent events. On the other hand, it would arouse suspicion if both of us should disappear from our quarters at the same time. Sasha realized the danger and consented to wait another week or two. The idea was for him to proceed to Minsk; I was to follow when he should have made the necessary arrangements. [. . .]

In the midst of the packing the long-expected letter from Germany arrived. It contained an invitation for Sasha, Schapiro, and me to attend the Anarchist Congress that was to take place in Berlin at Christmas. It sent me spinning round the room, weeping and laughing at the same time. "We shan't have to hide and cheat and resort to false papers, Sasha," I cried in glee; "we shan't have to sneak out like thieves in the night!" But Sasha did not seem elated over it. "Ridiculous," he retorted, "you don't mean that our Berlin comrades can exert any influence over Chicherin, the Communist Party, or the Cheka! Moreover, I have no intention of applying to them for anything. I've already told you that." I knew from experience that it was useless to argue with my stubborn pal when he was angry. I would wait for a more propitious time. The new hope held out by the letter had reawakened my objections to leaving secretly the land that had known the glory and the defeat of the great "October."

I sought out Angelica. She had told me that she would help us secure the consent of the Soviet authorities to leave the country. She herself was planning to go abroad to regain her health in some quiet spot. She, too, had reached the spiritual breaking-point, though she would not admit it even to herself. Dear Angelica immediately offered to get the necessary application blanks, and she would go to Chicherin and even to Lenin, if need be, to vouch for Sasha and me. "No, dear Angelica," I protested, "you shall do nothing of the kind." I knew what it meant to leave such security. We would not have anyone endangered for us, nor did we care to have the benediction of Lenin. I informed Angelica that all I wanted of her was to help quicken action if passports were to be granted at all.

In the space in the application reserved for the promise of loyalty and the signature of two party members vouching for the applicant I wrote: "As an anarchist I have never pledged loyalty to any government, much less can I do it to the R.S.F.S.R., which claims to be Socialist and revolutionary. I consider it an insult to my past to ask anyone to stand the consequences of anything I may say or do. I therefore refuse to have anyone vouch for me."

Angelica was considerably perturbed by my declaration. She feared it might spoil our chances of securing permission to leave the country. "Either we go out without any strings attached to us, or we will find another way," I declared. We would leave no hostages behind. Angelica understood.

I went to the Foreign Office to find out whether a request from our German comrades that we be permitted to attend the Anarchist Congress had been received. I was called before Litvinov,[48] who was acting in behalf of Commissar Chicherin. I had never met him before. He looked like a *commis voyageur*, short and fat and disgustingly content with himself. Reclining in an easy chair in his luxurious office he began to ply me with questions as to why we wanted to leave Russia, what our intentions were abroad, and where we meant to live. Had the Foreign Office not received any communication from the Berlin anarchists, I inquired. It had, he admitted, and he knew we had been invited to attend the Anarchist Congress in

Berlin. That was explanation enough, I told him; I could add nothing further. "But if you are refused?" he demanded suddenly. If his Government wanted it known abroad that we were being kept prisoners in Russia, it could certainly do so, for it had the power, I replied. Litvinov peered at me steadily out of little eyes bulging from his puffy face. He made no comment, but asked whether our Berlin comrades had made sure that the German Government would admit us. Certainly the latter would not be anxious to increase the number of anarchists in its territory. It was a capitalist country and we could not expect the reception there that Soviet Russia had given us. "Yet, strange to say," I replied, "the anarchists continue their work in most European countries, which cannot be said to be the case in Russia." "Are you singing the praises of the *bourgeois* countries?" he demanded. "No, only reminding you of facts. I have been strengthened in my anarchist attitude that all governments are fundamentally alike, whatever their protestations. However, what about our passports?" He would let us know. [. . .]

On the twelfth day, when I had about given up hope of hearing from the Foreign Office again, Angelica telephoned to me that passports had been issued to us. I should call for them at the Foreign Office, she said, and take with me dollars or English pounds to pay for them. Cabs were a luxury when so many of our people were in dire want, but I did not have the patience to walk. I wanted to see the passports with my own eyes before I would believe that they had actually been granted. It proved true, however, really true. Sasha and I would not have to hide and cheat to leave the country. We should be able to go as we had come—in the open, even if desolate and denuded of dreams.

Our comrade A. Schapiro had applied independently and I was happy to learn that his passport was also ready and awaiting his call.

I telegraphed Sasha: "This time I win, old scout. Come back quickly." It was probably cattish, but revenge was sweet. [. . .]

Passports on hand, I was now beset by other misgivings. Visas—how were they to be obtained? Our Berlin comrades notified us that they were trying their utmost to secure our admission to Germany. If we could somehow reach Latvia or Esthonia, it would be easier to get visas, they wrote.

Sasha burst into the house unannounced. He looked a fright, unshaven and apparently unwashed for days, tired and exhausted, and without the suit-case he had taken with him. "What's this?" he demanded; "just a hoax to get me back here?" He had made all preparations, he said, to cross the border and had come to fetch me. The papers would be awaiting us in Minsk and he had given fifty dollars' deposit on them. "Is the money to be lost?" he demanded. [. . .]

Triumphantly I held out the passports. He scrutinized them from every side. "Well," he drawled, "I was sure they'd refuse. A fellow may be wrong, sometimes."

But I could see he felt relieved that it would not have to be the Minsk route. His trip must have been ghastly. It took him a week to recuperate from it.

The Lithuanian visa was granted for two weeks. A transit through Latvia was obtained without much trouble. We could leave any day. The certainty made us feel doubly the plight of the comrades and friends whom we were leaving behind—in want, distress, fettered and utterly helpless in the Soviet void. [. . .] To ease the pangs of parting, our dear friends kept assuring us that by leaving our tragic Russia we should be aiding them, for we could do much more for the country abroad than in Russia, work for a better understanding of the chasm between the Revolution and the régime and for the political victims in Soviet prisons and concentration camps. They were certain our voices would be heard in western Europe and America to good advantage, and they were glad we were leaving. They pretended a gay mood to cheer us at our farewell party.

Belo-Ostrov, January 19, 1920. O radiant dream, O burning faith! O *Matushka Rossiya*, reborn in the travail of the Revolution, purged by it from hate and strife, liberated for true humanity and embracing all. I will dedicate myself to you, O Russia!

In the train, December 1, 1921! My dreams crushed, my faith broken, my heart like a stone. *Matushka Rossiya* bleeding from a thousand wounds, her soil strewn with the dead.

I clutch the bar at the frozen window-pane and grit my teeth to suppress my sobs.

CHAPTER LIII

Riga! Jostling crowds at the station, strange speech, laughter, and glaring lights. It was bewildering and it aggravated my feverish condition from the bad cold I had contracted on the way. We planned to go to our comrade Tsvetkov, who was employed in the Soviet transport department. [. . .] I needed a rest and I wanted to forget—to shut out the nightmare behind me and not to have to think of the void before me. We considered it inadvisable to go to a hotel: we would arouse too much attention and we were particularly anxious to avoid newspaper men. At Tsvetkov's we could live quietly.

Our first thought was to prepare a manifesto setting forth the appalling conditions of the politicals in the Communist State and urging the anarchist press in Europe and America to help save them from a slow death. It was our desperate cry after twenty-one months of forced silence, the initial step of fulfilling the pledge given our people to make known to the world the colossal fraud wrapped in the Red mantle of "October."

News from Germany was reassuring. Our comrades were working to secure our admission and they were confident of success. But they needed a little more time. [. . .]

When they returned, I knew the result without a word being spoken. Our application was refused.

Again it was necessary to procure a prolongation of our stay in Latvia. The sullen youngsters in office demurred, but finally permitted us another forty-eight hours. At the expiration of that time we must leave, they insisted, whether we procured any visa by then or not. "You'll go back to your own country," they declared peremptorily. Our country? Where was it? The

war had destroyed the ancient right of asylum, and Bolshevism
had turned Russia into a prison. We could not return even
there. Nor would we if we could. We'll go to Lithuania, we
thought, and we should have really gone there if we had not
missed the train on our arrival in Riga.

Our friend Tsvetkov would not hear of it. Lithuania was a
trap, he declared. It would be impossible for us to get to Germany from there, nor could we return to Riga again. He would
arrange a *sub rosa* route. He knew some freighters whose crews
were syndicalists, and he would manage the matter. But could
Emma stand being stowed away? I bristled at the implication
that I could stand less than the boys. "But your cough—it will
give you all away!" he retorted. I protested vigorously. To escape my feminine indignation our friend left to establish the
necessary connexions. But his scheme proved a bubble—luckily
for us all. For on the following day, the last we could remain in
Latvia, came Swedish visas that our syndicalist comrades in
Stockholm had obtained. Mr. Branting, the Socialist Prime
Minister, had proved more decent than his German comrades.[1]

Accompanied by Tsvetkov and Mrs. C., Secretary Shakol's
sister, who had befriended us and supplied us with a large
lunch-basket for the journey, we went to the railroad station to
board the train which was to take us to Reval. As it pulled out,
we heaved a deep sigh of relief. For a while, at least, our visa
troubles were over! But the train was barely out of the sight of
our friends when we discovered that we had an escort with us.
It proved to be three Latvian secret-service men. They demanded our passports, which they immediately confiscated, declaring that we were all under arrest. [. . .]

One by one we were taken into an inner office and examined
about our "Bolshevism." I informed the official that, though I was
not a Bolshevik, I refused to discuss the subject with him. He evidently realized that it was useless to threaten or coax me, and he
ordered me taken to another room, for later disposition. [. . .]

On the second day I was taken downstairs for examination. A
youth in his twenties was my inquisitor. He demanded to know
about our secret Bolshevik mission in Europe, why we had
stayed in Riga so long, with whom we had associated, and what

had become of the important documents he knew we had smuggled into the country. I assured him he still had much to learn to achieve fame and fortune as an interrogator of such an experienced criminal as he had before him. I would not take him into my confidence, I told him, even if I had any information that he might want. [. . .]

The day before Christmas he came to my cell to inform me that "it was an unfortunate mistake." I started at the familiar phrase. "Yes, an unfortunate mistake," he repeated, "and the fault is with your friends the Bolsheviki, not my Government's." I scorned his insinuation. "The Soviet Government gave us passports and permitted us to depart. What interest could it have to land us all in your jail?" I demanded. [. . .]

The guard did my Christmas shopping for me, bringing me fruit, nuts, cake, coffee, and a can of evaporated milk. Luxuries they were, but I was anxious to prepare a Christmas feast for my friends in the adjoining cells. In return for a tip the old guard's heart softened and he permitted me the use of the kitchen situated on the same floor. I took my time and found excuses for going back and forth to my cell, humming all the time: "Christ has risen, rejoice, ye heathen!" and finding a chance to whisper a few words to my invisible companions. Two neatly wrapped packages and a large thermos bottle of steaming coffee were carried by the guard to the two desperadoes next door in return for a little Christmas gift to his family.

We were finally released with profuse apologies. [. . .]

At last, on January 2, 1922, we departed from Reval, Esthonia. To avoid a repetition of our Riga adventure we went directly to the steamer, though the boat was not to leave until the following morning. We made good use of the free day to see the quaint town, much older and more picturesque than Riga.

Our reception in Stockholm was fortunately unofficial. Neither soldiers nor workers were ordered out to meet us wsith music and speeches, as on our arrival in Belo-Ostroy. Just a few comrades genuinely glad to see us. [. . .]

Letters from Berlin explained the sudden change of heart on the part of the German Consul in Riga after he had led us to believe that the visa would be issued to us. He had been warned by a Chekist that we were dangerous conspirators on a secret mission to the Anarchist Congress in Berlin. This also shed a light on the insistence of the Lettish officials that "our friends the Bolsheviks" had been behind our trouble in Riga. [. . .]

Our Swedish anarchists and anarcho-syndicalists were certain we could remain in their country as long as we pleased. We might as well live there as anywhere else and carry out our plan of writing about our Russian experiences. [. . .]

No sooner had our first article appeared in the *Arbetaren* than Mr. Branting had his secretary notify the Syndicalist Committee that had obtained our visa to Sweden that "it was inadvisable for the Russians to appear in print." [. . .] He would not drive us out, of course, his secretary assured our people, but we should try at once to find some other country for our abode.

Comrades in half a dozen lands were working hard to secure asylum for us. [. . .] The situation was rather desperate, made more so by several other circumstances. The cost of living in a Stockholm hotel had bankrupted us within a month. The hospitable Jensens invited me to share their two-room apartment, which I accepted in the belief that it would be only for a short time. Sasha had found a room with a Swedish family whose place was too small even for themselves. He regretted that we had not followed his original plan of going by the Minsk route. It had been stupid to ask Moscow for passports. At any rate, he would not apply for a visa any more and he was determined to leave without giving notice and to enter without permission. I could do as I pleased, he declared.

There was something else that had come between us—the question whether I should or should not permit the New York *World* to publish my series of articles on Soviet Russia. Stella had cabled me that the *World* was eager for the story of my Russian experience. [. . .] I wrote her that I preferred to have my say in the liberal and labour press in the United States, and that I should be willing to have them publish my articles without any pay rather than have them appear in the New York *World* or similar publications.

Stella tried the *Freeman* with an article on the martyrdom of Maria Spiridonovna.[2] It was declined. The other American liberal papers showed equal illiberality. I realized that in addition to being stamped an Ishmaelite I should also be gagged on the question of the Bolsheviki. I had kept silent long enough. [. . .] Now that I knew the truth, was I to be forced to slay it and keep silent? No, I must protest. I must cry out against the gigantic deception posing as truth and justice.

This I told Sasha and Schapiro. They also were determined to speak out, and, indeed, Sasha had already written a series of articles dealing with various phases of the Bolshevik régime, and they were being published in the anarchist press. [. . .] But Sasha knew that the bulk of workers, particularly in the United States, read nothing but the capitalist papers. It was they whom he wanted to enlighten on the difference between the Revolution and Bolshevism. His attitude hurt me very much and we argued for days. [. . .] He was my lifelong comrade in arms, my friend and fellow fighter in a hundred battles that had scorched our beings and tested our souls. We had gone our separate ways while in Russia regarding the question of "revolutionary necessity." There had been no break between us, however, because I also had been uncertain for a long time in my stand. Kronstadt had cleared our minds and had brought us closer again. It was harrowing now to have to take a position so divergent from my friend's attitude. Days and weeks went into the conflict, the hardest life had allotted me. All through the spiritual torture it beat against my brain: I must, I would be heard, even if it should be for the last time. Finally I cabled to Stella to turn over the articles, seven in all, to the New York *World*. [. . .]

I was too far away to witness the fury my articles aroused in the Communist ranks or to be affected by their poisonous venom. But from the descriptions sent me about Communist meetings against me and from their press I could see the similarity between their blood-lust and that of Southern whites at Negro lynchings. [. . .]

The stereotyped accusation that I had forsworn my revolutionary past, by people who had no past to forswear, was also nothing to worry about. What did trouble me was that the New York *World* had not rated my literary value as highly as did my

Communist admirers. It had paid me a paltry three hundred dollars for each article, or twenty-one hundred dollars for the series of seven. And it was being heralded by the Communist chorus that thirty thousand dollars had been paid to the traitor E.G. I was wishing it were true! I might have saved at least some portion of it for the Russian political victims who were suffering cold, hunger, and despair in the prisons and exile of the Bolshevik paradise.

Under pressure from the Swedish syndicalists Branting had extended permission for us to stay for another month. It was to be the last. Visas to other countries were not in sight, and Sasha and Schapiro decided to take matters into their own hands. The latter soon left and Sasha was to go next. A comrade in Prague had secured a visa for me to Czechoslovakia and I implored Sasha to allow our friend to do the same for him. But the mere suggestion of it aroused his wrath.

Sasha stowed away on a tramp steamer, but before the boat pulled out of Stockholm word reached me from the Austrian Consulate that a visa had been granted us. Sick with fear that the boat might leave before I should have the visa in my hands, I did not care if the chauffeur broke all speed limits. I found the visa ready for all three of us, but with it a demand of the Austrian Minister for Foreign Affairs that we give a written pledge not to engage in any political activities in his country. I had no intention of doing so, and I was confident that neither of the boys would consent to it. However, I could not disclose the clandestine departure of the one and the impending going of the other. I would consult my comrades, I told the Consul, and return with the answer the next day. It was not altogether a lie, as I still had time to reach Sasha. A blizzard had descended on the city, and the boat was held up for forty-eight hours. It afforded me the chance to send word to Sasha about the Austrian visa and the string attached to it. I did not expect him to accept it, but I felt he should be informed about it. A young Swedish friend, the one comforting association of my dismal sojourn in Stockholm, brought back word that Sasha had decided on his course and would not be swerved from it.

I hovered about the neighbourhood of the wharf in the deep
snow to be near our stowaway, whom fate had woven into the
very texture of my life. [. . .]

The next day, I found a letter from the German Consul. A
visa for ten days had been granted me.

CHAPTER LIV

[. . .] Five months after our comrades had begun the campaign to enable me to enter Germany, I landed in Berlin, with no more hope that I should be more successful than they in securing a longer stay. [. . .] Much to everybody's surprise, the Foreign Office made no difficulties about granting me a month's stay. At its expiration I was informed that two more months had been secured for me. [. . .]

With this respite, I decided on a little apartment. I had been driven about so much that I felt bruised in every bone and I was in need of a rest under my own roof. I wanted some peace to collect my thoughts before beginning my book on Russia. I longed for my flaxen-haired, blue-eyed Swedish boy, whose tender devotion had been my mainstay in the three and a half months of my existence in Stockholm.[1] I'd send for him and have two months of personal life in a lifetime that had never been my own. Vain hope! I realized it the moment I met my friend at the station. His fine eyes had not lost their friendliness, but the glow that had rekindled my soul was no longer there. They had come to see what I had known from the start, yet did not wish to realize—that he was twenty-nine and I fifty-three. [. . .]

There were various reasons why I could not tell him to go. He had avoided conscription and he had aroused the suspicion of the Stockholm police because of his attempt to help Sasha with some papers. He had no means and he would not be permitted to work in Germany. I felt I could not send him away. What if his love had died? Our friendship would still be sweet—my affection for him strong enough to be content with that, I reasoned. The rest and joy I had hoped for were turned into eight months of purgatory.

My misery was increased by Sasha's lack of sympathy with my struggle, the more surprising because he had been kind and solicitous when I fought against the growing infatuation for my friend. He had ridiculed the silly conventions regarding difference in age, and advised me to follow my desire for the youth who had come into my life. Sasha was fond of the boy, and as for the latter, he worshipped my old chum. But my young Swede's arrival in Berlin and his presence in the same apartment somehow changed their former fine comradeship into silent antagonism. I knew they did not mean to hurt me, and yet in their male short-sightedness they did nothing else.

I was in no state of mind for writing a book on Russia. [. . .] I had had no experience with publishers, our books in America having always been issued by ourselves through the *Mother Earth* Publishing Association. Albert Boni, representing Brainard and the McClure Newspaper Syndicate, did not find it necessary to enlighten me on their commercial methods. The result was that I sold to Mr. Brainard the world rights to my book on Russia for $1,750 advance against the usual royalties and fifty per cent for the serial rights. It seemed a very satisfactory arrangement to me, the most gratifying provision in the agreement being that nothing could be changed in my manuscript without my knowledge and consent.

My visa was renewed for another two months and the hope held out that I could have further extensions. My living-expenses were now also secured. I could proceed with my book. I had lived with it since Kronstadt and had worked it out in all its aspects. But when I came to write it, I was overwhelmed by the magnitude of my subject. The Russian Revolution, greater and more profound than the French, as Peter had rightly said—could I do it justice in one volume and in the limited time set? Years were needed for such a work, and a far abler pen than mine to make the story as vivid and moving as its reality. [. . .]

My immediate surroundings were anything but helpful. My young friend had got into the same slough as I. He had not the strength to leave, nor I to send him away. Loneliness, the yearning to be cared for in an intimate sense, made me cling to the boy. He admired me as a rebel and as a fighter; as a friend and companion I had awakened his spirit and had opened to him a new world of ideas, books, music, art. [. . .] But the difference, the ever present difference of twenty-four years, he could not forget. [. . .]

The arrival of my beloved Stella and Ian, my baby almost as much as hers, somewhat dulled my gnawing pain. I had not seen them for three years and I had longed for their coming. One week went by in sweet harmony with my own, in reminiscences of the past, with all its joy and travail, of what is admirable and what is hateful in my adopted land.

A dissonant note soon disturbed our idyll. Stella had always kept me on a pedestal. She could not bear to see my feet of clay. She had suffered through my relation to Ben, and now again my dear one resented that her adored *Tante* should "throw herself away." My young Swede was quick to sense the disdain of my niece. He became more contrary and went out of his way to be particularly disagreeable to her.

Ian, a beautiful youngster of six, wild and unbridled as a young colt, found our apartment too small for his energies. He knew no German and he could not understand why everybody should walk as on glass because "granny's" nerves were on edge. [. . .] Fortunately my sense of the ridiculous had not entirely forsaken me. I could still laugh at my own folly. But I could not write, or do as my Swede—run away!

He would go to the seashore for a few days, so that Stella and I could be with each other undisturbed, he said. I did not protest; I felt rather relieved. The two days lengthened into a week without a word to reassure me that all was well with him. My anxiety grew into an obsession that he had taken or lost his life. To escape the torturing thought I tried once more to start my book. As if by magic the load I had carried for months was lifted; the harrowing shadows disappeared together with the boy and my frustrations. I myself became dissolved into the picture that was taking form on the paper before me.

A storm began in the late afternoon and continued throughout the night. Thunder and lightning, followed by wind and rain, beat against the windows of my room. I wrote on, oblivious of everything except the storm in my own soul. I found release at last. [. . .]

The Swede returned hale and sound. He had not written because he was trying to muster up courage to go his own way. He failed. He was drawn back by his need of me. Would I accept him again? I did, certain that he could not consume me as before. I was back in Russia now, in her triumph and defeat, my every fibre intent on recreating the tremendous panorama I had witnessed for twenty-one months.

My dear old pal Sasha, though rarely sympathetic with my affairs of the heart, never failed me in our common activities or in his co-operation with my literary efforts. Just as soon as he saw me working in earnest, he came back with his old eagerness to help. I should have made considerable progress now but for a new disturbance.

[. . .] My secretary, an intelligent and efficient Jewish-American girl, and my young Swede could apparently not get on. [. . .] Soon I discovered the truth of the German saying: *Was liebt sich, das neckt sich.*[2] The two young people had fallen in love with each other and were fighting to distract my attention from their real feelings. They were too unsophisticated to be guilty of deliberate deception. They simply lacked the courage to speak and were perhaps afraid to hurt me. As if their frankness could have been more lacerating than my realization that their show of indifference was only a shield! At heart I had not ceased to believe that my love would rekindle his affection, so rich and abundant during our months in Stockholm.

I could not endure the silly hide-and-seek going on before my eyes. I assured them that nothing would change my affection for them, and that I wanted the girl to continue with me until the manuscript was typed, but I would ask them to find quarters of their own. It would be less wearing for the three of us. They moved out. [. . .] Their love was young, and it was unkind to cause it pain. [. . .]

I still had the hardest part of my book to do—an Afterword that was to set forth the lessons of the Russian Revolution which our comrades and the militant masses will have to learn if future revolutions are not to be failures. I had come to realize that with all the Bolshevik mania for power they could never have so completely terrorized the Russian people if it were not inherent in mass psychology to be easily swayed. I was also convinced that the conception of revolution in our own ranks was too romantic, and that miracles cannot be expected even after capitalism shall have been abolished and the *bourgeoisie* eliminated. I knew better now and I wanted to help my comrades to a clearer understanding. [. . .]

I wrote a closing chapter suggesting in general outline the practical, constructive efforts during revolution. I had reasons for a double celebration. I had regained my emotional sanity and I had completed the manuscript of "My Two Years in Russia." [. . .]

Our presence in Liebenstein brought to us many of our friends from America. [. . .] "Queen E.G. and her court," teased Henry [Alsberg] at the lovely surprise party my family arranged for my fifty-fourth birthday. This much life had given me: friends whose love neither faltered nor changed with the years, a treasure few possess.

Among the many birthday gifts and messages I received was also one from my faithful friend and counsellor, Harry Weinberger. It brought the good news that my manuscript had been sold by Brainard to Doubleday, Page and Company and that the book would be out in October of that year (1923). I cabled that page proofs be sent to me. The publishers replied that it would delay the issue of my book and assured me that they would keep strictly to the manuscript. [. . .]

Stella had hardly left when I received a blow that staggered me.[3] A copy of my book arrived with the last twelve chapters missing and with an entirely wrong title. As printed, the volume was an unfinished work, because the last chapters and particularly my Afterword, which represented the culminating essence of the whole, were left out. The unauthorized name was fearfully misleading: *My Disillusionment in Russia* was sure to convey to the reader that it was the Revolution that had disillusioned me rather than the pseudo-revolutionary methods of the Communist State. The title I had given my work was simply

"My Two Years in Russia." The spurious title was a veritable misfit. I wrote a statement for the press, which I sent to Stella, explaining that my manuscript had been amputated, and I cabled Harry Weinberger to demand of the publishers an explanation. I wanted the sales stopped till the matter should be straightened out.

In reply, Doubleday, Page and Company cabled that they had bought from the McClure Syndicate the world rights to the twenty-four chapters in the belief that they comprised my complete story. They had also been authorized to use their own title. They had known nothing about the existence of the other chapters.

Energetic Harry Weinberger would not give up. He succeeded in inducing Doubleday, Page and Company to publish the missing chapters in a separate volume, the cost of printing to be guaranteed by us. [. . .]

The reviews of *My Disillusionment in Russia* showed as much discernment as the representative of Doubleday, Page and Company who had bought three-quarters of a manuscript as a complete work. Among the scores of reviewers only one guessed that the book was an abortion. It was a Buffalo librarian, who pointed out in the *Journal* that Emma Goldman's narrative ended with Kiev, 1920, while in her Preface she stated that she had left Russia in December 1921. Had nothing happened in all the intervening time to impress the author? The man's perspicacity strikingly reflected on the dullness of the "critics" who presume to pass literary judgment in the United States.

The Communist response to my volume on Russia could have been foreseen, of course. William Z. Foster's "review" was to the effect that everybody in Moscow was aware that Emma Goldman was receiving support from the American Secret Service Department. Mr. Foster knew that I should not have lasted a day in Russia if the Cheka had believed such a thing. Other Communists, who wrote as kindly as Mr. Foster, also knew that I had not been bought. There was only one who had the courage to say so: René Marchand, of the French group in Moscow, who stated in his review that, though he regretted my misguided judgment, he could not believe that my stand against Soviet Russia was motivated by material reasons. I appreciated his giving me credit for my revolutionary integrity, and I wished he were brave enough to admit that he was unable to reconcile himself to some of the methods the Bolsheviki practised in the name of the Revolution. Commandeered to work in the Cheka, René Marchand had seen enough to plead for his removal, as otherwise he would be compelled to leave the Communist Party. Like many other sincere Communists he did not understand the Revolution in terms of the Cheka.

Not so Bill Haywood. As Sasha had foreseen, he easily took the Bolshevik bait. Three weeks after his arrival in Russia he wrote to America that the workers were in full control and that prostitution and drunkenness had been abolished. Lending himself to such obvious falsehoods, why should Bill not also credit me with motives he knew were absurd? "Emma Goldman did not get the soft jobs she was looking for; that was why she wrote against the Dictatorship of the Proletariat." Poor Bill! He began rolling down the precipice when he ran away to save himself from the burning house of the I.W.W. He could not stop himself in his fall.

My Communist accusers were not the only ones to cry "Crucify!" There were also some anarchist voices in the chorus. They were the very people who had fought me on Ellis Island, on the *Buford*, and the first year in Russia because I had refused to condemn the Bolsheviki before I had a chance to test their scheme.

Daily the news from Russia about the continued political persecution strengthened every fact I had described in my articles and in my book. It was understandable that Communists should close their eyes to the reality, but it was reprehensible on the part of people who called themselves anarchists to do so. [. . .]

The German Revolution was only skin-deep, but it succeeded in establishing certain political liberties. Our comrades could publish their papers, issue books, and hold meetings. The Communists carried on their propaganda with little molestation, condemning in Germany the abuses they defended in Russia. The reactionary nationalist elements were also not interfered with. Their arrogance knew no bounds, equalling that of the militarists of the old Prussian régime. With two such I had an encounter in a subway train. They were railing against the *verdammte Juden*[4] as idle vampires and the cause of the ruin of the Fatherland. I listened for a while and then remarked that they were talking nonsense. I had lived in a land where there were millions of Jewish workingmen, I told them, and many of them brave fighters for the betterment of humanity. "Where is that?" they demanded. "In America," I replied. It drew a volley of abuse from them. America had tricked Germany out of victory, they cried. As the train reached my station and I alighted, they shouted after me: "Wait till things change and we'll fix such as you just as we did Rosa Luxemburg."

Though in a desperate economic situation, Germany enjoyed considerable political freedom. That is to say, the natives. But I was not a German and consequently I had no right to express opinions. It was not a matter of mere arrest: it meant expulsion. There was apparently no other country willing to let me in. [. . .]

My friends Rudolf and Milly Rocker[5] favoured one of the two ways out of my dilemma: the legalization in Germany by marriage, or England. The first method had been a frequent practice among the Russian intelligentsia and revolutionists in the days when women had no political status apart from their husbands or fathers. In Germany Rosa Luxemburg had contracted such a nominal marriage to enable her to remain in the country and follow her work. Why couldn't I do the same? I, they said, should go through with the ridiculous ceremony and end my troubles. Such a step had long before been suggested in America. Several comrades had been willing to sacrifice themselves for the cause, among them my old friend Harry Kelly. It would have prevented the United States from deporting me, Milly reiterated. But I had been unable to do the ludicrous and inconsistent thing, having opposed the institution of marriage all my life. Moreover, there had been the lure of Russia, the glowing dream. That too was dead now, together with the notion that one could remain on earth without making compromises.

My difficulties in Sweden and other countries made me amenable to the suggestion of marriage in order to gain a foothold now in some corner of the world. Harry Kelly was still ready to keep his promise. On his visit to Sweden he had again offered to take me back to America as his bride. Good old scout! He had been unaware of the new law by which an American husband was no longer a protection for his foreign-born wife. [. . .]

England did not appear very enticing. Still, it might afford me asylum with comparative political freedom, and perhaps also an opportunity to earn my livelihood through lectures and articles. Frank Harris was in Berlin, keeping open house. His interest and kindness, as when I was in the Missouri prison, had not changed. It would be quite easy to get me to England, he said. He knew almost everyone in the Labour Government and he would try for a visa for me. Soon after, Frank left for France, and several months passed before I heard from him again. He informed me that the Home Office had asked no questions about my political views or intentions. It had merely inquired whether I had means of support. Frank had replied that I was an able writer who earned my living by my pen. Moreover, he could name a dozen persons who would consider it a privilege to support his friend and he was one of them. Shortly afterwards I was notified by the British Consulate in Berlin that a visa had been granted me.

Except for the parting from Sasha and from the other friends who had endeared themselves to me, I had no regrets on leaving Germany. [. . .] For the rest, I was glad to get away. England might let me take root, offer an outlet for my energies, respond to an appeal for the doomed and damned in the Soviet land. That was worth going to England for; it was a new hope to cling to.

With this thought to give me courage, I left Germany on July 24, 1924, via Holland and France, for England. [. . .]

CHAPTER LV

It was foggy and drizzling when I arrived in September, and it did not let up until May. Unlike my visit in 1900, when I lived in a basement, my quarters this time were on the heights: a bedroom on the third floor in the house of my old friend Doris Zhook. I even had the luxury of a gas-stove, which I kept going all day. The monster fog mocked my futile attempts to keep the chill out of my old bones, even when I tried to snatch a little cheer from an occasional ray of sunlight. [. . .]

I soon realized that physical handicaps would be the least of my difficulties. The anarchists of London were my friends of many years, solicitous and willing to assist in anything I wanted to do. [. . .] But there was no real movement in London or in the provinces, I soon learned. Coming as I did from the seething anarchist activities in Berlin, the situation in England was depressing. The general political conditions were worse than I had anticipated. The war had created greater havoc with traditional British liberalism and the right of asylum than it had in other lands. Getting into the country was extremely difficult for anyone of advanced social ideas. More difficult to remain if one engaged in socio-political propaganda. [. . .]

The older rebels were disillusioned by the collapse of the Revolution. The younger generation, as far as it was at all interested in ideas (which was little enough), was carried away by the Bolshevik glamour. Communist intrigue and denunciation were doing the rest to widen the chasm.

It was a disheartening picture. But I was in England and I did not propose to run away, notwithstanding the odds against me. My comrades agreed that my name and knowledge of Russian conditions might rally the radical and Labour factions to the support of the political victims of the dictatorship. [. . .] I did not know how to reach the British people, and the only suggestion I could make was a dinner at some restaurant as my début before the London liberal public. [. . .]

My note to Rebecca West[1] brought a kind of reply and an invitation to lunch. I was pleasantly surprised to find her anything but English in her manner. But for her speech I should have thought her an Oriental, she was so vivacious, eager, charming, direct. Her friendliness, the cosiness of her room, the hot tea, were grateful after a long, cold ride in the drab autumn afternoon. She had not read my writings, she frankly admitted, but she knew enough about me to add her welcome to that of the others and she would be happy to speak at the dinner. She would also arrange an evening to have her friends meet me. I was not to hesitate to call on her for anything I might need. I left my hostess with the comforting feeling that I had found a friend, an oasis in the desert London seemed to me.

The day of the dinner began in darkness and ended in a downpour. I went to the restaurant with a sinking heart. [. . .] There wasn't a baker's dozen present at seven o'clock. But at eight [. . .] two hundred and fifty people had crowded into the dining-room, and additional tables had to be laid for guests who continued to come, even after the speeches had begun. I was profoundly moved that so many should venture out on such a night to welcome me. [. . .]

With a feeling of gratitude I began my address on the purpose of my coming to England and the things I wanted to do. I have rarely had a more attentive audience until I mentioned Russia. Shifting of chairs, turning of necks, and disapproval on the faces before me were the first indications that all was not going to be so harmonious as it seemed at first. I went on with my speech. It was important that the main reason for my presence in England should be clear to everyone. I reminded my hearers of the Russian Revolution of 1905 and the horrors that followed it. [. . .] With whatever ability and voice I possessed I would cry out my *"J'accuse!"* against the Soviet autocracy responsible for political persecution, executions, and savage brutality.

The applause was interrupted by loud protests. Some diners jumped to their feet and demanded the floor. They never would have believed, they said, that the arch-rebel Emma Goldman would ally herself with the Tories against the Workers' Republic. They would not have broken bread with me had they known that I had gone back on my revolutionary past. It was growing late. The evening meant too much to me to have it end in a row. We were planning a meeting in Queen's Hall, I informed the audience, and there we all should have opportunity to discuss the matter in detail. [. . .]

Owing to the elections and the approaching holidays, our meeting had to be postponed till January. My friends insisted that the backing of a numerous committee was indispensable to the moral success of our undertaking. I chafed at the delay and resented the idea of a committee. [. . .]

In my public career I had been affiliated with groups only temporarily. I worked for them, not with them. Whatever value my activities had in America was due to my free-lancing and independent position. My London friends urged that my first large public appearance must have the proper support. The dinner had already called attention to my presence in London and to my purpose. The meeting would pave my way for further efforts. After all, they knew best how to reach the British public, and I was willing to follow their advice.

For two weeks I bombarded with letters every name on the list of the prospective committee, but the response was negligible. Most of them did not even reply. [. . .]

My circle of acquaintance kept enlarging, and invitations to luncheons, teas, and dinners began to pour in. Everyone was most hospitable, attentive, and cordial—all very pleasant if I had come to England for social entertainment only. But I had come for a purpose. I wanted to arouse the sensibilities of fair-minded Englishmen to the purgatory of Russia, to stir them to a concerted protest against the horrors parading as Socialism and Revolution. It was not that my hosts and their friends were not interested or that they questioned the facts I presented. It was their remoteness from the Russian reality, their lukewarmness to conditions they could not visualize and hence did not feel.

The Labour leaders were callous. In the words of a British Socialist, "It would spell political disaster to my party to declare
to its constituents that the Bolsheviks had slain the Revolution."
[. . .]

When I first called on Professor Harold Laski,[2] he expressed
the opinion that I ought to take some comfort in the vindication
anarchism had received by the Bolsheviki. I agreed, adding that
not only their régime, but their stepbrothers as well, the Socialists in power in other countries, had demonstrated the failure
of the Marxian State better than any anarchist argument. [. . .]
In America I had never met such lack of response to any appeal.
Laski thought I would find even the most radical elements reluctant to oppose the Bolsheviki. They were too enthusiastic
about the Revolution to draw lines of demarcation. In time I
might interest the labour ranks. He would do his best to aid me;
he would invite his friends for the next Sunday afternoon to
hear my story. Once more hope sprang from what seemed a
hopeless and futile quest.

It was impossible for me to speak dispassionately about Russia,
but on this occasion I sought to suppress all personal feeling. I
spoke in a conversational tone and as objectively as I could. At the
conclusion of my talk most of my questioners demanded whether
I could point out "any political group more liberal than the Bolsheviki, more efficient for establishing a democratic government
should the Soviet régime be overthrown." I replied that I did not
want the Communist State overthrown, nor would I aid any
group that attempted such a *coup*. [. . .] I believed that strong
radical opinion in the United States and Europe would affect the
Soviet government as it had that of the Romanovs. It might help
to curb their despotism, stop persecution for mere opinion, convictions without trial, and wholesale executions in the cellars of
the Cheka. Were not these simple human demands worth trying
for? "Yes, but it might lead to the return of autocracy."

The same evasions and objections, the same faint-heartedness,
I came across in every group I addressed. It was appalling. At
last realizing the futility of my efforts, I resolved not to waste
more time on the élite, the Labour politicians, or the ladies dab-
bling in socialism. Anarchists had always carried on their work

without so-called respectable backing and they would have to do so now. [. . .]

Professor Laski notified me that his friends were of the opinion that the I.L.P.[3] should abstain from attacking Soviet Russia. He added that Bertrand Russell, though he disliked the Soviet methods, doubted the advisability of my propaganda. [. . .] On the whole he agreed with Bertrand Russell that a campaign in behalf of the politicals must not be under anti-Bolshevik auspices "such as yours."

Bertrand Russell's stand was a disappointment to me. I had seen him and talked with him at length. While he had not promised to act on the proposed committee, saying he would have to think the matter over, he had shown no indication that he did not care to affiliate himself with an avowed anarchist. It was rather discouraging to find the brilliant critic of the State, the man whose spiritual attitude was anarchistic, fight shy of co-operation with an anarchist. And Laski, too, the bold exponent of individualism! [. . .]

Sasha had also not been idle; his *The Bolshevik Myth* now appeared, published in New York by Boni and Liveright. But the latter had eliminated the concluding and most vital chapter as being an "anti-climax." Thereupon Sasha issued it as a brochure under that very title and circulated it at his own expense. [. . .]

We kept our pledge to our suffering comrades in Russia. We made known their cause as well as that of all other persecuted revolutionists. We demonstrated the abyss between the Bolsheviki and "October." We would continue to do so, Sasha through the *Bulletin* of the Joint Committee for the Defense of Political Prisoners, and I whenever and wherever the opportunity presented itself. Now was the time for me to turn to other matters. After eight months' absorption in the Russian situation I felt justified in seeking different subjects for expression. This was especially imperative because I could not go on indefinitely accepting support from my family and American friends. [. . .] Now that I might become self-supporting by means of lectures on the drama, I decided to discontinue my Russian work, at least for a while. [. . .]

The Drama Study Circle I had organized in London was

planning several lectures on the origin and development of the Russian drama, and the anarchists in the East End of London asked for the same course in Yiddish. I could look forward to a busy time doing work I had always loved.

During my early days in England, when everything seemed bleakest, Stella had written me that London was a cold beauty that required much wooing before revealing her charms. "Who cares to woo a cold beauty?" I replied. Now I had been paying court to her for nine months. Could it be that I was beginning to touch her heart?

London was really beautiful now in its profusion of green and abundance of flowers and sun, as if it would never wear mourning or weep torrents again. One begrudged every moment indoors, knowing how short-lived the glory was. But six hours every day was the very least I needed to cope with the historic treasures I discovered in the British Museum on the Russian theatre and drama. This institution had been one of my objectives in coming to England, but it was only now that I had the time, the interest, and the need for availing myself of all it offered. The longer I worked in the museum, the more information I unearthed on stage arrangement, old plays, scenery, and costumes. This led to wider fields, embracing the political and social backgrounds of the dramatists of different periods, and their correspondence that reflected their feelings and reaction to Russian life. It was a fascinating study and so absorbing as to make me forget the closing-hour. [. . .]

My meetings with Havelock Ellis and Edward Carpenter stood out as the fulfillment of a wish cherished for a quarter of a century. Not that I learned to know them better through our fleeting personal contact than I had through their works. I saw Ellis for a bare half-hour in his London apartment and we were both rather tongue-tied. But if I had lived near him for years, I should not have realized better the oneness of the man with his life's labours, so expressive of his unique personality and lofty vision was every line that had spoken to me out of the pages of his liberating work.

My visit with Edward Carpenter lasted the greater part of an afternoon in his modest cottage at Guildford. [. . .] I attempted to tell him how much his books had meant to me—*Towards Democracy, Angel Wings, Walt Whitman.* He stopped me, gently putting his hand over mine. Instead I should rather tell him about Alexander Berkman, he said. He had read his *Prison Memoirs,* "a profound study of man's inhumanity and prison psychology, and of his own martyrdom, portrayed with extraordinary simplicity." He had always wanted to know Sasha and "the Girl" in the book. . . .

A friend had once said jokingly that I was like a cat; "drop her out of a sixth-story window and she'll land on her paws." [. . .] Two things brought me on my paws again. One was my plan of a volume on "The Origin and Development of the Russian Drama"; the other, a tour through Canada. The anarchists there had invited me to come, and a New York comrade promised to raise my expenses. I would go to some little place in France and devote the summer to writing and would leave for Canada in the fall. The two ventures, I hoped, might secure me for a year or two to live and be active in England. I made sure of my going to Canada by immediately reserving my passage.

The incentive to devote the next four months to writing had come from C. W. Daniel, my patron publisher. He had taken the keenest interest in my lectures on the Russian dramatists. [. . .]

I was about to leave London when the general strike was declared. I could not think of running away from an event of such overwhelming importance. Workers and helpers would be needed and I must remain and offer my services. John Turner was the most likely man to get me in touch with the people in charge of the strike. I explained to him that I was willing to do any kind of work to aid the great struggle: look after the relief of the strikers' families, organize the care of their children, or take charge of feeding-stations. I wanted to help the rank and file. John was delighted. It would dispel the prejudice my anti-Soviet stand had created in trade-union circles and would demonstrate that anarchists not merely theorized, but were capable of practical work and were ready for any emergency. He would take my message to the strike committee and put them in direct touch with me. I waited for two days, but no word came either from trade-union headquarters or from John. On the third day I again made the long trip on foot to see John and to inquire about the matter. He had been told that all help in the strike situation was drawn from trade-union ranks, and that no outside aid was needed. The excuse was flimsy; clearly the leaders feared it would leak out that the anarchist Emma Goldman had some connexion with the general strike. John was loath to admit my interpretation, nor could he deny that I might be right. It was the old story: the centralized machinery in every walk of British life left no room for individual initiative. It was torture to remain neutral where the line between masters and men was so sharply drawn, or to stand by idly while the leaders were making one blunder after another; nor would I leave by rail or ship manned by strike-breakers. I found some relief in being out on the streets mingling with the men and getting their reactions. Their spirit of solidarity was wonderful, their fortitude great, their disregard of the hardships the strike had already imposed admirable. No less extraordinary was their good humour and self-control in the face of provocation from the enemy: armoured cars rattling along the streets, taunts and ridicule from the young bullies in charge, and the affronts of the wealthy in their luxurious automobiles. A few encounters had taken place, but on the whole the strikers carried themselves with pride and dignity, confident of the justice of their cause. It was inspiring, but it also increased my misery at my own helplessness. On the tenth day of the strike, there still being no sign of a settlement, I decided to leave England by airplane.

CHAPTER LVI

Friends had unearthed a lovely spot in Saint-Tropez, an ancient, picturesque fishing-village in the south of France. An enchanted place it was: a little villa of three rooms from which one caught a view of the snow-covered Maritime Alps, with a garden of magnificent roses, pink and red geraniums, fruit-trees, and a large vineyard, all for fifteen dollars a month. Here I regained something of my old zest for life, and faith in my ability to overcome the hardships the future might hold. I divided my time between my writing-desk and my *ménage*. I even found time to learn to swim. I prepared the meals on a quaint, red-bricked Provençal stove in which only charcoal could be used. Many friends from America and other parts of the world found their way to my new home in Saint-Tropez. [. . .]

Peggy[1] and Lawrence lived not far from us in a village called Pramousquier and there I first met Kathleen Millay and Howard Young.[2] The latter reproached me for not writing my autobiography. "A woman of your past!" he exclaimed; "just think what you could make of it!" I would, I told him, if I could secure an income for two years, a secretary, and someone to scour my pots and kettles. He would undertake to raise five thousand dollars on his return to America, Young promised. In honour of my prospective benefactor, Peggy added a few more bottles of wine to those already emptied at dinner.

The four months in Saint-Tropez passed all too quickly in labour and play. A golden dream, not without its rude awakening, however. Mr. Daniels informed me that conditions in England since the general strike had grown from bad to worse;

there being no sign of coming improvement I should not feel bound to his firm with my manuscript on the Russian drama. That was the first ripple in my azure sky, yet not so disconcerting as the cable from the New York comrade who had promised to raise the initial fund for my Canadian tour. "It is off," he announced.

The Canadian Government had probably declared I would not be admitted, or our own people had reconsidered their invitation, I thought. But my conjectures proved false. Canada remained blissfully ignorant of the danger threatening it, and our comrades assured me they were expecting me without fail. [. . .]

While in Paris, I lunched with Theodore Dreiser.[3] "You must write the story of your life, E.G.," he urged; "it is the richest of any woman's of our century. Why in the name of Mike don't you do it?" I told him that Howard Young had put the question first. I had not taken it very seriously and I was not surprised that I had received no word from him, though he had been back in America several months. Dreiser protested that he was greatly interested in seeing my story given to the world. He would secure a five-thousand-dollar advance from some publisher and I would hear from him very soon. "All right, old dear, see what you can do! If you also forget or if you fail, I will not sue you for breach of promise," I laughed.

I entered Canada as unheralded as I had England two years previously. In Montreal I learned that no English anarchist had been heard in Canada for a great many years. The only active people were the Yiddish-language group, but they had no experience in organizing English lectures. [. . .] The Toronto anarchists were more numerous and better organized. They were carrying on intensive propaganda in Yiddish and exerting an influence in their community, but they sadly neglected the natives. They were eager, however, to assist me to any extent with my program of English lectures. [. . .]

Dear members of my family came to visit me from the States, and it was a great joy to be within their reach, even if they had to come to me instead of my going to them. Not that the opportunity was not offered me. Various friends were eager to smuggle me across the border. With my picture in every rogues' gallery in the United States, I could not have remained there long without being recognized, and there was no object in hiding. Those of my friends and comrades who could afford it would come to see me. For the rest, I never liked sensation for its own sake. There still was a large place in my heart for my erstwhile country, regardless of her shabby treatment. My love for all that is ideal, creative, and humane in her would not die. But I should rather never see America again if I could do so only by compromising my ideas. [. . .]

A note from Peggy Guggenheim on my return to Toronto expressed surprise that I had not answered Howard Young's letter regarding my autobiography. Had I changed my mind about permitting him to raise a fund to enable me to write the book? He was planning to proceed with it and she would open the subscription with five hundred dollars. I replied that I had never received Howard's letter, but it was all right for him to go ahead. Yet I should prefer to have my old friend W. S. Van Valkenburgh in charge of the hard work the appeal would entail. I knew that if energy and indefatigability could avail, Van was sure of success. With Peggy Guggenheim and Howard Young as my first sponsors, Kathleen Millay as the official secretary, and Van to do the heavy correspondence, the project was finally launched to secure funds for my writing the "masterpiece that would set the world afire."

Meanwhile my Toronto comrades kept on insisting that I was wanted in their midst. They had never believed that their city could respond so warmly to anarchist propaganda. They urged that I make Toronto my permanent home or that I remain there several years at least. [. . .]

My family sent cash as their birthday gifts. The two Bens, Big and Little, and other friends had also remembered me on the occasion. I would have enough to keep going for part of the summer. I thought I would rest up for a while and then buckle down to prepare a new lecture course. But I lost all desire for a rest with the impending murder of Sacco and Vanzetti.[4]

The first knowledge of their arrest had reached me in Russia;

then nothing more till I was in Germany. So overpowering were the proofs of their innocence, it seemed impossible that the State of Massachusetts would repeat in 1923 the crime Illinois had committed in 1887. Surely some progress had been made in America in the past quarter of a century, some change in the minds and hearts of the masses to prevent the new human sacrifice, I reasoned. Strange that I, of all people, should have thought so. I who had lived and struggled in the United States for more than half my life and had witnessed the inertia of the workers and the unscrupulousness and the inhumanity of the American courts! With our Chicago men innocently slain, with Sasha doomed to twenty-two years for an offence that legally called only for seven, with Mooney and Billings buried alive on perjured testimony, the victims of Wheatland and Centralia still in prison, and all the others I had seen railroaded! How could I have believed that Sacco and Vanzetti, however innocent, would escape American "justice"? The power of suggestion had taken me off my guard. The whole world had repudiated the monstrous possibility that Sacco and Vanzetti would be denied a new trial or that the sentence of death would be carried out. I had been influenced by it and had done little to help stay the hangman's hand reaching out for these two beautiful lives. Only after I had come to Canada did I fully realize my mistake. Talking seemed inconsequential and futile. Yet it was all I could do to call attention to the black deed about to be committed across the border, after the seven years' purgatory suffered by the two persecuted men. Alas, my feeble voice, like that of millions, cried in vain. America remained deaf.

My comrades organized a memorial meeting. I consented to speak, though I knew that no pæan of their valour and nobility could raise them to greater glory in the eyes of posterity than Vanzetti's own beautiful song or Sacco's last simple and heroic words. [. . .]

In January 1928 I delivered my final talk in a series of twenty, embracing various problems of our time. The last evening, on which I discussed Ben Lindsey's *Companionate Marriage,* brought out an audience equalling the total attendance of four other meetings. I was assured that I had performed a feat no public speaker had ever attempted in Toronto before. I had come as a stranger without funds or a manager. Within a year I had created enough interest to secure audiences twice a week for eight months. [. . .]

The call to arms for "E.G.'s Life" had not brought battalions to the fore, Van ruefully reported; no more than a thousand dollars had come in, though he had bombarded everyone within reach. His face lit up when he learned that the comrades of the *Freie Arbeiter Stimme* had, through the efforts of its editor, Joseph Cohen, B. Axler, and Sarah Gruber, raised nearly as much, and that Toronto and Montreal had not lagged behind. [. . .] In fifteen months I had raised over thirteen hundred dollars for the political fund, some money for the fight to rescue Sacco and Vanzetti and for similar causes. I had paid my debts, amounting to twelve hundred dollars, and I had enough left to cover my return passage, aside from the new fund for my autobiography.

I was returning to France, to lovely Saint-Tropez and my enchanting little cottage to write my life. My life—I had lived in its heights and its depths, in bitter sorrow and ecstatic joy, in black despair and fervent hope. I had drunk the cup to the last drop. I had lived my life. Would I had the gift to paint the life I had lived!

Notes

CHAPTER I

1. Johann Most (1846–1906): prominent German social democrat legislator, became American anarchist lecturer and publisher.
2. Hillel Solotaroff (1865–1921): Russian-born physician and anarchist lecturer and writer.
3. Alexander "Sasha" Berkman (1870–1936): Russian-born anarchist, publisher, and writer. Berkman had been in the United States for two years when he met Goldman in New York.
4. *My sister Lena*: Goldman's half-sister Lena, two years older than she, had preceded her to America.

CHAPTER II

1. Stella Comyn (Cominsky) Ballantyne (1886–1961): daughter of EG's older half-sister Lena; remained close to EG throughout her lifetime.

CHAPTER III

1. *Vera's venture in* What's [*sic*] to Be Done?: The widely influential novel *What Is to Be Done?* was published by the Russian intellectual Nikolai Chernyshevsky in 1863. His reform-minded, gentry-born heroine refuses the traditional safeguards of conventional marriage in order to work, study, and organize cooperative enterprises.
2. *Turgeniev's* Fathers and Sons, *and* Obriv (The Precipice): Ivan Sergeyevich Turgenev (1818–1883) published *Fathers and Sons* in 1862, a love story embedded in timely, social issues. Ivan

Alexandrovich Gontcharov (1812–1891) published *The Precipice* in 1869.

3. Modest "Fedya" Stein (1871–1958) was Alexander Berkman's cousin. An artist and later a successful illustrator, Stein was a major financial supporter of EG and Berkman in their exile.

4. Sophia Perovskaya (1853–1881) and Andrei Zhelyabov (1850–1881): Russian revolutionary heroes executed with their comrades for the assassination of Czar Alexander II in March 1881. Perovskaya was the first woman political prisoner to be executed in Russia.

5. *the opera* Trovatore: In Giuseppe Verdi's *Il trovatore* (premiere 1/19/1853), the star-crossed lovers Leonora and the troubador Manrico meet a tragic end.

CHAPTER V

1. Joseph Barondess (1867–1928): Russian-born Jewish socialist and anarchist, established the International Ladies' Garment Workers' Union (ILGWU) after the Triangle shirtwaist fire in New York City.

2. EG had befriended Annie Netter, a young labor and anarchist activist. Netter's home was an "oasis for the radical element, an intellectual centre" (see LML, 1970, 54–55).*

3. When Johann Most told EG that her blond hair and blue eyes were unusual for a Jewish woman, she recounted her father's mocking story that he had found her at a pig market (see LML, 1970, 35).

CHAPTER VI

1. Armes Aschenprödelchen: "poor little Cinderella."

2. Joseph Peukert (1855–1910): Bohemian-born anarchist. Influenced by Communist anarchism of Peter Kropotkin, he founded *Gruppe Autonomie* in London, favoring decentralized organization, small groups, individuals, and the revolutionary tactic of "propaganda by the deed," or *attentat*. Immigrated in 1890 to America, where he worked to clear his name of Johann Most's charge that he had acted as a political spy and was responsible for

---

* To provide the reader further reference, all citations to EG's autobiography in the endnotes are to the 1970 unabridged edition.

the arrest of the widely respected anarchist Johann Neve in Belgium in 1887. Called the "brothers' war," the feud between the Most and Peukert camps was "to a large extent the result of personal vanities," in Goldman's opinion (see LML, 1970, 75).

CHAPTER VIII

1. Andrew Carnegie (1835–1919): Scots-born American industrialist and philanthropist; organized the Carnegie Steel Company, which launched the steel industry in Pittsburgh. As a philanthropist, he argued later in life that great personal wealth should be administered as a trust for public welfare.
2. Henry Clay Frick (1849–1919): As chairman of Carnegie Steel, the largest producer of coke from coal, he formed the U.S. Steel Corporation. He bequeathed his private art collection housed in his New York City mansion As a public gallery.
3. See editor's introduction pages xvi-xix for an explanation of *Attentat* and its ideological history.
4. *Most's* Science of Revolutionary Warfare: The best-known pamphlet by anarchist Johann Most was subtitled "A Little Handbook of Instruction in the Use and Preparation of Nitroglycerine, Dynamite . . . Bombs, Fuses, Poisons, etc." (1885). Most's pamphlet confirmed the public impression of an anarchist as a fanatical bomb thrower.
5. Carl Nold (1869–1934) and Henry Bauer (1861–1934): German-born American anarchists, both were sentenced to five years in prison for conspiracy to murder in the attempt against Frick's life.
6. *Dostoyevsky's* Crime and Punishment: The novel, published in 1886, is an account of man's fall and redemption. Fyodor Mikhaylovich Dostoyevsky (1821–1881) explored the existential, moral, and psychological state of the human condition.

CHAPTER IX

1. *toy pistol:* Johann Most belittled Berkman's *Attentat,* suggesting that he had "shot off a toy pistol" (see LML, 1970, 98).
2. Berkman's assassination attempt had been lauded by Peukert and his anarchist group. Their support of Berkman enraged Johann Most, whose repudiation of Berkman's act became more public (see LML, 1970, 98).

CHAPTER X

1. *anniversary of the 11th of November:* On November 11, 1887, the Haymarket martyrs were executed in Chicago.
2. March Metzkow (1854–1945) was a follower of Johann Most.

CHAPTER XI

1. Edward Brady (1852–1903) elicted EG's immediate respect both as a revolutionary and as someone who had survived years in prison (see LML, 1970, 115).
2. Voltairine de Cleyre (1866–1912): American anarchist, prolific writer, and popular lecturer, admired by Goldman, although the two were not always in accord.
3. *Justus's den:* Located at 51 East First Street, Justus Schwab's Lower East Side saloon was a favorite gathering place in the late 19th century for Goldman and anarchist friends. Schwab (1847–1900) was a German-born anarchist and member of New York City revolutionary and working-class associations.
4. the Tombs: New York city prison built in 1835, modeled after a mausoleum with four distinctive massive columns. Built on a swamp, the prison was notoriously poorly ventilated, overcrowded, and foul.
5. Blackwell's Island Penitentiary: Today called Roosevelt Island, this 128-care, two-mile-long island east of Manhattan was home to a granite prison four stories high, built in 1832. Originally designed to accomodate 800 cells, but usually overcrowded, Blackwell's was closed by reform mayor LaGuardia in 1934. All inmates were moved to the new Rikers Island.

CHAPTER XII

1. Johann Most had been imprisoned earlier in Blackwell's Island and had described the penitentiary to EG as the "Spanish Inquisition transferred to the United States" (see LML, 1970, 63).

CHAPTER XIII

1. Thalia Theatre: Located in the Bowery district near Canal Street, it was a popular site for Yiddish theatrical productions in the late 19th and early 20th centuries.
2. Santa Caserio (1873–1894): Italian anarchist and assassin of Sadi Carnot, president of France, June 24, 1894.
3. Man kann nicht ungestraft unter Palmen wandeln: The literal translation of the proverb is, "One cannot walk under palm trees unpunished." More conventionally, the proverb implies, "You must pay for your sins," the image evoked by palm trees suggesting pleasure.
4. John Swinton (1829–1901): Scots-born New York journalist and Civil War correspondent, he achieved a national reputation as an editor for the *New York Times*.
5. Albert Parsons (1848–1887): one of the Haymarket martyrs, brought to the forefront of the labor movement in Chicago after railroad workers joined a mass strike for better wages and improved working conditions.
6. Dyer D. Lum (1839–1893): American anarchist-syndicalist, intellectual, and publisher. An advocate of violence, he called dynamite "the resource of civilization." Later he repudiated violence and published treatises defending conservative trade unionism (1892), for many years influencing the philosophy of the American Federation of Labor (AFL).

CHAPTER XIV

1. Friedrich Nietzsche (1844–1900): German iconoclastic philosopher whose anti-Christian writings and idealization of individual creativity and power were widely influential among artists and intellectuals in the late 19th and early 20th centuries.
2. Sigmund Freud (1856–1939): Viennese Jewish medical doctor and founder of the school of psychoanalysis; architect of the theory of personality in which infantile and early-childhood sexual experiences undergo repression in the formation of consciousness, shaping behavior in adult life.

CHAPTER XV

1. William Jennings Bryan (1860–1925): American political leader and reformer. In 1896 Bryan proposed unlimited coinage of silver

as a remedy to the economic ills afflicting farmers and industrial workers.

2. George Schilling: Goldman describes him as a "well-known Chicago comrade," "an ardent follower of Benjamin Tucker, the leader of the individualist school of anarchism" (LML, 1970, 179).

3. John McLuckie (1852–?): miner and steelworker, elected mayor of Homestead, where he established a virtual workers' government during the clash with Carnegie Steel. McLuckie had met with EG to ask her support for the free-silver campaign. He shared with her the widespread belief among the Homestead workers that Berkman was a company agent who had shot Frick to enlist sympathy for him. Learning that Berkman was still in prison, McLuckie apologized to Goldman and offered to help in the appeals to release him (see LML, 1970, 180–81).

4. James G. Huneker (1860–1921): an essayist and literary critic.

CHAPTER XVII

1. Moses Harman (1830–1910): American anarchist and publisher, exponent of free love, women's rights, and birth control.

2. Eugene Victor Debs (1855–1926): American socialist, labor leader, five-time presidential candidate. Debs was active in the formation of the Social Democratic Party, later the Socialist Party of America.

3. Max Baginski (1864–1943): German American anarchist and editor, publisher of the journal *Die Sturmglocken* in 1896. He met EG in Philadelphia in 1893; they became lovers in 1898.

4. Anthony Comstock (1844–1915): American reformer, founder of the Society for the Suppression of Vice in 1872. He successfully lobbied Congress for enactment of "Comstock" laws banning "obscene, lewd, or lascivious" material from the U.S. mail.

5. Lillian Harman (1870–1929): American free-love advocate and anarchist editor, she assisted her father, Moses, in publication of their journal, *Lucifer*.

6. Havelock Ellis (1859–1939): British doctor, sexual psychologist, Fabian socialist, eugenicist. His *Sexual Inversion* (1897) was one of the first scientific books not to treat homosexuality as a pathological condition.

7. Lucy E. Parsons (1853–1942): American anarchist, labor activist, lecturer, and editor.

8. Governor John Peter Altgeld (1847–1902): governor of Illinois (1893–97), pardoned the three surviving Haymarket prisoners

Samuel Fielden, Oscar Neebe, and Michael Schwab on June 26, 1893. Altgeld risked political suicide at the hands of powerful media giants such as the *New York Times* and the *Chicago Tribune* by exposing the miscarriage of justice in the state's original prosecution of the Haymarket men. The following year Altgeld's refusal to send in troops to end the railway workers' Pullman strike sealed his legendary heroic status in American labor history.

9. *Free Society* (1897–1901): San Francisco–based anarchist journal published by Abe Isaak. Most prominent English-language anarchist journal in the United States at the beginning of the 20th century. Abe Isaak (1856–1937) and Mary Isaak (1861–1934): Russian-born American anarchists, publishers and editors of weekly anarchist journal *Firebrand*. Their home was a center of local anarchist and radical political activity. EG later accused Isaak of political cowardice when he tried to "tone down" her sympathetic portrait of Leon Czolgosz, McKinley's assassin, published in Isaak's newspaper *Free Society* (see LML, 1970, 313).

CHAPTER XVIII

1. Ernest Howard Crosby (1856–1907): American reformer, "a leading single-taxer": single taxers were often libertarians who believed in minimal government, only enough to collect the single tax. EG and other anarchists found them politically congenial. "Tolstoyan anarchism": although Russian novelist and philosopher Leo Tolstoy did not call himself an anarchist, followers were influenced by his pacifism and sympathy for the poor.

CHAPTER XIX

1. Kate Austen (1864–1902): American anarchist, women's rights and free-love advocate.

CHAPTER XX

1. Robert Reitzel (1849–1898): German-born American anarchist, poet, critic, translator, defender of Haymarket anarchists. EG visited Reitzel in Detroit shortly before his death (see LML, 1970, 215).

2. EG had been invited to London to be one of the speakers at the Haymarket anniversary meeting (see LML, 1970, 249).

3. In their military engagement with the Dutch settlers in South Africa (the Boer War, 1899–1902), Britain sought to extend its imperial reach over the rich gold mines of the Boer republics of the Transvaal and the Orange Free State. After an initial success, two years of guerrilla warfare ensued until the Boer resistance was brutally put down.

4. Henry "Harry" May Kelly (1871–1953): American anarchist, printer, lecturer living temporarily in England when EG visited in 1898.

CHAPTER XXI

1. *Solidarity* (1892–1898): first English-language anarchist paper in New York. EG also helped to support the paper financially.

2. Tom Mann (1856–1941): British anarchist, trade unionist, popular public speaker, and organizer.

3. Hippolyte Havel (1869–1950): Czech anarchist, journalist.

4. Richard Krafft-Ebing (1840–1902): German/Austrian psychiatrist, authored widely influential *Psychopathia Sexualis* (1886).

5. Fernand Pelloutier (1867–1901): French anarchist and journalist who argued that trade unions or syndicates could be the primary force for social change.

6. Victor Dave (1845–1922): Belgian-born anarchist, writer, and advocate of *attentat* or revolutionary deed.

7. Michael Bakunin (1814–1876): Russian revolutionary and anarchist theorist who led anti-authoritarian opposition to Karl Marx, leading to his expulsion from the First International in 1872. He explored ideas of anarchist collectivism.

CHAPTER XXII

1. Nikolai Tchaikovsky lent his name to the influential Tchaikovsky Circles formed in St. Petersburg in 1872 to unify student revolutionary opposition and then to promote political propaganda in the countryside. EG called Tchaikovsky "the genius of the revolutionary movement of the Russian youth." Tchaikovsky had met EG in England at the home of the Kropotkins and had advised her against attempting to pursue medical studies while

doing political work, saying she could not do both well (see LML, 1970, 254–55).

2. Oscar Wilde (1854–1900): Irish playwright, poet, and writer known for brilliant and caustic wit in domestic comic dramas. Wilde was sentenced to two years' hard labor for homosexual practices; he died bankrupt in Paris.

3. Neo-Malthusian Congress: English political economist Thomas Malthus (1766–1834) believed unchecked population growth could produce global famine. He influenced Charles Darwin's development of principles of natural selection.

4. EG had come abroad under the name "Mrs. E. G. Brady," explaining she would not have been admitted under her own name (see LML, 1970, 171).

CHAPTER XXIII

1. While she was abroad, EG learned from friends and family that Brady had formed a new relationship and had fathered a daughter (see LML, 1970, 282).

2. Ed Brady had formed a partnership with an inventor of "a novelty in albums." On a previous lecture tour, Goldman had agreed to "take the contraption" on the road with her, and indeed she had been successful in soliciting "several substantial contracts" from stationery stores (see LML, 1970, 212, 230).

3. Leon Czolgosz (1873–1901): American self-proclaimed anarchist and assassin of President McKinley (September 6, 1901).

4. Jay Fox (1870–1961): Irish-born American anarchist and labor organizer.

5. Francis O'Neill (1848–1936): Irish American Chicago police officer and superintendent (1901–05). He was an active reformer of police corruption and collector and performer of Irish music.

6. Nellie Bly (born Elizabeth Jane Cochrane) (1864–1922): American journalist who pioneered in investigative journalism as a reporter for Joseph Pulitzer's *New York World*.

7. Clarence Darrow (1857–1938): American socialist, free thinker, single taxer, and lawyer. He achieved national recognition defending Eugene Debs and the American Railway Union during the 1894 Pullman strike.

CHAPTER XXIV

1. Harry Gordon (1866–1941): Lithuanian-born Jewish American anarchist.
2. Karl Heinzen (1809–1880): German revolutionary. The 1848 revolution brought radical social ideas to the foreground and laid the basis for expectations that a repressed peasantry and an exploited urban working class could combine with a new middle class to create conditions for democratizing Germany.

CHAPTER XXV

1. Joseph Roswell Hawley (1826–1905): representative and senator from Connecticut.

CHAPTER XXVI

1. Herbert Spencer (1820–1903): English philosopher, scientist, engineer, and political economist. He applied Darwinian theories of natural selection to human society, popularizing the notion of "survival of the fittest" and helping to found sociology as a social science.
2. Edward Carpenter (1844–1929): British socialist, writer, and poet; published *Love's Coming of Age* (1886) advocating sexual liberation for homosexuals and women.

CHAPTER XXVII

1. John Turner (1864–1934): British anarchist, journalist, lecturer, and union organizer.
2. *name of a Raines hotel*: After state Senator John Raines introduced a law to curtail prostitution in New York by imposing restrictions on saloons, only hotels with ten or more beds were permitted to serve alcohol. "Raines hotels" were saloons that subdivided rear or upper-floor space into small bedrooms to accommodate the law. Ironically, the law encouraged prostitution since the smaller bedrooms were more likely to be rented by prostitutes and their patrons than by other guests.

CHAPTER XXVIII

1. Catherine Breshkovskaya (1844–1934): Russian revolutionary, anarchist, and lecturer, sentenced to twenty years' hard labor in Siberia in 1878 for revolutionary activities. On her release she helped to form the Socialist Revolutionary Party.
2. Pavel Orleneff (1869–1932): Russian actor who specialized in comic simpleton, vaudeville, and character roles. He tried to establish a public theater for the peasantry.
3. Alla Nazimova (born Adelaide Leventon) (1879–1941): Russian Jewish stage actress and silent film star.

CHAPTER XXIX

1. Matushka Rossiya: "Mother Russia."
2. *Black Hundreds* was the popular name for the Union of the Russian People, a league of monarchists and nationalists who instigated pogroms and terror against the Russian revolutionaries.
3. Sir Herbert Beerbohm Tree (1853–1917): great English character actor and theater manager.
4. *the skin of Miss Smith:* EG had adopted the pseudonym of E. G. Smith to help her promote the Orleneff theater troupe among liberals who might otherwise rebuff her as the notorious anarchist.
5. Hull House: founded in 1889 by American reformer Jane Addams (1860–1935). Located in Chicago's Near West Side, the settlement house provided services for the neighborhood such as a kindergarten and day-care facilities, an employment bureau, art gallery, libraries, and classes in music and art.
6. In 1904 EG had rented part of an apartment at 210 East Thirteenth Street, which remained her home for ten years (see LML, 1970, 349–50).
7. *the historic revolutionary month of March:* Important events in the 1905 revolution in Russia occurred in March.
8. The Open Road: "The Song of the Open Road," by the American poet Walt Whitman (1819–1892), was first published in *Leaves of Grass* in 1900.
9. *the little farm:* Located three and a half miles from Ossining, New York, this "small place in the country" was a gift to Goldman from libertarian Bolton Hall to provide a refuge at a time when she "was being pestered by landlords" (see LML, 1970, 371).

CHAPTER XXXI

1. Henrik Ibsen (1828–1906): Norwegian playwright whose exposure of the hypocrisy of conventional Victorian values was considered scandalous at the time.

CHAPTER XXXII

1. In 1908 Lazarus Overbuch, a recent Russian immigrant, attempted to take the life of the Chicago police chief. The national press claimed the attempt was linked to a widespread anarchist conspiracy. EG denied knowing Overbuch.
2. EG had earlier corresponded with Russian American Dr. Becky Yampolsky, who offered EG room in her home in Chicago when it seemed unlikely hotels would admit Goldman (see LML, 1970, 414).
3. Ben L. Reitman (1879–1942): American social reformer, physician, and writer.
4. See note 1, "Overbuch."

CHAPTER XXXIII

1. Rudyard Kipling (1865–1936): English short-story writer, novelist, and poet who romanticized the heroism of British colonial soldiers in India and Burma.
2. John "Chummy" Fleming (1863–1950): Australian anarchist, lecturer, and labor organizer who agitated among the unemployed.
3. Johan Boyer (1872–1959): Norwegian novelist and dramatist who often wrote about the lives of poor farmers and fishermen.

CHAPTER XXXIV

1. William Buwalda: At the conclusion of an address the previous year in San Francisco on the meaning of patriotism, EG was publicly thanked by a man in uniform. He was later identified to her as William Buwalda, a soldier who was arrested for "attending Emma Goldman's meeting and for shaking hands with her" (see LML, 1970, 428–29).
2. *Among the sensational reports:* On their way to a speech in San Francisco, EG and Ben Reitman were arrested and jailed on

numerous charges, including conspiracy and disturbing the peace. The trial ended in acquittal with EG claiming that the arrest "did more for anarchism than months of propaganda might have accomplished" (see LML, 1970, 444–48).

CHAPTER XXXVI

1. Jack London (1876–1916): American novelist and short-story writer. He often wrote about the individual in a struggle for survival against the powers of nature. In 1910, London purchased a large tract of land near Glen Ellen in Sonoma County, California.
2. *the Ferrer Association:* The Spanish anarchist Francisco Ferrer (1849–1909) founded the journal *The Modern School,* influencing libertarian pedagogies worldwide.
3. In the *Kempton-Wace Letters,* Jack London argued against romantic love, saying mates should be selected for good breeding potential.

CHAPTER XXXVII

1. *House of the Dead:* Published in 1862 by Fyodor Dostoyevsky. In his work, Dostoyevsky drew upon his own experiences of imprisonment in czarist Russia (1850–54) for his liberal sympathies.
2. Gilbert Roe (1865–1929): lawyer and author; adviser to the American Civil Liberties Union (ACLU) after its founding in 1920.

CHAPTER XXXVIII

1. William "Big Bill" Haywood (1869–1928): American radical labor organizer, founding member of the Western Federation of Miners and the Industrial Workers of the World (IWW or the "Wobblies"). Convicted of violating Espionage and Sedition Acts, he fled to the Soviet Union in 1921.
2. Elizabeth Gurley Flynn (1890–1964): American socialist, feminist, and Communist; a lecturer and labor organizer for the IWW. Imprisoned after conviction of conspiracy under the Smith Act in 1952, she immigrated to and died in the Soviet Union.
3. In *An Enemy of the People* (1882), a doctor who warns townspeople that local water is contaminated is ostracized for threatening their economic interests.

CHAPTER XXXIX

1. Saul Josef Yanofsky (1864–1939): Polish-born Jewish anarchist. He criticized Emma Goldman's essay "The Tragedy of Buffalo" as contradictory and dangerous to anarchism.
2. *Chief Wilson:* Jefferson Ken Wilson (1862–1934) was chief of police in San Diego from 1909 to 1917. Earlier known for ending prostitution in San Diego's notorious "Singaree," Wilson steered the police department through the violent clashes between the "vigilance" committees and the IWW.
3. Eleanor Fitzgerald (1877–1955): American anarchist, lecturer, theater manager, and editor.

CHAPTER XL

1. Sons and Lovers *by D. H. Lawrence:* Published in 1913, Lawrence's partly autobiographical novel describes an enduring and emotionally wrought bond between the central character, Paul Morel, and his devoted and protective mother.
2. *Mother Jones:* Mary Harris Jones (1830–1930): Irish American labor organizer, orator, and labor advocate known as Mother Jones.
3. Leonard D. Abbott (1878–1953): American anarchist. Goldman had met Abbott earlier when she solicited help from prominent liberals who might help reduce Berkman's prison sentence (see LML, 1970, 233).
4. Mary G. Shaw (1854–1919): actress and feminist.
5. Fola La Follette (1882–1970) was a teacher and actress, daughter of Progressive senator Robert M. La Follette of Wisconsin. She was married to George Middleton (1880–1967), a playwright and copyright specialist.
6. *The Social Significance of the Modern Drama* was published in April 1914.

CHAPTER XLI

1. *the Ludlow massacres:* one of America's bloodiest assaults on organized labor. On April 20, 1914, the National Guard opened fire on a tent city of coal-mine strikers in Ludlow, Colorado. The resulting deaths, including women and children, precipitated widespread sympathy for the miners and armed resistance. Federal

troops, dispatched by President Woodrow Wilson, intervened and disarmed the strikers. John D. Rockefeller Jr. owned the Colorado company operating the mines at Ludlow.

2. *the Tarrytown campaign:* In response to the Ludlow massacres, Alexander Berkman had organized demonstrations of protest at the Rockefeller home in Tarrytown, New York (see LML, 1970, 535).

3. *Bresci's, Angiolillo's:* the Italian anarchists Michele Angiolillo and Gaetano Bresci were the assassins of the prime minister of Spain (August 1897) and King Umberto of Italy (July 1900), respectively.

4. *my dear nephew Saxe and my old friend Max:* Saxe Commins, son of EG's sister Lena, and Max Baginski.

5. *the Kaiser:* Wilhelm II, emperor of Germany, forced to abdicate as part of the armistice ending World War I.

CHAPTER XLII

1. Margaret Sanger (1879–1966): American nurse and pioneer of birth control movement; she founded Planned Parenthood in 1942.

2. *the fight for Caplan and Schmidt:* David Caplan and Matthew Schmidt were tried in 1915 for participation in the 1910 bombing of the Los Angeles Times Building.

3. Leon Bass (born Leon Malmed) (1881–1956): Russian American radical who met EG about 1906 and maintained a friendship with her until her death.

4. EG had met anarchist Ben Capes and his wife, Ida, while lecturing in St. Louis. Capes remained a lifelong friend (see LML, 1970, 464–65).

5. *Severance, . . . Anthony, Julia Howe:* Caroline M. Severance (1820–1914), American suffragist; Susan B. Anthony (1820–1906), pioneer women's rights advocate and suffragist; Julia Ward Howe (1819–1910), American writer and reformer.

CHAPTER XLIV

1. *Hearst's Examiner:* Newspaper magnate William Randolph Hearst (1863–1951) assumed control of the San Francisco *Examiner* in 1887. His editorship advocated sensational journalistic practices.

2. *Mooney . . . Weinberg:* Of these local radicals charged with complicity in the crime, Thomas J. Mooney, leader of the left wing of

the California Federation of Labor, and Warren Billings were convicted and would serve 23 years (1916–39) in California prisons, in spite of evidence that testimony against them was perjured.

3. Among others, EG enjoyed the company in Provincetown of Stella's actor husband, Teddy Ballantine, the playwright Susan Glaspell, the journalist John Reed (see note LII, 10), and his lover Louise Rryant.

4. Frank P. Walsh (1864–1939): distinguished lawyer who represented radical defendants like Thomas J. Mooney.

5. Frank B. Sanborn (1831–1917): His biography of American essayist, transcendentalist, and reformer Henry David Thoreau (1817–1862) was published in 1890.

6. *Woodrow Wilson campaign:* Nominated for the presidency in 1912, Woodrow Wilson advocated neutrality for America in World War I until 1917, when he asked Congress for a declaration of war against Germany.

CHAPTER XLV

1. Alexandra Kollontay (1873–1952): Russian revolutionary, labor organizer, and Soviet diplomat.

2. Leon Trotsky (born Lev Davidovich Bronstein) (1879–1940): Russian Jewish revolutionary who joined the Bolshevik revolution as an eloquent agitator for the social democrats. He was the first commissar of foreign affairs for the Soviet government under Lenin. Expelled by Stalin in 1926, he was assassinated by Stalin's agents in Mexico.

3. *The New Freedom:* economic reform program named in Woodrow Wilson's 1912 presidential campaign speeches. It was enacted in a series of congressional acts in 1914.

4. *Die Wacht am Rhein:* "The Watch on the Rhine."

5. *get Sasha to the hall on his crutches:* Berkman had sustained torn ligaments to his foot after a fall (see LML, 1970, 599).

6. Margaret Anderson: editor of the literary journal *The Little Review,* which EG had admired as "alive to new art forms." EG respected Margaret Anderson's freeing herself from "family bondage and bourgeois tradition" to form a new household with another woman (see LML, 1970, 530).

7. A Portrait of the Artist As a Young Man: Partly autobiographical, James Joyce's *Portrait,* published in 1916, describes a sensitive youth, harried by religious and sexual guilt.

8. *Jesus, Socrates, . . . Phillipses:* In addition to those martyred for their beliefs (Jesus, Socrates, Galileo, and G. Bruno), Goldman cites revolutionary architects of American freedoms (Jefferson and Patrick Henry), abolitionists William Lloyd Garrison and Wendell Phillips, insurrectionist John Brown, and civil disobedient Henry David Thoreau.

CHAPTER XLVI

1. *in Jefferson City:* EG was incarcerated at the Missouri State Prison in Jefferson City, there being no federal prison for women in the United States at that time (see LML, 1970, 625).
2. Louis D. Brandeis (1856–1941): U.S. Supreme Court justice, 1916–1939.
3. *what the Germans had done to the Belgians:* In August 1914 the German army invaded Belgium, terrorizing the population, looting and burning towns. "Easter uprising": On Easter Monday in 1916 about 1,250 Irish rebels attempted to capture the most prominent buildings in Dublin to challenge British rule.
4. EG identified the "Swede" as a friend named "Carl," a "staunch and dependable comrade" who helped arrange lecture tours and assisted in office work (see LML, 1970, 610).
5. Kronstadt: a naval fortress on an island in the Gulf of Finland, guarding the approach to Petrograd (today St. Petersburg). Detachments of sailors from Kronstadt were shock troops of both the February and October revolutions.
6. Labor lawyer, prominent Socialist Party theoretician Morris Hillquit (1869–1933) defended Eugene Debs and other antiwar activists against espionage charges. EG first met Hillquit at a Yom Kippur celebration held as a protest against Jewish orthodoxy, during which the young Hillquit held forth in the interior of the building while pitched battles raged between religious and nonreligious Jews outside (see EG's description in LML, 1970, 635).
7. *The new Espionage Law:* Enacted in June 1917, the law made interference with the military or obstruction of the draft illegal. Renamed the Sedition Act in 1918, its punishments were stiffened, and "disloyal" language about the government was prohibited.
8. Sam Gompers (1850–1924): English-born Jewish American labor leader, first president of the AFL (American Federation of Labor) 1886–1924.

CHAPTER XLVII

1. *The October Revolution*: In 1917 Russia underwent two revolutions. In February the czarist government was overthrown and replaced by a provisional government. In October the Bolshevik party led Russian workers and peasants to overthrow the provisional government.

2. Georgii Lvov (1861–1925): first prime minister of the provisional government. Pavel Miliukov (1859–1943): minister of foreign affairs in the provisional government.

3. Alexander Kerensky (1881–1970): prime minister of the provisional government from July 21, 1917, to October 1917; he fled St. Petersburg. He moved to the United States in 1940 and taught at American universities. Viktor Tchernov (1876–1952): minister of agriculture in the provisional government.

4. Helen Keller (1880–1968): Deaf and blind from early childhood, she achieved a remarkable literary and socially active career. After obtaining a bachelor of arts degree from Radcliffe College, she became a member of the Socialist Party of Massachusetts, publishing "Out of the Dark" in 1913, a series of essays on socialism. In subsequent essays she supported the IWW, antiwar activist and socialist Eugene Debs, and the infant Soviet Union. She was an outspoken supporter of the American volunteer Abraham Lincoln Brigade that fought in the Spanish Civil War against fascism, earning thereby her own FBI file under the administration of J. Edgar Hoover. A world traveler and advocate for the blind and deaf, Keller lectured in more than 25 countries and on five continents.

5. Alice Stone Blackwell (1857–1950): daughter of prominent female suffragists Lucy Stone and Henry B. Blackwell; a journalist, suffragist, and later a poet and translator. EG met Blackwell, whom she called "an energetic champion of liberty" (see LML, 1970, 360) when they both solicited American support for the Russian revolution. Blackwell was also active in the Women's Christian Temperance Union (WCTU) and the National Association for the Advancement of Colored Peoples (NAACP), among other progressive organizations.

6. *White generals*: in Russia, the color identified with anti-Communism, implying purity, harmony, and absence of violence, as opposed to red, the color of revolution. In czarist Russia, *whites* referred to the silk linings of the expensive uniforms worn by wealthy university students. After the October Revolution,

Bolsheviks used the term pejoratively to refer to czarist and counter-revolutionary troops.

CHAPTER XLVIII

1. Kate Richards O'Hare (1877–1948): American socialist and reformer, writer, journalist, antiwar agitator.
2. Ella: a fellow prisoner, a young American anarchist (see LML, 1970, 671).
3. Aggie: a fellow prisoner, a "piteous sight," "withered at thirty-three" (see LML, 1970, 673).

CHAPTER L

1. Mollie Steimer (1897–1980): a young Russian American anarchist who was imprisoned for distributing pamphlets opposing American intervention in the Russian revolution. EG admired Steimer's revolutionary zeal and severity (see descriptions in LML, 1970, 701, 704–5). Steimer was deported to Russia in 1921 where she was subsequently imprisoned as an anarchist. Steimer and her companion Senya Fleshin fled from Russia to Germany, then from Paris to Mexico.
2. Mitchell Palmer (1872–1936): U.S. attorney general and congressman. As attorney general in 1919, Palmer mounted an attack against political radicals in the United States, rounding up anarchists and Communists, arresting thousands of immigrant aliens whose political work was mostly social and educational.
3. *Federal deportation mania:* The Immigration Act of 1917 made any alien political radical deportable, no matter how nonviolent his speech or practice.

CHAPTER LI

1. Robert "Bob" Minor (1884–1952): a prominent American cartoonist whose work was an important influence on a generation of political artists. Minor impressed EG as "an artist and a socialist" (see LML, 1970, 477). Imprisoned under the Espionage Act for his antiwar cartoons, Minor continued his cartoon propaganda from the

Western front in Europe. Later as the Southern editor of the Communist *Daily Worker*, he was active in the black civil rights movement.

2. Morris Becker: Arrested at a peace meeting in Madison Square Garden, he was charged with conspiracy to resist the Conscription Law (see LML, 1970, 603).

3. Mikhail Kalinin (1875–1946): formal head of the Soviet state 1919–46.

4. Frank Harris (1856–1931): journalist and author who wrote a sensational autobiography, *My Life and Loves* (1922). Alexander Harvey (1868–1949): publisher and literary editor.

CHAPTER LII

1. S. S. "Zorin" Gomberg (1890–1937): secretary of the Petrograd section of Communist Party.

2. Anton Denikin (1872–1947), Alexander Kolchak (1873–1920), and Nikolai Yudenich (1862–1933): military leaders in the counter-revolution against the Bolsheviks during the civil war (1918–20).

3. William "Bill" Shatoff: friend and anarchist comrade who had been active in America organizing the return of mostly Russian anarchists to Russia after the 1917 Bolshevik revolution. Lenin appointed him commissar of railroads (see LML, 1970, 595).

4. Grigori Zinoviev (1883–1936): Jewish Russian revolutionary and Soviet politician and orator who served the Russian Communist Party in several positions. He was chairman of the Petrograd Soviet while EG was in Russia.

    Ellipses in the remainder of paragraph are EG's, not the editor's.

5. The All-Russian Extraordinary Commisson for Combating Counter-Revolution and Sabotage (the Veh Cheka) was a Soviet police organization intended after its establishment in 1917 to carry out investigative functions. Instead, the organization through its local branches (Cheka) were given greater powers by Lenin to combat counterrevolution, such as holding summary trials and executing sentences, including the death sentence.

6. Boris Savinkov (1879–1925): Russian revolutionary who joined forces with opposition to the Bolsheviks after the October Revolution.

7. Menshevik: after a division in the Russian Socialist Democratic Party, the group favoring a more evolutionary change, in opposition to the Bolsheviks.

8. George Lansbury (1859–1940): journalist, British Labour Party politician, and socialist historian. The founder of the *Daily Herald,* he was editor during 1919–1923.

9. Maxim Gorki (born Alexei Maximovitch Peshkov) (1868–1936): Russian short-story writer, novelist, autobiographer, and essayist. He was a spokesperson for writers during the Stalinist period and formulator of Socialist Realism school of Soviet literature.

10. John Reed (1887–1920): journalist and political radical who established his reputation as a writer and activist in dispatches written from Mexico about the revolutionary Pancho Villa. An eyewitness observer of the events in Russia, John Reed achieved international prominence with his *Ten Days That Shook the World* (1919), considered the best reporting of the Bolshevik revolution. Reed worked in the Soviet bureau of propaganda and died in Moscow of typhus. Honored by the Soviets, he was buried in the Kremlin wall.

11. Karl Radek (1885–1939): German socialist, Russian Bolshevik, and Trotskyist journalist. Elected to the Bolshevik Central Committee in 1920, he was expelled from the party after Lenin's death and purged by Stalin in 1937. Karl Liebnecht (1871–1919): German socialist and active anti-militarist, murdered by German soldiers in 1919. Rosa Luxemburg (1871–1919): Polish-born socialist, revolutionary, intellectual theorist, writer, and publisher. She was murdered by antirevolutionary soldiers in Germany in 1919. Gustav Landauer (1870–1919) German anarchist murdered by antirevolutionary soldiers in Germany in 1919.

12. Nikolai Bukharin (1888–1938): Bolshevik theoretician and leader, member of the Central Committee of the Bolshevik Party. He was tried and executed in the last Stalinist purges of old Bolsheviks.

13. izvostchik: the driver of a carriage.

14. Kharitonensky: Soviet guest house.

15. Soukharevka: main market in Moscow.

16. Anatol Lunacharsky (1875–1933): As commissar of education in the Soviet government, 1917–29, he directed the development of new socialist education and culture.

17. Angelica Balabanoff (1877–1965): Russian politician, active in Russian and Italian socialist movements. Elected secretary at the First International Congress in 1919, she emigrated from Russia in 1924 as an anti-Bolshevik.

18. Errico Malatesta (1853–1932): Italian anarchist and publisher.

19. *Makhnovtsy:* followers of Russian anarchist anti-Bolshevik Nestor Makhno; *ideiny* anarchists identified those who believed in

the principles of anarchism but were not committed to anarchist political action.

20. The Third International was convened in Moscow in March 1919 to implement the dictatorship of the proletariat.

21. Vera Figner (1852–1943): revolutionary socialist, one of the Russian revolutionary women who had inspired the young Emma Goldman (see LML, 1970, 362). Figner had joined in the successful conspiracy to assassinate Czar Alexander II, for which she was arrested in 1883 and released from Siberia in 1904. Figner was highly critical of the Bolshevik Revolution and for many years was in danger of being arrested. During her residence in the Soviet Union, EG met Figner and was moved by her resilience and animation (see LML, 1970, 894–95).

22. Ethel Bernstein: A fellow deportee and victim of the Palmer Raids, she had been assigned to EG as one of her roommates aboard the *Buford*. At EG's request, Bernstein and fellow roommate Dora Lipkin were given rooms near hers and Berkman's at the once fashionable czarist hotel, the Astoria (see LML, 1970, 711, 727).

23. Bakayev: Petrograd chief of the Cheka police. EG reported he was "known as very vindictive towards anarchists" (see LML, 1970, 785).

24. *a certain American journalist*: EG refers to John Clayton, who represented the *Chicago Tribune*, "one of the reactionary papers in the U.S." (see LML, 1970, 788).

25. Bertrand Russell (1872–1970): philosopher, mathematician, and social activist, he became critical of Bolshevism after visiting the Soviet Union in 1920.

26. EG had been introduced to Henry Alsberg earlier (see LML, 1970, 794–95) and had found in him "the best that was in America—sincerity and easy joviality." Allsberg arrived in the Soviet Union as a correspondent for the *Nation* magazine and the London *Daily Herald*, traveling with a British Labour mission. Less impressed by publisher Albert Boni, EG laughed after hearing of his arrest as a possible "counter revolutionary," saying he was "far from rebelling against any established institution, whether revolutionary or otherwise" (see LML, 1970, 832).

27. Nestor Makhno (1884–1934): anarchist leader of nationalist anticzarist and anti-Bolshevik movement in the Ukraine during the civil war (1918–20).

28. povstantsy: czarist term for Bolshevik rebels.

29. Vladimir Korolenko (1853–1921): Ukrainian short-story writer,

populist with international reputation for moral integrity. Protested against injustices after the October Revolution.

30. *The prophet of Yasnaya Polyana:* The Russian writer Leo Tolstoy (1828–1910) was born and lived in Yasnaya Polyana. The estate, a three-hour ride from Moscow, was made into a national museum by the Soviet authorities.

31. Ahasverus is one of many names given to the character of the "Wandering Jew," a figure from Christian folklore who represents metaphorically the Jewish Diaspora and its anti-Semitic subtext. According to this interpretation of the legend, the destruction of Jerusalem and the eternal homelessness of the Jewish people are divine retribution for their rejecting Jesus as the promised Messiah.

32. Georgii Chicherin (1872–1936): Russian revolutionary and diplomat who organized and trained a fledgling Soviet diplomatic corps.

33. pogromshtchik: one who advocates and participates in pogroms.

34. Peter Wrangel (1878–1928): Russian czarist general who fought the Bolsheviks in the Ukraine during the civil war (1918–20).

35. predsedatel: president.

36. Chaim Nachman Byalek (1873–1934): achieved international recognition with the publication of "The City of Slaughter," a Hebrew poem inspired by the Kushnev pogrom of 1903.

37. Yatmanov: commissar of the Museum of the Revolution. Kaplan: secretary of the Museum of the Revolution.

38. shkurniky: slang for someone who has betrayed you.

39. Tukhachevsky: EG refers to the "notorious" commander of the Kronstadt attack (see LML, 1970, 883).

40. In Moscow EG learned that Henry Alsberg had been released from jail after the intervention of a friendly guard. Once free, Alsberg returned a $200 gift EG had given him at the time of his arrest, which she commented "was a veritable fortune to us now" (see LML, 1970, 852).

41. Nep: the New Economic Policy launched by Lenin.

42. Ella Reeves Bloor, "Mother Bloor" (1862–1951): a socialist and labor organizer. She helped organize the American Communist Party after the Bolshevik Revolution. William Z. Foster (1881–1961): Irish Catholic American radical labor leader and Communist Party presidential candidate in 1924, 1928, and 1932.

43. Earl ("Jim") Browder (1891–1973): American labor leader and socialist, later Communist Party organizer.

44. Agnes Smedley (1892–1950): journalist and author who was active in the Indian independence movement. She gained national

prominence for reports from China in 1936. Chato: Indian nationalist leader Virendranath "Chatto" Chattopadhyaya.

45. Mikhail Tomsky (1880–1936): a Russian socialist and trade union organizer who led the Red International Trade Union in 1920. Elected to the Central Committee of the Communist Party in 1922 and later a member of the Politburo, Tomsky was purged by Stalin and committed suicide. A. Losovsky (1878–1952): a Russian Party and trade union official. Arrested under Stalin and died in prison.

46. EG met English anarchist and trade organizer Alexander Schapiro (?–1946) in 1907 at an international anarchist conference in Amsterdam (see LML, 1970, 403). Schapiro accompanied EG when she visited Kropotkin at his home outside Moscow (see LML, 1970, 769). Later an "intimate friend of the Kropotkin family" (see LML, 1970, 865), Schapiro assisted other anarchists in planning Kropotkin's funeral (see LML, 1970, 865).

47. Fanya Baron (?–1921): a Russian anarchist, rumored to have assassinated the head of the Czarist secret police. She lived in the United States from 1915 to 1917, returning to Russia after the Bolshevik Revolution. With Aaron Baron, she was among the first anarchists to meet with Goldman in the Soviet Union to inform her of the persecution of anarchists by Lenin (see LML, 1970, 812–13). While EG was traveling with the museum expedition in Kharkov, she was approached by Fanya, who was hoping to effect a meeting between EG and the peasant anti-Bolshevik leader Makhno. EG declined to leave the expedition, hoping for another opportunity to meet Makhno (see LML, 1970, 814).

48. Maksim M. Litvinov nominally subordinate to Chicerin, became People's Commissar for Foreign Affairs during 1930–39 (see LML, 1970, 923).

CHAPTER LIII

1. Hjalmar Branting (1860–1925): called "the father of socialism" in Sweden, served as prime minister in 1921 and 1924.
2. Maria Spiridonovna (1884–1941): Russian socialist-revolutionary activist and orator. She spent most of her adult life in prison or exile under czarist and Soviet regimes (see LML, 1970, 800–01).

CHAPTER LIV

1. Arthur Swenson served EG as a guide and translator while she was in Sweden.
2. Was liebt sich, das neckt sich: "He who loves himself mocks himself."
3. *Stella had hardly left*: EG's niece Stella Ballantyne returned to the United States, anxious about being separated from her family while the political situation was growing threatening in Germany (see LML, 1970, 952–53).
4. verdammte Juden: "damn Jews."
5. Rudolf Rocker (1873–1958): German-born Catholic anarchist, essayist, and intellectual.

CHAPTER LV

1. Rebecca West (1892–1983): English journalist, novelist, and critic.
2. Harold Laski (1893–1950): Jewish English Labour Party leader, author, and theoretician of democratic socialism.
3. ILP: Independent Labour Party.

CHAPTER LVI

1. Peggy Guggenheim (1898–1979): a patron of the arts, she married Lawrence Vail, an American writer, in 1922.
2. Novelist and essayist Kathleen Millay, younger sister of the poet Edna St. Vincent, was married to playwright Howard Young, when she befriended EG in Saint-Tropez.
3. Theodore Dreiser (1871–1945): author and social activist, architect of naturalism in American fiction.
4. Sacco and Vanzetti: In 1920 Italian anarchists Nicola Sacco and Bartolomeo Vanzetti were arrested and charged with murdering the guard of a shoe company in South Braintree, Massachusetts. Despite international protest against the obvious judicial bias during their trial, the two were executed in 1927. The case remains one of the most controversial in American history.

Index

FOR THE BEST IN PAPERBACKS, LOOK FOR THE

In every corner of the world, on every subject under the sun, Penguin represents quality and variety—the very best in publishing today.

For complete information about books available from Penguin—including Penguin Classics, Penguin Compass, and Puffins—and how to order them, write to us at the appropriate address below. Please note that for copyright reasons the selection of books varies from country to country.

In the United States: Please write to *Penguin Group (USA), P.O. Box 12289 Dept. B, Newark, New Jersey 07101-5289* or call 1-800-788-6262.

In the United Kingdom: Please write to *Dept. EP, Penguin Books Ltd, Bath Road, Harmondsworth, West Drayton, Middlesex UB7 0DA.*

In Canada: Please write to *Penguin Books Canada Ltd, 10 Alcorn Avenue, Suite 300, Toronto, Ontario M4V 3B2.*

In Australia: Please write to *Penguin Books Australia Ltd, P.O. Box 257, Ringwood, Victoria 3134.*

In New Zealand: Please write to *Penguin Books (NZ) Ltd, Private Bag 102902, North Shore Mail Centre, Auckland 10.*

In India: Please write to *Penguin Books India Pvt Ltd, 11 Panchsheel Shopping Centre, Panchsheel Park, New Delhi 110 017.*

In the Netherlands: Please write to *Penguin Books Netherlands bv, Postbus 3507, NL-1001 AH Amsterdam.*

In Germany: Please write to *Penguin Books Deutschland GmbH, Metzlerstrasse 26, 60594 Frankfurt am Main.*

In Spain: Please write to *Penguin Books S. A., Bravo Murillo 19, 1° B, 28015 Madrid.*

In Italy: Please write to *Penguin Italia s.r.l., Via Benedetto Croce 2, 20094 Corsico, Milano.*

In France: Please write to *Penguin France, Le Carré Wilson, 62 rue Benjamin Baillaud, 31500 Toulouse.*

In Japan: Please write to *Penguin Books Japan Ltd, Kaneko Building, 2-3-25 Koraku, Bunkyo-Ku, Tokyo 112.*

In South Africa: Please write to *Penguin Books South Africa (Pty) Ltd, Private Bag X14, Parkview, 2122 Johannesburg.*

CLICK ON A CLASSIC
www.penguinclassics.com

The world's greatest literature at your fingertips

Constantly updated information on more than a thousand titles,
from Icelandic sagas to ancient Indian epics, Russian drama to
Italian romance, American greats to African masterpieces

•

The latest news on recent additions to the list, updated
editions, and specially commissioned translations

•

Original essays by leading writers

•

A wealth of background material, including biographies
of every classic author from Aristotle to Zamyatin, plot
synopses, readers' and teachers' guides, useful web links

•

Online desk and examination copy assistance for academics

•

Trivia quizzes, competitions, giveaways, news on
forthcoming screen adaptations